Human Behavior
at Work

Human Behavior at Work

O. Jeff Harris
Northeast Louisiana University

Sandra J. Hartman
University of New Orleans

West Publishing Company

Saint Paul   New York   Los Angeles   San Francisco

Copyeditor: Deborah Cady
Text Design: John Rokusek
Art: Alex Teshin and Associates
Composition: Parkwood Composition Services, Inc.
Cover Image: © The Stock Market/Masahiro Sano, 1991
Cover Design: Kirsten Mikkelson Ford

Library of Congress Cataloging-in-Publication Data

Harris, O. Jeff.
  Human behavior at work / O. Jeff Harris, Sandra J. Hartman.
    p.   cm.
  Includes bibliographical references and index.
  ISBN: 0-314-93108-2
  1. Organizational behavior.   2. Corporate culture.   3. Personnel
management.   I. Hartman, Sandra J.   II. Title.
HD58.7.H3694   1991
658.3—dc20
                                                   91-29603
   CIP

Brief Contents

Preface, xiii

   1   Human Behavior at Work—With an
          Emphasis on Ethics, 0

Section I

The Climate in Which People Work, 17

   2   Organizational Culture and Informal
          Organizations, 18
   3   What Good Are Groups, Anyway? 46
   4   Technology—Its Impact In The
          Work Place, 68
   5   The Physical Surroundings Of The
          Work Place, 88

Section II

Individuals In The Work Place, 111

   6   Perception And The Individual, 112
   7   Personal Needs in the
          Workplace, 140

Section III

Managerial Actions, 167

   8   Stimulating Employees to
          Action–The Motivational Process, 168
   9   The Reinforcement View Of Motiva-
          tion, 196
  10   The Role of Leadership in the
          Organization, 220

Section IV

Interpersonal Communications, 249

  11   Communicating Concepts And Infor-
          mation, 250
  12   Counseling Employees, 282
  13   Managing Conflict, 308

Section V

*Managing The Problems Of Workers,
 337*

  14   Stress—Causes, Consequences, And
          Solutions, 338
  15   Chronic Worker Problems—Alco-
          holism, Other Drug Abuse, And
          Theft, 360
  16   Equity For Minorities, 384

Section VI

*Managing Growth And Development,
 413*

  17   Planned and Unplanned Change,
          and Organizational Development,
          414
  18   A Look Toward the Future, 442

Endnotes, 467

Glossary, 485

Index, 493

Contents

Preface, xiii

Chapter 1

Human Behavior at Work—With an
 Emphasis on Ethics, 0

Management Perspectives, 2
Ethical Issues and Social Responsibility, 4
 Ethics in the Workplace, 4
 Social Responsibility, 10
 Utilitarianism Versus Duty, 10

Section I
The Climate in Which People
Work, 17

Chapter 2

Organizational Culture and Informal
 Organizations, 18

The Culture of the Organization, 20
 Characteristics of an Organization's
 Culture, 21
 An Ideal Organization Culture, 23
 Cultural Realities, 24
 The Manager's Role in the Organization's
 Culture, 24
 Additional Sources of an Organization's
 Cultural Information, 25
How Organization Structure Influences
 Culture, 25
 Authority Relationships, 26
 Communication Channels, 28
 The Span of Supervision, 29
 Specialization, 29
 Centralization or Decentralization for
 Decision Making, 29

Informal Groups And Organizations, 30
 Functions of Informal Organizations, 32
 Characteristics and Activities, 33
 Informal Group Norms, 34
 Group Cohesiveness, 36
 Grapevine Communication, 38
 Management's Relationship to the
 Informal Organization, 40

Chapter 3

What Good Are Groups, Anyway?, 46

Formal Groups and Teams, 48
Traditional Groups and Teams, 49
Teamwork in an Automobile Plant, 49
How the Team Decision-making Process
 Works, 49
 Decision-making Groups. . . Or Is a Camel
 Really a Racehorse Designed by a
 Committee?, 50
 Problems with Group Decisions, 52
Nontraditional Groups, 54
 Interacting Conference Groups, 54
 Two More Nontraditional Decision Groups ,
 60
 A Different Kind of Group–The Quality
 Circle, 61
Team Building and Problem Solving, 62

Chapter 4

Technology—Its Impact in the
 Workplace, 68

The Flow of Technology Through An
 Organization, 70
The Chief Technology Officer, 73
What Technology Does for an Organization,
 73

Technology's Impact on Production, 73
Robotics, 74
Data Accumulation, Storage, and Decision Making, 74
Technology and Communication, 79
Working At Home—The Cottage Industries, 81
Neighborhood Work Centers, 82
Health and Safety Problems from Technology, 83
Clean-Air Activities, 84
Technology and the Manager, 84

Chapter 5
The Physical Surroundings of the Workplace, 88

Effects of Nature—Temperature and Humidity, 91
Other Weather Conditions, 92
Implications for Managers, 92
The Impact of Visual Stimuli, 93
The Effect of Color, 93
Beauty Versus Ugliness, 94
Levels of Lighting and Work Performance, 95
Auditory Factors—The Effect of Noise, 95
The Effects of High-Level Noise, 97
Reducing Noise Levels, 99
Physical Location and Placement, 99
The Open Office Versus the Conventional Office, 99
Working with the Open Design, 102
Where the Bosses Should Go, 103
What to Do If Centralization Is Necessary, 103
Other Causes and Results of Location, 103
The Status Impact of Physical Climate, 105
Smoking in the Workplace, 106
Managing Smoking in the Workplace, 107

Section II
Individuals in the Workplace, 111

Chapter 6
Perception and the Individual, 112

What You See Is What You Get, 114
Perceptions About Self and Others, 115
The Success-Failure Model, 117

The Johari Window, 120
The Transactional Analysis Model, 121
Summary of Self-Perception, 123
Managerial Actions for Better Self-Perception, 123
Role Perception, 127
Ways to Improve Role Perception, 129
Perception of Who Controls Outcomes (Locus of Control), 130
Behavioral Implications and Managerial Actions, 134
The Pygmalion Effect—Improving Performance Through Perception, 134
The Significance of the Pygmalion Effect, 134

Chapter 7
Personal Needs in the Workplace, 140

Can My Job Give Me What I Want?, 142
Needs Theories, 143
Murray's Manifest and Latent Needs, 143
The Maslow Heirarchy, 143
Alderfer's ERG Approach, 145
Herzberg's Motivation and Hygiene Factors, 145
Specific Human Needs, 146
The Physical Maintenance Need, 146
The Need for Security, 147
The Need for Affiliation, 149
The Competence Need, 150
The Reputation Need, 151
The Need for Power, 152
The Service Need, 154
The Achievement Need, 154
The Need for Hope, 155
The Degree of Need Fulfillment and the Urgency of Needs, 156
Discovering the Current Needs of Workers, 159

Section III
Managerial Actions, 167

Chapter 8
Stimulating Employees to Action—The Motivational Process, 168

Assumptions Underlying Needs-Based Motivation, 170

Where Do Motives Fit Into Motivation?, 171
Expectancy Theory, 173
Equity Theory, 179
  How Does the Supervisor Fit In?, 182
A Negative Motivational Model, 182
  The Role of the Boss, 184
Goal Setting as a Motivational Concept, 185
The Motivational Potential of Jobs, 187

Chapter 9
The Reinforcement View of
  Motivation, 196
Managing Reinforcement, 199
  Putting It All Together, 201
Guidelines for the Use of Reinforcers, 201
Reinforcement Schedules, 203
Comparison of Reinforcement Motivation with
  Cognitive Motivation, 207
Negative Reinforcement, Punishment, and the
  Disciplinary Process, 208
A Philosophy of Discipline, 209
Providing Fairness in Disciplinary Action, 211
Conducting the Correctional Interview, 214

Chapter 10
The Role of Leadership in the
  Organization, 220
How We Got Where We Are Today, 223
  The Trait Approach, 223
  The Behavior Concept of Leadership, 224
  The Style Approaches, 225
  The Situational View of Leadership, 228
Flexible Leadership—Adapting the Appropriate
  Leadership Style to a Situation, 236
  Determining Leadership Needs, 238
  The Problem of Consistency, 242

Section IV
Interpersonal Communications, 249

Chapter 11
Communicating Concepts
  and Information, 250
What Communication Does, 253

The Information Function, 253
The Command and Instruction
  Function, 253
The Influence and Persuasion Function, 254
The Integrative Function, 254
The Innovation Function, 254
The Perfect Organizational Communication
  Situation, 254
The Communication Process, 255
  Deciding on the Message, 255
  Analysis of the Receiver, 256
  Choice of Symbols, 256
  Selection of Medium, 257
  Receiver Responsibilities, 259
  Responsibility for Clear Communication of
    Messages, 260
Problems in the Communication Process, 260
  Problems in Conveying the Intended
    Meaning, 26
  The Problem of Filtering, 260
  The Problem of Distortion, 261
  Timing as a Problem, 261
  Inconsistent Actions and Messages, 262
  The Receiver's State of Mind, 263
  Overcoming Problems of Message
    Interpretation, 264
Creating Conditions for Effective
  Communication, 264
  How Does the Organization Chart Enter
    In?, 264
  Encouraging Upward Communication, 267
The Grapevine and It's Problems, 269
Telling It Like It Is—Assertiveness, 271
Additional Communication Problems, 275

Chapter 12
Counseling Employees, 282

Who Should Handle Counseling?, 287
Conditions for Effective Counseling, 289
  Set the Stage, 290
  What about the People Themselves?, 290
  Preparing for the Counseling Session, 291
Two Counseling Techniques, 293
  Directive Counseling, 293
  Nondirective Counseling, 294
Applying Contingency Theory to Counseling,
  300
The Ethics and Obligations of Counseling, 301

Chapter 13
Managing Conflict, 308

Management's Goals When Conflict
  Arises, 311
  Identifying What's Behind the Conflict, 311
  Redirecting Tensions and Hostilities, 312
  Integration of Ideas, 312
  Achieving Unity, 313
  Accomplishing Real and Permanent
    Solutions, 313
Sources of Conflict, 314
  Individual Differences, 314
  Perceptual Differences, 318
  Organizational Characteristics and
    Functional Differences, 319
The Degree of Conflict Development, 322
Dealing With Conflict, 324
  Robbins' Approach to Conflict
    Management, 324
  The Leadership Grid ® Approach, 324
  The Thomas-Kilmann Conflict Mode, 325
  Mediation and Arbitration, 329
  Choosing An Appropriate Approach, 330

Section V
Managing the Problems of
Workers, 337

Chapter 14
Stress—Causes, Consequences, and
  Solutions, 338

Type A and Type B Personalities, 341
Health As a Factor, 342
The Importance of Self-Concept, 343
Experiences with Family and Friends, 343
Age and Education, 343
Stressors—What They Are, Where They Are,
  and What They Do, 344
  Job-related Stressors, 345
  Other Stressors, 348
What Happens to the Person Under
  Stress?, 349
How Managers and Coworkers Can Help, 351

Chapter 15
Chronic Worker Problems—
  Alcoholism, Other Drug Abuse,
  and Theft, 360
The Problems of Alcoholism, 363
Other Drug Abuse Problems, 364
Dealing with Alcohol and Other Drug
  Problems, 365
  Drug Testing, 365
  Drug Policies and Procedures, 367
  Employee Rights, 368
  Employee Philosophy and Attitudes, 368
  Rehabilitation Programs, 369
  You as a Supervisor, 371
Employee Dishonesty and Theft, 373
  Who Steals and Why, 373
  Management's Role in Employee
    Theft, 374
  Dealing with Employee Theft, 374
  You as a Manager, 380

Chapter 16
Equity for Minorities, 384

Gender: Women as a Minority, 386
  Problems of Employed Women, 387
  Advantages for Women Employees, 394
  Dealing with the Problems Women Face,
    394
Older Workers as an Age Minority, 395
  Problems of Older Workers, 395
  Dealing with the Problems of Older Workers,
    397
Younger Employees—Their Strengths and
  Weaknesses, 398
Minorities Based upon Race, 399
  Organizational Problems Faced by Racial
    Minorities, 400
What Can Be Done?, 402
Workers with Disabilities, 403
  The Americans with Disabilities Act of
    1990, 405
Employees with AIDS, 405
Steps Toward Equity, 409

Section VI
Managing Growth and Development, 413

Chapter 17
Planned and Unplanned Change, and Organizational Development, 414

Internal Change, 416
External Change, 417
  The Economy and Its Effects, 417
  What About Technology?, 417
  Legal Changes Cause Organization Change, 418
  Society Calls for Changes, 418
Kinds of Changes, 418
The Effects of Change upon Employees, 419
  Behavioral Changes, 419
  Psychological Changes, 419
  Social Changes, 420
  Additional Effects of Change, 421
Why Change Is Often Resisted, 421
  The TA Approach, 423
  Tension, 424
  Fear, 424
Other Factors Influencing Response to the Demands for Change, 425
  The Initiator of Change, 425
  The Risk-Taking Tendencies of the Employee, 426
  The Necessity of Change, 426
Management's Goals for Change, 426
Leadership for Change, 427
Managerial Guidelines, 427
  Defining Objectives and Optimizing Mutual Benefits, 428
  Enlisting Employee Participation, 428
  Allowing for Early Planning and Advance Notification, 429

Guaranteeing Employee Protection, 429
Providing Resources and Training, 429
Using Groups to Help Employees Overcome Their Fears, 430
Applying the Tentative Approach, 431
Additional Means of Encouraging Acceptance of Change, 432
Summary of Guidelines, 433
Organizational Development, 433
  Role of the Change Agent, 435
  Helping OD Work Properly, 437
  OD, Attitude Change, and Training, 437

Chapter 18
A Look Toward the Future, 442

Characteristics of the Workforce of the Future, 445
Organizations of the Future, 447
  Dynamic Networks and Interorganizational Cooperation, 447
  Structure, Power, and Authority in Future Organizations, 448
  A Leadership Trend, 448
A Managerial Challenge—The Multinational Movement, 450
  Cultural Values, 450
  Societal Procedures and Methods, 451
  Multinational Language and Communication, 457

Endnotes, 467

Glossary, 485

Index, 493

Preface

The study of human behavior in the workplace is interesting, dynamic, and challenging. New things are being discovered daily about individuals and groups as they work together to accomplish personal and organizational goals. The material in this book is as up-to-date and as accurate as possible in a changing world.

Goals of This Book

One of the primary goals of this book is to provide prospective employees with knowledge and understanding of self and others so that they can interact in the workplace. Another goal is to provide prospective managers (this group includes many of you who as students will read this book) with guidelines concerning proper management actions and techniques. An additional goal is to provide opportunities to develop personal and managerial skills from the various techniques discussed in the book.

Chapter Structure

Each chapter begins with a list of objectives that establish the focus of the chapter. A case is provided to stimulate thought and to offer a means for illustrating ideas developed in the chapter. Key terms are defined as the chapter unfolds. Every chapter has a Self Test (Personal Feedback feature) designed to provide insight and understanding about personal habits, styles, beliefs, and preferences. Each chapter has a boxed highlight called Management-in-Action, which illustrates how actual managers or organizations have handled responsibilities discussed in the chapter. Some chapters have Insights boxes that describe processes or other supplementary thought. Some Insights provide background and philosophical explanations, such as how-to lists for putting a procedure in sequence. Each chapter ends with several study-discussion questions. The questions may call for reflection on ideas in the chapter, or they may stimulate and expand thought on related issues. Also at the end of each chapter is a case that allows sharpening of skills and the reinforcement of ideas. Some chapters have other exercises for the reader to use in developing further skills and insights.

This book studies human behavior and is concerned with the management of people in the workplace. Chapter 1 presents a brief history of the development of management thought. As the chapter points out, several schools of thought concerned with the management of people have developed. Some of the schools of thought have made their contributions and then faded. There are two schools, however, that remain especially relevant to contemporary thinking on the scope and content of managerial duties. One of the schools, the open system (discussed in detail in Chapter 1), is especially concerned with how the organization and the people in it relate to the environment outside the organization. The open systems concept is mentioned occasionally but is in the background, if not at the focal point, of each chapter.

The other contemporary school of thought used heavily in this book is the contingency-situational school. This approach is used in almost every chapter as applications of management responsibilities are identified. The contingency-situational school of thought states that there is no one best way of doing things in the management of human behavior. Not any of the managerial techniques will work 100 percent of the time. Perhaps the two concepts closest to working 100 percent of the time are goal setting (Chapter 8) and reinforcement (Chapter 9).

Because there is no one best way of fulfilling managerial duties, an important part of managing is the diagnosing of the managerial needs of a situation and responding to them. A large part of motivation, for example, is the discovery of a worker's need to which management can appeal. Providing the appropriate kind of leadership begins with an analysis of both the needs of the employee and the needs of the organization. Selection of the proper counseling procedure is dependent upon the ability of the person being counseled to communicate, to identify his or her own problems, and to formulate alternative solutions. As these managerial responsibilities illustrate, step 1 in almost any activity is the discernment of the needs of a specific situation.

The Book's Content

Chapter 1 begins with background information, showing how the development of management thought has progressed to its current status. It then turns to contemporary management issues—particularly to ethical behavior on the part of those who manage. Discovering what is right, what is fair, and what is socially responsible are all outstanding needs of managers. More than anything else, the study of ethical behavior in Chapter 1 is directed toward answering the question, Where can I look for help to determine what is ethical?

Part I of the book considers the surroundings of people in the workplace—the work culture, including the informal organization, the work groups, the level of technology, and the physical climate. In Part II, workers are viewed as individuals. Since the individual is the basic unit of behavior at work, Part II considers human nature, needs, expectations, perceptions, and other individual concepts.

Part III discusses the many responsibilities managers have as they work with individuals and groups. For the most part, Part III reveals how those in guiding positions go about stimulating behavior, maintaining performance, and providing leadership so that both personal and organizational goals are achieved. Communication is the focus of Part IV. Communication goals, methods, and procedures are discussed; listening and counseling techniques are presented; and the management of conflict is considered. Part V concerns itself with problems that individuals (including those who manage) face, along with techniques for handling problems. Problems of stress, alcoholism, other drug abuse, theft, worker illnesses, and inequitable treatment are all described, along with a number of solutions.

Part VI discusses helping an organization and its employees to become all they are capable of becoming while looking at future trends and needs. In particular, multinational management and leadership are discussed, an area that seems to be of major attention as the world gets smaller, businesses expand, and employees shift to new countries and work opportunities.

Supplements

An instructor's manual includes lecture outlines, presentation notes, teaching suggestions, and answers to the case and end of chapter questions. Experimental exercises included in the text are explained with suggestions for using the exercises in the classroom. Films and videos available through various sources are noted.

A test bank of approximately 1,000 essay, true-false, matching, and multiple-choice test questions is included. Suggested answers to the essay questions are provided in the test bank.

Key Contributors

Many people have been instrumental in producing this book. Our colleagues have provided invaluable ideas, constructive criticism, and suggestions. Some of them have actually contributed parts of some of the chapters. Professor Jim Logan of the University of New Orleans (UNO) provided many fundamental concepts and ideas to the technology chapter. Professors Pam Van Epps and Bill Galle of UNO prepared the test of conflict management styles. Professor Rose Knotts of the University of North Texas was the major contributor to the material concerning multinational behavior and management. Professors Greg Chachere, Jim McBeth, Robert Stevens, and David Loudon of Northeast Louisiana University (NLU) and Tom Blue of Fort Lewis College offered many ideas in addition to evaluation feedback.

We have benefited from the constructive criticism of a number of reviewers:

Thomas Allen
Appalachian State University

Kay Barchas
Skyline College

Mary Blalock
Southeastern Louisiana University

Deborah Brown
Santa Fe Community College

Stephen Bushardt
University of Southern Mississippi

J.E. Cantrell
De Anza College

Mike Farley
Del Mar College

Jan Feldbauer
Austin Community College—Northbridge

Samuel Gant
Nashville State Technical Institute

Larry Hill
San Jacinto College Central

Rhoda Jacobs
County College of Morris

Dorothy Jeanis
Fresno City College

Leo Kiesewetter
Illinois Central College

Mark Mallinger
Pepperdine University

C. William Roe
University of Southwestern Louisiana

Burl Worley
Allan Hancock College

We are grateful for the support we have received from the editors and staff at West Publishing Company. We are especially appreciative of Rick Leyh, the acquiring editor, who has been with us from prospectus to finished product. Jessica Evans, developmental editor, and Charlene Fields have worked with us patiently through the review process. In St. Paul, Emily Autumn has overseen the production process with editorial help from Deborah Cady. Elizabeth Grantham has effectively directed the promotional process. We appreciate the contributions of all these people.

Many graduate students have assisted us with the research. In particular, Richard Foshee, Sanjay Gupta, and Keith Kelley come to mind. Gloria Honeycutt, departmental secretary at NLU, has helped in many activities, as have members of the Division of Business Research at NLU. Student secretary Melissa Anderson typed a large amount of the early drafts.

We could write a book about the contributions Carolyn Harris has made in the preparation of this manuscript. She has performed many duties, including word processing, proofreading, and permissions tracking, and has served as a trusted critic. Both Carolyn Harris and Frank Malone, our spouses, have provided encouragement, inspiration, and sympathy throughout the process.

The Harris children (Larkin, Stephen, and Danielle) have all provided support and have faithfully helped to give Dad more time for writing. We are grateful for their sustaining hands.

OJH and SJH

Human Behavior
at Work

Chapter 1

Human Behavior at Work—With an Emphasis on Ethics

Objectives

- To recognize that the actions of individuals (specifically, those who manage) can make a difference in performance and goal achievement.
- To consider some assumptions about people in the workplace.
- To envision the challenges involved with being a manager.
- To discover ethical and social responsibility issues that must be confronted.
- To identify methods for determining appropriate ethical actions.
- To question the value of social responsibility.
- To consider the plans and purposes of this book.

The "Best Seller"

"Now, this item's a real bestseller for us—especially with the kids from the junior high school down the block," commented Bob Greenshaw, the manager of a small, locally owned convenience store, as he oriented Kassie Grigsby, a newly hired clerk-cashier, to her duties.

"But that's cigarette paper—and you know it's for drugs—marijuana and maybe even crack cocaine!" exclaimed Kassie. Kassie herself had reason to know. Her older brother Tom had been in and out of hospitals for years and had had several serious brushes with the law—all the result of a drug problem that had begun even before he'd entered high school. Her mother, heartbroken about the turn Tom's life had taken, had repeatedly warned Kassie about drugs. And now this! In effect, her new boss was expecting her to help supply the needs of drug users—many of them no older than Tom had been when he was first exposed to drugs. Kassie looked at Bob Greenshaw, visibly upset, and awaited an answer.

"Why the high and mighty attitude?" he responded. "Look here—we're a business, not the antidrug society or something. There's nothing illegal about selling cigarette papers. In fact, we have no right to ask our customers what they do with their purchases, or to tell them how to use them, for that matter. Join the twentieth century, young lady!"

Case Questions

1. Where does a business concern's social responsibility begin and end?
2. What are the ethical issues in this case?
3. What should Kassie consider before she decides whether she will continue to work at the convenience store? Should she stay? Why or why not?

As the title of this book suggests, this is a book about the behavior of people as they work together. The viewpoint is from the management perspective. Attention is focused on the attitudes, experiences, expectations, needs, problems, and changes in individuals and groups as they interact at work. Answers are sought to such questions as, Why do people do the things they do while at work? Why do people work anyway? What effects do groups have on individual behavior? Are managers and nonmanagers alike or different in their work motivations and responsibilities? To whom do those who manage have obligations and responsibilities? How should managers go about performing their duties effectively and efficiently? What changes and trends are occurring today within (and, to some extent, outside of) organizations that have a bearing on people at work? Why do people frequently resist change? Perhaps answers to some of these questions are obvious, but many will require serious searching.

Management Perspectives

Generally speaking, early managerial concern seemed to concentrate on increasing productivity, not on taking care of people. In the early part of this century, management pioneers such as Frederick Taylor, Frank Gilbreth, and their contemporaries applied scientific methods to design jobs and work conditions for optimal productivity. Work patterns were designed for efficiency. Incentives offered to workers were primarily monetary. It was believed that every worker could be good at something. It was management's job to help each individual find the best place for him or her to work. Time and motion studies were used to arrange each job more efficiently.

Since it was felt that managers had a responsibility to provide the very best working conditions, one of the most famous research efforts ever attempted in an organizational setting was begun in the 1920s at the Western Electric plant in Hawthorne, Illinois. The study was actually begun as an attempt to find the best level of illumination for workstations to achieve effectiveness (getting goals accomplished) and efficiency (using resources wisely).

In the process of researching lighting levels and other work conditions, the human side of organizations became the focus of attention. New questions were asked, and new assumptions were developed. It was felt that happy workers would be productive workers. Allowing and encouraging employees to work together in groups was considered important. Affiliation needs were felt to be a high priority. Unions gained strength as many believed employers were abusing and manipulating their employees. The Great Depression increased the desire of individuals for support from each other.

Many say that it was the Hawthorne studies that opened the door to consideration of the things people feel, need, and want from their work experiences. It was also seen as the introduction to group dynamics.

The Hawthorne studies were by no means the end of the development of management thought. When Koontz wrote his classic article published in 1961, he identified six different schools of thought. When he wrote a revisit article in 1980, he found eleven different management approaches.

Today's thinking about people in the workplace and the management of their behavior is really a blend of ideas from several approaches. To illustrate, Chapter 3 draws heavily upon the group behavior school for its content. Chapter 4 stresses as a central issue the need for technology and people compatibility. Chapters 8 through 13 are all about roles managers play. Practically every school is utilized in one way or another, even though each school may not be identified specifically. Perhaps the two most pertinent schools of thought utilized in this book are the systems and the contingency-situational approaches. The systems approach makes its greatest contribution in the structure it provides for the book. Figure 1–1 illustrates an organization (a system), its environment, climate, subsystems, processes, activities, inputs, and outputs.

The book begins by taking a look at the environment and climate in which people work (Chapters 2 through 5). It then discusses the basic sub-

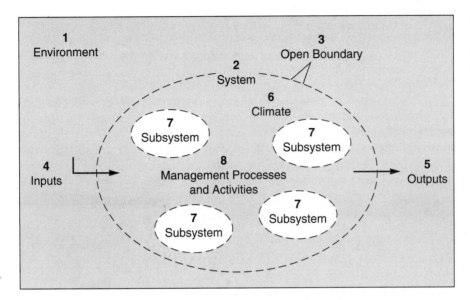

Figure 1–1

The Systems Perspective of an Organization

Components of the Systems View of an Organization

1.	Environment	everything that surrounds the system, including social, political, economic, legal, and technological components.
2.	System	a set of subsystems, relationships, and activities separated by a boundary from components of the environment. The organization, for example, may be viewed as a system.
3.	Open boundary	a wall, usually imaginary, surrounding a system which separates the contents of a system from the environment. The boundary is perforated so that inputs can be received from the environment and outputs can be issued to the environment.
4.	Inputs	items transported from the environment to the system and its parts. Resources, directives, information, and technology are examples of inputs.
5.	Outputs	items or things issued to factors in the environment by the system. Finished or semifinished products, information services, and even undesirable things such as pollution may be transferred outward.
6.	Climate	everything inside the system including formal, informal, physical, social, and psychological components.
7.	Subsystems	the groupings of components within the system. Different people see different subsystems within systems. For example, subsystems are sometimes viewed as the different departments within an organization. Or, subsystems might be the formal structure, informal relationships, etc.
8.	Management processes and activities.	duties such as controlling, training, leading, motivating, and so forth, that are performed by managers in the system.

system of organizational activity—the individual (Chapters 6 and 7). Chapters 8 through 13 focus on managerial activities. Chapters 14 through 17 talk about problems and adjustments that must be handled for a healthful workplace. Organizations want continuity and equilibrium, which is what systems want, too.

The other most influential school (the contingency-situational) provides the philosophy and the method for handling managerial roles. The contingency-situational approach teaches that there is no one best way of doing anything. There's no one best way of providing leadership. There is more than one way for providing authority relationships. There are different ways that can be useful in counseling with others. As Table 1–1 shows, diagnosis is a major activity in the management process. Employees have different needs; as a result, each requires unique attention.

Ethical Issues and Social Responsibility

ethical behavior
Actions consistent with society's code of conduct. Doing what is considered morally right.

Another key contemporary consideration is related to all schools of thought and to every managerial action mentioned above. That issue is, What is **ethical behavior? Ethics** is concerned with identifying and getting the "right" kind of behavior from people as individuals and groups.

Ethics in the Workplace

ethics
A set of values representing what a particular society believes to be right as well as what it considers to be wrong.

Experts are predicting that organizations and work relationships will change significantly in the future. One expert (Kanter) has written that there are already greater numbers and varieties of channels for taking action and influencing others than in the past. Relationships for influencing others are seen as shifting from the vertical to the horizontal—from the chain of command to peer networks. Top-down authority is becoming less important, and teamwork is taking its place. The distinction between managers and those managed is diminishing, especially in terms of information, control over assignments, and access to external relationships. This means that managers are having to use persuasion and participation more and commands and directions less.[1]

As a result of the many changes taking place and predicted for the future, decisions about ethical behavior and social responsibility are becoming increasingly complex. Ethics and social responsibility are interrelated though somewhat separate concepts. We'll discuss both, but let's start with the idea

Table 1–1
The Situational or Contingency Process

1. Identification of the sources of information or input (the environment, the climate, individuals, past experiences, etc.)
2. Gathering and diagnosing the needs of the situation
3. Planning of actions in response to diagnostic findings
4. Implementation of plans
5. Feedback from appropriate sources
6. Evaluation of actions and the beginning of the process all over again

of ethics and ethical behavior. Ethical behavior is activity that results in the right thing being done. But what is the right thing? Sometimes it is dictated by our **culture.** Most of the time, though, employees of an organization must determine for themselves what is right or wrong. In our rapidly changing world, there are many situations where there is no absolutely clear, indisputable course of ethical action.

How can we determine what is the ethically correct course of action? One way to seek the ethically correct action is to ask, Where can I look for guidelines on what's right and what's wrong? A starting point might be the question, What does the law say about this? Sometimes this is the only question that needs to be asked because constitutional laws, statutory laws, court decisions, and executive orders may clearly dictate what has to be done. For example, discrimination on the basis of race, color, religion, sex, or national origin is prohibited by the Civil Rights Act of 1964. A review of this legislation may quickly outline an appropriate course of action. Federal, state, or local laws frequently may be used as guidelines.

Some authors think that laws are depended upon too heavily as behavior guidelines. For example, a concept known as legal positivism (or positive law) has emerged. According to legal positivism, people have accepted the notion that if they have followed the laws that are on the books in a society, they have done all that society expects of them. When used in this manner, the laws of the nation, state, or local government become an ethical ceiling or limit.[2] Ideally, however, it seems better to look at laws as a minimal foundation—a starting place—with which to identify ethical behavior. Take a look at the case used to open this chapter. Bob uses the idea that selling cigarette paper isn't illegal as a justification for his actions. How does this tie in with our discussion to this point?

Another place to look for guidance for ethical behavior is to ask the question, What does my employer expect? Sometimes instructions will be clearly

culture
The social setting in which people live, including the values, norms, and procedures to be utilized. The culture develops over a period of time as individuals and groups interact and experience personal and social change.

Ethical and unethical behavior is often learned from supervisors or coworkers.

spelled out by the employer and representatives of the employer. Sometimes the behavior of an employer reveals an ethical position. What a supervisor does in a decision situation will usually be used as a pattern of behavior by employees. (Look again at the case that opens this chapter. What kind of statement might Bob's actions be making? Is Kassie likely to follow Bob's lead?)

Often, employers clearly spell out their expectations through an organizational code of ethics. Codes of ethics sometimes begin with a statement of an organization's values. For example, the credo of one national bank—Security Pacific Corporation—shows the corporation's values in six areas—the corporation's commitment to customers, employees, shareholders, and the community as well as the employees' commitment to each other and to the corporation (see Table 1–2).[3]

Table 1–3 lists three main categories or clusters found in corporate codes of ethics.[4] Cluster 1 includes guidelines for being a good organizational citizen. Cluster 2 covers legal obligations of an organization and its members. Cluster 3 identifies responsibilities to customers. There is also a set of miscellaneous responsibilities labeled "unclustered items." Clearly, a **code of conduct**

code of conduct
A set of guidelines specifying how the members of a unit (organization, profession) should behave.

Table 1–2
The Credo of Security Pacific Corporation

Commitment to Customer

The first commitment is to provide our customers with quality products and services which are innovative and technologically responsive to their current requirements, at appropriate prices. To perform these tasks with integrity requires that we maintain confidentiality and protect customer privacy, promote customer satisfaction, and serve customer needs. We strive to serve qualified customers and industries which are socially responsible according to broadly accepted community and company standards.

Commitment to Employee

The second commitment is to establish an environment for our employees which promotes professional growth, encourages each person to achieve his or her highest potential, and promotes individual creativity and responsibility. Security Pacific acknowledges our responsibility to employees, including providing for open and honest communication, stated expectations, fair and timely assessment of performance and equitable compensation which rewards employee contributions to company objectives within a frame work of equal opportunity and affirmative action.

Commitment of Employee to Security Pacific

The third commitment is that of the employee to Security Pacific. As employees, we strive to understand and adhere to the Corporation's policies and objectives, act in a professional manner, and give our best effort to improve Security Pacific. We recognize the trust and confidence placed in us by our customers and community and act with integrity and honesty in all situations to preserve that trust and confidence. We act responsibly to avoid conflicts of interest and other situations which are potentially harmful to the Corporation.

including all of these items will provide guidelines for many types of action and behavior.

A code of ethics might also include directives for dealing with conflict of interest, confidentiality of corporate information, misappropriation of corporate assets, bribes, kickbacks, political contributions, insider trading, government contracts, testing, privacy, and industrial espionage.[5] A code might spell out penalties for violation of the guidelines. Penalties can include such actions as termination, suspension, probation, demotion, and oral reprimand.

Although not every company puts its codes of ethics into writing, it is usually advisable to do so. The need for written policy is especially urgent in companies without a strong tradition of ethical behavior to draw upon or where a new way of thinking needs to be established.[6] Training programs on ethics, particularly for the new employees of an organization, are becoming commonplace. After employees receive written codes of ethics and hear the codes discussed and illustrated, the employees sign statements indicating they have read, have understood, and are committed to abide by the standards established.

Table 1–2
continued

Commitment of Employee to Employee

The fourth commitment is that of employees to their fellow employees. We must be committed to promote a climate of mutual respect, integrity, and professional relationships, characterized by open and honest communication with and across all levels of the organization. Such a climate will promote attainment of the Corporation's goals and objectives, while leaving room for individual initiative within a competitive environment.

Commitment to Communities

The fifth commitment is that of Security Pacific to the communities which we serve. We must constantly strive to improve the quality of life through our support of community organizations and projects, through encouraging service to the community by employees, and by promoting participation in community services. By the appropriate use of our resources, we work to support or further advance the interest of the community, particularly in times of crisis or social need. The Corporation and its employees are committed to complying fully with each community's laws and regulations.

Commitment to Stockholder

The sixth commitment of Security Pacific is to its stockholders. We will strive to provide consistent growth and a superior rate of return on their investment, to maintain a position and reputation as a leading financial institution, to protect stockholder investments, and to provide full and timely information. Achievement of these goals for Security Pacific is dependent upon the successful development of the five previous sets of relationships.

Table 1–3

Clusters of Categories
Found in Corporate
Codes of Ethics

Cluster 1

"Be a dependable organization citizen."

1. Demonstrate courtesy, respect, honesty, and fairness in relationships with customers, suppliers, competitors, and other employees.
2. Comply with safety, health, and security regulations.
3. Do not use abusive language or actions.
4. Dress in businesslike attire.
5. Possession of firearms on company premises is prohibited.
6. Use of illegal drugs or alcohol on company premises is prohibited.
7. Follow directives from supervisors.
8. Be reliable in attendance and punctuality.
9. Manage personal finances in a manner consistent with employment by a fiduciary institution.

Cluster 2

"Don't do anything unlawful or improper that will harm the organization."

1. Maintain confidentiality of customer, employee, and corporate records and information.
2. Avoid outside activities which conflict with or impair the performance of duties.
3. Make decisions objectively without regard to friendship or personal gain.
4. The acceptance of any form of bribe is prohibited.
5. Payment to any person, business, political organization, or public official for unlawful or unauthorized purpose is prohibited.
6. Conduct personal and business dealings in compliance with all relevant laws, regulations, and policies.
7. Comply fully with antitrust laws and trade regulations.
8. Comply fully with accepted accounting rules and controls.
9. Do not provide false or misleading information to the corporation, its auditors, or a government agency.
10. Do not use company property or resources for personal benefit or any other improper purpose.
11. Each employee is personally accountable for company funds over which he or she has control.
12. Staff members should not have an interest in any competitor or supplier of the company unless such interest has been fully disclosed to the company.

Cluster 3

"Be good to our customers."

1. Exhibit standards of personal integrity and professional conduct.
2. Racial, ethnic, religious, or sexual harassment is prohibited.
3. Report questionable, unethical, or illegal activities to your manager.
4. Seek opportunities to participate in community services and political activities.
5. Conserve resources and protect the quality of the environment in areas where the company operates.
6. Members of the corporation are not to recommend attorneys, accountants, insurance agents, stockbrokers, real estate agents, or similar individuals to customers.

Source: Donald Robin, Michael Giallourakis, Fred David, and Thomas E. Moritz, "A Different Look at Codes of Ethics," *Business Horizons*, January–February 1989, Table 1, p. 68. Reprinted from *Business Horizons*, January–February 1989. Copyright 1989 by the Foundation for the School of Business at Indiana University. Used with permission.

Even when codes are carefully spelled out and communicated, interpretation and action based on the statements may vary. For example, employees in different age groups place differing priorities on abiding by the guidelines established. Older workers interpret ethics codes more stringently than do younger workers.[7] The size of the organization in which individuals work also seems to make a difference in acceptance and implementation of standards. People working in small organizations seem to be more strict in matters relating to faulty investment advice, favoritism in promotions, permitting dangerous design flaws, misleading financial reporting, misleading advertising, and defending the healthfulness of cigarette smoking. On the other hand, people working in larger organizations seem to act more demandingly on padded expense accounts, tax evasion, favoritism in bidding, insider trading, discrimination against women, and copying computer software. Individuals who are self-employed seem to hold values similar to employees in small organizations.[8]

Up to this point, we've looked for ethical behavior guidelines primarily by looking at laws and by looking at organizational codes of conduct (whether they are written, shown by example, or otherwise communicated). There are other very important sources of ethical values. Professional groups frequently have codes of conduct members are expected to abide by. Rotary International, a worldwide service and civic organization, has suggested a four-way test to determine the ethical thing to do. The four questions to ask are (1) Is it the truth? (2) Is it fair to all concerned? (3) Will it build goodwill and better friendships? (4) Will it be beneficial to all concerned? Each potential decision/action can be judged using these four criteria. The more positive the answers, the more ethical an action is judged to be.[9]

Family members, teachers, coaches, and friends play a part in teaching correct and incorrect behavior.

Institutions such as churches and schools teach ethical guidelines. Family influences may also be strong conveyers of codes of conduct. Some feel that ethical training from family, religion, and education have less impact today than in previous years.

Two-career families, television, and the virtual disappearance of the dinner table as a forum for discussing moral issues have clearly outmoded instruction in basic principles at Mother's knee—if that fabled tutorial was ever as effective as folklore would have it. We cannot expect our battered school systems to take over the moral role of the family. Even religion is less help than it once might have been when membership in a distinct community promoted—or coerced—conventional moral behavior. Society's increasing secularization, the profusion of sects, the conservative church's divergence from new life styles, pervasive distrust of the religious right—all these mean that we cannot depend on uniform religious instruction to armor business recruits against temptation.[10]

While simple, easily applicable ethical guidance may not always be available, usually there will be guidelines from one source or another. If there are no sources to draw upon, basic questions such as Which benefits the most people? will need to be used.

Social Responsibility

social responsibility
The obligations a specific unit—an organization, for example—is perceived to have to act beneficially for the community at large.

A part of being ethical is being socially responsible. Where does social responsibility fit in? **Social responsibility** is the fulfillment of obligations to the society that surrounds the organization. (See the obligations listed by Monsanto in the Insights feature.) Some have said that management is "responsible for balancing the interests of the various stakeholders of an organization—stockholders; employees; customers; suppliers; the government; local, regional, and international communities; and various interest groups." The organization's obligation is to promote the common or social good.[11]

Usually, doing socially responsible things is beneficial to the organization doing them as well as to the community at large. Look again at the opening case. Is the convenience store being socially responsible? Bob points out that the sale of the cigarette papers benefits the store, and Kassie believes it won't benefit the community. Who's right? Is Bob necessarily right that the store is benefited?

Utilitarianism Versus Duty

enlightened self-interest
The belief that if an organization acts in a socially responsible way, everyone, including the organization itself, will benefit. The greatest good for the greatest number of people will be achieved.

There are two views on why organizations should be socially responsible. One view is called **enlightened self-interest,** or utilitarianism. According to this perspective, socially responsible acts reap benefits for everyone, including the organization itself.

By providing consumers with safe products of desired quality, consumer loyalty will be generated; by providing workers with pleasant and safe working conditions, absenteeism will be reduced and produc-

Insights

The Monsanto Pledge
of Social Responsibility

St. Louis-based Monsanto, the nation's fourth largest chemical producer, has adopted the following pledge:

☐ Reduce all toxic releases, working toward a goal of zero.
☐ Ensure no Monsanto operation poses undue risk to employees and communities.
☐ Work to achieve sustainable agriculture through new technology and practices.
☐ Ensure groundwater safety—making our technical resources available to farmers dealing with contamination, even if our products are not involved.
☐ Keep our plants open to our communities, bringing the community into plant operations. Inform people of any significant hazard.
☐ Manage all corporate real estate to benefit nature.
☐ Search worldwide for technology to reduce and eliminate waste from our operations, with the top priority being not making it in the first place.

Source: "Company Performance Roundup," *Business and Society Review,* Number 73, Spring 1990, p. 66, used by permission.

tivity will be increased; by working to be a good corporate neighbor in the local community, the quality of life will be improved, making it easier to attract a high quality work force.[12]

According to utilitarianism, the greatest good is the action in which the goals of the greatest number of people are achieved. In the opening case, could an enlightened self-interest argument be developed to support Kassie's position?

The other view of why organizations should be socially responsible is **deontology,** or the duty approach. According to this perspective, being socially responsible is something that organizations and their members are morally obligated to do. Caring for and meeting the needs of others simply go with the territory. Check your own social concern level by taking the Moral Anxiety Questionnaire.

In the future, as change continues to occur, we expect to see organizations respond. Departments or agencies within an organization may be initiated to be socially beneficial, and may include units such as the public affairs office, the affirmative action department, the consumer affairs office, and the corporate **ombudsman** (an advocate for employees, customers, or others who have complaints and disagreements with managers or management's positions).

It is not always easy to identify what is ethical and what is socially responsible. Preoccupation with personal gain may get in the way. It might be keeping up with competition, increasing the share of the market, or maximizing profits that overshadows social responsibility. Sometimes the feeling that

deontology
The view that social responsibility is a duty—an obligation to be fulfilled.

ombudsman
An individual who listens to the needs and complaints of employees (or other groups and individuals) and represents the employees or groups to management.

Self Test

Personal Feedback

Moral Anxiety Questionnaire

Read the statements below and decide whether each is true (T) or false (F) for you. Try not to spend too long thinking about any of the statements. Mark your answer in the appropriate space for each one.

_____ **1.** I sometimes worry that I may not be living up to the ethical standards I have set for myself.

_____ **2.** I have a tendency to worry about not following the teachings of my religion as closely as I should.

_____ **3.** I have a tendency to worry about having disappointed other people.

_____ **4.** I sometimes worry that I may be receiving special privileges that are denied to others.

_____ **5.** I sometimes worry about being more fortunate than someone else.

_____ **6.** I have a tendency to worry that I may do things which are inconsiderate of other people's feelings.

_____ **7.** I sometimes worry that I may be too selfish or self-centered.

_____ **8.** I sometimes worry about not always giving my help when it's asked for.

_____ **9.** I sometimes worry that I may be taking advantage of someone else.

_____ **10.** I sometimes worry that I may not be very cooperative.

_____ **11.** I have a tendency to worry about things I have done in the past.

_____ **12.** I sometimes worry that I may not do enough for others who are less fortunate than myself.

_____ **13.** I have a tendency to worry about breaking a promise to someone.

_____ **14.** I sometimes worry about having hostile feelings toward someone else.

_____ **15.** I sometimes worry about being too concerned with money or personal possessions.

☐ Total Score

Scoring the Questionnaire

Your score for the Moral Anxiety Questionnaire is the total number of times that you answered "true" for these statements. Place that number in the box labeled "Total Score." Your score on this questionnaire can range from 0 to 15.

It would seem that some worry about doing the morally correct thing should be helpful. That is, intention to do the right thing in a situation should help facilitate actually doing the right thing. A very low score on the moral anxiety scale (a score of 4 or less) may suggest an indifference to the needs of others, a kind of egoism and independence from concern about fellow human beings. A very high level of moral anxiety, on the other hand, may suggest too much concern for morally correct behavior to the point that inability to relax and enjoy life may result. A score of 10 or above would indicate high moral anxiety. Scores from 5 to 9 suggest a reasonable balance of independent motivation and socially responsible behavior.

Source: Adapted from Lawrence R. Good and Katherine C. Good, "Moral Anxiety Questionnaire," 1976.

bosses want results more than ethical action pressures employees toward less responsible actions. Sometimes a lack of reinforcement for doing the "right thing" discourages employees.

Not everyone agrees that an organization has much social responsibility. Some argue that:

1. Pursuing corporate social-responsibility policies reduces profits, the main purpose of a business.
2. Businesses aren't equipped to handle social activities.
3. Businesses already have enough power; they shouldn't be given social power.
4. The concept of corporate social responsibility would endanger businesses' international balance of payments by placing American business in a weak position when compared to foreign competition.[13]

These views appear to be a minority position, but, as we saw in the opening case, some managers hold to them—and that can present a problem to employees like Kassie who hold a broader view of social responsibility.

A real-life example of disagreement concerning how far to go in showing social responsibility is the plight of two restaurant employees who were fired for refusing to serve alcohol to a pregnant woman. News stories had just emphasized that a pregnant woman who drinks alcohol may harm the fetus she is carrying. The two employees felt it was their social responsibility to protect the unborn fetus even if the mother disagreed.

Changes at McDonald's

Management in Action

Stung by criticism that its Big Macs, thick milkshakes, and French fries were contributing to the "poisoning of America" because of their cholesterol and fat content, McDonald's is changing some of its food preparation. It's trying out an all-vegetable oil to replace the oil-and-beef-tallow mix now used to cook French fries, and it will use a new low-fat mix for its milkshakes. Claiming "a long history of responding to customers' concerns about nutrition," McDonald's noted that since 1986 it has been using a cholesterol-free shortening to cook its chicken, fish, and fruit pies and that it recently removed the chicken skin from Chicken McNuggets. Spokesperson Richard Starmann added: "Years ago we went to 2 percent low-fat milk and skim milk. We don't even serve whole milk anymore."

Source: "Company Performance Roundup," *Business and Society Review*, Number 73, Spring 1990, p. 65, used by permission.

In the future, ethical and social responsibilities will represent a major challenge to all managers and employees. Meaningful organizational direction in areas of ethics can only be attained through effort and perseverance.

Summary

The basic unit of human behavior in the workplace is the individual employee. When the employee goes to work for an organization, an agreement occurs (sometimes the agreement is subconscious commitment). The employee agrees to provide certain knowledge, skills, energy, and abilities in return for salaries, wages, benefits, and other rewards. As a result of this exchange, both employee and organizational needs are met. The needs of individuals and the methods used by organizations may change some through the years, but the same general contract continues.

One of the chief organizational issues lies in the area of ethics and social responsibility. Organizations usually want to do the things that are right (or socially acceptable) in the culture in which they exist. Being ethical simply means doing what society believes is right. Sometimes, what is "right" and what is "wrong" are easy to determine because there are specific laws and regulations pointing the way. Most of the time, however, what is right and what is wrong requires further study. Supervisors and employees have to consider inputs from a number of sources (bosses, family members, and industry practices, to name a few) to determine what the ethical way is. Normally, an organization that develops a code of ethics for its employees will provide a meaningful source of direction for the workers.

It is normally assumed that an organization has obligations for its employees, shareholders, customers, suppliers, the government, local, regional, and international communities, and other interest groups. Social responsibility is doing the things that will benefit each of these publics to promote the common good. As mentioned earlier, there are differences of opinion on how far social responsibilities should go.

Section I begins our journey into the management of behavior in the workplace with a look at the culture of the organization and its components.

Questions to Consider

1. Why do you think that many people have a low opinion of how ethical and socially responsible industry and businesses have been in the past? What is the general opinion about today's organizations?
2. Do you believe that people expect more social responsibility of organizations today than ever before?
3. Are there places other than those identified in the chapter to seek help in deciding ethical and social responsibilities?
4. What impact do professional codes of ethics have upon the professional for whom they are designed? Do people actually try to live by them? What about company codes—do employees abide by them?

5. Are the institutions of the family, religion, and education ineffective in teaching ethical responsibilities?

Key Terms

code of conduct	enlightened self-interest	ombudsman
culture	ethical behavior	social responsibility
deontology	ethics	

Chapter Case

Decisions, Decisions!

"Nobody ever told me things would be this complicated once I graduated and got out in the 'real world'," sighed Tony Gonzales as he pondered a problem that was on his mind more and more. "I've never thought of myself as a real straight-laced character. Live and let live has been my motto—keep your nose clean and keep out of trouble, that's the way I've always believed in handling things. And certainly I've not tried to play up to the boss or anything like that," thought Gonzales, continuing his interior dialogue, "but certain things get to me. What do you do in a no-win situation?"

In many ways, Gonzales's assessment that he was in a no-win situation was an accurate one. To begin with, the job was a great one—but only in terms of future prospects. Marschand Inc., the company Gonzales had joined after graduation, had a firm policy that *everyone* was to start at the bottom and work up. The philosophy at Marschand was that higher level people would be far more effective if they'd spent some time "in the trenches" and knew the business from the ground floor up. Gonzales had to admit that he really agreed with the policy in most respects.

Since Gonzales's career goal was in finance, that meant starting out as a clerk in the bookkeeping department, which had several other clerks like Gonzales who were assigned to assist the higher level employees—the records administrators and the senior accountants. The senior accountants especially were entrusted with a lot of authority and worked independently for the most part, with only an occasional oversight by Sharon Oldham, the department supervisor. Oldham herself seemed to be a hardworking, concerned supervisor who was simply too overloaded to give anyone in the department a lot of close attention. Although Gonzales had talked briefly to her several times, he didn't feel he knew her well at all.

That was part of the problem—"Whom to turn to? Whom to trust?" These were the thoughts that kept running around in Gonzales's mind, because Gonzales was pretty sure he'd uncovered a nasty problem. While helping John Wixmire, one of the senior accountants, he'd noticed that Wixmire seemed awfully nervous and kept trying to cover up some of the papers he was working on. It was payroll day, and Wixmire was drawing up the time sheets to pay the employees. Gonzales had been trying to ignore Wixmire's strange behavior, but as Wixmire turned in his seat to give some instructions, he swept some of the stack of payroll sheets he was working on to the floor. As Gonzales, mostly out of habit, picked the papers up, he glanced down and saw a new name—William Bennis—on the top sheet.

"No one by that name even works here," wondered Gonzales. "What's Wixmire paying him for?"

Wixmire could tell that Gonzales had seen his surprise and glared at him, "Look, kid, I'm going to give you some good advice. Just forget what you saw. I'm one of the guys who decides whether you move up or out around here!" Gonzales murmured something and moved quickly away.

That was yesterday. Gonzales had tried discreetly to find out if any of the other clerks had noticed anything funny about Wixmire and his recordkeeping. No one had. Technically, he didn't report to Wixmire. He reported to Sharon Oldham. But he didn't know her well. What if he was wrong? He didn't know any of the other analysts or accountants any better.

"What to do, that's the question," he sighed.

1. What should Tony Gonzales do? Give your reasons.
2. What are the pros and cons of any decision Gonzales may make?

Section I

The Climate in Which People Work

2. Organizational Culture and Informal Organization

3. What Good Are Groups, Anyway?

4. Technology—Its Impact in the Work Place

5. The Physical Surroundings of the Work Place

Chapter

2

Organizational Culture and Informal Organizations

Objectives

- To define an organization's culture and its purpose.
- To compare productive cultures with destructive cultures.
- To recognize the effects of the organization's culture on the actions of individuals and groups.
- To discover the inputs of the formal structure
- To learn to identify the informal organization and its role within the organization's culture.
- To learn the manager's role, opportunities, and obligations toward the culture, the formal structure, and the informal organization.

The Three Night Custodians

Edwin Armitage is superintendent of maintenance and sanitation at Audio Electronics Corporation, which manufactures and distributes electronic and sound equipment for a variety of functions. In his duties as superintendent, Armitage supervises the maintenance and repair of mechanical equipment involved in the production process and oversees janitorial and custodial work. The production shift at Audio runs from 8:00 A.M. to 4:30 P.M., five days a week. All of the maintenance and repair people work the day shift (except in emergencies) and are in constant contact with Armitage. They also perform limited cleanup work whenever their workload permits.

Three night custodians work from 4:30 P.M. to 12:30 A.M. They work independently; each one is responsible for cleaning one of the three production buildings. Armitage speaks with them briefly at the beginning of their shift and then departs for his home. He does not see them again until the next afternoon as they return to work. The custodians have been instructed to call the security guard with any serious problems, and aside from this the custodians work without any immediate supervision.

In recent weeks, Armitage has begun receiving complaints about poor janitorial performance. Most of the complaints have come from workers arriving to begin their day's work. Floors have been left unswept, glass coverings have been left grimy, and other custodial duties have been ignored. More complaints are coming in. In addition, Armitage has received word from supervisors who have been working after hours that the night custodians are spending a large amount of time together drinking coffee instead of working. One supervisor told Armitage that he knew of at least two hours spent by the custodians one night in which they "drank coffee, ate sandwiches, and laughed a lot." Rumors have also gotten back to Armitage that the workers may be napping on the job in the late evenings when no one else is around.

Occasionally in the early evenings Armitage has begun dropping in on the custodians. On each evening when he has visited the custodians, they have each been busily working in their own separate buildings, and everything has appeared quite normal. When he asks them about the reason for failing to do parts of their job, they have said that they need more help because there is too much work for them to do.

As Armitage arrived for work this morning, he was met by one of the production supervisors, who wanted to talk to him. The supervisor said:

Edwin, I think there's something you should know. You remember when you came out to the plant last Thursday night to talk with the custodians? I was working late that night and I couldn't help noticing what happened before you got there. At first the three custodians were all loafing around in the building, drinking coffee and gabbing. They got a call from someone, and I suspect it was the security guard at the gate. He must have told them you were coming, because two of them started running like crazy toward their own buildings, and the custodian assigned to our building sure got busy in a hurry. By the time you got to where they work, the custodians all appeared to be very busy. I think they are trying to put something over on you.

Case Questions

1. What type of work relationship appears to be developing among the night custodians?
2. What role does the night security guard appear to be serving for the work group?
3. Are there any explanations for the development of the informal work group? If so, what are the possible explanations?
4. What approach should Edwin Armitage take in dealing with the night custodians and security guard? Is there a way in which the informal ties can be used to the company's advantage?

The way an organization is designed to function and the way it actually functions are two different things. Within the boundaries of every formal organization is that organization's own unique culture and the informal groups that play a big part in determining how the organization actually operates.

The Culture of the Organization

When you first hear people talking about *organizational cultures,* you're likely to think that they're talking about an abstract concept. You might think of culture simply as something that anthropologists study when they visit exotic places and analyze the native people's behavior. What does culture have to do with the realities of life in an organization?

As soon as you've worked for a couple of different organizations, you'll quickly learn the enormous difference culture makes. Take the experience of Bill, a student at a community college in a large Southern city. Like many students, Bill works to pay his expenses while continuing his education. He had been working nights for the past year or so at a small, family-owned video store and going to school during the day. Recently, a new video store, part of a larger chain, opened closer to his home, and Bill resigned from his job at the small operation and went to work for the new, larger video store.

"Let me tell you, that was the biggest mistake I ever made," Bill remarked recently. "In the first store we felt like part of the family. There was a feeling of trust. Oftentimes the night manager would go out of town and leave the employees to handle things. As for scheduling, we'd get a basic schedule, but if anybody needed a change, they'd let us work it out. We felt like management respected us—they treated us like we had brains, not like children. We liked and trusted each other, too. I knew if I got behind I could count on the others to help me out. It was a real team effort! I hated leaving, but the new place was only five minutes from my house—and I figured video stores are all alike. WRONG! The new place has this dog-eat-dog atmosphere. Management is on us every minute. And to get in good with management, the employees report on each other. They'd die before they'd lift a finger to help anyone else. If I get behind, they report me to the boss. They hardly speak to each other, much less socialize. I'd go back to my first job in a minute, but they've already filled my slot. So it looks like all I can do is kick myself for making a terrible decision!"

One thing Bill's experience points out is that organization culture is real, and it really makes a difference. Organizations with strong, positive cultures can be great places to work, while those with negative cultures can be pretty grim. Most of the time, it's hard to get a feel for an organization's culture from the outside, such as when applying for a job. We will be discussing several aspects of culture that will be of importance to you in understanding **roles** and relationships of managers and employees. As Bill's experience points out, it's important to be sensitive to organization culture and to spot signs of problems when looking at an organization from the outside—as a job applicant, for example. Furthermore, if you serve as a manager, you'll find that you have responsibilities for shaping the culture through your own actions and through the way you deal with your authority as well as with the informal groups that make up the organization. This chapter deals with all of these aspects.

> **roles**
> A pattern of behavior expected of an individual.

Characteristics of an Organization's Culture

An organization's culture consists of values, norms, and attitudes of the people who make up the organization. Values show what's important. **Norms** reveal expected behavior. Attitudes show the mindset of individuals. The group selects symbols, slogans, and ceremonies to convey its values. Thus, the culture tells people what's important in the organization, how to behave, and how to perceive things.

> **norms**
> Standards of behavior to which group members are expected to conform.

At the beginning of a completely new organization, the formal structure, goals, and procedures may dictate the culture. What the organization and its founding bosses want may be pretty much the same thing that their employees want. As time goes on, however, the official values and patterns and the actual ones of the people in the organization tend to drift further and further apart. Someone has said that "left unattended, a company's culture almost always becomes dysfunctional."[1] In other words, the original ideals and the practiced behaviors frequently become separated to the point of becoming destructive. That's why it can be exciting and fun to be part of a newly forming organization. You can take part in forming its culture. Once an organization has been around for a while, cynicism and distrust may take over unless management actually takes part in managing the culture.

An organization's culture usually contains several characteristics, including the following:

Individual autonomy—the degree of responsibility, independence, and opportunities for exercising initiative that individuals in an organization have. (Bill's experience points out how differently autonomy can be handled in different organizations.)

Structure—the degree of rules and regulations and the amount of direct supervision that is used to oversee and control behavior. (Again, Bill's experience shows how different the number and the kind of rules and the amount of supervision can be, even in supposedly similar firms.)

Support—the degree of assistance and warmth managers provide for their subordinates. (Notice the difference in trust that Bill found in the two organizations.)

Identity—the degree to which members identify with the organization as a whole rather than with their particular work group or field of professional expertise. (In the first organization, Bill felt like part of the family. What about the second?)

Performance-reward—the degree to which rewards in the organization (salary increases and promotions) are based on employee work performance. (Notice that in the second organization, gaining favor with management came from informing on others.)

Conflict tolerance—the degree of conflict present in relationships between peers and work groups as well as the willingness to be honest and open about differences. (The key here is Bill's comment that management in the first organization would "let us work it out.")

Risk tolerance—the degree to which employees are encouraged to take chances. (This also deals with whether mistakes are punished or treated as learning experiences. How would you rate Bill's second organization in this area?)

Attitude toward change—the response given to new methods, ways, and values.

Focus—the vision of the goals and objectives of an organization's operations as communicated by those in control.

Standards and values—the levels of performance and behavior considered to be acceptable by formal and informal criteria.

Rituals—expressive events that support and reinforce organizational standards and values.

Concern for people—the degree of care and concern the organization shows for its employees, its management teams, its shareholders.

Openness, communication, and supervision—the amount and type of interchange permitted. The communication flow can be downward, upward, across the organization, and in other directions as spelled out by the culture.

Market and customer orientation—the extent to which the organization is responsive to its markets and customers.

Excitement, pride, and esprit de corps—a tangibly good feeling about the organization and its activities.

Commitment—the willingness of individuals to work toward goals on a continuing basis.

Teamwork—people working together for the common good.[2]

As you can see by quickly reviewing the above list, some of the cultural factors are spelled out by an organizational decree. Such factors as defined boss-employee relationships, job descriptions, and required performance reviews provide the bases for some of an organization's culture. Many of the factors, however, are determined by groups and individuals as they interact

The values and norms of a culture are passed from one person to another.

with one another on a day-to-day basis. As a manager, you will have some control over the formal aspects of the organization. Perhaps even more important, you can also influence a number of informal aspects. Let's look at how this can be done.

An Ideal Organization Culture

A starting point, of course, is knowing what an organization's culture is supposed to look like. If the ideas of Robbins and Kilmann (see notes 1 and 2) are pooled with the idealistic writings of Rensis Likert[3] (see Chapter 10), a perfected culture might develop. We could propose that an ideal culture for the accomplishment of an organization's goals might be one in which

- ☐ The organization's goals are established and reviewed periodically through the participation of all individuals and groups in the organization.
- ☐ Decisions are made at the appropriate level in the organization by the people who must live with the decision.
- ☐ Behavior is supportive of the organization's goals and purposes.
- ☐ The organization is supportive of the needs of individual employees.
- ☐ Individuals and groups show high levels of trust and respect for other individuals and groups.
- ☐ Superiors and subordinates have a high level of trust and confidence in each other.
- ☐ Cooperation and teamwork exist at all levels in the organization.
- ☐ Methods of reinforcement used are primarily rewards and participation.
- ☐ Individuals are cost conscious.
- ☐ Messages move upward, downward, or across the organization as needed to get information to the appropriate places.

- ☐ Downward communication is accepted with an open mind by subordinates.
- ☐ Upward communication is accurate and is received with an open mind.
- ☐ Changes are initiated to improve performance and goal attainment.
- ☐ Changes are received and accepted openly.
- ☐ Individuals speak with pride about themselves and their employer.
- ☐ The time individuals spend performing tasks is related to the contributions of the tasks toward the achievement of the organization's goals.
- ☐ Individuals are motivated through enjoyment from achieving the organization's goals.
- ☐ Conflict is seen not as a destructive force but as a potentially constructive activity.
- ☐ Where risks are necessary, endangered individuals and groups are given support.

Cultural Realities

The preceding ideals sound wonderful, don't they? Organizational realities, however, are often quite different. That's because the underlying premise in the ideal culture is that the formal organization's norms and values are to be consistent with those of the various individuals and groups within the organization. Often, however, the norms and values of individuals and groups to which they belong are antagonistic to formal goals. Also, the organization may not value the potential contributions of its workers. When this happens, the culture begins to send faulty "messages" to organization members. It's not unusual to see and hear some of the following guidelines. "Never disagree with the boss." "Never rock the boat." "Treat women as second-class citizens." "Put down (rather than speak favorably of) the organization (employer)." "Do not enjoy the work being done." "Do not share information with other groups." "Treat those you supervise as if they are lazy or incompetent." "Cheating on expense accounts is acceptable." "Look busy even when not." "Do not reward employees on the basis of merit." "Laugh at those who suggest new ways of doing things." "Do not smile much." "Openly criticize company policies to outsiders." "Complain a lot." "Do not trust anyone who seems sincere." "Do not be too explicit in establishing norms."[4,5]

It's evident that the attitudes and norms of the organization's culture can become very counterproductive. The basis of confidence and cooperation can be quickly undermined. One of the manager's most important (and most difficult) functions can be to bridge the gap between constructive needs of an organization and the informal, sometimes different norms that organizational members may establish. How can this be done?

The Manager's Role in the Organization's Culture

Much attention has recently been given to the manager's role in actively developing the organization's culture. This means that managers cannot afford to take a passive role and let culture develop naturally, since all too often this results in the negative messages listed above.

In managing a culture, the manager needs to do several things. He or she must first let employees know what's valued and then reward performance that supports organization values. Suppose, for example, that management decides that customer service is to be top priority. If you're a manager, you need to communicate this to your employees and let them know what's expected of them. If you expect them to take extra time explaining how a product works, tell them so. Reward your employees with praise or bonuses when they do what's expected of them. Do not send contradictory messages, such as telling them to take extra time with customers and then rewarding those who take shortcuts to get the job done quickly. People do what they're rewarded for—not what we "hope" they'll do.

Additional Sources of an Organization's Cultural Information

The stories we tell, the heroes we choose, and the actions we take can also provide powerful messages about what the organization values. During the late 1960s, nearly every telephone company plant office had a picture of a lineman at work during a howling blizzard. Virtually every employee knew that the man's name was Angus McDonald and that McDonald had almost singlehandedly kept the lines open during a severe storm. The stories and the picture served as a vivid reminder to employees of what was expected of them.

Not only can stories and pictures show employees what's expected, but managerial actions can also provide dramatic evidence. The old adage that actions speak louder than words contains an enormous amount of truth. In the early days of Marriott Corporation, J. W. Marriott, the founder, came into one of the firm's food service operations one day and found things in a real mess. The floor was dirty, and there were delays as the cooks tried to get food to the waiters and waitresses. Instead of giving the staff a dressing down, Marriott rolled up his sleeves and pitched in, cleaning the floor and then helping to get the food moving. As you might expect, the employees talked of little else for weeks afterwards. J. W. Marriott's actions had given a vivid message about his priorities.

Coworkers are another source of cultural information for employees. They are in touch with each other a significant part of each working day, and they tend to know the importance of cultural values. Because there is day-to-day contact between workers, frequent interactions influence their colleagues' perceptions significantly. Bosses also pass along cultural information through the communication of rules, regulations, and other managerial expectations. Customers and clients, through their own perceptions during their contact with employees, may further reinforce information about an organization's culture. Even an employee's friends and family can have input that shapes the employee's view of the culture in which he or she works.[6]

How Organization Structure Influences Culture

What about management's role in culture? Much of the responsibility for shaping organization culture rests with management, which can influence culture in two primary ways—through the formal structuring of the organization and through informal means. Let's look first at formal structures and how they can

Management in Action

Overcoming a Faulty Culture

People and events make up a major part of an organization's culture. Past events and the people who participate in them continue to affect the organization's culture for years. Changing a culture based upon past happenings and people may be a difficult task. A top Fortune 500 manufacturer had a history of poor quality, hostile labor relations, and terrible productivity. The company, with a desire to improve all of the aspects, hired a consultant to help them resolve the problems and develop a new, more achieving kind of climate.

The consultant began work by talking with the employees. They eagerly told him about Sam, the plant manager who was a 300-pound gorilla with a disposition that made King Kong look like Bonzo the chimp. One time Sam examined a transmission and smashed it to pieces. A worker summoned to Sam's office threw up on the way. Another time Sam drove his car into the plant, got up on the roof, and started screaming at his workers. One worker, fed up, poured a line of gasoline to the car and lit it.

The consultant, after hearing the stories about Sam, was stunned and made an appointment to see the plant manager. When he walked into the office he saw a slim, pleasant-looking man behind the desk. The plant manager's name was Paul. "Where's Sam?" asked the consultant. Paul, looking puzzled, replied, "Sam has been dead for nine years."

At this point, the consultant realized that the problem of improving performance and changing the employees attitudes and perceptions would be difficult. Paul, in trying to instill a sense of fairness and participation, was fighting against a strong history of abuse and autocracy established by Sam and others like him.

To deal with the past-history problem, Paul and his eight supervisors sat down with groups of eight to ten assembly workers to discuss Sam and the plant's history. In addition, Paul tried very hard to avoid doing things the way Sam would have done them. He sometimes could not anticipate how his actions would remind others of the culture Sam had established. Once, for example, he abruptly pointed at a worker, commanding him to throw away a coffee cup left near a machine. The workers on the floor, mindful of the hateful Sam, thought something like "Ah, he's just like Sam. He's a materialistic tyrant who likes spit and polish." It would have been better for Paul to have tossed the cup away himself—a small gesture, yet that and a thousand other subtle messages would help transform the culture to a more supportive participative climate.

It took four years for Paul to successfully transform the culture.

Source: Brian Dumaine, "Creating a New Culture," *Fortune*, Volume 122, Number 2, January 15, 1990, pp. 127–128, 130, 131.

influence culture. We say that organization structure traditionally deals with authority relationships and the level of centralization/decentralization.

Authority Relationships

The ultimate source of authority has traditionally been the top of the organizational structure (the board of directors, the owners, the general manager, or whoever may be at the highest level). The highest manager has a group of employees accountable directly to him or her; the employees have their own charges; and so the hierarchy goes until the lowest level in the organization is reached.

A look at a formal organization structure and some of the informal groupings active within it may help to understand how authority operates. The formal organization chart for the United Manufacturing Company shown in Figure 2–1 is a partial chart designed to show the formal location of office and secretarial personnel within the total structure. Only the formal channels connecting the office managers and secretaries with the lines of authority and communication are shown in the chart.

As can be seen in the formal structure, the company general manager has his or her own private secretary (Secretary I). However, in the departments of sales and marketing, accounting services, and personnel, a secretarial pool has been created in each department to serve all managers and supervisors working in these departments. The formal chain of command and **authority relationships** are clearly defined in the chart.

A key management principle—the unity-of-command concept—states that every employee should have only one boss to whom he or she is accountable

authority relationships
The situation in which an individual has the right to give orders and instructions to another individual and can expect the orders to be followed.

Figure 2–1   Location of Office and Secretarial Personnel in the Formal Organization Structure

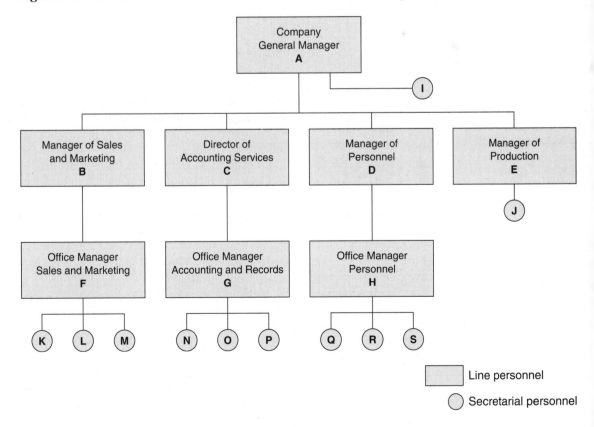

and through whom orders and directions should flow. Guidance and control bonds are strong when this principle is adhered to.

Can top management give orders to the people who work several layers (levels) below them? A traditionalist would say that upper-level managers influence the people who work for their lower-level supervisors, but they must do it through the chain of command. For example, they could tell the department heads what they want done and then have the department heads give the orders to their employees. The result is the same—the employees get the orders. From the traditional view, however, confusion is eliminated because employees get orders from only one person—their immediate supervisor.

The horizontal structure identifies peers, colleagues, or fellow workers across the organization. Individuals located on the same horizontal level normally have no authority over each other, and they tend to be about equal in terms of the amount of formal influence that they have. A key question that arises from a study of authority relationships concerns how closely management adheres to the traditional view. Is the chain of command followed without exception or is there a degree of flexibility for individual initiative? Management's decisions about how to handle the chain of command send important signals about the culture. Is it "We go by the book around here" or "We're a team, and each member has a say?" Glance back at Bill's experience in the two video stores. How does each store handle authority?

Communication Channels

Traditionally the path for communication coincides with the formal lines of authority. Messages downward must flow from superior to subordinate until the lowest level needing the information has received it. By the same token, messages moving upward go from employee to supervisor until the highest level on the ladder needing notification has been touched. Obviously, there's a lot of opportunity for messages to get lost or distorted in the traditional communication process. It's not unusual to hear employees complain about the slowness of the system. Traditionalists agree, however, that what's lost in timeliness is gained in order and lack of confusion. The same ideas apply to communication between peers or others at basically the same level. Again, the process may be cumbersome. Messages are expected to go to the immediate superior and then downward again.

communication channel
The path through which messages are expected to pass within an organization.

From the standpoint of organization culture, the issue is whether flexibility exists in the way the formal **communication channel** is used. The chapter opening case illustrates pretty clearly the possibilities. A lot of communication is going on, but NOT through formal channels. Notice, for example, that Armitage gets a tip-off from one of the production supervisors—a peer-level manager—as to what's going on at night. If the traditional view had been followed, the production supervisor would have reported the incident up the chain of command until Armitage's boss was notified. The boss would then have discussed the problem with Armitage. Instead, in our case, the supervisor took a short cut and talked to Armitage directly. We're guessing that the culture in this organization encourages such "nonhierarchical" communication.

The Span of Supervision

Another concept important to the traditional scheme is the **span of supervision,** consisting of the number of individuals who report directly to a specific superior. Each supervisor is accountable for the actions of the employees within his or her span of supervision. The number of people supervised is important in that it determines the amount of attention, the type of attention, the ease of communication, and the methods for decision making that supervisors will use with their employees. Look again at the chapter opening case. Armitage may have problems simply because he's stretched too thin. Perhaps the night custodians need more direct supervision. In any case, the tightness or looseness of supervision sends messages to employees about what management expects of them. Tight supervision expects more exact performance, while loose supervision provides more freedom and flexibility.

span of supervision
The number of people who are directly accountable to an individual supervisor or manager.

Specialization

Specialization of job assignments is another consideration from the traditional perspective. **Specialization** occurs when individuals are given assignments that are concentrated requiring a specific set of skills and knowledge. In the highly specialized job, the individual performs a limited number of tasks, often somewhat repetitively. High specialization involves limited task variety and may result in reduced task identities. Task identity is the completion of whole tasks rather than just parts of a task. A highly specialized person on the automobile assembly line might work on door handles all day long, where a less specialized person might assemble an entire door. In the chapter opening case, the night custodians are much more specialized than the day workers who perform custodial work and maintenance.

specialization
The structuring of a job that results in an individual's doing a small number of tasks repetitively. Only a limited number of skills are required. Training is simplified as a result of the use of this procedure.

Wherever job specialization occurs, workers tend to develop higher levels of expertise in a more limited number of categories. Efficiency and economy may be gained through specialization. Recent trends have suggested, however, that it is possible to specialize too much, so that skill development may be too restricted and activities can lack proper coordination. Employees may develop tunnel vision and show more concern for their specialized area than for overall organization goals. Notice again the cultural differences that may come about in highly specialized versus unspecialized organizations.

Centralization or Decentralization for Decision Making

Another issue addressed by organizational structure relates to the level in organizations at which decisions are made. In a centralized organization, authority for decisions and other activities tends to be held by a few people—usually individuals located at the top. Decentralization results when authority for decision making and other activities is pushed to lower levels in the organization. Once again, management communicates important messages for the organization's culture when deciding how centralized or decentralized the organization should be.

Informal Groups and Organizations

As already noted, every organization has formal communication patterns that result from the organization's structure. However, in addition to that which is formalized comes the culture that is composed of the general perceptions workers have of the acceptable behavior patterns and norms of the organization. Within the generalized culture of an organization, small groups of workers develop their own subcultures, their own set of goals, and their own set of behavior norms. These subcultures or supplementary groupings of individuals within the more formal structure of an organization are often called informal groups or **informal work organizations.** An informal group simply is an unprescribed affiliation of individuals whose relationships are not bound by formal authority. The purpose of the informal group is to pursue the fulfillment of goals valuable to the group and its members even if the values are contrary to those of the formal structure.[7] These informal relationships develop spontaneously and are initiated by the workers themselves.

When we talked about authority relationships, we looked at how an organization's chart specifies reporting relationships. Look again at Figure 2–1. The formal organization chart does not recognize or indicate the existence of a number of informal groups that interact within the context of the formal structure. In many cases, the social ties, loyalties, communication systems, and behavior norms of the informal groups appear to be more influential than those of the formal structure. The visible informal groups that exist on a fairly continuous basis are identified in Figure 2–2.

informal work organizations
The unplanned groups that develop spontaneously as workers interact. Sets of relationships not bound by formal authority that provide important support and fulfillment of needs for members.

Figure 2–2   Informal Organizational Relationships Among Office and Secretarial Personnel

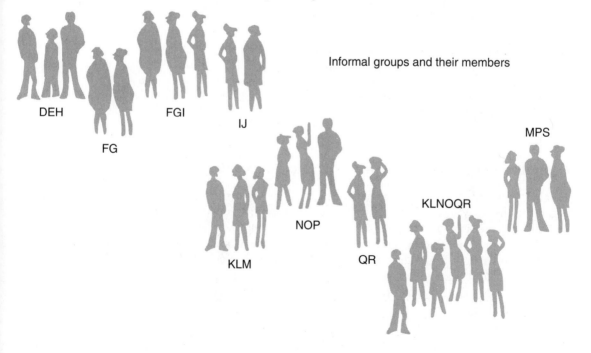

Informal groups and their members

DEH   FGI   IJ   MPS

FG   NOP   KLNOQR

KLM   QR

The list of informal groups includes only those groups of which office and secretarial personnel are a part. The following brief explanation of the content of each of the groupings attempts to provide some rationale for associations and ties that have developed.

The group including D, E, and H. D (Personnel Manager) and E (Production Manager) normally might not include someone of lower organizational status and responsibility in their informal associations. However, Office Manager H happens to be the only male office manager in the company. He works regularly with the personnel and production managers on a number of projects. He is included in their informal group because of his social acceptability as well as the frequency of his contact with the other two men.

The FG group. These two female office managers have many common interests and problems. They seem to need mutual support in dealing with the problems in their own departments. Office Manager H would be acceptable for membership in their group, but he has shown little interest in affiliating with them since he is a member of the DEH group.

The FGI group. This group is composed of the two women office managers and the general manager's executive secretary. The group is a high-status "club" as a result of the fact that two of its members are the only women managers in the company and the other member is strategically located immediately beneath the top-level boss as his chief assistant. These women have both on-the-job and off-the-job interests in common.

The IJ group. These people are the only secretaries who work directly for only one boss. They perform a wider range of duties for their superiors than do the people working in the secretarial pools. They enjoy more freedom than do the other secretaries. They often exchange work when one is rushed and the other has little to do.

The KLM, NOP, and QR groups. These groups have been formed in the respective secretarial pools because the members are together constantly, share many common interests, and perform related duties. The people in these groups are at the bottom of the authority hierarchy. Secretary S is not included in the informal group with Q and R because she is an individualist who seems to prefer her own privacy over affiliation with the group. She is considerably older than Q and R and has a set of personal values that do not concur with those of the other secretaries. The people in the secretarial pools do not include their bosses in their informal ties, because they are somewhat skeptical of their bosses' authority. They are not convinced that the office managers continually act in their best interests.

The KLNOQR group. The secretaries who compose this group come from the secretarial pools, share many common interests, and take their coffee break at the same time together each day. Their informal group not only is active in the company cafeteria but also spends time on the phone chatting with each other during work hours.

The MPS group. The workers in this group stay in their work departments while the others are out to coffee, then go to coffee together when the other secretaries have returned. Like the KLNOQR group, they share common interests, responsibilities, and coffee breaks. Secretary S, who is normally a loner, does participate in this informal group in a moderate way.

The grapevine is one of the best ways to spread messages. Only important messages are passed through the grapevine.

Functions of Informal Organizations

The informal organization exists to fulfill specific needs of the group and its members. It is the informal organization that many employees turn to for social affiliation and support.[8] The informal organization frequently is seen as a source of protection against threatening, oppressive forces. It was this desire for protection during World War II that caused soldiers under heavy attack to "bunch up" and get close to each other even though the togetherness actually increased the danger to each individual.[9] The point is, people are attracted to each other, especially under pressure. In the work organization, for example, members might bind themselves together to protect against the dangerously autocratic boss.[10]

grapevine
The informal communication network through which information is spread.

The informal organization through its **grapevine** is looked to for useful information and knowledge. A large percentage of the day-to-day communication received by most workers is from the grapevine. The grapevine is the informal communication network that knows no boundaries and cuts across all lines of authority.

The informal group may also seek to further preserve important values by demanding that members conform to group standards. Another important action of the informal organization is its involvement in helping members to find solutions to mutual and personal problems. As seen in the United Manufacturing illustration, the informal pact between Office Manager F and Office Manager G existed specifically to provide the two with a mutual exchange of ideas and assistance. Also, the informal ties between Secretary I and Secretary J revealed a concern for mutual help and support when job demands became too great.

The informal organization provides leadership to members in addition to what the formal structure provides. The informal organization does, therefore, serve a number of purposes for those individuals who desire membership and who are accepted into the group's ranks.[11]

Characteristics and Activities

Several things are noteworthy concerning the composition and behavior of the informal organization. The designs and actions of the informal organization have the capacity to be either supportive or detrimental to the goals of the formal organization. Look again at the chapter opening case, for example. The organization chart for Audio Electronics would undoubtedly show that there is no reporting relationship between the three night custodians and the security guard. But a very important *informal* relationship exists—and we can certainly say it's a detrimental one. What would cause the relationship we see in this case?

The informal organization exists to provide rewards, protection, and the preservation of members' values, among other things, for employees. Formal and informal goals may be complementary if the members of the informal organization perceive benefits from working in a unified way with the formal structure. For example, if working together might save the informal group's jobs, the informal group would be cooperative. If, however, it seems beneficial to work in opposition of the formal structure, the informal group has the capacity to do so. Such might be the case if the informal group were to cut back on production to protest an undesirable formal action.

Membership in an informal group is a selective process in which individuals are granted membership primarily on the basis of commonality of interests and willingness to be cooperative and to accept the group's values and norms. Individuals may have overlapping memberships in a number of informal groups, depending upon the frequency of contacts, the mutual interests shared, and other factors. In the United Manufacturing illustration, several of the people were members of at least two informal groupings, and some had the potential for belonging to even more (see Figure 2–3).

Informal groups select individuals to serve as leaders. The selected leaders are granted authority by the members to make decisions, take action, seek conformity, or take other steps that seem appropriate. The leaders are selected on the basis of their ability to perform for the informal group and usually are not individuals possessing a great amount of formal authority. In other words, their authority to serve as leaders is granted to them by their fellow members in order to fill a need. The leaders are expected to act in a way that

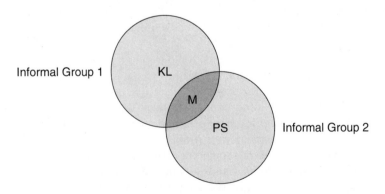

Figure 2–3
Illustration of Overlapping Membership in Informal Groups at United Manufacturing Company

Informal Group 1

KL

M

PS   Informal Group 2

Secretary M belongs to these two informal groups simultaneously achieves the goals of the group and protects the group's values. Informal leaders often are selected on the basis of respect, admiration, and the ability to perform advantageously for the benefit of the group. Some authors call informal leaders **"stars"**—individuals who are able to influence other members and are the center of much communication.[12]

stars (informal leaders)
Frequently those who are the center of much communication.

Quite often, a group may select numerous individuals to serve in specific leadership capacities. Leader A, for example, may be accepted as the production leader—the individual who sets and regulates the work pace (production standards, time standards, etc.) to which all members are expected to conform. Leader B may be expected to serve as the leader in charge of social and personal satisfaction; he or she is in charge of making work relationships pleasant and happy. Leader C may be selected as the public relations leader (sometimes called liaison); it is his or her role to represent the group in all verbal contracts with outsiders—supervisors, inspectors, and public visitors. Other leaders may be selected to serve in additional capacities. Many of these roles may be combined and assigned to a single individual. Of course, interest in the group plays a big part in who serves in what role in the group. Try the Social Interest Scale below for some ideas about your own basic orientation.

Certain characteristics and behaviors require an in-depth review, including group norms, group **cohesiveness,** and grapevine communication.[13] Of course, a basic orientation toward them is an important factor in how individuals respond to groups. But to really get a grasp of group functions, it's also critical to see how group norms, group cohesiveness, and grapevine communication fit us.

cohesiveness
The degree of strength or attractiveness a group has for its members. Where members find their group to be highly attractive, the cohesiveness level is said to be high.

Informal Group Norms

Each informal group characteristically establishes group behavior standards or norms to which members are expected to conform. Norms are designed "to regulate and regularize group members' behavior."[14] Typically, norms are not written down or even discussed openly. They do, however, serve as a powerful, consistent influence on members' behavior.

Norms are important for a number of reasons. They facilitate survival of the group and the pursuit of the group's goals. They simplify or make more predictable the behavior that is expected of members. Norms help the group to avoid embarrassing interpersonal problems. They express the central values of the group and clarify what is distinctive about the group's identity. Refer to the chapter opening case again. What norms have developed among the night custodians?

Norms generally are developed only for behaviors that are viewed as important by most of the group's members. If, for example, the goals of the group are to provide a pleasant, enjoyable work place for its members (to resist pressures for too much work or to fight back against rigid work controls), the group may establish maximum and minimum production standards. The standards may take the form of units produced, sales quotas achieved, or time required to do a certain job. To remain a member in good standing, each worker must adhere to the production guidelines. If a group working on an assembly-line job sets a maximum of 100 units assembled per day and a minimum of 75 units per day, workers who consistently exceed 100 units will be ostracized and eventually removed from the group if they fail to modify their

Personal Feedback

What Kind of Group Member Are You?
Social Interest Scale*

Below are a number of pairs of personal characteristics or traits. For each pair, underline the trait that you value more highly. In making each choice, ask yourself which of the traits in that pair you would rather possess as one of your own characteristics. For example, the first pair is "imaginative-rational." If you had to make a choice, which would you rather be? Draw a line under your choice in each of the pairs.

Some of the traits will appear twice, but always in combination with a different other trait. No pairs will be repeated.

"I would rather be . . ."

imaginative	rational
helpful	quick-witted
neat	sympathetic
level-headed	efficient
intelligent	considerate
self-reliant	ambitious
respectful	original
creative	sensible
generous	individualistic
responsible	original
capable	tolerant
trustworthy	wise
neat	logical
forgiving	gentle
efficient	respectful
practical	self-confident
capable	independent
alert	cooperative
imaginative	helpful
realistic	moral
considerate	wise
sympathetic	individualistic
ambitious	patient
reasonable	quick-witted

Source: James E. Crandall, "A Scale of Social Interest." Reprinted from *Journal of Individual Psychology*, Volume 31, Number 2, November 1975, pp. 187–195. Used by permission of the author and the University of Texas Press.

*The information on interpreting the results of this scale is at the end of this chapter.

behavior. The nonconformer is seen as a threat to the values of the rest of the group. The worker who frequently goes below the minimum 75 units will be pushed by the group to improve his or her performance to avoid penalties to self (and perhaps to the whole group).

The informal group may also establish behavior norms in other areas. Reaction norms, which may be defined as prescribed ways of acting when outsiders are around, may also be outlined. If a "big boss" (an influential and authoritative manager) is near, every worker is expected to look busy to avoid getting into trouble. If a time-and-motion-study person is around, everyone is expected to perform at a somewhat slower pace so that unreasonable time standards can be avoided. If a threatening company inspector is on the premises, everything is to be made shipshape for his or her review. Through these actions, desirable conditions can be ensured and penalties avoided.

The group can also establish norms and patterns to enhance its social interaction and affiliation through similarities of hair style and dress. The wearing of coats and ties may be begun by male members of an informal group in a sales force to provide group identification and to build status and prestige.

Norms usually develop gradually as the members of a group adapt to one another. It is possible, however, to cut short the development for things that are extremely important, for example, when a major change occurs, such as the sudden introduction of an outsider. Norms apply only to behavior—not to private thoughts and feelings. Norms do not always apply equally to every group member.[15] In other words, some people have a higher degree of independence from group norms than do others.

The degree of independence a person has from the norms of a group depends upon a number of things. For example, people who have lower levels of the affiliation need will be more independent of a group norm than will those high in the affiliation need. Low-affiliation individuals are simply less concerned about losing membership and acceptance by the group than are those who strongly need to belong to the group. Some norms don't lend themselves to enforcement as much as do others, because there are fewer standards that can be applied to measure conformity. Also, the prestige and power wielded by an individual influence the individual's independence from a norm. High-prestige, powerful individuals naturally have more freedom than do their opposites.[16]

Group Cohesiveness

conformity
The acceptance of group values and norms to the point that behavior is consistent with group directives.

Cohesiveness is the strength of the feeling of unity group members have for the group as a whole and for the other people in the group. It has also been defined as "the attraction the work group has for its members."[17] Cohesiveness is important because only cohesive groups are strong enough to enforce norms. A less cohesive group may attempt to get members to follow norms but may not be able to do so. The level of cohesiveness appears to vary significantly among informal work groups. Some groups seem to be tightly bound together for mutual support. **Conformity** to group standards and norms tends to be high among such groups. Other groups appear to have only limited control and conformity. Cohesiveness seems to be higher when a majority of the following conditions apply:

1. The members have a broad general agreement concerning the goals and objectives the informal group will serve.
2. There is a significant amount of communication and interaction among the participating members.[18]
3. There is a satisfactory level of homogeneity (similarity) in social status and social background among the members.[19]
4. Members are allowed to participate fully and directly in the determination of group standards.
5. The size of the group is sufficient for interaction but is not too large to stymie personal attention.
6. The members have a high regard for their fellow members.
7. The members feel a strong need for the mutual benefits and protection the group appears to offer.
8. The group is experiencing success in the achievement of its goals and in the protection of important values.

The level of cohesiveness appears to have a direct influence upon the behavior of the members of each informal group. For example, in groups where cohesiveness is high, members appear to be more attentive to each other, adherence to group goals is at a high level, pressure on violators of group goals is strong, and individual members find a strong sense of security and release from tensions as a result of their group affiliations.

Cohesiveness, of course, does not always have positive effects on group members. There is a tendency for highly cohesive groups to reject ideas and thoughts that come from individuals who express different opinions. This is how the groupthink phenomenon gets started. There is no guarantee that the norms of the highly cohesive group will be supportive of the formal organization. When this occurs, the efforts of the cohesive groups can be very harmful and counterproductive.

What can you do, as a manager, when group norms become counterproductive? The key is getting the group to put pressure on members to do what's wanted. In many situations, group pressure is far more effective than pressure from management in getting things turned around. But how do you do that in a situation where the group itself doesn't trust management or support its goals? That's where managerial skill comes in. As an example, here's how a manager we know handled a sticky situation.

Cathy was an experienced manager who worked for a large utility company. She was transferred to a new location and was told that help was needed desperately. And it was—productivity was far lower than at any other location. The employees involved were a group of thirty or so construction workers supervised by two foremen. The jobs were routine construction work connected with the utility's operations and involved laying cable and pipe. Because of the routine nature of the work, the foremen could accurately schedule times for each job. The only trouble was that most jobs, especially in the mornings, had enormous overruns—some taking as much as three times the estimate for completion. It was no wonder productivity was the lowest in the company.

The employees themselves formed a close group. In particular, they shared common interests in after-work sports activities such as hunting and bowling. As soon as work was over, they would go off as a group to enjoy one or the other of their favorite sports. They were all members of the union, and the union's strength made discipline difficult at best. Cathy explained that she first met with the foremen to try to see what the trouble was. The foremen were completely frustrated and asked Cathy to come to the work center the next morning to see for herself. The next morning at the work center Cathy found the workers loading equipment into their trucks. The foremen met with each worker—or, in some cases, pairs of workers—and gave the workers their first job assignment. As each job was given out, the workers jumped into their trucks and set off. After the last worker left, the foreman said, "Come on quick and hop in my truck. We've got to chase them!" When Cathy asked why, the foreman told her that the workers weren't really going to their jobs. In fact, what actually happened was that each evening they arranged to start the next day with an hour-long coffee break, where they relaxed and made plans for sports that evening. The spot changed each day, so the foremen couldn't find them. The foremen, in turn, tried to chase and catch them. In effect, what was going on was a version of hide and seek.

Naturally, we were intrigued. Cathy was up against a bad situation. Notice that she was dealing with a cohesive group. Just look back at the list of conditions for a cohesive group that we talked about earlier. Nearly all of them apply. The problem, of course, was the group norms, which supported socializing—not working. We were surprised when Cathy told us that she had productivity up to—and above—standard the next day. "What did you do?" we asked.

> "Well," Cathy explained, "I began by calling a group meeting for the next morning. When everyone had assembled, I told them that the rules had changed. From now on, the foremen would give the workers their full day's assignments in the morning. The assignments would be made based on the standard times provided by the company. But everyone knew that the times had a little extra built into them, and if you really pushed you could finish them early and still do a quality job. So I explained that if they could get their day's work done early, even by 2:30 or 3:00, they could leave for their sports activities and we'd pay them for the full eight-hour shift. The only stipulation was that they had to keep quality up. The foremen would stop chasing them but would spot check their completed jobs for quality. The workers jumped on the ideas—and they were able to leave early nearly every day. In fact, if anyone tried to slack off, they really put the pressure on. It got the job done, they got their sports activities—we were all winners in that one!"

Notice the key here. Like Cathy, you've got to find a way that makes the informal group want to meet management's goals. It takes some thought, but it can be done.

Grapevine Communication

An especially important means of achieving many of the goals and objectives of the informal organization is the development of its own communication network. The informal network is commonly known as the grapevine and is uninhibited by the formal communication networks. Messages are spread by the grapevine to members by word of mouth or by other means. Anything that seems to have interest or value may be transmitted through the informal network. Who's to be hired, who's to be fired, and other changes, for example, often move quickly throughout the grapevine. Seldom does the grapevine network operate in a rigidly defined pattern. Information may originate anywhere in the system and will be spread in a sometimes unpredictable manner. It has been suggested, however, that the cluster approach is the most frequently observable manner by which grapevine messages are passed along.[20] With the **cluster approach,** a message is communicated by an originator to two or three others who do the same thing. The result is a sort of ripple effect as the message is spread (see Figure 2–4).

Grapevine messages tend to be passed along rapidly and more selectively than many people expect. The grapevine may withhold or retard the giving of information to some individuals. The basis of withholding grapevine information may be the fact that the excluded individual lacks acceptable standing with the informal organization. The communication avoidance may also be a problem of lack of physical proximity (nearness) when messages are being passed along. For example, workers who labor in isolated areas often find themselves ignored or communicated to more slowly than workers in exposed positions. Grapevines tend to be accurate as much as 75 percent to 95 percent of the time. The levels of the grapevine's activity normally parallel those of the formal structure. The grapevine spreads only information that people are interested in hearing.[21]

cluster approach
The technique most frequently used by the grapevine (informal communication network) in which one person tells a few others (one cluster) and each subsequent person tells a few other members forming additional clusters.

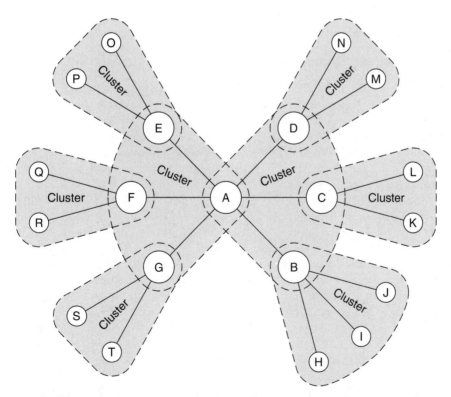

Figure 2–4
Cluster Pattern of Grapevine

Source: Adapted from Keith Davis, "Management Communication and the Grapevine," *Harvard Business Review*, Volume 31, Number 5, September–October 1953, p. 45

The informal organization acts similarly to a social fraternity in the sense that it develops secret codes through which it communicates. To the outsider or the uninformed, the codes will have little significance. To the informal group members, however, the symbols have important meaning. A college student employed part-time in a manufacturing concern reported that the work group in his department protected itself from outsiders by a novel system in which a certain worker who sat near the workroom's entrance was appointed the "warning" leader. It was his job to keep an eye on the door for the coming of individuals who might be threatening to the welfare of the group. If he spotted someone approaching who appeared to be dangerous, it was the warner's job to step on a foot pedal that released a blast of steam through a boiler valve. The steam blast was a warning to the other workers to be cautious because a possible enemy was entering. The warning system became even more sophisticated: one "toot" on the boiler meant the boss was coming in; two "toots" meant that a production expediter was in view; and so forth.

The returning prisoners of war from the Vietnam conflict apparently developed their own communication symbols. One of the first men released referred to the times in which the group's morale would get low. He said that someone would then begin humming the melody to "California, Here I Come." The tune, which was unknown to their captors, reminded the men that someday their imprisonment would be over and they would be returning home. The pleasant thought gave the men the encouragement needed to get through a bad time, and morale perked up accordingly.

These illustrations both show the importance of informal groups and their use of the grapevine to the individuals involved.

Management's Relationship to the Informal Organization

As previously discussed, the informal organization has goals, objectives, and methods of operation designed to benefit its members. These functions may or may not be beneficial to the formal organization, and they are not completely within the control of the formal structure. In this rather confusing state of affairs, a justifiable question seems to be, How should the manager with formally designated responsibility and authority go about the task of confronting the informal organization and working with it?

One concept to keep in mind concerning the informal organization is that it serves many useful purposes for its members. It usually provides a satisfactory amount of social affiliation and interaction as well as information to workers rapidly and, in many cases, it works accurately. The informal organization is capable of controlling or influencing the behavior of its members if their actions become so far out of line with formal organizational expectations that they tend to create problems and dangers for the informal group. In many cases, the informal group even works to support and achieve formal goals and objectives that are in harmony with informal ones. Since the informal group is capable of performing for its members many positive, constructive tasks that are desirable from the formal point of view, the group should be permitted and encouraged to perform these supportive functions. In meeting personal and group needs and in regulating worker behavior constructively, the informal organization can be a very helpful auxiliary to the formal manager.

Situations exist, however, in which the actions of the informal group are in opposition to formal goals and objectives and the behavior of individual members is detrimental to constructive organizational achievement. In Cathy's case, we've discussed a similar situation. If the workers have established lower production standards than are reasonable, if coffee breaks are being abused collectively, if legitimate supervisory instructions are being ignored, etc., the managerial task of working with the informal group becomes more complex.

The goal of every manager should be to unify the actions and efforts of the informal organization with those of the formal organization whenever possible. In addition, the manager usually wants to replace attitudes of hostility with those of trust and confidence. The existence of a set of positive conditions helps to unify the efforts and actions of formal and informal structures and to make them mutually more beneficial. In general, the two systems pull together more favorably under the following conditions:

1. The workers have a high level of confidence in their boss and believe that he or she consistently considers their needs and desires as decisions are made. This kind of confidence tends to build over a period of time as a manager's actions are discerned to be fair, considerate, and favorably oriented toward the worker. Usually, the more positive leadership styles (such as those of participative or free-rein leadership) build confidence more than do negatively oriented styles (autocratic leadership, etc.).

2. The workers know, understand, and accept the objectives of the formal organization. This condition calls for the communication of formal objectives to workers in clear, simplified terminology. If the objectives are reasonable and consistent with the values of the informal group, there will be general support of the goals. If the goals appear unreasonable, the workers may not support them. Normally, however, acceptance of reasonable goals can be attained.

3. The workers are allowed some participation in the determination of formal goals, objectives, and policies. This condition does not mean that every worker must be involved in every decision, but it does mean that some type of representation in matters that affect the workers will increase confidence and support for the decision or plan. Participation tends to increase confidence and support for the decision reached and reduces antagonism or mistrust. Workers tend to support decisions they help make.

4. The workers are kept informed regularly and accurately concerning facts and policies of interest to them. Workers receive the information needed through formal channels so that speculation and rumors become unnecessary.

5. The formal leaders (managers) listen for and seek out the feelings and sentiments of the workers.

When it is difficult for a formal manager to listen to every worker, to get participation from everyone, and to send messages directly to everyone, the identification and utilization of the informal leaders as representatives of the group may be effective. These leaders usually feel a great amount of responsibility for the well-being of their peers and perform conscientiously for them. The informal leader can serve in a capacity that will be beneficial for the group he or she represents and can at the same time be of assistance to the formal manager through participation in decision making and the communication upward of important messages.

Summary

Every organization has its own culture; that is, it has its own set of values, norms, and attitudes. The culture is shaped by the personal characteristics and needs of individuals as they interact within the formal and informal structures. The culture is sometimes constructive in its action, and at other times it is destructive. The ideal culture, of course, would be one in which everything that is said and done is positively beneficial, but that's unrealistic.

The formal structure of an organization's culture provides much of the authority relationship and patterns in which individuals work. The formal structure also establishes formal communication channels, the type of supervision that will be given (close versus general), the level of specialization employees will have, and the location where decisions will be made (centralized or decentralized).

The informal structure makes its cultural contributions by meeting many of the individual's and the group's needs—such things as social affiliation and support, a fast-moving communication source, supplementary leadership, collective goals, and norms.

Managers can enhance the culture of an organization in many ways. A manager who has the trust of the people in an organization will be more acceptable to individuals and groups. When formal organization values are consistent with individual and group values expressed, acceptance of organizational goals is more likely. When participative techniques are used to get worker involvement, formal and informal norms are more likely to coincide. When employees are kept informed on issues that concern them, there will be less speculation and fewer rumors.

Questions to Consider

1. Why does a cultural gap often develop in an organization? That is, why do the things individuals and groups within an organization want often counter the things the formal organization wants?
2. Why do subcultures (informal groups) develop within the context of the culture of an organization?
3. Besides the functions mentioned in the chapter, what are some other purposes for the informal organization's existence?
4. What are some things the informal organization may do that are detrimental to the formal organization?
5. What kinds of qualifications may be required of an individual to be accepted as a member of a group?

6. What happens when individuals find themselves isolated from an informal group? Can they find a way to belong to the group? If so, how?
7. Do you have to want to belong to an informal group to be a member?
8. How can the grapevine be constructively utilized by formal managers (or can they?)?
9. What should a manager do who discovers that the grapevine is spreading rumors that turn out to be false?
10. Is it ethical to give employees only selected information in order to manipulate their thinking?
11. Is it ethical for employees to withhold important information from their bosses if it benefits the employees?

Please go back to the case at the beginning of the chapter and answer the questions asked there.

Key Terms

authority relationships	grapevine	roles
communication channel	informal work	span of supervision
cluster approach	organizations	specialization
cohesiveness	norms	stars (informal leaders)
conformity		

Chapter Case

Marley Printing Company

Upon graduation, you go to work for Marley Printing Company, a locally based firm that provides all sorts of printing services to individuals and organizations. Your new boss will be Bob Marley, the son of the founder. Bob took over control of the firm several years ago upon his father's retirement and not too many years after his own graduation from college. He's known as a dynamic leader, and in the years since his arrival, Marley Printing has nearly tripled in size. You're told that it bears no resemblance to the sleepy, slow-moving, and rigid firm that Bob took over. You're anxious to work for Bob because you believe you can learn a lot—and furthermore, you're determined to keep your eyes open and to ask enough questions to ensure that you do learn.

You soon learn that Bob has considerable concern for his workers. One day Bob confides to you that he's particularly worried about the development of two groups of employees—the receivers and the boxers. "The rest of the groups in our organization are really catching hold—getting excited about their jobs and really participating," he explains, "but those two groups simply aren't turned on. Their productivity is low, their turnover is high. They simply aren't interested." You ask about what their jobs consist of. "Well," Bob continues, "they certainly aren't that exciting, I'll grant you. The receivers receive incoming shipments of materials—paper of all kinds, ink, and similar things, and stack them wherever management says to put them. The boxers box our finished product—printed materials of all kinds—and place them in a pickup area for delivery. The thing is that we offer jobs to people with real low educational backgrounds—this is the only job most of them could get—and they could move ahead in an organization like this if they'd show some get-up-and-go. I keep hearing about redesigning jobs. I wonder if that would help." You offer to look into the possibility and report back. The conversation about the two groups continues.

"The thing I really don't understand," Bob questions, "is why receivers and boxers don't encourage their fellow employees who show promise. Take Mable Hastings. We recently hired her into the receiving group, and I was really hopeful that we'd found the kind of worker we were looking for. At first, she asked to learn new things and volunteered to work on other stations. Then, suddenly she stopped. It's almost like she's afraid to show initiative. I just don't understand it."

1. You suspect that problems such as the one Bob described involving Mable may have something to do with group functioning. What are norms and cohesiveness, and how do they enter in? What should be done in a situation like this?

Self Test

Scoring the Social Interest Scale

Your score on the Social Interest Scale is the number of times that the trait you've underlined matches the one in italics in the key. Note that the key contains only 15 in italics traits. Nine of the pairs are called "buffer" pairs and are used to separate the pairs which Dr. Crandall uses to measure social interest. In effect, the buffer pairs make what the test is really trying to measure a little less obvious. To find your score, compare your answer to those on the Scoring Key. Give yourself one point for each matching word in italics.

Scoring Key

		Match
imaginative	rational	———
helpful	quick-witted	———
neat	*sympathetic*	———
level-headed	efficient	———
intelligent	*considerate*	———
self-reliant	ambitious	———
respectful	original	———
creative	sensible	———
generous	individualistic	———
responsible	original	———
capable	*tolerant*	———

		Match
trustworthy	wise	——
neat	logical	——
forgiving	gentle	——
efficient	*respectful*	——
practical	self-confident	——
capable	independent	——
alert	*cooperative*	——
imaginative	*helpful*	——
realistic	*moral*	——
considerate	wise	——
sympathetic	individualistic	——
ambitious	*patient*	——
reasonable	quick-witted	——
	Total Score	——

Interpreting Your Score

Low Scorers (0–6). People who score in this range are frequently seen by others as showing little interest, liking, or concern for other people. If you are a low scorer, values such as pleasure and excitement in life are probably important to you. There may be times when your emphasis on personal pleasure makes it hard for you to show concern, and feeling concern may not be the same for you. It is possible that some of your behavior that others see as self-centered is not intended to express the lack of social interest that it does. Your interpersonal relationships could improve if others had a better understanding of your interest in them.

Medium Scorers (7–11). Scorers in this range are seen by others as neither highly concerned about the welfare of humankind nor as extremely self-centered. You may actually be quite concerned about the welfare of others. Your social interest, however, may be focused on specific people, sometimes causing others to feel that you're not particularly concerned about the general human condition. If you are comfortable with how and toward whom you express your social interest, then any negative comments from others will not (and probably should not) concern you.

High Scorers (11–15). If you scored in this range, other people probably see you as genuinely concerned about humanitarian issues in your community. You emphasize in your dealings with others their concerns and feelings and are probably quick to help someone in need. High scorers generally value peace, equality, and family security more than they value personal pleasure or an exciting life. You most likely concern yourself with your loved ones, and those relationships serve as a source of satisfaction for you. In addition, high social interest people seem to be satisfied with life in general and report less depression and unhappiness than those who score low on this scale.

Chapter
3

What Good Are
Groups, Anyway?

Objectives

- To learn how and why groups make decisions.
- To discern advantages of group versus individual decision making.
- To spot problem areas in group decision making.
- To discover why groupthink occurs and how it can be managed most effectively (and avoided).
- To become familiar with some of the newer procedures suggested as creative decision methods.
- To identify how and why Quality Circles function.
- To become knowledgeable on methods for team building.

Arlin O'Keefe—The Director Who Wants a Group Decision

Arlin O'Keefe is director of the eastern district of the State Highway Department. He has under his jurisdiction all of the highways and state-maintained roads in a twelve-county region, and he reports directly to the deputy director of the State Highway Department. It is O'Keefe's responsibility to see that the district is maintained satisfactorily and to make recommendations concerning the construction of new roads, bridges, and other highway structures in the district.

To make his job more manageable, O'Keefe has divided his district into three subdistricts, each comprising four counties. He has put three of his assistants in charge of the subdistricts (one to each subdistrict) and has given them the title of assistant district director. Each assistant director is responsible for supervising the construction and maintenance activities in his or her own subdistrict.

One of O'Keefe's major responsibilities is to determine priorities for new construction projects. Resources are given to the most urgent projects. There is never enough money to do everything that is needed. This year, for example, O'Keefe has been told that his district will receive $46 million, and he knows of four major projects of urgent importance that would cost $62 million if all were undertaken at once. There are a number of minor projects to consider also, and a contingency fund for emergency projects in the sum of $500,000 is customarily set aside each year. The large number of costly, important projects and the limited availability of resources means that some difficult decisions must be reached concerning which projects to approve for this coming year and which ones to postpone.

To aid him in his annual priority allocation decision, O'Keefe calls in his subdistrict directors and his district research assistant to work with him as a decision-making team. The team meets in the first week of July each year to make priority decisions. It is nearing time for this year's decisions, and Tom Wittman (subdistrict A), Marlina Schell (subdistrict B), Roy Regis (subdistrict C), and Dale Edwards (district research) will soon be called in for the conference. O'Keefe observes that of the four major projects under consideration this year, two are in Wittman's subdistrict (an 18-million-dollar project and a 7-million-dollar project); one is in Schell's subdistrict (a 19-million-dollar project); and two are in Regis's subdistrict (a 12-million-dollar project and a 6-million-dollar project. The smaller projects are scattered throughout all three subdistricts.

O'Keefe has experienced some difficulties in past years in getting the directors to work together smoothly. Tom Wittman is the oldest person in the group and has more seniority with the highway department. He sometimes attempts to use his seniority to influence others to think the way he wants them to and to accept his position on issues. He is willing to make concessions at times, but he attempts to manipulate the group to follow his own line of logic. Roy Regis frequently has a very closed mind and fights for projects within his own subdistrict without much regard for the welfare of the other subdistricts. Marlina Schell, on the other hand, usually tries her best to remain objective in the decision-making process. Dale Edwards seldom does anything more than supply information and provide supportive material for consideration in making decisions.

In spite of these difficulties, O'Keefe feels that a group decision on the priorities for allocating funds is essential, and he is preparing to use team decision making this year. He hopes to be able to overcome the difficulties that have occurred with this group in previous years.

Case Questions

1. Why does Arlin O'Keefe prefer to have a group decision rather than to make the decision himself? What are the advantages of a group decision in the case?
2. What decision-making technique should O'Keefe use?
3. What preliminary steps can O'Keefe take prior to group meetings to smooth the way for more productive, more objective group discussions?
4. What criteria could be developed for use in these discussions?

Formal Groups and Teams

"Most of my time each day is spent in meeting with other executives and employees in which plans are made and organizational strategies are outlined."

"We seldom make decisions by individual action in our company anymore. Several people are involved in each decision."

"Our production process has become so interrelated that our employees must now work together as a team instead of as individuals."

"The most important training a young executive could receive today would be training on how to lead groups to work together to achieve goals" (spoken by an older manager).

The preceding comments from executives in different types of industries point out a very important pattern in today's organizations. More and more, people are working in groups within the formalized structure of the organization in which they are employed. An increasing number of organizational functions (e.g., planning, product development, production, distribution) are being handled by teams. Planning and decision-making responsibilities in particular are being given to teams rather than centralizing them in the hands of a few individuals acting independently.

In an era of increasingly complex organizations (resulting from mergers, takeovers, expansions, etc.) the importance of coordination and integration has progressed to new heights. Emphasis on teamwork has brought group effort to the forefront.

Traditional Groups and Teams

The group effort and teamwork we are talking about here refers to groups with formalized relationships (as opposed to informal work groups), where there are assigned duties and authority relationships that tie individuals together. These teams are in the structural chart of organizations. We will discuss at some length two types of groups: **decision-making groups** and **quality circles.** Other groups are important as well. These groups arise whenever people within the departments or units of an organization are called upon to work together.

A group could be a whole department or a smaller set of individuals working together. The public relations unit, for example, may function as a team, as may the legal department or a production group in a factory setting. Subgroups of employees, such as assemblers in the production department, may also function as a team to produce a part of the firm's final product.

Teamwork in an Automobile Plant

In more and more automobile assembly plants, teams are being used to perform specific production activities rather than having people do highly specialized single activities separately. There are several advantages to the team production concept. For example, the team concept provides much more flexibility in organizational structure. As individuals work together—usually in groups of five to twenty—each individual learns how to perform several jobs. Because the individuals are less specialized, each person can perform different jobs as the needs arise.

Groups are often more productive than individuals working separately. As a result of the broader abilities and the loosened rules, productivity has jumped 20 percent to 40 percent. Workers also seem more satisfied with their work in teams because there is greater variety in what they do and because each worker feels more in control.

One of the other advantages of working as a group rather than separately lies in the quality of products completed. Traditional approaches emphasize quantity, where the team approach plays up quality.[1]

How the Team Decision-making Process Works

In one way or another, you can be sure that as an employee, you will be involved with teams. When you talk to managers about how teams fit into their lives, you'll find that the subject of teams and decision making comes up over and over.

First, when you supervise others you are the leader of a team—the employees who work for you. You'll want to get them to work together in a variety of tasks, and you may want to involve them in the decision-making process. Second, you, as a manager, will be a member of the team reporting to your boss. Often, as a member of that team, you'll be involved in the

decision-making group
A team formally assigned to work together to solve a problem or make a decision.

quality circle
A voluntary grouping of a small number of individuals who work together within an organization. The group is joined together to pursue ways of improving and protecting the quality of the product on which they work. The circle originated in Japan.

Management in Action

Chaparral Steel Company

Recently a group of executives from a Fortune 500 manufacturer traveled to Midlothian, Texas, to learn how Chaparral Steel managed its teams. Efficient superteams have helped make Chaparral one of the world's most productive steel companies. During the tour, one executive asked a Chaparral manager, "How do you schedule coffee breaks in the plant?"

"The workers decide when they want a cup of coffee," came the reply.

"Yes, but who tells them when it's okay to leave the machines?" the executive persisted.

Why do Chaparral workers know when to take a coffee break? Because they're trained to understand how the whole business operates. Earl Engelhardt, who runs the company's educational program, teaches millworkers The Chaparral Process, a course that not only describes what happens to a piece of steel as it moves through the company but also covers the roles of finance, accounting, and sales. Once trained, a worker understands how his or her job relates to the welfare of the entire organization. At team meetings, many of which are held in the company's modest boardroom, talk is of backlogs and personnel hours per ton. Financial statements are posted monthly in the mill, including a chart tracking operating profits before taxes—the key measure for profit sharing.

In the early 1980s, the company sent a team leader and three millworkers, all of whom had been through The Chaparral Process, to Europe, Asia, and South America to evaluate new mill stands. These large, expensive pieces of equipment flatten and shape hot steel as it passes through the mill, much as the rollers on old-fashioned washing machines used to wring clothes. After team members returned from their first trip, they discussed with other workers and with top management the advantages and disadvantages of various mill stands. They then narrowed the field and flew off again. Eventually the team agreed on the best mill stand—in this case, a West German model—and top management gave its blessing.

The team then ordered the mill stands and oversaw their installation, even down to negotiating the contracts for the work involved. At other companies, it can take as long as several years to buy and install such a complicated piece of equipment. The Chaparral team got the job done in a year. Perhaps even more amazing, the mill stands—notoriously finicky pieces of machinery—worked as soon as they were turned on.

Source: Brian Dumaine, "Who Needs a Boss," *Fortune*, Volume 122, Number 9, May 7, 1990, pp. 52–59.

decision-making process. Decision making is often a vital element in teamwork. Let's take a closer look at how it works. Our examination will illustrate the common features of decision-making groups while providing insight into the nature of group problem solving.

Decision-making Groups . . . Or Is a Camel Really a Racehorse Designed by a Committee?

Many of the major decisions and some of the decisions of lesser importance in organizations are made through group deliberation. How to invest millions of dollars and what color to paint the walls in the hallway are representative of the variety of decisions frequently delegated to groups. Why not just let the boss, or the technical expert, or the manager of the department go ahead and decide what to do without involving others? As we will see, there are times when individuals should be making decisions rather than asking groups to do so. There are, however, some definite advantages to using groups for certain decisions and recommendations.

1. Team decision making usually results in the accumulation of a wider variety of facts and knowledge than individual decision efforts. Individuals working together as a team tend to supplement one another's knowledge as issues are considered.

2. Team interaction tends to result in the consideration of a greater number of alternatives before decisions are made. The nature of groups and their membership usually results in a broadened perspective for analysis and action.

3. Recommendations advanced through group problem solving frequently have a higher level of accuracy than do individually determined recommendations. It is important to note that decisions made by individuals in some situations may actually be more accurate than group decisions. ("Research tends to show that groups do better in making judgments than do individuals but fail to reach their potential as a result of interactional problems."[2]) Groups frequently do a better job of handling problems of moderate difficulty than do individuals. Individuals, however, may be superior when it comes to problems that are extremely easy or extremely difficult. Group efforts may be superior for problems that have many parts and where participants have different knowledge and skills.

4. If the acceptance of a decision by employees is important, group decisions have merit over decisions made by another person acting independently.[3] When the group comes to a decision that represents a high degree of consensus, individual members work harder to make it succeed. Even individuals who are not a direct part of the decision-making team will tend to look more favorably upon a decision if their views are represented in the deliberations.

5. Group decision making results in employees who are better informed and more knowledgeable concerning the decisions reached. The participants in the deliberation process are personally aware of problems, alternatives considered, and decision constraints as a result of their involvement in the decisions. Their knowledge can be shared with other employees to result in a well-informed group of workers in general.

6. The participants in the group interaction come to develop rapport toward one another. Goals, ambitions, interests, and concerns are revealed, and a better understanding is achieved.

7. There needs to be some kind of reward or reinforcement for acting together as a team or unit. Cespedes et al. suggest, for example, that sales groups that act as units or teams should have bonuses that are paid to all members participating in the team process. Bonuses should be split among group members when the group experiences successful

group efforts.[4] Along this same line, Paulsen suggests gain sharing as a good reinforcement for teamwork. With gain sharing, specific percentages of employee-related costs are calculated for all products and services. For example, the labor cost of a refrigeration unit might be considered to be 25 percent of the total production cost. Anytime unit members working together can cut the labor cost, the group members share the savings as bonuses.[5]

In brief, the positive effects of group decision making and problem solving may be better decisions and solutions, greater support and cooperation in the implementation of decisions, and better communication and understanding of decisions and personalities involved in teams. Notice, though, that we've qualified these statements with that all-important *may be*. Groups have potential to contribute a lot to the decision-making process. But they often don't live up to their promise. Why not? Let's see.

Problems with Group Decisions

It is important to note that decision making in groups has its drawbacks, some of which follow:

1. Group decision making usually works more slowly than decision-making processes performed by individuals acting separately.
2. Because team decisions are slower to process and involve several individuals, the decisions reached become expensive ones. Where one employee might be able to reach a decision working alone in twenty minutes, a group of five might take an hour. The salaries of the five individuals and the longer time period involved make the group decision a much more costly one (at least in terms of immediate expenses).
3. Group efforts frequently result in compromise decisions that are not always the most useful or most beneficial decisions. Members of the decision-making team often are more concerned about being good team members than they are about the quality of the final decision. As a result, groups tend to settle on the first generally agreeable solution rather than seek the best possible solution. Majority opinions also tend to be accepted regardless of whether or not they are logical and scientifically sound. Have you ever been a member of a group that was stalled—perhaps the group had spent a couple of hours working on a problem but felt it was going nowhere. Then, someone proposed a suggestion. Maybe it wasn't even an especially good one. But the group seized on it enthusiastically, glad to get off dead center. Such tendencies can hurt the quality of the group's work.
4. Group interaction is often dominated by one of the members of the team. This can happen because one of the team members is in a higher position of authority (in the authority hierarchy) than are the other members. (This may be you, if you're the boss working with your sub-

ordinates. It may also be your boss when working with you and your peers.) It might occur when some individual simply participates more, is more persuasive, or is more stubborn than anyone else. As a result, others concede to the individual's domination, which may destroy many of the positive effects of group decision making. The decision may be perceived as being unfair, and the dominant person may be rejected by others involved in the decision process.[6]

5. Conflict and disharmony may result if group actions are not handled properly. Because no two individuals think totally alike, group interactions may result in the airing of different feelings and different opinions. Individuals may begin to compete with each other to "win" their point of view rather than to find the best decision. This, of course, can result in the failure of the team's actions to be as useful as they should be. The disruptive effects may be deep-seated and enduring, as you know if you've ever been a member of a group that was divided up into disagreeing factions.

6. Too much dependence upon group decision making can hinder management's ability to act. In organizations in which teams are utilized for almost every type of decision, individuals who serve in managerial capacities may have almost no authority. A manager who encounters a problem that needs an immediate answer may not be able to provide it if team decision making has preempted this right. Teams might find themselves agonizing over whether to buy two dollars' worth of pencils and a dollar's worth of paper clips if organizations refer all decisions to teams. It is possible for organizations to vest too much power and responsibility in the hands of teams.

7. Groups are usually more willing to take risks than are individuals. More daring action coming from the group may be a mixed blessing. Whether it is the fact that individuals in groups try to outdo one another when they get together or whether it is the security in numbers that workers feel in groups, the larger-risks feature seems to be true of most groups.

8. Groupthink may occur in groups that are especially cohesive. Irving Janis, who coined the term **groupthink,** defines it as the mode of thinking that develops with people who are deeply involved in a cohesive group to the point that striving for total agreement overrides their abilities (and motivations) to realistically appraise alternatives.[7] Groupthink is a major problem that will receive further treatment in the Insights feature.

groupthink
The cohesiveness that develops in a group causing its members to seek a unanimous decision at the risk of failing to identify or consider factors that might result in a better decision.

Some people are beginning to question the concept of groupthink. It has been suggested, for example, that group decisions simply represent the positions held by the majority as the decision process begins. This way, it is not a matter of pressuring group members toward a position they initially reject. Instead, the majority position rules, and the decision process is one of convincing noncommitted members that the decision is right. Groups are inclined to take more risk-oriented positions than individuals acting alone would take.[8]

Insights

Groupthink: Why It Develops and What to Do About It

In his famous book on the subject, Irving Janis has popularized the perils of groupthink. In the analysis of a number of decisions made by groups (including some very famous ones—the Bay of Pigs fiasco, the decision to escalate the Korean conflict, and the Watergate coverup, to name but three), Janis identified the phenomenon. Groupthink is the team cohesiveness that develops, causing group members to seek a unanimous decision at the risk of failing to identify or consider factors that might encourage another decision. In groupthink, members of the team seem caught up in an esprit de corps that sacrifices reality for the desire for unanimity. There is a deterioration of mental efficiency, reality testing, and moral judgment resulting from in-group pressures. Individuals stop asking questions.

Specific conditions exist that lead toward the occurrence of groupthink: a high level of group cohesiveness, structural conditions that basically fail to provide the guidance that is needed (and the group composition of homogeneity), and situational conditions involving high levels of stress and low self-esteem.

As a result of the existing circumstances and conditions, the symptoms of groupthink evolve (see accompanying chart). Type I symptoms tend to overvalue the worth of the group and its status, Type II symptoms lead to closed-mindedness, and Type III symptoms are concerned with pressure for unanimity. Poor (defective) decision making is the outcome of the group's symptoms. In other words, the tendencies of the group lead toward incomplete, biased, frequently hurried evaluations of the available data. From these kinds of behaviors, of course, come decisions that have a high probability for being faulty.

The Groupthink Process

Conditions Leading to Groupthink	Observable Consequences
1. Highly or moderately cohesive group.	Concurrence (Agreement Seeking Tendency)
2. Structural conditions, or the organization, where	
2.1 The decision group is insulated from the judgments of qualified people from outside the organization.	**Symptoms of Groupthink**
	Type I—Overestimation of the group
	1. Illusion of invulnerability.
2.2 No tradition of impartial leadership.	2. Belief in inherent morality of the group.
2.3 Lack of prior norms requiring methodical procedures for information search and appraisal.	Type II—Close-mindedness
	3. Collective rationalizations.
2.4 Homogeneity in the social and ideological	4. Stereotypes of out-groups

traditional interacting group The most typical decision-making group, where group discussion is used as the method for reaching a decision.

Nontraditional Groups

Interacting Conference Groups

The focal point of the discussion thus far has been on the more traditional types of decision-making groups. The most typical decision group historically has been the **traditional interacting group** or conference discussion type.

3. Situational conditions.

3.1 High stress from external threats with low hope for a solution better than the leader's.

3.2 Low self-esteem temporarily induced by

3.21 Recent failures.

3.22 Excessive difficulties in making current decisions, lowering self-efficacy.

3.23 Moral dilemma: Lack of ethical alternatives.

Type III—Pressures toward uniformity

5. Self-censorship.
6. Illusion of unanimity.
7. Direct pressure on dissenters.
8. Self-appointed mindguards.

Symptoms of Defective Decision Making

1. Incomplete survey of alternatives.
2. Incomplete survey of objectives.
3. Failure to examine risks of preferred choice.
4. Failure to reappraise initially rejected alternatives.
5. Poor information search.
6. Selective bias in processing information at hand.
7. Failure to work out contingency plans.

Low Probability of Successful Outcome

Janis suggests the following actions that can be helpful in reducing the probability that groupthink will occur:

1. The leader of a decision group should assign all group participants to be critical evaluators of what will take place in the group. Objections and doubts that contributors have should be encouraged. The leader should be able to take criticism as well.

2. The leader, at the beginning of group deliberations, should take an impartial role, free of unbiasing comments. This allows participative freedom to be open to the exploration of several alternatives.

3. Groups should routinely establish several decision-making subgroups under separate leaders looking at some of the same issues and problems. While this may seem to be a duplication, it increases the breadth of data generation that will result.

4. During group considerations of alternatives, members should be divided into smaller subgroups with separate leaders. The result may be different perspectives that will be reviewed when the larger group reassembles.

5. Each group member should periodically discuss the group's progress with trusted associates outside the group, then report back their input.

6. One or more outside experts who are not core group members should be invited individually to group meetings and encouraged to challenge the views of the group.

7. At every meeting devoted to considering alternatives, at least one member should be assigned the role of the devil's advocate.

8. Whenever a competing organization is at the center of the problem, a significant amount of the time should be given to the analysis of signals and intentions issued by the rival.

Source: Irving L. Janis, *Groupthink*, Second Edition. Copyright © 1982 by Houghton Mifflin Company. Used with permission.

In this kind of group, several conditions conducive to most effective decision making have been suggested:

1. It is important for the participants in the group interaction to have a unity of direction—a common goal known and accepted by each individual. This becomes even more valuable when it is realized that each member has his or her own needs, past experiences, and developmental needs.[9]

2. In keeping with the previous point, it is helpful if each group member is able to envision personal benefits that will accrue to him or her if the group performs its duties successfully. Hampton et al. state that "in general, both the effectiveness of the group and the satisfaction of its members are increased when the members of the group see their personal goals being advanced by the group's success."[10] Think back on effective teams you've worked with in the past—with sports, perhaps, with such activities as getting out a school newspaper. In almost every case, it's interesting to see how your being a member of the team that performed well not only benefited you but also benefited the team.

3. More productive teams normally are those composed of individuals who are relatively equal in formal authority. One group of authors has called co-equal peers "hierarchically undifferentiated individuals."[11] Authority constraints are reduced by similarity of authority level. At work, you may notice that it's much easier to talk openly when management isn't there!

4. A state of open-mindedness on the part of every participant is critical to the success of group action. This component calls for receptivity to the views of others with a willingness to accept their ideas when the ideas seem to be valid. Group members, of course, will have ideas of their own, but it is a sharing of personal views and a consideration of the views of others that leads to success. To get a variety of ideas and to get them openly discussed, two things are necessary. First, there's a need for heterogeneity. Heterogeneous groups are ones where members have different backgrounds and ideas. (Homogeneous groups, on the other hand, where members are all alike, are prone to groupthink.) Second, an open, trusting atmosphere must develop so that group members aren't reluctant to give ideas, even if the ideas are different.

5. The size of the decision group seems to affect the performance of the team. While Slater, in his study, found the optimal group to be about five members in size,[12] others have suggested in a more general way the need to keep the group relatively small. Bray et al. indicate that it is the functional size of the group that is important. As the group gets larger, some members stop functioning.[13] Bales et al. conclude that as a group size is increased from three to eight members, the group is more likely to be dominated by one or two members.[14] Markham et al. reveal that as group size increases, more people are likely to be absent.[15]

6. Someone must accept the responsibility for leadership in the decision group. Frequently the leadership role is assigned in advance to a specific person. The leader can help the group to be successful by following procedures before group decision meetings and after the group has met as well as while the group is meeting. A suggested set of leadership activities is shown in Table 3–1

Other group discussion formats are available in addition to the traditional one just described. A good example of an innovation in interacting relations is the Social Judgement Analysis. The technique, advocated by experts such as

Table 3–1

Leadership
Responsibilities in
the Team Decision-
making and Problem-
solving Session

Before Session Begins

1. Review facts and symptoms; clarify problems, goals and objectives.
2. Encourage the collection of all pertinent data.
3. Assist in the selection of team participants who have an interest in the problem or task and are qualified to contribute.
4. Stimulate thought, provide information, and submit an interaction agenda to participants, if possible.
5. Make the appropriate physical arrangements.

During Session

1. Encourage a period of social introduction and development.
2. Help participants to become aware of group responsibilities and of pertinent information related to the fulfillment of responsibilities.
3. Lead the group in discussing problems, discovering and reviewing alternative solutions, and selecting the best available course of action.
4. See that individuals are rewarded for positive contributions.
5. Promise feedback and enlist the support of all participants

After Session

1. Communicate the results of group performance to all appropriate individuals and see that ideas are acted upon.
2. Lead in monitoring and evaluating the results of group efforts and continue to provide feedback to participants.

Sometimes groups become too large to make decisions easily and effectively.

Self Test

Personal Feedback

Manner of Communication
With Whom Do You Work Best?

This style indicator will give you an idea about how you communicate. You can use it to see with whom you work the best.

Word Groups

In each of the 10 groups of words below, choose 2 words in each numbered group of 4 words you feel most nearly describe you in your everyday environment. For example, in the first group underline two words from strong, smooth, critical, and cautious. Then do the same for groups 2 through 10.

1. strong	smooth	critical	cautious
2. centralized	verbal	studious	nonassertive
3. dominant	convincing	tenacious	willing
4. rigid	assuring	searching	adhering
5. guiding	compassionate	inquiring	imitating
6. regulating	motivating	probing	cooperative
7. governing	influencing	contemplative	listening
8. mastering	satisfying	organized	obedient
9. aggressive	inspiring	systematic	attentive
10. demanding	supportive	disciplined	dutiful
X total _____	Y total _____	W total _____	Z total _____

When you have finished underlining the appropriate words, do the following:

1. Add the words you've underlined down the rows and enter the totals in the spaces at the bottom of each row.
2. Add up the Total column to see if you have the right number of words. Your total score should add up to 20.
3. Place a point on each of the W X Y Z axes on the righthand chart below to reflect your W X Y and Z scores. Then connect the points to form a four-sided figure like the one in the lefthand chart. Suppose your X score is 6, your Y score is 4, your Z score is 8 and your W score is 2. Your figure will look like the one shown.
4. Now record your scores and draw the lines.

The Midwest Human Resource Systems who first developed this kind of test says that the size of the box in each quadrant determines the importance of the style as shown below.

> **Directors** have drive and initiative but don't attend to detail. They tend to run over others.
> **Persuaders** make others feel good but don't establish directions.
> **Analyzers** can pull a situation apart but usually can't make decisions.
> **Followers** are "good souls" and have loyalty but show little initiative.

Example

Number of W's	2	Number of W's	_____
Number of X's	6	Number of X's	_____
Number of Y's	4	Number of Y's	_____
Number of Z's	8	Number of Z's	_____

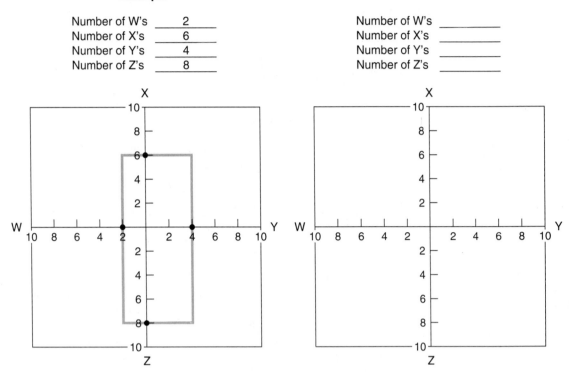

Interpretation: The size of the box in each quadrant determines the importance of the style.

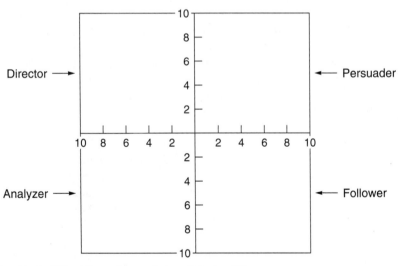

Source: Adapted in part from a test developed by the Midwest Human Resource Systems, Columbus, Ohio.

The Midwest Human Resource people further state that the best pairs for working together productively are directors with analyzers and persuaders with followers. However, especially in the case of directors and analyzers, they may not enjoy working together.

Hammond and Rohrbaugh,[16] requires a closer coordination of individual efforts through the weighing of decision factors, the determination of a sequence to tie factors together, and a definite organizing of all parts of the solution. Consensus as well as personal satisfaction is fostered by the use of this technique. (Please do the Self Test/personal feedback exercise to identify your behavior patterns toward others.)

Two More Nontraditional Decision Groups

The decision teams discussed previously were interacting groups in that there was a great deal of give-and-take among the participants in each group. In more recent developments, group decision techniques have been designed which, while not encouraging personal interaction very much, provide effective ways to make group decisions. Why the deemphasis on personal interaction if groups are so effective? As we've said, groups have their drawbacks. A key drawback is domination by one or more members.

Nominal Group Technique (NGT)
A group decision-making approach where individuals identify solutions, share them in round-robin fashion, and eventually vote to select the best choice. At certain points during the group's effort, members may discuss the votes before making other votes.

The Nominal Group Technique (NGT)   The NGT was developed in 1968 by Delbecq and Van de Ven as a part of their sociopsychological studies of decision conferences at NASA. There are normally about six or seven steps in the NGT process. First, the problem is identified for the participants. Then, group members silently and independently generate their ideas about the problem in writing. This period of silent writing is followed by a recorded round-robin procedure in which each group member, one at a time, in turn, presents one of his or her ideas to the group without discussion. The ideas are summarized briefly on a blackboard or poster board. After all individuals have presented their ideas, the ideas are discussed for clarification and evaluation. A preliminary vote on the best solution is then taken, with each person voting silently and independently. The preliminary vote is tabulated and discussed. The final vote is taken, with members again voting silently and independently. The voting is either by rank-order or by rating, and the group decision is the pooled outcome.[17]

delphi technique
A technique for making group decisions where experts are chosen as participants. Group members never meet together directly. They receive information, respond in written form, receive written feedback, vote, and so forth, until a consensus is reached.

The Delphi Technique   The delphi technique was first developed by Norman Dalkey at the Rand Corporation. Its stated purposes are to determine or develop a range of possible alternatives, to explore or expose underlying assumptions leading to different judgments, to seek out information that might lead to consensus, and to get ideas from experts.[18] The delphi method was originally designed for use through the mail. It has been adapted by some for local use, however, and the possibilities of FAX and similar applications are apparent. The process is a rather lengthy one. The steps to the delphi process are listed in Table 3–2.

The conclusions of several studies are that the NGT and delphi are superior to traditional interaction groups in their effectiveness for decision making.[19] Studies also conclude that the NGT and delphi techniques draw more ideas and creativity from members and result in more satisfied participants. On a separate note, it should be mentioned that these nontraditional techniques also seem to be a good way for avoiding groupthink.

Table 3–2

Steps in the Delphi Technique

1. Enlisting the cooperation of experts.
2. Presenting the problem to the experts.
3. Recording solutions and recommendations (from the experts).
4. Compiling the responses and reproducing them.
5. Sharing all responses with the experts.
6. Having the experts comment on the ideas generated and propose solutions.
7. Compiling the proposed solutions.
8. If a consensus is reached, announcing the decision.
9. Sharing responses with experts if no consensus is reached.
10. Again encouraging experts to respond and propose solutions.
11. Again compiling proposed solutions and comments.
12. Announcing the consensus (if reached) or continuing the process until consensus is reached.

A Different Kind of Group—The Quality Circle

In recent years, an organizational group called the quality circle (QC) has evolved. Actually, the idea for such a group began in Japan through some of the ideas fostered by Americans Edward Deming and Joseph Juran, blended with the nature of the Japanese culture. The QC is a small, volunteer group of workers who agree to meet together regularly to discuss, analyze, and propose solutions to quality problems. This type of group is more likely to exist in manufacturing and processing concerns, but there is application to service industries as well. QCs usually meet once a week, either during the regular workday or following work hours. The topics they discuss are limited to their own areas of performance.[20]

Quality circles begin with the training of leaders, usually at the initiative of levels of management higher up in the organization. The training the group leader receives includes (1) administrative skills development, (2) the learning of simple statistical methods, (3) technological training to aid understanding of the organization's process, (4) instruction on the use of the case study method to develop analytical skills, and (5) methods to use in teaching others.[21] The leader normally will begin working with volunteers from a single area of a factory. Most QCs include from five to ten members. If the circle gets too large, another leader is trained, and another group is formed.

When the QC meets (its average meeting time is between sixty and ninety minutes), all members are prepared as a result of assignments given them at the last meeting. This preparation is extremely important to the success of the session. Brainstorming is usually an important part of the meeting. Each member is encouraged to participate and put forth ideas. No idea is criticized, and members are encouraged to voice all of their ideas, no matter how trivial the ideas may seem. Topics for discussion are selected in part by the group itself and in part by upper management. Some groups get no pay for their work, although most organizations do provide funding. Some of the pay comes in the form of rewards for ideas generated. On the average, 50 percent of the QC's activities are related to quality control, 40 percent are concerned with productivity and cost matters, and 10 percent concentrate on safety and other miscellaneous considerations.[22] In Japan, QCs (or quality control circles, as they are called there) are very popular. At least one out of every eight workers is a member of a QC. The percentage of workers involved in QCs in the United States is lower than the Japanese level but seems to be growing steadily.[23]

In the United States, several kinds of QCs have formed. At Xerox, many QCs are special-purpose, one-time-only groups, assigned to solve a specific problem. For example, one group successfully solved a mail-routing problem involving a number of the company's operations. In other firms, such as several large oil companies, QCs are much closer to the Japanese mode and discuss any questions or problems that come before the group.[24]

The future of QCs seems bright as the ideas spread to other industries as well as to other nations.

Team Building and Problem Solving

For a group or team to perform effectively for a period of time, a large amount of effort goes into renewal, maintenance, and innovation activities. It is typical for any type of group—decision-making, operations, QC—to identify problem areas or areas where improvements are needed. A number of indicators exist that make groups aware that development is needed. Symptoms of group dysfunctioning include apathy and a general lack of interest; loss of productivity; increased grievances or complaints within a group; confusion about assignments; low participation in meetings; lack of innovation, imagination, and initiative; increased complaints from those outside the group; and evidence of hostility or conflict.[25] If you've ever been in a group with symptoms like these, you know that members quickly become turned off. Without some radical change, the group will stop making positive contributions.

team building
A concept including many stages where the intention is to improve the quality and effectiveness of performance in a specific group. Several exercises may be performed to build group cohesiveness as well as to produce more goal-oriented behavior.

A concept known as **team building** has developed for rebuilding and helping groups achieve an optimum level of effectiveness and efficiency. Team building does not require that a major crisis be in existence before it can be useful. Team building can be appropriate for any kind of organizational family (decision group, operational team, project groups, committee). Team building may be a part of a total program for growth and development (organization development, for example). It is an unending process.

Let's look at a team-building cycle that can help to put the stages of action into a sequence. Figure 3–1 is a modification of the developmental cycle that has been advanced. The process begins with the statement of goals for the group or the problem identification if it is known. Data are then collected to determine which may show potential for growth or for possible symptoms of problems. Specific developmental or change areas are identified (diagnosis). Planning for action or intervention occurs. The plans are implemented, and the whole team-building process is evaluated. After the completion of a cycle, the process is begun all over again.

William Dyer, an expert on team building, has suggested a method for discovering if problems do exist (see Table 3–3). This team-building checklist is a sample of the kind of document useful for identification and diagnosis.[26]

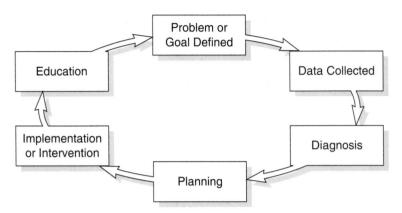

Source: William G. Dyer, *Team Building,* © 1987 by Addison-Wesley Publishing Company. Reprinted with permission of the publisher.

Figure 3–1

The Team-Building Cycle

Table 3–3

A Team-Building Checklist for Problem Identification

To what extent is there evidence of the following problems in your work unit?	*Low Evidence*		*Some Evidence*		*High Evidence*
1. Loss of production or work unit output	1	2	3	4	5
2. Grievances or complaints within the work unit	1	2	3	4	5
3. Conflicts or hostility among unit members	1	2	3	4	5
4. Confusion about assignments or unclear relationships between people	1	2	3	4	5
5. Lack of clear goals or low commitment to goals	1	2	3	4	5
6. Apathy or general lack of interest or involvement by unit members	1	2	3	4	5
7. Lack of innovation, risk taking, imagination, or taking the initiative	1	2	3	4	5
8. Ineffective staff meetings	1	2	3	4	5
9. Problems in working with the boss	1	2	3	4	5
10. Poor communication: people afraid to speak up, not listening to one another, or not talking together	1	2	3	4	5
11. Lack of trust between boss and members or among members	1	2	3	4	5
12. Decisions made that people do not understand or agree with	1	2	3	4	5
13. People feeling that good work is not recognized or rewarded	1	2	3	4	5
14. People not encouraged to work together in better team effort	1	2	3	4	5

Scoring: Add up the score for the fourteen items. If your score is between 14 and 28, there is little evidence your unit needs team building. If your score is between 29 and 42, there is some evidence, but no immediate pressure, unless two or three items are very high. If your score is between 43 and 56, you should seriously think about planning a team-building program. If your score is over 56, team building should be a top priority for your work unit.

Source: William G. Dyer, *Team Building,* © 1987 by Addison-Wesley Publishing Company. Reprinted with permission of the publisher.

If major change or innovation is needed, team-building methods most frequently used are individual consultation (counseling and coaching); instructional group training, including the use of T-groups and sensitivity training (these are loosely controlled group interactions); or structured group training, using readings, lectures, exercises, test instruments, MBO (Managing by Objectives is a participative technique to use for a degree of self-control), Grid training instruction on production—people emphasis, and transactional analysis (discussed in Chapter 6).

Process consultation, another method, features emphasis on technical, interpersonal, and communication procedures that are necessary to be effective. Analysis of the data collected in the earlier stages of the team-building process might be yet another intervention.[27] When this kind of approach is used, the group (any type of group) and the organization can remain dynamic and useful.

Summary

People in work settings are finding themselves more and more involved in teams and groups. They work cooperatively for such purposes as production planning and decision making. The importance of integration and coordination of effort is steadily rising. Groups come in all sizes and shapes.

Group work is being used as an alternative to highly specialized individual effort. Groups are also becoming more autonomous as members do more of their own decision making, motivating, and controlling. **Operational groups** have many advantages: they provide flexibility, increase productivity, result in greater personal satisfaction, and produce higher quality products.

operational group
A team of individuals formally assigned to perform a specific function or set of functions in an organization. This type of group may be a department or a set of functionally interrelated individuals.

Decision-making groups are also receiving recognition for their effectiveness. Decision groups, when properly composed, result in decisions made with a wider variety of facts and alternatives considered. Recommendations made by groups (such as those for problem solving) frequently have a higher level of accuracy than recommendations made by individuals acting independently. Decisions made by groups are more likely to be accepted by employees than decisions made individually. Group decisions, as a result of the information exchange they cause, make organizational members more knowledgeable which, in turn, may lead to more favorable mindsets. As people work together, they develop a rapport among themselves.

There are drawbacks to group decisions, too. Group decision making is slower and requires more individuals to spend time in the process. As a result, decisions can be expensive. If group decision making is not handled properly, compromise, win-lose, and other inferior decisions may result. Managers can also become too dependent on group decisions and as a result may avoid making their own decisions. Groups are more likely than individuals to make risk-oriented decisions. This, of course, can be either good or bad, depending upon the situation. There is also the danger that groupthink will result. Groups can be structured and conditioned so that they can be most effective. Keeping the group size small is important for best group results. Members of a group need to be compatible while bringing different skills and knowledge to the group. Participative, supportive leadership is normally more effective than dominant, controlling leadership.

Future trends include the development of new group techniques for decision making as well as new types of groups (like QCs). The future will find us also needing to emphasize individual efforts for some activities.

Questions to Consider

1. On a day-to-day basis, how can we tell when to use a group to do something or when to allow an individual to do something?
2. Why do many managers who are highly traditional in their philosophies oppose the use of teams, particularly for decision making and problem solving?
3. When would a decision made through individual effort probably be superior to one made through the group process? What kinds of decisions are involved?
4. Groups frequently tend to compromise in decision making. How can this be explained? How can it be improved upon?
5. If a single person is dominating a group and its efforts, what can be done to give the control back to the group?
6. What can be done about team members who fail to carry their share of the group's workload?
7. If you are a part of a group that you feel is headed toward groupthink and you're not the leader, how can you keep the group from making a mistake?
8. Why are the NGT and delphi techniques said to be superior to traditional interacting group processes? Explain.
9. What difficulties (if any) are likely to be encountered in the team-building process? Explain.
10. Is it ethical for a manager to ask a group to do something he or she is unwilling to do (like make an unpopular decision)?
11. Is it ethical for a group member to withhold information he or she knows might result in a decision he or she opposes?

Go back and analyze the case at the beginning of the chapter. What concepts from the chapter would be helpful if applied to the case?

Key Terms

decision-making group
delphi technique
groupthink
Nominal Group
   Technique (NGT)

operational group
quality circle
team building

traditional interacting
   group

Chapter Case

The Arrogant Architects

After graduation you go to work as a planner for a large architectural firm. The firm's offices have been moved to several large, luxurious floors in a spacious office building, a result, your new boss tells you, of rapid expansion. "It's hard to believe that only four years ago we were a struggling firm with only six employees," the boss tells you. "Now we stand at over two hundred and are considered one of the major firms of our type in the country!" You are impressed and ask what the boss believes is the secret to the firm's success. The boss responds:

> We are in the right place at the right time—no doubt about it! The situation is wild in our business. As you may know, competition is extremely intense among architectural firms, and gaining a competitive edge is the crucial issue. Things are especially rough because of the pressures on us—there are consumer groups, HUD and OSHA from the federal government, all kinds of state and local regulations, the environmentalists, and who knows what else, all involved in the way we do business. We've succeeded for two reasons, I believe. First, we've gained a competitive edge through the technology we've developed. Our design work is truly state-of-the-art. We can deliver a building that is environmentally sound and nearly twenty percent cheaper to heat and air condition for roughly the same costs as our closest competitors. We've been able to do that because of the team we've had—a second reason for our success. But I'm afraid that we may be looking at problems in that area now.

You ask for details, and the boss tells you, essentially, that in the early days the organization functioned as a loosely formed team where there really were no rules or real organizational structure. Everybody just simply came in and did whatever needed doing at the time. Even the most talented architect, for example, thought nothing of spending hours doing drafting work if that was what needed to be done. The boss goes on to say:

> But now, everything's changed. For one thing, we grew—and a large organization just simply can't run that loosely. And then our founding president left us, and the new one is a real organizational nut. Now everybody has a neat job description and a nice little slot on the organization chart—but it's not the same. Furthermore, we're losing ground—it just doesn't seem like we can respond to the competition the way we used to.

The boss tells you about a current problem involving the drafting group, the architects, and the architectural engineers. The architects and the architectural engineers are the "elitist" groups—highly educated and highly paid. They look down on all others in the organization and are known for being uncooperative. "Wait until you have to work with them," the boss adds. "We need lots of information from them to go forward with the long-range plan, and I'm willing to bet that they'll refuse to provide it. They're just like a bunch of spoiled children!"

The situation is particularly serious where the architects are concerned. You learn that they aren't even loyal to the company, and there is some evidence that they've given out proprietary information to competitors. Much of the work of building design requires close cooperation not only among the architects as a group but also between the architects and other groups, which is where the additional trouble set in. The architects work fairly well with the architectural engineers (though the architectural engineers disapprove of the architects' lack of loyalty to the company), but relations between the architects and drafting are terrible. The draftspeople, angered by the arrogant attitude of the architects, give them very little cooperation and actually try to sabotage their work when they think they can get away with it. "What a mess!" the boss moans.

1. What factors are contributing positively toward teamwork within the groups?
2. What factors are preventing the organization as a whole from functioning as a team?
3. What *needs* to be done to create teamwork? What *can* be done?

Technology—Its Impact in the Workplace

Objectives

- To consider the role that technology plays in an organization.
- To investigate the impact of technology upon people in the workplace.
- To discover reasons for employees' resistance to new technological ideas.
- To identify CIM and what it does.
- To become familiar with the meanings and effect of such concepts as robotics, artificial intelligence, the expert system, and electronic mail.
- To discover recent trends that technology is making possible in the way of work patterns.

What's in It for Me?

Samuel Jameson, Director of Information Processing , was heading for the Friday general staff meeting—and he was really fuming. "People must be crazy," he was thinking to himself as he walked down the hall. "Our new integrated data and information network has the capability to put all the information our top managers need at their fingertips, to cut way down on the clerical workload, and bring our company to the forefront technologically—but it's not being used! This is ridiculous!"

Jameson had asked for time on the staff meeting agenda to discuss the situation and the need to use the new system as designed. The new system that he was thinking about really WAS superb technologically. The database was updated nightly and contained up-to-the-minute information about all aspects of company operations, comparing plans to actual results. It also contained a wealth of supplementary data, including moves by competitors and other important information about events affecting the firm. There was a terminal on each executive's desk, and information could be retrieved in a matter of seconds. Furthermore, all of the executives were networked together so that they could use the system to communicate and to send information and reports to each other.

The latest analysis of system usage, however, showed almost no activity. The executives simply weren't using the system. The final straw had come yesterday afternoon when Jameson had discovered one of the secretaries laboriously retyping a printout that had been generated by the system. "So the execs can understand it," she'd commented!

"Talk about reinventing the wheel," Jameson growled to himself. "Anybody who's doing *that* has no idea how the system should operate!"

The meeting room filled quickly, and Jameson launched into his topic, trying once again to explain how important it was to make appropriate use of the new system and emphasizing that the company's enormous expenditure was being wasted without proper use. There were few comments after Jameson's presentation, and the meeting moved on to the next item on the agenda. The meeting adjourned, and Jameson walked out with Elena Ortiz, Director of Marketing and one of the most senior and most respected of the executives.

"I don't think I got anywhere with my presentation today," Jameson lamented. "I've never seen such a bunch of stony faces. What's with people, anyway?"

"It sounds to me like you need some advice," Ortiz commented. "Let me give it to you from a sales and marketing perspective. You have to SELL the new system just like any other product. You did a mighty effective job of pointing out the benefits to the *company* if we use the new system. But what about benefits to *us?* If you can't answer the question, What's in it for me? you won't be able to sell your product, that's for sure!"

"But the system is so easy to use," responded Jameson. "It saves all kinds of clerical effort."

"But that's not the point," Ortiz explained. "Sure, it saves clerical time—but it does it by making US—the execs—into clerks. Our time is valuable. Why should we spend time doing our own typing into those terminals you've installed in our offices—and trying to make heads or tails of the complex data displays and print-outs the system gives you? Frankly, we prefer the old way!"

"Now what?" thought Jameson in despair.

Case Questions

1. Why did the executives resist using the new technology?
2. What should Jameson do now?
3. Did the executives really understand how to use the system?

In its broadest sense, technology is the sum total of the ways through which societies provide themselves with the material objects of their civilization. In an organizational sense, technology is the sum total of ways the organization achieves its material goals. Technology refers in part to the organization's physical assets and capabilities of an organization, including such things as machinery, tools, and equipment. Technology is also the creative process through which new products and new processes are discovered (the primary work of a research and development unit). Another good view of technology is that it includes the tools, techniques, and activities necessary to transform organizational inputs into outputs.

The Flow of Technology Through an Organization

Innovation and creativity are important functions in many organizations, and the development of new goods and services is an important activity. "Building a better mouse trap," so to speak, is a strategy many organizations use to a competitive advantage. Organizations in the business of developing new products and procedures must take the necessary steps for creativity to emerge. The proper climate for innovation includes a general set of goals and guidelines, supportive leadership, resources and staff to draw upon, recognition when creativity is achieved, and appropriate rewards and reinforcements.

Raychem Corporation, for example, is supplier of technology-intensive products to industrial customers in aerospace, automobile, construction, telecommunication, and utilities areas. Since its founding in 1957, Raychem has pursued a consistent strategy: to master a set of core technologies and produce thousands of proprietary products based on those technologies. The company produces over 50,000 products, many of them manufactured only by Raychem.

Raychem's strategy has paid off handsomely. Raychem has annual revenues of over $1 billion, some 60 percent of which is generated outside the United States. The company consistently earns gross profit (amount earned before expenses are subtracted) of 50 percent, has no net bank debt, and has a price/earnings ratio of about 30 percent (30 percent of the price is earnings). For the first 25 years of Raychem's existence, the company's average growth rate was 25 percent. By any measure, this is a successful and innovative company.

Founder and CEO Paul Cook says this success is no accident and was produced by following a simple formula:

> To be an innovative company, you have to ask for innovation. You assemble a group of talented people who are eager to do new things, and put them in an environment where innovation is expected. It's that simple—and that hard. There is no one in any organization who can't be clever and imaginative about doing his or her job more effectively. We expect [and reward] innovation from our secretaries and the people on the loading docks as well as from the scientists.[1]

One of the biggest challenges managers face with new technology is to get it accepted by the culture of the organization and by the individuals who make up the organization.[2] Employees are resistant toward new technology for several reasons. Many employees, for example, fear that their skills will be made obsolete when new technological procedures are introduced. If new skills are called for, many are uncertain of their ability to develop those new skills. Some are afraid they will lose control of the way they work. Uncertainty raises fear of what the future will bring. Fear of physical harm is another concern. Some are afraid of computers, and change often involves working with computers. Of course, some workers fear being displaced by machines, robots, or computers. Check your computer concerns by doing the Personal Feedback exercise "What Bothers You about Computers."

Personal Feedback

Self Test

What Bothers You About Computers

Answer the questions below to identify the basis of concerns (if any) you have about computers. Rate the concerns on a scale of 1 to 5. A score of 5 indicates the item is of very high concern while a score of 1 represents no concern.

	Very High	High	Moderate	Little	No
I would rather write my thoughts on paper and let someone else type them or put them in the word processor.	5	4	3	2	1
I don't like having to learn the ends and outs of software every time I turn around.	5	4	3	2	1

The fact that computers get viruses sometimes bothers me a great deal.	5	4	3	2	1
I'm afraid I'll erase something when I'm working on a computer.	5	4	3	2	1
I'm afraid there will be an electrical interruption while my computer is on, and I'll lose a large amount of data.	5	4	3	2	1
The printers I've seen or worked with aren't very reliable.	5	4	3	2	1
No two software programs are alike and I find it frustrating to have to learn new procedures.	5	4	3	2	1
The manuals manufacturers put out are too confusing to be helpful.	5	4	3	2	1
I'm afraid that I'll do something that will damage the computer when I'm working with it.	5	4	3	2	1
I feel that the computer is like having a boss who makes you do what he/she wants you to do when he/she wants you to do it.	5	4	3	2	1
I'm afraid that computers will wind up replacing me and thus cost me my job.	5	4	3	2	1
I'm afraid I will never become competent at working with computers.	5	4	3	2	1
I'm afraid that if I put confidential matters in storage, someone will see the information who shouldn't see it.	5	4	3	2	1
It bothers me when people around me talk computer talk and I don't know what they are saying.	5	4	3	2	1
I'm afraid I will develop wrist and shoulder problems if I spend much time at the computer terminal.	5	4	3	2	1

This is not the kind of test you need to add for total points. Go back through and note the *items* to which you gave the highest scores. This will help you to pinpoint your concerns. For example, if you gave item number 1 a 4 or 5, you see computer work as too time consuming. If you gave item number 2 a high score, you dislike the unfamiliarity of different programs, and you may doubt your ability to learn new procedures. Once you've identified the causes of your concerns about computers, you can take steps to deal with the concerns.

The Chief Technology Officer

The increasing importance of technology is causing many organizations to appoint an individual to the position of **chief technology officer** (CTO), whose role has many dimensions. The CTO acts as link to the environment outside the organization. It is the CTO's responsibility to keep up with emerging technological advances to ascertain what might be used in his or her organization. The CTO spends a large amount of time talking with CTOs in other organizations, listening to sales personnel present their newest products and inventions, attending conferences with other professionals, reading technology-related journals, and cultivating contacts with university faculty and researchers.[3]

The CTO has several duties inside the organization as well. The CTO is responsible for identifying new technological developments and screening them to see if they can be useful. The CTO gathers the skilled staff needed to use new technology. He or she must link new technologies with top management. (Refer to the case at the beginning of the chapter. In effect, Sam Jameson is acting as CTO in his company. What are some of his activities?) Technology will join together different groups and individuals who will utilize it. The CTO is responsible for developing a climate supportive of the new concepts and techniques where cooperation thrives. The CTO is also responsible for assessing technology in relation to overall organizational strategy. Obviously, the CTO carries significant responsibilities.[4]

CTO (chief technology officer) The CTO in an organization is responsible for seeing that the technology appropriate for the organization is identified, implemented, and correctly utilized. This person's responsibilities are organizationwide.

What Technology Does for an Organization

Technology has its impact on an organization and its people in a number of different areas.

Technology's Impact on Production

Technology at the earlier stages of development was concerned with increased productivity and higher levels of efficiency. Mass production and assembly lines were some of the first technological developments. The idea was to take advantage of **economies of scale,** by which technology was used to spread fixed costs of production over a few products, processing them in large quantities. If, for example, the cost of machines was $10,000 and only one unit was produced, all costs would be charged to that one unit. If instead ten units were produced, the machine cost per unit would be only $1,000, greatly reducing the unit's production cost.

Some organizations began to take advantage of **economies of scope,** which are realized when it is less or equally costly to produce two or more products in combination rather than separately. The cost savings from using economies of scope are derived from spreading fixed costs of manufacturing equipment across several products.[5]

Recent advances in computer technology have enabled firms to enjoy the advantages of both economies of scale and economies of scope. Organizations

economies of scale Production of a larger quantity of units so that the cost per unit is reduced as fixed costs are spread over more units.

economies of scope Economies of scope occur when an organization can produce two or more products at a cost less than or equal to the cost of producing only one product.

can now manufacture large quantities of some items efficiently and then switch to other products without costly retooling and setup changes. This concept is called **economies of integration,** since it takes advantage of economies of scale and economies of scope. Through various computer techniques, an integration of manufacturing systems can be achieved. Several technologies controlled by computer when used in concert (see Figure 4–1) are called **computer integrated manufacturing** (CIM). CIM has four significant effects:

1. It allows the specialization that has normally been built into the hardware of conventional machine systems to be replaced by software that rapidly redesigns the production systems for different products.
2. It eliminates learning curve effects by removing the direct labor component through software that can repeat actions very precisely after they are accomplished only once.
3. It removes much of the confusion in manufacturing through integration of scheduling, machinery, materials flow, and tooling.
4. It allows setup changes to be accomplished rapidly, which reduces the economic batch quantity. This means that manufacturers can produce smaller quantities of products but still make a profit.[6]

Most studies of the effect on performance of a firm that uses CIM find that machine utilization is significantly more efficient, labor productivity increases, scrap rates decrease, and customer satisfaction increases because of improved quality and product variety.[7]

Robotics

The production process in recent years has been aided considerably in some cases by the development of **robotics**—the creation of mechanical units that act like humans and take the place of humans in the production process. First-generation robots are strictly motor in nature, limited to such routine functions as grinding, spray painting, welding, stacking, and loading. Routine, repetitive activities are the mainstay of first-generation robots.[8]

Second-generation robots are now arriving and are much more sophisticated. The more advanced robots have eyes to distinguish variations in color, shape, or location. The new robots have ears that can distinguish acceptable from unacceptable sounds. The robots have touch-sensitive skin that can distinguish acceptable from unacceptable materials. Recently, robots have even developed a sense of smell, whereby they can distinguish acceptable from unacceptable odors. Toxic materials or gases can be identified. Second-generation robots can be designed to work independently, or they can be designed to work with and under the direction of humans.[9]

As even more talented robots are developed, they are expected to be further skilled so that with the use of artificial intelligence they will become more humanlike and will make many of their own decisions.

Data Accumulation, Storage, and Decision Making

One of the earliest forms of activity for computers was the collection and storage of data. As time has passed, the capacity for acquisition and storage has

economies of integration
Computer technology enables organizations to concentrate on the production of one product efficiently and then switch to production of another product without costly retooling and setup. In this way, economies of scale and economies of scope can both be achieved.

CIM (computer integrated manufacturing)
CIM is achieved when computers and other technological devices coordinate the activities involved in a production process from the beginning of the process (planning and scheduling) to the end of the process (distribution).

robotics
The creation of mechanical units that act like humans and take the place of humans in the production process of an organization.

Figure 4–1   How Computer Integrated Manufacturing (CIM) Works

Computer integrated manufacturing (CIM) is meant to break down the barriers between customers, the corporate office, production, suppliers and product planning by allowing everyone to speak the same language. It also allows everyone to keep tabs on a product as it moves through the system. Here's an example of how CIM works—from customer order to delivery.

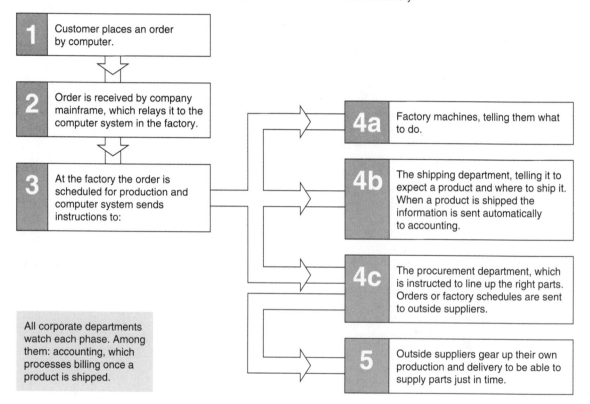

Source: Stephen Kreider Yoder, "Putting It All Together," *Wall Street Journal,* June 4, 1990, p. 24. Reprinted by permission of *The Wall Street Journal,* © 1990 Dow Jones and Company, Inc. All Rights Reserved Worldwide.

increased. With this increase, the decision-making skills of the computer have also grown.

In the Management In Action example from Frito-Lay, computers were fed data that went to a central location. The quick data collection and processing made data available for the appropriate person or persons to monitor activities and make adjustments using the company's new Decision Support System. In the Frito-Lay example, decisions mostly were made by those receiving the data. It is possible to program computers to reach decisions based upon the guidelines fed into them (as we will see in the next section).

Artificial Intelligence.   The term **artificial intelligence** is used to describe the way computers are developed with the ability to make humanlike decisions. To a limited degree, artificial intelligence has been around for a while as computers have exercised judgments in playing computer games, in musical and artistic fields, and in simulations.

At the highest level, artificial intelligence is a complex of computer hardware, computer programs, and robots. It possesses the faculties of

artificial intelligence
The capacity of computers to make humanlike decisions.

**Management
in Action**

Frito-Lay's Integrated Information System

Robert H. Beeby, president of Frito-Lay, describes the benefits of the company's new integrated information system.

Until recently, Frito-Lay had a centralized decision-making structure common to many corporations. Product information crept upward through the organization on what I thought was a timely basis. I soon discovered it wasn't timely enough.

It did not, for example, provide Frito-Lay enough time to respond quickly to its rapidly changing and complex markets or to fine-tune its inventory. It also did not allow us to shorten our business cycle enough to stay ahead of the competition. And it did not allow me, the CEO, to have the latest sales and profit information on the 14 million snacks sold weekly through our 400,000 sales calls.

So we changed—radically.

The catalyst was our Decision Support System, brought on-line last year. DSS kicks back to 200 managers detailed sales and inventory information fed into it by 10,000 route salespeople equipped with hand-held computers.

For example, one of our sales people who handles more than 50 stores for us in New Jersey no longer spends hours writing orders, invoices and sales reports. With his palm-sized computer, he now completes his "paper work" in a minute or two at each stop, running through a programmed product list complete with prices. At the end of each day, his sales report is transmitted in seconds to headquarters in Dallas. We save 30,000 hours a week for the entire sales force, and untold savings in clerical, postage and form costs.

Here's how the system serves us.

1. The system helps in tracking new products. In this area, DSS is invaluable. This spring, for example, Frito-Lay launched its new "Light" line of snack foods. DSS allows me to see if this new line is cannibalizing other Frito-Lay brands—and I get the information in a matter of days, not weeks as was previously the case. I also have easy access to data showing our performance vs. competitive brands'. For Ruffles Light Potato Chips, I can determine: total sales from the previous week; supermarket sales vs. smaller accounts; average sales on a particular route; and the success of our promo-

expert system
A knowledge-based program whereby rules, probabilities, facts, and relationships are entered into a computer database by a human expert

knowing, reasoning, and understanding. Proponents of this level see no reason why computers can't simulate every aspect of human intelligence, including the ability to invent, ask questions that go beyond orderly rational frameworks, and display "human" wisdom.[10]

The second level of artificial intelligence is the **expert system** (ES). (Robots are the third level.) E S is a sophisticated program that can diagnose a situation in a particular field, such as medicine, oil exploration, or business. E S is a knowledge-based program where rules, probabilities, facts, and relationships tions. Most important, the data allow me to make mid-course corrections to ensure the success of the Light line.

2. The system facilitates faster, more accurate decisions. Recently, I noticed red numbers (indicating reduced market share) for tortilla chips in our central business region. I punched up another screen display and located the problem: Texas. I kept punching up new screens and tracked the red numbers to a specific sales division and, finally to the chain of stores. The numbers pinpointed the problem area and, after additional research, revealed the culprit: the introduction of a generic store-branded product. We quickly formulated a counter-strategy and sales climbed again.

   Through information technology, even cardboard cartons used to transport our products become a business opportunity. Last year, 88 percent of all cartons shipped to our distribution centers were returned by our sales force for re-use. If we push the percentage up a single point, it saves Frito-Lay $700,000. So, through DSS, we are now tracking cardboard returns by individual sales route, and by store, and hope to push returns above 90 percent.

3. The system assists in "management by walking around." When Tom Peters coined that phrase he wasn't thinking of a computer tour of operations by the CEO. But that is what DSS allows me and other senior executives to do. I can, at a glance, view the performance of each of our managers and salespeople around the country. If I see something I don't like, I can fire off an electronic-mail memo. Conversely, if there is good news, I'm likely to contact the manager and congratulate him.

4. The system helps us to decentralize. I never thought a computer would be responsible for a total reorganization of Frito-Lay, but it has been. Last year we decentralized, breaking the company into four geographic business areas, each with its own business plan, structure, and profit-and-loss responsibility. We did so because DSS, and the detailed information it provides, allows middle managers to have a complete picture of what is happening in their regions. Now approximately 60 percent of the decisions that used to be made by top management are made by regional managers, leaving the decisions affecting the company as a whole at corporate headquarters.

Source: Robert H. Beeby, "How to Crunch a Bunch of Figures," *The Wall Street Journal,* June 4, 1990, p. A10. Reprinted by permission of *The Wall Street Journal,* © 1990 Dow Jones and Company, Inc. All Rights Reserved Worldwide.

are entered into a database by a human expert in a particular field. As a result of this input, the computer is able to generate expertlike responses to questions and issues. New data are continuously fed into the computer so that the knowledge base is constantly updated.[11]

One way E S works, for example, is a situation whereby a centralized help desk is established to assist employees in the field. When an employee has a problem, he or she calls into the help desk and electronically inputs the situational conditions. Usually the field worker will answer a series of questions the

in a particular field. The computer can then give expertlike responses to questions and problems that arise.

These are first-generation robots. Later generation robots can feel, touch, smell, and make decisions.

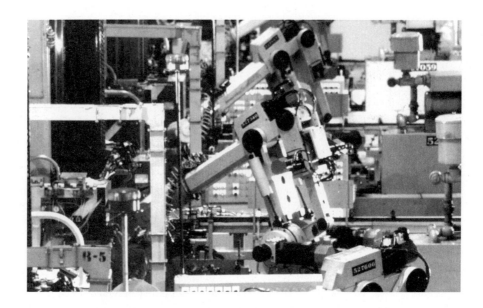

computer asks. After the input is complete, the computer, using the expert software, processes the information, makes a diagnosis, and suggests solutions.

An organization might benefit from the expert system for a number of reasons:

1. E S is an excellent way to distribute expertise across an entire organization.
2. E S makes possible uniform decision making. Since everyone uses the same expert system, everyone gets consistent information.
3. The program provides better service turnaround. With a central source of data, fewer callbacks are necessary.
4. Knowledge and expertise are preserved. Even if the expert leaves the organization, the expertise remains.
5. When problems are identified, training needed to handle a situation expertly can instantly be provided.
6. E S can be made to be user friendly. Patience can be built in so that an employee can learn skills and knowledge as time unfolds.
7. Employees diagnose some of their own problems as they provide input into the computer.
8. The E S program can provide contingency information to anticipate events that might occur. This is called what-if analysis, which anticipates possible unusual circumstances.
9. Better quality control is accomplished. Variations in outcomes are reduced; quality is improved.
10. Fewer workers will need to be on the payroll, since E S can process and analyze data thoroughly without much human assistance.[12]

Several research products are now being developed to further extend artificial intelligence. The products (shown in Table 4–1) range from a speech-activated typewriter that has a capacity of 1,000 words to an autonomous system that can take instructions, navigate, and carry out a military mission.

Employees can always benefit from an expert system.

Technology and Communication

Another area of major development in technology is communication. Messages can be sent, received, stored, or analyzed in several different ways. Many of the new communication developments will be computer related. Hooper writes, for example, that soon computers will no longer be connected by wires, but they will be able to communicate even more with other computers. Computers will never be turned off but will answer telephone calls, record and store data, and ask for replies from others.

Speech-activated typewriter with a capacity of 1,000 words.
Optical scanner that can distinguish among 100,000 pictures.
Automatic language-translating machine with a vocabulary of 100,000 words.
Computer acquisition and representation of world knowledge.
Common-sense reasoning.
Machine learning and adaptation.
Negotiation.
Computerized weapon systems that are able to see, reason, and plan as well as control actions.
Military assessment systems that are able to use, listen, understand, interpret, and represent information.
Autonomous systems that are able to take instructions, navigate, and carry out a military mission.

Table 4–1
Selected Artificial Intelligence Products Now Under Development

Source: Clark Holloway and Herbert H. Hand, "Who's Running the Store, Anyway?" *Business Horizons,* Volume 31, Number 2, March–April 1988, p. 71. Copyright 1988 by the Foundation for the School of Business at Indiana University. Used with permission.

electronic mail
Written information is exchanged between individuals at different locations by sending messages through their computers.

Electronic Mail.   Computers are being used more and more as a daily communication medium. **Electronic mail,** for example, is the sending and receiving of written information through the computer. A person sitting at a computer terminal can type in a message and send it to another person in the next room, in another building, in another city, or in another part of the world. If the receiver is not at his or her own computer at the time the message is transmitted, the information can be stored until the individual returns.

One of the problems up to this point with using the computer as a communication medium has been its lack of privacy. A top executive at U.S. Sprint Communication Corporation sent a very personal letter to his sweetheart, who was also an employee of Sprint. He, by mistake, made the "letter" available to 300 coworkers, who soon were reading about his love life.[13] There are, of course, ways to code messages so that only those who know the code can review dispatches. It is anticipated that computers will soon be responding to handwritten messages and voice commands. To be cautious about releasing messages only to the right parties, it may be that information will be given only after a thumbprint, retina scan, or voice analysis check has been completed.[14]

Electronic mail is also known for its release of inhibitions. People are much more likely to write something into the computer than they are to say it face-to-face or over the telephone. Electronic mail reduces status and power differences so that people aren't afraid to say what they want to say. A first-line supervisor might say something to his or her boss through the computer that the same individual would never say to the manager's face.

The average person speaks 125 to 200 words a minute, writes ten to twenty words a minute, listens and comprehends at the rate of 400 words a minute, and reads at the speed of 250 words a minute. Computers, of course, can outdo humans significantly in all of these areas. Computers can, for example, print a page of words in a single second.[15]

Computers as Integrating Devices.   Computers have excellent potential as integrating mechanisms tying together many activities and people related to an organization. For example, orders from customers can go from the customer to the mainframe to the factory to the factory machine to the shipping department to the procurement department to the outsiders who need time to prepare goods to be supplied (refer to Figure 4–1). This is the computer integrated manufacturing discussed earlier.[16] As a coordinating device, the computer has the ability and capacity to far exceed human efforts (refer to the Management in Action feature). Look again at the case at the beginning of the chapter. The computer system that Sam Jameson is working so hard on is an example of an integrated system in which data are linked to communications capability.

Computers have almost endless potential when conferring through video complexes, training through computers, desktop publishing, and other uses are considered.

Other Communication Devices.   Computers are not the only recent technological advancement. The telephone is being utilized in new and changing ways. **Voice mail**—the ability to send messages through a telephone network—has become a common method of communication. Voice messaging allows sending and receiving of messages through standard pushbutton telephones. Acting as an answering machine, incoming calls can be stored, replayed, forwarded, annotated, and distributed by the telephone network.

Telephone lines carry messages from facsimile machine to facsimile machine. Written messages can be sent from one location to another anywhere that sending and receiving machines and telephone lines exist. Telephones in the form of cellular phones have made communication possible between fixed and moving points. Even portable facsimile machines are readily available.

voice mail
Through a network (usually of telephone lines), messages are sent using pushbutton telephones. Machines record, store, replay, forward, or distribute messages for the appropriate individuals.

Working At Home—The Cottage Industries

The availability of computers and additional communication machines is opening up new work patterns. **Cottage industries**—which existed before industrialization began, as people assembled and processed products in their own homes—are making a comeback. With the existence of computers and the new communication methods, more and more people again are working at home. More than nine million Americans are now working at home full-time or part-time.[17] (For a look at the type of workers laboring at home, see Table 4–2) Working at home provides individuals with many advantages. Commuting and other traffic problems are limited. Family matters can be addressed, and the employee can spend more time with other family members. Interruptions from supervisors and coworkers occur less often than if the people were in the next room. Clothing, food, and transportation costs are reduced, as are childcare expenses sometimes.

cottage industry
A development in which individuals work in their own homes to produce or process products, materials, services, or information rather than working at a central location.

Occupation	Percentage of the 9.2 Million Workers
Construction trades	15.7
Executives, manager	9.2
Sales	8.7
Engineer, scientist	8.0
Business consultant	6.4
Technician, computer programmer	6.0
Government, public sector	5.0
Arts, music	5.0
Health-care professional	4.0
Precision production	3.0
Lawyer, accountant	2.9
Clerical	2.7
Teacher	2.0
Other manual and skilled occupations	21.4

Table 4–2
Occupations of the 9.2 Million Employees Who Work at Home, By Percentage

Source: Cynthia Crossen, "Workplace—Where We'll Be—At Home," *Wall Street Journal,* June 4, 1990, pp. R6–R8, R10. Reprinted by permission of *The Wall Street Journal,* © 1990 Dow Jones and Company, Inc. All Rights Reserved Worldwide.

The employer has advantages, also. No work space has to be provided. Good employees who might otherwise be lost can continue employment as a result of the flexibility working at home gives them. Workers often produce more because they have fewer distractions. There are disadvantages, too. For one thing, coordinating the efforts of employees is more difficult when they are scattered and away from one location. Monitoring work performance sometimes becomes difficult. Providing meaningful feedback may be more complex.

Significant costs are involved in outfitting the workstation at an employee's home. If computer work is the center of the home base, for example, it costs from $4,000 to $10,000 to equip the home for work. Any home-operated computer attached to the headquarters' computer will need a computer that is compatible with the one at headquarters, a letter-quality printer, an answering machine, a facsimile machine, a computer modem (the telephone link between a computer and another computer offsite), and a two-line telephone connection. The more high-powered home office may need a larger computer, a tape drive, a laser printer, a personal copier, and a more sophisticated facsimile machine. The appropriate software will be required. If telephone communication is important, having the call-waiting service, voice mail boxes, and an 800 number may also be necessary. If traveling is a part of the job, such items as a cellular car phone, a pocket cellular phone, a portable computer, and a portable printer may be needed.[18]

Working at home calls for much self-discipline and may require adjustments in family life. Since no boss is present to oversee work and provide motivation and instruction, the worker must monitor his or her own performance, seek out answers to unclear situations, and apply self-motivation. If children or other family members are at home during working hours, provision may need to be made for them. Many workers find it unsatisfactory to care for children and simultaneously keep up a work schedule. Employees have been known to leave their homes, get in their cars, drive around the block, and then walk into their homes again to help them make the adjustment to separate home life from work life.

Neighborhood Work Centers

neighborhood work center
A building located away from headquarters where people go to work rather than commute to the headquarters. Equipment and services are provided. Employees of several different organizations may go to a single work center.

Another trend has developed recently. **Neighborhood** office (or **work**) **centers** are being established and equipped with the appropriate technology—computers, printers, and facsimile machines, for example. An employee of a company with headquarters hundreds of miles away can leave home and within a few minutes arrive at one of these neighborhood centers in his or her own community. All of the equipment needed is available at such centers, and there may even be support staff to provide such things as duplication services, computer inputting, and other necessary backup. The space and the services are usually rented by the employer. Another firm leases the space and equipment to various employers, or the local or state government leases and runs the neighborhood center. An employer could establish its own satellite office in the same way and make it available to its own employees, although this hasn't happened much to this point.

The neighborhood work center provides many of the same advantages the home workstation makes available. In addition, the employee is removed from the demands of family, and other distractions are eliminated. Self-discipline issues, such as talking on the telephone too much and staying away from the refrigerator, are overcome.[19]

Health and Safety Problems from Technology

Along with the positive contributions from technological development come some negatives. For example, the use of computers has brought about a need to overcome the various problems related to **video display terminals** (VDTs). A number of illnesses and other problems have resulted from the regular use of video display units and their keyboards. Other forms of work—jobs on the assembly line, work in food processing, and employment as supermarket cashiers—can result in similar consequences.

The typical effects of these technology-related jobs are illnesses known as **cumulative trauma disorders** (CDTs). CDTs affect the soft tissues of the hands, wrists, arms, shoulders, and back. Two major studies of VDT operators have shown that this group of individuals has a much higher level of visual, musculoskeletal, and emotional health complaints than individuals who do not work with VDTs. Boredom, pressure, and management control cause additional stress. CDT injuries are a result of repetition, force, vibration, awkward posture, and extreme temperature.[20]

The repetition and other factors take an especially heavy toll on hands and wrists. Tendinitis and nerve injuries are the most frequent results, affecting sensing and motor functioning in particular. Numbness, tingling, and pain are typical effects. Eyestrain and backaches are also frequent results of sitting in front of a VDT for long periods of time.

One response to VDT-related problems has been the increase in **ergonomics** at work. Ergonomics is the label used to define the field of study that concentrates on the relationship between the worker and the worksite where he or she labors. Ergonomists (those who study the workplace and the worker) look for ways to increase worker comfort and productivity by redesigning workstations, tools, and job tasks. These scientists also work at eliminating health problems related to working with VDTs.[21]

Many organizations have voluntarily begun ergonomic efforts. Governmental regulators have also stepped in to evaluate employers' efforts to improve work in repetitive jobs. While OSHA, for example, does not yet have a well-defined set of ergonomic standards, it still monitors organizations and applies fines where inadequate efforts to improve the workplace exist.

Some cities and states have taken steps to regulate repetitive work, particularly where VDTs are involved. Some laws that were passed were eventually thrown out by the courts, so that only a few are now in place. Most laws have required employers with at least fifteen or twenty employees who use VDTs to provide annual eye examinations and to pay a major part of the cost and to use antiglare screens and antiglare lights as well as detachable keyboards and adjustable chairs and desks. Also required may be work programs to encourage better work habits (and as a result reduce eyestrain and backaches) and

video display terminal (VDT)
A technical term describing the screen on which desktop computer operators view the work they have put into the computer system.

CTD (cumulative trauma disorders)
Pain and stiffness of wrist, arm, and shoulder resulting from data input into computers over an extended period of time.

ergonomics
The study of the relationship between the worker and the workplace. In particular, the goal of ergonomics is to increase health, comfort, and productivity for each employee.

the provision of work breaks every two or three hours for employees working with VDTs. Such efforts are still in their early stages for the most part.[22]

Clean-Air Activities

In addition to ergonomic actions, there is a set of federal laws related to chemical and other potentially hazardous substances in the workplace. The Superfund Amendments and Reauthorization Act (SARA) of 1986, for example, required OSHA-controlled organizations to submit copies of material safety data sheets to state Emergency Response Commissions, the Local Emergency Planning Committee, and the local fire department. Each facility must also submit an Emergency and Hazardous Chemical Inventory to the same three agencies and supply lists estimating the amount of chemicals released into the environment each year. Some legislation also requires an employer to present a list of potentially hazardous materials present in the workplace to each employee who may be exposed to the materials. Training in the use of protective clothing and equipment may also be required. This information is sometimes known as right-to-know reports.[23]

Technology and the Manager

What is management's role in readying and supporting employees for technological change? Managers first must make decisions about whether to allow employees to be innovative. They must decide which innovation and technological changes are acceptable and compatible with the needs of their organization and its employees. Once decisions are made on what technology will be implemented, the managerial role becomes one of getting acceptance of the new technology by the employees who will utilize and work with the new procedures. The opening case in this chapter certainly makes that point clear. Where did Sam Jameson go wrong in his efforts to introduce the new system? What should he have done?

Often one of the biggest managerial challenges is securing acceptance of the new technology. As discussed earlier, many employees are resistant to anything new—particularly new work methods and procedures. New equipment seems to be a special source of concern. Chapter 17 discusses overcoming resistance to change. One of the biggest steps to overcome resistance is the securing of an open-minded trial of the new equipment or technique. Most of the time when employees actually get a chance to use a new machine or a new method, they see how they can be successful with the change. Allowing employee participation in the evaluation and selection of new technology can also be very reassuring to everyone involved.

With new technology, managers must provide training or retraining. Rewards need to be made available where new ideas are tried. A supportive climate in all matters is important.

Employees who are displaced by innovations can also be provided for. Retraining and relocation within the organization is appropriate when possible. Helping displaced employees find new employment is another organizational activity.

Preventive Measures for Avoiding VDT Discomfort

Here are some ways to avoid the discomfort frequently associated with the operation of computers and word processors:

1. Secure a desk that has some flexibility and can be used without strain. The standard desk height of 30 inches is comfortable for working and writing in longhand, but a lower desk is needed for the placement of a keyboard. Usually the proper arrangement calls for a separate typing table.

2. Arrange the height of the chair so that you are looking straight ahead with your chin down a bit. The position should be comfortable.

3. Wrists should be kept flat and unbent while typing. If the keyboard is too high or too low, wrists may be placed at an awkward angle, resulting in the harmful carpal tunnel syndrome (damage to wrists and arms).

4. The lower back should be supported by placing feet firmly on the floor so that hips are at a 90-degree angle with your torso.

5. Stop fairly often and stretch. Shake hands to loosen the tightness that might have developed.

Source: Adapted from material in *The Miami Herald*, March 26, 1991, p. 3C.

Many positive benefits take place through technology, and managers must be on their toes to meet the challenges and opportunities.

Summary

The level of technological utilization plays an important role in creating the climate in which employees work. Technology, in the first place, affects how and with what people work. Technology also influences the degree to which employees control their work pace and the amount of autonomy they can exercise. Technology influences the physical climate of the work environment. Technology can even impact the formal structure in which people work.

Technology also does many things from an organizational perspective. For example, technology provides a mechanism for integrating and coordinating all product-related activities. Technology aids (and in some ways dominates) the decision process and the monitoring of performance. Technology makes possible economies of scale, scope, and integration. This way, the production process not only can be improved but also can spread costs over larger numbers of products or services.

One of technology's greatest impacts has been in the area of communication. The computer has numerous communication capacities, including electronic mail, whereby messages can be sent and received instantly without the need for paper transactions. It is anticipated that in the near future, computers will become wireless, making them even more accessible. Voice mail, facsimile machines (both stationary and portable), and cellular phones are some additional methods that have improved and quickened the communications process.

Technology may change the location in which many people work and, in so doing, may change the family and personal lives of many workers. The movement to a new cottage industry pattern and the use of neighborhood work centers provide new opportunities for employees. Greater flexibility and reduced commuter time are indicative of the benefits that may occur from this trend. Working at home challenges an employee's sense of self-motivation and self-control.

Technology has a threatening impact on a number of employees. Many feel insecure out of fear that machines and computers will replace them or make their skills obsolete. Employees often fear loss of control over the work pace and the work flow that they will be required to meet. Sometimes their fears are realized as computers or machines step in and take control. Some workers actually feel that physical danger will result from technological processes, just as some people seem to have psychological fears when working with computers.

Managing the technology of an organization in a way that employees can accept and adjust to technological changes is a definite challenge. Employees need encouragement and support to get them through periods of difficult adjustment.

Questions to Consider

1. Is technology a good thing for organizations to utilize even if it means displacing employees? Why or why not?
2. What ethical considerations are involved in implementing technology within an organization?
3. Why do some individuals fear technology—including being fearful of computers?
4. Someone has said that technology tends to run ahead of the culture and society in which the technology was developed. What did the person mean by this? Do you agree?
5. Do you have any cautions about the direction artificial intelligence is moving—that is, are you concerned about the use of artificial intelligence as a replacement for human decision making?
6. What problems (if any) do you foresee with electronic mail? Voice mail? The use of robots?
7. What managerial problems and challenges do you see in the movement of some workers to work at home or in neighborhood work centers?

Key Terms

artificial intelligence
CIM (computer integrated manufacturing)

cottage industry
CTO (chief technology officer)

CTD (cumulative trauma disorders)
economies of integration

economies of scale
economies of scope
electronic mail
ergonomics

expert system
neighborhood work
   center
robotics

video display termi-
   nal (VDT)
voice mail

Chapter Case

Retooling the Dealers

"I'm sorry. There I go—flying off the handle again!" said Nancy Earhart to her husband Mark. Nancy's downcast eyes, her hangdog expression, and the way she twisted her hands were sure signs to Mark that she really meant the apology and that she was upset and confused by the series of violent outbursts that had recently cast a cloud on their relationship. Mark asked Nancy to try, one more time, to explain what was going on to cause the extreme change in her disposition that he was witnessing.

"Well," Nancy said, "I honestly think that part of it is a matter of circumstances—or at least I'd like to believe that that's the case. You know I love my job as a manufacturer's representative. It's exciting working between a major automobile manufacturer and the dealers, that's for sure. It really takes leadership—at least that's what I've told myself. I've got a group of independent dealers to bring into the manufacturer's programs to get cars sold. Change comes faster in the urban market than anywhere else. The dealers have to be ready to move fast to get ahead of their competition.

"Moving fast means analysis—the dealers need to keep up with the new automated forecasting and planning programs that are available today. There are many new things—things like the new program for custom specking (individually designing) each car so that it comes with a packaged system to meet the customer's need. That's the way to sell cars! But that's the problem.

"Two of the dealers in one of the metropolitan areas I work with are people who have recently come from small-town dealerships, and they've just plain gotten in over their heads. They're nice people, but they insist on going with their instincts rather than use computer data to make decisions. They don't trust the data generated by the computer. As a result they are one step behind their competitors in doing almost everything. I've talked with them several times, but they persist in doing things their way. I just don't know what I'm going to do with them."

1. Why are the small-town dealers having so many problems using the latest technology?
2. What should Nancy do?

Chapter 5

The Physical Surroundings of the Workplace

Objectives

- To discover the effects physical surroundings have upon employees.
- Specifically, to identify what the weather, visual stimuli, noise levels, office design and layout, location of bosses, seating locations, and other climate factors have upon worker performance and attitudes.
- To review the costs and other effects of having smokers in the workplace.
- To consider policies appropriate for regulating smoking at work.
- To identify and discuss managerial actions to be taken to provide a productive, pleasant set of surroundings in which employees can work satisfactorily.

The Superior Insurance Company

The Superior Insurance Company was experiencing phenomenal growth. Operations were being expanded to other states and territories, and sales efforts had been increased. As a result of the major client expansion, the physical plant facilities at the home offices were enlarged. On a space of land adjoining the existing offices of Superior, a large addition was constructed and passageways were opened to connect the new and old buildings.

The claims office was one of the areas that needed expansion. The claims office in the old building was housed on the third floor in a very conventional setting. Private offices for executive and supervisory personnel were provided. Computer terminals and printers were located in a room that was off-limits to everyone except statistical and computer personnel. Small groups of clerks and typists were located in spaces throughout the floor and were partitioned from other groups by room dividers.

When the new part of the building was constructed alongside the existing structure, a new office on the third floor was established for the expansion of the claims department. The old and the new claims offices were connected by a hallway. The design of the new claims office (a room with more than 18,000 square feet) was quite different from that of the old office. The new office was developed using the open floor plan where no permanent petitions were constructed, and only a few five-foot dividers were placed to hide some filing cabinets. Supervisors sat surrounded by those for whom they were responsible. Flowers and other plants were sprinkled liberally throughout the new area. The lighting was bright and colorful. It was decided that the old part of the building would be remodeled in a couple of years and would be reconstructed in the same type of design used in the new building.

Since the workers in each part of the building were performing similar types of duties, it was decided to take some of the more experienced workers from the old building and disperse them among newly hired and trained workers so that the ratio of old-to-new employees in each of the claims department areas would be about the same.

At the end of the first three months of operation in the new arrangement, some interesting statistics were beginning to take shape. Errors and mistakes in the handling of forms and other records were up noticeably. Absenteeism had increased over the prechange pattern. At the end of the second three-month period, the data were the same, and a turnover rate higher than in any previous period was noted. When the error-absenteeism-turnover figures were isolated by work area, it was discovered that it was the employees in the new room that were the ones making the errors and otherwise showing less desirable performances. A morale survey was taken, and workers in the new room were found to be less satisfied with their jobs and working conditions than the personnel in the older, more conventional workspace.

Case Questions

1. From the brief facts provided here, what would you expect to be the causes of low levels of accuracy in performance and the high rates of absenteeism, turnover, and job dissatisfaction?

2. What truths about the workplace should we be able to draw from this situation?

3. What are the advantages of the open-space plan? What are the disadvantages?

4. What are the advantages of the more conventional, closed-off kind of office design? What are the disadvantages?

5. What should the people at Superior do about their newly identified problem?

We've already talked about several aspects of the climate in which people work. There are the authority relationships (both vertical and horizontal) and the interpersonal relations (formal and informal) that make up a part of the organization's culture. We've been introduced to many technological innovations that affect people as they work. We've also viewed ergonomic activities related to technology. (Recall that ergonomics is the study of the relationship between the worker and the workplace.)

Now it's time to look at other workplace factors. Rather than discuss machines and equipment, let's consider such components as the weather, visual conditions (what people see), auditory factors (what people hear), as well as nonmachine-related things that people smell and breathe. Matters of location, building size, the orderliness with which things appear, and even the way furniture is arranged impact people.

The physical surroundings and their impact upon people and their behavior is one of the most overlooked, underestimated elements of an organization. In the days before the experiments at the Hawthorne plant of Western Electric were conducted (in the 1920s), it was commonly held that the **physical climate** played a role in affecting performance as well as in shaping attitudes. In the Hawthorne studies it was first believed that an optimum level of lighting in each work area would result in the highest level of performance. In the process of investigating the effects of lighting, the researchers discovered that no matter what the level of illumination, productivity kept increasing. When the lights were lowered, productivity improved, and when the lights were made brighter, productivity improved. As a result, the idea of the physical climate as a factor in performance and satisfaction was discounted. Today some argue that even the conclusions reached about the Hawthorne experiments were incorrect—that, in fact, the physical surroundings were instrumental in shaping the work activities, the relationships, and the communication patterns at Western Electric.[1] At any rate, for a time, the physical surroundings received little attention. Only in recent years have the physical factors and conditions around people been recognized for their potential to affect behavior.

Things such as noise, colors of walls, size of rooms, arrangements of furniture, and distance between workstations tend to serve as stimuli and create moods from which transactions are made. The effects of physical surroundings are not always conscious responses from individuals, but they exist, and

physical climate
The environment in the workplace. The elements surrounding employees as they work, including such things as air, temperature, noise, lighting, and humidity, as well as the physical objects, including furniture, machinery, and windows.

they influence behavior. In many situations, the affected employees have no control over the conditions that surround them.

Effects of Nature—Temperature and Humidity

The effects of nature have their beginnings outside the formal setting of the workplace. To an extent, some of the elements (temperature, for example) can be influenced through the use of controls such as air conditioning and dehumidifiers.

Stephen Rosen, one of the foremost experts on the topic of weather and its effects on human behavior, views the weather as a stressor.[2] As the level of stress in the body is increased by the movements of the weather, behavior becomes dysfunctional. Because the human body attempts to maintain equilibrium under all circumstances, it takes steps to bring about homeostasis. When the temperature is cold, for example, the blood vessels constrict to keep warmth in. The changes modify blood composition, body chemistry, and the supply of oxygen to the brain. As a result, the moods and behaviors of individuals are altered. Most of us are accustomed to thinking that it's an old wives' tale that weather affects our moods and behavior, but Rosen's views suggest that there is some truth to the idea.

What does temperature have to do with work behavior? Most of the studies done on temperature and its effect have shown that the extreme highs and lows in temperature cause differences in performances of all kinds of tasks (complex decision making, number checking, target tracking, and flight simulation).[3] Temperatures exceeding 90° for a high and 15° for a low were found to slow work behavior significantly. Other studies have shown that temperatures don't even have to be particularly extreme to affect performance levels negatively. Wyon discovered that temperatures of 80° or more had a slowing effect on typewriting performance.[4] In addition to reducing performance by 20 percent to 30 percent or more, the temperature and other weather conditions resulted in symptoms of tiredness, disinterest in work, headaches and head pressure, and moodiness.

We have known for some time that criminal activities such as theft and fighting are increased as the temperature climbs. Best thinking and best performance may occur when the temperature is cool and the weather is dry. Think about your own experiences. What temperature is best for you when you're involved in actions like reading or studying? Are there differences when you are engaged in more active duties (vacuuming a house or building something, for example)?

Another temperature level to be concerned about is the surface temperature of the tools and materials with which employees must work. Manual dexterity has been known to decrease (along with the accompanying productivity) as much as one-third to one-half as a result of the change in surface temperatures. Surface temperatures below 55° are all that is necessary in many cases to reduce performance levels.[5] Cold-impaired manual performance is assumed to be the result of a loss of sensitivity, changes in the fluids in the joints, or loss of muscle strength.

Employees who are dressed properly for the temperature and other conditions of the workplace can adjust comparatively well to the situation. Studies have shown that subjects wearing heavy clothing in low temperatures and light clothing in high temperatures perform at higher levels than individuals improperly dressed. Subjects properly dressed are more satisfied with their jobs and their working conditions than are those dressed inappropriately. In all fairness, however, some studies have found no particular difference in ability to handle difficult tasks based upon how people are dressed.[6]

The impact of humidity seems to coincide pretty much with the temperature level. In addition, depression levels of individuals seem to follow the level of humidity, and high humidity seems to cause higher levels of depression.[7]

Other Weather Conditions

Industrial accidents are at their highest when there are strong flows of warm-air currents or heat thunderstorms (positively charged molecules). On the other side of the weather, when cold-air movements are present, accidents and other undesirable types of behavior decline. Mountain air, with its cool content and a concentration of negative ions, results in higher levels of personal motivation and performance for many individuals.[8]

It is important to remember that not every worker is affected in the same way by weather conditions. Approximately 25 percent to 30 percent of the population is especially sensitive to weather conditions and will be significantly affected by changes. In addition, older and younger people seem to have more difficulty making adjustments to alterations in the weather than do people in middle-aged categories.

We have become aware that exposure to the same amount of sunshine twice a day (about 15 minutes morning and afternoon) also has positive effects on individuals. It seems that sunlight decreases the production of melatonen by the pineal gland in the brain, causing the body and its functions to become more stable (according to Alfred Lewy, Director of the Sleep and Mood Disorder Laboratory, Oregon Health Science University).

Implications for Managers

What does all of this mean to the manager? Obviously, it calls for temperature controls whenever possible, and it helps to justify the expenditure of money for air conditioning and heating. Where temperature itself cannot be regulated, workers need protection from the pain or discomfort that can result. Gloves may be necessary for intemperate situations. Uniforms appropriate to the situation (light materials that breathe for hot and insulated; heavier materials for cold) may be provided, and it may be cost-efficient for the employer to provide these for employees.

Not all of the sources of temperature problems are physical. Workers in enclosed areas without windows are more likely to complain about stuffiness. A good solution for this is to place paper streamers next to the air vents. The visible indication of air movement in most cases releases the anxiety over being without windows. Paintings of cool mountain streams placed strategically on walls can suggest psychological relief from heat, just as sunny desert scenes can provide a feeling of warmth.

The Impact of Visual Stimuli

What we see **(visual stimuli)** has a great deal to do with the way we behave and perform in the workplace. In particular, the predominant colors of the walls surrounding us have a major impact on our moods, attitudes, and behavior (see Table 5–1).

visual stimuli
Things seen by the eye that cause reactions, moods, or behaviors in individuals.

The Effect of Color

Every color sends out its own wavelengths when exposed to light. Each waveband stimulates chemicals in the eye, sending impulses to the pituitary and pineal glands near the brain. Stimulated by the response to a color, glandular activity may speed up or slow down heart rates, increase or decrease brain activity, and alter the moods of the recipient of the wavelengths.[9]

Bright red gets a very strong reaction when used heavily in a work setting. Red picks up the heart beat, overstimulates an employee, and may make the employee irritable, bad-tempered, and anxious. Blue tends to work in the opposite direction. Shades of blue reduce breathing and pulse rates, increase tranquility, and may even lead to depression if used in darker tones. Bright yellow, on the other hand, is another highly stimulating color (although not so much as red). Yellows are frequently used in restrooms, coffee break areas, and other places where people may gather during work. Because yellow tends to cause a desire to move to other locations, the color is used to discourage people from lingering too long in places where they are being nonproductive.

Table 5–1
Predominant Wall Colors and Their Effects on Behavior

Blue	Decreases breathing and pulse rate; causes tranquility; too much and rather dark shades of blue may cause depression.
Bright Red	Increases the heart beat; causes overstimulation; makes people irritable, bad-tempered, and anxious.
Bright Yellow	Raises blood pressure, pulse, and respiration. Keeps people from lingering too long in nonproductive areas (cafeteria, restrooms, lounges, etc.).
Drab Gray	Slows heart beat; causes lethargy and depression; makes people want to stay away from work.
Brown	A relaxing color, associated with comfort.
Dark Shades of Most Colors	Affect people's sense of time passage; makes time seem to pass more slowly.
Light Shades of Most Colors	Affect people's sense of time passage; makes time seem to pass faster; often used with monotonous jobs.
Pink	A temporary pacifier; after a short time period, it seems to foster aggressiveness.

Source: Adapted from *International Management,* Volume 32, Number 5, September 1977.

As mentioned, dominant colors sometimes affect the way employees feel about the temperature in the rooms where they work. Blues and shades of aqua cause some people to feel cold. Reds and oranges promote feelings of warmth.

The color of objects being handled can affect the attitudes and abilities of workers trying to manipulate them. Kane reports that workers had a harder time lifting light boxes painted black than they did heavier boxes painted white. Colors that are darker seem psychologically to suggest they are heavier than do lighter colors.[10]

Obviously, attention to the colors surrounding employees can make a difference in the behavior patterns of employees. There is no single suggestion covering all color situations, however. If tranquility is desired, blue tones are a good bet. If hostility is to be avoided, steering away from the use of red tones is helpful. If employees are in jobs that psychologically seem to drag, dark colors will need to be turned into light shades. In other words, it is possible to adapt color surroundings to the temperament and needs of a situation. Some fast-food stores, for example, have apparently made good use of yellow and yellow-related colors. In doing so, they encourage a faster turnover of customers.

It's important to remember that the color needs to be a dominant one to have a really large impact.

Beauty Versus Ugliness

beautiful room
As applied here, a beautiful work area—one that has pleasing colors, lights, and furnishings.

ugly room
A work location where the colors and other decorations are unattractive, the lighting is inadequate, and furnishings are poorly suited to the work situation.

Not only do the colors of the rooms and the objects with which people work influence people's attitudes and performance, but the general appearance of the places where people work has its impact as well. In the classic studies by Maslow and Mintz, a **"beautiful" room** with beige walls, indirect lighting, and pictures and other attractive furnishings was tested against an "average" room (a professor's office with typical furniture and battleship-gray walls) and an **"ugly" room** with only an exposed light bulb and ill-fitting furnishings in very messy condition. The first study revealed that work performed by individuals in the beautiful room was much more positive (the people evaluated photographs shown to them) than the work done by participants in the average and the ugly rooms.[11]

In the followup study, Mintz used just two rooms—the beautiful one and the ugly one. He had two examiners alternately test people in the two rooms. Findings showed that the examiners gave higher ratings to participants when they evaluated them in the beautiful room. They also discovered that the examiners finished their evaluations more quickly and left the room sooner when they worked in the ugly room. The examiners showed feelings of comfort, pleasure, enjoyment, importance, and energy while working in the pretty room. When they worked in the ugly room, they expressed reactions of monotony, fatigue, headache, sleepiness, discontent, irritability, hostility, and avoidance.[12] Clearly, it would seem that the different aesthetic conditions in the experiment had an impact upon personal judgment and self-worth and perhaps on the level of commitment to the tasks, cooperation, and interpersonal judgment.[13] It seems probable that a pattern exists. Pleasant work areas foster positive behavior, while grim and drab areas often lead to less inspired responses.

The message here is that attractive conditions facilitate the development of positive feelings, while visually offensive appearances can result in mediocre to poor responses. The effects of color may be a part of the picture here. The use of pleasant coloring along with the addition of such extras as paintings, draperies, carpeting, and adequate lighting may spell the difference between good performance and bad performance. Neatness and orderliness are important, too. Attention to the general appearance of a work area may contribute to levels of cooperation and satisfaction.

Levels of Lighting and Work Performance

In most cases, the level of illumination under which employees work has had a moderate level of influence on performance. In general, adjusting levels of lighting to more comfortable strengths (and those that allow for better concentration) tends to increase production an average of 3 percent to 15 percent. There are incidents, however, when the volume of performance has been altered as much as 35 percent as a result of lighting increases and decreases. The most important effect often comes with the removal of glare rather than with the changes in the level of illumination.[14]

Having windows in the workroom also affects the visual stimuli received by workers. In windowed rooms, workers seem more interested in their jobs, are more satisfied with what they are doing, and consider their physical working conditions to be superior to others when compared with the ratings of those who work in windowless areas.[15] In addition to the increased lighting from windows, the presence of windows affects perceived status, preferential treatment, and psychological conditions.

Glare can be alleviated by using indirect rather than direct lighting. Light directed towards the ceiling of a room and then back to a workstation is less likely to result in glare. Light fixtures that screen the light before spreading it can also be helpful. One architectural and office planning firm has suggested several steps as possible solutions to the problems of glare:

1. The use of new injection-molded acrylic lenses that fit on standard fluorescent fixtures and help spread light and eliminate the direct overhead source of glare.
2. Increased reliance on controlled-task lighting to supplement and overall lower the level of lighting, which provides appropriate lighting on a personal basis.
3. Increased use of electronic dimming control of indirect glare-reducing lighting, which makes it possible for workers to regulate and adjust the amount of artificial light used as natural light changes throughout the day.
4. The inclusion of distant views, preferably window views, for workers, which reduces constant eyestrain.[16]

Auditory Factors—The Effects of Noise

A major stressor in many jobs is noise—the sounds of the workplace. Noise is derived from many sources. Normally, however, it is not the source but the

Table 5–2

Protection for Noise
and Hearing

Firms covered by OSHA must

1. Survey noisy areas to establish the decibel-level exposures that employees in each area encounter.
2. Develop a hearing-conservation program to cover all employees exposed to continuing noises at or above 85 dB.
3. Give each worker with high-level exposure a baseline audiogram to establish the employee's level of hearing at the start of his or her assignment to the high-noise area.
4. Retest annually all employees working in the 85-dB and above areas to determine if there has been any measurable hearing loss at any tested pitch.
5. Offer hearing protectors to workers exposed to the 85-dB level and give protectors mandatorily to all workers receiving 90 dB or more of noise.
6. Train workers in the use and care of hearing protectors and enforce the wearing of them.
7. Refit hearing protectors regularly to employees incurring hearing loss and retrain individuals in their use.
8. Notify each worker suffering hearing loss within twenty-one days after a change in hearing is discovered. Send the hearing-loss individual to a specialist outside the organization if necessary for further testing.
9. Keep an ongoing training program on noise and hearing conservation and require each employee to participate at least once a year.
10. Maintain and make available to workers (and others requiring the information) records on the noise-level exposure of employees as long as they remain employed.

Source: Adapted from Janet Raloff, "Occupational Noise—The Subtle Pollutant," *Science News*, Volume 121, Number 21, May 22, 1982, pp. 347–350.

volume level that causes concern. In the Superior Insurance case at the beginning of the chapter, noise was a probable handicapping factor.

decibel (dB)
The unit used to measure the loudness of sounds.

Noise levels are measured in **decibels** (dB). To avoid hearing damage, the noise level should be no more than 74 dB for an average eight-hour day. Damage to hearing begins at 75 dB. The Occupational Safety and Health Administration (OSHA) requires that all noise levels in a work location not exceed 90 dB over an eight-hour period. Intensities higher than 90 dB may be acceptable, but for shorter periods of time. For example, the exposure to 105 dB is legal for a time period of up to one hour. Sounds of 115 dB are permitted for no longer than fifteen minutes. OSHA estimates that more than five million workers today are exposed to 90 dB or more for the eight-hour workday. Given the fact that people usually aren't aware of pain from noise until the 130-dB threshold is reached, a large number of employees today are suffering a loss of hearing without being aware of it (see Table 5–2).

As seen in Figure 5–1, a large number of noises both in and out of the workplace can be present and doing damage without people feeling pain. It is unfortunate that people don't experience pain until the noise level reaches several decibels above the damage zone.

Industrial Sounds	Hearing Effect
160	
	Harmful to hearing and painful
150	
Medium jet engine	
140	
130	
120	
Punch press	
Bulldozer	
110	
Cotton mill loom	Hearing loss begins to occur
Steel mill blast furnace	
100	
Newspaper press	
Road grader	
Subway train	
90	
Turret lathe	
Heavy-duty truck	
80	
One-ton truck	
Vacuum cleaner	
70	
60	
50	
40	
30 dB	

Figure 5–1

Intensity of Industrial Noise Levels and Hearing Effects (Measured in Decibels (dB)

Source: Adapted from Janet Raloff, "Occupational Noise—The Subtle Pollutant," *Science News,* Volume 121, Number 21, May 22, 1982.

The Effects of High-Level Noise

It is important to note that it is not necessary for noise to cause hearing damage in order for the sounds to influence behavior. Wohlwill et. al. discovered, for example, that continuous auditory stimulation will affect an individual's ability to cope with frustration. Where noise prevails over a period of time, a worker's tolerance for frustration declines. Employees affected in this way have problems continuing with an activity and give up more quickly when task difficulties occur.[17] Effects on performance don't always occur immediately.[18] It may take time for frustration and its impact to manifest.

Obviously, noise makes it more difficult for people to communicate with each other. Where noise levels are high, it is not unusual to find misunderstanding and confusion. Tasks that require significant amounts of concentration are also hindered by noise. You may have run into this kind of problem. For example, many students complain of an inability to concentrate on complex homework problems when others around them are playing distracting music or watching television. Even the level of cooperation is handicapped by increasing noise. People working together are less inclined to be helpful when noise levels are high. People who are in quieter areas are more likely to be friendly and to have more friends than people who are in noise-infested surroundings.[19]

People who have a predisposition to be aggressive are more likely to have their aggressiveness stimulated when loud noise levels prevail. On the other hand, all individuals are likely to be more positive and more approving of others in their evaluations when working in quieter areas.[20]

In summary, noisy environments are much more likely to result in frustration, the willingness to quit, the feeling of helplessness, decreased communication and understanding, lowered concentration, reduced cooperation and friendliness, decreased approval of others, and heightened aggressiveness than are quiet surroundings. Most of the effects of higher levels of noise are detrimental to the organization and to the people in it. (Do the noise sensitivity exercise to see how much noise affects you.)

The noise potential in a room like this is high.

Reducing Noise Levels

While it sometimes will be impossible to control or even reduce the noise level, in many instances, undesirable racket can be handled. Where the noise has a mechanical base, the revision of equipment, the replacement of extremely noxious machines, the use of lubricants, and the application of acoustical materials might make the noise level more tolerable. Work areas may need to be rearranged. Workers may need to be relocated, or the noise sources may be isolated away from workers. Where noise levels cannot be decreased to acceptable levels, protective hearing devices must be provided. Protective devices (ear plugs, etc.) serve as a last resort in some ways in that while workers may be protected, communication, cooperation, and other interpersonal conditions are not really aided.

Physical Location and Placement

Another important factor in the physical climate of an organization is the actual location and placement of the people in the buildings where they work. In the past twenty years or so, designers and researchers have juggled people and their workplaces in an attempt to find the optimal location to facilitate production, cooperation, and satisfaction.

The Open Office Versus the Conventional Office

One of the most tested and discussed concepts dealing with the physical arrangement of people at work has been the **open office** design. Refer to the Superior Insurance Company case at the beginning of the chapter. It's apparent that the open plan was a major factor in this situation. This fairly recent notion eliminates many of the boundaries around workers by removing all of the walls and doors in the workspace and putting all supervisors and workers into a single, open area. The open office concept was designed for enhancement of interpersonal relations by making it easier for people to be in contact with others. It was felt that communication would improve and barriers would be reduced. With the walls gone, flexibility in placing people would be improved. Open offices would be less expensive to construct and maintain. People would see themselves more as equals to the others in the building; cooperation would be encouraged.

Although this is a controversial subject, most studies of the open design compared to the conventional walled arrangement (where each office and most work areas are enclosed) indicate that the open plan has been inferior to the **conventional design.** The Superior Insurance Company case is typical in many ways of what has been reported after a change to the open plan. While open offices may be less expensive to furnish and maintain, and they sometimes do improve communication, most of the other yardsticks used for measuring the two approaches favor the conventional design.

Why have there been so many problems? For one thing, most workers prefer the conventional system. They complain about noise, the loss of status, and the lack of privacy of the open offices.[21] In their comparison of the two

open office
The office or room plan where there are no permanent partitions or dividers separating employees in a working area. Partial partitions may be used, but in most cases the plan is to allow people to be free to interact with others without structural interference.

conventional design
A floor plan or design where people are separated from one another by walls and other permanent partitions. In this procedure, the work locations of individuals and some groups of people will be set apart from the work areas of others by structural dividers.

Self Test

Personal Feedback

Noise Sensitivity

This exercise is designed to give you some feedback about how you relate to sounds and noises around you. Answer each question as accurately as you can. Each item is scored on a five-point range. Give the statements you strongly agree with a score of 5. Statements you strongly disagree with should be given a score of 1. In-between scores should be given as appropriate

	Strongly Agree	Agree	Neither Agree Nor Disagree	Disagree	Strongly Disagree
1. It is easy for me to concentrate on my studies when I have my stereo or radio on.	5	4	3	2	1
2. I find it difficult to concentrate on my studies when my spouse, roommate, or next-door neighbor has his/her radio on at a level where I can hear it.	5	4	3	2	1
3. I find it very distracting when I'm taking a test to have someone tapping his/her fingers on a desk, shuffling papers, clearing his/her throat frequently, etc.	5	4	3	2	1
4. When someone interrupts me with questions while I'm writing or studying, I find it easy to pick up again where I left off.	5	4	3	2	1
5. When I'm at a movie or play, I find it distracting to have someone in the row behind me whispering throughout the production.	5	4	3	2	1
6. I find it easy to fall asleep at night when there are noises nearby, such as other people's voices or automobile traffic.	5	4	3	2	1
7. I would say that when I play the radio/stereo in my home or in my car, I usually have the volume high.	5	4	3	2	1
8. When people are talking in a room near me, I find it	5	4	3	2	1

easy to tune out their
conversation.

9. When I'm watching television with someone else, I am the most likely one to ask that the volume be turned down.	5	4	3	2	1
10. I don't enjoy going to ballgames and other events where it is extremely noisy.	5	4	3	2	1

When you have answered all ten of the questions, record their scores in the following manner:

For the following questions, write down the score you gave as an answer:

```
2  ——
3  ——
5  ——
9  ——
10 ——
        Subtotal ——
```

Reverse score the following questions by subtracting the score you gave the statement from 6. If, for example, you scored item 1 as a 4, subtract 4 from 6 to get the adjusted answer of 2.

```
1  (6– —— ) = ——
4  (6– —— ) = ——
6  (6– —— ) = ——
7  (6– —— ) = ——
8  (6– —— ) = ——
        Subtotal ——
        Total    ——
```

Now add your two subtotals together. The higher your score, the more affected you are by the sounds around you. A score of 40 and above, for example, indicates a high sound sensitivity. A score of 30 to 39 indicates some sound sensitivity. A score of 20 to 29 indicates little effect from noise one way or the other. A score of 10 to 19 indicates you are absolutely free from the effects of noise (or that you need to turn your hearing aid up!).

plans, Oldham and Brass say that the conventional plan is better for the following reasons:

1. Boundaries (walls) help to provide privacy where there can be confidential conversations, the sharing of information, and better identification between employees and the tasks they perform.
2. Autonomy declines in the open arrangement because supervisors are more likely to interfere with employees (it is easier to observe employees).
3. Boss-worker feedback decreases because there is less privacy.
4. Fewer close friendships exist (thoughts and feelings are harder to share as a result of noise and loss of intimacy).
5. The feeling of task significance and concentration declines.[22]

An open floor plan
with wall partitions
provides little
privacy.

Another study has concluded that the open design does not improve flexibility, information flow, communication, or the elimination of internal barriers. In fact, communication, and flexibility became even more difficult.[23]

At this stage of observation, it appears that the conventional office plan accomplishes more desirable relationships and responses than the open plan.

Working with the Open Design

While there are still some strong advocates of the open design for working areas, the dominant position seems to be to modify or eliminate the design. Managers contemplating adopting the design would do well to reconsider. Managers where the concept is already being used have to consider alternatives to modify what they already have. A possible (and expensive) approach is to place full walls in areas to separate individuals from each other. Partial partitions are a less expensive (and less successful) alternative. The authors know of one case where "concentration rooms"—private, quiet areas permitting concentration—were added. Workers reported that they "escaped" to the rooms when privacy or concentration was needed. The addition of acoustical materials such as tile and sound reduction boards can serve to soften the noise. Use of draperies and plants can improve the atmosphere and at the same time reduce noise volume. Isolating major noise sources from the rest of the employees may also be helpful.

In the Superior Insurance case, the lack of privacy, the removal of status symbols, and the increased noise levels were some of the reasons that problems occurred in the open room. It is probable that for Superior Insurance, the solution will lie in the construction of walls or at least the placement of dividers to separate people and to decrease the noise input. In fact, almost all of the suggestions mentioned above could be used to improve the situation at Superior. Obviously, the open office is a controversial and highly debated topic at present. Other issues related to locating workers and managers are also receiving attention. Let's consider some of them.

Where the Bosses Should Go

Where should the managers' offices be located in relation to their employees? Would it be wise to put all managers in the same general area, or would it be better to place them in offices near the people they supervise? "An **executive row**," where all executives' offices are placed together and away from the employees, does offer some merit in making it easier for bosses to communicate among themselves. A closer spirit of teamwork among the managers may be promoted. But overall, the view is less encouraging. Steele says that the executive-row arrangement causes

executive row
Usually a series of offices occupied by managerial personnel. All managers are located within the series, and the offices are usually set apart from nonmanagerial personnel.

1. Executives to see less of the workings of other people and other parts of the system.
2. Greater compartmentalization unless specific places for interactions are provided for.
3. An increased degree of secrecy where executives give other people only very controlled information.
4. Less communication between supervisors and their employees.
5. Habit and precedent to become the method for acting rather than adjustment and flexibility.
6. Decreased control over what employees are doing.
7. Very little teamwork and identification between people.
8. Frequent boundary or jurisdictional disputes.[24]

Furthermore, the results when executives' offices are moved nearer those they supervise usually counter these findings.

What to Do If Centralization Is Necessary

The arguments for superiors to have their offices near their employees are numerous, while the points in favor of bosses being located centrally are few. If centralization is necessary, special arrangements are needed ·to be certain that boss-employee communications are not stifled and that teamwork is encouraged. Bosses need to move frequently among their charges. This is good advice under almost any circumstances and is called "management by walking around." Team sessions for giving and receiving feedback become a must. The open-door policy is appropriately cultivated.

Other Causes and Results of Location

An interesting set of observations has resulted after watching and interviewing people with regard to where they prefer to sit while interacting with others. Primarily through the efforts of Sommer, it has been discovered that when people are working on a cooperative project, such as proofing a script or watching a video together, they prefer to sit side-by-side (see Figure 5–2). Indeed, the side-by-side position is useful where coordination of effort is required. When people engage in casual conversations, they prefer sitting at

Management in Action

How Industrial Hygienists Increase Firms' Output and Efficiency

People testing tennis balls all day developed severe pains in their wrists. Employees at a silver mine began acting strangely. Computer-room workers started to have headaches and to tire easily.

These maladies were caused by conditions in the workplace. The sources of the problems were uncovered by industrial hygienists, whose specialty is finding, evaluating, and controlling health hazards where people work.

Eliminating health hazards can head off costly liability claims. Beyond that, industrial hygienists can assure that a business has optimum working conditions so that "employees do the best job they can," says William Ahearn, an industrial hygienist in Phoenix, Arizona.

Ergonomics, the science of adapting work and working conditions to suit workers, is one aspect of industrial hygiene. An industrial hygienist eliminated a situation that was giving a printing-plant worker aches and pains and making his job difficult. The remedy merely involved shortening the distance the employee had to reach to move heavy catalogs from one production line to another.

Attention to such details "can pay off in more productivity and higher efficiency," says Donald McFee, executive vice president of Occusafe Inc., Chicago.

Productivity can be affected by such simple things as whether chairs and desks and table heights allow people to work without discomfort. The tennis-ball testers suffered a tendon disorder as a result of clenching their hands when

adjoining sides located at a 90-degree angle if seated at a rectangular table. When two people are adversaries, they prefer to face each other across a table. These locations appear to be preferred by the participants and are utilitarian as well.[25] You'll find that such preferences occur naturally and are usually taken for granted. But think back to your own experiences. When you and a friend stop to eat somewhere, what seating arrangement do you most often use? Across the table? At a 90-degree angle? (We bet you select the 90-degree angle!) (See the Management in Action Segment for some additional climatic factors.)

Figure 5–2

Preferred (and Perhaps Most Useful) Seating Arrangements

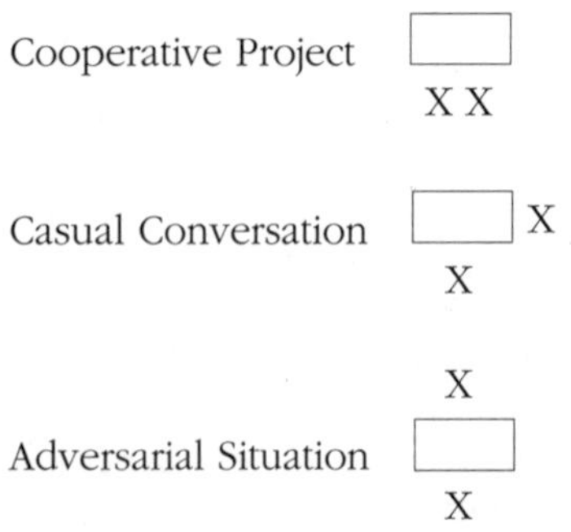

Source: Robert Sommer, *Personal Space: The Behavioral Basis of Design*, Englewood Cliffs, N.J.: Prentice-Hall, 1969, used by permission of the author.

they were cocked at an angle to the wrist. The solution was to change the work routine so that testers squeezed a ball only when their hands were in line with their wrists. Undersize tool grips can cause similar tendon troubles.

Chemicals, bacteria, and noise often cause work-related ailments. At a reactivated silver mine in the West, refinery workers got sick from something in the air. Their hands trembled, and some had what appeared to be crazy spells. A physician diagnosed the trouble as mercury poisoning. An industrial hygienist found the source: mercury vapors released when ore containing mercury was heated in the refinery. Improving ventilation and reducing workers' exposure to the refinery furnace solved the problem.

Even so-called clean industries can be hazardous. Lead poisoning is a common danger for workers soldering connections in electronics plants. "Temperature is an important factor," says Thomas J. Walker, a hygienist in Piedmont, California. Employees want to raise soldering temperatures to help increase their output, but higher temperatures produce more fumes.

Solder that melts at lower temperatures and soldering-irons tips that can melt solder at lower temperatures are two solutions. Other precautions are needed, Mr. Walker says, such as warning workers not to inadvertently ingest lead compounds by eating near soldering stations or by failing to wash up before they eat. Smoking increases the inhalation of the fumes and should be prohibited during soldering.

Source: Standford L. Jacobs, *Wall Street Journal*, March 5, 1984, p. 25. Reprinted with permission of the

The Status Impact of Physical Climate

Physical factors are also strong symbols of status and prestige. As Becker says:

> Settings communicate information about a user's level in the formal hierarchy, the kinds of functions he or she performs for the system, how a visitor to the setting is expected to relate to the system. . . .[26]

The most familiar function of the physical set surrounding a person is the status symbol message. "Various facilities and patterns of facilities form the basis for a visual language by which insiders and knowledgeable outsiders can tell at a glance an individual's status level in the system.[27] The following elements are used as status symbols:

- ☐ Size in square feet of personal space (more space usually signifies higher status).
- ☐ Luxuriousness of furnishings (carpet, drapes, thickness of carpet).
- ☐ A private office (being less visible to others usually signifies higher status).
- ☐ Desk (having one; the size, design, and materials out of which it is made).
- ☐ Location of office (on executive row, in a central place, or in a backwater area, etc.).

☐ Windows (having one or more, distance from them).
☐ Decorations (quality, whether provided by company or not).
☐ Secretary (private one or sharing one with others).
☐ Location of secretary (in a pool, inside or outside one's office).[28]

Smoking in the Workplace

One of the more recent controversies in the workplace has been over the issue of smoking. In spite of the Surgeon General's warnings about the effects of smoking, more than three out of ten adults still smoke cigarettes. A majority of today's smokers began smoking when they were in about the eighth grade.[29] Some have succeeded in quitting, but the majority have not.

Smoking is a major concern because its effects are so quickly recognizable and its impact is so pronounced. We know that cigarette smoking may result in such serious illnesses as chronic bronchitis, emphysema, and lung cancer. Unfortunately, the smoker is not the only person affected by the smoke. The sidestream, or secondary smoker—the person who breathes the smoke exhaled or generated by the smoker—may actually be affected as much as or more than the principal smoker. In a report issued by ASH (Action on Smoking and Health), it was stated that an idle cigarette generates as much as four times the toxic agents given off by a cigarette being puffed by a smoker. Toxic agents go into the air without being filtered.[30] As a result of others' smoking, the nonsmoker in a smoke-filled room may be forced to breathe the equivalent of several cigarettes a day.

The cost of having smokers as employees is significant. In one of the most comprehensive studies of the cost of smoking, the Weis study[31] estimated that the cost of the employee who smokes is as much as $4,600 a year. The costs of having a smoking employee are identified as

1.	Absenteeism from work	$ 220
2.	Medical care	230
3.	Sickness and early death	765
4.	Costs of insurance other than health	90
5.	Time lost on the job	1820
6.	Property damage—burns, stains, etc., and depreciation	500
7.	Maintenance	500
8.	Involuntary smoking	486

Employees who smoke one pack of cigarettes a day spend three and one-half hours a day with the smoking habit (smoking, lighting a cigarette, holding a cigarette, walking to and from an acceptable place to smoke, and so forth). Twenty percent of the smoking time is spent completely exclusive of all other activities. In other words, productive activity of the individual completely stops during exclusive smoking periods. An employee earning $6.00 an hour, for example, costs his or her employee at least $9.60 in lost time daily.[32]

Recently, some organizations have acted to limit or prohibit smoking in work areas. The General Services Administration, for example, has ruled that in all buildings under its control, direct smoking is to be held to a minimum in all areas where there are nonsmokers. Smoking is permitted openly only in areas where there are no nonsmokers. Smoking is not permitted in established areas, such as general office space, auditoriums, classrooms, restrooms, stairways, medical care facilities, and hazardous zones.

At least 15 states and 100 municipalities regulate the workplace to some degree or another. Smoking has been controlled in airline transportation with the federal ruling that smoking is prohibited on flights that reach their destination within six hours after starting. Northwest Airlines in March of 1988 banned smoking on all of its flights, and others have followed.

In a study conducted by the Administrative Management Society, 42 percent of the 336 respondents to the survey had a smoking policy. In the reporting organizations, smoking was prohibited in meeting rooms by 22 percent, in storage areas by 20 percent, in reception areas by 19 percent, and in hallways and aisles by 18 percent. Smoking was off-limits in 15 percent of the organizations' open areas, 14 percent of the cafeterias, 10 percent of security areas, and 8 percent of all areas in organizations.

The legality of managerial actions to restrict smoking is by no means clear. The courts have ruled that smokers do not have a constitutional right to smoke wherever they wish to do so, nor do nonsmokers have the inalienable right to expect a smokefree area in which to work (*Glasper* v. *Louisiana Stadium and Exposition District,* 1976). When workers labor in areas where smoking is present and as a result suffer physical problems, they may qualify for disability pay (see *Brooks* v. *Trans World Airlines,* California Workmen's Compensation Appeals Board, 1977). It is probable that a worker can be discharged for smoking in states that have the termination-at-will doctrine.

Managing Smoking in the Workplace

The need for control of smoking is obvious. The legality and fairness question must be given due consideration. It requires a balancing act. The organization must consider its smokers as well as its nonsmokers. If you or any of your friends smoke, you are undoubtedly aware that smokers have a number of frustrations. Many started smoking at a young age and feel unable to quit. At the same time, they feel that others are unduly hard on them. An organization that is insensitive to the concerns of smokers may alienate an important group of its employees. Some suggestions have evolved as organizations have gained experience. Some general policy statements are appropriate. For example, it is appropriate to state general policies that say that smoking is always off-limits in areas where there are

1. Flammable or otherwise hazardous material stored or in use.
2. Computers (not the desktop type) being used.
3. Sensitive materials in operation.
4. Critical records and supplies which, if exposed to smoke or ashes, would be damaged.[33]

Beyond these general policies, it would seem wise for management to

1. Limit smoking, where possible, to one area of the worksite.
2. Rearrange offices or other workplaces so that smokers are placed in one area and nonsmokers in another.

3. Separate smokers and nonsmokers with partitions.
4. Use smokeless ashtrays and room air filters.
5. Put smokers near exhaust fans and nonsmokers near fresh-air vents.
6. Ban smoking in common areas where everyone must mix and interact, including halls and conference rooms.
7. Allow smoking only in private offices or in other designated smoking areas.[34]

Managers in many organizations are not satisfied just to separate workers and create other physical conditions limiting space where smoking is permitted. Some are offering programs aggressively assisting workers who want to quit smoking. Employers sometimes offer programs to give employees direction and assistance in kicking the habit. If not offered in-house, the quitting program may be paid for fully or in part by the employer. Programs for the family or coworkers of the quitting smoker training them to serve as support are also offered as well as various forms of counseling.

Companies give rewards and offer incentives to help motivate the individual. Flat amounts of money are sometimes offered to individuals as a challenge to quit. A company might, for example, promise an employee a bonus of $1,000 if the employee quits smoking and continues to abstain for a period of six months. This kind of money is a justifiable reward when the savings gained by the employer is considered. A national survey of public (mostly governmental) organizations has revealed that a number of organizations are giving incentives and other favored advantages to employees in such things as preferred treatment in cafeterias or snack rooms; offices or workspaces; group life, disability, and health insurance programs; and even decisions about whom to hire in the first place.[35]

Back in the seventies, the Texas Division of Dow Chemical Company pioneered a unique program to encourage its employees to stop smoking. Dow established a special cash task force to help employees kick the habit. This group came up with a lottery as a central incentive. In the lottery, quitters had their names put into a drawing pool, not only when they pledged but also for each month they didn't smoke. Incentives were also proffered for "recruiters" (employees' workmates), who had their names put in a barrel for each month in which one of their pledged "quitters" didn't smoke. At the end of a year, names were drawn to award two $3,600 boats with motors, one to a quitter and one to a recruiter. Interim drawings were held to give away four 50-dollar bills "to help maintain interest" in the program until the drawing for the boats.

When the "I Quit" campaign began, 33 percent of the Texas Division employees were smokers. After four months, 24 percent of these smokers had enrolled as quitters. As an immediate result of the "I Quit" Program, Dow Chemical's cafeterias developed nonsmoking sections, some conference rooms became nonsmoking areas, and even the families of Dow Chemical employees were helped to quit.

Summary

Obviously the physical factors surrounding an individual at work can affect the individual physically and psychologically, and sometimes in productivity.

From a physical point of view, damage may occur to all of the sensing organs in particular but to the entire body in general. Hearing loss is one illustration, for example. While this chapter has not discussed the dangers of the pollution in the air, water, and materials around an employee, pollution obviously can cause illness, discomfort, nonproductivity, and even death. Health literally is affected by climate conditions. The ideal situation would be, of course, for the climate to be physically safe and comfortable for maximum effort to be extended.

Psychologically, the physical climate has the potential to promote tranquility or anxiety, coordination or dissension, friendliness or alienation, communication or confusion, the ability to cope rather than the feelings of helplessness, and openness rather than secrecy.

The physical climate does not always affect productivity insofar as *quantity* is concerned, though it sometimes does. Levels of productivity may be improved 35 percent or more as a result of physical climate factors. The *quality* of performance is also frequently touched by factors in the physical climate.

It is important for us to be able to identify factors in our surroundings that influence us. We need to be able to respond in a healthy way to these elements.

Questions to Consider

1. Should the goal of the management of an organization be to create a physical climate free of all detrimental objects and conditions? Why or why not?
2. What degree of responsibility does each employee have for providing and maintaining a safe, supportive work area around him or herself?
3. What should an employee do who feels conditions in the climate are not safe or conducive to good performance?
4. Since some things in the organization's climate cannot be completely controlled (the weather, for example), what should the response be toward such hazards?
5. In many cases, protective devices are available to defend workers from hazardous conditions. Sometimes it is very difficult to get workers to use what is available. Why is this, and what can be done about it?
6. What can an organization do (if anything) short of demolition and reconstruction if the open-office system or an executive row already exists and seems to be having negative effects?
7. When we observe an employee's performance, seldom can we say with absolute certainty that "the amount of noise she was exposed to caused her to make several mistakes" or "he becomes angry because it was too hot in the room where he was working." Why can't we be completely certain of the causes and effects? Is this set of conditions good or bad?
8. Is it ethical to require employees to work in areas where safety is uncertain?
9. Is it ethical to allow employees to smoke at work? What rights do non-smokers have? What rights do smokers have?

Key Terms

beautiful room   executive row   ugly room
conventional design   open office   visual stimuli
decibel (dB)   physical climate

Chapter Case

The Casino Crazies

At the end of the spring semester, you decide to take some time off and go to Atlantic City to visit Sam Chinn, an old high school friend who has recently taken a job with one of the large casinos in Atlantic City. Sam's title is Assistant Director, Governmental Relations; while taking a tour of the property, you ask Sam what his job entails.

"Well, government relations are crucial in the casino business," Sam points out. "I know that people have a preconceived notion that casinos are sleazy operations with all kinds of shady dealings. Here in Atlantic City, nothing could be further from the truth. Every aspect of our operations is under constant, close surveillance by state and federal authorities. I guess it's needed, but let me tell you, it can get terribly frustrating. It's up to me and the people in my department to handle governmental contacts and keep things moving along as smoothly as possible."

"I guess I'm not entirely clear about why you find government relations frustrating," you respond. "Can you give me an example?"

Just then an employee dashes up to Sam with an urgent memo. As Sam reads it, you watch him go into a slow boil.

"You want to know why this job is driving me crazy," he says. "Well, just take a look at this!"

You read over the memo that Sam hands you. It's from one of the regulating bodies, demanding that the newly repainted and recovered walls in the casino's restrooms and restaurants be redone.

"We decided to try to create a festive atmosphere," Sam explains. "So we literally spent a fortune on painting and papering—emphasizing bright reds, yellows, and oranges to create a party atmosphere. And some crazy government bureaucrat claims we can't do it. Just read this—they claim that the new colors are part of a plot to run people out of the restrooms and restaurants and back into the casino to spend money! They want a redesign in blue in ALL of those areas! I tell you, it's driving me crazy—it's a communist plot to destroy American business!" Sam wails.

1. From the standpoint of theory, why did the regulators insist on the change?
2. What should Sam do?

Section II

Individuals in the Workplace

6. Perception and the Individual

7. Personal Needs in the Workplace

Chapter

6

Perception and the Individual

Objectives

- To understand the importance of positive self-esteem as a factor in human behavior.
- To discover how self-esteem is developed.
- To identify managerial actions that will lead to more positive self-esteem.
- To consider the values of rewards and recognition.
- To see how role perceptions are established.
- To confront the problems occurring with role identification.
- To learn what locus of control is and how it influences behavior.
- To discover the value of communicating high expectations to others.

David Addison—An Unexpected Success Story

Brian McKenzie can hardly believe his ears. He has just been told by one of his friends who works at the Hidelburg Corporation (a local farm equipment manufacturer) that David Addison has been promoted to general supervisor in charge of welding and related activities. McKenzie had watched Addison grow up; they had lived next door to each other.

David was the son of Lucille and Mel Addison, who both held blue-collar jobs with area businesses. The Addisons left home for work each morning before their children, David and his younger sister Melanie, left for school. The children were required to get themselves ready and travel to school independently. David would pack their lunches. David was also responsible for watching after his sister when they got home from school until their parents arrived home from work. The Addisons showed little concern for their children and often did not get home until the early evening. McKenzie had heard rumors that the senior Addisons normally stopped at a local tavern and spent time with friends before going home.

The Addisons seemed to do very little to help or encourage their children. When they were at home, they spent most of their time watching television or talking on the telephone. The parents were frequently heard to criticize their children by saying such things as "You are as lazy as anyone I've ever known" or "You really are stupid."

McKenzie remembers the Addison children as shy, rather introverted, and lacking in self-confidence. He never really expected either of them to amount to anything. They both seemed to be pointing toward being nonproductive, incapable individuals who would probably wind up being cared for by the welfare system.

Two turning points in David Addison's life kept McKenzie's prediction from coming true. First, when Addison was a senior in high school, his guidance counselor showed an interest in him, discovered that he had mechanical abilities, and helped him to get admitted to a trade school when he finished high school. Addison gained skills as a welder and was employed by the Hidelburg Corporation upon completion of his trade school training.

Second, Addison's first boss at Hidelburg—Phil Turnley—identified Addison's potential and served as his mentor. Addison's skills developed rapidly under the expectant eye of Turnley. When Turnley was promoted to a higher position, he recommended Addison as his replacement. Again under Turnley's tutorage, Addison blossomed as a supervisor. His subordinates and peers saw him develop in confidence and ability under Turnley's approving guidance. When Turnley received another promotion, he again suggested that Addison follow in his previous position. Addison's performance is living up to the level Turnley had anticipated.

It was at this point that Brian McKenzie learned of David Addison's successes and his change in the way he viewed himself, his role, and his life opportunities. If the information McKenzie has received is correct, Addison is planning to take college classes at night. He seems to have set his mind toward other promotions.

As McKenzie reflects on what he has heard, he expresses an interest in knowing what Lucille and Mel Addison must think about their successful son. McKenzie would also like to know what happened to Addison's sister Melanie. The last time he heard anything about Melanie, she had just divorced her second husband, was unemployed, and was indeed living on welfare.

Case Questions

1. According to the clues given in the case, how would you describe the self-concept David must have experienced from his early years to the present? How did his self-concept change? Why?
2. How did the expectations of other people influence the way David behaved? How did expectations of others affect Melanie?
3. In what additional ways (besides their expectations) did the people around David affect his performance and behavior?
4. What lessons should we learn from the events in this case?

What You See Is What You Get

Behavior in the workplace is not only a result of the needs and drives of the people present, it is also a product of the perceptions of everyone involved. Employees, for example, have perceptions about themselves, the people around them, the roles that are to be played, the sources of control and power, among other things. These perceptions influence the outlook and the actions of each employee.

perception
A sensory experience in which an individual observes (experiences) a behavior, event, or condition, forms his or her own interpretation of the experience, develops an attitude or frame of reference toward the object observed, and allows the interpretation to be a factor influencing behavior.

Perception is a sensory experience in which an individual observes a behavior, event, or condition; forms interpretations of the factor observed; develops attitudes; and allows the processed observation to become a factor influencing his or her behavior. Perceptions are achieved for all aspects of the individual's environment (self, others, production components, customers, the general public, and so forth). Perception is not necessarily reality; that is, perceptions are not always accurate or correct. It is the worker's perception that influences his or her behavior, however, and not so much the real phenomena. Perceptions are real in their consequences.

If you have a job, it's likely you've heard an employee say something like this: "I can tell that the boss really doesn't like me. I've noticed that she never smiles or speaks to me—and she does to everyone else!" Notice that this perception came about from the employee's observation of the boss's behavior. The observation was "processed," and the perception, ("the boss doesn't like me") was the result. Notice also that this perception may or may not be true, but it will be what guides the hypothetical employee's behavior regardless of the objective truth. In this case, the employee may finally quit because the perception is that "the boss doesn't like me, and I'll never get ahead around here!"

Figure 6–1   How Perception Works

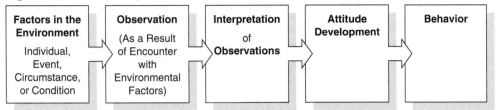

Source: Adapted from Arthur W. Combs and Donald Snygg, *Individual Behaviors: A Perceptual Approach to Behavior,* revised edition (New York: Harper and Brothers, 1959), pp. 240 ff.

Perception occurs in a fairly consistent sequence. First, the individual encounters environmental factors—other people, events, circumstances, and conditions. Observations are mentally photographed by the individual. From these observations, interpretations or judgments are made about the factor encountered and how the factor observed will be remembered by the person. Attitudes are formed as a result of the encounter and the subsequent analysis. From the attitude comes a behavior pattern. Figure 6–1 summarizes the perceptual process.

The objects in the environment may be continually changing. As a result, perceptions must be constantly reforming, although perceptual changes may be slower to occur than actual physical or interpersonal modifications. To illustrate perception and how it affects attitudes and behavior (performance levels), three major areas of perceptual influence will be discussed. The first is a review of self-perception and how individuals come to view themselves. Self-perception directly relates to the perceptions of other individuals in the work environment, as will be seen momentarily. The individual's perception of roles to be played is the second area of focus. The individual employee's perceptual view of who or what is in control of his or her fate is the third area of investigation.

Perceptions About Self and Others

Perhaps the most fundamental set of observations and interpretations is related to self-perception (the development of self-concept or self-esteem). **Self-esteem** (which comes from self-perception) has been defined as "an attitude of approval or disapproval, an indication of the extent to which the individual believes self to be capable, sufficient, and worthy."[1]

Self-esteem, or positive self-perception, results when two things occur. First, the individual experiences times of achievement in which good things are accomplished. After accomplishments are completed, the individual sees the successes and accepts them, attributing some of the accomplishment to such things as skill and effort that he or she has contributed. The positive evaluation of self leads to a chain of attitudes and behaviors.

In one study of self-esteem, it was revealed that individuals high in self-esteem also have the ability to quite successfully work independently. High self-esteem individuals become more self-governing and do not require as much in the way of attention and motivation from external sources. Low self-

self-esteem
An attitude of approval or disapproval or an indication of the extent to which the individual believes self to be capable, sufficient, and worthy.

esteem individuals, on the other hand, tend to (1) perform less effectively under stress, (2) be more easily influenced through persuasion, (3) engage more frequently in role modeling (following the behavior of others), (4) show less initiative and confidence, (5) be less ambitious, and (6) are more likely to be influenced by peer group interaction and situations where teamwork is a common pattern.[2] In addition to being able to be independent when needed, the high self-esteem person usually knows when to call upon others for help and does so without hesitation. Colleagues and peers as well as supervisors and subordinates are seen more as helpers than as threats. On the other side of the issue, the high self-esteemer is more likely to offer to help others than is the low-esteem person. He or she recognizes contributions that can be made and is willing to provide assistance without being personally threatened.[3]

Think back on high and low self-esteem people you know. Are these statements true of them? How is your self-esteem level? Do the personal feedback exercise to measure your self-esteem.

Self Test

Personal Feedback

Test for Self-Esteem

Your Perception of Yourself

How good is your self-esteem? By truthfully answering the following questions, you can get an estimate of your self-esteem. This is a relative measure of how you feel about yourself. In the blank space next to the number that appears by each question place the number of the following statement that most accurately reflects your feelings.

4   if the statement is always or completely true
3   if it is usually or mostly true
2   if it is occasionally or partly true
1   if it is seldom or rarely true
0   if it is never or not true

  1.   _____   I get along well with most other people.
  2.   _____   I am growing and changing positively.
  3.   _____   I have good friends.
  4.   _____   My physical health is sound.
  5.   _____   I am satisfied with my physical appearance.
  6.   _____   I handle difficult interpersonal relations well.
  7.   _____   I listen to others.
  8.   _____   The people who count listen to what I say.
  9.   _____   I make good decisions.
10.   _____   My life has been a good one.
11.   _____   My sex life is good.
12.   _____   I have a sense of humor.
13.   _____   I enjoy my work (or school).
14.   _____   I am happy most of the time.

15. ——— I have important objectives to accomplish in life.

16. ——— I have already accomplished a lot at this point in life.

17. ——— I am highly motivated.

18. ——— If I had my life to live over, there are only a few things I would do differently.

19. ——— I control my own destiny.

20. ——— I listen to other people, but I make up my own mind.

21. ——— I let people know what I think about an issue.

22. ——— Each day's experiences are worth the time I have traded for them.

23. ——— People seek me out as a friend.

24. ——— People seek my opinion.

25. ——— I am happy with my physical surroundings at home.

26. ——— I really wouldn't want to be anybody else.

27. ——— I feel comfortable meeting new people.

28. ——— I like doing something different.

29. ——— I handle stress well.

30. ——— I don't worry about things I can't change.

31. ——— I'm organized.

32. ——— I'm persistent and don't give up easily.

33. ——— I am not overly sensitive to others' opinions of me.

34. ——— I relate well to people of all cultures.

35. ——— I am flexible.

36. ——— I like to stop and smell the roses.

37. ——— I do not yield to excesses; for example, I do not eat too much, drink too much, or smoke too much.

38. ——— I'm a kind person.

39. ——— I can laugh when the joke's on me.

40. ——— People of the opposite sex find me attractive.

After you have responded to each statement, add the total points to determine your self-esteem score. A score of 130 and above indicates a good, positive self-perception. If you scored yourself at 145 or more, you may want to question whether you have been unrealistically high in your evaluation. Scores of 129 or lower may suggest that you need to work on your self-esteem to increase it.

Source: James M. Higgins, *A Manual of Student Activities in Human Relations,* copyright 1982, Random House, pp. 8–9. Reprinted by permission of McGraw-Hill, Inc.

The Success-Failure Model

A fruitful exploration of self-concept is the success-failure model (see Figure 6–2). In keeping with the basic model of perception in Figure 6–1, the success-failure model begins with the interaction of an employee with his or her environment. If the interaction is good, the individual will normally experience success. If success is the interaction outcome, the individual perception of self is positive. The individual views self as being liked, wanted, acceptable, able, and worthy. A self-concept based upon dignity and integrity is

Figure 6–2   The Success-Failure Model

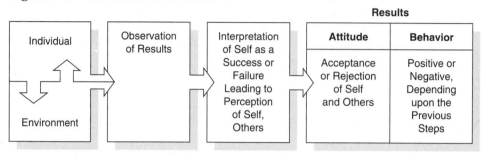

implemented. Self is seen as capable of meeting the challenges that one may encounter.[4]

If an individual perceives the interaction with the environment as successful, attitude and behavior will be affected in many ways. Success seems to breed success because the individual who has experienced success develops an optimistic outlook and anticipates future success. This optimism tends to aid in the achievement of positive expectations. In addition, the optimistic outlook coupled with previous successes builds a reservoir of strengths to draw upon when negative experiences are encountered. Because of positive experiences and perceptions, the successful person:

1. Is open and ready for new experiences.
2. Has the ability to admit to and cope with the existence of unflattering things.
3. Can remain more objective in analyzing data because there is less need for self-defense.
4. Is capable of tolerating unsolvable problems.
5. Is capable of experimentation and creativity because of inner security and strength.
6. Achieves a higher degree of independence from social and physical forces as a result of previous successes.
7. Has a high regard for others.

In other words, the adequate personality (the one who has experienced success) has a high perception of self and others, and this perception results in an open, positive set of attitudes and actions (see Figure 6–3).

Think back on our discussion of David Addison in the chapter opening case. One explanation for this "unexpected success" may be that the successes David experienced as a result of his high school counselor and his mentor served to raise his self-esteem. Do you think he's now performing as a high self-esteem person?

If the interaction experience results in failure, however, a completely different set of perceptions and behavior patterns may result. The individual who, through an assessment of personal experiences, sees self as unsuccessful eventually comes to feel unworthy, unwanted, unacceptable, and incapable. A low self-concept results in difficulty in accepting self and in identifying with

Figure 6–3 The Successful-Performance Model

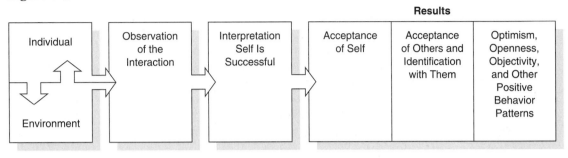

others. The resulting behavior is evidenced in several ways. The self-condemned individual may enter into a continuously belligerent, aggressive pattern to enhance self and overcome negative perceptions. On other occasions, the failure-oriented individual may withdraw from interaction and may give up in despair. Sometimes the experiences and perceptions become so traumatic that the individual behaves neurotically or psychotically. Whatever the case may be, the level of self-confidence, self-acceptance, and interpersonal identification is very low, and the resulting behavior tends to be uneasy and disturbed (see Figure 6–4).[5]

When you have managerial responsibilities, you will quickly notice that some of the nonmanagement people who work for you will closely fit this pattern. One of the authors remembers Charlie, a typical example. Charlie was working for a large utility company and after nearly thirty-five years had never been promoted beyond a semiskilled job. Charlie was one of the belligerent, low self-esteem people. Nothing management did was right. All of his coworkers were "stupid," and even the safety rules established by the organization were "dumb." Why did Charlie act this way? We can guess that he was trying to bolster his lagging self-esteem by putting others down.

As can be readily seen, the results of an individual's interaction with the surrounding environment determines to a great degree the individual's self-perception. The self-concept that develops shapes attitude and behavior.

Figure 6–4 The Failure-Based Model

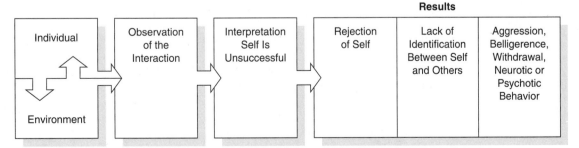

The Johari Window

Luft and Ingham have developed a concept, known as the Johari Window, that helps individuals discover more about their perceptions of themselves. The concept also helps individuals understand the behavior of self and others.

According to Luft and Ingham, there are four parts of a personal window that account for self-perceptions. There is the public arena, which includes the individual's knowledge of his or her own attitudes and behavior. This knowledge is also recognized by the people who surround the individual. The private arena contains perceptions the individual has about self that are not known to others. A third part, the blind arena, is not recognized by the individual but is known to others. Finally, there is the unknown arena, where neither the individual nor others are aware of perceptions that may be held about the individual (see Figure 6–5).

The more we can recognize our own perceptions of ourselves, the more we can alter, improve, or support the way we think and act. Since we know about our public and private arenas, we can let positive perceptions guide us to constructive performance while we work to improve the negative we find.

The feedback that we can get from others about our blind arena gives us insight into the perceptions that others have so that we can enhance or alter our behavior or take whatever steps are needed to have positive attitudes and behavior. The more we can cultivate this type of feedback, the more we will benefit. The way we react to feedback and the way we reward it will influence the willingness of others to confide in us what they see. From feedback we may also discover perceptions we wish to change or clarify. We may engage in public relations programs to change the perceptions others have of us.

The unknown perceptions are difficult to define and analyze. If we wish to influence our attitude and behavior, we need to dig around to discover as much as possible about the unknown. We need to engage in self audits as well as seek assistance from those around us.

Figure 6–5

The Johari Window— A Means for Analyzing Perception

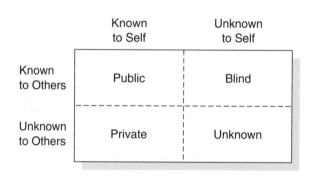

Source: Joseph Luft, *Group Process: Introduction to Group Dynamics,* 2nd edition (Palo Alto, Calif.: National Press Book, 1970).

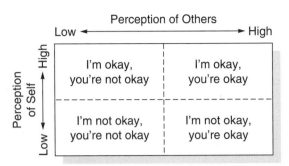

Perception of Others

Source: Excerpts from *I'm Ok—You're Ok* by Thomas A. Harris. Copyright © 1967, 1968, 1969 by Thomas A. Harris. Reprinted by permission of HarperCollins Publishers

The Transactional Analysis Model

Another important approach related to the development of self-perception and its impact upon behavior is the **transactional analysis** concept. According to the theory, as first proposed by Eric Berne, much can be discovered about an individual by analyzing the type of interactions (transactions) he or she engages in.[6] According to Thomas Harris, who has popularized the concept, the type of transaction an individual uses in relating to other people is a consequence of the individual's **life position** at a particular moment (life positions do change at times).[7] Life positions are really types of perceptions of self and others. In the Harris scheme of things, there are four basic life positions (see Figure 6–6)—I'm not okay, you're okay; I'm not okay, you're not okay; I'm okay, you're not okay; and I'm okay, you're okay.

The transactional analysis life position is a function of the performance of an individual and the stroking received from the other party or parties involved in a situation. **Stroking** is the receiving of attention from the other participant in a transaction. The assumption is that all people want stroking—preferably positive stroking (praise, encouragement, promotions); but if positive stroking is not given, people seek negative stroking (penalties, reprimands, etc.). The worst possible consequence would be to receive no stroking at all from a transaction.

The "I'm not okay, you're okay" life position is the starting life position for most people in this society (see Table 6–1). It results when the individual is doing little or is doing poorly but nevertheless receives positive stroking from a parent or other supportive individuals. Some individuals may never break out of this life position. "I'm not okay, you're okay" individuals are likely to participate in game playing, giving up and withdrawing, or being compliant to the wishes of others. Emotional reactions are frequent, as the child part of the personality is dominant. Other people are perceived positively because they provide attention, but the individual feels that his or her actions are unworthy of attention.

The "I'm not okay, you're not okay" person basically receives no stroking from others (or perhaps negative stroking to a small degree). Because there is no good reinforcement received, this type of individual develops a negative perception of self and others. "I'm not okay, you're not okay" individuals tend to feel useless, give up hope, and struggle through life.

Figure 6–6

The Life Positions of Transactional Analysis

transactional analysis
A method of studying and analyzing behavior that concentrates on the type of interactions an individual has with other individuals. Three parts of the human personality (parent, adult, and child) provide the mechanism for looking at past and present behavior. Recordings of past experiences are stored away for future reference.

life position
A form of perception where interpretations of one's previous performance and the manner and amount of stroking received from others lead to interpretations of self and others.

stroking
The giving of attention psychologically, physically, or both to another individual. Stroking can be positive when the attention given is supportive and rewarding, and it can be negative when the attention is in a chastising or penalizing form. Stroking fulfills a common need among human beings.

Table 6–1

Transactional Analysis
Life Positions—How
They Are Developed
and What the
Behavior Becomes

Basis of Development	Interpretation	Effects of Interpretation
Stroking from others received for behavior that is not particularly deserving.	I'm not okay; you're okay.	Game playing, withdrawal, being compliant to the wishes of others.
Actions that receive no stroking.	I'm not okay; you're not okay.	Giving up hope, resigning self to just getting by, game playing.
Heavy negative stroking at an early age.	I'm okay; you're not okay.	Self stroking, growing hardened toward others, getting tough, blaming others, committing crimes.
Good performance that receives positive stroking.	I'm okay; you're okay.	Intimacy, openness, helpful behavior toward others, constructive actions.

Source: Excerpts from *I'm Ok—You're Ok* by Thomas A. Harris. Copyright © 1967, 1968, 1969 by Thomas A. Harris. Reprinted by permission of HarperCollins Publishers.

"I'm okay, you're not okay" is a position that results from very unfortunate circumstances—too much negative stroking—to the point of being abusive—while an individual is young. The child may be beaten or given such treatment that other people become perceived as "not okay," and the "I'm okay" feeling is really a false assessment that develops as a defense mechanism. "Everyone else is out of step, and I'm the only one that is right" is the position reached here. Also, "I'll pat myself on the back and take care of myself, since no one else will" becomes a part of this philosophy. The "I'm okay, you're not okay" position leads to self stroking, false pride, a hardened attitude toward others, and the tendency to blame others for things that happen. The habitual criminal is often said to have an "I'm okay, you're not okay" feeling about self and others.

The most desirable life position is "I'm okay, you're okay." This positive perception phenomenon results when two things occur: the person involved *performs satisfactorily* and *people nearby give positive stroking* as a result of the performance. In this way, both self-perception and the view of others are affirmative. When this set of perceptions occurs, people can establish open, honest relationships. People communicate accurately, decisions are made objectively, and constructive transactions take place on a very positive plane. The ultimate goal for transactional analysis would be to reach the "I'm okay, you're okay" state of self/other perception.

Summary of Self-Perception

Self-perception obviously is an important factor shaping attitudes and behavior. The effects of the way individuals view themselves cover a wide spectrum of relationships and behaviors. If acceptance of self, ability to accept and relate to others, openness, objectivity, increased rationality, greater capacity for dealing with unsolvable problems, stronger inner security (to name a few)

This man is receiving positive stroking as a result of having just completed a good presentation.

are desirable outcomes, those who manage other people should attempt to foster positive views of self for each employee.

Managerial Actions for Better Self-Perception

Let's now think from a managerial perspective. What can a manager do to help promote a positive view of the self on the part of each employee? There are, in fact, several constructive managerial steps, and all of them are ones you can readily do as a manager:

1. Since it is important for success to be experienced, it is imperative to assign to each individual work that he or she can perform correctly. It is essential to carefully match the skills and abilities of individuals with their assigned jobs.
2. Every individual should have job responsibilities clearly identified for him/her before beginning a task. Energies can be devoted more carefully so that successful outcomes are more likely.
3. Essential skill and attitudinal development can be provided through training prior to performance.

Insights

How Self-Concept Shapes Performance

After World War II, an interesting finding came to light that triggered today's managerial revolution. In comparing the output of West German and British automobile manufacturing plants, it was found that the Germans were producing as much as four times what the British were producing.

It wasn't a result of the Germans having newer factories after rebuilding from the war. Researchers compared brand-new British plants with brand-new West German plants, and old British plants with old German plants, and found a four-to-one productivity difference throughout. They also found, as they extended these studies (which are now updated every year), that within Britain there was a difference of four-to-one between the best-managed and the worst-managed plants. Within Germany, there were the same great discrepancies, as with the United States and Japan.

Now, over and over again, we find companies manufacturing the same products, in the same markets, with the same number of people, with the same technology, the same level of unionization, but with differences in productivity ranging from 100, 200, 300, 500, and up to 1,000 percent. Why?

In individual performance, we also find, especially in sales, some people outproducing others by 20, 30, 40, 50 times. Again, we ask, why?

The answer can be found in the psychological factor. Thus, it is not latent talent and ability of people that makes the difference, but what is going on in people's minds.

The best-selling works that have been written in the past few years on excellence all come to the same conclusion. Excellent companies have certain psychological characteristics, and wherever you find these characteristics, you find high performance, high productivity, high job satisfaction, high output, lower costs, and higher profits.

The great challenge that we as managers have is to instill those psychological qualities in our organizations. We must become psychologists ourselves and create high-performance environments.

People perform the way they do as a direct result of patterns laid down in early infancy. The bundle of beliefs that people have about themselves is called the self-concept, and the discovery of self-concept is the single most important discovery in psychology in this century.

Your self-concept is the way you see yourself, think about yourself, and feel about yourself. You perform in a manner consistent with it. As adults, we have two to three hundred self-concepts. Each one of us has many self-concepts that govern, regulate, and control every area of our lives.

For instance, you have a self-concept of how you dress, and you always dress in a manner consistent with your self-concept. When we are not active in a manner or situation that is consistent with our self-concept, we are said to be out of our "comfort zones." If we move too far out of our comfort zones, we feel stress, anxiety, nervousness, and fear, and the natural human tendency is to withdraw to the comfort zone.

In their upbringing, children learn two basic fears—fear of failure and fear of rejection. First, they learn fear of failure—parents discourage them from touching, tasting, smelling, and feeling new things. The child soon learns that it's not a good idea to try anything new, to take risks, to do what is not approved of, or to take a chance. Later, as an adult, when a person is asked to take on a new job or enter into a new relationship or risk a certain amount of money, the instant response is, "I can't, I can't . . . I've got to play it safe . . . I've got to be careful because I'm afraid . . . I'll get spanked . . . I'll get punished . . . I'll be sent to my room."

This basic fear of failure is the greatest single obstacle to success in adult life. The fear of taking a risk and of moving out of the comfort zone is what holds us in a rut.

Fear of rejection is learned when a child's parents make their love conditional upon the child's performance. To be free from the feeling of guilt, punishment, and withdrawal of love from the parent, the child has to do what Mommy and Daddy like.

We transfer these same habit patterns to our work. For instance, if the manager asks the person to do something challenging, the employee naturally feels, "I can't . . . what if I fail . . . if I fail, I'll be punished . . . if I'm punished, I might lose my job . . . therefore the best thing to do is not to volunteer for anything."

Peak-performance organizations, on the other hand, overcome these negative patterns. They create an environment where people feel terrific about themselves, feel valuable, and feel like winners.

Peak-performance organizations nurture three aspects of self-concept:

1. Self-ideal, allowing people to make decisions and adjust their behavior to be more like the person they want to be.
2. Self-image, letting people see themselves as peak performers.
3. Self-esteem, where people like themselves.

When people like themselves, feel valuable and respected by others, and feel like winners, they will perform the very best they possibly can. Excellent corporations find that the more people feel like winners, the less they fear failure and rejection. The more people like themselves, the less they have those basic subconscious fears that hold them back and impair performance. Everything you do as a manager boosts other people to improve their performance, increase their output, and increase their contribution to the organization.

Your main role as a manager is to create a task-focused environment where everybody feels great about himself or herself. When people feel like winners, they'll perform to the very best—you will not have to supervise, monitor, or control them, not lie awake at night grinding your teeth over the way things are going. You'll just have to get out of their way, and they will perform in ways that will astonish you. This is the key to peak-performance management.

Source: Reprinted from Brian S. Tracy, "I Can't, I Can't," *Management World,* Volume 15, Number 4, April–May 1986, pp. 1, 8. Copyright 1991, Administrative Management Society, Washington, D.C.

**Management
in Action**

Stopping the Revolving Door

Research has shown that the loss of an employee through turnover costs the employer approximately $6,000 per individual. From 50 percent to 60 percent of new employees leave a new job within seven months of accepting the job. The message behind these statistics is that employers must find ways to recruit and retain workers.

People leave their jobs soon after starting them for many reasons. Some new employees find themselves performing tasks incompatible with their skills and interests. Some find themselves bogged down in bureaucratic red tape. Some find their energy and drive go without reward. Many are lacking in information about their jobs, their roles, and how they fit into the overall picture. Others discover office politics wields a powerful hand.

One thing almost all new workers need to do when they arrive in new jobs is to master their job tasks and achieve feelings of competence. Different employees find different ways to learn their organization and become competent for the demands of the job. Affiliations with other individuals who are also new hires can be a real source of information and support. Others find that attaching themselves to a mentor helps them to learn the organization, the job, and the work climate. While these are good ways of gaining orientation and confidence, there are other workable opportunities.

In the mid-1980s, the U.S. Department of Education found itself with a shrinking budget, layoffs, and floundering morale. The department developed the CIP (Career Internship Program) to help its new employees through uncertainty to bring them into the mainstream of the organization. Each year's new

4. Workers can be allowed to see the positive results of their efforts so that they can achieve a state of motivation to perform better. The viewing of good results can be a strong encouragement to the worker.

5. Feedback based upon performance outcomes is absolutely essential. Reports presented on successful performance build a correct mental state. Evaluations of substandard performance must also be communicated so that future improved performance will result.

6. Rewards and commendations for good performance provide the positive stroking that significantly affects self-perception. It should be remembered that when commendation is not appropriate as a result of poor performance, constructive criticism and negative feedback are useful in that negative stroking is preferred over no stroking at all.

7. Arrangements can be made for individuals with lower self-perception to work in interactive groups where teamwork is called for. Group interaction enhances an individual's opportunity for improvement in self-concept while receiving support and encouragement from peers.[8]

8. Managerial actions affecting the physical appearance of employees will also affect the worker's self-esteem. Good grooming may be a contributing factor. Research has shown that the wearing of uniforms that identify the employee with the employing organizaton may be a step to good esteem as well as to the feeling of being a part of a team.[9]

employees (called interns) were brought in as a group and went through the transitions and orientation process together.

Major features of the program included supervisory action planning, where the supervisors of new employees used their own organizational entries as the foundation for developing written action plans for physical, social, and work climate orientation. Another feature was the development of personnel teams and career intern councils. These councils, taken from human resources staff and representatives in the organization units where interns were placed, planned program activities, reviewed progress and goals, and solved problems.

Monthly one-day training sessions were held to teach new employees about the organization, to ensure the new employees met together regularly, and to respond to their concerns. Project teams were developed within each group to research and report on issues important to the group and its members. Employees working with career counselors developed plans for training for the next two years.

Each new intern was teamed with a recent intern who sponsored the new employee and made him or her feel welcome.

The organization reduced turnover, while the interns benefited in many ways. New employees learned about their department, took responsibility for their own informational needs, built contacts and visibility throughout the organization, developed relationships with peers, and developed confidence and presentation skills. They learned by doing things for themselves with the help and support of others.

Source: Adapted in part from Zandy B. Leibowitz, Nancy K. Schlossberg, and Jane E. Shore, "Stopping the Revolving Door," *Training and Development Journal,* Volume 45, Number 2, February, 1991, pp. 43–50.

Role Perception

A **role** is a pattern of behaviors expected of an individual by others who have contact with that individual. The more relationships an individual encounters, the more roles the individual will be expected to play. A woman who is in a middle management position, for example, will have a role as a follower to one or more higher level managers, will be a leader to one or more employees, will be a colleague to other middle managers, may serve a role as a consultant to managers in other departments, and may be a member of an informal group of managers who have lunch together frequently. In her off-the-job hours, this woman may have other roles, such as mother, wife, daughter, and community volunteer. Each of these roles carries its own unique demands and expectations.

role
A pattern of behavior expected of an individual by others.

Role perceptions are an individual's view of the obligations he or she has to fulfill the expectations of others. In the managerial situation mentioned above, the manager may get formal information from each of the groups or from individuals in specific ways (job descriptions, departmental memoranda, notes left on a bulletin board, letters, etc.). In many situations the expectations will be communicated through less formal means (a frown, a raised eyebrow, a whispered conversation).

role perception
An individual's view of the obligations he or she has to fulfill the expectations of others

Role perception is the interpretation of responsibility to each of the relevant publics that an individual serves. The perception may be accurate at times and inaccurate at others. Nevertheless, it is the individual's perception of his or her role that becomes the major factor influencing the individual's behavior. As shown in Figure 6–7, the role perception pattern fits the mold of other types of perception. There must be some kind of interaction resulting in an observation that is interpreted by the receiver. The recipient then transforms the interpretation into attitude and behavior patterns.

Several problems may surface for the role player in the perceptual process. Problems may include ambiguity, unrealistic or conflicting demands, demands inconsistent with personal values, and role overload. **Role ambiguity** simply means uncertainty about what an individual is expected to do for one or more individuals or groups. Ambiguity can be a result of many factors—those that are a fault of the communicator as well as those for which the receiver may be to blame. It is management's responsibility to give clear information on what's expected. "John, I'll need you to take over on the Cheever account" may not be enough information about role expectations. It's your responsibility as receiver of unclear information to reduce ambiguity by asking questions to determine what's really expected of you.

Unrealistic demands can be expectations that are impossible to fulfill because the requests contain inconsistent features—requests that are illegal, that demand unavailable skills, and so forth. In one organization, for example, the boss's secretary was put into an extremely unrealistic situation when her boss insisted that she type 500 pages of manuscript in a few days' time—never suspecting that the task was impossible.

Conflicting demands occur when the expectations of one group are at odds with the demands of another group. If a mid-level manager asks a supervisor for a speed-up in the performance of a set of tasks, while employees ask for more time to accomplish a related project, a conflict may develop for the supervisor. Simultaneous demands may be difficult to integrate. Many women have recently become concerned that their roles as business people may be inconsistent with their roles as wives or mothers.

Demands inconsistent with personal values would be incongruencies between personal goals or priorities and the demands of others. An employee

role ambiguity
An individual's uncertainty about what he or she is expected to do for other individuals or groups.

Figure 6–7   The Process of Role Perception

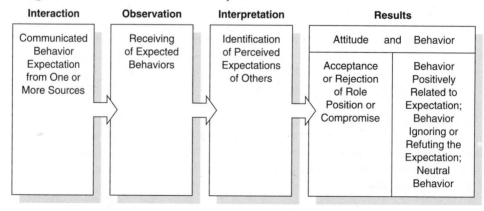

Interaction	Observation	Interpretation	Results	
Communicated Behavior Expectation from One or More Sources	Receiving of Expected Behaviors	Identification of Perceived Expectations of Others	Attitude and Behavior	
			Acceptance or Rejection of Role Position or Compromise	Behavior Positively Related to Expectation; Behavior Ignoring or Refuting the Expectation; Neutral Behavior

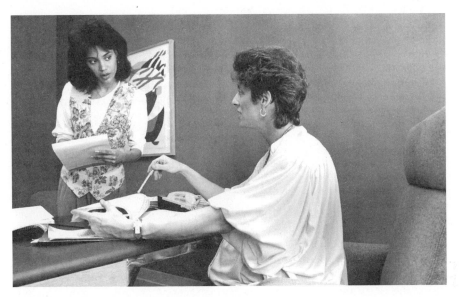

What roles are these women playing? Does each of them know what the other is expecting?

might be asked to postpone personal goals for the good of the company, or an employee may be requested to do something not in keeping with his or her conscience. Role overload would occur when the expectations of different groups and individuals collectively reach the point where performance cannot be completed within a satisfactory time frame, within a permitted budget, or in the quantity desired.

Ways to Improve Role Perception

A manager can do many things to help others improve their perceptions of roles. Job descriptions can be communicated in enough detail to explain specific job responsibilities and organizational expectations. Employees may be given assignments in keeping with their abilities and value systems insofar as these are known. A manager can serve as a buffer to keep others from unreasonable volumes of demands from organizational groups—other managers, outside clients, and spans of supervision beyond the abilities of the worker (to name a few). Managers can also help others negotiate more realistic responsibilities where needed. Counseling and support programs may be beneficial where the problems are personal in nature.

If you are on the receiving end, you can do much to help yourself where role perceptions are involved. Assertiveness, which has been defined as communicating significant information to others for the mutual benefit of all parties, may clarify and mediate responsibilities. Assertiveness may involve raising questions, asking for more information, or giving opinions so that positions and issues can be clarified.

All of us know of cases where people never learned what was expected of them because they were reluctant to ask. Realistic, compatible demands may be negotiated. Unrealistic demands can be rejected in many instances. Suppose it's your boss who's making the unrealistic demand. Even then, the demand can be tactfully rejected. Lydia, for example, was a real expert at doing just that. When her boss gave her one more job, Lydia would look at her work assignments, decide which ones were most appropriate for her to do, and approach her boss with a realistic schedule of what she could do and a plan for handling the remaining work, either by deferring it or delegating it to someone else.

Because role perception shapes the sense of responsibility and obligation toward others, these views become an extremely influential factor in shaping attitudes and behavior.

Perception of Who Controls Outcomes (Locus of Control)

In recent years, it has been recognized that another perception is very important in shaping behavior at work—the perception of who or what controls outcomes of behavior. This concept has come to be known as the internal-external issue or the **locus of control** concept. Before going any further, take the Rotter Locus of Control test. The individual who perceives that the things he or she does and the results of personal actions are really within his/her control is known as an **internal person.** This person feels that fate is a result of personal efforts. On the other side of the pendulum is the **external person.** This person feels that the things that happen to him or her (promotions, commendations, penalties) are controlled by external factors (the boss, the economy, competitors, etc.) and that he or she has no control over these influential elements. The external individual sees self as a victim of the environment, while the internal individual sees self as the initiator and source of influence. The internal person is more likely to have positive self-esteem as well.[10] An individual's perception of the locus of control is readily measurable through a process of testing (see the Rotter Locus of Control Scale).[11]

The locus of control process of perception is shown in Figure 6–8. The procedure is a relatively simple one, whereby the individual interacts with environmental factors, makes observations about influencing factors, and translates observations into an attitude, which in turn is translated into behavior patterns.

As a result of research performed on the locus of control, it is possible to identify several different behaviors for internal and external individuals, as illustrated in Table 6–2.

locus of control
An individual's perception of who or what controls the events in his or her life and affects the outcomes related to his or her efforts.

internal person
An individual who feels that his or her own behavior and the consequences are controlled by himself or herself.

external person
An individual who thinks things happening to him or her are controlled by external factors, such as the boss or the economy.

Figure 6–8
The Locus of Control (Internal-External) Perceptual Model

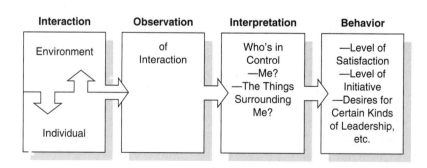

Table 6–2

Comparison of
Behaviors Between
Internal and External
Individuals

The internal (I control my fate) individual:	*The external (things in my environment control me) individual:*
☐ Is more satisfied with the results of his/her efforts.	☐ Is less satisfied with the results of his/her efforts.
☐ Would feel more satisfied in working under a participative leader and would be less satisfied with directive supervision than would externals.	☐ Would feel less satisfied with a participative leader and would be more satisfied with a directive leader than would internals.
☐ Would see a strong relationship between personal effort and personal output. The internal individual, as a result, would be more responsive to need-fulfillment motivational processes.	☐ Would see a weak relationship between personal effort and personal output.
☐ Will use personal persuasion and rewards to influence others.	☐ Will use coercive power to influence others.
☐ Will be more responsive to situations involving individual decisions.	☐ Will be less secure in individual decisions.
☐ Will be more open to input from the environment.	☐ Will be more concerned about environmental change.
☐ Will be more considerate of the needs of others.	☐ Will be more concerned about self-welfare than the welfare of others.

Source: See Terence R. Mitchell, Charles M. Smyser, and Stan E. Weed, "Locus of Control: Supervision and Work Satisfaction," *Academy of Management Journal,* Volume 18, Number 3, September 1975, for some ideas about the effects of locus of control on behavior. See also M. W. Pryer and M. K. Distefano, "Perceptions of Leadership Behavior, Job Satisfaction, and Internal-External Control Across Three Nursing Levels," *Nursing Research,* Volume 20, Number 6, November–December 1971, pp. 534–537; and L. A. Broedling, "Relationship of Internal-External Control to Work Motivation and Performance in an Expectancy Model," *Journal of Applied Psychology,* Volume 60, Number 1, February 1975, pp. 65–70.

As you reviewed the list in Table 6–2, something may have occurred to you—most managers are internals, and many of their subordinates are externals. How does this happen? Of course, it would be impossible to determine this for certain, but we can predict that the experiences that shape self-esteem (as discussed earlier in the chapter) are contributors. Perhaps managers simply have more experiences than do nonmanagerial employees that lead them to believe that they can control their fate.

Regardless of how it happens, if an internal manager attempts to discuss a problem with an external employee, miscommunication is likely to occur. One of the authors, an internal, recalls having the following conversation about attendance with Julie, an external employee who was frequently late for work:

Manager: *Julie, I'm concerned. You've been late several times this week. A pattern like that isn't meeting job standards.*

Julie: *But my clock didn't go off. . . .*

Self Test

The Rotter Locus of Control Scale

Instructions for the Locus of Control Scale   This is a set of items to find out the way in which certain important events in our society affect different people. Each item consists of a pair of alternatives lettered "a" or "b." Please select the one statement of each pair *(and only one)* which you more strongly *believe* to be the case as far as you are concerned. Be sure to select the one you actually *believe* to be more true rather than the one you think you should choose or the one you would like to be true. This is a measure of personal belief: obviously there are no right or wrong answers.

Your answers to the items on this inventory are to be recorded on the answer spaces which follows.

Please answer these items *carefully* but do not spend too much time on any one item. Be sure to find an answer for *every* choice. Mark your choice for either A or B for each item.

In some instances you may discover that you believe both statements or neither one. In such cases, be sure to select the *one* you more strongly believe to be the case as far as you are concerned. Also try to respond to each item *independently* when making your choice; do not be influenced by your previous choices.

1. a. Promotions are earned through hard work and persistence.
    b. Making a lot of money is largely a matter of getting the right breaks.

2. a. In my experience I have noticed that there is usually a direct connection between how hard I study and the grades I get.
    b. Many times the reactions of teachers seem haphazard to me.

3. a. The number of divorces indicates that more and more people are not trying to make their marriages work.
    b. Marriage is largely a gamble.

4. a. When I am right I can convince others.
    b. It is silly to think that one can really change another person's basic attitudes.

5. a. In our society a man's future earning power is dependent upon his ability.
    b. Getting promoted is really a matter of being a little luckier than the next guy.

6. a. If one knows how to deal with people they are really quite easily led.
    b. I have little influence over the way other people behave.

7. a. In my case the grades I make are the results of my own efforts; luck has little or nothing to do with it.
    b. Sometimes I feel that I have little to do with the grades I get.

8. a. People like me can change the course of world affairs if we make ourselves heard.
    b. It is only wishful thinking to believe that one can really influence what happens in society at large.

9. a. I am the master of my fate.
    b. A great deal that happens to me is probably a matter of chance.
10. a. Getting along with people is a skill that must be practiced.
    b. It is almost impossible to figure out how to please some people.

Locus of Control Scale

1.	a.	_____	b.	_____
2.	a.	_____	b.	_____
3.	a.	_____	b.	_____
4.	a.	_____	b.	_____
5.	a.	_____	b.	_____
6.	a.	_____	b.	_____
7.	a.	_____	b.	_____
8.	a.	_____	b.	_____
9.	a.	_____	b.	_____
10.	a.	_____	b.	_____

Add up the number of times you marked choice *a* and the number of times you marked choice *b*. The *a* items stand for internal and the *b* items represent external. Your inclination is reflected by the column you chose most frequently. If you checked each column five times, you are middle of the road.

Source: Julian B. Rotter, "External Control and Internal Control," *Psychology Today,* Volume 5, Number 1, June 1971, p. 42, used by permission of the author.

Manager:	*Julie, you're going to need to take more responsibility. Get a backup clock if necessary.*
Julie:	*My mother's supposed to call me, but she forgot.*
Manager:	*Julie, you've got to get control of your life.*
Julie:	*Besides that, the bus was late.*

In this instance, no real communication is taking place. The manager is oriented toward taking responsibility, while Julie believes that outside factors control her fate.

Behavioral Implications and Managerial Actions

The behavioral consequences of internal individuals seem superior in several respects to the external category. From a managerial perspective, it would seem desirable to facilitate development of an internal perception as much as possible in supervised individuals and to encourage the continuation of this philosophy in those who have already attained it. Delegating tasks to be performed individually, providing feedback and reinforcement as a result of specific actions, and the clarification of job responsibilities are a few methods of enhancing development of the internal control position.

The Pygmalion Effect— Improving Performance Through Perception

Pygmalion effect
A concept named after a character in Greek mythology in which people give back to others performance consistent with the others' expectations. Those who sense high expectations give back high performance, for example. This concept is also known as the self-fulfilling prophecy.

The perceptual process can be used very advantageously for the employing organization and the employee through use of the **Pygmalion effect.** The Pygmalion idea (also known as the self-fulfilling prophecy) is named for the character in Greek mythology who saw a female figure carved in ivory brought to life because he thought of her as a living being. The Pygmalion effect as we know it today suggests that people give back to others the behavior they sense others expect of them. A football player executes a play in a superior way because the coach expects it of him; a student excels in the classroom because her teacher communicates the belief and expectation that the student is capable of performing that way.

While the expectation-to-behavior cycle may be positively oriented, negative expectations also result in negative performance. A parent who believes a child to be untrustworthy and communicates such a perception to the child may eventually reap a juvenile delinquent. A boss who communicates lack of confidence in an employee may wind up disciplining or dismissing the employee receiving the negative perception. See Figure 6–9 for a picture of how the Pygmalion effect works.

The Significance of the Pygmalion Effect

The significance of the Pygmalion effect lies in the idea that people frequently receive back from others (employees, children, colleagues, and so forth) the kind of behavior consistent with communicated perceptual expectations they send out. The manager who wants positive results must communicate positive perceptions of others to stimulate positive performance. The managerial implementation suggests that capable people should be selected for tasks and that the superior must communicate a positive belief in the ability of the capable subordinate. Frequently, performance may be below the potential of the individual because the individual has received low-level perceptions of ability. Too often, communicated expectations are below the actual capabilities of the performer, leading to performance below the employee's potential. Challenging expectations stimulate outstanding performance. Substandard perceptions tend to produce substandard performance.

Summary

There can be little doubt that perception plays a major role in shaping the behavior of people in the workplace. Perception is how people sense something or somebody to be—even if the perception is not accurate. Perception occurs in a fairly consistent pattern. An individual encounters environmental factors—other people, events, circumstances, or conditions. Observation results that in turn leads to interpretations or judgments. From these judgments come attitudes that eventually lead to behavior.

Figure 6–9   The Perceptual Process of the Pygmalion Effect

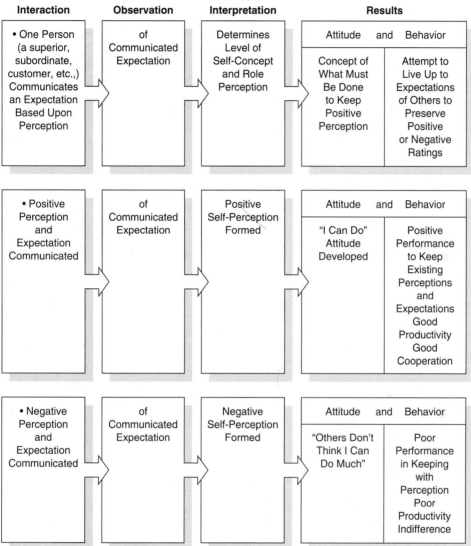

A very important perception is self-assessment. From self-assessment comes self-concept and self-esteem. Self-esteem means looking at self and judging that there is value and capability. Positive self-esteem results when an individual experiences successes and accepts self for having been successful. Self-esteem allows individuals to accept others as well. Others are seen as less threatening when self-esteem is positive.

Transactional analysis provides a mechanism for self-analysis as well as a means for analyzing other individuals. The ultimate life position based upon transactional analysis is the "I'm Okay, You're Okay" position because this reveals self-acceptance as well as the acceptance of others. The "I'm Okay, You're Okay" life position is achieved by an individual when he or she does something good and receives positive stroking or recognition from others.

Role perception is another important perceptual event. A role is a pattern of behavior others expect of an individual. Role perception is the individual's assessment of what others expect of him or her. Role perceptions that are clear and realistic are likely to allow an individual to function more effectively. When the expectations of others are realistic, nonconflicting, consistent with personal values, and manageable, the end result is normally positive.

Locus of control, another perception, is the sensing of whether an individual controls his or her own fate in life. The internal person feels in control of the sources and outcomes of life, while the external person feels life events and circumstances are a result of outside forces. These perceptions also affect attitudes and behavior.

It is possible to use perception to an advantage when relating to other people. With the Pygmalion effect, positive expectations of another person are communicated. The positive message tends to build the self-esteem of the other person. This individual will usually try hard to live up to the positive expectations communicated by someone else. Perception plays a major role in shaping future behavior.

Questions to Consider

1. "Perception is more important than reality." What does this statement imply? What effect would the truth in the statement have upon a manager? If the statement is true, what problems do you see for those who manage?

2. Do perceptions stay the same, or do they change over a period of time? Is this good or bad?

3. Since self-perceptions and life positions are so important, what can managers do to help their development in working toward positive interpretations? What can individuals do to develop good self-perceptions and life positions?

4. "Individuals who have negative self-perception and life positions do not have to continue with those perceptions." Is this true? Why or why not?

5. How can we learn more about our unknown self?

6. What kind of behavior would you expect from an "I'm not okay, you're not okay" leader? An "I'm not okay, you're okay" leader? An "I'm okay, you're okay" leader? Explain.

7. What kind of attention would an "I'm not okay, you're not okay" employee need? An "I'm not okay, you're okay" worker?

8. What are the most likely causes for incorrect role perceptions? Why do people make erroneous perceptions of the roles they are to play?

9. What factors and circumstances might lead an individual to become an external person? An internal person?

10. What messages does the Pygmalion effect concept have for today's manager?

11. Is it ethical to communicate high expectations of others just to get higher levels of performance?

Key Terms

external person	perception	role perception
internal person	Pygmalion effect	self-esteem
life position	role	stroking
locus of control	role ambiguity	transactional analysis

Chapter Case

The State Highway Review Board

You have just completed your education and have been offered what seems to you to be a great opportunity. You will be working for a federal government agency that investigates safety-related complaints involving the highway system. Your unit is specifically charged with going out to local, state, and federal highway departments when complaints are filed, investigating problems, and finding solutions. Your new boss tells you:

> One of the reasons we hired you is the heavy-duty course load you took while in college—especially that course in human behavior. I'm sending you out to investigate what's going on at the State Highway Board Review Group. We've been called in on a sticky case there, and I'll be waiting for your ideas when you get back.

You tell your boss you can hardly wait to get started, and you set off for the Highway Review Board's offices. When you arrive, you are met by Harold Macinac, who introduces himself as the director of the group. Macinac explains that the organization, while it is housed in an impressive-looking office complex, really has only two small groups of employees. The section heads are Margaret Ambrosini and Colleen Kinoshita.

The group itself functions as a coordinating body for highway boards throughout the state. Its mission is to coordinate review and expense practices for the individual boards to ensure consistency and legality of operations. It provides a number of informational programs for the reviewers and, more importantly, provides two services—legal research and zoning compliance information.

Because of the technical nature of the services it provides, the organization is generally valued and heavily used by the individual boards wherever they encounter zoning or legal problems. Macinac tells you:

> The problem is those two crazy supervisors we have working for us. Margaret handles legal affairs, and Colleen handles zoning. It seems like I can't communicate with them. They're always making demands, and they say I don't understand them. I don't get it—here they are—in beautiful offices, working a short, easy 35-hour workweek, and they say they're unhappy. People must be nuts!

You ponder Macinac's statements and set off to begin your investigation. You ask about the supervisors' backgrounds and are told that Ambrosini is an attorney, while Kinoshita is a high school graduate who has worked her way up through talent and willingness to work. A similarity is that both believe, in a sense, that they serve two bosses. One boss is Harold Macinac, but the other is Mal Dodson, Chairman of the Association of Highway Employees, a unionlike organization designed to protect the interests of highway employees. You are puzzled at the arrangement but set off to talk to the employees.

You begin your investigation by talking to Ambrosini, and you quickly learn that she has a totally different perception of the situation than you have heard before:

> I love my job. This was the first job I took out of law school. We had a single organization director then—doing both Mr. Macinac's and Mr. Dodson's jobs. He's since retired, but he was absolutely wonderful. He taught me all the ins and outs of the legal investigation job, and then, as he could see that I was eager to learn, he taught me his job as well— administration, a bit about zoning, and how to represent our organization in a whole variety of spots, like at the state legislature. When he left, there was no one to do his work so I just sort of took over. The work is great. Besides running a legal investigation group completely on my own, I represent the association with the legislature, speak before the legislature, and things like that. On the outside, I'm recognized as a real leader in the legal aspects of highway work. But not here! I get absolutely no recognition from the association. They think I'm still just a paper pusher, filling out forms and answering telephones and working a seven-hour day. Who do they think took over all the other work? And do you have any idea what my typical work week is? It's between 50 and 60 hours, that's what! And when I complain, Mr. Macinac tells me I must be disorganized! How does he know? He knows nothing about my work.

You next talk to Kinoshita. Her situation is somewhat different:

> I was brought in here as a receptionist, but it certainly hasn't worked out that way. I'd been here a couple of years when they changed my job, and I was told that I was to be trained to be the backup person for the zoning job. Before long, I was named acting zoning supervisor, and finally I became supervisor. When I was offered the temporary job, I asked about a raise and they said no. For some reason, they think it's an honor to be trained for management. I finally did get a little more money when I got the supervisory appointment, but it really isn't what I want. The problem is that I haven't been married long, I have a new baby, and I really want to spend time with my family. Worse yet, there are all kinds of new developments in zoning, and I have to take stuff home every night just to keep up. I've been trying—because I really need a job—but I'm just not sure how long I can take this!

1. What does role perception have to do with the problems in this case? What differences in role perception exist?
2. Are there any indications that role overload, role ambiguity, or conflicting demands exist? Explain.

3. What kinds of stroking, if any, seem to exist? What is the effect?
4. From the limited information given, is Harold Macinac—an internal or an external person? What is Margaret Ambrosini? What is Colleen Kinoshita?
5. What needs to be done to correct problems in this case?

Chapter 7

Personal Needs in the Workplace

Objectives

- To become familiar with the terms used to describe human needs.
- To be able to identify individuals' needs.
- To discover methods to fulfill existing human needs.
- To learn how human needs affect behavior in the workplace.
- To identify your own urgent needs.
- To be able to apply the different needs theories to people in the workplace.
- To benefit from the experiences of managers as they have worked to provide needs fulfillment.

Lisa Lanigan, C.P.A.

Lisa Lanigan, C.P.A., has reached a crossroads in her life. She has just been offered the position of managing partner of the Buffalo office of a major national accounting firm. She finds the offer to be rewarding in many ways. For one thing, the invitation recognizes the twelve years of hard work she has given to her job with the firm. The opportunity is satisfying, too, because it puts to rest some of her fears about being treated fairly as a woman in a very competitive organization. In her company, very few women work in major managerial capacities.

While the offer is flattering, it is not without its problems. For one thing, the position would require Lisa to move from her Midwestern home area several hundred miles to a location where she knows only a few people and where she has no family. One of the nice things about her present position has been that it has allowed her to be near her family—her parents and her sister and family. While Lisa is quite independent of her relatives in many ways, she still looks to them for support. Because she works long hours on her existing job, her social life is limited. Her parents and sister are her best friends. She fears that the Buffalo position would curtail this closeness with her family

Lisa has been thinking for some time now that she needs to give more attention to her personal life. Because she is a family-oriented person, she has given thought to marriage someday. Right now she is not romantically close to anyone. Lisa is concerned that her heavy commitment to her work is keeping her from a deeper relationship with someone else. The Buffalo job, if she should decide to take it, would demand even more of her time and concentration. She fears that developing her own family would be further jeopardized.

There's one other worry Lisa has—is she equal to the managerial requirements of the job she has been offered? She has previously exercised her supervisory skills on a small scale, but she's never had total responsibility for more than three or four people at a time. Can she provide the leadership a larger group of people would need on a continuing basis?

With these doubts and concerns weighing on her mind, Lisa isn't sure what she should do. Her decision is more than just a job decision—it's a decision about her life.

Case Questions

1. What are Lisa's career goals? Life goals? How well-defined are they?
2. What needs is Lisa's job now fulfilling?
3. How should Lisa go about analyzing the opportunity that has been offered to her?
4. Whom, if anyone, should Lisa involve in establishing her priorities and in making her decisions?
5. What actions might cause Lisa's concerns to subside?

Can My Job Give Me What I Want?

human need
A personal, unfilled
vacancy that exists
within an individual.

Each of us as a human being has needs and personal goals. We recognize some of our needs and take care of them objectively, while we may respond to other needs subconsciously and spontaneously. A **human need** is a personal, unfilled vacancy that determines and organizes mental processes and physical behavior so that fulfillment can occur. Each of us possesses many needs, and those needs differ from person to person. The needs we individually have are quite varied, as are the way our needs are triggered. For example, most of us have known children—and adults, too—who "act up" to get attention. For these people, the "unfilled" vacancy is for attention. This vacancy in the person's life leads to action—in this case, "acting up" aimed at filling the vacancy.

From a managerial perspective, the needs of individual workers are very important. In the first place, it is unfilled needs that bring prospective workers to an organization for employment. What kinds of needs can work fulfill? If we think for a moment, we recognize that there are many of them. Some people work primarily for money. Money in turn can be used to satisfy many other needs—for a new wardrobe or for a decent place to live, for example. Other people may tell you that besides money, work meets other needs—for creativity, for social contact, or for power. Thus, work can be a major source for meeting a variety of needs. Every new hiree brings a set of expectations with him or her at the beginning of a work affiliation. It is these unsatisfied goals that provide mechanisms for motivating workers. Employees respond to opportunities to fulfill personal goals and objectives.

Need fulfillment opportunities are a primary factor in keeping turnover at a low level.[1] Employees whose needs are being met and whose continuing desires are promised future fulfillment are likely to want to stay with an organization. The degree of fulfillment of past and existing needs is also a method for measuring personal satisfaction. Satisfaction is gauged by identifying the strength of a need, then comparing the need strength to the amount of fulfillment provided (satisfaction equals the strength or desire for a need minus the amount of fulfillment actually provided).

The type of needs an employee has will in many ways shape the individual's behavior. The degree of individual initiative, the level of willingness to take risks, and the desire to climb the organizational ladder are specific results of the type and strength of unfilled needs. Even though what we know about needs is neither perfect nor complete, the role and importance of needs cause us to give serious, in-depth attention to the subject. For example, you may have noticed as you read the case that opened this chapter that Lisa Lanigan is a person with a complex mixture of needs, like most of us. Furthermore, needs may conflict with one another, as you may have felt was the situation with Lisa. Lisa is proud of her work, and doing well has been a central concern in her life. The promotion and move are important because they recognize her efforts in the past and provide the advancement and challenge that will permit her to continue to meet the needs that are satisfied by her work. But what about her other needs—for security and love, for example? It appears likely that the move could threaten those needs. And what effect could threats to other vital needs have on Lisa's performance and satisfaction if she accepts the new job? As a leader, you will need to consider these issues both in managing your own career and in guiding the careers of others.

Needs Theories

Murray's Manifest and Latent Needs

A fairly significant amount of information about needs has been cultivated by a number of authors. One of the earliest investigators of needs theory was Henry Murray, with his **manifest** and **latent need** categories. To Murray, a manifest need is a desire that has been activated by a stimulus or cue. The manifest need is at work shaping the drives and behavior of the individual. For example, a particular work environment may stifle risktaking and creativity but encourage workers to meet the need to be with others by encouraging lunches in the company cafeteria or sponsoring a bowling league. Under such circumstances, workers' needs to take risks and to be creative may remain latent. Latent needs are those desires that lie dormant as a result of lack of stimulation by the environment. Latent needs can become manifest needs at any moment, however, if factors in the environment arouse them.[2]

manifest need
A need, according to Murray, that has been activated by a stimulus or cue.

latent need
A need, according to Murray, that lies dormant because nothing has happened to stimulate it.

The Maslow Hierarchy

Perhaps the best-known approach to needs is the one developed by Abraham Maslow.[3] Maslow identified at least five different types of needs and drew some conclusions about their relationship to each other. The five most pronounced needs as he defined them are the physiological, security, love (or social), esteem, and self-actualization needs (See Figure 7–1).

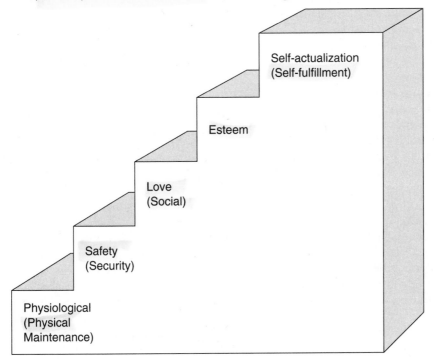

Figure 7–1
The Maslow Needs Hierarchy

physical maintenance (or physiological) need
The seeking of biological survival for food, clothing, and shelter.

love need
Sometimes called the social need. The desire to give and receive affection from others.
Belongingness and acceptance by others are important here.

esteem need
The desire to be respected (considered to be valuable) by self and others.

self-actualization need
The desire or yearning to become self-fulfilled, to achieve one's potential, to excel at something.

Maslow's theories suggest that there is a hierarchy to these needs. The **physiological need** (the need for such things as food, clothing, and shelter), for example, is the most necessary of the needs and the one that captures first attention. As this need is relatively well provided for, security (physical and psychological security) needs become more urgent. As security needs are fulfilled to a satisfactory degree, love needs (both giving and receiving) become more important. When **love** needs are met, **esteem** (self-respect and respect from others) needs become urgent. When esteem needs are met, **self-actualization** (fulfilling what an individual is capable and desirous of becoming) is of major importance. A filled need pushes the individual to a higher level of needs concern.

Needs are seldom, if ever, 100 percent fulfilled; as a matter of fact, the physiological need is usually best satisfied, and the level of satisfaction diminishes as the hierarchy is ascended. Research has questioned the relationships between needs that Maslow proposed. The value of Maslow's hierarchy, however, is that it leads managers to recognize that different employees may be at different needs levels. Thus, one single set of motivators won't work, and the manager must use different motivational tactics with different employees.

This problem is particularly acute at lower levels in the organization. Managers who supervise nonmanagement employees (such managers are referred to as first-line supervisors) often find that they are supervising a number of employees who would be classified as being at Maslow's social needs level. Employees at the social needs level are among the hardest to supervise. For them, the important thing is to fit into the group. Usual motivators such as praise will not work with these employees because it makes them stand out from the group. Pressure from the supervisor is often ineffective with social needs employees, while pressure from the work group can be highly effective.

In contrast, employees at the next level—esteem—respond positively to praise because they want to stand out from the group, but they may be unmoved by group pressure. For example, the authors recall the case of Jill, a young secretary who was clearly at the social needs level. While Jill was a good and conscientious worker, she would be quick to tell you that her primary motive for working was to enable her to have money for an attractive wardrobe for evenings out with her friends. Those evenings were important to Jill, and Jill literally lived for them. One afternoon there was a particularly complex typing and setup job that came up at the last minute. Worse yet, the boss was on her way out of the door to an evening seminar that couldn't be cancelled. She left the job with Jill, instructing her to keep at it until it was finished, since it was due at 8:00 the next morning.

Poor Jill! She cancelled her plans most reluctantly and worked until nearly 10:00 that evening. The work was hard, but she did a good job. The next morning Jill handed the report to her boss. The boss looked it over and was delighted at what she saw. She smiled and said, "This is great, Jill! You've done so well on this report, I'm going to give you the next one!" The question here, of course, is whether praise of this type will be an effective motivator for Jill, a social needs level employee.

Alderfer's ERG Approach

Clayton Alderfer[4] took the Maslow concept and modified it in a couple of ways. First, Alderfer condensed the types of needs into three categories:

1. The existence need (E) consisted primarily of the physiological and security needs proposed by Maslow.
2. Relatedness needs (R) were mostly love needs and the esteem needs involving recognition from others.
3. Growth needs (G) were composed of self-esteem needs and self-actualization needs.

The ERG approach as developed by Alderfer departs from Maslow by hypothesizing that while the fulfillment of lower level needs may cause an individual to seek fulfillment of higher level needs, so the lack of fulfillment of a higher level need (growth, for example) will cause a lower need (relatedness) to be sought to a fuller degree (see Table 7–1). This theory is helpful in explaining why employees who have been repeatedly denied promotion opportunities will say to you that they don't want to advance. It's common to hear, "I don't care about all that stuff! Just give me my paycheck," from such people. The hierarchy not only works upward but also progresses downward when circumstances cause this to happen.

Herzberg's Motivation and Hygiene Factors

Another perspective on human needs was provided by Frederick Herzberg. In 1968 he wrote an article entitled, "One More Time: How Do You Motivate Employees?" The article identified some factors about jobs that are motivational, including the desire for achievement, recognition, the performance of the job itself, responsibility, advancement, and growth. These are pretty much the upper level needs identified by Maslow and Alderfer. It is through the fulfillment of these needs (according to Herzberg) that satisfaction is achieved.

Table 7–1

Maslow and Alderfer Categories Compared

Maslow	*Alderfer*
Self-actualization	
	Growth
Esteem	
	Relatedness
Love (Social)	
Security	
	Existence
Physiological	
Needs must be filled before new needs become motivators.	Filled needs may cause concentration on higher level needs.
	Needs that cannot be filled may focus attention on lower level needs.

Table 7–2

Herzberg's Motivator (Satisfier)-Hygiene (Dissatisfier) Model

Dissatisfier (Hygiene Maintenance) Factors	Satisfier (Motivator) Factors
Security	Growth
Status	Advancement
Relationships with subordinates	Responsibility
Personal life	Work itself
Relationship with peers	Recognition
Salary	Achievement
Work conditions	
Relationship with supervisor	
Supervision	
Company policy and administration	

SOURCE: Adapted from Frederick Herzberg, "One More Time: How Do We Motivate Employees?" *Harvard Business Review*, Volume 57, Number 1, January–February 1968.

On the other hand, hygiene factors (the extrinsic elements of a job), such as company policy and administration, supervision received, relationships with coworkers, working conditions, salary, and job security, are neither motivational nor satisfying. Instead, when these items are not available in a work situation, they become dissatisfiers—that is, they cause people to be unhappy (see Table 7–2). In more recent research, Herzberg has found similar patterns of satisfiers and dissatisfiers among workers in other countries—in Europe, Israel, Japan, Zambia, South Africa, and India.[5]

Specific Human Needs

While research has not clearly identified the relationship between separate needs categories, several specific needs have been clearly identified and their effects have been pinpointed. In particular, there are nine needs that seem prominent as expectations held by employees as they work: physical maintenance, security, affiliation, competence, reputation, power, service, achievement, and hope needs.

The Physical Maintenance Need

physical maintenance (or physiological) need
The seeking of biological survival for food, clothing, and shelter.

Each of us possesses the **physical maintenance** need—the need for biological survival. Adequate food, water, oxygen, and shelter are essential, of course, if we are to continue to live. As children, we had to depend upon others to provide for these needs. As we mature, we accept responsibility for procuring these things ourselves.

How Organizations Fulfill Physical Maintenance Needs. Most of us today look to our jobs to provide the means (the necessary resources) to satisfy the physical maintenance needs for ourselves and our dependents. As mature adults, it is our responsibility to use earnings wisely so that these critical needs can be satisfied.

Some believe that organizations bear a responsibility to see to it that pay scales are developed so that the lowest level full-time employee is paid at a rate that allows him or her to at least provide for the physical maintenance of self and dependent family members (this assumes an average-sized family). The concept behind this is that every worker who is devoted to a full-time job should receive compensation adequate to meet these basic needs. Think about the arguments on both sides of the issue. The wage level needed to be sufficient varies from community to community, as cost-of-living levels vary. Most organizations want to establish a foundation wage well above the minimum standard-of-living figure.

The Need for Security

The need for **security** is partially related to the physical maintenance need. The certainty of a continuing supply of resources to meet physical needs is a security concern, but this need category goes much further. Each of us has a need to feel safe, secure, and protected from those elements around us that can harm us. Our security concerns may include fear of bodily harm and distress over threats of psychological pain as well.

security need
The yearning for safety or for the ability to overcome threats and dangers.

Insecurity is one of the realities of life. As long as there are people and factors independent of an individual's control, security will be challenged. A dynamic society filled with politics, pollution, disharmony, dissension, and change makes security difficult to provide in a consistent way. It is normal for every employee to seek protection for self and family over the elements of insecurity. We buy life and medical insurance, use seat belts, vote for political candidates, open savings accounts, and choose friends in ways that provide security potential and improve the probabilities that we can control external threats.

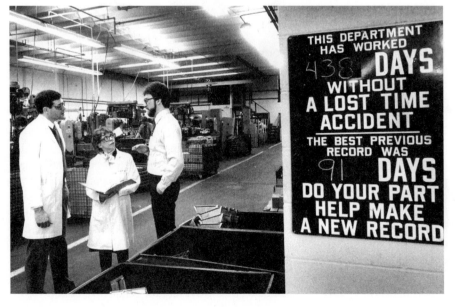

Employees' physical maintenance/security needs are met in this workplace.

Management in Action

Where You Can't Get Fired

Few companies today have a no-layoff policy. In effect, what this policy does is say to the workers in these companies, "Whether business is good or bad, you've still got a job. Even if we should have to down-size, you won't lose your employment." Companies that provide this kind of security are, indeed, rare. Perhaps there are as few as eight major organizations still using this policy—Delta Air Lines, Digital Equipment, Eli Lilly, Federal Express, Hallmark Cards, Hewlett-Packard, IBM, and Lincoln Electric.

The companies who have used the layoff-free plans have sometimes struggled to honor their commitments, but they have been rewarded when they've kept their promise to their employees. Delta Airlines, for example, has received as much back from its workers as it has given. When a sluggish economy forced Delta to curtail flights in the early 1970s, pilots pitched in to handle baggage. When fare wars decimated profits in 1983, flight attendants staged a fundraiser to buy a 40-million-dollar jet to give to the company. As a result of the dedication of its employees, Delta has survived and grown. Delta, for example, has added 200 flights in the past two years and is hiring pilots, mechanics, and flight attendants at a time when competitors are shutting down or retrenching.

At Hallmark Cards, when consolidations occur that would normally result in layoffs, employees who are misplaced are allowed to declare themselves "surplus" employees if they wish to stay with the corporation. "Surplus" workers float among departments as the workload demands. One worker, Jim Manker, for example, recently went "surplus," learned new skills, gained a promotion, and has become an even more loyal Hallmark employee. As Manker says, "When Hallmark told us the presses were leaving, they said we still had our jobs. I thought that was really neat."

Source: Mary Lord, "Where You Can't Get Fired," *U. S. News and World Report*, January 14, 1991. Copyright 1991, *U. S. News and World Report*.

How the Need for Security Can Be Fulfilled. While it would be unrealistic to expect to conquer insecurity completely, organizations can provide respectable levels of it. Through the trustworthy, fair, considerate actions of a manager come increased feelings of safety. On the opposite side, hastily made, arbitrary, inconsistent managerial actions increase the level of insecurity.

Economic insecurities in the face of potential health problems, possible loss of employment, future retirement, and other difficulties must be reckoned with. Most businesses provide medical and hospitalization insurance, disability compensation, pension plans, Social Security contributions, and other programs to offset workers' economic insecurities. The use of seniority (even with some of its undesirable attributes) as a method for making decisions about layoffs and the granting of privileges gives long-term employees additional job security. Companies that use only the safest of equipment and implement policies that encourage safe practices are aiding the physical security of workers. The Management in Action feature ("Where You Can't Get Fired") presents a good illustration of an organization's present way of providing for security needs.

When it comes to physical safety, there's no doubt that some jobs are much more threatening than others. The blue-collar occupation that experiences the highest rate of work-related fatalities is the timber cutter-logger, where there are 129 deaths each year per 100,000 workers. Asbestos-insulation workers and structural metal workers are next in line for being in hazardous positions. The most fatality-related white-collar job is that of the airplane pilot, where there are 97 deaths per 100,000 employees annually. Most other white-collar jobs are much lower in physical risks.[6]

We probably should note that some people actually seem to thrive on risk taking. We'll talk more about risk taking when we discuss achievement needs.

The Need for Affiliation

The need for **affiliation** is really an other-related type of desire. It is the need for belonging, for association, for acceptance by others, or the need for giving and receiving friendship. The affiliation need appears to be at least partially inherent, since even newborn babies respond to affiliation and tend to vegetate without it. Affiliation needs can also be cultivated and can be affected by a number of cultural and social factors. It would appear, for example, that urban workers may have stronger needs for the approval and support of others than do rurally raised individuals. First-born children seem to be joiners of organizations (clubs, civic groups, etc.) more than are later borns, possibly indicating a stronger affiliation need.

affiliation need
The desire to belong, to be accepted, to be able to associate with others.

As children, each of us looked more to family members as the source for affiliation fulfillment. As we grew older, peer groups and friends became more and more the center of affiliation expectations (note the stronger peer influence among teenagers, for example). Adults who are a part of a work organization seem to carry affiliation expectations with them to work.

Affiliation need level has an impact upon our behavior at work. Those of us who are high in the need for affiliation tend to be more conforming to the wishes and norms of others. We highly value membership in informal groups and pursue careers that provide for us more interpersonal contact (sales, personnel administration, counseling, and the like). There is some indication that high affiliation need causes people to have lower absenteeism and turnover patterns. High affiliation people are motivated by opportunities to earn the recognition and respect of others. It is also possible that these individuals are able to cope with stress more effectively if they have successfully cultivated the support and interest of other people. Look back at the Lisa Lanigan case, for example. One of Lisa's fears is that away from the support of her family she may have difficulty dealing with the stress of a new and challenging job.

Encouraging and Fulfilling Affiliation. While workers cannot be forced into social affiliations beyond their own personal desires, it is possible to provide people who want affiliation with opportunities to interact with others. Where there is flexibility in workstations, individuals can be placed near one another to allow for conversation and social exchange. Simultaneous work can be scheduled to provide several employees with the opportunity to strengthen their contacts. Organizationwide or departmental picnics can enhance social ties. Group assignments can be utilized for affiliation seekers.

Supportive feedback (as opposed to critical, task-related feedback) can be provided.

Workers who are low in affiliation needs may be happier and more productive in individual assignments where interactions are less necessary. Duties that must be performed in isolation will probably be better handled by low affiliation individuals. Managers faced with unpopular decisions affecting others may be able to perform more effectively if their affiliation needs are not restrictively strong.

It seems probable that workers who have a high need for affiliation may respond favorably to bosses who lead them using consideration and approval techniques rather than heavy task orientations. Workers who are less affiliation bound may be more open to productivity-centered leadership. They may be happier and more productive working in a group if the group has high productivity goals and can exert pressure on them to comply with group standards.

The Competence Need

competence need.
The desire to feel adequate to meet the expectations and requirements that one must face.

The **competence** need is the desire to feel adequate to perform the tasks and assignments expected of us. In the workplace, this will mean a drive to capably fulfill the roles and obligations inherent with the job. The average human being desires to be a success rather than a failure. Studies have shown that very often, particularly for young people, this drive for a feeling of competency is stronger than any other drive.[7] In the Lisa Lanigan case, some of the satisfaction Lisa gets from her work comes from mastering a complex and demanding set of job skills. Lisa feels adequate for her current job, but what about the new one? Thus, competence needs may enter into her decision.

Nonsupervisors seek competence as they use materials, equipment, and their own physical and mental resources to meet performance standards under time and quality pressures. Managers seek competence as they direct the efforts of others toward useful achievement. In almost every situation, competency involves self-judgment—judgment where we evaluate our own performance and are able to reach a favorable conclusion. The judgment of others (bosses, colleagues, etc.), of course, will influence our own feelings.

One author said:

> The competent individual feels potent and worthy of being taken seriously by others. The person who lacks the attitude of competence may not dare to hope to achieve. The competent person may experience conflict, disappointment, and frustration, but he (or she) is not likely to think of self as being bored or defeated.[8]

Providing for Attainment of Competency. The best way to develop a feeling of competency is to actually perform job assignments capably and adequately. When we perform successfully, our confidence in our own abilities develops, and we come to view ourselves positively.

Supervisors can help those with whom they work to develop a feeling of competency by properly assessing the capabilities of each employee and then giving each worker job assignments within the boundaries of the employee's ability. Feelings of futility will result when employees are given tasks beyond their capabilities. Bosses can also help by providing the necessary training, communication, and material assistance needed by the worker to increase ability to perform.

Feedback on successful performance is also helpful in the attainment of competency. Workers benefit when methods are available to measure performance levels in ways that provide knowledge of results pointing out successes as well as needed changes.

As is true of most need fulfillments, managers can do only a part of what is needed to help workers achieve competency. Workers must exert their own effort and possess a certain level of skill to attain competency.

The Reputation Need

In many ways, the **reputation** need is an extension of both the affiliation and the competence needs, for the reputation need calls for the recognition of one's competencies by others. Maslow defined the reputation need as a desire for status, recognition, and deserved respect from one's colleagues. The implication is that we are not satisfied simply to recognize our own adequacies; we want others to realize our capabilities and respond to us with admiration.

Workers, like everyone else, seek praise and recognition when they have performed well. A supervisor who says, "I don't see why I should have to commend a worker for just doing what he or she is supposed to do when I'm paying $9.00 an hour for them to do it," is showing a lack of sensitivity to this need. In reality, workers want recognition in addition to monetary rewards they are receiving.

A by-product of fulfillment of the reputation need is **status.** As an esteemed reputation is acquired, status very often is an outward form of calling attention to this accomplishment. In a realistic sense, status is an earned distinction that provides the individual with unique recognition—something above the ordinary, the commonplace. Earned status calls for symbols to portray the status and requests further recognition on the part of those who see the status symbols. Attempts by some business organizations and some political philosophies to destroy status positions and status symbols have been basically unsuccessful. Where one symbol has been removed, another symbol has risen to take its place.

When channeled properly, the desire for a good reputation and high esteem (and status also) can be a very useful drive. Of course, it is imperative that all workers be given the opportunity to achieve this goal when their actions deserve recognition.

Providing Workers with Fulfillment of the Reputation Need. One of the simplest, most helpful ways of fulfilling the reputation need is for supervisors to identify and commend good performance whenever it is given. Most workers respond enthusiastically to praise. Praise can be given easily and can mean much to a worker, yet it is interesting to note that many managers realize that they do not use praise as often as it is earned. It is important to note that to be effective, praise must be genuine and must recognize a real accomplishment. Empty praise, such as "You're doing fine, Sally," may appear meaningless and may be resented by workers.

Promotions and salary increases based upon merit are other forms of managerial response to the needs of workers for esteem and recognition.

reputation need
The desire to have the respect of others, to have one's competencies recognized by others.

status
A form of recognition in which an individual is esteemed in a way that distinguishes him or her from other individuals and groups. A high-status person is held in positive esteem. A low-esteem person is given little recognition.

As these men interact, reputation and affiliation needs are met.

Techniques such as employee-of-the-week awards and the giving of watches or pins for service rendered are other ways of extending symbols of esteem. These techniques do not appear very sophisticated, but they are rewards that provide recognition and enhance reputation. There are, of course, many status symbols (a private office, a large desk, a reserved place in the company parking lot) that provide esteem and reputation recognition. Many workers are self-conscious about their esteem ambitions, but the need continues to surface. Managers have an abundance of ways to provide for this need.

In providing recognition rewards and status achievement, it is important that opportunities to attain rewards and status are made known to all employees. Equitable reward systems provide everyone with equal opportunities to attain the benefits. The giving of rewards and recognition is something that should be earned by the recipient to satisfy his or her reputation and competence needs.

The Need for Power

power need
The seeking of the capacity to control people or things in one's environment. To wish to be dominant, influential.

Power is the capacity to influence or control the objects and forces in one's environment. Power is sometimes blended with the concept of authority, but they are really different things. Power is the ability to control or influence others, while authority is the right that an individual has earned or has been given to control or direct others. On a personal basis, power describes the ability of an individual to be dominant over or control the utilization of physical objects and the actions of other people. While power may make possible the fulfillment of other personal goals and objectives, many individuals seem to seek power primarily for the sake of being dominant and forceful. The need for power does not appear to be of the same intensity in all individuals—power is a chief concern of many and of less interest to others.

It has been observed that power is an important need of many politicians and may be a vital part of the makeup of many supervisors and managers. There is little doubt that many administrators climb the organizational ladder in search of power, often at the sacrifice of other goals (such as those of affiliation).

Many types of power can be acquired in the work climate. Perhaps the most definitive view of power types and how each type may be utilized is the one that French and Raven have given us.[9] The authors suggest five types of power that people at work may possess:

1. **Reward power** is the influence exercised by an individual as the individual controls the reinforcements that others desire—promotions, wage increases, recognition, and so forth.
2. **Coercive power** is the ability to influence others through fear, threats, or punishment.
3. **Legitimate power** is really formal authority: it is the right that an individual has to demand obedience from others based upon an official role or position held.
4. **Referent power** is a personal strength gained by an individual because the individual is attractive to the point that others wish to be identified with him or her. The person influenced wants to be accepted by the power holder so that the interpersonal relationship will continue. Individuals with high affiliation needs may be especially affected by referent power.
5. **Expert power** is the respect earned by an individual based upon superior knowledge or abilities. Others accept this power by acknowledging the unique characteristics of an individual.

These five types of power have differing degrees of influence. Expert power seems to have the largest impact on performance and satisfaction. Legitimate power seems to cause the highest level of conformity from others. Referent power seems to be strong among professionals. The impact of coercive power seems weakest overall.

Fulfilling the Need for Power. Officials in organizations control the giving of power only to a limited degree. Power resulting from formal authority comes with the delegation of duties and responsibilities (especially power through rewards, coerciveness, and legitimacy). These and other types of power may be won by individuals as they informally relate to others. The power of expertise may be enhanced through training and practice.

Managers face one of their greatest challenges in properly providing those workers who have a desire for power with opportunities for fulfillment in the work organization. A major element of the problem is the fact that not all individuals who desire power have the credentials and qualifications for handling it. Managers must assess not only the needs of their employees for power but also the workers' ability to use power. It has been pointed out that many people have unsocialized power needs and are likely to exploit others. Individuals with socialized power needs will work hard to make sure that others grow in capabilities and in ability to use their own power. Obviously, people with

reward power
The right to dominate people or things as a result of control over desirable reinforcements.

coercive power
The right to dominate people or things based upon the ability to give out undesirable reinforcements.

legitimate power
The right to dominate and control based upon an offered role or position held.

referent power
The ability to dominate others based upon attractiveness such that the person(s) dominated want to be associated with the power holder on a continuing basis even when the cost is heavy.

expert power
Respect earned by an individual based upon the possession of supervisor skills, knowledge, or abilities.

socialized power needs have much more ability than do those with unsocialized power needs to use power in ways that benefit organizations.

The Service Need

service need
The desire to do things that will be helpful or supportive of other people.

The **service need** is a yearning to give aid to others. To provide nurturance is one of the major aims of this need. We're not sure how it develops, but this other-related drive seems strong among certain groups of people. Individuals in the health care field would appear to be very strong in this desire. Educators and personnel administrators are identified with an abundance of this need. Some very evangelical sales personnel seem motivated to convey the benefits of their products to the aid of others. Obviously, individuals in clerical positions may possess this need to a high degree.

Providing Opportunities for Service. A genuinely service-oriented individual will be unhappy without opportunities to help others. Human contact is essential here. A human resources administrator, for example, may be gratified as he or she helps a new worker find a job that is well-suited to the worker's personal qualifications. A trainer will find satisfaction in seeing a trainee grow and develop. A counselor will get good feelings as the problems of a client are resolved.

A service-directed employee can feel satisfied with the end product in a company that provides, for example, surgical supplies. In educational and health care organizations, nearly any daily activity may be viewed as an opportunity for service. For an especially service-oriented individual, organizations need to be able to provide one of these opportunities for fulfillment.

The Achievement Need

achievement need
The desire to accomplish feats or tasks that are very challenging. The desire to do things that have an element of risk involved.

The **achievement need** is the human desire to accomplish a feat or task through the individual's efforts in the face of opposition and challenge. David McClelland, who has studied achievement needs in depth, indicates that the achievement need involves an emotional risk in which pleasure is sought with the realization that pain is an immediate threat.[10] The achievement need differs from the competence need in that the competence need is satisfied by the ability to cope with routine situations, while the achievement need is fulfilled primarily with the confrontation and mastery of extraordinary situations. Individuals with a desire to blaze new frontiers in a pioneering spirit may be responding to their need for achievement. Highly innovative, creative individuals may be motivated by the desire to do things no one else has done before.

The high achievement need individual has several specific traits. First, high achievers are responsive to situations where there is some risk involved.[11] Risks, however, must be at moderate levels. Extreme risks will be considered as too uncertain, and low risks will be thought of as unchallenging. Take one more look at the Lisa Lanigan case. Is Lisa an achievement-oriented person? What is her assessment of the risks involved in accepting the new position? How do you think this could affect her decision process?

Second, clear, unambiguous feedback must be forthcoming as a result of performance for a high achiever to get involved. The high achievement need person will not be satisfied with a situation where there is no way to identify whether one's performance has been a success or a failure. High achievement need individuals thrive on being personally responsible for performance. There is no challenge to a task that is someone else's responsibility.

Zemke shows the difference in high achievement need and low achievement need managers by saying that high achievers tend to be optimistic, favorable toward employees, participative, inclined to attempt personal fulfillment for employees, open with bosses and workers, and concerned with both people and productivity. By contrast, low achievement need managers are more pessimistic, distrustful of workers, unlikely to delegate, likely to avoid interaction, and more concerned about self-preservation.[12]

Providing the Opportunity for Achievement. Recognizing those individuals who have definite interests in achievement at a specific point in time and providing them with opportunities for fulfillment is another of the more demanding tasks faced by supervisors. The achievement-oriented worker often can be identified by a willingness to assume responsibility and a desire to be innovative and to take risks. As each manager discovers this desire on the part of one of his or her employees, the opportunity is there to encourage the worker's initiative and to provide the desired challenge through greater delegation of decision-making duties. In other cases, workers are given assignments where high-risk performances are involved. Wherever workers are encouraged to be innovative through the existence of reward structures, achievement is being encouraged.

It is highly important that workers' desires and abilities be compatible with the risk-taking and creativity demands of the jobs they hold. The worker with high-level needs for achievement will thrive on challenge, while a less achievement-oriented worker may feel nothing but anxiety and frustration while working in a high-risk job.

The Need for Hope

The **hope need** is the desire we all have to believe in the possibility that the future will bring conditions or circumstances that are better than those now existing. Hope is optimism based upon perceived opportunities for improvement or expectations that conditions and circumstances will improve. Without hope of improvement, the psychologically, socially, or economically depressed individual becomes increasingly listless, distressed, and sometimes even violent.

People at work are no different from other humans in their need for hope. They respond with optimism if hope is possible and may even tolerate deplorable conditions for a time if improvement is in view. On the other hand, those who work in less than ideal conditions become either passive or hostile if hope is denied them. Hope-oriented persons will seek methods to bring the world more in line with their desires even if only remotely possible.

Encouraging Hope. Hope would, of course, be unnecessary if all conditions were perfect, but perfection is rarely achieved. Because hope is partially an intangible state of mind, managers must first provide an environment where optimism can exist. Workers acquire a spirit of optimism when they

hope need
The desire to be able to believe that future conditions or circumstances will be better than those existing presently or in the past.

experience improvement in areas that have previously been unsatisfactory. While workers may normally be reluctant to accept change, they may welcome it when existing conditions are intolerable.

When workers have confidence that their superiors are sincerely interested in the workers' personal welfare, they more readily feel that improvement is a real possibility. Workers are prone to believe that their bosses will therefore act in their best interests. To some extent, trust is involved. Workers who have seen their bosses go to bat for them in the past tend to believe and trust that they will get support when needed in the future.

Perceptive managers have discovered that listening agencies such as grievance committees or other appeal boards serve an important role in encouraging hope. Workers often respond to the opportunity to present their feelings and concerns to a fair grievance committee if they know the grievance committee has a sympathetic ear as well as the power to act when improvement is possible. The promise of improvement is not enough to continue the desire for hope. Hope will be furthered only if tangible evidence exists to show that previous concerns have sometimes been fulfilled and that resources are available to provide real fulfillment in the future.

The Degree of Need Fulfillment and the Urgency of Needs

Needs are present in all individuals, but some needs seem to be activated to a greater degree than others. Some individuals experience a much higher level of fulfillment of their needs than do others. Individual needs and levels of satisfaction vary according to previous accomplishments, present conditions, and future opportunities.

Studies support the position that needs do indeed vary on the basis of such factors as what the individual has already experienced and what an individual's responsibilities are. In a Department of Labor study, for example, it was discovered that the composite goal hierarchy for American employees put "interesting work" above all other goals. "Enough information to get the job done" was second in importance (see Table 7–3 for other rankings).[13] In the composite figures, more than 50 percent of the employees were white-collar personnel (professional, technical, managerial, clerical, and sales workers). Distinct differences in the job expectations of the composite worker and blue-collar workers became evident in the analysis performed by Fein.[14] "Good pay" and "job security" appear to be more important for the blue-collar workers than for white-collar employees. On the other hand, "interesting work" and "enough authority" appeared particularly to be of lesser importance to most blue-collar workers than was true of the composite.

In an international study of employees in seven occupational levels performed by Hofstede (including employees from sixteen different countries), clear differences were shown in the goals being sought by the different classifications of workers (see Table 7–4).[15] The professionals in the Hofstede study exhibited urgent needs for self-actualization and esteem (achievement and reputation). Managers had self-actualization, esteem, and social needs. Technicians had a mixture of self-actualization, esteem, social, security, and physio-

Table 7–3   Order of Importance of Working Condition Factors for Composite Worker and Blue-collar Worker

Working Condition Factor	Composite Worker Ranking	Blue-collar Worker Ranking		
		Factory Worker	Construction Worker	Miscellaneous and Truck Drivers
The work is interesting	1	7.5	5	3
Receive enough information to get the job done	2	2	4	5
Receive enough help and equipment to get the job done	3	1	6	1.5
Good pay	4	4	1	1.5
Enough authority to do the job	5	11	12	6.5
Friendly and helpful coworkers	6	5	3	4
Work where the results are visible	7	9	11	8
Good level of job security	8	3	2	6.5
Opportunity to develop special abilities	9.5	13	16	9
Job where responsibilities are clearly defined	9.5	6	7	10

SOURCE: Mitchell Fein, "The Real Needs and Goals of Blue Collar Workers," *The Conference Board Record,* Volume 10, Number 2, February 1973, p. 28.

logical needs. Clerical workers were most concerned about social needs, and unskilled workers sought the basis of security and physiological needs. Again, the moral here is that it's important to know your workers and what their individual needs are. Only then can we, as managers, develop an effective motivational approach for each one.

In a study with a slightly different focus, Mitchell was able to identify the degree of need fulfillment and the satisfaction of personnel (in this case, Air Force officers) by their rank in the organization. The security, social, esteem, autonomy, and self-actualization needs of generals and colonels were better fulfilled and more satisfied than were those of personnel at the next organization level surveyed (lieutenant colonels and majors). With the exception of satisfaction with autonomy, lieutenant colonels and majors had more satisfaction and fulfillment than did captains and lieutenants. Mitchell was also able to note that line personnel (those in the chain of command) had more fulfillment and more satisfaction in just about every need category than did staff (support) personnel.[16]

According to surveys done by the American Association of Retired Persons (AARP), needs change as workers age and their life circumstances are modified. When broken into subgroups for purposes of analysis, the AARP survey shows classifications of mid-life career changes (ages 50 to 62), displaced

Table 7–4   Ratings of Goals by Various Worker Groups

Goals Ranked in Needs Hierarchy	Professionals (Research Laboratories)	Professionals (Branch Offices)	Managers	Technicians (Branch Offices)	Technicians (Manufacturing Plants)	Clerical Workers (Branch Offices)	Unskilled Workers (Manufacturing Plants)
High							
Self-Actualization and Esteem Needs							
Challenge	1	2	1	3	3		
Training		1		1			
Autonomy	3	3	2				
Up-to-dateness	2	4		4			
Use of skills	4						
Middle							
Social Needs							
Cooperation			3–4			1	
Manager			3–4		4	2	
Friendly department						3	
Efficient department						4	
Low							
Security and Physiological Needs							
Security				2	1		2
Earnings					2		3
Benefits							4
Physical conditions							1

SOURCE: Geert H. Hofstede, "The Color of Collars," *Columbia Journal of World Business,* Volume 7, Number 5, September 1972, p. 78. Reprinted with permission of the *Columbia Journal of World Business.* Copyright 1972.

workers 62 and younger, retirees ages 62 and younger, retirees who are between the ages of 62 and 69, and retirees who are 70 and older who are on Social Security. The mid-life career changers have plateaued or believe economic conditions threaten their jobs. This group looks primarily for growth needs and, to some extent, financial security.[17]

The displaced workers 62 and younger have work experience but currently are without a job. Security needs are strong among the individuals in this category. With full-time workers, good benefits, good health maintenance coverage, and the opportunity to build retirement security are the primary concerns. Retirees age 62 and younger often seek employment again because they are bored with retirement, are looking for more structure in their lives, or have a desire for belongingness and meaningfulness in life. For some, full-time jobs are attractive. For others, part-time work is satisfactory.

Retirees ages 62 through 69 on Social Security find their incomes are fixed, but they can work only a limited number of hours as a result of Social Security income ceilings. They often feel that their skills are becoming obsolete. Health problems are adding up, too. People in this grouping usually want part-time, flexible work hours and supplementary group insurance. Retirees 70 and older share many of the same needs younger retirees have, particularly the need for more income. Chapter 16 presents some ways of providing for the needs of older workers.

Discovering the Current Needs of Workers

Each of us has our own set of needs and expectations. We have some general information about the classifications of needs and how they may exist among workers in different industries, by different professions, and at different levels in an organization. To effectively use needs as techniques for motivation, placement, and best performance, we must identify the specific needs of each individual. Because needs do change, the urgencies of an individual's needs must be constantly monitored.

Managers frequently have a difficult time discovering the needs of their subordinates. A good illustration of this is the recent survey of 100 supervisors and 1,000 of their subordinates (see Table 7–5). Bosses were asked to identify what they felt their subordinates wanted from the jobs and work experience. The subordinates were then asked to identify what their personal needs from their jobs were. The employees ranked interesting work first, full appreciation of work done second, and a feeling of being in on things third. None of these items appeared at the top of the supervisors' estimates of what their subordinates wanted. Instead, the supervisors listed good wages, job security, and promotion and growth in the organization as their estimates of what their subordinates most wanted. Obviously, a mismatch existed between the employees' real wants and their bosses' beliefs about what they wanted. Such a mismatch can lead to problems with job satisfaction and motivation if no adjustments are made.[18]

Job Feature Wanted	What Supervisors Said Workers Want	What Workers Said Workers Want
Interesting work	5	1
Full appreciation of work done	8	2
Feelings of being in on things	10	3
Job security	2	4
Good wages	1	5
Promotion and growth in the organization	3	6
Good working conditions	4	7
Personal loyalty to employees	7	8
Tactful discipline	9	9
Sympathetic help with personal problems	6	10

Table 7–5

What Motivates Employees: Different Answers from Workers and Supervisors (by Rank Order)

SOURCE: Kenneth A. Kovach, "What Motivates Employees? Workers and Supervisors Give Different Answers," *Business Horizons,* September–October 1987, adaptation of Table 2, p. 61. Reprinted from *Business Horizons,* September–October 1987. Copyright 1987 by the Foundation for the School of Business at Indiana University. Used with permission.

Perceptive managers look for clues to discern an employee's needs in every manner possible. What a worker complains about, for example, may be an indication of unfilled or threatened needs. How an employee responds to an incentive may reveal the existence and strength of a need. Straightforward inquiries to subordinates may reveal needs and desires. In other cases, nondirective interviewing (discussed in Chapter 12) may be necessary to uncover the real needs of a worker.

It is possible to analyze the needs of a worker through the use of tests and questionnaires. One of the best known techniques for discovering the strength of needs is the Thematic Apperception Test developed by Murray (see Figure 7–2). In this test, individuals are shown pictures of people in different settings and are asked to write a story about each picture. By analyzing the stories written, the strength of needs (especially achievement, power, and affiliation can be diagnosed).[19]

Scales such as the one shown in the following self-test may also be useful in identifying the strength of needs levels. Try out the Needs Importance Questionnaire and identify the strength of your needs. The questionnaire can be adapted so that employees in a specific organization can answer the same basic questions.

Figure 7–2

Thematic Apperception Test Exercise

Look over the picture of the man in the photograph below. What is the man thinking? Compose a story telling what he is doing and what he is thinking about. Take ten minutes to write your evaluation of his thoughts and actions.

What did you talk about in the picture? Did you talk mostly about the work the man is doing and what he's trying to accomplish? If so, you might be considered achievement-oriented. The true Thematic Apperception Test works in this way to identify achievement-affiliation orientation.

Personal Feedback   # Self Test

Needs Importance Questionnaire

Please evaluate the following eighteen items according to how important you feel they will be to you as you look for a job upon graduation. Circle the score that is appropriate. The number 1 is the least important; 7 is the highest in importance. You may indicate importance within the range of 1 through 7.

1. It is very important to me to find a job where problems will be corrected when they are discovered.
   1 2 3 4 5 6 7

2. It is very important to me to find a job where I have authority and responsibility.
   1 2 3 4 5 6 7

3. It is very important to me to find a job where I can do things that are helpful to others.
   1 2 3 4 5 6 7

4. It is very important to me to find a job where I can do things no one else has had the opportunity to do before.
   1 2 3 4 5 6 7

5. It is very important to me to find a job where I can win praise and the respect of others.
   1 2 3 4 5 6 7

6. It is very important to me to find a job where I can feel good about myself and what I am able to accomplish.
   1 2 3 4 5 6 7

7. It is very important to me that I find a job that allows me to adequately feed and clothe myself and those who depend upon me.
   1 2 3 4 5 6 7

8. It is very important to me to find a job where I will receive the guidance and instruction I need.
   1 2 3 4 5 6 7

9. It is very important to me to find a job that provides the opportunity to develop close friendships.
   1 2 3 4 5 6 7

10. It is very important to me to find a job where my superiors will treat me with fairness.
    1 2 3 4 5 6 7

11. It is very important to me to find a job that has prestige within the organization.
    1 2 3 4 5 6 7

12. It is very important to me to find a job where I can develop a feeling of belongingness as I relate to others.
    1 2 3 4 5 6 7

13. It is very important to me to find a job where it appears that the future is brighter than the present.
    1 2 3 4 5 6 7

14. It is important to me to find a job that is challenging.
   1 2 3 4 5 6 7
15. It is important to me to find a job where I will have control and influence over other people.
   1 2 3 4 5 6 7
16. It is important to me that I have a job where I can help others to find solutions to their problems.
   1 2 3 4 5 6 7
17. It is important to me to be able to handle whatever the demands of my job turn out to be.
   1 2 3 4 5 6 7
18. It is important to me to find a job where I have a paycheck that will meet my essential needs.
   1 2 3 4 5 6 7

To find the importance of each need for you, add the two answers listed below together and divide by two to get the average score. Seven is the highest score possible.

Physical Maintenance
  Scores on 7 + 18   _____ + _____ = _____ = _____
                                                    2

Security
  Scores on 8 + 10   _____ + _____ = _____ = _____
                                                    2

Affiliation
  Scores on 9 + 12   _____ + _____ = _____ = _____
                                                    2

Competence
  Scores on 6 + 17   _____ + _____ = _____ = _____
                                                    2

Reputation
  Scores on 5 + 11   _____ + _____ = _____ = _____
                                                    2

Power
  Scores on 2 + 15   _____ + _____ = _____ = _____
                                                    2

Service
  Scores on 3 + 16   _____ + _____ = _____ = _____
                                                    2

Achievement
  Scores on 4 + 14   _____ + _____ = _____ = _____
                                                    2

Hope
  Scores on 1 + 13   _____ + _____ = _____ = _____
                                                    2

Summary

The more we can discover our own goals and ambitions, the more we can direct our behavior toward their fulfillment. The more we can learn about things that are unimportant to us, the more we can manage our time and effort to avoid wasting them in the pursuit of insignificant goals. The more we can learn about the needs of others, the more we can help others to succeed in matters that are vital to them. The more a manager can discover about the needs and ambitions of subordinates, the more he or she can provide attractive incentives and guide the subordinates' efforts along the most beneficial path.

One thing many organizations are doing more of to keep an eye on employee needs is to take employee surveys. In past years, companies undertook surveys primarily to keep unionization away or to find out why employees were griping. The more recent trend is to use surveys to discover what an organization can do to meet the manifested needs of employees. Comprehensive employee surveys can be very costly. In large organizations the price tag for polling employees can be a $50,000 to $125,000 expense. Surveys, of course, may serve purposes other than discovering employee needs—such things as gathering information for decisionmaking and collecting data to help in the implementation of policies. Such surveys encourage more bottom-up communication and may facilitate downward and cross communication.[20]

Questions to Consider

1. To what extent are companies and supervisors responsible for the fulfillment of each of a worker's needs?
2. In considering each of the needs listed in this chapter, are there any legitimate reasons for management to avoid trying to fulfill these needs?
3. What risks, if any, are involved in encouraging workers to affiliate with one another?
4. What problems, if any, do you see in helping workers to fulfill power needs?
5. Can you think of real situations that support the statement that an individual's needs change over a period of time?
6. Can workers who have different personal needs work compatibly with one another? Explain.
7. What problems do you see in the process of identification of an employee's needs?
8. After an employee's needs have been diagnosed, what are some of the problems an organization may have in fulfilling those needs?

Key Terms

achievement need	competence need	hope need
affiliation need	esteem need	human need
coercive power	expert power	latent need

legitimate power	power need	service need
love need	referent power	status
manifest need	reputation need	
physical maintenance (or physiological need)	reward power	
	security need	
	self-actualization need	

Chapter Case

Motivational Problems at the Environmental Improvement Unit

You've been out of school for only a short time when you are offered a job with a large government agency that oversees environmental improvement policies. You accept the job with pleasure.

"Now I can settle in and really practice management in a well-organized, stable atmosphere," you think. Unfortunately, life is never that simple, and it turns out that government agencies have problems of their own, and worse yet, your boss expects *you* to solve them.

You are put in charge of what is loosely described as the "administrative unit." The unit's responsibility, you learn, is to provide all of the clerical support and backup for several divisions of the agency. Several primary tasks are performed. One group of workers classifies and files the complaints and action reports dealing with environmental improvement infractions. Another group does word processing; most of its work involves typing reports and letters discussing charges. In both cases, there is a tremendous volume of work. The work is collected by a third group of employees—the mail processors. This group receives incoming mail, sorts it, delivers it to the proper departments, picks up incoming work for your group, and brings the work back to the word processors and the filing group.

The workers are primarily young and have limited education. Most are high school or vo-tech school graduates, and most seem to have little ambition.

"I know I'll never get anywhere," one of them tells you. "I never was much for schoolwork, and I can't see myself getting more education, and that's what it takes to get ahead around here. What they do is bring in college folks like you for the big jobs. So I just put in my time. After all, it's no better anywhere else, and I really like the gang around this place."

You quickly learn that that attitude is typical—the workers seem to be willing to put out minimal effort but primarily try to find any excuse to sneak out to take a break with their friends in the group. The only positive aspect you can see is that they aren't actively antimanagement. Instead, they seem to view management (including you) with indifference—sort of as a hindrance to the fun and games they would like to enjoy all of the time.

The only exception is a small group of complaint classifiers. This group reviews complaints and actions and classifies them into several categories before turning them over to the filing group. These workers are slightly more skilled than the others and much older—most have been with the agency for at least twenty years and have been doing the classifying job for ages. This group is actively dissatisfied, with a whole catalogue of complaints for you.

"Now it's nothing against you, honey," the unofficial spokesperson tells you. "We're used to young whippersnappers like you. They come and go, and we've had dozens of them over the years, but we're fed up with those other kids in the unit. They have no respect for us, no morals. Why, look at their crazy clothes and hairstyles—and they have no idea of doing a fair day's work. They're lazy and no good, and worse yet, they're at the same pay grade as we are. It's not fair, and we want you to straighten them out!"

1. What needs are manifest needs in this case? What needs are pretty much latent?
2. According to Maslow's theory, what are the problems in this case? What solutions would Maslow suggest?
3. According to Alderfer's theory, what's wrong here? What solutions would Alderfer propose?
4. What other problems do you see?
5. What additional solutions would you suggest?

Managerial Actions

8. Stimulating Employees to Action—
   The Motivational Process

9. The Reinforcement View of Motivation

10. The Role of Leadership in the Organization

Chapter 8

Stimulating Employees to Action—The Motivational Process

Objectives

- To discover how the needs of the worker can be used as motivators.
- To question the psychological state of employees when cognitive needs-oriented motivational techniques are used.
- To identify the questions an employee asks and the decisions employees make when needs-centered motivation is being applied.
- To become aware of the significance of reward action following successful performance.
- To analyze the importance of perceived fair treatment (equity) in the motivational process.
- To recognize how negative motivational techniques can provide incentives for good performance.
- To discover how the setting of challenging goals stimulates performance.
- To learn to analyze the motivational potential of the jobs being performed in an organization in order to enhance each job.

Brent Templeton—The Uninspired Draftsman

Brent Templeton is a draftsman for a large industrial equipment manufacturer. He has been with the company for more than seven years and is well respected for his abilities. In a recent conversation with one of his friends, Brent revealed the following thoughts about his work.

I really shouldn't complain about my job, I guess. The money is good. The working conditions are excellent. I have good friends who work with me, and that's important. While retirement is a long way off, I'm putting aside funds to help me live comfortably then. I'm also setting aside money to put our children through college when the time comes.

My problem is this: I just don't see anything different in the future. I have already reached the top of the pay scale for draftsmen. Except for cost-of-living adjustments, my income will never be much greater than it is now. More importantly, I've reached the top level for promotions that a draftsman can achieve. To get into a higher level design or engineering job, the company requires you to be a college graduate. Since I don't have a college degree, I have no real hope of advancing. Even if I could go back to college to get a degree, it would take years for me to get one. I must support my family; so I can spare neither the time nor the money that would be necessary to get a degree.

As I view the alternatives available, I just don't see many within the company itself. Perhaps what I should do is get involved in something off the job that would be stimulating. One of the boys' clubs in town needs someone to teach the kids how to do carpentry and woodwork, and I'm pretty good at those things; so I may volunteer to work in the program.

I guess it's not really important that I be all fired up about my work with this company. Just so long as I do my job and stay out of trouble, that's all that's really important, isn't it?

Case Questions

1. On the basis of material presented in Chapter 7, which of Brent Templeton's needs are being fulfilled by his employing organization?
2. Which of Brent's needs, goals, or expectations are not being met by his employer? Why is this particularly discouraging to Brent?
3. Is it important that an employee be fired up about his work, or is it enough to expect him to do his job and stay out of trouble?
4. What steps could Brent's employer take that would result in a change of attitude and improve his inspiration to perform?
5. With a partner, role play this case with one person playing Brent's role and the other acting out the role of Brent's boss. Seek to identify the causes of the problems that have developed and the possible solutions.

For those serving in supervisory capacities, a major responsibility is goal achievement. Goals are attained by working with and through bosses, workers, and fellow employees. Managers are expected to stimulate employees to perform their own duties and responsibilities usefully and constructively. The function of stimulating others toward productive performance is called the motivational process. Motivation has also been defined as the process of arousing action, sustaining the activity in progress, and regulating the pattern of activity.[1] Thus, the motivational process attracts and initiates action and serves as a factor in assuming that activity continues until objectives are attained. But how does one do it? That's the trick isn' it? You undoubtedly can think back to times in the past when you were motivated and eager to accomplish a goal. How could you get others to want to do it? That's what this and the next chapter will be considering.

There are two contemporary views of the motivational process. The approach discussed in this chapter is usually known as the needs view, or the cognitive approach. The other approach—the conditioning (or reinforcement) view—is discussed in the next chapter.

Assumptions Underlying Needs-based Motivation

The cognitive (needs) concept of motivation is based upon several assumptions about people and what people think and do. More specifically, the needs view of motivation seems to assume the following:

1. Individual workers are aware of their own personal needs in a conscious manner. Each individual knows whether affiliation needs are important to him or her, whether power needs are greater than security needs, and so forth. People recognize urgencies and are capable of putting them into priority.
2. Motives are primarily internal needs and not those things that are created by the environment.
3. People are capable of assessing activities available to them to determine that if they do well and receive rewards for their performance, the result will be the fulfillment of known internal needs.
4. Individuals are future oriented in their motivational drives. Instead of looking to past performances and past rewards, individuals are concerned about existing and future unfilled needs, not past fulfilled ones.[2]

cognitive motivation
The view of how people are stimulated to action that believes that individuals make rational choices based on the incentive opportunities they will respond to. Cognitive motivation is needs oriented, looking to future fulfillment.

The cognitive approach to motivation believes basically that people are mentally aware of how things around them appeal to their needs. At the same time, people recognize the consequences (effects) of their own personal actions as those actions result in rewards and penalties. The key to **cognitive motivation** is the fact that the performer senses or comprehends what is taking place. Although these seem like logical assumptions, they contrast in important respects with the cognitive approach (discussed in Chapter 9).

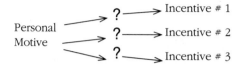

Which incentive offers the best need fulfillment?

Figure 8–1

Motive in Search of Fulfillment

Where Do Motives Fit into Motivation?

By using the assumptions of cognitive-needs theories, it is possible to build a model of motivation. The model begins with the **motive** of the prospective performer. One definition of the motive states that it "is an inner state that energizes, activates, or moves. . . and directs or channels behavior toward goals." Environmental factors influence the development and expression of motives, but the motive (or need) is centered within the individual human being. Motives cause individuals to reach out, to seek fulfillment, to begin searching for gratification. Figure 8–1 shows that motives initially may look for fulfillment in a number of ways.

You have undoubtedly seen this in your own life. Suppose you've been cooped up at home with the flu for the past week. You are now well and motivated to get out and socialize. What will you do to meet your need for socialization? A number of things might come to mind: stopping by a friend's house, participating in a sports event, or going driving. You will select the alternative that best meets your needs at that time.

The **incentive** enters the motivational process as Phase 2. The relationship between an incentive and a motive is very similar to the relationship between a magnet and a metallic object. The metallic object represents the need or needs an individual has, while the magnet represents the incentive that can be received in return for the appropriate action or effort. If an unattractive incentive is offered, it will have no appeal (will have no magnetic attraction). The motive seeks a means to accomplish need fulfillment, and the incentive appeals to the motive and attempts to mobilize it into action by promising the attainment of the urgent need (see Figure 8–2).

motive
An inner state that energizes, activates, moves, directs, or channels behavior toward goals.

incentive
The reward offered to a worker to stimulate him or her to act.

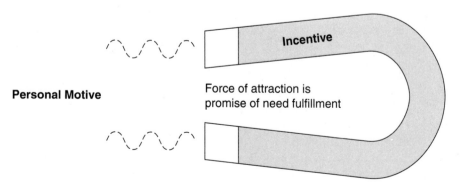

Personal Motive

Force of attraction is promise of need fulfillment

Figure 8–2

Magnetic Effect of the Incentive

Figure 8–3   Positive Motivational Model (Cognitive-needs View)

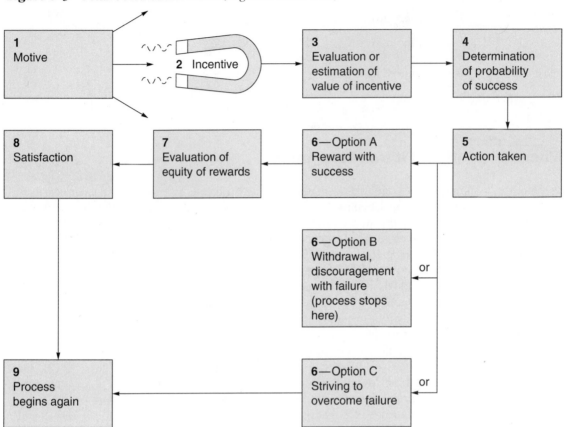

Just as a magnet must be directed toward the metal object, so the incentive must be directed so that it appeals precisely to the personal motive. This means that the incentive must be tailored to the motive. Continuing with our example, if you're longing to socialize, the prospect of spending a quiet evening at home with a good book just won't work! In the organizational setting, if the urgent motive of an individual is, for example, the need for power, an incentive in the form of better working conditions will not draw out the desired result. However, if the promised reward is a promotion with increased authority, the individual can be expected to respond with the appropriate effort to earn that which was promised by the incentive.

As the power-oriented individual may respond to the opportunity to gain more power, so may the friendship-starved individual be appealed to by the opportunity for socialization. Other motives (such as the needs discussed in Chapter 7) create the same need-action sequence. What does this mean? Incentives that are relevant to a particular person will attract that person's attention. This in turn, may lead to action. Incentives that are not relevant will be ignored or rejected. At this point, the first of our cognitive models of the motivational process comes into play. Let's see how expectancy theory enters in.

Figure 8–4   Relationship Between Perceived Personal Cost and Perceived Value of Obtained Monetary Rewards

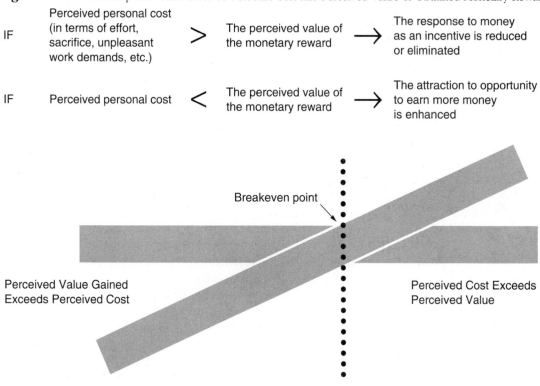

Expectancy Theory

One form of cognitive motivation is known as **expectancy theory.** Simply stated, expectancy theory operates on the premise that people behave as they do in response to their expectations about the future. People do things if a positive, valuable reward can be expected as an end result but will do little for unattractive, irrelevant rewards or no rewards at all. They respond to opportunities that have reward, utility, or reinforcement value. People have preferences and desires about the future that affect what they will and will not do in an organizational setting.[3] An easy way to think about this is to look back at the opening case. It's obvious that Brent Templeton's lack of motivation had a lot to do with his expectation that the future had little for him in the way of rewards—promotions and raises, for example.

According to the **positive motivational model** (see Figure 8–3), supposing an incentive appears to offer a means for satisfying the motive, the individual considers the *value* of the incentive as a means for fulfilling the motive. This is Phase 3 of the motivational process. The chief consideration at this point is on the value of the incentive or reward which is offered for performing. The value of a particular incentive or reward is considered on the basis of two criteria: (1) to what degree will the unfilled need be satisfied, and (2) will the reward (if attained as promised) be equal to or greater than the effort required to perform successfully and to earn the promised reward? Figure 8–4

expectancy theory The model of motivation that operates on the premise that people do the things they do because they believe their actions will result in future rewards to fulfill their important needs. People "expect" their efforts to result in good things they will earn.

**positive
motivational model**
A view of the way to
stimulate people to
action that is very
similar to expectancy
theory. Behavior
results from the
perception that
incentives offered are
worthwhile and
attainable.
Satisfaction occurs
after rewards are
received and
evaluated favorably.

shows a breakeven analysis an employee might use when considering the value of additional monetary rewards. This analysis sometimes is done subconsciously. The issue here is, Will the reward I get be worth the time and effort it cost me to get it? In Brent's case, we would expect little extra effort— the breakeven analysis says it's not worth it.

How do people decide what they value? The process is both complex and subjective, of course. People consider previous experience, existing urgencies, and future needs in an attempt to determine what the potential for satisfaction will be. There's also the relevance of the incentive to the felt need and the demands in terms of mental and physical effort. For example, consider the case where management offered to promote Tom, a skilled and talented non-management employee, to the position of foreman. The employee's managers were surprised when Tom flatly refused the offer.

"My leisure time means too much to me," Tom said. "The extra pay's not worth having to take on the hassle of being a manager!"

One thing is clear. The reward—promotion—wasn't *valued* in this situation.

Suppose the reward is valued. Then what? If the promise of reward is perceived to be acceptable, the motivational process moves to another pre-action phase—the probability that the individual can perform in such a way that the reward promised can be successfully earned (Phase 4). In effect, the person is asking, "Can I actually *do* what's wanted of me?"

People think about the probability of successful performance in several ways (see Figure 8–5). The worker surveys (often subconsciously) personal knowledge and skills related to the demands of the job to determine if he or she feels capable of performance that would earn the anticipated reward. The worker analyzes accessible resources (including machinery, materials, etc.) to determine their availability and adequacy. The individual also considers the amount and type of support that can be expected from superiors, colleagues (peers), employees, and other personnel on whom the employee may be dependent. The availability and support of others may be an extremely important part of the success-potential analysis.

Another factor that enters into the assessment of the probability of success is time. The worker reviews (again perhaps subconsciously) the time available for performance in an effort to judge whether the amount of time is sufficient. To illustrate, a manager offered a group of workers a 1,000-dollar bonus if they would load out fifty trucks in a ten-hour period. The group refused to try. Why? The members of the group believed it was impossible to do what was asked.

The final factor involves whether the person will actually receive the reward if the performance is successful. In effect, the person asks about the intent and sincerity of the agent offering the incentive. Is the employee's supervisor genuinely interested in having the worker achieve a successful performance so that the reward can be earned? Will the organization actually deliver the promised reward? In a recently overheard conversation, an obviously disgruntled employee said, "I don't see any point in killing myself to get that job out. Even if I do, I'll never see an extra dime in my paycheck!" In effect, the employee believes he *can* do the work, would like the extra money, but *won't* do the work because he doesn't believe management will deliver the reward.

Figure 8–5   Evaluating Probabilities of Successful Performance

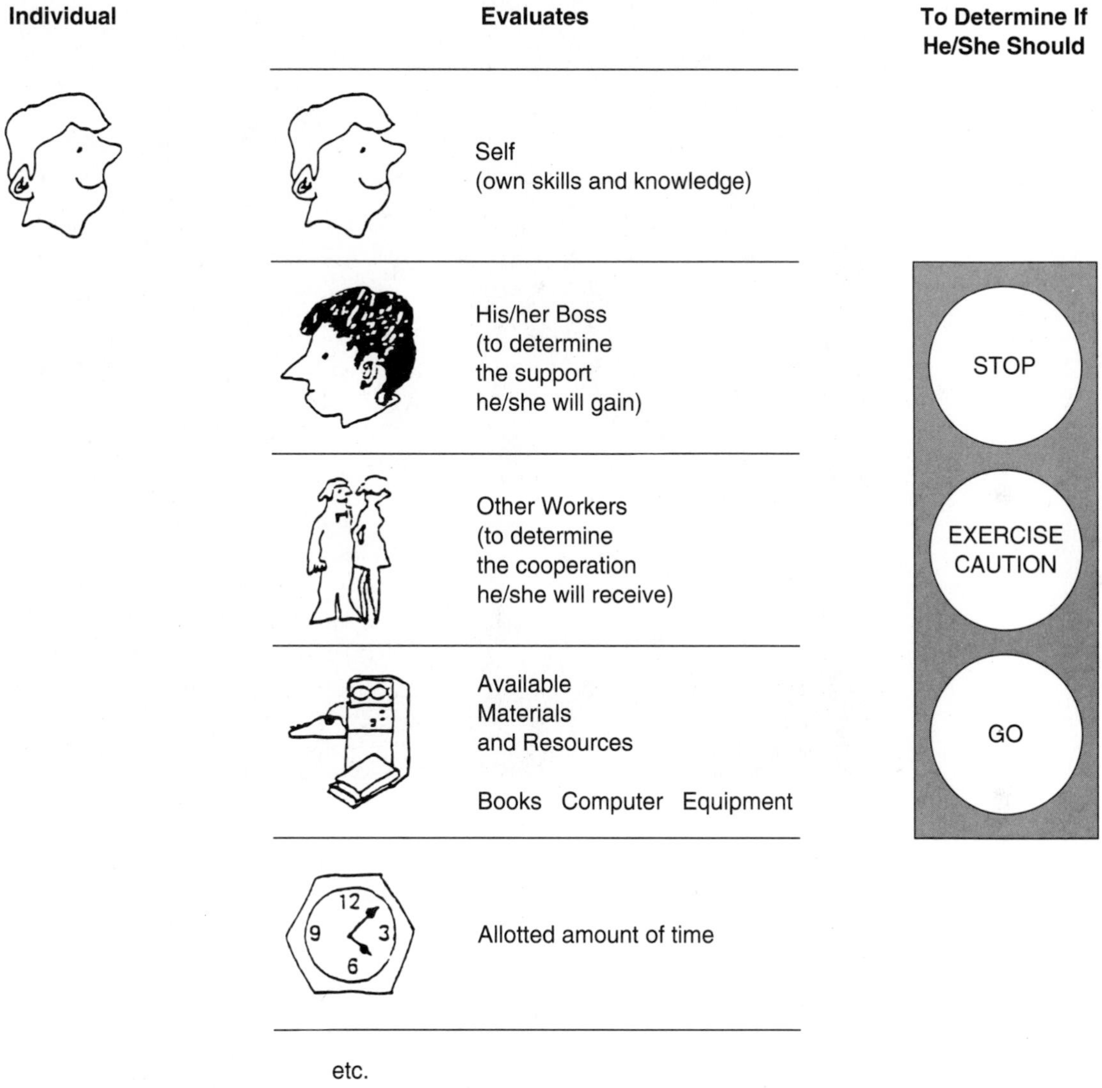

Individual	Evaluates	To Determine If He/She Should

Self
(own skills and knowledge)

His/her Boss
(to determine
the support
he/she will gain)

STOP

Other Workers
(to determine
the cooperation
he/she will receive)

EXERCISE
CAUTION

Available
Materials
and Resources

GO

Books   Computer   Equipment

Allotted amount of time

etc.

Overall, these and other factors help the individual worker determine whether there is a reasonable chance to perform in a way that would make possible the earning of the reward promised by the incentive. How can we analyze Brent Templeton's situation based on the chapter opening case? Brent values opportunities for increased responsibility and new job challenges. He'd like to move up with the company to better pay and a more stimulating job. So Phase 3 of our model looks fine. Brent values the reward. How about Phase 4? We can't be sure, of course, but Brent may believe that he could meet the demands of more responsible work even without a college degree. Brent believes that management won't give him the rewards, and the motivational process stops right there—at Phase 4. Based on expectancy theory, we'd have to predict low future performance from Brent unless management

This man may be
concerned about his
ability to do his job,
or, he may be con-
cerned about having
adequate time to
complete the task.

does something to convince him that he has an opportunity to move up. Take the Personal Feedback test to learn some things about the motivational model and yourself.

If the value of the benefits offered by the incentive, the probability of successful performance, and the likelihood of a reward appear to be positive, the worker usually decides to expend the effort in order to achieve the promised rewards. Action on the part of the worker (Phase 5 of the model) is a voluntary step entered into with optimism and a sense of expectation. An action-result relationship is anticipated in which the adequate performance of the worker is expected to result in need fulfillment.

Quite often, theorists discussing the motivation process stop their analysis at the point where action is taken by the worker. However, post-action events are extremely important if immediate satisfaction is to be gained by the worker and future receptivity to incentives is to be provided. Workers who perform as managers ask them to, should receive the promised reward (Phase 6—Option A). When anticipated rewards are given, motives are *potentially* fulfilled, and the employee's confidence in future performance-reward situations is increased.

Adequate performance that does not receive the promised reward will result in skepticism about future rewards as well as immediate disappointment. This is where the distrust of management's motives noted earlier comes

Personal Feedback

Self Test

What The Positive Motivational Model
Can Tell You About Yorself

One of your professors needs a student to spend some time (up to twenty hours) entering data into a computer. The professor asks you if you would be willing to do the work. The professor gives you the following information. You will need to attend a three-hour training program before you begin your entry work. You will be paid five dollars an hour for up to twenty hours of work. If the work takes you more than twenty hours, you must finish on your own time. The work must be completed within the next two weeks. You will need to get a friend to help you. The friend will be responsible for coding the information gathered from questionnaires.

If you were using the positive motivational model to decide how to respond, Step 3 of the model would call for questions to determine if the rewards being offered are of value to you. You would answer questions such as:

> If it takes me twenty hours to do the work, I will be paid $100. I will undergo three hours of training. That means I will earn approximately $4.35 an hour for my time. Is that amount of money worth the effort?"
> Yes _____   No _____

Would I earn less if I spent my time working somewhere else?
Yes _____   No _____

Will my friend receive the same amount of money for his or her time?
Yes _____   No _____

What if it takes me more than twenty hours to do the job, and I must work on my own time? Will it be worth it?
Yes _____   No _____

Will the experience be good for my computer skill development?
Yes _____   No _____

Will the experience look good on my résumé?
Yes _____   No _____

Will I enjoy the experience of working with my friend?
Yes _____   No _____

Would I rather do this job than do something else with my time?
Yes _____   No _____

A *yes* answer to a majority of these questions is important if you are going to say yes to the job.

Then step 4 of the model would ask questions about whether you believe you can handle the job. You would ask questions such as:

Do I know enough about computer data entry to handle the job?
Yes _____   No _____

Can I learn enough in three hours to do the job?
Yes _____   No _____

Will the instruction be adequate (will the instructor be helpful)?

Yes _____   No _____

Can I do the job within the twenty hours allotted?

Yes _____   No _____

Do I have a friend who can be counted on to do a good job?

Yes _____   No _____

Will the professor give me help if I need it?

Yes _____   No _____

Do I have enough free time in the next two weeks to do the job?

Yes _____   No _____

A *yes* answer is needed to most if not all of these questions if you are to feel confident about your probability of success.

Now stop and consider what you've learned about yourself.

Would the money you earned be enough satisfaction if you got nothing else out of the project?

Yes _____   No _____

Would helping the professor out provide enough satisfaction if you got nothing else out of the project?

Yes _____   No _____

Would the experience be satisfaction enough?

Yes _____   No _____

Would a line on your résumé be satisfaction enough?

Yes ——   No ——

Do you have confidence in your computer skills?

Yes _____   No _____

Do you have confidence in your ability to learn this task?

Yes _____   No _____

Do you have a friend you can trust to do his/her part?

Yes _____   No _____

Are you over-scheduled for the next two weeks?

Yes _____   No _____

You can learn much about yourself by considering your answers to these questions. Take time to think about your values and your confidence in yourself and others.

from. And it's around a lot! How often have you overheard someone say, "Around here, it's not *what* you know, but *who* you know?" If employees have come to that conclusion on the basis of their experience with management, what they're really saying is that they believe that there will be no relation between their doing the work and getting the reward. Instead, it's all politics. Clearly, there's a message for all of us here: *If you offer a reward, make sure you deliver!*

If on the other hand, the worker fails to perform adequately and does not earn the reward expected, the effects are less certain. Sometimes the worker who fails in performance becomes bitter and antagonistic toward external factors felt to have caused failure. The worker may lose self-confidence. In effect, what's happened in this case is that the employee doubts whether he or she is capable of doing what's asked. If performance leads to failure, future use of the model may be in doubt. In most situations, the employee will view future motivation-incentive situations more critically, and the value and probability factors will need to be strongly positive before the employee will take action to attain the rewards (Phase 6—Option B).

In some situations, however, failure makes the worker even more determined to succeed. In these reactions, the worker reassesses the motives, incentives, values, and probability of success factors and puts forth additional effort to perform satisfactorily in order to gain the rewards sought (Phase 6—Option C). Through additional effort, the employee may achieve performance deserving the reward.

Equity Theory

When performance is successful and rewards are received, motive fulfillment or satisfaction (Phase 8) does not always occur immediately. Instead, individuals move to Phase 7, which is the assessment of the equity of the rewards. In effect, we say, "I got the reward, but is it really what I want?" Perhaps you've heard someone say, "Sure, I got what I expected, it's just wasn't worth it." This was what we were getting at when we said we looked at Phase 6—Option A and said that when rewards are given, motives are potentially filled. If it wasn't worth it, the motive wasn't fulfilled, even if the reward was received. Tricky? Let's look into this a little further.

A major motivation concept known as **equity theory** concentrates primarily on the assessment of the fairness and appropriateness of rewards received. When thinking about equity, one can start with the idea of using a reference point as a means of comparison. The point of comparison is a reference person—someone in similar circumstances with inputs (effort, skill, experience, etc.) and outcomes (salary, wages, promotions, etc.) against whom one's inputs and outcomes can be compared. Equity would occur in this framework if the input/outcome ratio of the person observed was similar to that of the observer (see Figure 8–6).

If both employees worked forty hours and got about the same amount of pay, they would probably consider themselves equitably treated. In many situations, perfect equity doesn't exist. If the ratio is seen by the observer to be favorable to self, the stage would be set for satisfaction to occur (Phase 8). If the ratio is seen as unfavorable (i.e., the input is greater or the outcome is less than that of the other worker's), dissatisfaction may result. With satisfaction, the employee is open to continual motivation. In fact, the employee may display motivation by working hard to prove he or she is *worth* the heavy outcomes. If the employee is dissatisfied, it may become more difficult to get him or her to be receptive to future incentives (Stage 9).

equity theory
A concept of motivation in which each performer evaluates rewards received against the rewards received by other employees as well as against inputs required to earn the rewards. Outcomes (rewards) equal to inputs are considered against the outcomes and inputs of others. Where outcomes and inputs differ from those of reference persons, results will be perceived as inequitable.

Insights

Who Is Responsible for Seeing That an Employee Achieves Job Satisfaction?

For an employee to achieve the feeling of satisfaction about his or her work, several things must happen. First, the individual must have goals or objectives that are expected to be fulfilled through work. Second, performance must occur that is deserving of rewards. Third, rewards must be given that have the potential for fulfilling the employee's personal needs. Fourth, the employee must evaluate, accept, and feel good about the reward received.

Satisfaction requires a number of efforts on the part of the individual employee as well as the employing organization. The following are some of the responsibilities:
The individual is responsible for

1. A rational code of values, including values that do not contradict needs, reality, or the individual's abilities. To illustrate, an employee cannot rationally advocate contradictions such as a merit system for others and favoritism for himself or herself. Nor can one expect a promotion if one lacks the ability to perform the job in question or a higher salary than either the market price or what the organization can afford to pay.

2. Rational expectations (for example, that value attainment cannot be guaranteed; that rewards are not always automatic or immediate). Every effort does not always pay off. Hard work does not always result in success, and success does not always result in a reward being received. A deserving employee might not receive a promotion if there is no place to promote him or her.

3. Proper choice of job and willingness to change jobs or careers when previous choices do not work out. The individual is responsible for making a good match between skills and abilities possessed with those needed by the organization. If career and job choices do not work out, flexibility in seeking other opportunities is important.

4. Conscientious efforts to obtain values on the job through sustained, competent performance and rational persuasion. There are some individuals who have the neces-

Figure 8–6
Equity Ratio and
Questions

Equity Ratio

$$\frac{Outcome_{self}}{Input_{self}} = \frac{Outcome_{other}}{Input_{other}}$$

Questions of
Comparisons with others:

Is my outcome   >,<, or = the outcome of others?
Is my input   >,<, or = the input of others?

Comparisons with personal criteria:

Is my outcome >,<, or = my input (the cost/benefit question)?
Is my outcome >,<, or = the promised outcome (reward)?

sary abilities but are not willing to take the necessary actions to be successful. Also, some people don't seem to expect much and, as a result, don't get much in the way of rewards.

Just as the individual employee has responsibilities, so the employing organization has duties to help the employee find satisfaction. The organization's responsibilities include the following:

1. Realistic job previews given to job applicants along with the keeping of preemployment promises. Employees need to know what they can reasonably expect upon employment. If there are modifying conditions and contingencies involved, they need to be communicated. After employment, commitments made by the organization must be kept.

2. Proper selection and placement and willingness to make changes when selection and placement errors occur. The organization needs to see to it that people with the necessary skills are matched with the correct jobs and that the long-term goals of individuals are compatible with those of the organization.

3. Proper identification of what the individual wants; provision for the individual's values as competent performance occurs. The organization must attempt, within reason and limitations of cost, to fulfill these wants.

4. Giving honest and justifiable reasons for inability to provide certain job values. If needs cannot be met, employees will respect the inability if the problem is communicated.

No organization can satisfy all job values of employees. Not all employees want the same things. An organization cannot use all resources to make employees happy while trying to provide goods and services. Not all employee values are rational. Employees also change their values over time.

Source: Edwin A. Locke, David M. Schweiger, and Gary P. Latham, "Participation in Decision-Making: When Should It Be Used?", *Organizational Dynamics,* Volume 14, Number 3, Winter 1986, pp. 65–79. Reprinted, by permission of publisher, from *Organizational Dynamics,* Winter/1986 © 1986. American Management Association, New York. All rights reserved.

In addition to asking questions about input/outcome and reference persons, the worker may have questions about the cost/benefit ratio and the compatibility of the outcome received with the promised outcome (please refer to Figure 8–6). Satisfaction is likely only when outcome is equal to or greater than personal input. Also, if outcome is less than what was promised, dissatisfaction will probably be the result.

What actions can management expect from the employee perceiving inequity? Obviously, the results won't be good! For one thing, the employee may quit and look for a more equitable situation. Another possibility is *lowering* production. In effect, the employee is saying, "If they won't give me what I'm worth, I won't produce!" If all equity questions have positive answers, however, there is evidence that both satisfaction *and* commitment might be increased. There is good evidence to show that feelings of equity/inequity may be related to such items as turnover, absenteeism, increased or decreased quantity of performance, and quality of performance.[4]

Let's return to the Brent Templeton case. What insights can equity theory give us into Brent's actions? Obviously, part of the problem is with inputs.

Brent knows he's missing a vital input—the college degree—to permit his advancement. Our guess is that he's in an equity situation when he looks at other drafters—after all, he's at the top level and believes that the company's treatment is fair. A situation like this calls for the status quo which is exactly what we see from Brent: such things as not rocking the boat and "doing my job." But will this state of affairs produce *real* motivation? Obviously not, in Brent's case.

How Does the Supervisor Fit In?

Most employees will need help in utilizing the motivational process. In each situation, the employee's immediate supervisor will usually be the person to identify current needs, select incentives to be offered to attract interest in performance, and deal with the pre-action questions of value and probable success. The immediate supervisor is responsible for seeing that promised rewards are conveyed when they are earned. The manager may need to provide information to the employee so that the employee can make good judgments about equity. Satisfaction should be communicated in some way, and dissatisfaction should be transformed into the desire to do better in the future. In the Brent Templeton case, for example, it's possible that an insightful supervisor could spot Brent's feelings and help by exploring options with Brent. Maybe there's some way to help Brent get the education he needs, for example!

A Negative Motivational Model

The motivational model that we've discussed is primarily based on positive motives and constructive rewards. The implication of the model is that people want improvement over existing conditions (fulfillment of existing needs) and are willing to direct their efforts and actions toward organizationally useful behavior if they believe that doing so will help fulfill existing needs. There are times, however, when managers use motivational techniques that are negatively based as opposed to positively oriented. The use of negative motivation, therefore, deserves investigation.

negative motivational process
A view of the way to stimulate people to action where fear is used as the incentive. Employees are threatened with punitive action if they do not perform successfully. If performance is successful, the penalty is avoided. If performance is not successful, the penalty is applied.

The cognitive-needs negative motivational process is primarily the inducement of the desired behavior or performance from an employee through the use of fear. The fundamental assumption behind the **negative motivational process** is that people are protective by nature—they wish to preserve and protect what they already have and maintain the status quo in terms of their existing possessions and previous achievements. Thus, the worker's basic motives include the protection and preservation of his or her previous attainments so that already fulfilled needs are not jeopardized by future action (see Figure 8–7). It's worthwhile to speculate about Brent Templeton in our introductory case, for example. Isn't fear of getting in trouble or losing his job a factor that keeps Brent doing his work? The effect of this protectiveness is to maintain and hold securely rather than to enrich and fulfill.

Under negative motivation (Phase 2) the "motives" are threats to reduce or restrict existing levels of attainment and satisfaction. If a worker is presently earning a good wage and is achieving personal goal satisfaction, the negative approach threatens to reduce the worker's income level if the worker does

Figure 8–7   Model of Negative Motivation

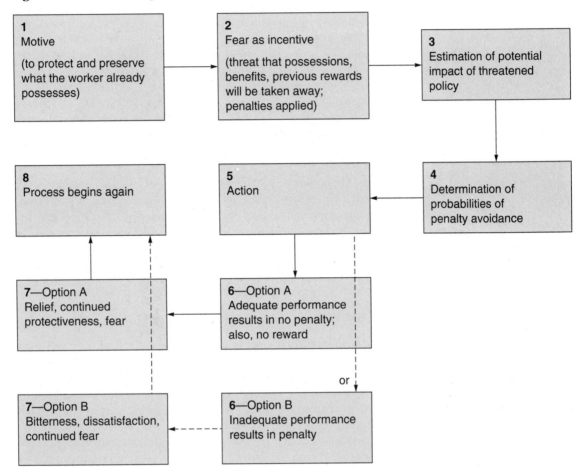

not achieve or maintain a certain performance level. If the worker presently enjoys respect and admiration, the negative motivational approach may threaten to destroy or reduce reputation if the worker does not adhere to a certain performance. Other motive-need categories may be threatened in a similar manner. In cases where an employee has alcohol or drug problems, fear may be the only motive that will get the employee's attention. The threatened penalties are analyzed in terms of the potential discomfort and pain they will cause (Phase 3). The more punishment and suffering that is anticipated, the more urgent the desire to avoid the threatened penalty. The penalty must be avoidable, however, if the individual is to be enticed into an attempt to escape its predicted effects. As a result, the worker must be convinced that he or she has the ability to perform successfully to avoid the penalty, and he or she must also have confidence in the support received from superiors, peers, and subordinates (Phase 4).

Under negative motivation, workers take action (Phase 5) with the specific purpose of performing adequately to avoid receiving the penalty that threatens the worker's goal of keeping secure what he or she already possesses. The action usually takes place with apprehension and resentment. If the individual's performance meets the standard imposed upon the individual, the penalty is avoided (Phase 6—Option A). If performance falls below the behavior expected, the penalty occurs (Phase 6—Option B) and the worker loses something valued (wages, prestige, security, the opportunity for achievement or advancement, etc.).

The effect of penalty avoidance (Phase 7—Option A) is temporary relief but a continued protectiveness and a fear that the threat of penalty will become a reality sometime in the future. The results of receiving a penalty (Phase 7—Option B) may include disappointment, bitterness, dissatisfaction, and continued fear. Psychologists have stated that if the negative motivational approach is to be successful in the long run, penalties and threats of penalties must be constantly present to reinforce the fear. For example, we've all seen cases where workers go right back to their "old ways" as soon as the boss turns his or her back. The worker also must feel a dependency on the organization so that he or she cannot readily escape from the threat by leaving (or sabotaging) the organization.

The Role of the Boss

The role of the manager--supervisor in the negative motivational process once again begins with the discovery of the worker's motives. From the negative viewpoint, these motives are achievements, values, or possessions the worker is seeking to protect and preserve. The supervisor suggests the possible penalty (applies the incentive) and outlines the specific performance that is expected if the penalty is to be avoided. The boss who wishes to impress the individual with the seriousness of the penalty may emphasize the potential effects of the penalty upon the factors the worker is attempting to maintain. The supervisor also helps the worker to realize that penalties can be avoided by acceptable performance. After the worker takes action, the supervisor is a primary participant in the evaluation of the worker's performance. Actions must be judged to determine whether they meet or fall below expectations. Penalties are meted out or withheld depending upon the assessment of the performance. For maximum effectiveness, necessary penalties are applied rather rigidly as threatened. It does no good to threaten and then not carry out the threats. The process then begins again.

The negative motivational approach has been the center of great controversy. Traditionalists have taken the position that the "stick" approach is essential with some individuals in specific situations. Behavioralists have often called the approach old-fashioned, brutal, and unnecessary. There is no question that positive motivation is infinitely more desirable, more pleasant, and usually more effective. It is possible, however, when the positive approach has been tried and has not worked, that conditions may call for the use of negative motivational techniques. From a realistic point of view, the negative approach should be utilized only temporarily with the goal of shifting to the positive approach as a central factor in future planning. Because it has such harmful potential, negative motivation is a last resort. It should be used only after all positive approaches have been explored.

Nordstrom Incorporated's Motivational Methods

Nordstrom Incorporated is a family-owned department store chain based in Seattle, Washington. The company has experienced extraordinary success and is now opening new stores in the East and Midwest. One of the reasons for Nordstrom's success is the way it handles and motivates its employees. For one thing, the Nordstrom family creates an intensely competitive atmosphere by setting ever higher sales goals and pitting employees against one another in contests. Store managers, for instance, must publicly declare their sales goals at regional meetings. A top executive then unveils what he calls the "secret committee's" sales target for each store. Unlucky managers who set goals below the committee's goal are booed. Those who exceed them are cheered. To egg on the crowd, John Nordstrom, one of the family owners, dons a letter sweater emblazoned with a big "N".

Executives hand out monthly cash prizes to stores that provide the best service. The choice is made on the basis of scrapbooks bulging with letters from customers, copies of thank-you notes that salespeople write to their customers, and notes, called heroics, that salespeople write about each other.

Salespeople who do especially well are honored monthly as All-Stars. A Nordstrom executive shakes their hand and gives them $100 and the right to large store discounts. The most productive salespeople are inducted annually into the Pace Setters club, which also entitles them to big discounts. The best managers get their names engraved on a plaque in the executive suite.

To promote service, employees are allowed to do almost anything to satisfy shoppers. Billie Burns, a former men's clothing department manager, once got a call from a regular customer who was racing to the airport and needed some clothes. Mr. Burns gathered up a bagful of blazers, slacks, and underwear, charged them to the customer's account, and met the man's car outside the store for a handoff. A saleswoman at the same store once soothed a frantic executive who had a run in her stocking by delivering some nylons to the woman's office in time for her to change for a big meeting.

Virtually every new employee at Nordstrom begins on the sales floor. Career-oriented college graduates are attracted to the company partly because Nordstrom pays, in combination with an hourly wage, commissions from 5 percent to 10 percent after employees meet certain sales quotas. The average salesperson earns around $25,000 a year, while a top performer earns $80,000. Nordstrom is highly decentralized, and it promotes only from within.

Employees are encouraged to write upbeat slogans, called affirmations. They are then asked to repeat the phrases to themselves. Slogans include such things as, "I enjoy being a store manager at Nordstrom" and "I feel proud about being a Pace Setter."

Source: Francine Schwadel, "Nordstrom's Push East Will Test Its Renown for the Best in Service," *The Wall Street Journal*, August 1, 1989, pp. A1, A9. Used by permission.

Goal Setting as a Motivational Concept

An additional approach to motivation—known as goal setting—is compatible with positive motivation in that it begins by defining what each employee is expected to do. This expectation is then communicated to each individual employee. If contributing factors are managed properly, the process of conveying performance expectations is enough to cause an employee to work hard to achieve the standard expected.

According to the goal-setting concept of motivation, the following holds true:

1. A goal (standard) is whatever an individual is consciously trying to do.
2. Goals that have greater difficulty will stimulate the individual to higher levels of performance than will more easily attained goals.
3. Goals that are specifically stated and difficult to achieve will result in higher performance than if no goals are assigned or a generalized challenge to "do your best" is issued.
4. Goals assigned to a person by a supervisor will affect the individual's behavior only to the degree the goals (standards) are consciously accepted by the performer.[5]

If goal setting is a valid concept, the importance of establishing individual goals for workers is vital to optimum performance in organizations. While Locke, who first researched the concept, had evidence to support his theory, a large amount of research has been done to test various aspects of the theory since it was first presented. Answers have been sought to the following questions:

1. Does the establishing and communicating of individual performance goals really act to increase the level of individual output?
2. Do goals that are difficult to attain spur performance that is superior to more easily attainable goals, or to generalized "do your best" statements?
3. For a goal to influence an employee's behavior, is it essential that the employee accept the responsibility for working to accomplish the goal?
4. Does allowing an employee to participate in setting goals enhance the influence of the goal or the employee's behavior?

The giving of specific performance goals to individuals seemingly does have positive results in a majority of cases. In a 1981 position paper, Locke stated that "goal setting is the only current approach to work motivation that claims a beneficial effect on performance in 90 percent of the reported cases."[6] Latham and Yukl state that ten out of eleven studies they analyzed gave support to the effectiveness of goal setting.[7] The general conclusion seems to be that in more cases than not, the setting of goals and communicating them to the performer really do result in higher levels of performance.

Goals that are specifically stated and have a reasonable level of difficulty are, indeed, more likely to result in higher levels of performance than generalized goals such as "do your best." Latham and Yukl observe that in six out of seven studies concerning goal difficulty and performance, hard goals definitely led to higher performance than easier goals and generalized ones.[8] This finding is particularly important when one considers what goes on in many organizations. Often, managers do almost the opposite of what's needed. Instead of clearly stating exactly what's expected, managers often give very general guidelines, or maybe none at all. Think about organizations you're familiar with—how often does the employee really receive a full description of what's wanted? Notice how, when the worker is told what's expected, the worker's confidence and self direction are enhanced. Many managers are missing a vital tool here!

An important overall point coming out of the Latham and Yukl research, however, is that the goals need to be accepted if they are to affect performance. The relationship between acceptance and performance is not always clear. Sometimes the acceptance is expressed; sometimes it is only implied. An employee is more likely to accept performance goals (standards) under the following conditions:

1. The employee feels the goal is reasonable.
2. The employee has a degree of self-confidence.
3. The employee has been successful in accomplishing previous performance goals.
4. An adequate, desirable reward is provided for accomplishing goals.
5. An objective performance appraisal will follow the performance effort.[9]

As you review the above conditions for gaining acceptance of goals, notice that they provide guidelines for supervisory behavior. It is important that goals be reasonable, the employee feels capable, the incentive structure is in place, and constructive performance appraisals occur.

The question of whether or not the employee must participate in the setting of goals for his or her performance to be affected is less certain. Chang and Lorenzi found that "participative and assigned goal setting have no significantly different effects on performance if goal difficulty is held constant."[10] Further, they say that "participation in goal setting has been shown to affect performance only if it leads the subject to a higher goal than that which is assigned by the supervisor or experimenter unilaterally."[11] Again, goal difficulty is the more important factor. Once a high goal is established, the high goal leads to high performance regardless of who established it.

Steers[12] found that people low in need for achievement must participate in goal setting for goal setting to influence their performance. In addition, Schuler and Kim noted that participation in goal setting can increase workers' satisfaction levels with performance.[13] Participation could also enhance the feeling of autonomy. Umstot et al. found that goal setting with an existing job may need participation, but participation on new jobs was less necessary for goal setting to be effective.[14]

Obviously, the findings on participation aren't clear-cut. Generally, we conclude that participation in goal setting may be needed in certain conditions (for example, when employees are low in need for achievement), but in many cases, goals may be set for the employee and be just as successful. As a general statement, it is clear that performance goals are important standards, but goals are equally important in stimulating performance. Effective goals are those that are reasonable, clearly stated and communicated, and defined with some degree of difficulty. Employee participation may sometimes enhance performance and will frequently result in a high level of satisfaction.

The Motivational Potential of Jobs

In using both positive and negative models of motivation, it is important to note that some jobs have high levels of motivational potential, while other positions may have limited motivation potential. Some jobs are simply more motivating than others. Jobs with high potential are those with many components that make possible high levels of need fulfillment. Low-potential jobs have little to attract an employee's attention and will result in little stimulation. In the Brent Templeton chapter opening case, what do Brent's comments about the work he's doing have to do with his motivation? How would you rate his job in terms of potential for motivation?

Perhaps one of the most useful techniques for diagnosing the motivational potential level of a job is the Hackman-Oldham model of analysis. The model assumes that three critical psychological states influence the motivational potential of a job—the meaningfulness of the work, the responsibility for the outcomes of work, and the knowledge of actual results of work activities (often called feedback). Jobs that provide much of all three states are called high-potential jobs, while jobs with little in any area are said to have low potential.[15]

Three factors are involved in diagnosing the meaningfulness of a job:

1. *Skill variety.* The degree to which a job requires a variety of activities involving a number of different skills and talents. High-level jobs, such as managerial ones, tend to have lots of variety, as do some nonmanagement jobs, such as hotel desk clerk in a small hotel, for example.

2. *Task identity.* The degree to which a job requires a complete, "whole and identifiable piece of work," that is, doing a job from beginning to end with a visible outcome. Wide differences exist here. The autoworker in a traditional Detroit auto plant who does one limited activity (e.g., attaching a window frame) over and over is low in this factor, for example, while a craftsperson making pottery probably does the whole job from start to finish.

3. *Task significance.* The degree to which the job has a substantial impact on the lives of other people, whether these people are in the immediate organization or in the world at large. Doctors and other professionals, such as counselors, immediately come to mind. An office manager or similar employee who is literally keeping an important part of an organization running may feel equally vital to the organization.

The second psychological state influencing a job's motivational potential—responsibility for work outcome—is measured by the amount of autonomy that is present. Autonomy can be defined as "the degree to which the job provides substantial freedom, independence, and discretion to the individual in scheduling the work and in determining the procedures to be used in carrying it out."[16] The key is whether you work on your own or whether you feel you're continually monitored and must check every step.

The final area—knowledge of work results—is calculated by considering feedback received from doing a job. Job feedback is "the degree to which carrying out the work activities required by the job provides the individual with direct and clear information about the effectiveness of his or her performance."[17] A person can learn how well he or she is doing from the job itself (e.g., counts of how much the person's produced) or from others, such as a supervisor.

The job rating form developed by Hackman and Oldham provides the mechanism for analyzing a job on the basis of its skill variety, task identity,

What would be the motivating potential score for a job like this?

motivating potential score
A number arrived at by using the Hackman-Oldham test of job design that reveals the degree of skill variety, task identity, task significance, autonomy, and feedback of a specific job. The larger the number of these characteristics of a job, the greater the motivating potential score.

task significance, autonomy, and job feedback. By answering three questions on each factor and calculating the average scores of the items, a numerical score is established for each factor. On a scale of 1 to 7, a job with an average of 1 would have very little potential for fulfilling that factor, while a score of 7 would indicate high motivating potential in that area (see Figure 8–8). The **motivating potential score** for a specific job can be calculated by using the following formula:

$$\text{Motivating Potential Score (MPS)} = \left(\frac{\text{Skill Variety} + \text{Task Identity} + \text{Task Significance}}{3} \right) \times \text{Autonomy} \times \text{Job Feedback}$$

The range of scores possible when using the Hackman-Oldham formula is from 1 (very low potential) to 343 (very high potential). In addition to acquiring a total score for motivational potential, it is possible to diagnose the caus-

Figure 8–8

Sample Questions
from the Hackman-
Oldham Job Rating
Form

Determining the task identity level of Job C:

1–3 To what extent does the job involve doing a whole and identifiable piece of
     work? That is, is the job a complete piece of work that has obvious beginning
     and end? Or is it only a small part of the overall piece of work which is finished
     by other people or by automatic machines.

1	2	3	4	5	6	7

The job is only   The job is a   The job involves
a tiny part of   moderate sized   doing the whole
the overall piece   "chunk" of the   piece of work
work.   overall piece   from start to
                                    of work.   finish.

How accurate are the following statements in describing the job you are rating:

1	2	3	4	5	6	7

| very | mostly | slightly | un- | slightly | mostly | very |
| inaccurate | inaccurate | inaccurate | certain | accurate | accurate | accurate |

2-11 The job provides a person with the chance to finish completely any work he or
      she starts.

2-3 The job is arranged so that a person does *not* have the chance to do any entire
     piece of work from beginning to end.

Suppose that you answered Question 1-3 with a 4, Question 2-11 with a 3, and
Question 2-3 with a 5. To calculate the task identity of Job C, average the items:

$$1\text{-}3 \quad 4$$

$$2\text{-}11 \quad 3$$

$$2\text{-}3 \quad \underline{3} \text{ (reverse scoring by subtracting 5 from 8)}$$

$$10 \text{ divided by 3 to get the average score of } 3.33.$$

This is the task identity potential of Job C. This factor would be added to the formula

$$\left(\frac{\text{Skill Variety} + \text{Task Identity} + \text{Task Significance}}{3} \right) \times \text{Autonomy Job Feedback}$$

to get the total Motivating Potential Score

Source: J. Richard Hackman and Greg R. Oldham, *Work Redesign*, ©1980 by Addison-Wesley Publishing Company. Reprinted with permission of the publisher.

es of a job's motivational strengths or weaknesses by plotting the individual
components on a diagnostic graph (see Figure 8–9). Job A in the figure, while
showing a total score of over 300, indicates that all factors of the job are highly motivational. Job B, with a total score of about 30, shows high motivation
from a task significance perspective but average to low amounts of autonomy
and job feedback. Attempts to make Job B more motivational should be
focused on the areas of weakness. By redesigning (when possible) those jobs
with low motivational potential by including more autonomy, for example,
the motivational potential can be increased.

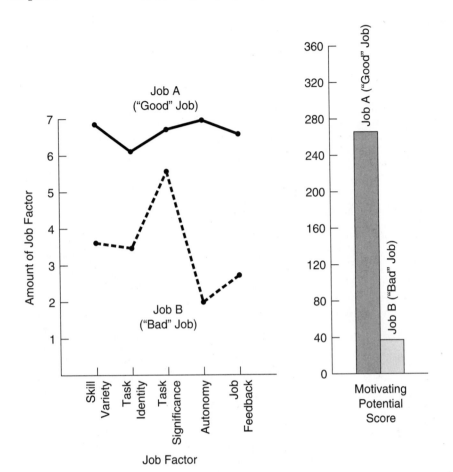

Figure 8–9
Job Diagnostic Profile for a "Good" Job and a "Bad" Job

You may want to look back at the opening case and speculate on how Templeton would answer questions like those on the Hackman-Oldham job rating form.

Summary

Motivation has been defined as the process of arousing action in individuals and sustaining the activity until a project has been completed. Many different methods exist for motivating people.

One of the most frequently used methods is known as expectancy motivation. With the expectancy concept, the opportunity to satisfy unfilled needs is offered to the individual employee. The employee must make a number of decisions before electing to accept or reject the opportunity to try for need fulfillment. If the individual decides to try, he or she accepts the opportunity and works to perform a task to earn rewards. The actions determine whether rewards will or will not be given. Other decisions need to be made before satisfaction or dissatisfaction occurs.

Insights

Job Design: Approaches, Outcomes, and Tradeoffs

According to research by Campion and Thayer, there are at least four ways jobs can be designed. Mechanistically designed jobs, for example, are patterned so that they are simplistic and specialized. Motivationally designed jobs, on the other hand, are designed for enrichment and enlargement in keeping with organizational psychology. Participation, involvement, and recognition are important so that employees will be stimulated to perform.

A third way jobs can be designed is biologically—structured to minimize the physical costs and biological risks of work. The goal here is to see that an employee's physical capabilities and limitations are not exceeded by the demands of the job. Physical fatigue, safety, and threats to health are important considerations.

The fourth way to organize jobs is the perceptual/motor job design. The emphasis on perceptual/motor design is to ensure that an employee's mental capabilities and limitations are not exceeded. The goals of this approach are to decrease the chances of mental overload and stress, reduce training time, and improve the percentage of workers who can perform jobs with little or no training.

A summary of job design approaches and their positive and negative outcomes follows:

Job-Design Approach	Positive Outcomes	Negative Outcomes
Mechanistic	Decreased training time Higher utilization levels Lower likelihood of error Less chance of mental overload and stress	Lower job satisfaction Lower motivation Higher absenteeism
Motivational	Higher job satisfaction Higher motivation Greater job involvement Higher job performance Lower absenteeism	Increased training time Lower utilization levels Greater likelihood of error Greater chance of mental overload and stress
Biological	Less physical effort Less physical fatigue Fewer health complaints Fewer medical incidents Lower absenteeism Higher job satisfaction	Higher financial costs because of changes in equipment or job environment
Perceptual/Motor	Lower likelihood of error Lower likelihood of accidents Less chance of mental overload and stress Lower training time Higher utilization levels	Lower job satisfaction Lower motivation

Source: Michael A. Campion and Paul W. Thayer, "Job Design: Approaches, Outcomes And Trade-Offs," *Organizational Dynamics*, Volume 15, Number 3, Winter 1987, pp. 66–79. Reprinted, by permission of publisher, from *Organizational Dynamics*, Winter/1987 © 1987. American Management Association, New York. All rights reserved.

Negative motivation is the opposite of expectancy theory in many ways. The individual worker is threatened with the loss of something important unless he or she works hard enough to avoid the penalty. Effective work performance may be successful in avoiding punishment and protecting possessions. Negative motivation leaves a certain amount of fear and bitterness no matter what happens.

The equity concept of motivation is compatible with expectancy theory in that people who consider themselves to have been rewarded fairly will respond favorably to rewards, while those who feel treated inequitably usually will behave in undesirable ways.

The simple task of setting and communicating challenging goals to workers usually results in raised levels of motivation. Another view of motivation calls for the designing or redesigning of one's job to make it more meaningful. Five job components have been identified in a model developed by Hackman and Oldham which, when provided for, will raise the motivational potential of a job.

Bosses play important roles in clarifying opportunities, setting challenging goals, selecting appropriate incentives, supporting workers through times of uncertainty, providing promised rewards, and being equitable in the entire motivational process. Some jobs, as a result of their strong motivational potential, will be highly attractive. Other jobs may have low motivational potential unless redesigned.

Questions to Consider

1. When a manager attempts to motivate a worker so that the worker will be more productive, is the manager manipulating the worker to do something the worker doesn't want to do?
2. Is it true that a satisfied worker often is not a productive worker? Why or why not?
3. This chapter stated that motives are within individuals. Can managers have an effect upon the development of these motives?
4. How can a manager who wishes to apply the positive motivational model discover the need motives of his or her workers?
5. Discuss in detail the role of a manager in helping a worker determine the value of an incentive. Discuss a manager's role in helping an employee determine the possibility of successful performance in order to earn a reward.
6. If a worker fails to perform successfully and therefore does not earn a reward, what can the manager do to help the worker decide to try again rather than to withdraw?
7. What problems and complications do you see with the use of the negative motivational model?
8. When negative motivation is utilized, a certain amount of fear and bitterness often remains after penalties have been applied or avoided. What can be done, if anything, about the bad effects that may be present?

9. Is negative motivation an ethical managerial practice? Why or why not?
10. What problems do you see with the use of the Hackman-Oldham Motivating Potential Score and its application to typical jobs? Why might it sometimes be difficult to use?

Key Terms

cognitive motivation	motivating potential	positive motivational
equity theory	score	model
expectancy theory	motive	negative motivational
incentive		processs

Chapter Case

The Case of the "Hungry" Actress

After finishing school, you set out to look for a job and are determined to get something really different, something with a challenge. Of course, that's what everybody wants, but in your case, it turns out that that's exactly what you got! The only problem is that now you're wondering if a really challenging and different job is all that great. What occurred is this. You had just happened to see an ad in the paper for positions in a newly forming company, and you called to see what it was about. The organization (if you can actually call anything that disorganized an organization) is Talent Unlimited, and its founders describe it to you as "the world's first talent management organization run entirely by the talent themselves."

Talent, in this case, refers to theater-related talent—actors, actresses, directors, bit players, and the like. You learn that with the recent emphasis on the culture of your area, there is a steady stream of films being made where you live, and gradually a nucleus of performers, even beyond the local talent, has settled here. It's that group that has started Talent Unlimited. You ask what job is open, since they've already told you that they run everything themselves. "Well, it's not exactly management," says Lola LaRue (you suspect that that's her stage name; in any case, she is more or less taking on the role of spokesperson for the group). "You see, we want an administrator," she continues. "We want to make all the major decisions, but nobody wants to be concerned with the day-to-day running of things. In fact, I'm afraid things are in a bit of a mess."

You are hired on the spot. In fact, the group is amazed when they learn you have a business degree.

"You mean you can do numbers and all that?" asks Lola, eyes open wide. You quickly learn what "a bit of a mess" really means. Not only are the books in chaos, the schedule a disaster, and plans nonexistent, but there's considerable dissension in the organization. There appear to be two main factions. At the very top, acting as a sort of "kitchen cabinet" making decisions, are five or six performers who have really made it. They're living the lifestyle of the rich and famous and are interested in using the organization as an easy way to advance their careers without running into heavy agent's fees. Lola is typical of this group, and one day you run into her having a discussion with Marla Mallory, who's decidedly in the other camp.

The other camp consists of the vast majority of members—hopefuls who haven't yet had a break. Like most, Marla lives a hand-to-mouth existence, supplementing her meager theatrical earnings by hourly work as a cashier in a local supermarket. Most of this group—with Marla among them—are pretty discouraged and see Talent Unlimited as a last hope—that maybe by banding together they can get some work. Marla is telling Lola that she wants Talent Unlimited to try to get some bit parts for her in a Broadway road show that is coming to town soon.

"Now, really, you must stop being so childish," exclaims Lola. "All you people do is think of yourselves. Look at me. I've devoted my LIFE to this profession, and I'm literally STARVING to death? Why, I've just learned that upstart Kitty Kelly is getting $750,000 for a five-minute cameo slot, while I only get $425,000 for a similar one. Those are the REAL problems Talent Unlimited is going to have to deal with?"

1. Which steps of the positively based cognitive-needs concept are shown in this case so far as Lola is concerned? What does this case reveal about expectancy theory?
2. How would the director of a play or movie motivate Lola? What incentives could be used?
3. What does this case illustrate that is in keeping with equity theory? Lola says she is "starving to death." Has she lost her mind? Explain according to equity theory.
4. Marla is currently working as a cashier in a grocery store. Suppose her boss decides she needs to become more motivated and wants to redesign her job. Briefly discuss Hackman and Oldham's theory and apply it to Marla's situation.

Chapter
9

The Reinforcement View of Motivation

Objectives

- To compare reinforcement theory to cognitive-needs theory to discern their compatibility.
- To study the Law of Effect in order to use it when working with others.
- To discover the circumstances required for conditioning or reinforcement to work.
- To become acquainted with the four reinforcement techniques so that the appropriate technique can be chosen for the appropriate situation.
- To learn other rules for effective conditioning.
- To consider the four different schedules for reinforcing behavior.
- To develop a positive philosophy for disciplinary action.
- To develop skill in providing fair disciplining.
- To learn how to provide constructive criticism when the behavior of others requires it.

Marinell Clayton—The Full-time Nurse Who Seldom Is

Patrick Osborne is the owner-manager of Rest Manor Nursing Home, a facility for elderly or infirm patients who require constant care, including medical treatment. The home is located in a community of about 5,000 residents and is somewhat isolated from major cities and population centers. The town has, in addition to Rest Manor, a full-service hospital, a small medical clinic, and several doctor's offices that require staffing by nurses. As a result, trained nurses are in heavy demand in the small community. It is especially difficult to hire and keep good registered nurses.

Rest Manor is small by most nursing home standards; it contains twenty-eight beds, which remain filled constantly. Osborne indicates that he has a waiting list of applicants wishing to enter the facility whenever a vacancy occurs. One of the state laws regulating nursing homes requires the presence of a qualified registered nurse at all times. Practical nurses, orderlies, and other assistants may be used for treatment, service, and other care purposes, but an R.N. must be present constantly and in charge of nursing care.

Osborne has been able to hire three registered nurses, each of whom works an eight-hour shift five days a week. On weekends, two nurses from a local doctor's office and a semiretired nurse fill in while the regular nurses have their time off. This arrangement has been the best one Osborne has been able to organize because of the shortage of registered nurses. He has unsuccessfully tried to attract nurses from other communities to come in to work. Seemingly, there are no other qualified nurses locally who are willing to work at the nursing home.

This arrangement might be reasonably satisfactory except for the fact that one of the regular registered nurses, Marinell Clayton, is creating a problem. Clayton works the 3 p.m. to 11 p.m. shift Monday through Friday. She is in her late forties, is married, and has three grown children. Her husband is self-employed as a clock and watch repairman.

Clayton is an excellent nurse when she is present and working. She is extremely considerate of the patients; they all respond to her favorably and with admiration. The workers Clayton supervises indicate that she treats them fairly and helps them whenever they need it. The problem is that Clayton has a habit of taking off from work a day or two almost every other week to accompany her husband on a trip he is taking.

Because Clayton's husband is self-employed, he sets his own workdays and hours. He is an avid sportsman and takes off a few days regularly to hunt, fish, or travel some distance to see a special sporting event. Clayton could seldom go with him while their children were at home, but now that the children are grown, her husband wants her to go with him whenever possible. Because Clayton shares her husband's interests, she usually goes with him. This practice requires her frequently to stay away from work on a Friday (or sometimes a Monday) so that she can be away for a long weekend.

Clayton doesn't ask for a day off before she leaves. She just tells Osborne she won't be in the next day because her husband wants her to go with him. She never asks to be paid for the days she is away—money is not important to her. She and her husband have an adequate income and enjoy themselves. In addition, she feels that her job is secure because Osborne can't find anyone to replace her and because he wouldn't fire her under any circumstances. She also believes that the other nurses can fill in adequately for her when she's out of town. She has frankly stated that if she can't go places with her husband when he asks her, she'll give up her job to make it possible.

Clayton's absences upset the work schedules and attention given to the patients. One of the other registered nurses has to fill in extra hours in Clayton's place, or the shift goes along without a registered nurse. The operating license of the nursing home is in jeopardy because of her actions.

Case Questions

1. What alternatives does Osborne have?
2. In what ways can the positive and negative motivational models from Chapter 8 be applied to this case?
3. From a behavioral reinforcement approach, what parts of Clayton's behavior need to be discontinued? How are employees encouraged to keep doing what they are doing? How can they be encouraged to stop undesirable behavior?
4. In the past, Osborne has been very flexible concerning absenteeism and tardiness among workers. He gives each worker a two-week annual paid vacation and one week of paid sick leave. What rules and regulations are needed to cover absenteeism and tardiness at Rest Manor?
5. If an organization has rules and regulations concerning absenteeism or other types of worker behavior, can the rules and regulations be ignored in special cases?
6. Role play the conversation that might occur between Osborne and Clayton about this problem.

reinforcement
Providing either a reward or a penalty following an employee's behavior to encourage the continuation of desirable behavior or the elimination of an undesirable behavior.

In Chapter 8, people were assumed to know what they wanted, and they rationally made choices to respond to certain stimuli (incentives) to fulfill their needs. In this chapter, let's assume that employees either are not really aware of their motives or don't need to be aware of them. Instead, the rewards and reinforcements they receive *after* doing something serve to motivate them. The **reinforcement** approach to motivation, while not altogether in opposition to the cognitive approach, begins with a different concern.

The first responsibility of management from the reinforcement perspective is to discover the behavior needed by the organization to accomplish organizational goals. When organizational goals and the related essential behavior are known, everything necessary to achieve goals can be put in place and employees perform to achieve the goals. When employees perform in ways consistent with the organization's needs, their behavior is given positive reinforcement. When individuals behave in ways counter to organizational needs, their behavior is discouraged through the use of other types of reinforcement.

Conditioning or reinforcement has its foundation in the Law of Effect, which E. L. Thorndike proposed back in 1911. The law says that behaviors that appear to lead to positive consequences tend to be repeated, while behaviors that appear to lead to negative consequences will not be repeated.[1] The pleasure-pain principle is the idea here. Contrary to what the cognitive approach suggested about working toward future fulfillments, the orientation of the reinforcement view is toward the past. Future efforts are a response to results from the past. Those things given attention will be repeated. This is why some people refer to reinforcement as a learning process rather than a motivational technique.

The sequence of events for reinforcement runs in this manner: stimulus → response → consequence or reinforcement. A continuing cycle then begins. The consequences lead to future behavior, which in turn leads to new consequences, and so the pattern goes. Reinforcers or consequences are usually described in two categories: **primary,** which includes food, water, and other items for basic survival; and **secondary,** things we learn to want because they offer fulfillment of the primary needs—such things as promotions, praise, recognition, and money, among other things.

Managing Reinforcement

The manager who wishes to influence the behavior of employees and provide motivation for them must be able to influence and control the consequences of behavior. In other words, when an employee does "the right thing," the manager needs to be able to provide desirable consequences to follow the effort.

There are four methods of reinforcement. Two are used to continue or increase desirable behavior: positive and negative reinforcement. Positive reinforcement uses rewards to follow good performance so that good behavior continues. Negative reinforcement, sometimes called avoidance, begins with the threat of something bad happening (such as the loss of something important to the performer). The employee who performs in an acceptable manner avoids unpleasant consequences. Both of these patterns encourage good behavior to continue. Past behavior has provided desirable consequences.

We see the operation of positive and negative reinforcement around us all the time. Let's first look at an example of positive reinforcement, suppose a friend tells you that she hasn't kept up with her class reading assignments as well as she should and she's intending to stay up all night and do a crash review just before the exam. You act uncertain that the plan will work, and your friend responds, "Well, it's worked for me in the past!" In effect, what your friend is saying is that because she believes that this set of behaviors (staying up all night studying) has met with positive consequences in the past,

primary reinforcer
Basic items such as food, clothing, and shelter that are used to provide the continuation of a desirable behavior or the elimination of an undesirable behavior.

secondary reinforcer
Reward or penalty following a behavior where the reward takes the form of a promotion, praise, or recognition.

she's doing it again! By staying up all night, she hopes to avoid a negative consequence—such as making a bad grade. If she does well, she will receive something good and avoid something bad. In the same way, employees tend to keep doing behaviors that are rewarded by the manager, other employees, or customers. Think of the kinds of rewards that are available—praise, pay raises (or maybe tips from customers), and even a friendly smile of approval.

As an illustration of negative reinforcement, consider a football coach in the National Football League. Typically, if a coach has more than one losing season in a row, he is fired from his job. (Actually, a coach sometimes is released from his job following one losing season.) Let's assume for the moment that you are a coach in the NFL who has just experienced a losing season. Before and during the next year, you will do everything within your power to ensure that your team has a winning season. Let's suppose that you accomplish your goal and have a winning season. As a result, you avoid being fired. This is exactly what happens with negative reinforcement. Performance occurs at a satisfactory level, and a bad consequence is avoided. This is why negative reinforcement is frequently called avoidance behavior.

Positive reinforcement is a pleasant experience, while negative reinforcement causes fear and often results in a feeling of bitterness. Since negative reinforcement can be pretty problematical in its application, it's no wonder that both William Whyte and B.F. Skinner[2] argue that positive reinforcers are the most effective ways to influence the behavior of others.

The other two methods of reinforcement are used to stop undesirable behavior: extinction and punishment. With **extinction,** reinforcements are withheld following an undesirable behavior. As a result, the behavior that does not receive reinforcement (is ignored, or is not rewarded), may cease. If, for example, an individual demands a large amount of his or her boss's time but the boss goes ahead without paying attention to the demands (and therefore does not reinforce the demands), the demands for excessive attention very likely will stop. Extinction not only causes bad behavior to cease but also sometimes causes good behavior to die as a result of lack of attention. The manager who says, "I know that Giulia's performance is improving, but I think I'll wait to see that the improvement is permanent before I commend her," unwittingly is risking using extinction. If several weeks pass and the boss ignores the improvement, the improved performance may stop.

The other technique for stopping undesirable behavior—**punishment**—works by following poor performance with unpleasant consequences. Criticism, being shunned by others, loss of pay, demotion, and removal from membership in a prestigious group are examples of punishment. To break the unpleasant cycle, an individual ceases the behavior that results in the negative consequence. Punishment has drawbacks, however. It is usually effective in stopping behavior, but it may be accompanied by undesirable side effects, such as anger or resentment by an employee. You may recall situations where you received a punishment, such as strong criticism. You may have stopped doing whatever it was that caused the criticism, but you may have become angry and resentful as well. In fact, you may have been tempted to do something to "get even" with the person who criticized. Obviously, this same kind of problem can occur when managers use strong criticism to stop certain employee behaviors.

extinction
A form of conditioning where behavior goes unrewarded as a method of getting that behavior discontinued.

punishment
A form of reinforcement where penalties are applied to get a behavior decreased or stopped.

Putting It All Together

We see the effects of positive and negative reinforcement, extinction, and punishment around us every day. Sometimes the techniques are under careful control by management. More often, they're not. To see some of the difficulties, let's analyze the Clayton case at the beginning of the chapter. From Osborne's standpoint there's definitely an undesirable behavior going on. Clayton is missing a lot of work. But let's look at the situation from Clayton's perspective. Why does she miss so much work? Because she's being *rewarded* for staying away. She gets a hefty does of positive reinforcement in the form of weekends with her husband fishing, hunting, and traveling—all activities she enjoys. Because her staying-away behavior is rewarded, we should expect it to continue. There's a moral here, and it's one we've hinted at before. Reinforcement works as expected only when the manager is in control of the rewards and punishment—and poor Patrick Osborne *isn't!* He isn't in control of a key source of reward, from Clayton's standpoint—those out-of-town trips. It's true that he some power to punish, but how effective will the punishment be? Since Clayton says she would quit rather than lose her weekends off, we can guess that threats of being fired won't be very effective. Osborne could scold and criticize Clayton, but we've already seen that criticism can backfire—Clayton might react as one would in a negative reinforcement situation and avoid coming to work even more. Osborne is in a bind that he's unlikely to escape from. The moral is this: As a manager, you must find ways to gain control of the important sources of reinforcement influencing employees.

Guidelines for the Use of Reinforcers

If you plan to use reinforcement, you must be able to control the consequences of your employees' behavior; that is, you must be able to provide positive and negative reinforcers to a worker's actions. How do you do that? Bandura indicates three steps managers must take to effectively control the consequences of an employee's behavior:

1. To maintain the worker responsiveness while the desired behavior is established and strengthened, managers should select reinforcers that are sufficient, powerful, and desirable. Money is often used as the reinforcer but other things can be used as well. It is important to note here that the strength of the reward or reinforcement should be in keeping with the strength of the performance that has earned the reward (or penalty). This is where Osborne runs into trouble in the Marinell Clayton case. What this principle suggests is that Osborne needs to find a reward for being-on-the job behavior that is stronger than the reward (the pleasure of the weekend vacation) that Clayton now gets from missing work. Clearly, that can be difficult to do in cases like Clayton's.
2. Make the reinforcer contingent. The idea of contingencies means that reinforcement is made to depend upon the desired behavior. It should be clear what an individual must do and what the consequences will

The Importance of the Merit Raise

Over the past twenty-five years or more, the automatic adjustment of the employee's salary every twelve months has become a standard procedure. Cost-of-living adjustments and union contracts have come to make the anniversary increase a routine occurrence for many employees. Even where so-called merit programs are used, the spread between salary increases for best performers and just-average ones is too narrow to be meaningful. Recent surveys of 459 companies show top performers averaging 7.7 percent annual increases, while satisfactory performers average 4.7 percent. The difference in earnings between the two groups of workers turns out to be just a few dollars a week.

Up to this time, there has been little or no evidence to show that merit-increase programs have improved individual performance or a company's financial performance.

Ira Kay, managing director of a compensation consulting firm, suggests some new approaches to replace or reduce fixed salary programs with performance-based rewards. According to Kay, *the rewards must be constructed to pay out significantly more than the typical merit increase if performance is high and less than the typical merit increase if performance lags*. The measure by which the reward is determined may be performance by the company as a whole; results for a small group or unit; an individual set of objectives; or a combination of these.

To illustrate the reward technique, in a department at the DuPont Company, a client of Kay's, the merit increases for the next three to five years will be lower than usual. In exchange for accepting salaries and wages lower than might be expected, employees have been given the opportunity to earn bonuses as high as 18 percent of their salaries—12 percentage points more than they would have received under traditional merit-increase plans. The bonus is determined according to outstanding performance based upon quantifiable results.

For the bonus type of program to be successful, employees must have confidence in management. Employees must know how the plan works and why it was instituted.

Source: Adapted from Ira Kay, "Do Your Workers Really Merit a Raise?" *The Wall Street Journal,* March 26, 1990. p. A10.

be following the performance. Then follow-through is important. Among other things, this means that the reward isn't given *unless* the employee performs the behavior. A managerial mistake from this perspective is giving rewards to everyone rather than only to those who perform.

3. Make sure that there is a reliable procedure for bringing about the desired response. If the desired behavior never occurs, there will be no opportunities to reinforce good performance. Training, modeling or other methods may be necessary to set the stage for proper actions. When correct performance is elicited, reinforcement can appropriately follow. If good performance is already being given, reinforcement of that performance can be applied without preliminary preparation.[3]

Other rules for conditioning behavior include the following:

1. Don't reward all people the same. In other words, don't give rewards indiscriminately without considering the performance level of each individual. Instead, make reinforcements variable and related to the degree of performance. Individuals performing at higher levels will have their performance extinguished by treating everyone alike, while lower performers will have their sub-par performance strengthened.

2. Remember that failure to respond and recognize performance has reinforcing consequences. Behavior that is not responded to will be modified regardless of its positive or negative nature. This is particularly true where managers fail to recognize good performance. The manager who says, "There's no reason for me to recognize good performance in my employees—that's what they are being paid for!" is making a big mistake. It's likely that extinction is occurring.

3. Be sure to tell each employee what to do to get reinforcement. A part of this communication is the giving of standards on which performance will be judged. All employees can benefit from clear guidelines.

4. If behavior is outside the desired boundaries, the performer should be informed of the inadequacies so that reinforcements (which should be punishing, in this case) can be interpreted properly as they are received. Even extinction can be misinterpreted if there is no information exchange.

5. If punishment is required for inadequate performance, it should be done privately. The punishing reinforcement should be enough of an affecter without the public condemnation and damage to the self-image that would occur if done in front of others. Praise for good performance can be given publicly in most situations.

6. Workers should not be cheated out of earned rewards. Workers should feel equitably treated. Workers who feel under-rewarded become angry or upset with the inequity of a situation. Workers who feel over-rewarded may lock themselves into poor performance levels if reinforcement is more positive than is deserved.[4]

Reinforcement Schedules

A major issue with the reinforcement method of motivation or conditioning is the frequency with which the reinforcement is given. One way to apply reinforcement, of course, can be continuous reinforcement. If this technique is used, it requires that every appropriate action be rewarded each time the action takes place. In other words, reinforcement is on a 1-to-1 ratio of performance-to-reward. One thing in favor of this approach is the fact that learning or beginning to practice a new, desirable behavior increases rapidly when reinforced this way. In fact, most experienced managers find that it is quite appropriate when employees are learning new skills and need heavy doses of encouragement. Long-range reinforcement can have its problems. Sustained effort is difficult to maintain. Under long-range continuous reinforcement, if continuous reinforcement is slowed or stopped, good behavior quickly

Insights

The Platinum Rule

While the Golden Rule says "Do unto others what you would have others do unto you," the Platinum Rule states, "Motivation is the result of recognizing and rewarding performance improvements in a meaningful and timely way." The Platinum Rule is a behavioral approach based upon the premise that employees are more productive when the manager provides frequent, meaningful, and positive consequences for their performance. The approach places little emphasis on internal states of motivation, emphasizing instead the role the environment plays in motivation and performance.

The process involved in the Platinum Rule is as follows:

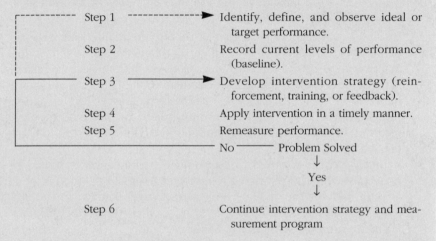

Step 1	Identify, define, and observe ideal or target performance.
Step 2	Record current levels of performance (baseline).
Step 3	Develop intervention strategy (reinforcement, training, or feedback).
Step 4	Apply intervention in a timely manner.
Step 5	Remeasure performance.
	No —— Problem Solved
	↓
	Yes
	↓
Step 6	Continue intervention strategy and measurement program

The Platinum Rule can be taught to virtually all levels of management, irrespective to the amount of education a manager has. It does not require an indepth understanding of complicated internal states or psychological considerations many other theories rely on.

---

decreases. Also, from a practical point of view it may be extremely difficult to reinforce *every* good behavior of an individual.

Because continuous reinforcement has its limitations, it is usually wise to consider partial reinforcement (see Table 9–1). **Reinforcement schedules** can be based on two primary criteria: *by interval,* which means over a set period of time; or *by ratio,* which is done after a specific number of performances is achieved. Each category has two frequencies; fixed and variable. Fixed frequencies are specified ahead of time and known to the rewarder and the rewardee. Variable frequencies operate on average figures but are subject to fluctuation within the averages.

Using these two classifications, there are four partial reinforcement schedules. *Fixed interval* reinforcement is the rewarding of performance on the basis of a predetermined, precommunicated time period. A worker receives a salary every two weeks or a boss receives a monthly paycheck, for example. Fixed interval reinforcement affects performance at certain times. Higher lev-

reinforcement schedule

A designated pattern by which behaviors will be rewarded or penalized. The sequence and frequency is determined usually by ratio or interval on a variable or fixed basis.

Defining the performance desired as the first step can be difficult for some jobs. It is hoped that each job can be broken down into its meaningful components, which can then be used as the basis for performance evaluation. For this rule to be applied, it must be possible to tabulate activities and units of productivity that need to be accomplished. The time period for which accounting is based may be hourly, daily, weekly, or monthly, for example.

When the manager clearly understands what employee performance is to be expected, the next steps are to accurately observe and record present performance to establish a point of reference against which future performance will be compared (this is called the developing of a baseline). Once the current level of performance is determined, observed, and recorded, it is time to intervene and tackle the performance problem. Simplicity is important. A simple intervention might be a token system where an employee earns points and exchanges them for a tangible gift.

As the desired behavior is witnessed by the manager, reinforcements are given. Social reinforcers that can be applied include verbal praise, a special job title, recognition in front of coworkers, and a picture in the company paper. Material reinforcers may be plaques, fringe benefits, raises or bonuses, and a larger office, to name just a few. Special privileges given may include a personal parking space, the employee's birthday off, longer coffee breaks, and training for a better job. Tokens given may be telephone credit cards, points backed by prizes, coupons redeemable at local stores, and chances to win a prize. The intervention must fit the degree of employee effort necessary to generate performance.

The only way to determine whether the intervention is successful is through monitoring and measuring performance over a sufficient period of time.

The rewards of the behavioral approach are many. Overall communication between bosses and their subordinates should increase. Employees will soon see that good things happen to them when they exhibit an acceptable level of performance.

Source: Rodney R. Nordstrom and R. Vance Hall, "The Platinum Rule," *Training and Development Journal,* Volume 40, Number 9, September 1986, pp. 57–58. Copyright 1986, the American Society for Training and Development. Reprinted with permission. All rights reserved.

els of performance usually occur just prior to the predetermined reward, but a decline occurs quickly after the reward is received.

Some argue that salary is not a good reinforcer, because the time period is too lengthy to be effective. Also, some feel that salary techniques are really avoidance conditioning. This view sees employees working enough to avoid being discharged rather than to get a reward.[5] Fixed interval reinforcement usually is short-lived if its application is stopped. In other words, extinction takes place rapidly when reinforcement is curtailed.

Variable interval reinforcement is still based upon time periods but with less specific scheduling. Rewards may be received, for example, on an average of every two weeks but at random times unknown to the performer ahead of time. Random appraisals and bonuses might fit this category. Of course, they must still be tied to correct performance. Imagine the problems that could be created if a bonus is given to an employee who has just made a major error, for example. Variable interval reinforcement usually achieves

Table 9–1

Partial
Reinforcement
Schedule

Reinforcement Type By Interval	When Applied	Effects on Behavior	Effects If Stopped	Typical Application
Fixed	After pre-determined period of time—weekly, biweekly, etc.	Overall, performance is average; performance increases just prior to reinforcement date, then decreases thereafter.	Quick extinction.	Salaries; pay by the hour.
Variable	Over a period of time on an average but at a time unknown specifically to the performer.	Moderately high, fairly stable performance.	Slow extinction.	Random monthly performance evaluations and rewards.

By Ratio	When Applied	Effects on Behavior	Effects If Stopped	Typical Application
Fixed	After a certain output level is achieved.	High, very stable performance.	Quick extinction.	Piece-rate.
Variable	After some average number of performances.	High, stable.	Slow extinction.	Bonus given on an average number of performances.

moderately high, fairly stable performance. Extinction occurs comparatively slowly.

Fixed ratio reinforcement is applied after a predetermined number of performances, such as after every 100 units of something is produced or after every 100,000-dollar sales quota is met. The smaller the ratio (after every third unit, for example), the more effective the reinforcement. Fixed ratio reinforcement gets quick performance increases that tend to be stable over a period of time when the number of units is small. Extinction moves quickly when performance is no longer reinforced.

Variable ratio reinforcement is based on an average but less structured number of performances. Reinforcement can occur on an average every 100 units produced but at more random levels that are not clearly known ahead of time by the performer. Extinction when variable ratios are used is slow, and performance usually remains high all through the time the technique is used.

Figure 9–1

Comparison of
Similar Stages of
Reinforcement
Motivation with
Positive and Negative
Cognitive Motivation
Models

Reinforcement Approach

	Stimulus————	Response ————	Reinforcement
Cognitive Approach Positive Model			
Motive————	Incentive ————	Action taken———	6A (success and reward) or 6B and C (failure and no reward)
Cognitive Approach Negative Model			
Motive———— (to protect and preserve what the worker already possesses)	Fear as Incentive——— (threat that possessions,benefits, previous awards will be taken away; penalties applied)	Action ————	6—Option A (adequate performance results in no penalty; also, no reward) or 6—Option B (inadequate performance results in penalty)

Comparison of Reinforcement Motivation with Cognitive Motivation

Positive motivation was viewed in Chapter 8 as internal in origin. Motives were seen as unfilled needs, assuming that individuals were aware of unfilled needs. Chapter 8 also assumed that each individual was capable of evaluating the incentives offered. Values of rewards were evaluated in advance, as was the probability that successful performance could occur. Action was voluntary. Success resulted in rewards being received, while failure meant no rewards. Satisfaction occurred only after rewards were judged to be equitable. Dissatisfaction came if rewards were viewed to be inequitable. The process was to be repeated so that future rewards could be earned. Positive cognitive motivation was said to be future oriented. Work and other performances took place to gain future benefits.

Negative motivation from the cognitive view was seen in Chapter 8 as somewhat internal in origin. In this case, of course, the motivation was the fear of the loss of something important to the performer. Possible losses were evaluated on the basis of their worth, and probable successful performance was again estimated. Performance was based upon the hope of success so that losses could be avoided. The fairness and appropriateness of successes and failures were judged after rewards or penalties became apparent.

Cognitive motivations and reinforcement motivations may seem poles apart in their natures and origins, but the two concepts don't need to be kept separate. As seen in Figure 9–1, each phase of reinforcement motivation has its parallel in the cognitive models. There are stimuli, responses, and reinforcements in the cognitive model. The main differences are in the assumptions about the performer's thought processes as the steps occur. The reinforcement approach believes that either performers do not think about the different stages or the thoughts are dismissed as being unimportant.[6] Reinforcement motivation theory assumes that reinforcement (past rewards) causes future motivation, while cognitive motivation theory feels that incentives (future opportunities) result in future motivation.

The negative model of cognitive motivation closely parallels the negative reinforcement and punishment concepts. If there is fear that something will be lost, the condition exists for negative reinforcement. If there is fear of loss, if performance is unsatisfactory, and if the loss is experienced, the employee receives punishment. This illustrates that the reinforcement and cognitive approaches differ in what people are perceived to think about as each step in the process occurs.

Negative Reinforcement, Punishment, and the Disciplinary Process

The disciplinary procedures that many organizations use are basically implementations of negative reinforcement (avoidance) and punishment. The chief goal of the disciplinary process is to show the employee the consequences of undesired behavior. Once employees are aware of the consequences, it is assumed that they are conditioned to give desired behavior and to avoid undesirable actions. Good efforts will avoid punishment, while bad actions will result in penalties.

discipline
The process by which an individual learns self-control that leads him or her to do the correct things so that rewards are earned and penalties are avoided.

The term **discipline** often connotes the giving of rewards or punishment after the fact when, in reality, discipline in its proper context should be visualized as the development of the ability to analyze situations, to determine what is the correct behavior, and to decide to act favorably in advance of the receiving of specific rewards or penalties. The worker eventually should become goal oriented voluntarily and under his or her own power. The employee becomes "disciplined" to do what is desired by the organization rather than to do something that would be incorrect or "wrong" in terms of the organizational aims.

On a personal basis the healthy and well-disciplined individual is the one who can both discuss what is right and wrong and have his or her own emotions, feelings, and desires so well under control that the individual performs the organizationally appropriate action even when it might be easier not to. Ideally, no worker would ever be called upon to sacrifice important moral values for the benefit of the organization, but workers sometimes do find discipline necessary in order to follow the course charted by organizational planners. Rules, regulations, procedures, and guidelines are a necessity in any organization. Adherence to these controls may require discipline on the part of each worker. Psychologists have indicated that discipline provides structure to our lives. It is an essential part of living and working and does not have to be viewed with total skepticism.

A Philosophy of Discipline

Before discussing the details of a disciplinary program, let's talk about the development of a philosophy of disciplining. Perhaps an analogy to the philosophy behind an entirely different managerial activity will be helpful in establishing the positive frame of reference needed as a foundation for disciplining. While the setting involved in the analogy is totally different from a situation requiring employee disciplining, the philosophy is illustrated.

Wayne Housey is the credit and collections manager for Landmark Department Store, a major retail establishment in a large metropolitan area. Landmark handles its own credit and collections in addition to accepting other credit cards. Whenever Housey (or one of his assistants) receives an application for credit, he completely reviews the credit record of the applicant. When a decision is made to issue a credit card, Housey or his assistant is indicating that he is confident that the customer is willing and able to meet the financial obligations of the credit extension.

When the customer makes a purchase using his or her card, the purchase is recorded. A statement is sent at the end of the monthly billing period to remind the customer that it is time for a payment to be made on the account. The department store (through its credit manager) has confidence that the customer will meet the obligation and that only a simple reminder (usually an impersonal bill) is all that is necessary to secure the payment.

If no payment is made, Housey sends another brief statement the next month restating the obligation. The statement is handled very positively; it is still expected that the customer will pay his or her account.

If no response is received on the basis of the reminders, the collection procedure progresses to the "should pay" stage, in which Housey sends a note discussing the terms of the original agreement and suggesting that the customer "should pay" the account to protect his or her credit rating or out of a sense of fair play or some other line of logic. The individual is still seen as a valued customer, one whom the store wishes to keep as a customer. It is expected that the customer will respond to logic, reason, and the desire to act fairly and honorably. Perhaps more than one "should pay" letter is issued over a period of time.

If a customer fails to respond to the appeal to reason and honesty, Housey eventually decides that the customer has no intention of living up to the obligation. The customer is no longer welcomed as a credit risk. A letter threatening to take steps harmful to the customer (through a legal suit, the loss of all credit privileges, etc.) is issued. Continued contact is not considered desirable if the customer is unwilling to meet the obligation. The threat of action is made and exercised if necessary.

The philosophy behind Wayne Housey's approach to collecting his company's credit payments is that qualified people who are knowledgeable concerning their responsibilities normally will willingly fulfill their obligations. Housey's role primarily is one of selecting qualified people and reminding them of their obligations at the appropriate time. Only when individuals do not fulfill their obligations does the role change. If the conditions behind nonpayment appear to be beyond the control of the customer, Housey is helpful in attempting to find agreeable terms and adjustments. If, however, the individual shows that he or she has no intention of meeting his or her obligations and fails to respond to reason and logic, the procedure moves to a negative, threatening stage. The customer is urged to action through fear of what might happen to his or her credit rating if responsibility is not assumed for the obligations.

The similarity between this case and the proper handling of disciplining is striking. Individuals selected and placed in jobs ideally are chosen because they are qualified to perform adequately—they have the skills and abilities required to do the job, or they are considered to be trainable. Training is provided as needed. Their supervisor instructs employees in their duties so that there is a clear understanding of the job demands. Organizational rules, regulations, and procedures should be spelled out, and the reward and penalty system should be clarified in advance. Understanding and acceptance of goals and expectations from the beginning is extremely important. It is these factors that workers must discipline themselves to observe or to work toward.

If a worker is to be disciplined to obligations, requirements, and demands, regular feedback must be given concerning the strengths and weaknesses of performance. The supervisor and other qualified personnel help discover progress and assist in overcoming difficulties that are encountered. Rewards are given whenever possible following an individual's successful performance.

Normally when a worker's performance falls below the standards expected, the worker will catch his or her own errors and correct them. If this does not occur, a reminder from the supervisor usually receives a positive response, and inadequate behavior is corrected. If for some reason the worker does not immediately correct inadequacies in performance, other constructive reminders may be appropriate. If there is still no noticeable response to the oral reminders, the disciplinary process may enter a phase very similar to the "should pay" stage in the collection process. With this, the supervisor may need to explain to the worker the importance of specific actions and may need to review the worker's understanding of personal obligations. If the employee is willing to perform satisfactorily but is being hindered by other factors, the supervisor may be able to help the employee overcome obstacles to performance. At this stage of the disciplinary program, good will prevails, and the supervisor's intent is to help the worker meet obligations and continue employment.

If, however, the worker shows no intention of living up to the obligations accepted when he or she agreed to take the job, the negative phase of the process begins. The worker may receive a warning that penalties will be applied if job responsibilities are not fulfilled. The penalties may vary depending upon the nature and degree of the poor performance.

If a worker fails to exercise self-control and self-discipline, the phases of the disciplinary process proceed progressively. For example, the worker first

Advance warning is an important part of the disciplinary process.

receives one or more gentle reminders of the performance obligations that were accepted, and the need for correction is stressed. If the worker needs help in correcting actions, the supervisor provides the appropriate assistance. If the worker still fails to respond and to fulfill responsibilities, he or she then may be made aware of the positive contributions personal performance can make to the organization and the benefits that will come personally from performing satisfactorily. Sometimes a written warning is given at this stage to clarify the seriousness of the problem and to notify whatever unions may be involved.

Eventually, if the worker shows no desire to improve or to perform adequately, penalties will be threatened and applied. A disciplinary approach, therefore, can be conducted on a very positive, constructive level. It is assumed that workers will live up to goals and standards if they are known and accepted. The performance evaluation and control procedures are kept on a positive plane unless the actions and intent of the worker call for negative action. Disciplining is much more than the application of penalties. It is the training and regulating of behavior (preferably through self-control) so that work performance contributes to organizational and personal achievement.

Not everyone agrees that procedural disciplinary action is most useful. Some say, for example, that (1) for punishment to be effective, there must be continued surveillance, which can waste expensive time; (2) punishment only temporarily suppresses wrongdoing; and (3) punishment has bad side effects.[7]

Providing Fairness in Disciplinary Action

Douglas McGregor, in developing the **hot stove** approach to **disciplining,** suggested that criticism and penalties should occur (1) immediately after the employee does the wrong thing, (2) with advance warning in the sense that the worker knows what is expected and what the action will be if he or she does not live up to expectations, (3) consistently against all individuals who

hot stove disciplining
The process used by an organization to get "correct" behaviors from employees by the use of immediate, consistent, impersonal, prewarned penalties.

Self Test

Personal Feedback

Disciplinary Style Questionnaire

Instructions: Please read the following cases and check the action you would take in each instance. Please answer with the response you feel would fill the correct action for each situation.

"The unauthorized possession of company property is an offense that will result in the immediate discharge of the offending employee."

While taking inventory and matching the orders to repair invoices, it was found that Walker, one of the mechanics, was ordering more parts than were needed to fix the cars that he was repairing. After talking with Walker, the supervisor learned that the mechanic was taking the parts and using them to fix cars at his house, thus picking up a little extra money.

What would you do as a supervisor?

———————— Ignore the infraction this time

———————— Informal oral warning

———————— Oral warning that goes on employee's record

———————— Written warning that goes on employee's record

———————— Suspension with pay for remainder of day

———————— Suspension with pay for longer than one day

———————— Suspension without pay for longer than one day

———————— Discharge employee

"Sleeping, reading, etc., during company time is expressly prohibited. An employee guilty of the above will be subject to a three (3) day suspension for the first offense."

Reed had a history of minor violations during his three years of employment with the firm, although he was a hard worker and the violations never amounted to enough to result in a formal disciplinary action. One day as he was waiting to pick up a crew of men out working, Reed became drowsy and fell asleep in the truck. This caused the work crew to have to call a man from the plant to come get them. Reed was discovered asleep about three miles from the work crew.

What would you do as a supervisor?

———————— Ignore the infraction this time

———————— Informal oral warning

———————— Oral warning that goes on employee's record

———————— Written warning that goes on employee's record

———————— Suspension with pay for remainder of the day

———————— Suspension with pay for longer than one day

_____ Suspension without pay for longer than one day

_____ Discharge employee

"An employee found by his supervisor to be unfit for the performance of his duties as a result of excessive drinking of alcoholic beverages will be suspended for five (5) days for the first offense."

Lyons, one of the workmen in the telephone repair department, was building a house with the help of his friends. Many times Lyons would provide beer and drinks after they had finished working on the house. The department supervisor noticed that since the house had been started, Lyons' work had suffered due to the excessive amount of drinking he was doing plus the added physical labor. The supervisor had jokingly referred to the problem one time because he knew Lyons was a good worker and was not accustomed to drinking so much. However, one day Lyons could not climb a high power pole safely because the night before he had stayed up too late drinking.

What would you do as supervisor?

_____ Ignore the infraction this time

_____ Informal oral warning

_____ Oral warning that goes on employee's record

_____ Written warning that goes on employee's record

_____ Suspension with pay for remainder of the day

_____ Suspension with pay for longer than one day

_____ Suspension without pay for longer than one day

_____ Discharge employee

"Any employee guilty of disorderly conduct, including horseplay, fighting, etc., during working hours will be suspended for three (3) days for the first offense."

Davis and Williams, both machinists, worked in the same general area under one supervisor. Monday morning, about ten-thirty, Williams walked over to Davis and, without saying a word, began hitting him. The supervisor learned in the interview that the two men had a fight Saturday afternoon in a local bar. The fight had been broken up and seemingly forgotten until Williams attacked Davis on Monday.

What would you do as supervisor about Williams?

_____ Ignore the infraction this time

_____ Informal oral warning

_____ Oral warning that goes on employee's record

_____ Written warning that goes on employee's record

_____ Suspension with pay for remainder of day

_____ Suspension with pay for longer than one day

Self Test
continued

_____ Suspension without pay for longer than one day

_____ Discharge employee

Source: David H. Hovey Jr., *Disciplinary Philosophy of First-Line Supervisor as a Function of Work-Unit Technology and Personal Values,* Unpublished dissertation, 1978.

Evaluating Your Answers

1. After you have answered each situation, check your answer by the hot stove rules.

   Have you been   consistent?
                      impersonal?
                      with warning?
                      immediate?

2. What additional information would you like to have about the situation before deciding what to do?

3. What would be the consequence of your action on the behavior of each person involved? What would the effect be on other workers who find out about it?

commit the same shortcoming under the same conditions, and (4) impersonally in that personalities are not criticized but the deed or action receives the corrective or punitive attention.[8]

Taking action immediately following the identification of performance inadequacies is important because the employee needs to relate the undesirable behavior to the penalty or the need for correction. A major managerial mistake from this perspective occurs when managers decide to wait and not immediately discuss poor performance by employees, hoping it will go away by itself. Chances are it won't! The need for advance warning makes certain that goals and penalties have been communicated before any action is begun. Consistency in disciplining is designed to provide fair treatment and to avoid favoritism to certain individuals. The need for impersonality of correctional action removes the subjective, more emotional element of discipline so that corrective action can be handled objectively and constructively. Guidelines such as these can help managers assure that they are administering discipline as constructively as possible.

Conducting the Correctional Interview

When it has been established that a worker needs correctional assistance and constructive criticism, the manager points out inappropriate behavior and sees that necessary changes are identified. The purpose of the discussion is to achieve improved performance, concentrating primarily upon future needs and future behavior. Notice our emphasis on the future and on *new* behavior.

Private disciplining or correcting is more effective than public criticism. However, public praise may be very effective.

Several approaches and conditions can help to transform the session from a potentially negative and subjective review of a worker's shortcomings into a constructive, objective analysis that can result in improved performance.

1. It is extremely helpful if the supervisor-worker conversation concerning performance needs and inadequacies can take place in a private, confidential climate. The old adage, "Commend in public, but criticize in private," is exactly what comes into play here. Privacy tends to remove the threat of making individual imperfection a matter of public record. Workers usually respond more favorably to constructive criticism that is confidentially given than they do to public criticism. Resentment and resistance build when a supervisor broadcasts the deficiencies of one individual to the individual's coworkers and employees.

2. Before any criticism is given, the manager determines whether the worker understands the duties and expectations the job requires. If goals and standards are not understood, the correctional process must clarify them.

3. Any criticism that occurs dwells upon performance standards and the worker's inability to meet those standards. Criticism concentrates upon the job to be done and avoids personal references and accusations. Another adage is related to this: "Criticize the problem and not the person." Instead of saying to a worker, "You must not want to do what's right because your performance is always lacking" (or worse yet, "You messed up because you are so dumb"), a much better approach would be to say, "Your job makes these contributions and requires these actions . . . You seem to be having some difficulty with this area . . . What can be done to correct the problem?"

4. The initiative for identifying and correcting problem areas is given to the worker to every degree possible.

5. Constructive criticism searches for tangible steps that can provide solutions for improvement. The worker is not criticized, penalized, and then left to flounder around aimlessly. If you've ever been in a situation in which someone told you what you were doing wrong but didn't let you know how to do it right, you know what we mean. Positive steps for improvement need to be discussed, explained, and implemented.

6. The tone of constructive criticism is forward looking rather than dwelling upon past actions. The damage from yesterday's mistakes has been done, but tomorrow's errors can be avoided. Any good coach, for example, will tell athletes that if a mistake is made, the offender should recognize the mistake, determine how it can be corrected, then forget about it. The same situation is true with the worker and the boss. When a problem is identified and a solution is found, the mistake should not be continually brought up. In other words, the error should be forgotten after a positive plan of action is developed, as long as performance stays at the desired level.

7. Constructive evaluations include praise and affirmative recognition of good performance as well as criticism and penalties for inadequate performance. Recognition of adequate performance frequently is overlooked by managers, but as we well know, it's vital to the performer.

8. When penalties are involved, they are applied objectively and explained. Methods and means for avoiding future penalties are reviewed.

Use of these concepts will help to make criticism and correction constructive rather than destructive.

Summary

Reinforcement motivation is based upon the premise that people repeat behavior that is treated positively and cease behavior that is penalized or ignored. There is a large amount of research support behind this premise. The process, sometimes known as conditioning, would appear on the surface to be a technique in opposition to cognitive motivation. In reality, however, the concepts may be compatible. The stimulus → response → reinforcement sequence of this conditioning approach is accomplished in the cognitive method, also. The cognitive approach fills in details of the thought in people's minds more than the reinforcement position does.

There are four types of reinforcement available: (1) positive reinforcement, which strengthens behavior with its use of rewards; (2) negative reinforcement, which strengthens performance as it avoids losses; (3) extinction, which withholds reinforcement to get unacceptable performance stopped; (4) and punishment, which applies penalties to bring a halt to undesirable actions.

Organizations use disciplinary action, a form of conditioning to increase or decrease behaviors. Disciplinary action can help individuals to be more self-regulating. Disciplinary action can be made fair and constructive if correct procedures are used.

Questions to Consider

1. Reinforcement or conditioning frequently is viewed as unrelated to cognitive motivation. Do you see the two concepts as related or unrelated? Why?
2. Is reinforcement inappropriate as a managerial technique because it manipulates employees to do things they may not wish to do? Explain.
3. What risks and dangers do you see with extinction as a means of getting behavior discontinued? With penalties as a means of getting behavior discontinued?
4. What risks, if any, do you see with conditioning as a behavioral control technique?
5. What are the strengths and weaknesses of the different reinforcement schedules?
6. What are the assumptions behind the procedural discipline concept as a philosophy of discipline?
7. What are the ethical issues of reinforcement in the workplace? Is reinforcement fair to the employee?
8. Do organizations have the right to punish employees for doing things they should not have done? For failing to do things they should have done? Explain.

Key Terms

discipline	primary reinforcer	reinforcement
extinction	punishment	schedule
hot stove	reinforcement	secondary reinforcer
disciplining		

Chapter Case

Management in the Fast Track

Upon graduation from school, you get accepted into the management training program of a large international hotel company. The offer is particularly exciting because you're put into an exclusive, fast-track program the firm has developed for high potential new employees. The program works like this: You are brought in at a high salary—approximately 30 percent higher than other college graduates entering the standard management training program—

and over a three-year period, you will be rotated through a series of six-month assignments aimed at giving you background in all of the hotel chain's functions. You are expected to prove yourself, of course, by demonstrating outstanding performance in each assignment. At the end of the period, assuming you do well, you can look forward to an immediate promotion, either to hotel manager or into a second-level slot at headquarters—a position that will take people entering into the standard training program years, if ever, to attain. You're excited by the challenge and vow to do well.

Your first assignment is in St. Louis, at a large convention property. You will be supervising the housekeeping staff—a group of fifty-three workers. Of this group, thirty-three are housekeepers, ten are inspectresses, and the other ten work in the laundry, doing washing, ironing, and related laundry activities. The housekeepers do the actual room cleanup; the inspectresses are leads—nonmanagement employees, but half a grade higher than the housekeepers—and they work behind the housekeepers, inspecting rooms, correcting minor problems, and, if there's a major problem, reporting to you so you can take action with the employee.

You quickly discover that things aren't all sweetness and light. There is constant bickering and arguing among the three groups, with each accusing the others of trying to act "better" than they. The laundry workers feel that they have the hot, nasty job and that none of the others respect them. The housekeepers feel that the inspectresses look down on them, and they in turn look down on the laundry workers. The inspectresses are torn—most have recently been promoted from housekeeper and feel ties to their friends in housekeeping but are afraid they'll lose their jobs if they pretend to overlook poor work.

Then, there's you. EVERYBODY looks at you funny. Word is out that you're on some kind of fancy program and won't be there long. Your own subordinates clearly don't know what to make of you and are highly suspicious. The other managers are suspicious at best and overtly jealous at worst. Everybody gives you the cold shoulder.

You decide there's nothing to be done about it and get on with your work. Since the morale problem among the inspectresses seem to be the most critical problem, you decide to start by talking to them individually. You start with Susie, the newest appointee to inspectress. No sooner do you start talking to her than she bursts into tears.

"I just want to go out and shoot myself!" she sobs. "I desperately need the extra money, or I'd go back to housekeeper in a minute! All my housekeeper friends hate me! At first, when they messed up, I'd try to do it over for them so no one would know and they wouldn't get in trouble. But as soon as they found out that I'd do that, they'd just mess up more. So I started turning them in, and now nobody's speaking to me!"

At this point, Susie collapsed into uncontrollable sobs, and you were left wondering what to do.

1. According to the disciplinary approach recommended in the chapter, how should Susie have been handling the housekeepers? Compare how she should have been handling the situation with the way she *was* handling it.

2. If Susie is to use reinforcement theory properly, what does she need to do with the housekeepers? What should you as her boss do?

3. What kind of reinforcement are you as the management trainee receiving? What's wrong with this?

4. Does reinforcement come only from one's superiors? How does this case illustrate this?

Chapter 10

The Role of Leadership in the Organization

Objectives

- To identify the roles leaders play in contemporary organizations.
- To review the development of thought concerning leadership to see where we've been and how we got where we are now.
- To discern why trait, behavior, and one-best-style approaches are being set aside.
- To see what contemporary situational leadership approaches offer to managers.
- To learn what factors to consider in selecting the appropriate leadership approach to fit the situation.
- To confront the dilemma of the need for consistency in leadership that operates concurrently with the need for flexibility.

Ted Gunderson—The Construction Supervisor

Ted Gunderson is a general supervisor for a large custom house-building concern. The company he works for is known for its quality work; most of the homes it builds are large, expensive, and individually designed. It is Gunderson's job to oversee the construction of five or six houses being built at the same time. During each workday, Gunderson moves from one building site to another checking on progress. A foreman is in charge of each house; the foremen spends all of his time at one site and works directly with the crew there. The foreman of each job reports directly to Gunderson, who in turn is accountable to the owner-manager of the company.

Gunderson came up through the ranks to get to his present job. He started as a carpenter's helper, then worked for several years as a carpenter, spent three years as a foreman, and was recently promoted to general supervisor.

Gunderson describes his job in the following manner:

> As I view my job, I think my primary duty is to see that each foreman has the materials, equipment, and personnel needed to do his job. The foreman and I consult together on what is reasonable in terms of work schedules. The rest of the responsibility is completely in the hands of the foreman. He runs the whole construction job. He has a completely free hand to do things as he wishes. I try to interfere as little as possible. That's the way I preferred things when I was a foreman, and that's the way that seems best to me.

Ralph Cannister, one of the foremen working under Gunderson, has been with the company as long as Gunderson has. He has been a foreman for about five years himself. These are his comments concerning Gunderson's supervisory abilities and actions:

> Ted is an excellent boss to work for. He lets you run the show completely on your own. He doesn't bug you all the time, like some bosses I've had in the past. He just puts you in charge of a crew and tells you to get the job done. That suits me fine.

Rudy Grantham, another of the foremen working under Gunderson, was recently promoted to the job of foreman to fill the vacancy Gunderson had left. Grantham came up through the ranks like Gunderson. He has a different reaction toward the supervisory skills of Gunderson.

> Frankly, I don't think too much of Mr. Gunderson. He comes out on the construction site for a few minutes, and then he's gone, and I don't see him for the rest of the day. Some days he doesn't come out at all. I don't think he's interested in me. He's never available when I need him. I'm getting along all right with the men working for me, but I am having some trouble coordinating all of the work and in doing the paperwork. I've never had to do some of these things before. Mr. Gunderson just is no help to me personally.

Case Questions

1. What leadership style is Ted Gunderson using?
2. Why does this style seem to be working with Ralph Cannister?
3. Why does this style seem to be unsatisfactory for Rudy Grantham?
4. How does a supervisor discover the type of leadership and supervision needed by each subordinate?

During the Biblical days, the children of Israel needed someone to guide them out of their bondage, and Moses stepped forward to lead them in their journey to the promised land. During the Great Depression, the American people needed someone to restore their confidence in their government and to provide a way to overcome the economic crisis they were facing, and Franklin D. Roosevelt became their leader to accomplish these tasks. During World War II, the British people were suffering severe losses and appeared to be unsuccessfully combatting their foes when Winston Churchill came to the forefront and guided the British efforts to victory. Lee Iacocca provided Chrysler Corporation with the leadership it needed to rescue the company from financial disaster and turn it into a profitable organization. Other leaders have done the same type of things.

People working together in organizations have a need for leaders—individuals who will be instrumental in guiding the efforts of groups of workers to the achievement of goals and objectives. The objectives may not be as far-reaching as those mentioned above, and the actions of the leaders may not be so dramatic, but the successful performance of the leadership role is essential to the survival of the business. Goods and services have to be provided, products and customers need to be united, and worker efforts require integration and coordination. The needs of workers have to be met. The leader guides the actions of others in accomplishing these tasks.

There is by no means a universal concept of the role of the leader in an organization. Some have said simply that "leadership is an organizationally useful behavior by one member or members of the same organizational family."[1] Others say that "leadership can be described as a process through which the supervisor structures reinforcement contingencies that modify the behavior of employees. Stimuli preceding behavior and rewards following behavior serve to motivate employees to work according to standards of performance."[2] In the eyes of others, the leadership function is a matter of pushing or prodding people until they do what the leader-supervisor wishes them to do. This, of course, applies primarily to formalized leaders. To others, leadership is primarily a matter of removing barriers so that workers can act with freedom and independence. In the next section, we suggest that leadership is providing followers with the knowledge, tools, equipment, and incentive to allow them to attain mutually beneficial goals. While the definitions of the leadership role vary widely, there is general agreement that someone is needed to serve as the agent for guiding and encouraging people to work together.

How We Got Where We Are Today

The Trait Approach

In preindustrial years, a person's possessions often determined whether the person was to be a leader. As a result of their great material resources, the wealthy usually held the right to give directives to those of lesser fortunes. The "rights of kings" is, or course, legendary. Those with power could command obedience.

After the Industrial Revolution occurred, and additional source of the right to have a leadership possession was noted. Individuals having essential personal traits were identified as desirable to fill leadership roles. Fayol, an important early management theorist, noted that more effective managers would be those possessing specific traits:

1. Physical qualities–health, vigour, address (charisma),
2. Mental qualities—ability to understand and learn, judgment, mental vigour, and adaptability,
3. Moral qualities—energy, firmness, willingness to accept responsibility, initiative, loyalty, tact, dignity,
4. General education—general acquaintance with matters not belonging exclusively to the function performed,
5. Special knowledge—that peculiar to the function, be it technical, commercial, financial, managerial,
6. Experience—knowledge arising from the work proper.[3]

> **trait approach**
> The theory of leadership that states that individuals are granted the right to give direction because they possess certain respected traits, such as physical and mental qualities, knowledge, and skills.

In more contemporary times, people still talk about needed leadership qualities or qualifications. Qualities such as perceptual skills (abilities to observe and discover realities), objectivity (ability to look at issues and problems rationally), the ability to establish priorities, and the ability to communicate are frequently listed requisites for effective leadership.[4]

The success of political leaders such as Roosevelt and Churchill was said to lie not only in their power through election but also because they possessed the ability to communicate and because they had a rapport with their constituents. This theory—the great man theory of leadership—explained that the possession of certain traits in a person determined the success that person would have influencing the attitudes and behavior of others.

As recently as 1948, Stogdill observed that based on a review of 124 research studies into leadership, it was his conclusion that individuals who were in leadership capacities tended to be more fluent, more original, more adaptable, more responsible, more popular, and more capable of getting work done than were their subordinates or followers.[5]

House has recently argued that there is need for continuing study of trait theories of leadership.[6] Even when trait theories were extremely popular, people began to note that no one set of traits was useful in different leadership circumstances. Think back over your own experience with leaders—in clubs and work settings you're familiar with, for example. As you think about the leaders' personalities and traits, we suspect that you'll be startled at the variety of traits you've seen.

One friend of ours underscored this point in an unusual way. He was talking to a group of people about leadership and asked everyone in the group to name at least one great leader. Here's the resulting list:

Franklin Roosevelt
George Patton
Martin Luther King
Joan of Arc
Adolf Hitler
Margaret Thatcher
Mahatma Gandhi
Attila the Hun

Is this a joke? Should someone like Hitler be on the list? Think about it? Certainly under the definitions of leadership that say that leaders are able to get others to follow their wishes, people like Hitler would be included even though very few twentieth-century Americans would agree with where Hitler was leading. Look again at the list. Maybe you can even add a few names to it. Notice the enormous variety of traits and characteristics of the people on the list. Clearly, great leaders don't possess a single set of traits. As Stogdill himself noted, "the pattern of characteristics of the leader must bear some relevant relationship to the characteristics, activities, and goals of the followers."[7]

The Behavior Concept of Leadership

behavior theories of leadership
Explanations of why individuals are followed by others based on the concept that successful leaders perform activities or duties differently from other less successful individuals.

As the researchers and theorists in leadership discovered that no single set of traits could be identified that could be universally applied, their thoughts turned to the possibility that it was the behavior of leaders rather than their traits that made them effective. Could it be that what leaders did rather than what they possessed was what made them successful? As a result, this research approach, the **behavior theories of leadership** began to observe the activities that more successful leaders engaged in as a comparison against the activities of less successful leaders. Studies conducted at Ohio State in 1955 identified and observed four behavior patterns: consideration (friendship, trust, warmth, and respect for others), initiating structure (the process of planning and organizing activities in support of organizational objectives), emphasizing production (emphasis on getting the job done), and sensitivity (the awareness of social relationships and pressures). After considerable analysis, it was decided that consideration and initiating structure were the two factors that differentiated successful from unsuccessful leadership behavior.[8] Even though there was general agreement that the two factors were important, it was difficult (if not impossible) to describe a combination of these activities that would be appropriate for every leadership situation.

Studies done in Michigan around 1950 were similar to the Ohio State studies in several ways. They looked primarily at supervisory behavior and identified employee orientation and production orientation as two major sets of thoughts and behaviors that distinguished the more successful from the unsuccessful. Employee orientation represents concern for the needs and satisfaction level of subordinates, while production orientation emphasizes organization output.[9] In addition, the Michigan findings played up the difference between loose (general) supervision and close supervision.

System 1 Exploitative Autocrat	System 2 Benevolent Autocrat	System 3 Consultative	System 4 Participative	**Table 10–1** The Four Systems Developed by Rensis Likert
Rules by being bossy. Is very centralized. Top-down is the primary communication pattern. Subordinates uninvolved in decisions. Mistrust and antagonism are common. Mediocre performance results.	Sometimes allows a slight amount of participation. Follows most of the System 1 ideas, except less extreme. Still top-down oriented. Performance is fair.	Allows more participation and involvement in decision making. Some delegation of authority. Moderate to good performance patterns.	People who must live with decisions have a hand in making those decisions. Groups make decisions. Good two-way communication. Excellent productivity. Self-guidance is practiced where possible.	

Source: Adapted from Rensis Likert, *New Patterns of Management,* New York: McGraw-Hill, 1961; and Rensis Likert, *The Human Organization,* New York: McGraw-Hill, 1967, pp. 4–11.

The Style Approaches

From the research based upon the behavior patterns of leaders came **leadership approaches** that we now call **style** positions. The style theorists said that while a number of different leadership behaviors are possible, one set of behaviors is more ideal than others. That is to say, there is a method of leadership that will achieve long-range, more desirable results than other patterns of behavior. Two of these stylized approaches are Likert's System 4 concept and Blake and McCanse's Leadership Grid®.

System 4 Approach　　In the 1960s Rensis Likert, one of the participants in the Michigan studies, took the position that when successful organizations are discovered and analyzed, a large majority of the time a single style of leadership is in use. He called the "most successful" style the **System 4** approach. For descriptive purposes, he perceived four different types of leadership as possibilities.[10] The System 1, which Likert called the exploitative management system, would be the most centralized type of authority of all. Somewhat less centralized but still very authoritative would be the System 2, a benevolent autocrat type of management. The System 3, which Likert called the consultative approach, would be slightly autocratic but would be somewhat more open. Likert viewed the System 4 as participative, with something of a team view of management. The teamwork, the participation, the delegation, and the self-guidance factors are critical to the System 4 approach. As Likert saw it, the closer the leadership in an organization to the System 4 position, the more effective the performances of the organization and its members. (Table 10–1 presents details of the four systems developed by Likert.)

leadership approaches or styles
A pattern of interacting with others for leadership purposes that consistently uses the same methods or techniques.

system 4
A leadership style proposed by Rensis Likert that calls for participative leadership using a team-oriented concept of people in organizations.

leadership grid®
A leadership style concept developed by Robert Blake and Anne McCanse for purposes of diagnosing leadership styles and proposing an idealistic style (the 9,9 approach).

Look back at the Ted Gunderson case at the start of this chapter. Gunderson emphasizes that he consults with the foremen but tries to leave them as free as possible to manage their own people. We suspect that Gunderson's style would be close to a System 4—a style that Likert suggests is ideal. It does seem ideal to Ralph Cannister, one of Gunderson's subordinates. The question is, Why isn't Rudy Grantham responding positively to Gunderson's style? Grantham's comments suggest that he's looking for something different from what Gunderson is providing. We'll return to this issue as we go along.

The Leadership Grid   The **Leadership Grid®,** which was presented in book form in 1964 as the Managerial Grid (see Figure 10–1) looked at leader-

Figure 10–1   The Leadership Grid® Figure

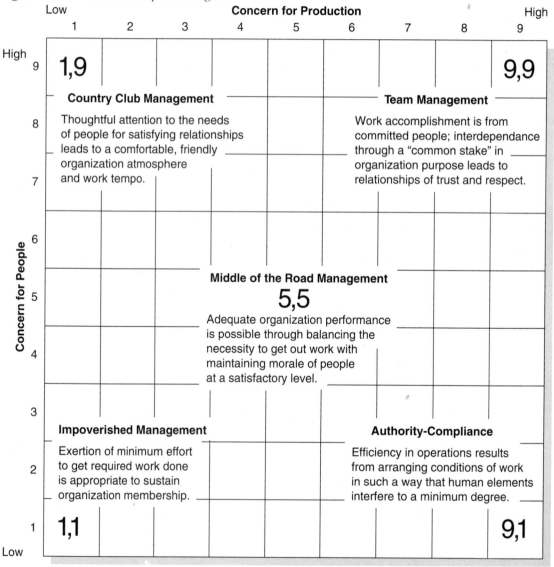

Source: The Leadership Grid® figure from *Leadership Dilemmas—Grid Solutions,* by Robert R. Blake and Anne Adams McCanse, Houston: Gulf Publishing Company, p. 29. Copyright © 1991, by Scientific Methods, Inc. Published by permission of the owners.

ship behaviors based upon two criteria: the leader's concern for production (getting the job done) and the leader's concern for meeting the needs of the employees working in his or her area of influence.[11] The effort and concern for each factor was charted on a grid, with at least nine intervals in each dimension. Eighty-one different combinations of activity would be possible in charting leadership behavior. The ultimate leadership behavior or style would be the **9,9 approach**—an emphasis on maximizing both task and human achievement. How can a leader be *both* task oriented and people oriented at the same time?

Blake and McCanse point out that the 9,9 leader designs work so that meeting work goals will also meet employees' needs for growth, experience, and participation. If a leader applies 9,9 behavior instead of one of the less ideal behaviors, it would be likely that the following would occur:

1. Organizational profitability would be good.
2. Intergroup relations would be strong.
3. People would work together as a team.
4. Frictions would be reduced and understanding increased.
5. Employee commitment and personal effort would be high.

The 9,9 leader's responsibilities include the following:

1. Providing for better direction and control through helping subordinates understand and agree with organizational purposes.
2. Helping people to realize that mistakes should be regarded as educational so that future errors can be avoided.
3. Meshing individual goals with organization purposes insofar as this is possible.
4. Developing teamwork so that everyone's efforts are synchronized.
5. Providing opportunities for participation and involvement so that people will support what they have helped to create.
6. Serving as a advisor, coach, and helper to subordinates as needed.
7. Creating conditions so that people will have mutual trust, support, and respect.
8. Fostering open communication so that individuals will send messages to others as needed.
9. Encouraging experimentation and innovation.[12]

In short, 9,9 leadership is team oriented, providing participation and involvement rather than domination. The leader creates an environment for open exchange that is to be beneficial for all parties involved.

Look again at the Ted Gunderson case. Gunderson certainly comes across as production oriented. While he is concerned with giving the foremen the freedom to act on their own, he doesn't come across as especially people centered.

Grantham's remarks suggest that he doesn't respond well to Gunderson's rather production-centered style, which is right in line with Blake and McCanse's theory. But what about Cannister? According to Blake and McCanse, Gunderson's style shouldn't work with Cannister, either, yet Cannister's remarks sound as though Gunderson's approach is highly effective with him! Maybe what the case is suggesting is that we can't simply prescribe

nine-nine (9,9) leadership
The idealistic style of leadership proposed in the Leadership Grid® in which the best leader pursues task and human goals to the fullest degree possible.

one leadership style as best for all situations. In fact, problems such as this have led some to view the System 4 and 9,9 approaches (which are very similar) to be rather idealistic, somewhat utopian positions. This is not to say that they're wrong. In fact, each has many supporters, and each approach is seen by its authors to be effective and advantageous. Rather, the question is, do *all* situations call for the same leadership style?

The Situational View of Leadership

Many of the more recent models of leadership have taken the position that there is no one best way of leadership that will be appropriate for all situations. Instead, there are a number of types of leadership possible, and the conditions or circumstances present (including the characteristics of the people involved) determine which type would be the most effective. The challenge to the manager is to discover the type of **situational leadership** needed and then to find the way to provide the correct leadership behavior.

situational leadership
The view of leadership activities that suggests that there is no single best way leaders should perform. Each leadership situation must be judged and responded to based upon its own unique needs.

The Fiedler Contingency Approach   One of the earliest and best-known situational leadership models was the one developed by Fred Fiedler in the mid 1960s.[13] Fiedler felt that there were two types of leaders: the task-oriented leader and the relationships-oriented leader. The task-oriented person focuses primarily on the completion of work. Esteem and satisfaction come from getting the job done. Relationship-motivated people seek good interpersonal relationships with group members and get work done through good working relations. It is possible for managers to discover their leadership preference by using the Least-Preferred Co-Worker (LPC) Scale developed by Fiedler. Individuals scoring low on the LPC Scale are labeled task-oriented, while high LPCs are said to be relationship-oriented.

The needed leadership for a specific situation is determined by using three identification criteria: (1) leader-member relations, (2) task structure, and (3) position power. Leader-member relations refers to the interpersonal relationship between the leader and his or her subordinates. This most important aspect of the work situation is concerned with how completely the followers accept the leadership of the lead individual. When leader-member relations are said to be good, the leader has the high acceptance of subordinates. When leader-member relations are poor, the followers respect the leader's authority very little.[14]

Leader-member relations can be identified by asking such questions as, Is the leader trusted by subordinates? and For what boss in your organization would you prefer to work? Fiedler created a ten-item semantic scale, called the Group Atmosphere Scale, to help calculate leader-member relations. The leader is asked to describe his or her work unit by rating the group on an eight-point scale. Bipolar adjectives on the scale include such items as pleasant-unpleasant and friendly-unfriendly.

The second most important factor according to Fiedler in identifying the proper leadership for a situation is task structure. Task structure involves the degree to which task requirements (performances) are spelled out for workers. Structured tasks are, or course, those that detail the duties of the performer, while unstructured work provides a wide range of behaviors in an undesignated fashion. Questions to ask to determine the degree of task structure include, To what degree are the requirements of a job clearly stated and known to the people performing the job? To what degree can different methods and procedures be used to perform a task? To what degree are different solutions—i.e., different results—acceptable as the end product of a task? Jobs that are spelled out in detail, where specific job methods must be used and very exacting results must be achieved, would be called *structured.* Jobs described only in terms of general directions, where many different procedures might be used and where any one of several solutions would be appropriate, would be identified as *unstructured.*

Position power is the remaining component in Fiedler's scheme of things. Position power refers to the right that the leader possesses in his or her job to demand the followership of employees—as a result of being a boss. Answers are needed to such questions as, Can a supervisor punish or reward subordinates personally? Can the supervisor promote or demote subordinates on his or her own? How specifically can the leader give instructions and expect them to be followed? Where the leader has much authority to direct others, the position power would be called *strong.* If the leader had little control over subordinates, position power would be *weak.*

Table 10–2 shows how the conditions present at a specific moment are related to the appropriate leadership approach. Generally, in situations where leader-member relations are good, the task is structured, and the position power is strong, task-oriented leadership will be most useful. When leader-member relations, task structure, and position power are low, task-oriented leadership is also useful. When the situation favorableness is moderate (neither high nor low in leader-member relations) relationship-oriented leadership is needed. Some conditions are exceptions to these, but you can see how

Table 10–2   General Guidelines for Determining When to Use Task-Oriented and Relationship-Oriented Leadership

Leadership style to be used	Use task-oriented when favorableness exists	Use relationship-oriented when situation favorableness is moderate	Use task-oriented when situation is unfavorable
Condition calling for leadership style	Leader-member relations are high	When the three factors leader-member relations, task structure, and position power are in intermediate ranges	Leader-member relations are low
	task is structured		task is unstructured
	group is open to leadership (high position power)		group is not open nor receptive (low position power)

Source: Adapted from Fred E. Fiedler, "A Contingency Model of Leadership Effectiveness," in L. Berkowitz (Editor), *Advances in Experimental Social Psychology,* New York: Academic Press, 1964; Fred E. Fiedler, *A Theory of Leadership Effectiveness,* New York: McGraw-Hill, 1967; Fred E. Fiedler and M. M. Chemers, *Improving Leadership Effectiveness,* New York: John Wiley and Sons, 1984, and Fred E. Fiedler, "Situational Control and a Dynamic Theory of Leadership," In Bert King, Siegfried Streufert, and Fred E. Fiedler (Eds.), *Managerial Control and Organizational Democracy,* Washington, D.C.: V. H. Winston and Sons, 1978.

Fiedler's concept works. More recently, Fiedler has suggested that other factors such as leader intelligence, and amount of stress, may also enter in.[15]

Fiedler is pessimistic about individual leaders developing flexibility in their leadership approaches. He suggests that leaders, instead of being expected to change their approach, be placed where their orientation matches the needs of the situation.

The Vroom-Yetton Decision Tree Approach   Another popular leadership model is the one developed by Vroom and Yetton. The model is sometimes perceived as a guideline for making decisions as well. In the original model introduced in 1973, four leadership categories were portrayed: (1) *A* leadership (autocratic leadership, where decisions are made by the leader without considering inputs from others), (2) *C* leadership (consultative leadership, where information from others is sought and accepted or rejected), (3) *G* leadership (group leadership, where members work as a team and the leader serves to facilitate the group's actions without being dominant), and (4) *D* leadership (delegative leadership, where a follower is handed a task to be performed under his or her own initiative). Subsequently, the model was reduced to three leadership categories: autocratic, consultative, and group.[16] (Check your leadership preferences by answering the questions in the accompanying Self Test.)

Self Test

Personal Feedback

Leadership Decisions Questionnaire

Please read the following situations. Then review the four courses of action you might choose. Check the one course of action in each case that best describes what you feel you would do.

1. A group of workers who are your subordinates are experiencing conflict among themselves. The source of disagreement is over some work responsibilities (who is supposed to perform which activity). In the past, you have left the workers alone, and they have always worked out their own problems. Group performance and interpersonal relations have been good in the past. You don't know the extent of their disagreement in this situation, however.

    As their boss, would you?

    _____ a. Sit down with the group and work with them to evaluate possible courses of action. Your role would be more like that of a chairman. You would not force "your" decision upon them but would accept the solution that had the support of the whole group.

    _____ b. Identify to the whole group what you considered to be the problem. You would obtain the collective suggestions of the group. Then you would make a decision that might or might not reflect the influence of the group.

_____   c.   You would ask for information from you subordinates without telling them why you want the information. You would then decide what to do about the subordinates' problem. You would view the subordinates only as sources of information.

_____   d.   Let the group recognize and solve its own problem. You would, of course, provide the group with any information that you possess.

2.   It is your job as the manager of a project group to select a new member of the work team to replace a member who has resigned. Members of the team work closely together both mentally and geographically on a constant basis. All of the team members are highly trained and skilled. The group is a self-motivating group in that they take the initiative in solving problems and in creating new procedures when needed. The last time a vacancy in the group occurred, you selected a member by yourself and assigned him to the group. Shortly after the new member joined the group, he was rejected by the group and you had to make another choice (whom the group eventually accepted). You have a high level of confidence in the group. You, of course, are accountable for the group's performance.

Would you:

_____   a.   Consult with the members of the group collectively to review possible new members. You would receive the recommendations and suggestions of the group and consider them before making the final decision yourself. Your decision may not reflect the recommendations from the group.

_____   b.   Act quickly to replace the resigned member using data you have collected yourself without consulting with group members.

_____   c.   Bring the team together and identify the need for selecting a new member. You would then leave the room and let them decide who they would select as a new member. Their decision will be accepted and implemented.

_____   d.   Bring the team together and show them the problem as you see it. You would encourage the group to be involved in selecting the right person. You would work with the group to make this correct decision without dominating the group.

3.   As the boss, it is your responsibility to select the brand and model of the car you would like to have to replace the company car you have driven for the past four years. You make this type of decision every four years as company policy prescribes. You are well versed on the subject, since you have received literature and have test-driven several cars. You drive the company car most of the time yourself, although you occasionally allow one of your employees to use the car.

Would you:

_____   a.   Delegate the decision to your subordinate and let him/her make it. You would, of course, pass along the information you have collected.

—— b. Explain the decision need to your subordinate and ask for his/her opinion. Together you would arrive at a mutually agreeable solution.

—— c. Explain the decision need to your subordinate and ask for his/her ideas and suggestions. Then you would make a decision, which might or might not reflect his/her influence.

—— d. Make a decision yourself based upon the data you have without consulting anyone.

4. Some equipment needs to be replaced in a department supervised by one of your most trusted subordinates. The work done in that department is of a very technical nature known only to the people who work in the department. The supervisor of the department (your subordinate) knows the budget limitations for new equipment. He/she is a cooperative-team member—one who contributes well to the organization and its goals.

Would you:

—— a. Let the supervisor of the technical department make the decision, using whatever technique he/she wishes to arrive at a conclusion. You accept his/her recommendation as being final.

—— b. Discuss the problem with the supervisor, get his/her suggestions, and make the final decision yourself. You may choose to accept his/her suggestions or you may reject them.

—— c. Share the need for a decision with the supervisor, then sit down with him/her and together evaluate the alternatives and reach a mutually agreeable decision. Neither individual would dominate the decision.

—— d. Make the decision yourself based upon the facts you have without consulting with anyone else.

5. You have two important projects under your direction with three subordinates assigned to each project. One of these projects is three months behind schedule, with only six months remaining before the work must be completed. The project has been under way for about twelve months. The subordinates seem to be trying hard but are not getting sufficient results.

Would you:

—— a. Meet with the people in the group that is behind schedule and get information from them without telling them why you want the information. Then, based upon the information collected, you would make some procedural changes and announce some new schedules that they would be expected to meet.

—— b. Share your concerns individually with the members of the team experiencing problems. After considering their ideas and yours, make decisions on actions that will affect them. Your decision may or may not reflect what they have told you.

—— c. Share your concerns with the group, then let them work out their own problems so that they can meet schedules.

_____ d. Meet with the three members and discuss the problem. Together you would arrive at conclusions on adjustments on their actions and the schedule.

6. As principal of an elementary school, you often handle disciplinary cases. Over the past six months, one of your fifteen teachers has referred an unusually large number of cases to your attention. This fact, combined with other information you have received, leads you to believe that there is a serious breakdown of discipline in that teacher's room.

Would you:

_____ a. Ask the teacher to be more conscious of the problem and to take steps to remedy the situation. Leave the future steps to him/her.

_____ b. Decide to reassign the teacher to a group of students where fewer disciplinary problems have existed, using the information you already have in hand.

_____ c. Consult with the teacher to find out his/her explanation of the problem. You would then make a decision on the appropriate assignment or disciplining of the teacher, using your own opinion of what should be done.

_____ d. Sit down and discuss the problem at length with the teacher. Together you would try to find problem sources and solutions.

7. You are the district supervisor of a large sales distribution organization. You are opening up a new sales territory in a state where you have never had a sales force before. You have just hired a person to be the manager of the state sales office in one of the state's three major communities. The data that have been collected indicate that no one of the cities offers a clear advantage over the other cities so far as your company is concerned. The new person you've hired has his/her own thoughts about which city should be chosen.

Would you:

_____ a. Ask the new state sales manager what his/her thoughts are on the best location, then decide on a location which seems best to you. Your decision might or might not reflect his/her suggestions.

_____ b. Tell the new state sales manager to choose the location he/she prefers. His/her decision would then be accepted.

_____ c. Analyze the problem together with the new state sales manager and reach a decision together that you both feel is appropriate.

_____ d. Make the decision yourself with the information already available to you. Then you would announce it to the new sales manager and the other people affected.

8. The marketing research department of your company has told you (as a manager of product design) that your customer would prefer to buy your products in three specific colors—blue, green, and yellow. Your current product is produced in none of these colors. The cost of producing the new colors is the same as the cost for producing the present colors.

Self Test

continued

Would you:

_____ a. Consult with your production employees about the problem and make a decision as a team effort.

_____ b. Ask for the opinion of some of your subordinates, then make a decision. Your decision might or might not reflect the opinions of your subordinates.

_____ c. Let the production people decide which colors they wish to produce. You would, of course, share the information with them that you received from marketing research.

_____ d. Make a decision yourself using the data available to you without consulting with anyone else.

Interpretation

Four leadership styles are involved as choices for each situation. They include autocratic (A), consultative (C), group (G), and delegative (D), much like the original Vroom-Yetton model. Accordingly, the choices in the eight situations are

1.		2.		3.		4.	
a.	G	a.	C	a.	D	a.	D
b.	C	b.	A	b.	G	b.	C
c.	A	c.	D	c.	C	c.	G
d.	D	d.	G	d.	A	d.	A

5.		6.		7.		8.	
a.	A	a.	D	a.	C	a.	G
b.	C	b.	A	b.	D	b.	C
c.	D	c.	C	c.	G	c.	D
d.	G	d.	G	d.	A	d.	A

If you used one style more frequently than other styles, this may be your dominant or preferred style. If you used each type at least once, this may indicate that you are flexible in the ability to adapt to a situation.

To determine which leadership approach is appropriate in a particular situation, a series of eight questions must be answered. The questions, included in Figure 10–2, must be answered in sequence. The first question (Question A), is, Does it matter from a quality point of view what is decided? If the answer to the Question A is yes, question B must be answered. If the answer to A is no, questions B and C are bypassed, and Question D must be answered next.

At the end of the question sequence, the leadership styles appropriate to a situation are revealed. Styles appropriate are listed in the order of the time involved to fulfill the style, with autocratic, consultative, and group listed in that order according to time needed for implementation.

The Hersey-Blanchard Situational Approach   Another popular situational leadership model was developed by Hersey and Blanchard. In this leader-

Figure 10–2   Questions and Sequence Used to Determine the Appropriate Leader-Decision Style
A. Is there a quality requirement such that one solution is likely to be more rational than another?
B. Do I have sufficient info to make a high quality decision?
C. Is the problem structured?
D. Is acceptance of decision by subordinates critical to effective implementation?
E. If I were to make the decision by myself, is it reasonably certain that it would be accepted by my subordinates?
F. Do subordinates share the organizational goals to be attained in solving this problem?
G. Is conflict among subordinates likely in preferred solutions? (This question is irrelevant to individual problems.)
H. Do subordinates have sufficient info to make a high quality decision?

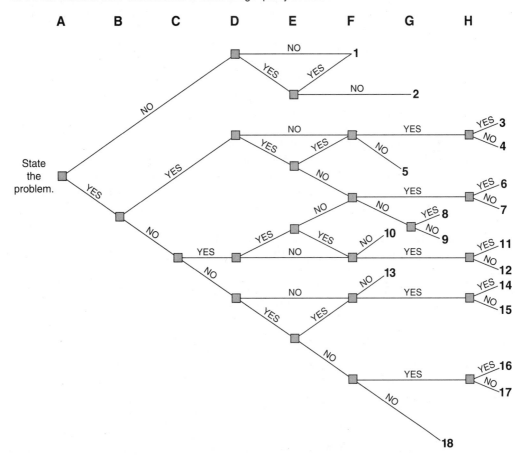

The feasible set is shown for each problem type for Group (G) and individual (I) problems.

1 { G: AI, AII, CI, CII, GII
    I: AI, DI, AII, CI, GI

2 { G: GII
    I: DI, GI

3 { G: AI, AII, CI, CII, GII
    I: AI, DI, AII, CI, GI

4 { G: AI, AII, CI, CII, GII
    I: AI, AII, CI, GI

5 { G: AI, AII, CI, CII
    I: AI, AII, CI

6 { G: GII
    I: DI, GI

7 { G: GII
    I: GI

8 { G: CII
    I: CI

9 { G: CI, CII
    I: CI

10 { G: AII, CI, CII
     I: AII, CI

11 { G: AII, CI, CII, GII
     I: DI, AII, CI, GI

12 { G: AII, CI, CII, GII
     I: AII, CI, GI

13 { G: CII
     I: CI

14 { G: CII, GII
     I: DI, CI, GI

15 { G: CII, GII
     I: CI, GI

16 { G: GII
     I: DI, GI

17 { G: GII
     I: GI

18 { G: CII
     I: CI

Source: Victor H. Vroom, "A New Look at Managerial Decision Making," *Organizational Dynamics,* Volume 1, Number 2, Spring 1973, p. 70. Reprinted, by permission of publisher, from *Organizational Dynamics,* Spring/1973 ©1973. American Management Association, New York. All rights reserved.

ship approach, the appropriate leadership for a situation is based upon the readiness (and maturity) of an employee. Readiness is determined by the employee's ability and willingness or level of confidence or security. An R1 person is one who is unable and unwilling or insecure. An R1 needs a *telling* kind of leadership which provides guidance, direction, and structure.

An R2 person is one who is unable but willing or confident. The R2 person needs a *selling* kind of leadership which explains, persuades, and clarifies.

An R3 person is one who is able, but unwilling or lacking in confidence. The R3 needs a *participating* leader who will collaborate, facilitate, and commit.

The R4 person is able and willing or confident. This type of person needs leadership that is *delegating*. There is little need for guidance; so the leader mostly observes and monitors.[17]

The leadership approach is chosen to fit the ability, willingness, and confidence level of the employee.

The Path-Goal View of Leadership   One of the most recent theories of leadership from the situational perspective is the path-goal model (See Table 10–3). According to this view, the primary roles of the leader are to provide stimuli and reward opportunities to keep the followers motivated while making the path to payoffs easier to travel. The path is kept clear by clarifying the path, reducing roadblocks and pitfalls, and increasing the opportunities for personal satisfaction along the way.[18] The leader behavior is dependent upon the needs of the follower, the rewards that are available, and the obstacles confronting the follower.

As Table 10–3 shows, there are four leadership types related to the path-goal framework. The appropriate style is chosen based upon the needs of the situation. Leadership here, simply stated, is providing the motivation, instruction, and assistance that will enable a subordinate to be productive and fulfilled. A new employee in an uncertain situation with hazy performance guidelines might need directive leadership, while a long-term employee performing a familiar task might be better served by the supportive approach. The leader must change his or her method of dealing with subordinates based upon the conditions present.

Look back at the Ted Gunderson case. We bet that Rudy Grantham, as a struggling new foreman, may need a directive approach, while Ralph Cannister, the experienced employee with high goals, may respond best to the achievement-oriented style that Gunderson appears to be using. No wonder Cannister is so much more satisfied that Grantham.

Flexible Leadership—Adapting the Appropriate Leadership Style to a Situation

By now you may be saying to yourself, "That's a lot of theories! Sure, they all suggest a need for flexibility in leadership style, but how do I put them together to form a basis for MY style?" Let's talk about that!

The leader wanting to use flexible leadership will be confronted with two major challenges. First, the leader must determine the type of leadership

Table 10–3 Types of Path-Goal Leadership with Appropriate Conditions for Use

Leadership Type	Description	Appropriate Time for Usage	Inappropriate Time for Usage
Directive or initiating	Planning, organizing, structure controlling, and coordination of subordinate activities.	When task is ambiguous and procedures and policies are unclear or conflicting.	When task, procedures, and policies are clear.
Supportive	Considering the needs of subordinates; displaying concern for the subordinates' well-being, status and comfort; and creating a friendly, pleasant environment.	When work is stressful or dissatisfying.	When work is satisfying and conditions are good.
Participative	Sharing information, power, and influence between supervisors and subordinates. Treating subordinates as equals, allowing them to influence the leader's decisions.	When tasks are ego involving, where subordinates are independent and nonauthoritarian involved.	When subordinates are not ego involved.
Achievement-oriented	Setting challenging goals, expecting high performance, showing confidence in subordinates, seeking continually for improved performance.	When individuals are working on ambiguous, non-repetitive tasks.	When goals are clearly defined and subordinates are self-motivating.

Source: Adapted from Alan C. Filley, Robert J. House, and Steven Kerr, *Managerial Process and Organizational Behavior,* Glenview, Ill.: Scott-Foresman, 1976.

needed in a specific situation. This determination will come through analysis of the prevailing circumstances. Second, the leader will be required to adjust his or her style to fit the present needs, or according to Fiedler, the leader must be replaced with the appropriate type of person if the leader's own personal style doesn't match the situation.

The analytical process involves a number of questions regarding decisions. Let's suppose for the moment that we have decided that there are three styles of leadership to which we've given primary attention. There is the autocratic leadership, which is a very direct, close type of supervision. With autocratic leadership, the leader makes decisions without input from anyone else. The second style of leader—the participative leader—consults with others before making a decision. The third—the delegative leader—delegates the authority to and places the responsibility on someone else for carrying out the decision. (See Figure 10–3).

Figure 10–3

Autocratic,
Participative, and
Delegative
Leadership Styles

Autocratic Leader

"Look, I'm the boss around here. I'll make the decisions and I'll tell you what I want you to do. You'd better do your job because I'll be watching your every move."

Participative Leader

"I'm sure you understand that the final responsibility for making a decision is mine, but I'd like your thoughts and ideas. I'd like your help in the implementation of the decision once it's been made."

Delegative Leader

"Here's a job for you to do. Do it any way you want to so long as it gets done. I'll expect to hear from you only when you are experiencing unusual difficulties."

Determining Leadership Needs

By combining the questions raised in the situational theories and those from the decision tree along with the ideas from the path-goal theory, it is possible to develop a fairly comprehensive evaluation to determine appropriate leadership needs. The combination of questions results in a set of materials in four major categories: (1) factors in the organization, (2) factors in the leader-supervisor, (3) factors in the subordinates, and (4) task situation.

The factors chosen represent four significant influences upon the appropriateness of a leadership style. Factors within the organization provide the framework for all supervisory action. Factors within the leader-supervisor

Emergencies are a good example of circumstances calling for autocratic leadership. Urgency rules out the time for participative leadership and the need for coordination doesn't allow for complete delegation.

recognize the effects of the leader's own abilities, attitudes, and goals upon superior-subordinate relations. Factors within the subordinates reflect the needs of the subordinates for large or small amounts of direction and control. Factors in the task situation explore the effects of job complexity and the time element upon leadership decisions.

The four major factors are shown in Table 10–4, and a list of questions probing for clues to the proper choice is shown beneath each factor. The three leadership styles are then tested against the questions to find the conditions under which that leadership style is most appropriate, other things being equal.

To illustrate the appropriate adaptation of the right leadership style to the right situation, a review of the factors in Table 10–4 indicates that autocratic leadership is the appropriate style when there is a set of conditions in which the subordinates lack knowledge of the company goals and objectives, where the company endorses fear and punishment as acceptable disciplinary techniques, where the workers are inexperienced and somewhat lacking in training, and where there is little room for error in the final performance. These conditions, other things being equal, would suggest the appropriateness of rather strong, autocratic leadership to provide the needed force, direction, and control.

Participative leadership might be more appropriate under conditions in which the company has communicated its goals and objectives to the subordinates and the subordinates have accepted them, where the company practices the use of rewards and involvement as the primary means of motivation and control, where the leader-supervisor truly desires to hear the ideas of others before making decisions, where the leader wishes to develop analytical and self-control abilities in subordinates, where workers are reasonably knowledgeable and experienced, where subordinates desire involvement in matters that affect them, and where the time for task completion allows for participation. If other conditions are relatively neutral, these conditions would suggest the appropriateness of the participative style in meeting existing demands. Of the various leadership patterns available to managers, we can guess that idealistically, the participative approach is probably the most popular. It continues to generate a significant amount of study and support.[19]

The delegative style of leadership would seem to be most appropriate under conditions in which company goals have been thoroughly communicated and are highly acceptable to those who must abide by them. In fact, the company's goals and the employees' goals need to be highly compatible. In addition, delegative leadership is most appropriate when the leader desires to delegate decision making fully, when the leader has a high degree of confidence in the abilities of his or her employees, when the employees themselves are will trained and highly knowledgeable concerning their jobs and are willing to assume responsibility for decision making and self-control, when the employees have a high need for independence, when the workers derive large amounts of personal satisfaction from their work, and where performance demands allow some room for error if mistakes occur in the rather decentralized arrangement. Under these conditions, where workers are highly competent and self-motivated and organizational conditions are nearly ideal, delegative leadership may be utilized most successfully.

Table 10–4 Factors and Primary Determinants in the Selection of the Appropriate Leadership Style

Factors in the Selection of a Leadership Style	Leadership Style		
	Autocratic Leadership	Participative Leadership	Delegative Leadership
Factors in the Organization			
1. How clearly are organizational goals defined?	Clear definition is is helpful.	Clear definition is a requisite.	Clear definition is a requisite.
2. How thoroughly have goals been communicated to subordinates?	May or may not have been communicated.	Must be communicated rather thoroughly.	Must be thoroughly communicated.
3. How adequate are formal communication channels? Are both upward and downward channels provided for?	Downward channels are definitely provided for.	Two-way communication is provided for and encouraged.	Two-way communication is provided for but used infrequently.
4. Does company philosophy support the predominant use of (1) fear? (2) threats? (3) punishment? (4) rewards? (5) involvement?	Mostly 1, 2, and 3 are encouraged.	Mostly 4 and 5 are used.	4, 5, and sometimes 3 are used.
5. How wide is the normal span of supervision and control?	Is usually narrow.	Must be moderately narrow.	Can be wide.
Factors in the Leader-Manager			
1. What are the leader's inclinations in terms of communicating to, listening to, and emphathizing with employees?	Tends to be somewhat self-centered.	Is keenly aware of and interested in employees.	Tends to observe only highlights and trouble spots.
2. What are the leader's attitudes toward involvement in decision making?	Prefers own decisions to decisions of others.	Wants ideas from others before deciding.	Prefers to let others make decisions on their own.
3. What degree of confidence and trust does the leader have in the abilities and knowledge of his or her subordinates?	Has a questionable amount.	Has a reasonably high degree.	Has a high degree.
4. How knowledgeable is the leader concerning decisions that must be performed?	Must be highly knowledgeable.	May be moderately to highly knowledge-able.	May or may not be knowledgeable.
5. How important to the leader is the development of analytical skills and self-control abilities in the subordinates?	Is unimportant.	Is important.	Is highly important.

Table 10–4   *continued*

Factors in the Selection of a Leadership Style	Leadership Style		
	Autocratic Leadership	*Participative Leadership*	*Delegative Leadership*

Factors in the Subordinates

	Autocratic Leadership	Participative Leadership	Delegative Leadership
1. To what degree do subordinates accept the goals of the company, and how loyal are they to these goals?	Accepted to a questionable degree in both areas.	Some degree of acceptance and loyalty is evidenced.	High degree of acceptance and loyalty is essential.
2. Do the subordinates have a relatively high need for independence?	No, they prefer dependence.	At least moderately, yes.	Yes.
3. Are the subordinates willing to assume responsibility for decision making and self-control?	May not be willing.	Should be at least moderately willing.	Must be willing.
4. How much personal satisfaction do workers derive from the performance of their jobs?	A questionable degree is derived.	A moderate to high degree is attained.	A high degree is achieved.
5. Are the subordinates well trained, knowledgeable, and experienced at their work?	Usually are not.	Yes, from a moderate to high degree.	Yes, they must be of necessity.
6. Have the subordinates shared in decision making and control processes previously?	Probably not much.	Probably, to some degree.	Yes, they should be well acquainted with decision making and control responsibilities.
7. Are the subordinates' personal goals and objectives compatible with those of the organization?	Questionably so.	Normally this is necessary.	Yes, this is essential.
8. Do subordinates have mutually positive respect for each other?	May or may not have any.	Yes, this is very helpful.	Yes, this is vital.

Factors in the Task Situation

	Autocratic Leadership	Participative Leadership	Delegative Leadership
1. How much room for error is there in the task to be accomplished?	Little or no room available.	Is limited to moderate amount.	Moderate amount is possible.
2. How much time is available for making decisions and completing tasks?	Very little is available.	A moderate to large amount of time is available.	(Not applicable)
3. How important are new ideas and innovations to the successful task completion?	Is considered unimportant.	Is thought to be important.	Is felt to be very important.

The individual leader-supervisor who is to be proficient in the application of leadership styles must be well informed on organizational policies, plans, and structures that influence the choice of style. The adaptive leader must practice introspection to discern his or her own inclinations, desires, and motivations. The leader must also be keenly empathetic to the needs, desires, abilities, and knowledge of the subordinates being led. The leader must be able to size up task situation factors that might influence a subordinate's need for leadership.

The use of adaptive leadership becomes a demanding yet interesting challenge to the conscientious leader. Adaptive leadership demands much from the leader, both perceptively and actively, but the results of such efforts are beneficial to the leader, the employees, and the company. Each human aspect of the organization receives the proper amount of attention and guidance when adaptive leadership is practiced.

The Problem of Consistency

In applying adaptive leadership, the leader often finds it necessary to change approaches in dealing with certain followers. This shift in leadership approaches ordinarily is effective in accomplishing its purposes, but the use of this flexible approach may sometimes cause confusion and misunderstanding. Worker A may believe that his or her leader is erratic when autocratically supervising him or her in an emergency and then later in the same day giving the worker a free hand to do as he or she pleases on a less urgent

Some leadership situations require over-the-shoulder support. Employee and task situations may be keys to choosing this type of leadership action.

W. Graham Claytor of Amtrack

In a day when some say there's no place for strong disciplining and somewhat autocratic leadership, the head of Amtrack is proving the naysayers wrong. Amtrack's head, W. Graham Claytor, eight years ago was called from retirement from the Southern Railway to provide direction and control of the nation's passenger system. At the time Claytor took over Amtrack, the federal government was subsidizing the system at $896 million annually which accounted for 52 percent of Amtrack's operating costs. Most recent figures under Claytor's leadership show federal subsidizing at $604 million covering only 28 percent of costs.

Claytor's approach to leadership is completely hands on. He rides the rails himself, investigates and inspects every facet of each train's condition and performance, and writes scathing reports to managers when he feels the reports are needed. One vice president says "Mr. Claytor leads by being vociferously demanding, and he doesn't hesitate to chew people out." Others say, "Claytor is an arrogant aristocrat . . . he runs Amtrack like the military, and that's a morale killer."

Claytor now has employees working forty hours a week for full pay where previously workers would get a full day's pay for traveling only a hundred miles.

Claytor defends his tough discipline by saying that in his opinion, a railroad system is like a military organization and must be run like one. Compliance to rules is absolutely essential.

It's possible that the day will come where federal subsidation of Amtrack will no longer be necessary. And that day may not be far into the future.

Source: Daniel Machalaba, "Stern Boss of Amtrack Pushes to Wean Line of Federal Subsidies," *Wall Street Journal*, April 5, 1990, pp. A1 and A8.

project. Worker B may feel unfairly treated when the boss gives a free rein to one of the worker's colleagues, Worker C, and then spells out in detail what worker B must do in performing his or her own tasks.

Changes in leadership style when dealing with one specific employee usually are a result of change in the task. The factors involved in the leader, the employee, and the organizational setting tend to remain more constant. Task changes may result from modifications in the tolerance of errors, the amount of time available to act, or the need for creative thinking. If the task changes, the leader might be well advised to inform the worker of the change before modifying the leadership style. For example, when supervisor A finds it necessary to retract the freedom given to an employee because of time, it would be helpful to inform the employee by saying, "John, you know I normally would have discussed this with you before taking action. But I had to tell our customer what we could do for her while I was talking to her on the phone. I had to make a decision before talking with you." Most subordinates will accept changes in leadership exercised toward them if the modifications are explained adequately and appear to be reasonable.

The use of different leadership styles simultaneously toward different employees is a more difficult problem to handle. Supposedly, the change is not made necessary by organizational factors or leader-supervisor factors, which remain fairly constant. If there is a need for a variation of the leadership style applied to two different subordinates, factors regarding the task and the subordinates usually account for the style change. In analyzing our opening case, we've suggested that Ted Gunderson might need to use a more directive approach with Rudy Grantham than with Ralph Cannister based largely on Grantham's inexperience. Abilities and motivation also enter in. If a supervisor has little confidence in the abilities of a worker and the project must be completed without error, the supervisor might become highly autocratic. If, on the other hand, the leader has high confidence in a worker and the performance level is flexible, a more participative style might be used.

Some workers recognize the leadership they are receiving as the kind of leadership they need to get their work done. In such situations, the difference between the leadership style applied to them and that applied to other workers may be quite acceptable. However, a worker who feels unfairly treated or discriminated against by the unequal leadership actions of his or her superior might develop concern or resentment.

Some recent work does suggest that workers are well aware of differences in supervisory behavior toward different people. It is known for example, that employees the boss treats as part of the "in crowd" are the recipients of more assistance, more patience, more open communication, more responsible tasks, and so forth. People the boss treats as part of the "out group" on the other hand, receive no more attention than is absolutely required by the job. These employees must literally protect themselves and their rights.[20]

If a worker is unhappy because the boss seems more autocratic with him or her than with other workers, the leader should sense this and help the subordinate to understand the reasons for the difference in treatment. If the difference is related to task factors, the communication of this fact may resolve the employee's unhappiness. If the reason for the difference is a factor within the employee, the leader may be able to point out that the employee who is given more freedom of movement has won freedom on the basis of long years of experience, concentrated effort to develop skills, or other factors of merit. The worker in question can be encouraged to devote efforts in the same way if he or she wishes to attain greater autonomy. A typical leadership reaction in this situation might be, "Susan has performed this task so many times she can almost do it backwards. She doesn't need my assistance. As you repeat the job, you'll be the same way, and I'll not stick as close to you, either."

If the worker, on the other hand, feels neglected because the boss does not give him or her as much attention and help as the supervisor gives to others, the leader-supervisor may be able to point out that the worker is believed to be capable of directing self. Assurance should be given that the supervisor is interested in the worker and stands ready to help when needed. Look at Rudy Grantham's reaction in our opening case for an example of what can happen when employees feel that their manager is neglecting them!

Other problems may also develop in the application of leadership techniques, but with effort the problems can be overcome. Leadership techniques and styles properly applied are a major factor in the success or failure of organizational achievement. Adaptive leadership is an invaluable aid in the accomplishment of organizational objectives.

Summary

This chapter has gone through several schools of thought concerning leaders and what they should do in organizations. The contemporary view seems to embrace the situational approach in particular. From this view, it is the leader's responsibility to analyze the factors present in each set of circumstances. From the analysis, the appropriate leadership actions can be determined. Fiedler says to look at leader-members relations, task structure, and position power. By using these factors, a decision can be made about the use of task-oriented or relationship-oriented behavior. Vroom and Yetton formulate a more lengthy list of eight considerations guiding toward selection of autocratic, consultative, or group leadership. Path-goal leadership uses the clarity of task definition, the ego-involvement of the subordinates, the repetitive nature of tasks, and the level of a subordinate's motivation along with other clues to determine whether directive, supportive, participative, or achievement-oriented leadership is needed. It is possible to develop an analytical grid to evaluate the leadership needs.

Fiedler would suggest changing leaders to fit situational requirements. Other models would call for the leader to adjust his or her technique to fit the circumstances. Most models suggest the value of consistent treatment of employees.

The idea that leadership is providing an employee with the support, information, and guidance to do the job effectively seems pertinent. Some workers, of course, need lots of support, while others need very little.

Questions to Consider

1. Why is it that some individuals with seemingly attractive leadership qualities are not leaders? In other words, why aren't some people who seem to possess leadership qualifications not in leadership capacities?
2. Is it possible for individuals who are not leaders to develop skills and attributes so that they can become leaders?
3. What are your own preferred styles of providing leadership for others?
4. What leadership preferences do you have for receiving support and guidance from others?
5. Is it realistic to believe that an individual can change his or her own style of leadership to meet the needs of a specific situation? Why or why not?
6. How can an appropriate level of consistency be achieved in the face of a need for adaptability and flexibility?
7. Is it ethical to treat people differently, that is, to give individuals different directions, rewards, punishments, and so forth? Why or why not?

Key Terms

behavior theories
    of leadership
leadership
    approaches
    or style

leadership grid®
nine-nine (9,9)
    leadership
situational
    leadership

system 4
trait approach

Chapter Case

Seeing Through Things in Radiology

Upon graduation, you go to work in the personnel department of a large hospital in the area. You immediately learn that your boss is frustrated and unhappy. You ask why.

"You have no idea what this job is like!" the boss responds.

It's always a bad situation being in personnel—you've got all of the problems but none of the power to do anything about them. But this is ridiculous. Those radiologists are going to drive me crazy!

Naturally, you ask what's going on. The boss responds:

I'll tell you what. Why don't you go over to the Radiology Department and see for yourself? They have a departmental thing this morning, and the department head has asked me to come over and try to straighten things out. I'll call him and tell him that I'm tied up but that I'm sending you instead. Maybe a fresh view point will help—and at least it will give you a chance to try out some of those wild ideas about organizational behavior that you picked up at school.

You arrive at Radiology and are taken to the office of Edward Ogden, the department head.

"I hope you can give me some ideas," he says, shaking his head in despair. "I just don't know what to do next."

Again, you ask what the problem is.

"It's the people," Ogden responds.

You have to realize that radiologists are all prima donnas. They're extremely smart or they would never have gotten out of medical school. But they just don't have any human relations skills. They fight with everyone in the hospital—the other doctors, the nurses, the staff, and each other. And as far as trying to manage them goes—well, forget that. Anytime I try to give them any orders at all, they simply refuse—they say that they're bound by the Hippocratic Oath they took to practice medicine according to dictates of their consciences and that no one else can tell them what to do. Imagine trying to manage in a mess like that!

You ask for some background on how the department is set up, how it operates, and what it does. Ogden explains that there are twelve radiologists in the department and that Pat Burns is the informal lead person. Pat has been in the department longest and has the most outstanding reputation—in fact, Pat is often out of the office and the area consulting on tricky cases or giving speeches at conventions and meetings. Pat is supposed to make assignments to remaining staff members and be available to consult with them. In Pat's absence, assignments either aren't made or are informally split up by the group members themselves. Considerable confusion and animosity results.

"Why don't you step in and give direction in Pat's absence?" you ask Ogden.

Ogden responds:

That's part of the problem. You have to remember that I've been in administration for years. My skills simply aren't state of the art any more. I'm not really in a position to be of help in technical areas. Worse yet, we're in an extremely dynamic situation here. The hospital gets all of the most advanced and problem-filled cases, and the doctors are continually overworked just trying to stay up with the patient load and to keep up professionally.

Obviously, there is a problem with leadership in this situation.

1. How would researchers like Likert and Blake and McCanse analyze this situation? What would they recommend? Discuss their theories, comparing and contrasting them. Show specifically how each would work.
2. What would the situational theorists, especially Fiedler, Vroom-Yetton, and the path-goal model say about this specific situation? Again, be specific and draw on the theories.
3. What, then, are your suggestions to help Edward Ogden?

Interpersonal Communications

11. Communicating Concepts and Information

12. Counseling Employees

13. Managing Conflict

Chapter
11

Communicating Concepts and Information

Objectives

- To identify the contributions made by effective organization communication.
- To consider the optimal conditions and circumstances for good communication.
- To study the communication process.
- To clarify managerial responsibilities for each step of the communication process.
- To identify problem areas in the communication process and to consider solutions and alternatives.
- To discuss methods for the selection of communication media.
- To learn how to be assertive for the benefit of everyone.
- To consider the actions, methods, and purposes of the communication grapevine.

Communication Policies at Central Food

Central Food Processing Corporation is a young, diversified processor and distributor of agricultural products for human consumption. The company has been in business only two years. It purchases raw food materials, processes them to fit the needs of the consumer, packages the finished products for the customer's convenience, and distributes the products to wholesalers and retailers.

At the beginning, the organization was small and had a limited number of personnel. The management of the corporation did not feel it was necessary to draft a long list of detailed policies and procedures, because most policies could be spread by word of mouth when necessary. Also, it was felt that there would be more flexibility in handling policies if the policies were oral rather than written. However, with the tremendous growth in the company during the two years it has been operating, management now feels that more written policies are necessary. Accordingly, new statements of policy are periodically distributed in memorandum form to all supervisory personnel. The supervisors are expected to inform their employees of the policy through whatever means they feel is appropriate. A few days ago, the company issued the following statement of policy concerning disciplinary action:

> Disciplinary action shall be taken by supervisors for just cause whenever necessary. Each supervisor shall be certain to establish that the worker to be disciplined has actually committed an offense worthy of a penalty before the penalty is applied. Whenever possible, four steps shall be followed in disciplining a worker. First, the worker shall be given an oral warning following the first commission of a mistake. Second, if the poor behavior continues, the worker shall be given a written warning that future errors will result in the application of serious penalties. Third, if no improvement in performance is evidenced, a penalty such as a disciplinary layoff without pay will be implemented. Finally, if no change in behavior is exhibited, discharge will occur. All of the preliminary steps may be bypassed in the case of serious offenses such as fighting or actions that endanger the health and safety of other workers.

The company director of personnel is curious to know the reactions of supervisors and their employees to the new policy statement. He circulates through the plant interviewing different people to see what they think of the policy. He gets a variety of reactions. From one supervisor, he hears:

> I think this is what we've needed for a long time. This new policy gives me the authority to knuckle down on some guys that have been getting away with murder. I try to run a tight ship. I want my workers to know who is the boss. With this policy in effect, I'm going to give some people written warnings in the next day or two. I should be able to discharge some poor workers pretty soon.

Another supervisor has these comments:

The policy statement doesn't give me much help. From what it says, I don't really know when I'm supposed to give a written warning or when I'm supposed to deal out a penalty. And I don't know how severe a penalty should be. This only seems to complicate my job. I could use some help in interpreting the policy, but nobody has offered any.

A worker (a nonsupervisor) with a history of work infractions (for which he already has been disciplined) has this to say:

Well, I haven't actually seen the policy statement, but my boss said that I'd better be on my toes from here on because he has the company's okay to fire me if I do anything wrong again. I feel like I'm pretty well under the gun. I'm kinda shook up about it all.

Another worker (a nonsupervisor) with a good work record (and in another department) makes this statement:

I've read the statement, and it seems fine to me. As long as I do my job, I've got nothing to be afraid of. I've got a good boss, one who treats me well. I personally feel the policy is a protection for me.

The director of personnel is struck by the diversity of reactions to the new policy statement. It appears to him as if the four individuals interviewed have been looking at four different policy statements instead of the single one issued by his office.

Case Questions

1. To what factors do you attribute the different reactions to the policy statement? Take each individual who was interviewed and analyze the causes for his or her reaction.
2. Analyze the way in which policy statements were introduced to the workers. What problem areas exist in the communication methods?
3. What steps could the company take to improve its methods of communicating important matters such as policy statements?
4. Someone has said the distortion of communication messages is likely to occur when there are intermediaries who relay messages from one individual to another. What situation in this case supports this statement?
5. What lessons can be learned about interpersonal communications from this case?

Providing the proper leadership, determining the appropriate incentives to appeal to employees' motives, and giving careful attention to workers' morale are essential responsibilities of ever manager. Another important duty of every manager is to see that there is an efficient exchange of ideas, information, and knowledge among all individuals who work together.

One of the most vital activities in an organization is the **communication** of ideas between individuals as they interrelate with each other. When people communicate, they are exchanging messages upon which action can be taken. Communication has sometimes been defined as the transferring of a mental concept from the brain of one individual to the brain of another. Communication can occur between two or more people anywhere. This book is mostly concerned with the communication that takes place between people in the work setting.

communication
The transfer of a mental concept from the brain of one person to the brain of another.

What Communicating Does

Proper interpersonal communication does a great deal for the people who make up work organizations. Lee Thayer, for example, divides the purposes or functions of organizational communication into four specific categories: (1) the information function, (2) the command and instruction function, (3) the influence and persuasion function, and (4) the integrative function.[1]

The Information Function

The **information function** serves to provide knowledge to the individuals needing it for guidance in their work. The information function also fulfills workers' desires for awareness of things that affect them. Employees are hungry for information about anything that is related to their job.

Employees want to know about their company—its background and present organization. They want to know what its products are—how they're made and where they go. They are interested in knowing what the company's policies are—especially new policies—as the policies affect them and their fellow workers. They are concerned about the reasons for changes in methods, and they are interested in information about new products. They want this information in advance. They are eager to learn what is expected of them and how they are measuring up. They want to know what the outlook is for the business and what their prospects are for steady work. They are interested in knowing about profits and losses. Should circumstances make layoffs necessary, employees want as much advance notice as possible, and they want to know the reasons for the layoffs and how they might be affected.

Look back at the Central Food case that opened this chapter. Notice that one function that was *intended* (regardless of how effective it may or may not have been!) by the policy statement was to give information to supervisors and employees about how the company wanted to handle discipline of its employees.

information function
One of the purposes of communication provides knowledge to individuals, including data concerning jobs, the organization, and other related materials.

The Command and Instruction Function

The **command and instruction function** serves to make employees aware of their obligations to the formal organization and to provide additional guidance and assistance on how to correctly perform their duties. Greenbaum, in speaking of what he calls the informative-instructive function, stresses that this function's importance lies in helping not only each worker individually but

command and instruction function
A function of communication that makes an employee aware of his or her obligation to the organization.

also the organization collectively. Higher performances, better morale, greater adaptability, and increased effectiveness result as people learn more about what is expected of them.[2] Most of this type of communication appears to flow downward in the organization. In the Central Foods case, the second supervisor apparently believes that this is the purpose of the policy statement. Furthermore, the supervisor's comment, "The policy statement doesn't give me much help," suggests that for that particular supervisor, the policy statement isn't performing its intended function.

The Influence and Persuasion Function

influence and persuasion function
One of the purposes of communication primarily known as motivation, used to encourage individuals to perform or behave in specific ways.

The **influence and persuasion function** is sometimes known as the motivational function because its main purpose is to encourage the appropriate individuals to perform or exhibit a certain behavior. Messages communicated are used to convince individuals that their actions can be personally or organizationally beneficial, or perhaps both.[3] In the Central Foods case, the supervisor of the employee who has made previous errors may have been trying to use the policy statement as the basis of an influence and persuasion communication with this employee. Was the communication successful?

The Integrative Function

integrative function
The purpose of communication used to relate the activities of workers so that they complement rather than detract from one another.

The **integrative function** of communication refers to the fact that the communication of messages and ideas, if handled properly, should help to relate the activities of the workers so that their efforts complement rather than detract from one another. Work efforts are unified rather than fragmented as a result of properly integrative communication.[4] Take another look at the Central Foods case. Clearly, the director of personnel had hoped that the policy would unify and integrate the supervisors' approaches to discipline. Was the communication a success?

The Innovation Function

innovation function
The purpose of communication intending to help the organization and its members to adapt to internal and external influences as they occur.

To this list of communication functions, at least one other can be added—the **innovation function.** This is the communication duty that works to ensure that the organization can adjust to various internal and external influences (such as those from technology, society, education, economics, and politics). This function is concerned with problemsolving, adaptation to change, and the processing of new ideas.[5] Notice, for example, in the Central Foods case, that the switchover to written policies is part of the organization's effort to adapt to changes brought about by the recent tremendous growth.

The Perfect Organizational Communication Situation

Within Likert's System 4—the rather idealistic kind of organization mentioned in Chapter 10—are some "perfect" conditions for communication within an organization. The four considerations Likert mentioned for effective communi-

Table 11–1

Characteristics of an
Ideal Organizational
Communication
System

1. Three-directional communication that moves downward, upward, and sideways throughout the organization.
2. Downward communication that is accepted with an open mind by those receiving it.
3. Upward communication that is accurate.
4. Superiors (supervisors) who know very well the problem faced by their employees.
5. The things people communicate to each other are for the benefit of everyone, not just one person or a few people.
6. Employees, peers, and bosses communicate what others need to know in order to perform effectively, not just what they want to know.
7. Problem areas and subjects where there are differences of opinion that are identified and handled rather than avoided and swept under the rug.
8. People receive and interpret messages in such a way that the intended meaning is given to the message.
9. Individuals receive feedback regularly so that they know results of their efforts.
10. Information arrives for recipients when it is needed rather than before or after it is needed.

Source: Some of the components were derived from Rensis Likert, *New Patterns of Management,* New York: McGraw-Hill, 1961, pp. 225–227.

cation are added to other characteristics to describe a model for communication. The workplace where these factors are present would be an open, stimulating environment (see Table 11–1).

While perfection in communication is impossible to attain, it is useful to recognize what ideal communication would look like. With the ideas mentioned in mind, we can envision what is desirable and strive for the best possible levels of performance. The closer we come to the ideal, the better will be our results in a number of areas. Let's now turn to a brief description of the communication process, after which we'll look at stumbling blocks to ideal communication. Finally, we will consider methods for achieving better communication performance.

The Communication Process

There are many phases to the communication process.[6] The model in Figure 11–1 illustrates the many steps in the complete communication process.

Deciding on the Message

The **sender** begins the communication process by recognizing the need to convey a message to someone else. The sender has information guidelines, motivational material, or coordinative concepts that may be important to the **receiver.**

sender
The person in an organization who begins the communication process by issuing symbols with meaning.

receiver
The person in the organization who takes in a message issued by the sender in the communication process.

Figure 11–1   Model of Purposeful Communication

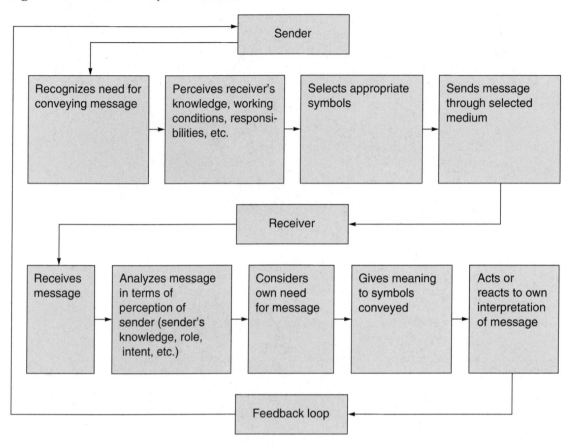

Analysis of the Receiver

As the sender plans the message, he or she considers the knowledge that the receiver has of the subject matter to be communicated, the working conditions of the receiver, the job responsibilities of the receiver, and other background information. Look again at the Central Foods case at the beginning of the chapter. Notice that each receiver of the information has a *different* background. Did the personnel director *plan* the message to take this into consideration?

Choice of Symbols

The sender analyzes the receiver to determine the meaning that the message will have as it is received and interpreted. People communicate through symbols. Words, gestures, expressions, etc., are all symbols in the communication process, although we aren't always accustomed to thinking of them in this way. As a result, the sender must anticipate the meaning a symbol may have for the receiver and choose the symbol that will best be interpreted in the way the sender intends. Thus, the sender looks for clues that will help gauge the receiver's interpretation; the appropriate symbol is then communicated. This is often called the **encoding** process.

Groups of individuals sometimes develop their own unique set of symbols or language—known as jargon—for communicating. Jargon generally lacks meaning for outsiders. To airline pilots, for example, to "grease a landing" is to make a smooth arrival. A "pudknocker" is a beginning pilot who doesn't have an instrument rating. "Sky Goddesses" are female flight attendants, and "Sky Mama" is the lead female flight attendant. Boeing 727s are "three-holers" (three engines), Boeing 747s are "whales," and Boeing 757s are "Coleco cruisers" as a result of their electronic flight systems.[7]

If you were a youth during the late 1980s to early 1990s, you may know what a "bowhead" or a "Clydesdale" or a "Bifftad" or a "dweeb" is. A bowhead is a girl who wears ribbons in her hair. A Clydesdale is a good looking guy. A Bifftad is a preppy boy (these boys are often named Biff or Tad). A dweeb is a nerd or a geek (terms from an earlier era).[8]

When communication is simple and only one message needs sending, the encoding process is simple. When more than one message needs forwarding, the encoding process becomes complex and time consuming as symbol selection and sequencing are accomplished.[9]

Sometimes our symbol selection is subconscious, particularly in nonverbal message sending. We even send message when we don't speak. Body language conveys a message just as surely as a spoken word. As Table 11–2 shows, such actions as rolling the eyes, deep sighing, and continuing to read a report when someone is talking can convey messages—messages that often are not very positive.[10]

encoding
The process where the sender of a message selects symbols to communicate to the receiver so that a message will be interpreted correctly.

Selection of Medium

Selection of the proper medium through which to send the message is the next step. Lengel and Daft have said that the truly good communicator is not the best speaker or the best writer, but the person who knows how to select the right medium (channel or instrument) through which to communicate. The key is to select the medium with the right degree of richness. A rich medium is the one through which the most learning can be accomplished. A lean medium, on the other hand is one where only bare information is given without any help.[11]

Richness of a communication medium can be determined by analyzing the medium's ability to handle multiple information cues simultaneously, facilitate rapid feedback, and establish a personal focus. As Figure 11–2 on page 259 shows, the communication medium with the highest level of richness is the physically present (face-to-face) communication. Interactive media such as telephone conversations come next. Personal, static media, such as letters, memoranda, and reports, come next. The media with the least richness—the impersonal, static type, including bulletins, flyers, and generalized reports—come last. Learning, in other words, occurs best in direct, personal message giving.

Lengel and Daft declare four rules for matching media richness to the communication situation:

1. Send nonroutine messages through a rich medium (such as face-to-face).

Table 11–2

Nonverbal Cues
and Their Effects

Nonverbal Communication	Signal Received	Reaction from Receiver
Manager looks away when talking to the employee.	I do not have this person's undivided attention.	Supervisor is too busy to listen to my problem or simply does not care.
Failure to acknowledge greeting from fellow employee.	This person is unfriendly.	This person is unapproachable.
Ominous glaring (i.e., the evil eye)	I am angry.	Reciprocal anger, fear, or avoidance, depending on who in the organization is sending the signal.
Rolling of the eyes.	I am not being taken seriously.	This person thinks he or she is smarter or better than I am.
Deep sighing.	Disgust or displeasure.	My opinions do not count. I must be stupid or boring to this person.
Heavy breathing (sometimes accompanied by hand waving).	Anger or heavy stress.	Avoid this person at all costs.
Eye contact not maintained when communicating.	Suspicion and/or uncertainty.	What does this person have to hide?
Manager crosses arms and leans away.	Apathy and closed mindedness.	This person already has made up his or her mind; my opinions are not important.
Manager peers over glasses.	Skepticism or distrust.	He or she does not believe what I am saying.
Continuing to read when employee is speaking.	Lack of interest.	My opinions are not important enough to get the supervisor's undivided attention.

Source: Michael G. Barton, "Manage Words Effectively," *Personnel Journal*, Volume 69, Number 1, © January 1990, p. 36. Reprinted with permission from *Personnel Journal*, Costa Mesa, California. All rights reserved.

2. Send routine, simple messages through a lean medium.
3. Use rich media to extend your presence throughout the organization.
4. Use rich media for implementing company strategy.[12]

The general rule is to apply rich media in nonroutine situations and lean media in highly routine situations.

The computer is becoming more and more of a communication medium. Computer communication is rapid and serves as an excellent method to gath-

Media
Richness

Highest

↑ Physical presence
   (face-to-face)
Interactive media
   (telephone, etc.)
Personal, static media
   (memos, letters, reports)
Impersonal, static media
   (flyers, bulletins,
     generalized reports)
↓

Lowest

Figure 11–2

Matching Media Richness to Communication Situation

Source: Robert H. Lengel and Richard L. Daft, "The Selection of Communication Media as an Executive Skill," *Academy of Management Executive,* Volume 2, Number 3, August 1988.

er, synthesize, organize, monitor, and disseminate messages. On the richness scale just discussed, computers have the potential to be rich or lean, depending on how they are used.[13] A message sent from one person to another through the computer would be a rich message, since the communication occurs directly through the computer. Simultaneously communicating the same message through the computer to one hundred different people would be communicated in a lean manner.

Receiver Responsibilities

After the symbol is sent, the burden of interpretation and action then is placed upon the receiver. The receiver takes the message and attempts to discover its meaning by analyzing the sender and his or her intent by looking at the

Telephone communication, while not face-to-face, is still a rich communication medium.

sender's role, knowledge, experience, and authority. The receiver also considers his or her own need for the message and the message's significance. The receiver places meaning on the symbols conveyed and acts or reacts to the message as it has been interpreted. This is called **decoding.** Feedback is then given to the sender in the form of another message, an action, or a body motion or through some other method of communication.

decoding
The process by which the receiver of a message takes the symbols communicated and gives meaning to them.

Responsibility for Clear Communication of Messages

Most of the time we tend to think of communication as a simple matter. How often have you heard people say things like, "Of course John knows how to do that—I just told him how!" But the model we've just reviewed suggests that communication is much more complex than most people realize, and in a work environment, it's a process where heavy responsibility falls on the manager. Only the correct interpretation of messages will be useful. Faulty interpretation will often cause more harm than good. If the supervisor-manager is the sender of messages, he or she must prepare and convey the message so that it can be interpreted as it was intended to be. The manager must also help others know how to communicate so that messages they send will be understood and acted upon properly.

Problems in the Communication Process

Problems in Conveying the Intended Meaning

As the sender communicates a message, several difficulties may get in the way of proper interpretation of the message communicated. Some of the problems are perceptual and psychological; others occur primarily as a result of the specific situation.

The Problem of Filtering

filtering
The action of a receiver in which the receiver hears only what he or she wishes to hear.

Objectivity in receiving and interpreting messages is often difficult to achieve. Receivers have a tendency to hear what they wish to hear in messages directed toward them. The **filtering** of messages occurs both in what the receiver is willing to acknowledge receiving and in the interpretation the receiver gives to the message. Messages that are consistent with the receiver's self-image and provide useful knowledge may be received and interpreted carefully. Messages that threaten self-image or negatively affect desires and expectations may either be ignored or be interpreted in a less threatening way. This may happen in the performance appraisal situation when the message of the appraisal is negative. Let's listen in on the end of a discussion between John, a manager, and Fred, a poorly performing employee:

John: *Fred, I honestly believe you can do the work. And I know you're interested in the job. That's good. But I've got to see those things translated into performance. You simply aren't getting the work out, and I've got to see improvement immediately!*

Fred: *Sure thing, John.*

After the discussion, Fred runs into Sally, a coworker, and this discussion ensues:

Sally: *How'd the appraisal go, Fred?*

Fred: *Not bad! I think the boss is really catching on to what I have to offer. He commended me for my ability and my interest.*

Did Fred hear what he wanted to hear?

The Problem of Distortion

Distortion is another form of message interpretation. It is usually an unintentional manipulation of messages. Distortion is the wrong interpretation of meanings that may result from misleading circumstances or conditions. Distortion frequently occurs, for example, when a message must go through several individuals in order to reach the intended recipient. Anyone who has played the parlor game "Telephone" understands the potential for distortion. As a message is passed through a long chain of individuals, the content and order of the message undergo a transformation.

> **distortion**
> Giving an incorrect meaning to communicated symbols. Is sometimes the result of misleading conditions or circumstances.

The hearing problem is especially compounded when the message is received out of context. Distance between the sender and the receiver normally results in such difficulties. Furthermore, differences in background may enter in. Words may mean different things to different people, depending upon people's past experiences and education. The authors recall a student who had become increasingly fond of big words. "Let's interact!" the student said to a female acquaintance one day. She slapped him vigorously. "I don't do things like that with men I hardly know!" We hope the point is clear. Avoid use of big or impressive sounding words unless you're *sure* your receiver knows what they mean!

Distortions can also occur when the receiver is distracted from the intended message by other noises (symbols without significant form or value). The employee receives many messages while at work. Sometimes messages and rumors pour upon the recipient from all directions—supervisors, employees, and colleagues. Frequently, one source sends out too many messages; some of the messages sent may even appear to be contradictory. Overcommunication may be as much a problem (resulting in distortion) as other sources of difficulty.

Sayles and Strauss say that another form of distortion is exaggeration.[14] With exaggeration, the message is received and then overstated or overreacted to. The message is interpreted to mean more than it really does. Often this results from the perception of the large amount of authority carried by the sender of the messages—particularly a high-level official. We ask ourselves, "What did he or she *really* mean by that?" Then we may add our own interpretation.

Timing as a Problem

On occasion, the stumbling block to the proper interpretation of messages is the fact that the message reaches the receiver at a time when he or she is not ready to utilize the message (it is premature), or the message is too late to be helpful, or the message is received at a time when the receiver is preoccupied with other matters, and the receiver therefore misinterprets the meaning.

The difficulties of receiving messages before or after they are needed are fairly obvious. The more unique problem, however, is the one of sending a message when the receiver has other thoughts in mind. If, for example, a worker is feeling insecure because rumors are flying around that a large number of workers are to be laid off, the boss's request for data concerning that person's performance over the past year may be viewed as a request for data to find grounds for his or her dismissal. The boss, in fact, may have been looking for data to use in considering the employee for a promotion, but the timing has caused the request to be misinterpreted.

Inconsistent Actions and Messages

The receiver's interpretation of messages is significantly influenced by the receiver's perception of and attitude toward the sender. If the sender is consistent, the receiver will find the development of a set of perceptions and attitudes toward the sender much easier than if the sender constantly says one thing and does something different. If the sender appears steady, competent, and knowledgeable, the receiver may learn to respect the information sent and to place high value on receiving it. If the sender appears flighty, erratic, and uncertain, the receiver will come to be apprehensive toward messages received. Even more important may be the consistency of information passed along by the sender. If information is regularly useful and dependable, the receiver learns to trust it and give it attention. If the messages are variable and sometimes inadequate, the receiver becomes skeptical rapidly. The level of confidence in the sender as a result of consistent actions and messages, therefore, has its own impact upon message interpretation.

The discussion of transactional analysis (TA) in Chapter 6 adds another dimension of consistency. According to TA, three personality parts make up the psychological composition of each individual—the parent, the adult, and

complementary transaction
An exchange between two individuals where both parties are correctly aware of the personality parts doing the communicating.

crossed transaction
An exchange between two individuals where the parties involved incorrectly determine the personality part doing the sending, the receiving, or both.

the child. The parent is the guidance-filled part; the adult is the rational, objective part; and the child is the emotional part. Both sender and receiver have the three personality parts at work. If sender and receiver both recognize which part of their personality (parent, adult, or child) is sending or receiving messages, interpretation of each message will be more accurate. When each party is aware of the personality part sending or receiving messages, the **transaction** is said to be **complementary** (see Figure 11–3). When either or both parties expect the other to be communicating from one personality part but other parts are actually used, a **crossed transaction** occurs. Neither sender nor receiver may get what was expected.

Here's an example of a crossed transaction:

Manager (from the adult): *We're going to have to give this proposal some serious consideration.*

Employee (from the child): *Oh, don't be serious about everything. Let's just run through it and get out of here!*

Have these two people really *communicated* about this project?

Complementary transaction

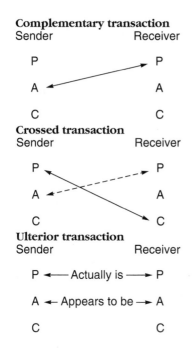

Crossed transaction

Ulterior transaction

sender and receiver are both aware of the parts of the personality being used to send or receive messages.

unexpected parts of the personality are used to send and receive messages.

a hidden agenda exists; one or both parties deliberately hide source of or receiver of communication.

Figure 11–3
The Transactional Analysis View of Communication

Note: P=Parent, A=Adult, C=Child.

When sender or receiver or both purposefully hide the source of sending and receiving messages and a hidden agenda exists, the **transaction** is called **ulterior**. When communication transactions are complementary, messages are more likely to be received openly and objectively. When crossed or ulterior transactions occur, reception is likely to be faulty.

ulterior transaction
An exchange between two individuals where one or both parties deliberately hide personality parts sending and receiving a message.

The Receiver's State of Mind

Running through all of the previously mentioned barriers is the perception the receiver holds of the sender, and vice versa. One of the overall determining

Transactions may occur so rapidly and voluminously that they may be difficult to identify.

factors of the success of communication is the state of mind of those involved. If the participants' minds are optimistic, forward looking, and free of bias, the communication and interpretation of messages will probably be unbiased, objective, and realistic.

Anxiety, as many psychologists call the state of mind where someone is worried and apprehensive, tends to be detrimental to either the sender or the receiver. The sender who is anxious tends to overcommunicate (often including a lot of unnecessary information) or to remain silent when there should be communication. The receiver who is apprehensive tends toward overreaction, distortion, or bias. Individuals may even fail to listen because of tension or mental strain. The individual's mind may be closed to useful receiving and interpretation. You can probably recall times when this has happened to you. When you were anxious, were you as good a sender or receiver as you usually are?

Overcoming Problems of Message Interpretation

The sender of a message has at least partial control over the communication process. As a result, there are several actions that may improve interpretation of and reaction to the messages sent. Following is a list of suggestions to be considered by senders in the communication process:

1. The sender should attempt to remove biases and tensions that may cloud his or her own mind. While it may be impossible to remove them completely, identification and acknowledgement of the existence of personal biases and tensions go a long way in managing the effects they will have. At least they may be compensated for or overcome.

2. Before communicating, the communicator should attempt to determine the real purpose of the communication. What reasons does the sender have for sending messages, asking for actions and reactions, or requesting return information? What is the receiver's need for communication? Once the need has been determined, it is wise to send only necessary communication and refrain from sending nonpurposeful messages. This will help check massive flows of communication that can result in distortion and insensitivity.

3. It is desirable to learn as much as possible about the receiver before the communication occurs. This will help in determining how the receiver is likely to interpret or react to the message received. In addition to looking for clues concerning communication needs, the sender should look for signals relating to the receiver's state of mind, background, previous experience, organizational responsibilities, self-perceptions, and anything else that might indicate how messages will be decoded and understood. The sender should empathize with the receiver as completely as possible.

4. Also desirable is consistency in thought and action. The receiver can learn to receive and react to consistent messages from a consistent sender more readily than to fluctuating messages from an unpredictable sender.

5. The sender will be assisted in the communication process if the activated personality part (parent, adult, or child) of self and the receiver are known. The sender who knows where his or her own thoughts are arising and where they are going insofar as the receiver is concerned will be more effective in communicating. This is also true when the receiver is upset. Filtering and distortion become serious problems when the receiver is emotional. In such cases, don't continue with the message. Allow time for the emotional period to pass before continuing.

6. In issuing the message, it is important to have the receiver's attention so that the receiver will be sensitive to what is being sent. If the receiver is preoccupied with other thoughts or the noise level is high, the receiver may fail to hear the message sent.

7. The sender should communicate as directly with the intended receiver as is practical. While it is not always possible to give the message directly to the person intended, the fewer go-betweens involved, the more the chances of distortion or other forms of misinterpretation are reduced.

8. The use of symbols (words, gestures, etc.) that are simple and uncomplicated is helpful. The more complex the communication symbols, the more likely the misinterpretation of their intended meaning.

9. Repetition of messages may be helpful in conveying the intended thoughts. Often a single transmission of an idea may not be received or decoded properly. A second or third repetition of the message may assist the receiver in the understanding and use of the concept. Communicators are frequently reluctant to repeat themselves because they feel repetition is either unnecessary or insulting to the receiver. However, after a communiqué fails, the sender is often aware that a second or third repetition would have been useful. A good technique is to send the message again but do it in a different way. If you tried sending a communication in writing and it didn't work, don't try a written form the second time. Instead, try speaking the communication or even using pictures!

10. Messages should be timed so that they are received when they are needed and are not misconstrued as a result of other thoughts on the receiver's mind. As the sender, you must put yourself in the receiver's place (empathize with the receiver) if timing of messages is to be handled properly.

11. Get feedback. Ask your receivers to repeat back to you what they understood to be your message. After giving a lengthy message to Amy, you might say something like this: "Amy, I want to make sure we both understand what needs to be done. How about giving me a rundown of what I've said and what actions you're to take?"

When you are the receiver, of course, you are responsible for putting messages into the context in which they were intended. The receiver should also attempt to be aware of personal biases as well as those of the sender, recognize his or her own needs for the message as well as the needs of the sender, size up the sender and self in terms of activated personality parts, and listen for all intended meanings. The receiver must be aware of the conditions existing in the environment as messages are interpreted.

Creating Conditions for Effective Communication

How Does the Organization Chart Enter In?

The preceding section emphasized sender-receiver relationships and the communication process in general. It is important to recognize that the formal organization structure will also have an effect upon the successful transmission of concepts and ideas from the appropriate sender(s) to the appropriate receiver(s). A firm's organization chart offers many clues about the firm's communication patterns.

Chapter 2 pointed out that the formal hierarchy with its accompanying lines of authority determines to a large degree how communication channels are set up. If the employees of an organization are clearly aware of manager-employee relationships and horizontal networks, the employees will know with whom they should communicate directly and what communication needs and expectations the receivers will have. If lines of authority and channels of communication are not known, excessive communication or lack of communication will occur. Difficulties with who is accountable to whom and how messages are to be spread are most likely to occur when organization structures are altered frequently or when organizations are established and grow without proper defining of authority relationships.

Looking more closely at the pair of organization charts below, let's see what we can determine about the communication patterns in the two firms.

Of course, our example is exaggerated, but think for a moment about the communication pattern you would expect of Firm A versus that of Firm B. What would be the pros and cons in each case?

Here's how we see it. Notice that the two firms have the same number of employees, but Firm A features a narrow span of control (there are few reporting directly to a boss), while Firm B has a wide one (many reporting to a single boss). Wide spans of supervision tend to restrict the amount of time a supervisor can spend with each of his or her subordinates and may result in hurried communication on the part of both supervisor and employee. Communication can easily become impersonal if the interests of supervisors are

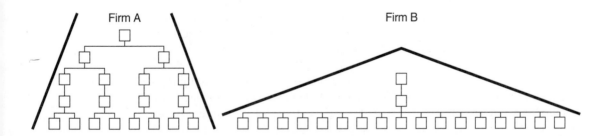

spread too widely. Employees who work for bosses with wide spans, such as the manager in Firm B, may come to feel that their boss has no direct, personal interest in communication with them.

On the other hand, the chances of upward-downward distortion are decreased in flat structures such as Firm B, with wide spans of supervision and few levels in the hierarchy. There are fewer distortions because messages flow through fewer levels in getting from the top to the bottom, and vice versa. In contrast, in tall structures, such as Firm A, that have narrow spans and many levels, communication becomes more manageable. Each supervisor has fewer employees to communicate with and listen to and more time to devote to communication. However, the possibility of upward-downward distortion increases as the number of levels in the hierarchy grows. So we would expect more distortions in Firm A than in Firm B, but ironically, employees may be more satisfied with communication in firm A than in Firm B.

What about horizontal-sideways communication? Surprisingly, relatively little research has been done on communicating effectively with others at the same level in an organization. However, a glance at the organization chart for Firms A and B suggests that the organization chart will probably affect horizontal communication. In Firm A, employees at the same organization level may report to different managers. When this happens, they may find it more difficult to communicate with each other, especially when it comes to resolving problems. Instead of simply talking out problems and resolving them at their level, employees may find themselves getting their supervisors involved and "kicking problems upstairs," possibly by as much as two or three levels. Obviously, this can be a cumbersome and time-consuming process.

Firm A may have the potential for better horizontal communications—but only if the supervisor is skillful. Ideally, in organizations like Firm B, the manager will establish clear job descriptions and will make clear to employees how much authority they have, what problems they are to work out among themselves, and which problems should be resolved by the boss. This may involve the principle of management by exception—where managers look at exceptions (departures) from expected performance rather than watching every little step the worker takes. Routine things should be manageable by the workers themselves. If principles such as management by exception are in effect, if subordinates have the proper training, and if they are motivated to take responsibility for it, horizontal communication can be very effective in firms such as Firm B.

Encouraging Upward Communication

Much of the previous discussion has pointed to the importance of the supervisor in communication. The initiative for downward communication is in the hands of the supervisor in charge of a group of people and their activities. Supervisors are expected to know the people for whom they are responsible and to provide downward communication.

Encouraging workers to communicate upward is another matter. Upward communication is more difficult because much of the initiative in this direction is in the hands of the employee. For upward communication to take place, employees must feel the need to communicate and must have a certain amount of confidence and security in their relationship with the boss. What erodes the boss-employee relationship, and when are employees likely to be reluctant to communicate upward? Several things can lead to problems:

1. An employee will be hesitant to send upward any messages that may result in negative, punitive actions toward the employee by bosses. The employee will tend to suppress or slow down messages that he or she feels the boss will not be happy about. The employee will be tempted to distort or rearrange negative information about self to reduce the probability of receiving negative response from his or her supervisor.[15] As Gemmill states, "a subordinate who believes that disclosure of feelings, opinions, or difficulties may lead a superior to block or hinder attainment of a personal goal will conceal or distort the message."[16]

2. The employee who feels a boss is autocratic, unsympathetic, and task oriented will develop a distrust for that supervisor which may cause the withholding of useful information. The more trust and confidence the employee has in the supervisor, the more likely that messages will be given to the boss freely and openly.

3. The employee who feels unimportant or feels that the job and information he or she has is not vital will be unlikely to communicate messages to a supervisor. A direct relationship appears to exist between one's feelings of importance and responsibility and one's willingness to communicate upward.

4. Employees keep their boss better informed when they know what will be done with their work, when they share common references with their supervisor, and when the supervisor is readily available to them.[17]

5. The employee's perception of the boss's attitude toward the employee (the amount of interest the boss has in him or her) and the openmindedness of the boss will affect upward communication. If the manager regularly shows a desire for messages from employees, practices an open-door policy, and provides feedback on information received, upward communication will be enhanced.[18]

The implications of these conditions are clear for the supervisor who needs and wants upward communication.

1. The supervisor must make known the need for messages from employees and his or her personal interest in hearing from them.

2. The supervisor needs to reward employees for their upward communication efforts whenever possible. Rewards don't have to be financial. An adequate reward may be a sincere thanks and an expression of appreciation for the worker's efforts at communication.

3. The supervisor should cultivate a relationship of mutual understanding with employees. The key here is getting to know the employees as individuals. By gaining the trust and respect of workers, the supervisor can encourage more open, complete communication.

4. Managers should emphasize to employees the positive as well as the negative uses make of their messages.

5. Supervisors should delegate authority and encourage employees to feel responsible for specific actions. The importance of upward communication will normally be felt under such conditions.

6. If upward communication is still below desired levels, other steps may be necessary in order to gain needed information. Formal questionnaires, reports, and other information sources may be called for.

As Table 11–3 reminds us, the proper climate for upward communication (or a communication in any direction) to occur is supportive, promotes equality, is descriptive, is spontaneous, is problem oriented, is provisional (adaptive), and is empathetic. This means that to be truly successful in getting open communication, the manager bears a responsibility for promoting the courage, trust, and willingness to communicate that will encourage employees to send and receive messages freely.[19]

The Grapevine and Its Problems

Chapter 2 discussed the informal communication network (the grapevine) and identified several of its effects. As pointed out, the grapevine can make many

---

The supportive communication climate encourages open message exchanges, while the defensive one results in distortions, exaggerations, and even the withholding of messages. The following columns show the two poles in the communication climate:

Table 11–3

The Supportive Versus Defensive Communication Climates

Supportive Climate	*Defensive Climate*
(encourages communication)	(puts receiver on guard)
1. Promotes equality ("We're all in this together.")	1. Promotes feelings of superiority ("I'm the boss; you listen to me.")
2. Seeks descriptive information, (asks for information, feelings, perceptions, participation)	2. Seeks information on which to pass judgment (asks for information on behavior levels, motives, etc.)
3. Promotes spontaneity (encourages individuality; also seeks latest information)	3. Uses strategy (has a predetermined plan along with rules and regulations)
4. Is problem oriented (seeks solutions without intruding on the receiver's goals, decisions, and progress)	4. Is control oriented (has predetermined solutions to sell to the subordinate)
5. Is provisional in nature (is adaptive, flexible, and willing to experiment)	5. Projects certainty (indicates decisions have already been made)
6. Has empathy (shows respect for the worth of others and a willingness to share feelings others may have)	6. Maintains neutrality (shows no feelings and concern for others)

Source: Charles E. Beck and Elizabeth A. Beck, "The Manager's Open Door and the Communication Climate," January–February 1986, adaptation, pp. 15–19. Reprinted from *Business Horizons,* January–February 1986. © 1986 by the Foundation for the School of Business at Indiana University. Used with permission.

positive contributions to the organization because it does tend to convey messages rapidly and it often accurately supplements the workings of formal communication channels. Grapevine communication can flow in three directions (up, down, and sideways) within the organization, but its pattern is normally more unpredictable than is the formal pattern. Much of the flow of messages is uncontrollable by the formal authority structure.

Grapevines tend to act rapidly and selectively (refer to Chapter 2). This means that some people get grapevine information while others do not. Superiors and subordinates alike may discover that they are being left out of the informal network, often to their own personal disadvantage. Grapevines, therefore, cannot be depended upon to disseminate messages faithfully throughout the organization in the place of formal communiquês.

The messages spread by the grapevine may be in support of the formal organization and its goals, or the messages may be antagonistic. A large number of variables determine whether the messages of the grapevine will support or work against the formal organization. As usual, much responsibility rests with the manager. There are several questions the manager may want to consider as a part of "grapevine management."

The manager might ask, "Am I included in grapevine information, or am I being completely bypassed?" This question is significant because it is, in part, a gauge of the confidence and acceptability of the manager in the eyes of superiors, subordinates, and peers. A manager who discovers that isolation exists will need to work toward gaining the respect and confidence of those around him or her so that he or she will receive important messages. No manager, of course, will be able to overcome completely the authority barrier of being a supervisor. However, supervisors who talk with individuals about matters other than official business can cultivate the grapevine more effectively and can be included in grapevine communications more frequently.

Another question a manager might ask is "Are individuals who need information being left out of the grapevine without their knowledge?" Where the answer to this question is yes (and it often is), formally appointed supervisors will need to issue messages of significant importance in ways that will reach the parties needing the information. In other words, important messages should be issued formally, monitored to see that they reach all appropriate individuals, or both.

A third question could be, "Is the information being spread accurate?" Because the answer in normally yes, there typically may be no cause for concern. However, to avoid the danger of inaccuracies and to counter false rumors, several actions may be necessary. If managers decide to utilize informal networks to spread information, messages should be given to individuals who have the respect and confidence of both the sender and the prospective receivers. Messages should be given to several respected messengers throughout the grapevine so that distortion will be less likely to occur. When false rumors are spread, formal networks should immediately send out the correct information with the appropriate supporting evidence. Sources of incorrect information should be traced, and individuals sending such information should be asked to take part in the correctional process. When false rumors tend to occur frequently, managers may need to consider whether they are giving out enough meaningful information to all individuals who need the messages.

Because people tend to spread rumors about things of personal concern, rumors may indicate specific informational needs that are not being met.

Another question could be, "Is the grapevine typically supportive of or antagonistic toward the formal organization?" The answer to this question may be a revelation of the general feelings and sentiments of informal organizations toward the formal organization. If grapevines normally remain on a positive plane, formal organization-informal organization relations are usually good. If the informal grapevine continually acts in a manner derogatory to the formal, relationships between the two need careful attention.

Formal managers should never expect to control completely the workings of informal grapevines, but they can learn to sense the activities and effects of grapevines. Managers can learn when additional formal actions and personal efforts are needed to make formal and informal relationships mutually beneficial. They can then identify trouble spots and take corrective action more quickly.

Telling It Like It Is—Assertiveness

In listing the ideal communication conditions and circumstances, several factors are notable. Effective communication calls for very open, honest, forthright interactions between organizational members. Upward communication must be accurate. Managers must know the problems of employees. Communication must be done for the benefit of everyone. Information that is needed must be communicated rather than only information that is wanted. Areas where disagreement exists must be identified and addressed. Communication that accomplishes these goals requires cultivation and effort. In recent years, this open, complete type of communication has come to be known as **assertiveness**.

One definition of assertiveness states that it "involves standing up for the personal rights and expressing thoughts, feelings, and beliefs, in direct, honest, and appropriate ways which do not violate another person's rights."[20] There are two kinds of respect involved in assertiveness—respect for self and respect for others. Assertiveness is not selfishness, nor does it result in complete deference to others. It is simply communicating those things that need to be communicated to the people who need the information for the benefit of everyone. As Lange and Jakubowski have said:

> The goal of assertion is communication and mutuality; that is to get and give respect, to ask for fair play, and to leave room for compromise when the needs and rights of two people conflict.[21]

Or as Dawley and Wenrich state:

> The intention of assertiveness is to result in decreased anxiety and hostility; increased interpersonal understanding; the ability to establish close and meaningful relationships; and the skill to improve overall quality of social interaction and personal esteem.[22]

Behaviors that are alternates to assertiveness are **nonassertiveness** (passive behavior) and **aggressiveness.** Nonassertiveness is allowing rights to be

assertiveness
Communication in which the rights of self and others are respected. As a result, communication is honest and forthright.

nonassertiveness (passive behavior)
Communication where the rights of self or others are infringed upon. Passive behavior tends to be self-denying. Inactivity rather than activity tends to occur.

aggressiveness
Directly standing up for one's own rights at the expense of others' rights.

Management in Action

A New Open-door Approach—Operation Speakeasy

Managers through the years have tried almost every technique imaginable to encourage subordinates to communicate what's on their minds. Suggestion boxes have been used with only minimal success. Open-door policies have been declared as a means of showing receptivity to the ideas and needs of subordinates. Managers have even been known to take their doors off their hinges to illustrate constant openness to communication. Even this has had little success.

A consulting firm has recently developed a technique designed to overcome any reluctancies subordinates may have to communicate their thoughts and needs. The technique the firm has developed and is now being used in several companies is called Operation Speakeasy. The technique works something like this:

1. A group of employees is brought together once a month with two or three top managers. The employees, who change each month, serve as presenters from their departments rather than as originators of the suggestions, concerns, and questions.
2. All questions, suggestions, and responses are recorded in writing so that employees can refer to a "speakeasy notebook," which is kept in each department. This is an ongoing, written, accessible record that serves as the heart of the program and is the measure of its success.
3. A one-month maximum time is set for answering each question asked. While many questions are answered on the spot, others need research or consideration before a response is given.

Speakeasy Notebook Entry

Operation Speakeasy—January 5, 19--

Attending: Sam Evans (representing drivers), Sue White (administration), Ellen Steward (customer service), Richard Sloan (day operations), Ted Sandowsky (night operations), Selma Ward (sales), Don Butcher (purchasing), and A. B. Elliot, Steven Edwards, and Craig Lewis representing management.

Suggestions and Actions

1. Suggestion: Upstairs ceiling; when will it be completed?
   Action: The ceiling has been replaced and new lighting fixtures installed.
2. Suggestion: We need more soap for pressure washer brushes and sponges for washing the trucks.
   Action: Bob has ordered them, and most items are in already. Contact him.
3. Suggestion: Why do people with less seniority get promoted faster than others?

    Action: Promotions are not based on seniority but on people's taking the extra steps. Consistently giving 100% when 85% would be acceptable. Aptitude, behavior, and cooperation with management, peers, and subordinates. Excellence at current level.

4.   Suggestion: What about job descriptions?

    Action: Thank you for your reminder and concern. They will be out by the end of the month. We are all looking forward to the entire performance review system being in place.

5.   Suggestion: Parking schedule—what happened to it?

    Action: Parking lot is paved. We are making progress. It will be ready as soon as weather permits. Parking spaces will be assigned. This should eliminate any complaints. Remember, the employee of the month gets the best spot.

6.   Suggestion: Importance of the word *communicate*. Do not guess that some know what to do. Supervisors should explain what they want done.

    Action: Management agrees completely with this. The most important thing we need to do is communicate clearly what needs to be accomplished in terms of results.

7.   Suggestion: We should have a safe-driver program.

    Action: We are developing one with our insurance company. It should be ready by April 1.

8.   Suggestion: We should have a first-aid kit for the upstairs office.

    Action: Joan will order one.

9.   Suggestion: The wooden step in front of the plant is cracked.

    Action: Tim Harding will fix it this week.

10.   Suggestion: Can we look into eyecare as part of our Blue Cross/Blue Shield plan?

    Action: A representative is coming to talk to us about this. Jerry Roberts is doing the background work and will report his finding at the next meeting.

Source: Joyce S. Anderson, "Blueprint for Real Open-Door Communication," *Personnel Journal,* Volume 68, Number 5, © May 1989, pp. 32, 33, and 36. Reprinted with permission from *Personnel Journal,* Costa Mesa, California. All rights reserved.

Insights

A Sample Training Exercise

Refusing Requests

The exercise on making and refusing requests might be supplemented by the following exercise created by Rita Whiteley (personal communication, 1975). The trainer asks each person to identify a personal belonging that is important or precious to him or her. The trainer than attempts to borrow that object using all conceivable manipulations (flattery, crisis, guilt, pressure, condescension, helplessness). Each participant gets to practice refusing assertively and to persist in that refusal. The trainer might also request something that the participant agrees to lend and then introduce new information, making the agreement progressively more demanding or unreasonable than the original request. For example, one participant agreed to loan his ten-speed bike to enable the trainer to get home. By the end of the interaction, the trainer had asked to keep the bike for an unspecified period of time and to have the participant drop the bike off at his office across the campus at an inconvenient time.

In another example, the trainer might use flattery by saying, "You are a caring individual. This request should be right in keeping with your caring attitude." In still another case, the trainer may play up a crisis by saying, "If you don't let me borrow your car, the store will be closed before I can get there, and they will charge me a penalty for not getting this rental back on time." This last appeal plays on guilt and pressure.

An important caution is in order for this type of exercise: Trainers should be very careful that these interactions do not lead to a self-depreciating, negative experience for the participant. The trainer should stop the interaction before the participant experiences considerable difficulty in responding assertively. The purpose is not to push the participant until he or she gets anxious, but rather to raise some important issues regarding refusals and to help the participant to develop and practice assertive responses.

Source: Arthur J. Lange and Patricia Jakubowski, *Responsible Assertive Behavior,* Champaign, Ill.: Research Press, 1976, p. 114.

infringed upon (either one's own rights or the rights of others). It doesn't adapt well and is self-denying. Nonassertiveness generates anxiety and negative feelings about self and others, and it leads to strained relations.

Aggressiveness, on the other hand, does involve directly standing up for one's personal rights, but it is coupled with expressing thoughts in ways that are often dishonest and usually inappropriate and in ways that violate the rights of other people. Aggressiveness usually involves the display of hostile, offensive behavior against others without regard for their rights.

When a group working together to make a decision, for example, gets off the subject and strays into unrelated areas an aggressive boss might say, "As usual, you people are goofing off again." A passive boss might say, "I'm sorry; I must have let us get off track. I just don't know what to do." The assertive boss, on the other hand, might say, "What we are talking about is interesting; however, I feel we need to get back to the original subject."

While some individuals seem to develop a wholesome assertiveness fairly naturally and without much effort, training and practice are necessary for most people. The training process for developing assertiveness includes several aspects:

1. Developing an understanding of what assertiveness is and what it can help accomplish. At the same time, nonassertiveness and aggressiveness are identified.
2. Learning to identify comments and behaviors that represent each of the three types of communication. This is usually done by reading or viewing statements made by others, and then analyzing which type of behavior each one represents.
3. Acting out each of the three types of behavior through role playing and modeling.
4. Using assertive behavior as a response to different situations in a rehearsal, behavior modeling, or coaching technique, where the learner acts out responses assertively, models the behavior using assertiveness, and receives coaching and feedback. The procedures learned often include (a) learning how to give and receive compliments, (b) learning how to say no, (c) learning how to identify the rights of self and others, (d) learning how to make and refuse requests, and (e) dealing with persistent people.
5. Receiving reinforcement for modeling assertive behavior. Some of the reinforcement may come from the trainer or other organizational representatives. Some of the reinforcement is self-rewarding when performance is recognized to be consistent with assertive models.
6. Continuing to practice and to apply assertiveness until it becomes a habit.

Through the development and application of assertiveness, many of the ideals of communication become achievable. To determine your existing level of assertiveness, take the Assertiveness Inventory and see if you need to give further attention to your own skills.

Additional Communication Problems

We've talked about the communication process as well as the most common communication problems and offered some suggestions for dealing with them. However, communication problems not specifically identified previously may arise as a result of such factors as differences in perceptions, physical distances, and psychological and emotional barriers. A problem-solving approach is essential in the handling of each problem as it arises. Specific underlying causes must be identified, alternative solutions considered, decisions made on courses of action, solutions implemented, and followup analyses conducted to determine continuing communication needs.

As a result of position and responsibilities, the manager-supervisor is primarily responsible for the successful resolution of communication problems and the proper activity of communication networks. This does not mean that other parties may be excused from concern about communication exchange, but it does establish the ultimate responsibility for effective communication in the workplace.

Self Test

Personal Feedback
Assertiveness Inventory

The following questions will be helpful in assessing your assertiveness. Be honest in your responses. All you have to do is draw a circle around the number that describes you best. For some questions the assertive end of the scale is at 0, for others at 4. Key:

0 means "no" or "never"
1 means "somewhat" or "sometimes"
2 means "average"
3 means "usually" or "a good deal of the time"
4 means "practically always" or "entirely"

1. When a person is highly unfair, do you call it to his or her attention?
   0   1   2   3   4

2. Do you find it difficult to make decisions?
   0   1   2   3   4

3. Are you openly critical of others' ideas, opinions, behavior?
   0   1   2   3   4

4. Do you speak out in protest when someone takes your place in lines?
   0   1   2   3   4

5. Do you often avoid people or situations for fear of embarrassment?
   0   1   2   3   4

6. Do you usually have confidence in your own judgment?
   0   1   2   3   4

7. Do you insist that your spouse or roommate take on a fair share of household chores?
   0   1   2   3   4

8. Are you prone to fly off the handle?
   0 ·1   2   3   4

9. When a salesperson makes an effort, do you find it hard to say no even though the merchandise is not really what you want?
   0   1   2   3   4

10. When a latecomer is waited on before you are, do you call attention to the situation?
    0   1   2   3   4

11. Are you reluctant to speak up in a discussion or debate?
    0   1   2   3   4

12. If a person has borrowed money (or a book, garment, thing of value) and is overdue in returning it, do you mention it?
    0   1   2   3   4

13. Do you continue to pursue an argument after the other person has had enough?

    0 1 2 3 4

14. Do you generally express what you feel?

    0 1 2 3 4

15. Are you disturbed if someone watches you at work?

    0 1 2 3 4

16. If someone keeps kicking or bumping your chair in a movie or lecture, do you ask the person to stop?

    0 1 2 3 4

17. Do you find it difficult to keep eye contact when talking to another person?

    0 1 2 3 4

18. In a good restaurant, when your meal is improperly prepared or served, do you ask the waiter/waitress to correct the situation?

    0 1 2 3 4

19. When you discover merchandise is faulty, do you return it for an adjustment?

    0 1 2 3 4

20. Do you show your anger by name calling or using obscenities?

    0 1 2 3 4

21. Do you try to be a wallflower or a piece of furniture in social situations?

    0 1 2 3 4

22. Do you insist that your landlord (mechanic, repairman, etc.) make repairs, adjustment, or replacements that are his or her responsibility?

    0 1 2 3 4

23. Do you often step in and make decisions for others?

    0 1 2 3 4

24. Are you able to openly express love and affection?

    0 1 2 3 4

25. Are you able to ask your friends for small favors or help?

    0 1 2 3 4

26. Do you think you always have the right answer?

    0 1 2 3 4

27. When you differ with a person you respect, are you able to speak up for your own viewpoint?

    0 1 2 3 4

28. Are you able to refuse unreasonable requests made by friends?

    0 1 2 3 4

Self Test

continued

29. Do you have difficulty complimenting or praising others?

0   1   2   3   4

30. If you are disturbed by someone smoking near you, can you say so?

0   1   2   3   4

31. Do you shout or use bullying tactics to get others to do as you wish?

0   1   2   3   4

32. Do you finish other people's sentences for them?

0   1   2   3   4

33. Do you get into physical fights with others, especially with strangers?

0   1   2   3   4

34. At family meals, do you control the conversation?

0   1   2   3   4

35. When you meet a stranger, are you the first to introduce yourself and begin a conversation?

0   1   2   3   4

Scoring Instructions

1. Add the scores for questions 1, 4, 6, 7, 10, 12, 14, 16, 18, 19, 22, 24, 25, 27, 28, 30, and 35.   _____ Total Score
2. Add the scores for questions 2, 3, 5, 8, 9, 11, 13, 15, 17, 20, 21, 23, 26, 29, 31, 32, 33, and 34.   _____ Total Score
3. Subtract the total score in No. 2 from the total score in No. 1. The net result is you assertiveness score.   _____

A score less than 0 indicates that you are low in assertiveness.
A score of 0–10 indicates that you are somewhat assertive.
A score of 11–20 indicates that you are usually assertive.
A score over 20 indicates that you are very assertive.

Source: Robert E. Alberti and Michael L. Emmons, *From Your Perfect Right.* Reprinted by permission of Impact Publishers, Inc., San Luis Obispo, Calif., 1982. The Assertiveness Inventory is not a validated psychological test.

Summary

Communication is the exchange of ideas or concepts for purposes of information, command and instruction, influence and persuasion, or integration. Without some type of communication, no organization will exist long. Without accurate, meaningful communication, no organization will be successful.

Managers bear a heavy responsibility for the creation of a proper environment for communicating and for establishing and maintaining the necessary organizational communication channels. Senders and receivers both bear a responsibility for the successful interpretation and understanding of messages communicated. For one thing, the sender must choose the correct medium through which messages will be sent. Some messages are sent directly and personally to other individuals (through a rich medium), and some messages can be sent impersonally to a large group of people (through a lean medium).

The communication process itself involves several stages in addition to choosing the right medium. The receiver's need for and knowledge of the message have to be considered. Messages have to be placed in the proper code. Messages must be transferred properly, and symbols must be interpreted. Action or reaction occurs, and feedback is given. This process repeats itself as new messages are needed.

Some idealistic goals for communicating within organizations have been established by Likert in his System 4 concept, but these perfected targets are difficult to achieve. Many problems stand in the way of ideal communication. There are problems of message interpretation, filtering our messages needing to be heard, and message distortion; problems with improper timing of messages, and actions inconsistent with messages sent; and perceptual problems, to name a few.

We know several management steps that help to convey messages appropriately. We also recognize the importance of establishing the right conditions in which communication takes place. Organizational communication works best when messages mesh three ways—upward, downward, and across an organization. Upward communication is difficult to achieve most of the time and requires special attention to accomplish. Message sending that is rewarded will probably be repeated. When the need for information is known, messages are more likely to be sent upward, also. A number of steps exist that usually are helpful in stimulating upward communication.

Assertiveness is an important part of the communication process. Assertiveness is speaking or acting in a way that benefits everyone in the long run. This includes standing up for the personal rights of self and others.

Formal communication networks are not the only communication taking place in an organization. There is also a communication grapevine functioning within the organization. The grapevine supplements the formal network, often getting information more quickly to people and places than the formal channels.

Questions to Consider

1. The comment was made in the chapter that employees desire large amounts of information about their organization, economic and competitive influences that affect their employer, and a host of additional information. Do you think this statement reflects the interests of the majority of today's workers? Why or why not?
2. How does the upward flow of communications help to achieve the integrative function of communication?
3. Is the sender more responsible for the successful exchange of an idea through the communication process than the receiver? Explain your answer in detail.

4. Someone has said that words have no meanings in themselves. How do you interpret this statement?
5. In most organizations, downward communications are given more attention and emphasis than are upward communications. If this trend continues to be true over a long period of time in one specific organization, what will the effect be? Why are downward communications usually handled more effectively than upward communications?
6. Anxiety and other personal factors can be barriers to effective communication. What can the concerned manager do to overcome these problems?
7. What communication barriers do large organizations have that are less of a problem with smaller organizations? Why?

Key Terms

aggressiveness	crossed transaction	information function
assertiveness	decoding	integrative function
command and	distortion	nonassertiveness
instruction	encoding	(passive behavior)
function	filtering	receiver
communication	influence and	sender
complementary	persuasion function	ulterior transaction
transaction	innovation function	

Chapter Case

Is He Communicating?

At the end of the spring term, you decide to take a break before fall term starts. You set off for Chicago, where your friend, Pat, who graduated several years ago, is working for a firm that manufactures specially designed steel and aluminum fittings for a variety of industrial uses. You're anxious to see Pat for several reasons. First, you're anxious to hear about Pat's impressive new job—Pat has recently been promoted to an executive vice-president's position, reporting directly to the chief executive officer. In addition, you've had little first hand experience in manufacturing and are anxious to see what a manufacturing operation is like.

As you sit and talk to Pat on the evening of your arrival, you get a funny feeling that all isn't well, and you question Pat closely to see what's going on. Pat responds:

> There are a couple of things. First of all, I really enjoy my position, I can tell you that. But things don't function at my new level in the way I've always imagined they should. The top management—the other managers and me reporting to Rae Arbuckle, the CEO—have a couple of major issues on the table to be resolved right now, but I'm afraid we're not making much progress. Maybe the meeting tomorrow will be better.

Naturally you're curious and ask if you could observe the meeting as a spectator/visitor. Pat checks, and you're invited. In fact, Rae asks if you could give your thoughts after the meeting. The meeting begins, and you listen intently as several related ideas are under discussion. There is evidence of problems with the workforce—low morale, heavy turnover, and a moderate decline in productivity. There is agreement that the workers themselves are part of the problem. As a result of an economic slump in the area, most are overqualified for the unskilled, repetitive production jobs they are hired to do. While most of the workforce have completed high school and have several years of college, the work is an assembly-line operation, where each person performs a tiny segment of a total job under close supervision. You are surprised at how quickly the management team comes to an agreement about what the problem is and how to deal with it.

> "It's obvious," one of them says. "Young folks these days have no gumption. All they do is talk about how dissatisfied they are with the work. They should be glad they have jobs in this economy! There are plenty of people out there who like this kind of work. Let them quit, I say, and let's bring in some less-educated people who will be satisfied with a good, well-paying job like we have to offer."

The others immediately agree, and the "decision" is made. Pat says nothing. The subject moves on to economics and competition in more general terms. Things sound gloomy to you. The corporation has traditionally been a slow-moving specialty manufacturer servicing a number of long-term contracts. Not only have the shop floor jobs been highly specialized, but so have the individual departments and the work generally. There have been close supervision, carefully prescribed lines of authority, and all of the traditional controls.

Recently, things have begun to change radically with challenges from foreign competition. Purchasers no longer are willing to sign long-term contracts for thousands of identical pieces. Instead, they are insisting on flexibility and may order only a few pieces made to a particular specification. The firm itself is threatened not only by a group of domestic competitors who have suddenly appeared on the scene but also by foreign competition. Again, the top management group quickly comes to an assessment of the situation. One of them says, "There's only one thing to do—keep doing what we've always done, but do it better. We've got to tighten up, establish more controls, and get things on an even keel."

Again, Pat says nothing. As the two of you walk out, you ask, "Why didn't you speak up, Pat? I'm not sure those ideas were really examined in the meeting."

Pat responds, "Oh, I couldn't speak up. Those people are really pros, and I'm just the new kid on the block. They really know what they're doing."

By now you're getting a headache and wonder what to say to Rae.

1. Why didn't Pat say anything about his feelings, thoughts, and position?
2. What additional conditions and circumstances are making communication difficult at this firm?
3. What advice would you give the management of the company to improve their communication skills, patterns of communication, and analysis of problem areas?
4. Are the managers making good decisions? Explain in terms of communication as well as other areas.

Chapter 12

Counseling Employees

Objectives

- To identify the goals and potential outcomes of counseling.
- To consider who should do the counseling in most organizations.
- To identify and learn how to create the optimal climate for counseling.
- To focus on specific counseling skills and aptitudes.
- To review the two major counseling techniques and to discern their strengths and weaknesses.
- To learn how to determine the appropriate kind of counseling for the situation.
- To develop skills for being a good listener.

Danny Tabor—The Salesman Who Won't Admit His Problems

Bruce Clover began Commercial Security, Inc. three years ago on a very small capital investment he was able to scrape together from personal savings and a loan from the bank. He saw an opportunity for a company that provides television cameras and monitoring devices, alarm systems, and other security equipment for banks, commercial enterprises, and industrial firms. The security equipment leased or sold by Commercial Security assists businesses in protecting themselves against thefts, burglaries, and robberies on their premises.

Bruce began his business as a two-person operation. Bruce did all of the sales contact work himself, designed the security systems to meet the needs of each customer, and kept all records. He hired a technician to install the systems (and help with their design) and to service and maintain all equipment. Business has been good and the demands of the work have grown until Bruce has had to add six additional employees in his home office. He now serves as the general manager; his original helper now manages installation and customer service. Bruce has hired a sales manager, an additional salesperson, two installation and service technicians, a systems design specialist, and a secretary-bookkeeper.

As soon as Bruce got the home office operating efficiently, he decided that it was time to open a branch office in a nearby city that had an excellent market potential. Bruce decided that at the beginning he would drive to the branch office each week and spend one or two days managing the business personally. In addition, he felt that a salesperson, an installation-service technician, and a secretary-bookkeeper would be necessary to complete the branch office staff. Any specialized help could be supplied by the main office as necessary. Telephone communications would make possible other contact as needed. Everyone would report directly to Bruce until the branch office grew big enough to hire a full-time manager. In Bruce's absence, each employee was to be self-controlling.

The branch office has been in operation for more than a year, and business there has been excellent. An assistant service technician has been added to the staff to meet the heavy volume of installation and maintenance demands. The original salesperson resigned about two months ago to take another job, and Bruce hired a replacement, Danny Tabor, as the new salesperson. Danny came well recommended as a salesperson from a music and electronics equipment company. He is in his thirties, has been in sales since high school graduation, and indicated a strong interest in security systems when he was hired. He has been at Commercial Security for five weeks now.

When Bruce hired Danny, it was agreed that Danny would be on a straight salary for eight weeks until he learned the business and developed his own clientele. At the end of the eight weeks, Danny will be placed on a commission earnings basis. During the eight-week training program, Bruce is meeting with Danny at least once a week to help him get acquainted with customers and to learn how to uncover prospects.

Bruce is now quite worried about Danny's performance. Danny regularly has been late for their weekly meetings—often by an hour or more. He has reported very few new sales agreements each of the five weeks of his employment. The secretary-bookkeeper reports that she hardly sees Danny—Danny spends very little time in his office and appears to be staying at his home an unusually large amount of time.

Bruce has begun to suspect that he is getting very little in return for the straight salary he has paid Danny the past five weeks. He has asked Danny about his work and has gotten unenthusiastic answers, such as "It's taking me a while to learn, but I eventually will get the hang of things" or "It's taking me more time than I expected to begin to show any good results." When Bruce has asked what specific problems Danny has experienced, Danny's only response has been, "Oh, nothing in particular. Just the problems any new employee experiences."

What Bruce has not been able to uncover is the fact that Danny has been working only a few hours a week on his new job. In addition to the time Bruce and Danny have spent together, Danny has averaged only eight to ten hours a week at his work. The main reasons for his lack of work lie in health problems. Danny's wife, in particular, has been very ill for the past two months. She suffers frequent dizzy spells and faints unexpectedly. Because they have no relatives living near them, Danny must stay with her except for the time their teenaged son is at home to help. In addition, Danny himself has been sick for the past few days, and it now appears that he may be diabetic. Danny also has had dental problems since beginning his employment with Commercial Security. He needs the money from his job badly, but he has not felt well, and he needs to be at home to care for his wife.

Bruce has another meeting with Danny scheduled for tomorrow morning. He has decided that he must get more information from Danny (remember, he doesn't know anything about the health problems) so that he can help Danny with his job and so that he can protect Commercial Security's investment in Danny's training. Bruce's previous inquiries have been unsuccessful, but he feels that it is imperative that he get more information from Danny.

Case Questions

1. Why is Danny unwilling to tell Bruce what his real problems are?
2. Is it possible for Bruce to get more helpful information directly from Danny concerning Danny's progress, problems, and goals? If so, how can Bruce help Danny discuss his concerns more openly? How can supervisors help their subordinates to be more open and complete in their communication?
3. Suppose that through counseling Danny finally tells Bruce about his family health problems. What should Bruce do then?

Counseling is a concentrated form of interpersonal communication. With most types of counseling, the interchange of ideas between the parties involved (the counselors and those being counseled) is directed toward a problem or a need that requires in-depth attention. Counseling may have obvious benefits in dealing with problems such as those discussed both in previous chapters and in the chapters that follow.

To be more specific, counseling may serve at least four functions. Counseling, in the context of work organizations, is **corrective,** or remedial, if it identifies conditions, attitudes, or behavior patterns that precipitate problems and if it advances a set of actions that result in improved performance. Counseling is **therapeutic** if it diagnoses personal ills and applies "medicine" to wounds so that normalcy results. A number of employees in the typical organization suffer from emotional stress. In particular, upper-level managerial employees feel pressure that results from their obligations. Top-level officials may have few, if any, peers to confide in. Such pressure may be relieved by therapeutic adjustive counseling. Managers at all levels can benefit from supportive counseling that may seem to take the form of coaching.[1]

Any employee, of course, can benefit from such therapeutic counseling to deal with specific emotional—or even physical problems.[2] Look back at the Danny Tabor case that opened this chapter. It seems pretty obvious that Danny would benefit from such counseling, doesn't it? Danny's problem is typical in another way as well. Some of the problem is probably temporary, brought on by a specific set of circumstances, and is likely to lessen as the circumstances change. However, while most maladjustments are temporary, they can be devastating to the employee experiencing them. This is certainly true in Danny Tabor's case.

Counseling may be primarily a means of conveying information and exchanging ideas. Such **informational** counseling may serve more to prevent problems than to diagnose those already in existence.

Counseling may also be **developmental** in nature, helping individuals to more fully utilize their capabilities and to more completely achieve their potential. Developmental counseling may accelerate the growth of an individual so that the individual achieves higher levels of efficiency or productivity more rapidly than would otherwise be the case. This type of assistance, when given to the employee, helps in the determination of existing capabilities, the establishment of future developmental goals, and the evaluation of the compatibility of potential skill development with goals being sought.[3]

To illustrate how developmental counseling works, let's suppose that Leslie, a young college graduate, wishes to advance into a managerial position with her employer. Leslie sits down with her superior, and they review her present skills and abilities compared with the abilities she will need to achieve her goals. They analyze her present skills by looking at her operative, interpersonal, and decision-making abilities. Operative skills are the technical requirements people need for fulfilling their jobs. Interpersonal skills are the abilities individuals need to relate effectively to other individuals. Decision-making skills refer to the ability to gather facts, review alternatives, and make effective choices.

To complete the illustration, Leslie and her boss analyze Leslie's strengths and weaknesses in the three areas (see Figure 12–1). Together they attempt to help Leslie verbalize her goals and ambitions. The two then view Leslie's goals in the light of the additional skills and knowledge Leslie will need to achieve her goals. If they determine that Leslie's aptitude and motivations are

corrective counseling
A type of interpersonal communication where the listener seeks to discover a counselee's problems and the underlying causes, with the goal of eliminating or overcoming the problems.

therapeutic counseling
Consultation between counselor and counselee in which problems are diagnosed and "healing" solutions are provided.

informational counseling
Communication between two or more persons primarily to convey ideas.

developmental counseling
The activity of a counselor that attempts to help the counselee perform up to the level of his or her capabilities.

Figure 12–1

Existing Skills Compared to Required Skills in Developmental Counseling

	Areas of Skills and Abilities		
	Technical Skills and Abilities	*Human Relations Skills and Abilities*	*Analytical Abilities*
Goal position skills and abilities needed	0 0 0	0 0 0 0 0	0 0 0
Skills and abilities already possessed by counselee	0 0	0 0 0	0
Skills and abilities that must be developed to achieve counselee's goals	0	0 0	0 0

Each circle 0 represents a skill.

Source: This chart is a modification of one developed by M. I. Gould, "Counseling for Self Development," *Personnel Journal,* Volume 49, Number 3, March 1970, p. 230.

realistic, they may plot a course of training and development for her. If the goals are unrealistic, this will be acknowledged, a substitute set of new realistic goals will be defined, and a course of development toward those goals will be charted.

If counseling serves its purposes well, everyone will benefit. Counselors will gather needed information, the people being counseled will be helped, and organizational goals will be achieved more effectively.

Schuh and Hakel suggest that for the individual, counseling can result in the following:

1. Greater stability of employment (reduced absenteeism and turnover).
2. Improved ability to relate with people in positions of authority.
3. Development of better, more friendly coworker relationships.
4. Improved personal mood and disposition.
5. Reduction of anxiety.
6. Improved ability to communicate with others.
7. Increased willingness to assume responsibility for decision making and activity.
8. Elimination of feeling of aloneness.[4]

Employees with special needs, such as those who are facing retirement, moving to new positions, or experiencing health problems, will be greatly assisted through well-performed counseling. The personal value of these advantages is obvious, but they may also be translated into organizational advantages. Counseling can help to reduce absenteeism, employee turnover, lack of cooperation among workers, interpersonal anxiety, and poor communication patterns and may otherwise result in overall improvement for the organization. (See the Management In Action feature for a rather comprehensive program to benefit employees.)

Who Should Handle Counseling?

The question of who should perform the counseling duties with an organization may have several answers. It is obvious that psychological problems, deep-seated personality difficulties, and some personal matters require the attention of well-trained psychiatrists or psychologists if the needed help is to be provided. A good piece of advice from an experienced manager the authors know well is this: "It's a great temptation to try to act like a psychologist. But I resist it. I keep telling myself that I DON'T have the psychological training and that I can do more harm than good. I see my role as a resource person helping the employee get needed help."

Many organizations have hired full-time counselors qualified to handle the more profound problems of individual employees. Other organizations have chosen to pay a retainer to trained counselors so that they can be available to help workers when their skills are needed. Some organizations have sent selected employees to counselor training programs so that they can come back to the organization and handle many of the counseling needs. These individuals are often placed in staff positions or are otherwise placed so that their services will be available to people throughout the organization. In still other cases, and especially in smaller organizations, the organization itself may not be able to provide the needed help directly. In such situations, you as a manager may need to use all your ingenuity to ensure that employees get specialized treatment when they need it. You will find that you may be able to refer employees to a number of community agencies or to specialists within their religious preferences, for example. As our experienced manager puts it, "Help is out there. It just takes a lot of persistence and determination to find it sometimes!"

The truth of the matter is that professional counselors and psychiatrists (whether inside or outside the organization) have not been utilized in any great numbers for organizational counseling purposes.[5] Perhaps managers in most organizations have never fully appreciated the services available through these counseling duties, or perhaps some have thought that the expense involved in having specialists available could not be justified on a cost-benefit basis. At any rate, the majority of problems in today's organizations typically are channeled into the hands of line managers. Supervisors are expected to be a "first line of defense" and to handle the corrective informational, developmental, and, to some extent, therapeutic needs of their subordinates through counseling or other appropriate actions.

This is not at all a bad idea. From many points of view, the manager may be better suited than anyone else to communicate with employees and to counsel with them. An employee's own boss is in a position to know more about the employee's abilities, strengths, weaknesses, ambitions, and needs than most outsiders or staff specialists would be because the supervisor and the employee work together regularly and communicate on a wide range of

Management in Action

Wellness Programs

Some organizations are taking their concern for the well-being and productivity of their employees beyond the talking stage. They are adopting active plans, sometimes called wellness programs, to lift employees to healthful lives and then help them stay there. One of the leaders in the wellness movement is the Johnson and Johnson Company, which began its program over eleven years ago.

Enrollment in the Life for Life program, as it is called at J. and J., is voluntary. When an employee first enrolls, he or she must answer a 19-page questionnaire to establish his or her general health status and need for change. The new member ponders questions such as, "How many times a week do you add salt to your food?" "How many flights of stairs do you climb a day?" "Have people annoyed you by criticizing your drinking?" "How many close friends do you have?" The program is concerned about both mental and physical health. The questionnaire is evaluated by computer; then a counselor, who in Johnson and Johnson's case is a nurse, discusses findings and lays out a program of physical activity and mental conditioning.

The program is expensive for Johnson and Johnson (they pay all of the fees) in that the checkups and counseling cost about $200 for each employee each year. Johnson and Johnson, however, figures the program saves at least $378 per employee by lowering absenteeism and by slowing the rise of health-care expense. Officials at Johnson and Johnson indicate that it takes about two years before the program breaks even.

The Coors Brewing Company runs a program with a slightly different focus. The kind of program at Coors is generally known as the Health Risk Assessment (HRA) plan. The HRA program is administered by a company that specializes in the planning and implementation of such procedures. Employees voluntarily participate in the program. When the program begins, all employees are mailed a 105-question appraisal form for themselves and their spouses. The company encourages the employees to complete and return the form by offering an incentive. The company rewards employees who complete the form and meet the health-age-chronology guidelines by assuming more of the health insurance premiums.

The information about each employee's medical history and lifestyle (information gleaned from the assessment form) is compared against national statistics for the appropriate age group and life pattern. The employee than receives the analysis results. Individuals are accessible by telephone or in person to discuss and help clarify the data. High-risk employees are consulted every six to twelve months. The assessment shows each employee possible problem areas.

The risk assessment program is supported by special programs to meet specific employee needs: a mammography program for women employees, a companywide seat-belt campaign to encourage employees to buckle up, skin cancer screenings, onsite cholesterol testing, smoking cessation program, obesity management, and alcohol education programs. This type of program results in better employee health, and it lets employees know the company cares about them.

Sources: Neal Tomplin,, "Johnson and Johnson 'Wellness' Program for Workers Shows Healthy Bottom Line," *Wall Street Journal,* May 21, 1990; and Shari Caudron, "Assessments Rescue Health Programs," *Human Resources Magazine,* (formerly *Personnel Administrator*) Volume 35, Number 4, April 1990, pp. 64–68. Reprinted with the permission from HRMagazine published by the Society for Human Resource Management, Alexandria, VA.

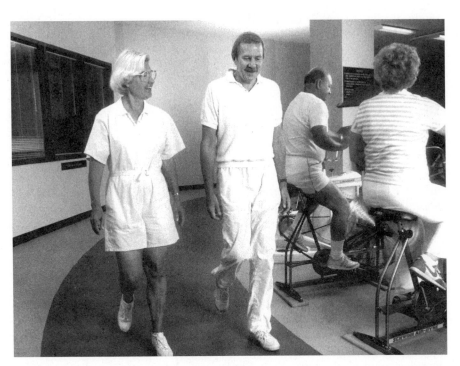

A combination of counseling and exercise programs may be part of a total wellness program.

matters. Supervisors also may have the authority to take action on organizational conditions that are creating employee problems. Supervisory counselors may help activate organizational opportunities that could help an individual develop abilities and fulfill both personal and company goals and ambitions.

Perhaps the main handicap in having supervisors counsel their own workers lies in the fact that workers may wish to avoid revealing some of their personal problems, feelings, and ambitions to their bosses. Look back at the Danny Tabor case that opened the chapter. Why isn't Danny opening up to Bruce? Employees such as Danny may feel threatened by the authority of their supervisors, and they may be afraid to confide in them. This reluctance to open up and discuss problems freely with one's supervisor may seriously impede managerial attempts to assist the employee. Notice Bruce's frustration in the opening case, for example.

Because in more cases than not, the manager will find it appropriate to counsel with his or her own workers, the comments and suggestions in this chapter concentrate particularly on the manager's role as a counselor. It is important to remember, however, that some forms of counseling, particularly therapeutic counseling, are usually done best by trained counseling specialists. Therapeutic counseling can be very dangerous and very delicate.

Conditions for Effective Counseling

Many types of counseling can occur spontaneously, and this is often a desirable way of coping with a problem or plotting a course of action. Other counseling sessions, however, are planned in advance and are instigated deliberately and methodically. In either case, certain conditions are conducive to a higher degree of success and effectiveness. Some of the conditions are environmental; others are within the participants themselves.

Set the Stage

The location (setting) of the counseling session is vital to the type of discussion that will occur. Ideally, when a supervisor and a worker are talking together in a counseling session, the location should be a room that will be nonthreatening to the person receiving the counseling and one that is private, free of noise, and removed from potential distractions.[6] The manager's office may not be the best place for a discussion to take place, because in psychological terms, the territory belongs to the boss and may result in domination by the manager/counselor. The counselee may feel intimidated as a result of being on the counselor's turf. A conference room where both the counselor and the counselee sit as equals across a table (or, as suggested in Chapter 5, at right angles to each other) may be more conducive to an open exchange of ideas.

Additional environmental conditions that might help to overcome authority barriers are desirable. Counseling should occur in an interruption-free atmosphere. Ideally, conversations should take place in an area free of interference from phone calls, people knocking on the door, or other distractions. Another intruder could be the time clock. Serious counseling sessions should be held when both the counselor and the counselee have the sufficient time to give complete attention to the issue before them. These and other ideal climate factors, while not always possible to achieve, aid the counselor and the counselee as they endeavor to achieve their common goals.

What About the People Themselves?

Perhaps even more important than climate factors are the attitudes, perceptions, and abilities of the participants themselves. It is especially important that the counselor have a positive outlook on the potential usefulness of counseling and the abilities of the counselee to contribute meaningfully as counseling takes place. In a National Defense Education Act study, it was discovered that "good" counselors have a set of values and perceptions that differ from less effective counselors. Study results showed the following:

1. In general perception orientation, good counselors are more likely to perceive:
   a. from an internal view rather than an external one
   b. in terms of people rather than things
2. In their perceptions of other people, good counselors see others as:
   a. able rather than unable
   b. dependable rather than undependable
   c. friendly rather than unfriendly
   d. worthy rather than unworthy
3. In their perceptions of themselves, good counselors perceive themselves as:
   a. identifying with people rather than being apart from them

    b.   having enough rather than wanting

    c.   self-revealing rather than self-concealing

4. In their perceptions of goals and purposes as counselors, good counselors are:

    a.   freeing rather than controlling

    b.   unselfish rather than self-serving

    c.   concerned with larger rather than smaller meanings[7]

Many of these attitudes and beliefs are very similar to those stressed by Douglas McGregor in his description of the "Theory Y manager." McGregor proposes that managers can be classified into one of two categories, based on their beliefs about workers—Theory X managers or Theory Y managers. Managers holding Theory Y beliefs take the position that employees are capable, willing, and able to participate. They have faith in their employees in the sense of believing that they want to do a good job without needing to be prodded. McGregor also finds that people with these beliefs are more effective managers. Apparently, as suggested by this study, similar beliefs can also contribute to effectiveness as a counselor.[8]

Preparing for the Counseling Session

The following section looks at counseling techniques. One of those techniques (the one that is given the most emphasis) stresses the value of allowing the counselee to identify personal problems or goals and arrive at actionable conclusions. If this approach is to be used, it has been suggested that the counselor's attitude toward the person being counseled (an employee, for example) should include the following:

1. A belief that the individual is responsible for self and is mature enough to keep that responsibility.

2. A belief that a person is capable of solving his or her own problems once he or she recognizes them.

3. A belief that people want to be understood, not judged. True feelings can be expressed only by developing a permissive atmosphere.

4. A belief that the individual is important, hence, the creation of a feeling of acceptance.

5. A deep-seated respect for the feelings of the employee (counselee). Disagreement and argument will not enhance this respect. Only by trying to understand the individual's feeling can a mutual respect be created.[9]

In preparing for counseling, the counselor needs to do some attitude development about self as well. The counselor must prepare his or her mind so that there is a desire to be helpful, since the desire to be of service is a key ingredient in successful counseling. Carl Rogers has suggested that some soul-searching should go on within the counselor's mind. He suggests that questions such as the following should be asked by the counselor:

1. Can I be perceived by the other person (counselee) to be trustworthy, dependable, or consistent in some deep sense?

2. Can I be expressive enough as a person that what I am will be communicated unambiguously?

Counseling requires
empathy and respect
for the counselee on
the part of the coun-
selor.

3. Can I let myself experience positive attitudes toward this other per-
    son—attitudes of warmth, caring, liking, interest, respect?
4. Can I be strong enough as a person to be able to empathize with the
    counselee while maintaining my role as an independent person?
5. Am I secure enough as a person to permit the counselee his or her
    separateness (individuality)?
6. Can I let myself enter freely into the world of others' feelings and
    personal meanings and see things as they do?
7. Can I receive the counselee as he or she is? Can I communicate with
    this attitude?
8. Can I act with sufficient sensitivity in the relationship that my behav-
    ior will not be perceived as a threat?
9. Can I free the counselee from the threat of external evaluation? (This
    is a very difficult step to achieve.)
10. Can I meet this other individual as a person who is in the process
    of *becoming,* or will I be bound by the counselee's past and by
    my past?[10]

As can be seen, preparation on the part of the counselor is extremely
important. It is hoped that the counselee is prepared and capable as well. If
the counselee can be objective, feels secure, has confidence in the counselor,

is a skilled communicator, and desires improvement, it will be more likely that counseling will succeed and worthy objectives will be accomplished.

Two Counseling Techniques

While there are many approaches to counseling, the two most discussed techniques are very different indeed. They are known as directive and nondirective counseling.

Directive Counseling

Directive counseling is a structured interaction controlled and led by the counselor. If the purpose of the counseling is corrective or remedial in nature, the counselor pointedly asks (or tells) the counselee what the problem is, asks (or tells) the counselee what the alternatives are, and asks (or tells) the counselee the course of action to be taken for improvement. If the counseling session is for developmental purposes, the counselor leads (again through asking or telling) the counselee into what the goals are or should be, leads in the analysis of the capabilities of the individual to develop those skills, and charts a course of action. If the counseling purpose is therapeutic, the counselor guides in the diagnosis of weaknesses and the prescription of solutions. If the purpose is to provide information to or gather information from, the counselee, straightforward communication results in the inclusion of little superfluous material.

> **directive counseling**
> A structured communicative interaction where the counselor leads in the identification of problems, alternatives, and solutions by asking questions and giving answers.

Directive counseling may include a large amount of advice giving, admonishment, exhortation (motivational pep talks on how and why the counselee should improve or change behavior), explanation, and reassurance (the giving of encouragement).[11]

Directive counseling is counselor-centered to a large degree. It is the counselor who activates and controls the thought processes of the interaction. If the counselor is unusually skillful, it may be possible to draw the counselee into the discussion, but seldom does the counselee become wholeheartedly involved in seeking solutions or development. Counseling that is too direct and too forceful may tend to choke off involvement and may push the counselee into a defensive, protective position.

These comments should not be taken as a complete rejection of the use of directive counseling in every situation, because there are places in which forceful leadership is required to compel individuals to think and act. There are times when individuals (counselees) are incapable of discovering problems, objectives, and courses of action on their own. Some counselees respond better to a more directive approach. There are also situations in which time permits the use of only direct, to-the-point counseling. The directive technique may be the answer to such needs.

Directive counseling may be the only technique that supervisors who tend toward an authoritative leadership style will adopt. Nondirective techniques may be out of character for such supervisors and may result in role inconsistencies. Bosses who are oriented toward participative or free-rein management may prefer the nondirective approach. Even for these managers, however, there will be times when it is necessary to be more directive.

One instance the authors vividly recall involved Edward. Edward was bright—no doubt about it. He was well trained—he had done well in school and had been out of school for over five years. He had begun his career with a large government agency on the East Coast. His work record was excellent, and when he decided to move to Houston, he was promptly granted a transfer to the agency's office there. It was then that the problems began.

As Edward's new boss (the agency manager in Houston) told it to us, Edward ran into problems almost immediately. Edward's work required careful analysis of records furnished by the companies that came under the agency's jurisdiction. Unfortunately, Edward wasn't thorough. It looked like he often took the easiest approach rather than devoting the time and attention that the cases required. In addition, Edward was in the habit of talking rather than listening. When his boss would ask why he had taken a particular approach to a case, Edward would respond with a whole battery of excuses for his actions.

"I've never been so frustrated!" Edward's boss told us. "I'm committed to working WITH employees and helping them to solve their problems. But that approach simply wasn't working with Edward. Every time I tried to get him to talk about his performance, he would give me a list of excuses—reasons, he called them—and end by saying, 'That's not how we did it in my old office!' I knew I'd have to change tactics."

"What did you do?" we asked.

"Well," responded the manager. "I took a directive approach. I walked Edward through the procedures as WE do them HERE! Then I discussed—as objectively as I could—what I saw to be his deficiencies when compared to the standards of our office. Finally, I told Edward I expected his cooperation in meeting those standards if he intended to keep working for the agency *here*."

"What happened?" we asked.

"It was amazing," responded the manager. "Edward came right around. He said he'd just never realized the difference in expectations—though I still don't see how he could have missed that! In any case, he assured me I'd see a difference right away. And I'm delighted to say that I have—he's turning into a fine employee."

Why would a directive approach work so well with Edward? It's hard to say. People really are different, and managers need to use flexibility in searching for the counseling style best suited for each individual.

Nondirective Counseling

The alternative approach is the nondirective approach. **Nondirective counseling** is counselee-centered. When this technique is used, the counselor plays a supportive role. The counselor is present primarily to listen and to help the counselee verbalize his or her thoughts. The *counselee* is encouraged to act as leader in the counseling discussion so that it will fit his or her needs and personal ideas. The counselor adopts the philosophy that the counselee is responsible for self, is capable of solving personal problems, wants to be understood, is an important human being, and has feelings that deserve to be respected.

nondirective counseling
Communication between counselor and counselee in which the counselor listens and encourages the counselee to identify problems, alternatives, and solutions. The role of the counselor is supportive rather than dominating.

In the pure form of nondirective counseling, the counselor does not diagnose the employee's problems, offer solutions to the employee's problems, or give advice.[12] In the role of a supportive listener, the counselor reflects the counselee's thoughts back, attempts to increase perspective, and helps to explore thoughts that may not have been previously considered. Although nondirective counseling is not closely structured, the counselor would like to help the counselee do the following:

1. Identify current features—the problems, attitudes, and capabilities of the counselee.
2. Determine what is to be achieved through counseling—what are the objectives or goals of counseling.
3. Discover specific actions to achieve those objectives or solutions.

By most accounts, nondirective counseling began accidentally. At the Hawthorne, Illinois, plant of Western Electric, where the famed Hawthorne studies took place, researchers were extremely interested in finding out more from workers about their motivations and feelings. The direct approach was being used, but without the desired results. The procedure was then relaxed, and employees were allowed to talk about whatever they wanted instead of being asked specific, predetermined questions. Answers became revealing as more personal data were provided. The technique of nondirective counseling then became the standard method for communicating with employees in most organizations.[13]

The counselor using the nondirective technique helps the counselee in a number of ways. Before the counseling begins, the counselor tries to arrange environmental and personal conditions so that they will facilitate the counseling interaction. The counselor tries to provide an interruption-free place, the necessary time, and his or her own mental preparedness so that he or she can give the counselee support and assistance.

The nondirective interview has basically three parts: an initiation phase, an exploration or development phase, and a closing phase. In the initiation phase, the counselor's role is mostly one of trying to help the counselee feel at ease and to establish rapport so that a good discussion can occur. Together the counselor and counselee briefly explore their previous relationship and their mutual interests. The counselor wants the counselee to know that he or she cares about and is interested in the counselee's growth and welfare. The early stages of nondirective counseling may involve encouraging the counselee to get feelings and emotions out in the open. Once this is done, it seems easier to move to facts and solutions. In fact, there is one type of therapy designed to sort out emotions and rational thoughts.[14] If the counselee has initiated the interaction, the initiation phase may be extremely brief because the appropriate desire is already there.

Good Listening Skills. Active listening needs to be exercised by the counselor. **Active Listening** is not "passive absorption of words, but actively trying to grasp feelings and fact in such a way that the speaker can be helped to work out personal problems."[15] Active listening involves listening for total meaning, response to feelings, and the noting of all cues, such as facial expressions and body posture.

active listening
Making a concentrated effort to hear what the communicator is attempting to convey rather than passively absorbing the message. Seeking the purpose and intent of someone else's messages.

It is possible to develop good listening skills with training and practice. Here are some helpful suggestions that welcome messages from another individual:

1. Maintain eye contact with the speaker.
2. Use an open body stance, including leaning forward, which indicates an interest in what is being said.
3. Acknowledge the individual's presence promptly with a warm smile or nod of the head.
4. Avoid facial expressions that indicate anger, displeasure, or hurriedness.
5. If in an open area, walk toward the speaker to indicate interest.
6. Avoid long periods of silence that may leave the impression that you're not listening.
7. Be aware of gestures or other nonverbal cues that may send negative signals (e.g., finger tapping, rolling of the eyes, shrugging shoulders, and jiggling change).[16]

The counselor cannot fulfill the role of a good listener, of course, unless the counselee is saying something. If the employee is not talking, the counselor may extend an interested invitation to talk about whatever is on his or her mind. This can be done in the form of a soft question: "After working here for six months, how do you feel about your job?" "What thoughts do you have about the new work routine?" "You mentioned some concerns you had about your future when we talked last month. What are your thoughts about the future?" These questions indicate that the counselor has an interest in the counselee, and they open the door to bring thoughts out into the open. (See the Self-Test).

probe
An effort to get the counselee to talk about problems, alternatives, and solutions that seeks to be stimulating without being too demanding.

Probes.   *Probes* are slightly more direct questions used to stimulate discussion and obtain more information: "I'd like to know more about your thinking on this subject." "What did you have in mind when you said that?" "Is there anything else that might be affecting this situation?" The counselor must be careful to word probes so that they are not too pointed, do not put the employee on the defensive, and do not reveal any biases on the counselor's part. Probes serve to motivate the counselee to communicate more fully so that he or she enlarges, clarifies, or explains reasons behind what has previously been said.[17] Probes also invite attention to areas not previously identified or explored.

restatement
A technique used by the counselor to get the counselee to talk more by repeating what the counselee has just said.

Restatement.   Another extremely effective technique for encouraging the further revelation of ideas is the **restatement** by the counselor of points already made by the counselee in an attempt to encourage in-depth consideration of the thoughts. As Benjamin states, the restatement tells the counselee:

> I am listening to you very carefully, in fact, so that I can restate what you have said. I am doing so now because it may help you to hear yourself through me. I am restating what you have said so that you may absorb it and consider its impact, if any, on you. For the time being, I am keeping myself out of it.[18]

If an employee tells his boss, "I can hardly wait until I get old enough to retire—this job has gotten to be a regular monster," the boss as a counselor

Personal Feedback

Exercise in the Use of Restatement as a Means of Accomplishing Nondirective Counseling

Restatement has been identified as one of the more effective ways of encouraging counselees to talk further about things they want to say. In the following illustrations, which one of the responses is the best example of the restatement concept? What is wrong with each of the other responses? Be specific.

1. Jason McCall stops in the office of Bill Snowden the coach of the school basketball team, with a complaint. Jason, a forward on the team, tells Coach Snowden:

    "I just don't know what to do. The fellows on the team just don't accept me as an equal member. Instead of passing the ball to me, they look for someone else. Instead of talking to me, they only talk among themselves. I'm thinking of quitting."

    Coach Snowden responds by saying:

    a.   "Just don't pay any attention to them. You're new here. It takes time to be accepted by others."

    b.   "Why do you think they don't like you?"

    c.   "Maybe if you get a different haircut they will like you better."

    d.   "You say you feel they don't accept you?"

    e.   "I want you to ignore what others do and just do your best."

2. Jill Stanwick, product manager for a new line of merchandise with a large distribution firm, tells her boss:

    "You've got to give me more authority so that I can carry out my job in a better way. The people in my project group look to you instead of me, as their superior. I keep telling them to do things, and they tell me that they have to talk to you before they can do anything. I find it very frustrating to be bypassed in this way."

    Her boss responds by saying:

    a.   "You go out there and tell them to pay attention to your directions or else."

    b.   "I'll have a talk with them and see what we can work out."

    c.   "You say you are very frustrated?"

    d.   "If you were older than the people you are supervising, you wouldn't be having this problem."

    e.   "No job's perfect, is it?"

might use restatement by saying, "You say your job has gotten to be a monster?" When a worker tells her supervisor, "I don't feel this job utilizes my abilities and knowledge fully," the boss could reflectively restate, "Your job doesn't utilize your abilities and knowledge fully?" Usually, the boss pauses to allow the worker to think about the restatement and to encourage the worker to elaborate. Doing this usually provides the necessary amount of encouragement to bring important ideas to the surface.

Table 12–1

Steps to Remember in Conducting a Nondirective Counseling Session

1. Be prepared.

If you—either as a professional counselor or as some type of supervisor—are aware that a particular individual is coming in later in the day to discuss a problem, it is always wise to know as much about the individual as possible. In most companies, handy reference can be made to a person's personnel folder. If the employee appears unannounced and no advance preparation is possible, it is always best to be prepared for such happenings by a periodic review of your subordinates. In this way, some knowledge of your people is always with you.

2. Put the counselee at ease.

There are many ways to achieve this. Hold the interview in comfortable surroundings where you can both sit and relax. People are always willing to talk more fully in surroundings conducive to personal comfort.

3. Establish a rapport.

This refers to establishing a friendly, rather close relationship between yourself and the counselee. Let the counselee know that you want to listen and that what is said will be held in the strictest confidence. In Himler's words, there must be a mutual feeling of friendliness and sympathetic unity. You need to convey to the individual that you want to share his or her problem and aid in deciding on a definite course of action.

4. Don't argue or admonish.

If you start one of these, immediately the counselee will assume a defensive position. If the counselee senses that he or she is in the wrong in any way, this can cause a higher level of emotionalism than may have been present at first. Any kind of negativism may defeat the purpose of the interview. Defensiveness in attitudes causes issues to become hazy and more involved.

5. Don't display authority.

Avoid exerting any authority before this individual, not only organizational authority but also intellectual authority. People resent social subordination, so do not command

Closing the Session.   If ideas have been explored fully, the counselee has identified the problem or goals, all angles have been considered, and solutions have been discerned or conclusions reached to the mutual satisfaction of the counselee and the counselor, the counselor can help the counselee to close the immediate conversation gracefully. There is no established formula for winding down a counseling session. The counselor should attempt to keep the relationship an easy, open one. If a concluding summarization of facts and resolutions is appropriate, the counselor can see that this is accomplished. For example, towards the end of a session, the boss might begin by saying to Linda, the employee, "You've made several important points in our discussion this afternoon, Linda. As I understand it, here's how you feel. . . ." The boss will often promise interest in the counselee's progress and emphasize a desire to give continuing support and assistance.

Table 12–1
continued

or confuse. Talk *with* the counselee, not *to* the counselee. Seek to understand and be understood.

---

6.   *Listen carefully.*

This is essential to nondirective interviewing. Listen critically for negative and positive feelings. Don't interrupt. Encourage the counselee to speak fully and openly without fear. Echo statements back through careful questioning, and the use of facial expressions and body movements. And remember to listen with the eyes as well as the ears. Seek to understand through good listening.

---

7.   *Don't advise.*

Try to avoid giving the counselee advice, even though he or she may emotionally ask, "But what should I do?" Keep encouraging the counselee to speak; in this way, emotions are cleared away. Sooner or later the counselee will come up with solutions. Seize upon this and encourage more probing. You can perhaps answer some questions about company policies and procedures but offer as little as possible direct advice for solving the problem. Keep the talking going so that self-awareness and insight can begin occurring.

---

8.   *Help clarify positive courses of action.*

When the counselee does start making positive suggestions, encourage continuance so that the consequences of his or her behavior are understood. An occasional suggestion might help after this stage is reached. Let the counselee know you agree when the right courses of action are identified. Ask questions to be sure that alternatives are considered but let the counselee make the choice.

Source: I. L. Heckman Jr., and S. G. Huneryager, *Human Relations in Management,* Cincinnati: South-Western Publishing Company, 1960, pp. 508–509, used by permission of the authors.

For another view of how to conduct a nondirective counseling session, note the suggestions of Heckmann and Huneryager in Table 12–1.

An Example of Nondirective Counseling.   When is nondirective counseling most useful? Let's look back at the Danny Tabor case that opened this chapter. Suppose Bruce and Danny have sat down in a quiet room, free of interruptions. Let's see one way Bruce could handle the interview:

Bruce: *Danny, several days ago you mentioned to me that you're concerned that your progress isn't as quick as you'd hoped it would be. I'm here to give you support and assistance, and I want to be of help to you. Overall, how are you feeling?*

Danny: *Oh, I don't know. . . .*

Bruce: *(Pause, looks concerned)*

(Incidentally, we should point out that a well-placed pause can be vital in discussions such as this one. In effect, Bruce is waiting for Danny to collect his thoughts rather than jumping in and asking questions. The signal to Danny is that Bruce is really concerned and will wait to see what Danny's ideas are.)

Danny: *I feel like there's so much on me.*

Bruce: *You feel there's a lot on you?*

(Note Bruce's effective use of restatement here. Bruce signals Danny that he's heard him, lets Danny hear his own words, and opens the door for further exploration.)

Danny: *Well, you know there* are *times when nothing seems to go right.* . . .

Bruce: *Nothing seems to be working out?*

(*Another* effective restatement.)

Danny: *Well, it all started with my wife's dizzy spells a month or so back.* . . .

(Now Danny is really starting to open up!)

Bruce: *I see.* . . .

(This is called an *understanding listening response*—it signals that you're concerned and want the speaker to continue. Often, a nod, eye contact, or a sympathetic smile can serve the same purpose.)

Danny: *Actually, it's been a* horrible *period. I didn't want to worry you with this, but I'm concerned it could really be serious. The doctors don't know what it is. I've tried to be with her all I can.* . . .

We can safely leave Bruce and Danny now. Bruce's effective use of the nondirective technique has let Danny start the dialogue he so badly needs. We should expect that as Bruce listens and expresses concern and sympathy, Danny will be able to talk about his feelings. Once the problem is out in the open, Danny will be able to look for solutions, again with Bruce providing support and minimal guidance. Obviously, nondirective counseling can be a powerful managerial tool when effectively used.

Applying Contingency Theory to Counseling

We've seen situations where both types of counseling—directive and nondirective—have advantages. Each has occasions or situations in which it is most useful. The same concepts that were applied to the selection of leadership styles in Chapter 10 are appropriate for the selection of a counseling technique. While Table 12–2 fills in the important details, we can generalize by saying that a combination of variables based upon organizational conditions; counselor preference, attitudes, and abilities; counselee attitudes and abilities; and task situations may influence the choice of the proper counseling technique as the vehicle for accomplishing organizational-personal goals. Directive counseling usually is more appropriate when the end result of counseling is already known and the means to achieve it are easily visible.[19] The nondirective approach works best when the desired end result is not known from the beginning and the intermediate steps to success are still open to debate. There are of course, a number of additional considerations.

Froehle and Broadwell focus only on the counselee in developing their situational approach. They suggest three central questions to ask in identifying the right kind of counseling (they call it therapy) to provide for the counselee. The first question is, Does the individual (employee) have the *ability* to do what is needed or to find solutions that are needed? The second question is, Does the individual have the *willingness* (desire or motivation) to do what is necessary? The third question is, Does the individual have the *confidence* in his or her own ability to do what is necessary?[20]

Figure 12–2 shows that the results of the Froehle-Broadwell study are based along two axes—one axis is directive behavior of the therapist, and the other axis is supportive behavior of the therapist. In the first quadrant, the individual is unable, unwilling, and lacking in confidence, and the *telling* style, which is high in directive counseling and low in supportive counseling, is appropriate. In the second quadrant, the employee is unable and unwilling and needs the *teaching* style. In the third quadrant, the employee is able and willing but lacks confidence. The employee needs *supporting* here but not telling or teaching. In the fourth quadrant, the employee has everything needed and just needs *delegating*. Recall that the Hersey-Blanchard model in Chapter 10 used this approach. Froehle-Broadwell have built upon the Hersey-Blanchard foundation

Most supervisory personnel who attempt to perform counseling may find it difficult to adhere to a pure form of nondirective counseling because it may appear awkward and have a tendency to drift and ramble. However, if managers make the effort to listen rather than dominate the conversation, to be open rather than overly restrictive, and to be helpful instead of forceful, a useful form of nondirective counseling can be achieved. Most experienced counselors believe that nondirective counseling will provide many longer lasting results for the counselee and the employer than will directive counseling. Nondirective counseling will be a particularly natural style for those with staff positions, because the role of the staff specialist usually coincides precisely with the role of the nondirective counselor. Few adjustments may be necessary for the staff specialist, because he or she may already be cast in a helping role.

The Ethics and Obligations of Counseling

Because counseling often probes into the ambitions, attitudes, and personal problems of individual employees, questions are frequently raised concerning how ethical it is for the manager-counselor to pry into the personal matters of an individual. The position is often expressed that counseling invades the privacy of personal lives and enters areas where managers have no right to delve. In many cases, this is probably a valid position.

Managers who serve as counselors to their subordinates have the right to be concerned only with behavior and attitudes that affect the employee's level

Table 12–2

Factors in Selection of a Counseling Approach

Factor Variable	Counseling Method	
	Directive Factors in the Organization	Nondirective
1. Is the organization concerned about achieving organizational goals and helping employees to achieve their own goals?	Tends to be more organizationally oriented, although not always planned that way.	Fits best in organizations that are both performance and people oriented.
2. What kinds of communication networks are maintained within the organization?	Works more easily in organizations with stronger downward communication channels.	Good two-way communication systems helpful.
3. What kind of spans of supervision and control exists?	May be applied with either wide or narrow spans.	Because a large amount of time is involved and personal rapport is important, narrow spans of supervision make application easier.

Factors in the Manager-Counselor

Factor Variable	Directive	Nondirective
1. For what purposes does the manager-counselor view the use of counseling?	As a means of increasing control over the subordinate, as an important method of achieving an organizational goal.	As a means of simultaneously helping the individual involved and the organization.
2. How important is it to the supervisor that his or her own authority position be maintained?	The counselor who constantly prefers this approach tends to regard the maintenance of authority positions as very important.	The counselor using this approach normally feels fairly secure in his or her own authority and tends to be unconcerned about threats to it.
3. What attitude does the manager-counselor have toward counselees?	Typically has a limited amount of confidence and trust in the counselee's abilities and intentions, tends to be somewhat insensitive to the feelings of the counselee.	Holds a high assessment of the abilities and intentions of counselees, believes people are capable of identifying their own goals and supplying their own solutions, is sensitive to the feelings and attitudes of others.

Table 12–2
continued

4. How well trained is the counselor as a discussion leader? as a listener?	Usually a capable, forceful leader; listening skills not required in this approach.	Must be a particularly capable listener; it is helpful if he or she is skilled at helping others to talk.

Factors in the Counselee

1. Is the counselee self-motivating and self-controlling, or is external pressure necessary to get the counselee moving and on the right track?	Since this approach does not require self-motivation and self-control, it is usually assumed that the employee needs external pressures.	It normally is assumed that the employee is self-motivating and and self-controlling.
2. Is the counselee articulate, knowledgeable, and otherwise capable of identifying problems and goals and finding desirable courses of action?	Need not be particularly articulate, knowledgeable, or capable; may be offended by this approach if he or she is.	It is helpful if the if the counselee is articulate, knowledgeable, and capable.
3. Does the counselee need and want a degree of independence and self-determination, or would he or she prefer to let others lead?	Works best when the counselee would prefer to let others make decisions.	Usually is more satisfactory when the counselee wants a degree of independence and self-determination.

Factors in the Task Situation

1. How well defined are the counseling and consultation?	Normally most useful when the desired end result is known, the means to achieve it are available, and little or no variations are desired.	Most useful when the end result is not completely known in advance and individual initiative is highly desirable in uncovering the end and the means to achieve it.
2. How much time is available for counseling and consultation?	Since objectives are more clearly stated and methods to achieve them are more prescribed, this approach can move more quickly to completion.	Normally unfolds slowly, deliberately; as a result, significant amounts of time are required.

Figure 12–2

Matching Counseling
to Individual Needs
and Characteristics

Source: Thomas C. Froehle
and Gilda Broadwell,
"Therapy Duration: Inde-
pendence of Field Practi-
tioners," *Counseling and
Human Development,* Vol-
ume 21, Number 5, January
1989, pp. 1–16. Adapted
from G. S. Howard, D. W.
Nance, and P. Myers, *Adaptive Counseling and Therapy: A Systematic Approach
to Selecting Effective Treat-
ments,* p. 45 (table). © 1987
by Jossey-Bass Inc., Pub-
lishers.

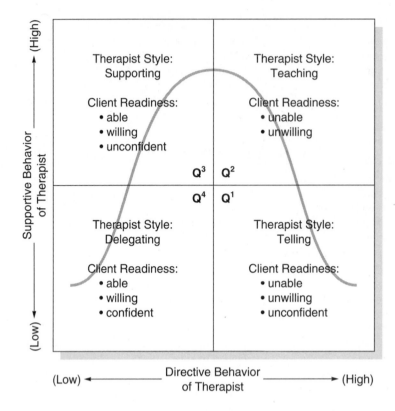

of performance at work—how well the employee is contributing to the organization, whether or not the individual is carrying a fair share of the workload,
and whether the person is preparing for future responsibilities. As stated earlier, managers have the right to help individual employees examine their organizational needs, responsibilities, and problems and to focus on the negative
consequences of an employee's actions. If counseling discloses that personal
attitudes or personal needs are the source of concern, the ethical manager's
role is to listen, reflect, and support but not to enforce or command. The
manager-counselor may even find it necessary to caution the counselee about
going too far in unveiling private details of his or her life that are best kept
secret.

    Another important ethical consideration should be the confidential nature
of ideas exchanged and feelings communicated during counseling. Information given in confidence should be kept in confidence. When important personal information is to be communicated to other individuals (up the chain of
command, for example), counselors do indeed have a heavy burden of
responsibility for the ethical use of information collected during counseling
sessions. A general guideline may be that direct work-related information may
go forward and that other, personal information should not.

Summary

Counseling can serve a number of purposes in an organizational setting. Counseling can be corrective, therapeutic, informational, developmental, or a combination of these. As a part of their duties and responsibilities, many managers will find themselves in a position where an employee needs their help through a counseling relationship. Sometimes, especially where therapeutic counseling is needed, counseling specialists may be called upon.

Two counseling techniques are used in working with employees: directive and nondirective counseling. In many situations, nondirective counseling is more successful because it allows the person being counseled to do most of the problem identification and the development of solutions. There is no one set technique for all counseling situations, however. The ability, willingness, and confidence level of the person being counseled may be determining factors for the selection of the appropriate counseling style.

One of the most important steps in any counseling situation is the creation of the right atmosphere for counseling. The right atmosphere is one that is neutral and nonthreatening and free of interruptions. Sufficient time also needs to be available.

It would be a miscalculation to assume that counseling is the key that opens the door to all personal problem-solving and developmental tasks that managers face. Counseling only provides a mechanism whereby attitudes, interests, objectives, and problems and their causes can be brought to the surface. Skillful counseling can unlock some doors, identify some attitudes, present some alternative courses of action, and help individuals to outline programs of development.

While a number of conditions must prevail for counseling to be successful, the counselor can go a long way in securing such success through adequate preparation for a counseling session. The counselor's own attitude is important. The more the counselor is counselee oriented, the more helpful he or she will be when actual counseling takes place. Both directive and nondirective counseling have their place in the fulfillment of organizational and personal goals. The choice of a particular technique for a particular situation may be aided by the use of contingency theory.

The ethical responsibilities of the manager-counselor must be recognized and observed. Counselors should go no further than they have a right to go. The confidentiality of information exchanged is also of primary importance.

Questions to Consider

1. A professional counselor's time is expensive. Is it really the organization's duty to provide professional counseling?
2. The effects of counseling are very difficult to measure. What are some things that can be done to evaluate the effects of counseling?
3. What problems may exist for the manager-counselor in formal, planned counseling sessions that might not exist in informal, unplanned

counseling? What problems may develop for the manager-counselor in spontaneous counseling that might not occur in planned counseling?

4. One of the conditions for optimum counseling is said to be a desire on the part of the counselee to improve self and the organization. Do employees universally wish to improve themselves and to rid themselves and their employers of problems? Explain your answer.

5. Why do most of the experts recommend the nondirective counseling technique most of the time over the directive approach?

6. What should the counselor do if all of the techniques mentioned in the chapter are tried to get the counselee to talk (under nondirective counseling) and the counselee refuses to respond?

7. When nondirective counseling reaches the stage where alternative solutions are being reviewed, what should the counselor do if the counselee asks for an opinion concerning which course of action to take?

8. How are counseling sessions best closed? What should be done? By whom?

9. How can a counselor learn to listen more and talk less in counseling sessions?

10. What if the counselee reveals information that members of the management really need to know but asks the counselor to keep the information confidential? What should the counselor do?

11. What kind of information can counselors ethically attempt to get from counselees?

12. Role play a situation in which a worker has a problem that is keeping him or her from peak performance, for example, because of lack of interest in the job or personal problems at home. How would a counselor using the directive counseling technique go about dealing with the employee? A counselor using the nondirective technique?

13. Role play the case at the beginning of the chapter by applying the concepts discussed in the chapter using the directive and nondirective techniques.

Key Terms

active listening	directive	probe
corrective	counseling	restatement
counseling	informational	therapeutic
developmental	counseling	counseling
counseling	nondirective	
	counseling	

Chapter Case

Terry the Dispatcher

This is a case that can be role played effectively. You are Terry Cleburne, and you are a dispatcher in the shipping department of a large supply house. It is annual performance appraisal time, and your boss wants to see you. You're pretty sure that it's about the appraisal. You have mixed feelings about how this session will turn out. There are some positive things—you generally like the job and respect your boss. You consider your boss to really know the job and believe that your boss is basically a fair, reasonable person.

There are some things that worry you, however. For one thing, you have had some difficulties and disagreements with the people in the repair department. Your boss has talked to you several times about improving your relations with them. You have tried, to some extent at least, to get straightened out with the repair people, but things haven't really gone well. You feel that the repair employees are a bunch of showoffs who have no respect for dispatch personnel. The repair people act like spoiled children whenever things don't go their way. You wish your boss would support you and go to the supervisor of repairs to try to iron things out, but your boss doesn't seen interested in doing that at all. Instead, your boss stays on you to do it yourself. Lately, you've decided that the only thing to do is to show the people in the repair department, indirectly that they can't get away with bullying you. You're just polite enough to them that they can't complain. To get back at them, you try to do little things like assigning them long driving times.

You are also concerned that home problems are affecting your work. Your teenaged daughter has been running around with a wild crowd and has had some scrape with the law. Now, worse yet, you suspect that drugs may be involved. When all of this gets on your mind, you sometimes feel that you've lost all ability to concentrate. You also get irritable, which adds to the problem with the repair people. Your boss has seemed concerned and has tried to draw you out several times in the past, but you haven't opened up—partly because you're embarrassed and partly because you feel as an adult that you should solve your problems on your own. You have decided that if your boss seems sincerely concerned, you will open up.

1. Role play the counseling session (performance appraisal) that might have occurred between you and your boss. Let's let your boss lead off.
2. Would directive or nondirective counseling be the appropriate managerial style to use? Why?
3. What preparations would be needed before directive counseling could be used? Before nondirective counseling could be used?
4. As Terry's boss, how would you go about getting Terry to talk if you used the nondirective way? Show the pattern this approach would follow.
5. Do the same for the directive approach. What would you say and do?

Chapter 13

Managing Conflict

Objectives

- To ascertain a manager's goals when conflict occurs.
- To identify typical causes of conflict.
- To recognize that the presence of conflict is not always destructive.
- To identify constructive processes for the resolution of conflict.
- To see the strengths and weaknesses of the different conflict management techniques.
- To develop skills for handling conflict when it arises.

Elizabeth Reynolds—The Secretary Everyone Wants

Aaron Slade is regional sales manager for World-International Airlines. He administers a wide range of responsibilities and has three district sales managers (in the same office) who cover smaller territories within the region to help him fulfill his duties. One of the district sales managers, James Calton, is retiring at the beginning of next month. The retirement of this district manager has created something of a crisis between the two remaining district managers in a unique way. Each of the managers wants Calton's personal secretary to become his or her own secretary.

Calton's secretary, Elizabeth Reynolds, is a long-time employee of World-International and knows its operation from the inside out. She is exceptionally knowledgeable, capable, and skilled as an executive secretary. Reynolds has been an employee of World-International for almost twenty-five years, the past eighteen of which she was Calton's secretary. She is totally familiar with the responsibilities and functions of a district sales manager's office. Her vast knowledge of the office duties and her superior abilities create the keen demand for her skills. As a result, a clash has developed between Charles Wong and Marilu Powell, the two remaining DSMs.

Both Wong and Powell have demanded of Don Bright, the regional personnel director, that Reynolds be assigned to them as personal secretary upon Calton's retirement. Wong has told Bright that he should be entitled to Reynold's assistance for the following reasons:

1. Wong has the longest seniority with World-International, both in years of total service and in rank. He has been with World-International for twenty years and has been a district sales manager for nine years. Powell has been with the organization only fourteen years and has been a district sales manager for only three years.
2. Wong is out of town almost constantly and needs someone in his office who can handle matters competently in his absence. His present secretary has made a number of mistakes and appears incapable of performing well in his absence.
3. Wong has spoken with Ms. Reynolds about making the move to his office, and she has indicated her willingness to do so.

Powell has also argued her case before Bright. She states that

1. She requested Ms. Reynolds be transferred to her office at an early date, several days before Wong made his request.
2. Her secretary resigned a few weeks ago to move to a different city. She has no secretary, therefore, while Wong already has one.
3. Ms. Reynolds could be of invaluable assistance to her (because of her knowledge and experience) as she formulates new plans for the district that she supervises. Powell, too, is out of town a large percentage of the time.

Both Wong and Powell have been rigid in their demands, and hostility seems to be developing between them. Bright has been unable to resolve the problem, and there is no precedent upon which he can base a decision. He has no authority over either Wong or Powell. When vacancies have occurred in secretarial positions in the past, it has been Bright's responsibility to screen applicants and forward qualified prospects to the manager in need of replacement personnel. Mr. Bright has been searching for an appropriate replacement of Powell's secretary for nearly a month and has sent two candidates to Powell's office. However, Powell is adamant in her wish to have Ms. Reynolds as her secretary. Mr. Bright also realizes that he must find a personal secretary for the new district sales manager as soon as one is appointed.

Because Bright lacks the authority to decide which DSM will have Reynolds as his or her secretary, he has requested that the regional sales manager (Aaron Slade) step in and handle the situation, and Slade has accepted this responsibility.

Case Questions

1. As Slade (the RSM) assumes responsibility for resolving the differences between the two DSMs, what should his goals include? Please be specific.
2. What are the specific, underlying causes of the conflict that is developing. In other words, what's to blame for this situation?
3. The hostilities between Wong and Powell have already begun to develop. What should Slade do to resolve these hostilities?
4. Does Reynolds have any rights in the matter? What about her preferences? Is she merely the object of the decision, or is she an integral part of it?

traditional view
An attitude toward conflict that anticipates that each situation of dispute and disagreement can have only bad results. Since this is expected, conflict is considered to be something to avoid or eliminate.

contemporary view
An attitude that considers conflict to be inevitable when people work together. The role of the manager, therefore, is to attempt to turn conflict into desirable consequences with constructive results for the organization and its people.

One of the primary purposes of the organization is the coordination and integration of the efforts of a number of people to attain mutual goals and objectives. As people work together, tensions sometimes develop that result in dissension and hostility. Traditionally, conflict has been considered to be something that does not have to take place but frequently does. It has been viewed as a consequence of greed, self-centeredness, and competition. Conflict has been seen as a disruptive force that keeps organizations from being optimally productive. In the **traditional view,** managers are supposed to eliminate conflict from the organization. Conflict is seen to be harmful in its consequences.

A more **contemporary view** sees conflict as inevitable when people work together. Conflict occurs as a consequence of many factors, including the struggle to excel and achieve. Conflict, while sometimes working in a detrimental way, can also have constructive effects on organizational and personal performance. A certain amount of conflict and tension may even be essential for optimal performance to occur. Managers must control conflict so that the result is positive and beneficial to the organization and its members. The difference between successful and unsuccessful outcomes from conflict is partially a result of the leadership skills of the supervisors involved. Constructive conflict management may also be a product of the proper identification and treatment of problem areas.

Look back at the Elizabeth Reynolds case that opened this chapter. It's easy to see that there is conflict between the two DSMs over which one—if either of them—will get Reynolds as a personal secretary. It's also easy to see that this conflict can be harmful to the organization. While the conflict is in progress, both DSMs may be paying more attention to it than to other, more important issues—such as increasing sales in their units. But could it be possible to constructively manage conflict such as this? For example, could it be possible to find a solution that strengthens the individuals and departments involved and leaves the organization in a better position to meet its competition and sell its product? Such possibilities make the ability to skillfully manage conflict essential for managers at all organizational levels.

Management's Goals When Conflict Arises

If conflict is to be managed positively and constructively, those who manage need a set of goals and objectives. While the goals discussed in the following sections may not always be attained, they provide a helpful set of guidelines to pursue. When conflict arises, managers and supervisors who are in a position to influence and affect the attitudes and actions of those in disagreement may find it helpful to (1) identify the causes and feelings of the parties involved, (2) redirect the tension and hostilities, (3) work to integrate ideas rather than accept a compromise, (4) achieve unity between the parties in conflict, and (5) accomplish real and permanent solutions.

Identifying What's Behind the Conflict

Conflict may be symptomatic of more deep-seated problems that may need attention and corrective action. The underlying causes of conflict, if left unattended, can fester and develop into even deeper, more severe problems. Resolution of conflict that deals only with surface tensions and not with actual causes can be considered only a temporary treatment of conflict. A more thorough approach to conflict is to identify and deal with the causes of conflict rather that the symptoms.

It may take real detective work to identify the underlying causes of a conflict. Often, those involved aren't fully aware of the underlying causes themselves. Or they may be aware of the causes but reluctant to deal with them openly. Take the case of Sonia, a bright but unmotivated case handler in a large government office. Sonia's work was below acceptable standards. When her supervisor transferred from the unit, one of Sonia's fellow case handlers with several years less service but a far better work record received a promotion to the supervisor's slot. Almost immediately, conflict broke out between Sonia and Elena, the new supervisor. On the surface, Sonia claimed that the reason for the hostility was a personality conflict. "Besides, I can't work for Elena—her supervisory style is terrible."

Anyone witnessing this situation as it developed is likely to have other questions entering his or her mind. Questions such as, Are there deeper reasons for the conflict? Does Sonia resent Elena's appointment? If Sonia is a bright and potentially capable employee, why is her work so poor? Issues such as these must be dealt with before a lasting solution to the conflict is to be found.

Redirecting Tensions and Hostilities

It's important to avoid the statement, "Provide for a release of tensions," because it has been discovered that people are often more highly motivated when a "healthy" amount of tension prevails.[1] If an individual feels strongly enough about about something, it would be more helpful to channel interests and feelings in a positive direction rather than simply to release feelings and emotions. In other words, when tension is felt, the channeling of that tension toward the discovery and resolution of the problem rather than toward the simple venting of emotions may be a productive endeavor.

In the case of Sonia, management needs to look for ways to redirect her energy into productive channels. Could Sonia be used for special assignments that would be motivational, would give her an opportunity to show what she can do, and would possibly start the process of preparing her for her next promotion?

Integration of Ideas

It is better to achieve an integration of ideas from the conflicting parties rather than reach a compromise as a solution. Mary Parker Follett first suggested that decisions involving more than one person do not have to be reached on the basis of pure compromise in which each party states a position and then the two extremes are conceded to a purely middle-ground position between the two poles. The middle-ground position tends to represent not the most satisfactory resolution of conflict but simply the most expedient solution. In place of the compromise position, as Follett saw it, conflict is best resolved with a solution that is most beneficial both *for the organization and for the parties involved*. Integration is better than compromise—it represents the best possible position. By integrating the ideas of the conflicting parties, the best ideas and concepts are utilized rather than the most easily agreed upon ideas.[2]

When a conflict occurs, this integration can sometimes be accomplished by redirecting the attention of the parties in conflict from their proposed solutions to thoughts about what it would take to make them feel like winners. If we were to ask Sonia for her proposed solution, she might say, "I want Elena to lay off and quit nagging me!" But if we could get Sonia to focus on what it would take to make her feel like a winner, she might ask for more recognition and more challenging assignments. As Sonia's work improves, both she and Elena could feel like winners.

Achieving Unity

Unity can be achieved through a meeting of the minds between the parties in conflict. This desired result of the proper handling of conflict is not absolutely essential, but it is helpful. Through unity, the efforts and interests of individuals can be coordinated, and cooperation tends to progress.

The parties to a conflict tend to distance themselves from each other, and communication diminishes both in amount and in quality. We've all felt the release in tension that results when we talk over a problem during a conflict. When we clear the air, it becomes easier to find solutions. It's hard to remain angry at someone you're talking with honestly and openly. Undoubtedly, Sonia and Elena need to make a start by talking privately, candidly, and objectively about what their real problems are.

Accomplishing Real and Permanent Solutions

Artificial, temporary solutions are quickly recognized by individuals and will not be respected or supported. Only genuine resolutions that attend to the causes of the conflict will be supported by those affected.

In Sonia's case, a temporary solution such as transferring her to another supervisor most likely won't work, since it doesn't deal with the resentments and causes of poor performance that lie below the surface.

Conflict can occur at any time at any place.

Sources of Conflict

The sources of interpersonal conflict are numerous and varied, but problems tend to group themselves into general categories—problems based upon individual variances, difficulties resulting from perceptual differences, and issues arising out of characteristics of the organization and functional differences.

Individual Differences

No two people are identical. People's temperaments vary. Some individuals are aggressive, others are passive, and still others are assertive. Some individuals are extroverted; others tend to be introspective and self-centered. Some people are highly ambitious and upward-bound, while others seek primarily to preserve and protect what they already have. One worker may want to work with other people, while another will prefer working alone. One individual will prefer independence in decision making, while another will seek out the opinions and ideas of others before acting. One worker may be able to withstand criticism and difficulty with a high degree of tolerance, while another may react emotionally at the slightest personal challenge.

The attitudes and actions of individuals also differ on the basis of background, involving educational, cultural, social, and ethnic dissimilarities. The differences in workers' backgrounds tend to influence the philosophical values of the workers. An individual's philosophy provides a set of guidelines or principles by which the individual's life is conducted. Because individuals' backgrounds are different, their philosophies tend to differ. Differences in philosophies will have a direct bearing on individual behavior and may be a significant cause of interpersonal conflict when incongruent philosophies interact.

One type of philosophical difference centers on styles of handling conflict. We will discuss conflict-handling styles in detail later, but for now you might look at the Conflict Management Style Survey (Self Test), which measures the most commonly used method of dealing with conflict. The five possibilities are (1) avoiding it, (2) acting as a competitor and trying to win it, (3) acting as an accommodator and letting the other party win it, (4) trying to find a collaborative, or win/win solution, and (5) trying to find a compromise. It's probably clear that someone with a competitor style of handling conflict will approach a conflict much differently from someone with an avoider or accommodator style.[3]

Krupar and Krupar say that it is possible to identify the individuals who are likely to be difficult to work with. Table 13–1 lists the characteristics of ten types of "difficult" people. In using this information, a manager should be able to identify the general category into which an employee might fall and then respond in a way that helps both the employee and the organization. One would expect conflict from some of these types of people (the hostile/aggressive, for example), but the know-it-all, the complainer, and the plagiarist, among others, require special attention and support as well.[4]

Conflict based upon **individual differences** (personality and philosophy) is often the most difficult type of conflict to manage as a result of its embedded, ingrained nature. Specific causes and effects may be obscured by circumstances and conditions.

individual differences
In this context, variances in temperament, background, and philosophy of employees are seen as sources of conflict.

Table 13–1
Ten Types of
Difficult People

Type of Difficult Person	Characteristics
Hostile/aggressive	☐ Bullies, overwhelms, and intimidates. ☐ Criticizes and argues relentlessly. ☐ Believes there's only one way to handle a situation. ☐ Can't accept feedback. ☐ Reacts even more strongly to resistance from others.
Wet blanket	☐ Uses negativism ("It won't work; we tried it that way last year"). ☐ Feels those in power don't care or are self-serving.
Know-it-all	☐ Feels and exhorts the impression of absolute certainty, power, authority. ☐ Is usually right. ☐ Cannot be dissuaded once on a course. ☐ Treats others as irrelevant.
Balloon	☐ Speaks with great authority or pretends to be an expert on subjects he or she has little knowledge of.
Staller	☐ Is pleasant and supportive but avoids decision making until the decision is made for him or her. ☐ Hints and beats around the bush. ☐ Is quality oriented; can't let go of something until it's perfect, which means never.
Complainer	☐ Acts self-righteous, blames and accuses others. ☐ Makes no effort to solve problems (feels powerless).
Clam	☐ Uses monosyllables or silence to avoid conflict. ☐ May feel backed into a corner.
Super agreeable	☐ Is often personable, funny, outgoing. ☐ Tells you what *you* want to hear, but lets you down in a crisis.
Deadwood	☐ Doesn't contribute anything to the actual team effort. ☐ Is often in a power position.
One who takes all credit (Plagiarist)	☐ Steals credit for others' achievements, ideas, roles, organization abilities.

Self Test

Personal Feedback

Conflict Management Style Survey

Instructions: Allocate 10 points among the five alternative answers given for each survey item.

Example: When one of my subordinates becomes involved in an interpersonal conflict, I usually:

__ 0 __   a) Step in to settle the dispute.
__ 3 __   b) Call a meeting to discuss the problem.
__ 4 __   c) Offer to help any way I can.
__ 2 __   d) Don't do anything, they can handle it.
__ 1 __   e) I get each party to give in some, to get some.
   10

1. When I observe conflicts in which anger, threats, hostility, and strong opinions are present I tend to:
    _____   a) Attempt to help in working out solutions.
    _____   b) Become involved and take a position.
    _____   c) Try to soothe feelings to preserve relationships.
    _____   d) Act as negotiator to help both parties.
    _____   e) Mind my own business, if possible.

2. When I perceive other people as meeting their needs at my expense, I tend to:
    _____   a) Work to do anything I can to change that person's behavior.
    _____   b) Work to find a benefit for myself, also.
    _____   c) Do nothing, because helping others is important.
    _____   d) Work hard to focus on all aspects of our relationship.
    _____   e) Just ignore the situation.

3. When involved in an interpersonal dispute, I tend to:
    _____   a) Wait and hope the problem will work itself out.
    _____   b) Try to satisfy the other party's expectations.
    _____   c) Argue my case to show the merits of my position.
    _____   d) Win some and lose some.
    _____   e) Examine the issues between us as logically as possible.

4. The feedback I receive from people about how I behave when faced with conflict indicates that I generally:
    _____   a) Try to bring all concerns out in the open to find the best possible way.
    _____   b) Try hard to get my way.
    _____   c) Try to stay away from disagreements.
    _____   d) Am easy to satisfy and take an accommodating position.
    _____   e) Am a real "horsetrader."

5. The cliches I am inclined to use most often include:
- —— a) "Let's split the difference."
- —— b) "Leave well enough alone."
- —— c) "Two heads are better than one."
- —— d) "Kill your enemies with kindness."
- —— e) "Might makes right."

6. When communicating with individuals with whom I am having serious conflicts, I tend to:
- —— a) Search for solutions we can both live with.
- —— b) Listen passively, often withholding personal opinions.
- —— c) Take time to tell my ideas and feelings and ask the other people for theirs.
- —— d) Try to overpower the others with my speech.
- —— e) Listen attentively, frequently agreeing with the other people.

7. When involved in an unpleasant conflict situation, I generally:
- —— a) Try to satisfy the needs of the other party.
- —— b) Try to integrate my ideas with others to come up with a joint decision.
- —— c) Propose a middle ground for breaking deadlocks.
- —— d) Avoid being put "on the spot."
- —— e) Don't hesitate to use my power to set things right.

8. A consequence of the way I deal with interpersonal conflict is:
- —— a) Others seem afraid to share their views and opinions with me.
- —— b) People complain about being unable to get my input on issues.
- —— c) Sometimes my constant bargaining seems to undermine the trust of others.
- —— d) My trust and openness are being over utilized.
- —— e) My ideals and concerns are not getting the attention they deserve.

9. When trying to resolve interpersonal conflicts I have noticed that:
- —— a) I admit when I am wrong and know when to give up.
- —— b) I frequently see differences as opportunities for joint gain.
- —— c) I am comfortable using my authority.
- —— d) I find it relatively easy to make concessions and I tend to enjoy bargaining situations.
- —— e) I refuse to address issues I feel are inconsequential.

10. The qualities that I value the most in dealing with conflict would be:
- —— a) Neutrality and professional detachment.
- —— b) Compassion and tolerance.
- —— c) Maturity and openness.
- —— d) Strength and security.
- —— e) Cooperativeness and fairness.

Self Test
continued

Conflict Management Style Survey Score Sheet

	Avoiding	Dominating	Accommodating	Compromising	Collaborating
1.	e _____	b _____	c _____	d _____	a _____
2.	e _____	a _____	c _____	b _____	d _____
3.	a _____	c _____	b _____	d _____	c _____
4.	c _____	b _____	d _____	e _____	a _____
5.	b _____	e _____	d _____	a _____	c _____
6.	b _____	d _____	e _____	a _____	c _____
7.	d _____	e _____	a _____	c _____	b _____
8.	b _____	a _____	c _____	c _____	d _____
9.	e _____	c _____	a _____	d _____	b _____
10.	a _____	d _____	b _____	e _____	c _____
Total	_____	_____	_____	_____	_____

To check your scoring, each item added across all five styles should equal 10 and your totals should add to 100 points.

Then discover what your dominant style is according to which one has the highest score. The five dimensions used here are the ones described in the Thomas-Kilmann Conflict Mode.

Source: Pamela D. VanEpps and William P. Galle, Jr., used by permission.

Perceptual Differences

perceptual differences
In this concept, perceptual differences are assessments individuals make about the authority they possess, the role they play, the treatment they receive from others, the status they possess, the rights that accompany their status, and the goals being pursued that may be construed in ways that would put individuals at odds with each other.

Individual perception is the conscious awareness of occurrences, events, or happenings in one's surroundings. As most people view the activities in their environment, they have a tendency to classify those events as either supportive and beneficial or threatening and derogatory. The perceptions workers have of the events that surround them in their work environment have a direct, important bearing upon the development or avoidance of conflict. When a worker views something in his or her environment that appears to be supportive or favorable, that occurrence will be accepted, but when an event appears to be threatening, there is an almost instinctive reaction to fight back, to resist, to attempt to master or overpower the threatening force. It matters not whether the perception is accurate or inaccurate. If the action or force is perceived to be threatening, tensions and resistances will build. We see this frequently during performance appraisals. A supervisor may be trying to point out a weakness and give pointers to improve performance. The employee may react defensively and negatively because, from the employee's perspective, the suggestions represent a threat, not help.

There are many events that are potential causes of the perception of a threatening situation, with resulting tensions and antagonisms. Some examples of **perceptual differences** that could lead to conflict include perceptions of

1.   Loss of authority. If a worker sees the actions of another as a threat to freedom and the right to act and make decisions, increased tensions

and potential hostilities will usually result. Jurisdictional disputes often take place on these grounds.

2. Role conflict. If a worker perceives that the expectations and demands of others overlap, the demands may be resisted. For example, if a supervisor feels that his or her boss and subordinates are making incompatible, irreconcilable demands, the demands may be resented and will not be accepted. Recall ideas from Chapter 6 about role conflict, role overload, and role ambiguity.

3. Unequal or unfair treatment. If an employee feels that discriminatory treatment is favoring someone else, this negative perception will usually result in tensions toward the discriminator and sometimes against the employee being favored. Jealousy, in particular, precipitates conflict between individuals. In addition to the feelings of unequal treatment, the threatening actions of another worker may be perceived in a derogatory manner. A worker who senses an unfair penalty, an improper reward, or arbitrary actions from others may develop resentment and hostility.

4. Status difference. Every worker has a perception of his or her position in relation to social standing, esteem, and reputation. When the actions of others are perceived to be a threat to self-perceptions, the actions and the sources of these actions will be fought against.

5. Goal differences. Each worker has his or her own set of personal goals. Actions from others that are perceived to hinder fulfillment of goals will cause tension and resistance.

Organization Characteristics and Functional Differences

Several **organizational characteristics** contribute to the development or avoidance of conflict. For example, the *size* of the organization can be a factor in conflict development. As the number of people increases in a department or unit of the organization, the individuals in one area lose touch with individuals in other departments. The people in each unity may come to think of themselves as separate from others rather than as a part of a team. All of this, of course, leads to individual thinking and actions.

> **organizational characteristics** Sources of conflict resulting from size, departmentation, spans of supervision, and other structural factors.

Another characteristic affecting conflict is the *method an organization uses for determining the financial performance* of its units, departments, and divisions. While there are many advantages to judging units on the basis of separate profit centers, this technique is more likely to result in competition between units. This, in turn, is more likely to lead to conflict. If the earnings of an individual are determined by the profit success of the individual's unit, an additional reason for conflict arises. When units are judged on the basis of total organizational performance and when individual earnings are shared based upon this performance, cooperation is more likely to occur.

The *kinds of employees* an organization hires can also affect the level of conflict (see the Insights feature for some prevention techniques). If an organization hires employees with specialized expertise in major numbers, the specialized individuals are likely to group together with similar personnel. For example, the small group of lawyers in a large organization are likely to develop a close-knit group, often to the exclusion of others. Remember the

Insights

Ways to Avoid Conflict with the Boss by Asking the Right Questions Before Accepting a Job

A major retail outlet had just hired a young executive with a solid track record to head its new product division. The young executive was made the division's president, and within a year the enterprise was off the ground and set to fly on what subsequently proved to be a successful trajectory. However, in the twelfth month of the division's life, right when everything seemed destined for success, there was suddenly a clash of styles between the president and the company's chief executive officer.

Managers are not usually fired for incompetence; more often than not, the culprit is bad chemistry with a new boss. Results, capability, or future potential will not provide much protection when a new relationship with a boss deteriorates before it ever gets off the ground. The past—prior successes, dedication, loyalty—is the past. Look around at the people you know who have been fired. How long had they been working for the boss who fired them?

There are ways to minimize the risk:

Before you say yes to an "opportunity of a lifetime," try to uncover the potential differences that could undermine your success. A financial expert was brought in from a top blue-chip corporation to become a planning director for a growing billion-dollar business. He was let go before completing three years in his job, even though his planning system, which he was hired to install, is still being used to manage the business. He assumed that his role was to impose greater control of the operating managers. However, this clashed sharply with the chief executive's style of giving his line executives wide latitude.

Four kinds of boss-subordinate conflicts can run deep enough to result in termination:

1. Differences in style or values that cause people to be natural antagonists.
2. Conflicts over where the business should go and how to get there.
3. Contrary ideas about how people should be managed.
4. Not fitting in with a boss's expectations about the subordinate's role in the organization.

The sorts of questions you need to ask about your prospective boss are the following: What is his or her style of doing things and dealing with people? How does this fit in with your style? (For example, is a fanatic over details going to tolerate a free spirit?) Does the boss have strong beliefs about the business? About how the organization should

informal groups we talked about in Chapter 2. Individuals joined together because they had characteristics in common with other individuals. They sought to fulfill needs and protect values that were important to them. Sometimes their goals ran counter to the goals of other groups. This grouping is a very natural phenomenon. Individuals narrowly focused in their training are also less likely to understand and communicate with individuals with other skills and responsibilities. On the other hand, individuals recruited as generalists (no single set of skills) and those who share responsibilities for more than one function in an organization are more likely to have broad interests and more universal communication skills. Conflict is more likely to occur between specialists and others than between generalists and others.

function? About your respective roles? If you are far apart on any of these issues, are the differences reconcilable?

Take an active role in the interview process. Employers may not feel it is their obligation to reveal much about themselves, but you should treat the interview as a two-way street. A billion-dollar communications corporation recruited a top-flight human-resources professional to update its personnel practices. After eight months of pushing hard for the very changes the company had asked for, the man was fired. What this individual didn't bother to ask during his interviews was how hard the company wanted to push for change. It turned out the management was exceedingly sensitive about disrupting the organization and therefore wanted to make the changes gradually.

Formal interviews across a boss's protective desk are not conducive to the boss's letting you get to know him or her. Suggest a meeting in a relaxed setting, perhaps over lunch or dinner, where the conversation may be more revealing.

Talk to other people who know the boss. You should meet with others in the company; ask them directly about what it's like to work for him or her. You could also conduct the equivalent of reference checks, seeking out contacts who could help you verify your impressions.

Be objective and critical in your evaluation. It's too easy—and tempting—to shift prematurely from "Why should I take this job?" to "I sure hope I get it." You stop looking for pitfalls, and the unknowns get filled with hopeful expectation. Don't ignore your instincts. Too often candidates shrug off seemingly irrelevant reactions, only to discover, in the midst of a fatal clash, what the warning meant.

When you enter a new organization, you can take steps to reduce the risk of being done in by an intolerable conflict. If you are about to take the offer, make sure you have a clear agreement about your role, the results expected, and how you will accomplish them. If you proceed and conflicts arise, such a conversation can provide a foundation for getting things back on track.

The best way to keep relationships from going haywire is to have open communication right from the start. If you sense conflict, get it out in the open. Left unspoken, conflict can fester, distort perceptions, and become irreversible. If the boss isn't making a move to deal with the problem, take the initiative to talk about getting a better understanding of how each of you sees things and what might be getting in the way.

The type and strength of external pressures can affect the level of conflict within an organization. Where there is great pressure from competitors or from the environment, for example, the people within an organization are more likely to pull together. When there are few or limited pressures, the individual and units are not forced to work together.[5]

Conflict can result when the resources allocated to each worker seem inadequate to do the job. Competition may be fostered between workers to obtain shared resources. The authors remember a situation in which a large organization was preparing to open a new operation. A number of legal clearances were required, and that called for extensive typing of legal documents. At the same time, hiring and training of hundreds of new employees was also under way. Unfortunately, the typing pool that had been set up for the new opera-tion consisted of only two typists. Needless to say, there was considerable conflict between the legal and personnel training departments as they vied for these scarce human resources. Return to the Elizabeth Reynolds case that started this chapter. Can Reynolds be thought of as a "scarce resource"? What effect would this interpretation have on your analysis of this conflict?

Conflict between workers may result when individuals are placed on a win-lose competitive basis for rewards (such as salary increases or promo-tions). When a worker recognizes that his or her success is gained at the expense of another worker, the potential of interpersonal conflict is present.

functional duties
In this context, sources of conflict result from varying job responsibilities, disputes over access to limited resources, intraorganizational competition, and goal incompatibility related to the job being performed.

Conflict may be encouraged by the **functional duties** of the workers. A production foreman who is being pressured by his or her supervisor (the pro-duction superintendent) to produce more units of the company's product may not concur with the recommendations of the quality control supervisor if achieving higher quality means producing fewer units. Goal incompatibility can be a very real problem between workers on a purely functional, account-ability basis.[6]

Other possible organizational sources of conflict include unclear jurisdic-tions, communication barriers, the degree of interdependence workers have for each other, the degree to which consensus is required, and unresolved prior conflict.

For the most part, the pressures for performance and achievement set off the reactions resulting in conflict when organizational forces are involved. This recognition leads to an important observation: *Conflict often arises when a worker sincerely is attempting to do his or her best*—when he or she is trying to perform to meet the worthy expectations that have been established. Con-flict does not necessarily result because a worker wishes to be disruptive and destructive. Quite to the contrary, many individuals enter into conflict as a result of the pursuit of goals considered valuable and important. The recogni-tion by managers of this important concept may cast a new light on the han-dling of some types of conflict. Over the years, a number of suggestions have been made for avoiding unnecessary conflict or directing a conflict that has already arisen toward a constructive resolution.

The Degree of Conflict Development

Another factor to consider before we talk about methods of handling conflict is the stage of development to which conflict has progressed. Conflict that has just surfaced, for example, might be treated very differently from conflict that has continued for a long time. Phillips has designated five stages of conflict running from just-surfaced conflict to well-cultivated conflict (see Figure 13–1). The first stage of conflict is that which has has *just begun*. Phillips says that when conflict is first identified, it is usually easy to handle. The parties involved want to know why there are differences and what is the best solu-tion possible. They believe resolution that will benefit everyone is possible. The parties freely exchange information and show respect for the values of others.

Stage 5	All-out War
Stage 4	Limited Warfare
Stage 3	Contention
Stage 2	Dispute
Stage 1	Just Begun

Figure 13–1
Stages of Conflict Development

Source: Adapted from Ronald C. Phillips, "Manage Differences Before They Destroy Your Business," *Training and Development Journal*, Volume 42, Number 9, September 1988, pp. 66–71.

If conflict is not resolved in the first stage, the *dispute* stage follows. The parties consider that the possibility of successful resolution is somewhat diminished. Egos become more of a factor. The hope now is that conflict can be handled so that the losses to the parties will be as few as possible. It is assumed that some losses may occur for everyone but that they can be held to a minimum.

If conflict resolution still has not been attained, the third stage begins. This is the *contention* stage, where win-lose is present. The whole process is designed to help the person who is "right" to win and the person who is "wrong" to lose. Parties exchange less information and begin to play dirty tricks on each other. Often, a third party enters the scene to select a "winner" and a "loser."

The fourth stage of conflict's progression is called the *limited warfare stage*. The goal is to diminish the adversary's power so that he or she is no longer a threat. Personal security is threatened by this struggle. Hurt, anger, disgust, and bitterness often result. Again, a third-party mediator will probably be necessary to resolve difficulties that reach this level.

What stage of conflict development has this situation reached? The all-out-war stage has not been reached yet.

The final, most severe stage of conflict is *all-out war.* Power positions have polarized so that individuals feel strongly about the issue and try to limit or completely dominate the opposition. Who gets hurt and who benefits are no longer important. Victory and justice are openly sought.

The stages of development are important because they determine the ease by which conflict can be resolved. Generally speaking, the early stages of conflict—the just-begun, dispute, and contention levels—can be handled much more easily than the warfare levels. What this is saying is that the sooner conflict receives attention, the more likely harmonious resolution will occur.[7]

Dealing with Conflict

Many attempts have been made to describe the managerial responses that occur when conflict develops in organizations. Two of the most useful descriptions of techniques for handling conflict were done by Robbins and by Blake and McCanse.

Robbins' Approach to Conflict Management

problem solving
Terminology used for the technique of managing conflict in which causes are identified, alternative solutions are sought, and a course of action believed to be optimal for everyone is chosen.

In his description of managerial actions related to conflict, Robbins identifies nine possible responses: **problem solving, development of superordinate goals,** expansion of resources, avoidance, suppression, **smoothing,** compromise, authoritative command, and alteration of the behavior of one or more of the parties involved.[8] Each of these techniques is defined and described in Table 13–2.

The Leadership Grid® Approach

superordinate goals
A way of avoiding, reducing, or handling conflict where the sharing of common purposes unifies the efforts of the parties involved.

Another very descriptive approach to managing conflict is provided in the Leadership Grid® developed by Blake and McCanse (refer to Chapter 10 for the introduction of the Grid). If you will recall from the discussion about Grid leadership, the Grid consists of five different degrees of emphasis (on two nine-point scales) on productivity (task) and people orientation.

smoothing
A technique for handling conflict where common interests are talked about but discussions of differences are avoided so that conflict can be minimized.

Each of the Grid positions represents a different philosophy and a different set of priorities. The 1,1 type of leader is afraid that performance goals and people-related efforts are in conflict; the supervisor's role is to remain neutral and not get involved in the struggle. The 9,1 leader has a primary concern for productivity. The 9,1's efforts are all directed at getting work done whatever the cost may be. The 1,9 leader has a low concern for performance but a high desire to have happy, satisfied people. Whatever makes people happy is what the 1,9 leader concentrates upon. The 5,5 leader has a moderate concern for performance and for human needs simultaneously. A middle ground is what the 5,5 leader seeks. The 9,9 leader believes that high performance results from the integration of task and human requirements. Through participation and involvement, the supervisor is to attain high performance as well as a high level of satisfaction.[9]

Technique	Characteristics	
Problem solving	Solutions to conflict problems use the scientific process. Causes of problems are sought, alternative solutions are considered, and an optimal course of action is chosen. Individuals affected by the conflict are involved in decision related to the conflict's resolution.	**Table 13–2** Robbins' Conflict Resolution Techniques
Development of superordinate goals	Conflict is avoided or reduced because individuals share common goals that require the efforts of all parties related to them.	
Expansion of resources	The acquisition of more of the needed supplies (of materials, people, machines, money, or whatever) so that an adequate amount is available which, in turn, reduces competition over limited resources.	
Avoidance	A refusal to acknowledge the existence of conflict by withdrawing from the arena of confrontation.	
Suppression	A refusal to deal with symptoms, causes, and other solutions to situations of conflict by not allowing issues to surface.	
Smoothing	Playing down differences that exist between individuals and groups while emphasizing common interests. The issues upon which differences exist are not openly discussed.	
Compromise	External or third-party intervention as well as internal agreement between conflicting parties where a midpoint is found between the opposing positions. Each party gives up something.	
Authoritative command	The use of formal authority to stop conflicting expressions and activities.	
Altering the behavior of one or more of the disagreeing parties	A long, slow process whereby single or multiple behaviors (and attitudes) are changed through education, laboratory training, and so forth.	

Source: Stephen P. Robbins, *Managing Organizational Conflict: A Nontraditional Approach,* © 1974, pp. 59–72. Adapted by permission of Prentice-Hall, Englewood Cliffs, New Jersey.

The Thomas-Kilmann Conflict Mode

Before you read this section, take the Conflict Management Style Survey if you haven't already done so. In keeping with the philosophy of the Grid, Thomas and Kilmann have identified five main conflict-handling styles by thinking of conflict management as having two components—assertiveness and cooperation. Figure 13–2 shows the new model that results.

Look over your results on the Conflict Management Style Survey. What is your natural conflict-handling style? Suppose you find yourself in conflict with your boss. Here are the ways you could use the different styles to handle the conflict:

Avoider: Keep your mouth shut and don't express any dissent. Neutrality continues to be important. Keep a low profile. Be at least outwardly compliant with the boss and make no demands.

Competitor: Take a win-lose approach and fight to win your own points as long as possible. You would probably do this only if you believe the cause is important and your position is correct. In this case you fight to win your own position.

Accommodator: Avoid conflict by conforming to the thinking of the boss. Seek knowledge of the boss's position and never "go out on the limb" against the boss. Never give the boss any information that would be upsetting. Try to keep the boss pleased and happy.

Compromiser: Concentrate on compromises and tentative statements. To the boss you might state, "We could do this . . . or we could do this. . . ."

Collaborator: Confront conflict directly. Communicate your feelings as well as facts so that there is a basis for understanding and working through the conflict.

The approach to be used in handling conflict may be altered somewhat if you as a supervisor perceive conflict between two workers or between yourself and a worker. In such situations, as supervisor you can also utilize the

Figure 13–2
The Thomas-Kilmann
Conflict Model

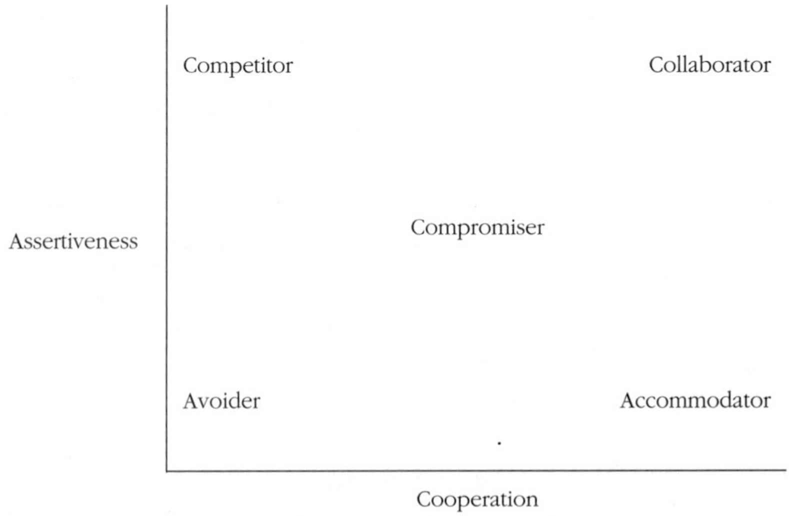

	Competitor		Collaborator
Assertiveness		Compromiser	
	Avoider		Accommodator

Cooperation

Source: Kenneth Thomas and Ralph H. Kilmann. Adapted from "Conflict and Conflict Management." In Marvin Dunnette (Ed.), *The Handbook of Industrial and Organizational Psychology,* Chicago: Rand McNally, 1975.

authority of your own position to influence the resolution of conflict. Not every style involves use of formal authority as a means of resolving conflict, but the following statements suggests some of the possibilities:

Avoider: Don't get involved. Avoid issues that might give rise to conflict by not discussing them with subordinates.

Competitor: Suppress conflict by the use of authority. You fear the disruptive effects of conflict on organizational achievement, so you beat down the impending threats.

Accommodator: Smooth over conflict. Attempt to encourage people to relax and forget about their troubles. Suggest that some troubles have a way of disappearing or resolving themselves. Encourage those involved to "count their blessings" and be happy with what they already have.

Compromiser: Split up parties in conflict and keep them separated. Talk with each party individually. Discuss their positions and blend their ideas to reach a solution. Attempt to get acceptance of the compromise, even though each party tends to be only moderately satisfied with a compromise.

Collaborator: Confront conflict directly and work it through at the time it arises. Conflict is accepted so that the clash of ideas and people can generate creative solutions to problems. Those involved are brought together to work through differences.

The collaborator approaches conflict by bringing together the parties in conflict (this is the only approach in which the parties are brought together). He or she stresses the importance of both (or all) parties to the organization and attempts to emphasize the desirability of mutual cooperation and understanding. This leader indicates a genuine interest in the parties individually and collectively. The collaborator attempts to inspire the participants to communicate fully the causes of the disagreement and the tensions felt in relation to the conflict. Individuals are encouraged to present and review all feasible alternative solutions to their problems. The emphasis is placed upon reaching a decision that will be most beneficial to the individuals in conflict and to the organization as an entity.

If the individuals seem to be sliding into a situation of pure compromise, the collaborator raises questions and issues to stimulate a more complete review of facts and the decision. The alternatives presented and the decision reached should be the agreed-upon choice of the parties originally in conflict. Only on this basis will the parties support the ultimate outcome. The role of the manager is one primarily of coordinator and stimulator. In many ways, this approach parallels the nondirective counseling approach discussed in Chapter 12.[10]

As an example of the collaborator, consider the Elizabeth Reynolds case at the beginning of the chapter. As soon as Aaron Slade accepted responsibility for the secretarial decision, he would call for a meeting between Wong and Powell. He might consider having Bright and Reynolds also attend the meeting. At the meeting, he would express his interest in each individual present as well as for the airline company. He would stress the role each person plays in the organization and the contributions each one makes to the organization

Management in Action

Getting to Know the Conflict Options

The decision at General Insurance Company has been made to increase the company's market orientation by changing the Management Information System from product to customer-based systems. Some new software must be selected. Paul, the software group manager, and Sara, the planning group manager are the logical people to be involved in making decisions about software. Jack, the division manager, is the person to whom both report. Sara has worked under Jack for several years. Paul, who has ten years of experience as a software manager, has just become assigned to Jack's division.

Paul and Sara have had some serious problems recently. Paul has tried to avoid allowing Sara to be involved in some sales support decisions. Sara has wanted to get some identification codes changed, but Paul has resisted because the changeover would be costly. Jack is aware of the disagreements between the two.

Jack reviews his options for dealing with the needed software decisions. He has the traditional choices available to him. He can ignore the previous problems Paul and Sara have had in hopes that they can find solutions to their problems. He can change the structure, transferring one or both of the managers. He can make a decision himself and tell Paul and Sara what will be done. He can explain the logic of the situation to them in hopes that if he talks to Sara and Paul together or separately they will see the light and will come to work together. He can also use the collaborative problem-solving interaction, letting Paul and Sara make their decision by working together in a cooperative atmosphere. Paul and Sara could then come to an agreement on their own. Jack rejects this last technique, however, because the two have demonstrated no ability to work together and he (Jack) is not sure that he has the skill and time to make collaboration work. Jack also eliminates ignoring the conflict and restructuring the reorganization.

This leaves making the decision and clarifying the issues. Jack, however, wants to avoid three problems: missing important facts, appearing biased, and setting up future dependence on himself. He now considers two more options that might be helpful—arbitration and mediation. In arbitration, issues are presented by the involved parties to the decision maker, who in this case is Jack. Positions are stated and defended, and the arbitrator decides what to do.

Arbitration has some positive points and negative points. In its favor, more facts get to the decision maker, the solution is seen as less one-sided as a result

and the team. He would restate the issue at hand as he understands it, then ask for input. He would encourage each person to describe the problem as they see it.

Slade would serve as a facilitator encouraging everyone to talk openly about their needs and their perspectives. He would ask Wong and Powell not only to define the alternatives but also to evaluate them. He would seek to get a group decision reflecting what's best for each person and the organization itself. Slade would be actively involved to the degree necessary to get alternatives identified, reviewed, and decided upon. The more Wong and Powell do on their own initiative, the less active will be Slade's role.

of the participation, and the decision can be timely. On the negative side, arbitration may limit itself to only one or a few issues. Arbitration takes more time than individual decision making. Arbitration keeps others dependent on the decision maker.

Mediation might help to overcome some of the problems of arbitration. In mediation, the manager brings the parties together to get them to identify the issues where they disagree. Each side then is asked to draw up a proposal suggesting solutions to these issues. Then the discussion between the parties begins. The manager can either play an active role or serve as an orchestrator until a decision is reached. Through mediation, all parties can maximize joint gains, the process will develop negotiating skills for the future, and the participants will be more likely to accept a decision they have made.

Jack, like all managers, benefits from having ways to determine which conflict strategy to use. Three dimensions can be used in making the selection of techniques. The first dimension raises the question, Is the issue simple or complex? A simple issue has few characteristics similar in content, is clearly delineated in the participants' minds, and is not emotionally charged. Complex issues are just the opposite.

The second dimension is concerned about past and future relationships. When parties have had minimal contact in the past, are unlikely to work closely in the future, have unequal status and power, and have different communication and negotiation skills, their past-future relationship is considered divergent. Again, the opposite experiences would be convergent.

The third dimension is, How much control does the manager need over the outcome? The more control is needed, the more unilateral decision making will be called for. The less control is needed, the more others will be allowed to make the decision. The figure below shows the stages of conflict resolution using the issue and relationship factors. In the first method, the manager makes the decision and tells others. Somewhat more involving is arbitration. Next more open is mediation. Finally, where participants can do so and the situation allows it, parties involved can make their own decision without outside help.

Source: Deborah M. Kolb and Priscilla A. Glidden, "Getting to Know Your Conflict Options," *Personnel Administrator*, Volume 31, Number 6, June 1986, pp. 77–89. Reprinted with the permission from HRMagazine (formerly *Personnel Administrator*) published by the Society for Human Resource Management, Alexandria, VA.

Mediation and Arbitration

Frequently discussed as management activities for handling conflict are two additional procedures—mediation and arbitration. Mediation is sort of a cross between compromise and collaboration. It's like compromise in its result—it aims to bring about a middle-ground, mutually acceptable decision or solution. It's similar to collaboration in that people are brought together to talk about their positions and to find a solution. The manager's role in this is to act as a leader in bringing the parties and their views together. The leader does not make decisions for the parties involved. The parties themselves make decisions (with help from the leader).

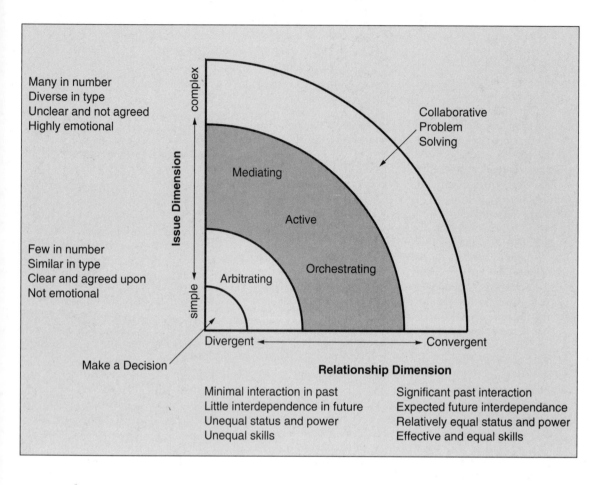

Arbitration is unlike any of the concepts we've discussed. In arbitration, the arbitrator listens to all sides of an issue as the different parties in conflict are encouraged to state their position. The arbitrator reviews the evidence and then makes a decision or agrees to a solution. Usually, the arbitrator's decision is binding on all individuals and groups involved.

Both mediation and arbitration are useful techniques in management-union disputes as well as in individual-to-individual disagreements (see the Management in Action feature).

Choosing an Appropriate Approach

The approach selected from the five styles for dealing with conflict can be determined by factors in the situation in addition to the philosophical desires of the manager. The decision concerning the approach to use may be similar to the overall choice of leadership style discussed in Chapter 10 in connection with adaptive leadership. The choice of approaches will be dependent upon forces within the leader, within the subordinates, within the organization, and within the task situation.

Thomas and Kilmann point out that there is no one best way to handle all conflict, since each situation is different. The manager needs to be able to use different styles and to use them at the appropriate times. While the collaborative approach to the resolution of conflict has the potential for accomplishing all of the objectives outlined earlier in the chapter, it also requires skill and commitment to this approach from the manager. Executing it consumes a large amount of time. It demands maturity, patience, and tolerance from the participants. For example, if one of the other parties to a conflict is an extremely aggressive person who holds a win/lose (I win-you lose!) view of conflict, it may be necessary to adopt a competitive style to convince him or her that you are serious about what you want. It may also be most appropriate when you have better information than others and when time is tight. Accommodating may be advantageous for political reasons. At times, by being accommodating now on an issue that is important to another individual, you may be able to enlist accommodation later on a topic of concern to you.

Collaboration, as we have defined it, involves meaningful exchange with the other party to the conflict. In this exchange, a win/win solution is sought—a solution that meets all of the needs of both parties. No wonder collaborating is time consuming! Sometimes, however, collaborative solutions simply aren't possible, and important differences remain between the parties. At this point, the parties begin the kind of bargaining that, in effect, says, "I'll give in on this point, if you'll give in on that point." If a solution is found that both parties can accept, compromise has been effectively used. Thus compromise can be thought of a style that can be employed when a collaborative solution isn't possible.[11]

A danger is that conflict-handling styles may be used inappropriately. Since the traditional position discussed at the beginning of the chapter sees conflict as potentially very destructive, techniques such as suppression and authoritative command as well as the competing approach would all be very much in keeping with traditional procedures and practices. Since injury and dissension are feared, avoidance, smoothing, and compromise (or avoiding, accommodating, and compromise) might be used just to see that conflict is out of the way, even though solutions are only temporary. These techniques usually do little to deal with the actual causes of conflict.

The more contemporary view wants to get positive results from conflict. Conflict is viewed as an opportunity to direct energies and knowledge toward improvements in the organization. Problem solving and superordinate goals in particular are a part of the contemporary view. In the Thomas-Kilmann scheme, the collaborating view of conflict would be contemporary in its techniques.

Where problems exist that have available solutions (the resources, the knowledge, the skill needed for resolution), the changes that will provide the necessary correction should be implemented. If conflict is over limited resources and more resources are available under acceptable circumstances, for example, the acquisition of more resources is desirable. If conflict is a result of an inaccurate perception, attempts to correct the perception are appropriate. If the worker's perceptions are accurately based upon an actual loss of authority, a real role conflict, unequal or unfair treatment, and so forth, the corrective action should be to modify the conditions so that the problem no longer exists. An employee who feels unjustly treated can file an appeal through the grievance process so that corrective and compensatory action can

collaboration (nine, nine—9, 9— conflict handling) A technique for achieving positive results from conflict through bringing together people with disagreements, encouraging open discussion, confronting differences, and seeking outcomes beneficial to the parties as well as for the organization.

result.[12] In other words, conflict caused by issues needing resolution benefits from corrective action.

Some solutions to conflict cannot be identified, and some identifiable solutions cannot be accomplished. However, when the conflict resolution technique works for a mutual understanding and good intraorganizational communication is stimulated, many of the tensions may be softened. Team effort can replace some of the individualistic efforts that tend to separate rather than unify workers. The use of win-lose competition can be abolished in favor of competition that rewards "winners" but does not punish those who "lose." The problem solving, superordinate goals, and collaborating leadership techniques all seem to work for what is best for the organization and for all of the people who are a part of it.

In his book on conflict management, Robbins goes one step further than the traditional and contemporary approaches. He suggests that the interactionist approach to conflict is appropriate today. Robbins sees conflict as absolutely essential for growth and change. He suggests creating conflict if necessary, but he expects conflict to occur naturally in vibrant, thriving organizations. His view (1) recognizes the absolute necessity of conflict, (2) explicitly encourages opposition, (3) defines conflict management to include stimulation as well as resolution methods, and (4) considers the management of conflict as a major responsibility of all administrators.[13] Few would argue with the fourth point. Others would feel uneasy about the first three.

Summary

Conflict and tensions may develop between people working together. Some people would encourage the creation of conflict so that an organization can grow and develop. Most people would not suggest the deliberate creation of conflict; many would say that conflict shouldn't be something to fear and run from. The tensions resulting from conflict can be channeled and redirected toward constructive, positive results.

The model in Table 13–3 shows the many facets of conflict. Every organization should have predetermined goals for the handling of conflict when it occurs. The full identification of causes and feelings, the integration of ideas, a spirit of unity, real solutions that can be supported by the parties involved, and, at the appropriate time, the reduction of hostilities and tensions may be some of the planned goals.

Sources of conflict can be identified according to differences between groups and individuals: individual personality differences, background differences, perceptual difference, and organizational differences. The sources of conflict can usually be found within these many differences.

Another important matter in the management of conflict is the stage or degree to which the conflict has progressed. The most elementary (and usually the least developed) stage of conflict is the *just begun* stage, followed in progressional order by the dispute, contention, warfare, and all-out war stages. Generally speaking, the least developed the stage of conflict, the easier the conflict will be to resolve.

Goals for Conflict When It Arises	Sources of Conflict	Degree of Conflict Development	Methods of Handling Conflict	Table 13–3
Identification of causes	Individual differences	Just begun	Avoidance	Components of Conflict Management
Redirection of tensions and hostilities	Background differences	Dispute	Accommodation	
Integration of ideas	Perceptual differences	Contention	Competition	
Unity through meeting of the minds	Organizational factors	Warfare	Compromise	
Real solutions that can be supported by parties involved		All-out war	Collaboration	

Source: Kenneth Thomas and Ralph H. Kilmann, Adapted from "Conflict and Conflict Management." In Marvin Dunnette (Ed.), *The Handbook of Industrial and Organizational Psychology,* Chicago: Rand McNally, 1975, and Ron C.Phillips, "Manage Differences before they Destroy your Business," from *Training and Development Journal,* Volume 42, Number 9, September 1988, pp. 67–71.

An array of conflict management techniques are available. In many ways, the collaborative approach, in which there is full communication and participative solution discovery, has the most to offer as a conflict resolution technique. Avoidance, competition, accommodation, and compromise are additional approaches.

Conflict, when it arises demands attention because sources of tension left unattended tend to smolder or fester until larger explosions erupt.

Questions to Consider

1. Why is it so many managers and employees are afraid of conflict and attempt to avoid it at all costs?
2. Some authors have said that interpersonal and intergroup conflict will inevitably result whenever people must work together. Do you agree with this statement? Why or why not?
3. Is it ever wise to avoid getting the causes of conflict out in the open? Is it ever useful to avoid the issues conflict presents?
4. Is it possible to predict when background differences of individuals will be likely to result in conflict? If you answer yes, explain how this can be done.
5. Is it ever desirable to handle conflict in the competing manner? The accommodative way? The compromise approach? Support your answers.

6. Is it ethical to create a situation involving conflict to get individuals and groups to make changes? Explain your answer.

7. Role play a situation in which conflict develops between a production manager and a sales manager over production requirements for the following month. The sales manager wants more units produced than the production manager believes is reasonable. How would a collaborative general manager handle this conflict?

8. Look again at the chapter opening case. How might the conflict that developed have been handled most effectively? Role play the situation as an avoider, an accommodator, a competitor, a compromiser, and a collaborator regional sales manager might handle the situation.

Key Terms

collaboration (nine, nine— 9, 9—conflict handling)	individual differences	problem solving
	organizational characteristics	smoothing
contemporary view	perceptual differences	superordinate goals
functional duties		traditional view

Chapter Case

Poor Sid Rosen—The Engineer and Manager

Your education is complete and you have graduated from college. You get what appears to be a real break. You are hired by Monmouth Incorporated, a major defense contractor. The federal government has shown a new interest in the Star Wars defense system and is pumping new money into the program. At Monmouth, this new effort means an enormous amount of management training. Literally hundreds of engineers and highly trained technicians, many of whom know nothing whatsoever about management, are being trained as managers to head up various aspects of the work.

Your boss, the vice president of Personnel and Human Resources, explains your job as follows:

> We know, of course, that you're not an engineer and that's not what we expect. What we need is what we call a "big ear"—someone to visit on a regular basis with our newly trained managers, listen to their problems, and give them on-the-job training in the form of suggestions and ideas about how to manage as they get started on their new jobs.

You feel a bit intimidated about trying to counsel all of these super-bright, highly trained people, but you set out to give it a try.

Your first new manager to counsel was Sid Rosen. When you entered Sid's office, your first instinct was to run out screaming. The whole situation was intimidating, to say the least. The office looked like a mad scientist's workshop, with piles of paper, graphs, computers, and incomprehensible formulas everywhere. You were nervous about saying the first word to Sid. He, too, looked like the stereotype of a mad scientist—wild, scraggly hair, disheveled clothing, and an aloof, distracted gaze that made you fear that you were interrupting a great thought simply by entering the room. It took very little time, however, for you to discover, much to your horror, that first impressions mean almost nothing where Sid is concerned.

Sid's subordinates have complained to you that Sid is incompetent. Even ten years ago when Sid graduated, his engineering skills were not very good, and apparently he's been afraid to upgrade them. By now he's not only a poor engineer but also ten years out of date. One of Sid's subordinates moans:

> How he ever got the job, I'll never know. You can't imagine what it's like working for someone like that—none of us respects him, and most can't stand him. And we really need help. This project is vital, and we really have no idea how to approach some of the most critical engineering features of it. Needless to say, Sid's worthless as far as giving the direction we need is concerned. Our only hope is that maybe top management is getting wise to him. After all, *you're* here—we're hoping you'll get word back on how bad things are.

You explain that you're there as an impartial party but that you hope to help them all. Then you sit down for a private talk with Sid. You feel a certain sympathy for Sid. It's clear he feels lost. He states:

> I know everybody thinks I'm a total incompetent, and I admit that I've gotten a bit rusty. But it's not just that. For one thing, I have no power— what can I possibly do to the high-priced, highly trained specialists who report to me? I surely can't fire them, that's for certain!

In fact, you discover that Sid tries to be everybody's buddy. He tries to encourage coffee breaks and bowling matches to promote friendly relations among the group but finds the group is much more interested in getting the job done. Furthermore, Sid is reluctant to give any direction—even on the rare occasions when he has a good idea.

A good example of Sid's ineptness is a recent discussion Sid had with Lucinda, a highly specialized expert in sound transmission systems. Lucinda insisted that there was only one solution to a problem involving voltage regulation for the sound system under design—and that was *her* way—virtually undoing a whole lot of work that had taken months to complete. You sense that Sid didn't really agree with her, but Sid's only comment was, "Well, if you say so, we'll have to respect your professional opinion." From the grumbling you hear later, you begin to believe that Lucinda was wrong and Sid was right in this instance. When you try to discuss the matter with Sid, he admits that he really wasn't sold on Lucinda's idea but felt it was best to just go along with it.

By this time, you're really getting concerned about Sid and wonder what to do.

1.   Using concepts from this chapter, what are the sources of conflict in this case?
2.   According to the Thomas and Kilmann Model, what kind of conflict approach did Sid use?

3. What kind of approach *should* Sid have used in the situation in this case?

4. What was the role of perceptions in determining your initial reaction to Sid? Explain in terms of theory.

5. What problems does Sid have in terms of power? Be specific, draw on theory and make recommendations.

6. Sid's subordinates are clearly dissatisfied and want to get their concerns known at higher levels. What advice would you give them based on what is known about communication? What advice would you give based on politics?

Managing the Problems of Workers

14. Stress—Causes, Consequences, and Solutions

15. Chronic Worker Problems—
Alcoholism, Other Drug Abuse, and Theft

16. Equity for Minorities

Chapter 14

Stress—Causes, Consequences, and Solutions

Objectives

- To identify potential stressors (factors contributing to the development of stress).
- To learn how the overload-underload concept of stress works.
- To identify personal characteristics and traits that influence how an individual will react to stress.
- To learn ways to cope with stress and to make productive use of it.
- To identify your own personal level of stress.

Who Has Stress, Anyway?

"I'll admit that 8:30 on a Saturday morning is a strange time to ask my three oldest friends to come over for coffee and talk," comments Lindsey Ferrara, "but this is the ONLY time we could get together, and I need help fast!"

Lindsey is a young registered nurse in the intensive care unit of Metropolitan Hospital who has been jarred into reality by a comment her shift supervisor had just made. The comment was something like, "Lindsey, are you feeling okay? I've noticed for several days now that your performance just hasn't been up to standard. What's the problem?"

Lindsey's only explanation was that she just hadn't been feeling well recently. As she drove home from work, she realized that she has been feeling depressed and discontented. For several months, she has sensed this feeling creeping up on her. Maybe she needs to take a vacation and get out of town for a few days. Maybe she should get a physical examination. If she could just sleep better, everything else might look brighter.

Lindsey is a very conscientious member of the intensive care team at Metropolitan. She began work in the ICU when she graduated from nursing school and became a qualified RN almost three years ago. She was originally attracted to intensive care because she recognized the impact she could have on other people's lives. She immediately found her work to be gratifying. In the past few months, however, she hasn't felt enthusiastic about her job—or anything else. She always seems to be tired, physically and psychologically depleted. Her job seems so demanding.

"I just don't know where to turn next," she says to Jill, Buddy, and Fred. "I know you have problems of your own, but you're the only people I can really talk to. After all, we've been close friends since high school and have gone through a lot—good and bad—together. What's wrong with me, anyway? I never used to be like this. I was a carefree, happy-go-lucky person. But now . . ."

Jill knits her brow and tries to concentrate. But it's hard. She DOES have problems of her own. Jill was promoted two months ago to district manager for marketing in a large consumer products company. Since her promotion, Jill's life has changed considerably. Before the promotion, her job seemed simple—she was merely responsible for contacting customers and selling them the company's offerings. Now she has many decisions to make—important decisions that involve big money. Her job entails developing an advertising budget, analyzing markets to determine new territories for expansion, and hiring new personnel. Her nights and days are filled with apprehension.

"Am I doing the right thing? Will I succeed or will I fail? If only I had someone to talk to who understands marketing!" These are the thoughts flooding Jill's mind as she tries to concentrate on what Lindsey is saying.

Buddy's dilemma is just the opposite. His job as corporate accountant for a building supply company is so boring he can hardly make himself go to work each day. When he graduated from a university two years ago with an accounting degree, he was eager to apply his knowledge and develop his abilities. He took what he felt was a job with a great deal of promise with a new, growing company. Buddy has been with the same business since graduation, and all he has been assigned to do has been simple bookkeeping work. He's had no opportunity to make decisions, instigate new procedures, or use his training in any constructive way. He hates going into the office. But there's an economic slowdown in the area, and opportunities in other firms are simply nonexistent.

"I guess I'm a fool not to pack up and move somewhere else. Somewhere with better opportunities—but what about my family? The folks are getting older, and they need help. My sister is ill. I can't just walk out." These are the thoughts on Buddy's mind as he listens to Lindsey.

Fred is a draftsman in a large manufacturing concern. He is very confused and frightfully hesitant about his boss. One day the boss will be very open and supportive in his dealings with Fred, the next day the boss will be very autocratic and restrictive toward him. As a result of the inconsistencies and the sometimes very negative actions of his boss, Fred has become increasingly reluctant to show any initiative and indeed has stopped almost all activities except those things that are demanded by his boss on a given day.

"There are times I'd just like to punch him in the jaw," thinks Fred as he tries to concentrate on what Lindsey is saying. "But I can't. Everyone says I've got a super job in terms of money, prestige, benefits . . . I can't just walk out on something like that—or can I?"

stress
A state or condition wherein external factors (time pressures, social norms, success-failure conditions, and so forth) interact with an individual psychologically or physiologically so that tensions develop inside the individual.

negative stress
The state or condition wherein the pressures applied to an individual cause a threatening, fearful sort of tension within the individual. Often in this kind of stress, the individual feels incapable and inadequate to meet the challenges lying ahead.

Case Questions

1. From the details given in the above paragraphs, what clues are available concerning the probable cause of Lindsey's performance and feelings about herself and her job?
2. What can Lindsey do at this point that would be constructive and beneficial? What can her supervisor do? What can her friends do?
3. What about Jill, Buddy, and Fred? How are their problems similar to Lindsey's? How are they different?

What do Jill, Buddy, Fred, and Lindsey have in common? While their jobs and work circumstances are very different, each one of them is in a position where **stress** has come to be a dominant factor in their jobs. Job stress has been defined as a situation wherein job-related (or external) factors interact with a worker to change the employee's psychological or physiological condition so that the worker is forced to deviate from normal functioning.[1]

Stress has become a major element in the work lives of many employees. **Negative stress** occurs when circumstances and characteristics of the job environment are perceived as a threat to the individual.[2] It usually evolves when demands are made on an individual beyond that which he or she feels capable of meeting. Stress and its related problems are estimated to cost businesses more than $150 billion dollars annually, mostly in health insurance disability claims and lost productivity.[3]

The stress process has several components. The unit in which stress builds, of course, is the individual employee. Each employee brings his or her unique characteristics to the job, and these individual facets determine in part how the individual will respond to stress. Individuals bring to their work such factors as personality traits; physical condition; feelings about self; experiences with family, friends, and the community; age; and education. Each of these individual characteristics affects how a person responds to stress.

Type A and Type B Personalities

One approach to personality definition suggests that the **Type A personality** responds with more agitation to stress than does the **Type B personality.** The approximately 40 percent of the population who are Type A tend to be explosive in speech, live at a fast pace, be impatient with slowness, be self-preoccupied, be dissatisfied with life, make all situations into competitive events, and have free-floating anxiety. You may have experienced free-floating anxiety yourself at some major stress point in your life—during an unusually heavy exam period, for example. Such anxiety is characterized by depression and worry not related to any specific thing. It may shift from one thing to another. You feel anxious and upset but can't really say why.

Type B personalities are inclined toward less overreaction, less desire to compete, less status consciousness, and less insistence on recognition.[4] Needless to say, the Type A personality has more problems in dealing with stressors than does the less aggressive Type B individual. While Type A's move ahead rapidly in organizations, they may pay later through increased physical problems, including heart trouble.

Type A personality
The nature and disposition of an individual to be fast living, impatient, self-preoccupied, competitive, accepting of more and more responsibility, and so forth. The Type A person drives himself or herself to the point that health is threatened.

Type B personality
The nature and disposition of an individual to take things slowly, to avoid unrealistic demands, and to be deliberate rather than reactive.

This man's relaxed appearance indicates that he is likely to be a Type B person.

Are you a Type A or a Type B? Before continuing, complete the Self Test exercise to find out.

Self Test

Personal Feedback

Type A-Type B Test

Indicate your level of agreement with each of the following statements:

5   means you *strongly agree* that the statement describes you
4   means you *agree* that the statement describes you
3   means you feel the statement is *somewhat characteristic* of you
2   means you *disagree* that the statement describes you
1   means you *strongly disagree* that the statement describes you

_____   **1.** I get impatient if the car in front of me doesn't move quickly when the light turns to green.
_____   **2.** I leave the door to my office or room open when I am working.
_____   **3.** I willingly volunteer for new assignments and accept all of those given to me.
_____   **4.** I find myself completing sentences for people around me who talk slowly.
_____   **5.** I eat very rapidly.
_____   **6.** I am happier when I'm working than I am when I'm loafing.
_____   **7.** I do two things at a time such as using my electric razor while eating or driving.
_____   **8.** I get impatient when watching people do things I can do faster.
_____   **9.** I grind my teeth or clinch my fists often.
_____ **10.** When I'm playing things such as tennis and golf, I think about my work frequently.
_____ **11.** I like to take charge of conversations.
_____ **12.** I seldom look at paintings, plants, and other things in offices.
_____ **13.** I don't read things outside of my occupational field except summaries or condensations.
_____ **14.** I don't like to wait in lines such as those encountered while waiting to be seated at a restaurant.
_____ **15.** I find it difficult to let other people do things I can do for myself.

Add up the total points to get your score. Your score can then be interpreted as follows:
15 to 25 points=Mild Type B
26 to 50 points=Moderate Type A
51 to 75=Type A

Health As a Factor

While stress may contribute to health problems, the status of an individual's health may influence a person's reaction to stress. Studies have shown, for example, that anxiety levels seem to be higher in individuals with health problems than in individuals who are in good health. Cause-and-effect sequences are not always clear, but it has been shown that people in good health are more likely to maintain low heart rates under stress than are individuals in poorer physical condition.[5] Good physical health seems to be an ally in combatting stress symptoms.

The Importance of Self-Concept

The esteem with which an employee regards himself or herself may also influence an individual's response to stress. Normally, the individual who possesses a positive self-concept will find stressors less threatening than will the individual with a low self-perception.[6] With positive self-perception comes confidence in one's abilities to cope with challenges and problems. When threats occur, the potential harm is received with less fear by the person with a positive feeling about personal abilities and strengths. Individuals who already consider themselves vulnerable will find pressures from stressors to be even more threatening. Look especially at Buddy and Fred in the opening case. What threats to their self-concepts are present?

Experiences with Family and Friends

If experiences with family or friends are supportive and constructive, the individual who is exposed to stressors will be able to react favorably to the stressors, while the individual who has primarily negative, nonsupportive experiences with family or friends will find stressors to be more distractive and upsetting. Family and friends can act as a source of support to sustain and encourage when threats come along. By the same token, unsympathetic, indifferent relatives and peers can weaken and make an employee even more vulnerable to the pressures in the workplace. Absence of encouraging relatives and friends can result in lack of support during periods of stress.

Recent family and friendship experiences are of particular importance. Also, changes in relationships have a major impact.[7] You've probably noticed, for example, how helpful it is to have friends and family around to lean on when things aren't going well. Have you ever noticed how students congregate and compare notes after a particularly difficult exam? This venting of feelings with others in the same situation can provide a meaningful release valve in times of stress. That certainly is the situation with Lindsey in our opening case. We can only hope that her friends aren't under too much stress themselves to be able to provide the sympathetic ear she needs.

Age and Education

While the age and the level of education of an employee have been researched less than most other factors, it is felt that the two factors do have an influence on an individual's response to stressors. Studies conducted some years ago, for example, suggested that people in some age groups are more likely to develop high blood pressure when stressors are applied.[8]

Education can either benefit or handicap. The highly educated individual in a job demanding highly polished skills and technical abilities may respond well to stressors, while underprepared individuals might crumble under the attack. It is possible, of course, to be overeducated for some jobs—a factor that could result in increased pressure. The lack of challenge can result in boredom, which may in turn lead to stress. For example, when we discussed Buddy's dilemma in our opening case, you may have noticed that underemployment was a factor. During hectic days at work, many of us might dream of having a job that makes no demands on our skill or our intelligence, but continually working under slow schedules can be just as stressful as working in a high pressure job.

As all of the above factors indicate, the state (conditions, characteristics, and circumstances) that an employee brings with him or her to the workplace will affect responses to stressors. Some individuals obviously will be more immune to stressors, while others will be more vulnerable.

stressor
Factor that causes tensions to build within an individual to the point that stress occurs. A strong command from a superior or a rapid decline in the market may be an externally caused stressor. A strong achievement need or a demanding growth need may be an internally originated stressor.

Stressors—What They Are, Where They Are, and What They Do

Stressors are around each of us most of the time. A negative **stressor** is any condition or circumstance that an individual encounters that seems to threaten the physical or psychological well-being of the individual. As Holmes revealed in his well-known Life Change Index Scale, the threat of change surrounds all living beings regardless of whether or not the individuals are in work organizations. In the Holmes index, the impact of each stressor is measured as it relates to other stressors. The death of one's spouse is calculated to

Table 14–1
Selected Items from the Holmes Life Change Index Scale

Event	Points on Stress Scale
Death of spouse	100
Divorce	73
Major personal injury	53
Marriage	50
Retirement from work	45
Pregnancy	40
Changing to different kind of work	36
Son or daughter leaving home	29
Troubles with boss	23
Taking on mortgage of more than $10,000	17
Vacation	13

Adapted from Thomas H. Holmes M.D., "Life Exchange Index Scale," School of Medicine, Seattle, Washington.

have the biggest impact. However, you may have noticed positive events, such as vacations are treated as stressors on the scale. While it's true that negative events such as divorce or financial problems are the ones that we usually think of as stressors, positive events can be too. In fact, anything that causes a jolt to an individual, whether positive or negative, contributes to stress. Family circumstances dominate the list to a large degree, indicating that *as people come to work, stresses and strains already exist for most of them.*

Job-related Stressors

One of the most popular approaches to the identification of job-related stressors is the overload-underload method. According to this technique, each employee has a comfort zone in which demands made from a job's climate and environment are perceived as neither dangerous nor threatening. For example, a job with a "reasonable" amount of mental challenge may not be threatening to an employee who wants a mentally demanding job, so long as the demands remain within comfortable limits. These suitable boundaries become the comfort zone.

Overload occurs when the job becomes too demanding in its mental requirements (thinking, planning, decisionmaking, etc.). When a job has little or no mental requirements, the employee can face **underload.** Albrecht suggests eight factors that can become stressors as a result of overload or underload, and others have been added to the list (See Figure 14–1).[9] The areas of potential stress defined by Albrecht include workload, physical variables, job

overload
A situation in the workplace wherein the demands made by a work-related component are so high that tensions develop.

underload
A situation in the workplace wherein the demands of a work-related component are less than normal or expected so that tensions develop.

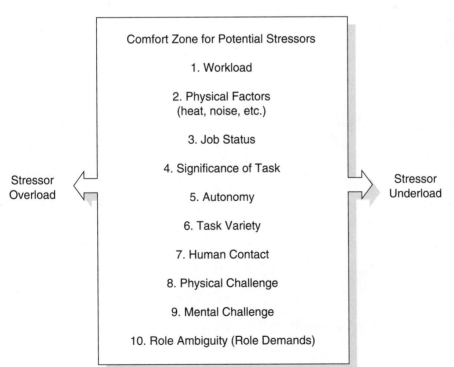

Figure 14–1
The Comfort Zone, Potential Stressors, And Overloads-Underloads

Source: Karl Albrecht, *Stress and the Manager,* 1979, includes eight of the ten items shown.

status, accountability (or significance of task), task variety, human contact, physical challenge, and mental challenge. Other factors that may be added to this group are autonomy and role ambiguity, or role demand.

No two jobs have the same degree of potential stress. By the same token, no two individuals have the same comfort zone. Some individuals can tolerate more pressure than others and, as a result, have a larger comfort zone. Under differing conditions, those who can normally tolerate stress may not be able to handle it.

Workload includes the number and complexity of the tasks an employee must perform to fulfill job responsibilities. An overload in this area means that an individual has either too many tasks or tasks that are too complex (or a combination of the two) to accomplish in a given period of time. An underload would be a situation where the tasks performed were too few or too simple (or both) to keep the employee feeling useful and worthwhile. Either overload or underload can cause stress to occur. Look back at our opening case. Consider Lindsey's and Jill's situations and compare them with Buddy's situation. Notice that while they are in very different situations, all three are showing signs of stress.

Workload can also be considered in the context of the number of hours worked daily, weekly, and so forth. Many people work significantly beyond a forty-hour workweek, and the more these people work, the more they are prone to stress. Entrepreneurs—in particular, small business owners—put in long hours of work. One study showed that most new business owners as a group put in more than forty hours a week. Only 23 percent of the owners worked fewer than fifty hours weekly, while 23 percent worked fifty to fifty-nine hours, 28 percent worked sixty to sixty-nine hours, 13 percent worked seventy to seventy-nine hours, and 12 percent worked eighty or more hours a week.[10] Working such long hours can impact personal health, family life, and many other important things.[11]

This woman seems to be experiencing workload overload.

The Entrepreneur

George Johnson* went into the interior decorating business in a major southeastern city in 1947. Sales and profits have increased every year. Sales in 1988 were approximately $6,000,000.* Of forty people on the payroll, 90 percent have been employed for more than five years. Four employees recently retired after twenty-five to thirty-eight years with the company. In the past five years, eight of twelve new employees are still with the firm.

How does Johnson manage stress to keep this relatively stable workforce? "Honest up front," he says. Everyone is on a trial basis for sixty days. So the stress is primarily whatever the new employee perceives is needed to prove his or her worth. However, the new employee is made aware that Johnson's style is to have "you work with me, not for me." The team concept seems to be a strategy that has helped to keep his organization growing and prosperous.

Johnson's financial policies have managed stress, too. He relates the fact that he has never missed a discount. He buys selectively after a contract has been signed. He has consistently capitalized profits. All of these policies—taking all discounts, selective buying, capitalizing profits—have the ongoing effect of reducing the stress of meeting financial responsibilities. In summary, Johnson manages personnel turnover stress in two ways: (1) he uses a trial employment period; (2) he builds the team concept. "You are working with me, not for me." He manages financial stress through conservative fiscal policies; (1) he takes all discounts; (2) he buys selectively; (3) he reinvests profits in the business.

*The name and sales figures are fictitious, as requested by the contributor.

Source: R. Frank Harwood, "Seven Successful Stress Managers: Their Strategies/Tactics," *Bulletin of the Association of Business Communication*, Volume 53, Number 1, March 1990, pp. 10—14. Used with permission of the author.

Status is the social rank given to a person or given in relation to other persons or things. *Job status* is the rank or value assigned by individuals in an organization to each job or set of work responsibilities. High-status jobs are those that command much respect or attention, while low-status jobs are considered to be beneath the social recognition given to most other jobs. Usually we think of low status as a stressful condition; and low status does tend to be a stressor for most individuals when they fail to win respect from other employees. Extremely high-status jobs may be stressful, too, as high-status employees struggle to keep the status of their jobs and to fulfill obligations related to a high-status job. Fred, in our opening case, is feeling some of those pressures.

Accountability has been divided into two factors—significance of the task and autonomy—in this chapter. *Significance of the task* refers to the effect an assignment has if it is performed properly. A job that involves the issue of life or death, such as that of a brain surgeon, would have a high level of task significance and could result in stress overload. A task that makes little difference if performed or not performed might be considered low in task significance. It is easy to see how low significance can lead to pressures of boredom and a lack of meaningful contribution.

Autonomy is the degree to which a job provides freedom, independence, and discretion to the holder so that decisions, schedules, and procedures can be self-determined. A job that has been completely delegated to an employee would be high in autonomy, whereas a job that is closely supervised and constantly evaluated would be low in autonomy. Overload might occur when an untrained worker is left alone in a challenging job, while underload could occur when an experienced worker serves under a prying, very autocratic boss who dictates every move. Look again at Fred's situation in our opening case. Autonomy is certainly a factor here.

Task variety is exactly what its name suggests—the degree to which a job provides the opportunity to perform different, dissimilar duties. A completely repetitive, rather short-cycle job would perhaps create a stress underload, while a job that is constantly changing and completely unprogrammable could result in *variety* overload.

Human contact as a potential stressor can be defined as the regularity with which a job provides the opportunity for interaction and affiliation with other people. A certain amount of contact with others is necessary for most individuals so that messages, support, and psychological stroking can occur. An isolated job providing no opportunity to relate to other people might result in a human contact underload. A job with constant interaction to the point that privacy is never possible might cause an overload.

The *physical challenge* of a job is determined by the position's demand for dexterity, physical skill, endurance, strength, risk of danger, and opportunity to use tools and equipment. A job with a combination of requirements for strength and endurance could result in an overload. Physical underloading would be void of physical activity or danger (which may not cause a significant stress problem in some people).

The *mental challenge* of a task relates to the degree of thought and deliberation an employee must perform. Jobs that require much observing, evaluating, interpreting, and decision making might be prone to an overload, while a completely mechanical, no-decision type of job might cause an underload.

Role ambuigity involves uncertainty about what others expect of an individual in terms of scope of responsibility, the amount of authority, methods that will be used for evaluation, degree to which company rules must be followed, and expectations of informal groups. If responsibility, authority, role definition, and informal expectations are poorly described, this can lead to role ambiguity underload. If the role is specifically prescribed to a high level of great restriction, this would be an overload of job definition.

Other Stressors

Other experts offer additional stressors. Johnson and Indrik say that stress is a product of uncertainty, perceived control, and emotional level. The more uncertainty (ambiguity, complexity, information unavailability, lack of perceived control, and unpredictability of the boss), the greater the probability that stress exists.[12]

Others suggest that emotional exhaustion, depersonalization, and the level of feelings of personal accomplishment also contribute to stress. Emotional exhaustion is an internal thing that leaves the worker psychologically (and perhaps physically) drained. A worker who is emotionally exhausted is especially vulnerable to the effects of stress. Depersonalization refers to the viewing of workers, clients, supervisors, and employees more as numbers or robots than as individuals. Once an employee becomes only a Social Security number or a patient in a hospital becomes "the kidney in room 609," stress is more likely to build than if individuals are known personally and are treated with respect. Feelings of low levels of personal accomplishment leave an individual with feelings of low self-worth.[13] On a daily scale, interruptions by telephone, by employees, by colleagues, and by others can also be very stressful, as they hinder the employee's productivity.[14]

What Happens to the Person Under Stress?

In reality, more than one stressor is usually at work at a given point in time. The individual employee, with his or her own set of conditions and circumstances, is thus impacted by more than one stressor. The strength of the stressors and the degree of the comfort zone combine to determine the individual's first reactions to the presence of stress. Involved is the employee's *perception* of the stressors and the possible consequences that may result or the damage that may be received from the stressors. As discussed in an earlier chapter, the interpretation of events or conditions is important from a behavioral point of view. The interpretation of the strength of the stressors and one's own ability to deal with the stress will largely determine the resulting consequences.

Look back at what Lindsey Ferrara in our opening case is saying. Lindsey is now in the first stage—she has *perceived* stress and is feeling its consequences. Notice that she had been under stress for a while before perceiving it. Now her ability to cope will be critical.

As soon as the perceptual process is accomplished, the first consequences and reactions are set in motion. These effects may continue unless adjustments and other coping measures are utilized. The initial personal consequences have been divided into three categories: psychological health, physical health, and behavioral consequences. Some psychological responses to stressors include anxiety, tension, depression, anger, boredom, mental fatigue, low self-esteem, repression, and loss of concentration. Physical consequences sometimes are the development of health complications, such as cardiovascular and gastrointestinal disorders, headaches, skin disorders, and physiological fatigue. Behavioral effects might include drug use, over- or undereating, aggression, stealing, vandalism, and poor interpersonal relationships with others.[15] The employee may be absent or tardy more frequently, have more difficulty making decisions, miss deadlines, forget appointments, and make more mistakes.[16]

The impact of stress on the individual also takes its toll on the organization in which the individual works. Effects on costs, efficiency, quality, and quantity may all be observed in relation to productivity. Strikes and grievances may be increased. Absenteeism and turnover may be high. Health care costs and workers' compensation payments may go up. The price of goods and services sometimes has to be raised.

If allowed to continue without coping responses, the initial consequence can result in serious, permanent damage. Normally, the individual under stress undertakes procedures to reduce the negative impact of the stressor(s) and perhaps to turn the experience into a positive encounter.

The coping mechanisms used by the individual may take two directions. First, the individual can attempt to increase his or her tolerance of stress by expanding the comfort zone so that stressors will have less impact. The majority of personal coping techniques used today are attempts to expand the tolerance zone and to increase the individual's capacity for controlling stress. Comfort-zone and capacity-increasing techniques include physiological efforts such as getting more rest, improving one's diet, and increasing the level of physical exercise. Perhaps, in our opening case, Lindsey's body is trying to tell her something. Psychological procedures can include meditation, increased spiritual activity, better planning of daily activities and responsibilities, the changing of personal values (such as the acceptance of less-than-perfect performance and reduction of psychological importance of work), the management of personal desires and ambitions, and the setting of more realistic goals. Other people can be called upon for support. The learning of relaxation techniques and the use of feedback require both physical and psychological involvement.

Second, the individual can seek changes in the demands and pressures of the job so that the strength of the stressor(s) will be reduced. Unrealistic time schedules can be negotiated toward more feasible periods. Duties can be delegated to others. Greater use of staff support can be sought. Clarification of ambiguous information can be pursued. Jobs in keeping with abilities can be matched.

This man perceives something bad will happen if he's late again.

Relaxation Therapy

Insights

Relaxation therapy is a technique for both widening one's comfort zone or tolerance for stress and improving the ability to cope with stress when an overload or underload is present. Through a process of self-awareness, the body muscles can be monitored and levels of relaxation rather than tension can be provided. While biofeedback can help in the monitoring process, self-analysis also can be achieved. Relaxation, thus, can be secured to handle potential stress conditions more effectively or relaxation can be reached as a postencounter combatant.

One form of relaxation, for example, involves a breathing exercise. Start by finding a comfortable position either lying down or sitting. Become aware of parts of the body, beginning with the top of the head, then the forehead, lower jaw, the neck, shoulders, arms, hands, back, hips, thighs, calves, ankles, feet, and then the toes, releasing and relaxing tightened muscles wherever they are found. Practice letting each muscle go limp.

Once this is accomplished, begin concentrating on your breathing. Take a deep breath by inhaling through the diaphragm. Expand the lower level of the respiratory system first, then gradually let the lungs and chest fill by enlarging from the bottom to the top. Let the upper chest be the last part to expand (to the point that the shoulders feel the extension themselves). Hold your breath as long as reasonably comfortable, then exhale, letting the upper part of the chest sink first, then gradually let the air move out of the midchest area. Finally, let the diaphragm relax completely. Rest in the relaxed position before beginning the breathing process again. Start the expansion of the lower chest-abdomen area first, spreading slowly until the chest is fully inflated again. And so the process goes.

Concentration on breathing is the key. Each deep breath should be counted. If the cycle is done properly, the count will soon become vague and will eventually be lost. Once this state of relaxation has been achieved, continue for several moments.

When the time available has been expended, begin to move rather slowly. When you are fully mobile, you should feel very rested, ready to move back into the day's activities with vigor.

How Managers and Coworkers Can Help

Ideally, the individual employee will receive help from his or her employer. Organizations can assist individuals in the expansion of comfort zones and stress tolerance levels through the provision of health services and exercise facilities, better communication of information, career-path planning, the use of teamwork, and the encouragement of interpersonal involvement. In our opening case, Jill is in special need of this kind of assistance. Stressors can be reduced by redesigning jobs, changing the authority and responsibility relationships, modifying work schedules, making changes in evaluation and reward systems, matching individual abilities with job requirements, and providing training for skill development.

Supervisors, staff specialists, policymakers, colleagues, and training officials may be key individuals who can alter some of the stressful conditions as well as provide personal support to the individual under pressure. Some of the organizational alterations can take place before stressors act so that the potential stress "bomb" can be defused before the pressure builds.[17]

Notice that the manager has a key role as the person who may recognize stress in employees. Recall that it was Lindsey Ferrara's supervisor who first recognized signs of stress in Lindsey. There are other things an employer can do to provide personal help. Securing time to consider alternatives can be helpful. Planning adequately before something takes place or a duty is fulfilled can be stress reducing. Working to build a team effort may lessen stress as responsibilities and accountabilities are shared.[18]

Help for coping with stress at work can come from individuals and groups outside the organization. Counselors especially trained in methods for overcoming negative effects of stress can help to widen an employee's comfort zone. Family members and friends can provide psychological and social support and nurturing. Physicians and psychologists can provide technical assistance, resulting in physical and psychological strength. The entire healthcare network may be needed at one time or another to provide therapeutic as well as preventive help. Training experts can provide innovative methods for handling problems as they come up. Professional groups can instigate change to correct stressful practice in occupational categories. Lawmakers can also legislate laws regarding quality of work life, health care, and mandatory retirement.

In a study dealing with the presence of heart disease in Japanese men, it was found that heart disease in Japanese men living on the West Coast of the United States was ten times greater that in Japanese men living in Japan. Other reasons for the difference between sample groups were sorted out, and it was finally concluded that Japanese men in the United States had more heart disease because they were more isolated and had less effective support systems. When a support system of friends and family members is present, stress can be buffered. The men in Japan were receiving more cushioning from stressful elements around them from friends and family. As a result, the men in their "home" environment experienced less physical distress and illness from surrounding pressures.

Charles Roppel points to the Japanese example to illustrate the importance of sympathetic support groups in the form of family members and friends. Roppel suggests that each of us should evaluate our existing support systems by answering the survey questions in the accompanying self test.

In short, stress can be handled in one of two ways—the ability to tolerate stress (the comfort zone) can be increased or the impact of a stressor can be softened. Conditions and circumstances can be channeled and rearranged appropriately. The individual, the organization (employer), and outside factors all play a role in causing and treating stress at one time or another.

Figure 14–2 summarizes the stress process. An individual brings several characteristics to a situation. Stressors impact the individual, and those stressors outside of the comfort zone create discomfort as their dangers are perceived by the individual. Personal and organizational consequences begin to take effect. The immediate consequences are sometimes moderated as a result of adaptive responses from the individual, the organization, and factors and influences outside the organization.

Figure 14–2   The Stress Cause and Reaction Model

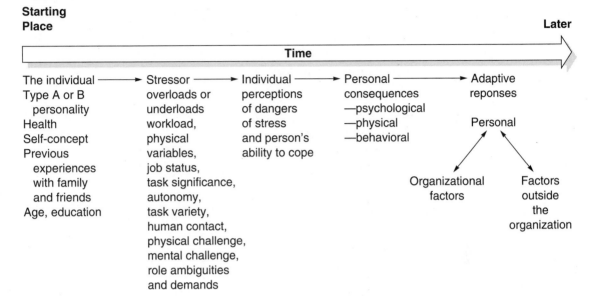

Personal Feedback

The Roppel Support Test

Self Test

Circle one response for each item. Then add the scores next to each item you circled and write your total in the box.

1. At work, how many persons do you talk to about a job hassle?

    None (0)

    One (3)

    Two or three (4)

    Four or more (5)

2. How many neighbors do you trade favors with (loan tools or household items, share rides, babysitting, etc.)?

    None (0)

    One (1)

    Two or three (2)

    Four or more (3)

3. Do you have a spouse or partner?

    No (0)

    Several different partners (2)

    One steady partner (6)

    Married or living with someone (10)

Self Test
continued

4. How often do friends and close family members visit you at home?

   Rarely (0)

   About once a month (1)

   Several times a month (4)

   Once a week or more (8)

5. How many friends or family members do you talk to about personal matters?

   None (0)

   One or two (6)

   Six or more (10)

6. How often do you participate in social, community, or sports groups?

   Rarely (0)

   About once a month (1)

   Several times a month (2)

   Once a week or more (4)

   [ ]   Your Score

If your support network is :

Less than 15:

> Your support network has low strength and probably does not provide much support. You need to consider making more social contacts.

15–29:

> Your support network has moderate strength and likely provides enough support except during periods of high stress.

30 or more:

> Your support network has high strength, and it will likely maintain you well even during periods of high stress.

> If your support system is weaker than needed to give strength and encouragement, work on developing more personal, trusting contacts.

Source: Charles Roppel, California Department of Mental Health, as quoted in *The Baton Rouge, LA. State Times,* March 17, 1984.

Stress does not have to be a destructive force. Frequently, if managed properly, the results of stress can be positive and constructive. The manager has a key role in the stress management process by recognizing and dealing with job-related stressors and by helping employees deal with them.

Getting off the Fast Track

Insights

Some managers in high-stress career paths are stepping off the **fast track** to release some of the pressures of jobs that often demand sixty to seventy hours of work each week. The move to get off the fast track and to move to what one Carnegie-Mellon professor calls the **sanity track** is not without stress itself. To step away from climbing the corporate ladder is a dramatic step for many highly achievement-oriented, ambitious persons. With the step frequently occurs the giving up of long-held personal goals.

One problem of moving to the sanity track is the loss of the respect of many colleagues and associates who are on the fast track. To many people, the move is interpreted as an admission of failure. The in thing is to move upward and be successful and not to set lower goals.

Switching to the sanity track requires the development of a new routine and other personal adjustments. Individuals who have been working sixty- to seventy-hour workweeks often experience guilt feelings as they find themselves putting in shorter days and weeks. "Working fewer hours seems to shortchange the employer," is the first general feeling. A related factor is the problem of finding things to do to fill the newly available free hours.

Some employees step off the fast track, they suppose, by going into business for themselves. The thought is that by being one's own boss, there will be more autonomy and self-determination. While self-control may be accomplished, along with it come many pressures. There may be less security in a self-owned situation. The owner-manager has to make a wide range of decisions and must fill several roles in the organization. Most self-owned and operated organizations are small in size, and with smallness comes less economic and social clout, which can be frustrating in itself. Self-ownership may aid or worsen the stress situation, depending on how it is handled.

Another trend toward getting off the fast track has developed for another reason. This newly defined pattern, sometimes called the **mommy track,** is designed to temporarily shift mothers (usually with small children) to less demanding, slower track, flexible job assignments until the children are old enough to be in school or to attend day care. In such programs, the mother works only two or three days a week, for example, or half days, or some other flexible arrangement, allowing more time for children and other family responsibilities. The career is then picked up in full measure when the development of the children is sufficient to allow the mother to give her best to her job.

fast track
The career path designed to let an employee climb the organizational ladder in a short timespan or the quickest way possible. In this track, the employee is expected to place first priority on doing whatever his or her job requires to benefit the organization most.

sanity track
The career path where an employee usually deliberately opts to take a slower route in moving up within the organization. The path is usually taken to eliminate some of the stress involved in being on the fast track. Other personal goals are often given priority.

Sources: Carol Hymowitz, "Stepping Stones Off the Fast Track," *Wall Street Journal.* June 13, 1989, p. B1; "The Mommy Track," *Business Week,* March 20, 1989, pp. 126–129, 132, 134; and Roger Rickless and Udayan Gupta, "Traumas of a New Entrepreneur," *Wall Street Journal,* May 10, 1989, p. B1.

Summary

Stress is an individual's reaction to perceived threats regardless of the source of danger. Stressors are viewed as the cause or source of the impending danger. Stressors carry with them varying degrees of danger, and individuals have

mommy track
A term used to describe situations where employees—usually mothers—choose to temporarily slow down their organizational career progress while raising small children. During the time of being away from the fast track, the woman works part-time. She returns to the fast track when the children no longer need constant care.

within themselves differing abilities to respond to stress. Some individuals have a high level of tolerance for stress, while others have a very low pain threshold when it comes to stress. In the underload-overload concept of stress, there are at least ten factors that have the potential to result in an underload or overload: workload, physical factors, status, task significance, autonomy, task variety, human contact, physical challenge, mental challenge, and role ambiguity and/or demand. Stress has its consequence for individuals—psychological, physical, and behavioral. Its consequences for organizations include less efficiency, more expense, lower quality, lower quantity, and sometimes increased grievances and strikes.

There are usually two approaches to take for handling stress. One approach is to increase the individual's ability to tolerate and cope with stress. The other technique is to decrease the causes of stress existing around the individual.

Questions to Consider

1. What are some effective ways to develop a supportive group of friends and family members who help an individual cope with stressors? How can existing social contacts be utilized in a more supportive manner?
2. Is it possible for an individual who is a Type A personality to change to a Type B personality? Explain.
3. An individual who is low in self-esteem will have more problems with stressors than an individual who has a positive self-concept. What are the implications of this truth? What can individuals, superiors, and outsiders do to help improve the self-concept? Discuss in detail.
4. According to the Life Change Index Scale, what are the sources of most stress-related problems? What are the implications of these sources insofar as managers are concerned?
5. How can each of the potential stressors identified in Figure 14–2 be dealt with so that underload or overload does not occur? Is it possible to cope with each of these stressors adequately? What can an employee do about each one? What can an employee's boss do about them?
6. As individuals suffer from the consequences of stress overload or underload, in what ways do organizations feel the effects of stress that are present in their employees?
7. Consider at length what a superior can do to help a subordinate cope with stress. Consider preventive and curative actions.
8. Is it ethical behavior for management to allow known stress in an employee to continue at high levels?

Key Terms

fast track	sanity track	Type B
mommy track	stress	personality
negative	stressor	underload
stress	Type A	
overload	personality	

Chapter Case

The Automobile Manufacturer's Representative

Does stress run in organizations? Here's evidence that it does. Both of the following situations involve a large automobile manufacturer. This manufacturer hired bright, young graduates with associate's or bachelor's degrees and assigned them as dealer representatives in its regions. The new dealer reps are in charge of representing the manufacturers with the local dealers who sell the cars. They are to line up promotions, encourage dealers to order certain cars, and generally serve as go-betweens, working between the dealers and the manufacturer. Unfortunately, the problems that follow will only give you a taste of a very stressful job.

John's Problem

"There are times when I just don't know where to turn," John McIntosh confided to Tom Jenkins. It was late on a Saturday afternoon at the apartment complex where they both lived. John had stopped by the pool, and Tom had mentioned that he hadn't seen John for a while.

"You mentioned that you hadn't seen me. Well, here's why," John continued. "In my job, I'm getting to feel like one of those marionettes that jumps every time you pull the strings. The only trouble is that there are too many strings being pulled. I think I've told you that I consider myself an organized guy—I like to accomplish; and I feel that the best way to do that is to put together a reasonable plan, establish priorities, and set about doing what needs to be done in priority order. Well, that's hard to do in a job where you travel, no matter what. And, as you know, I'm on the road five days a week, moving from one of our dealer operations to the next. To get anything done, you've got to have a plan for your activities at each spot—and, for an ambitious person like I believe I am, you also plan to get as much as possible into each day. That would be fine. I'm not afraid of hard work."

"The trouble is all the other signals I get. I'll be partway through the first day, and the office will get hold of me with about two dozen changes—most of them little petty things. When I try to protest or suggest putting them off, what I usually hear is that it's some new thing from headquarters, and it's got to be done. So there I am—priorities completely gone. And it gets worse as the week goes along."

"Naturally, as the extra work piles up, I start running behind. But the work doesn't stop. Instead, it gets worse, because later in the week some of the changes apply to locations I've already visited, and I'm faced with going back. And that's how it goes, week after week. I feel like I'm getting in deeper and deeper and that there's no end in sight. If I could even see some relief, I think I could take it, but let's face it, I'm getting discouraged. And to tell the truth, it's affecting me. I don't have the zip I used to, I'm having trouble concentrating, and I'm getting the feeling that I overreact—the least little thing and I feel like I'm about to fly off the handle. The trouble is, what to do?"

1. From the materials in the chapter, what are the causes of stress in John's situation?

2. What can John, using his own power and skills, do to confront the stressors and the stress?
3. What are some things John can do little, if anything, about? What can he do—what should he do about them?
4. What does the future hold if nothing is done by anyone in this case?
5. What are some problems, other than stressors in this case?

Terry's Problem

"Okay, Terry, out with it," said Roy Ainsworth, one of Terry Juneau's fellow managers after he had spotted Terry, visibly upset and driving aimlessly through the back roads in the area where their territories adjoined. Roy had flagged Terry down and persuaded him to come to a nearby restaurant for a cup of coffee and some talk. After they had arrived at the restaurant, Terry seemed relieved and immediately followed Roy to the table.

"I'm afraid I'm cracking up," Terry began. "I've just had it out with Jack Tobias. You know him, at least by reputation, don't you? He's the dealer with the giant chip on his shoulder. He always has had it in for headquarters, and he's made it clear since I came on board that he has no use for me either. According to him, I'm just some second-rate kid who's been sent in to bring him a million complications he doesn't need. You know how he can be— pick, pick, pick, argue, argue, argue, until I've come to dread visiting him. I know he wants me to stay away, but I've got my job to do, too; so I've kept coming and kept trying, even though I think I've hated it worse than he has. Well, recently I let myself feel a little encouraged. After all this time, Jack actually went along with one of my ideas.

"I just got back today to see how it was going, and he was literally lying in wait for me. I've never seen anyone so furious. He claims the whole thing was a total disaster and that I'd set him up to get back at him. Then he grabbed me by the arm and physically ran me out the door and into the street, screaming and cussing. The last thing he said before he slammed the door was that if I ever tried to get near his operation again, he'd call the police! And he's not kidding, either. I don't even know where to begin. What can I tell them back at headquarters? Will anyone believe me? What about my other dealers? A lot of them respect Jack, and this will get around. Maybe it's overwork, but I've slipped up several times lately, and feel like everyone— dealers and headquarters alike—is starting to wonder about me. The question is what to do?"

1. "Terry himself is responsible for the shape he's in." Do you agree with this statement? Why or why not?
2. Looking back at the counseling techniques in Chapter 12, what should be Roy's response to what Terry has told him?
3. Identify the stressors in this situation.
4. In what ways can Terry's employer help him and the situation that has developed?
5. What other problems in this case need attention?

Chapter 15

Chronic Worker Problems— Alcoholism, Other Drug Abuse, and Theft

Objectives

- To identify and evaluate the impact on organizations of alcoholism, other drug abuse, and theft.
- To review techniques presently being used to deal with alcohol and other drug abuse problems.
- To consider the effectiveness of drug-testing techniques.
- To discuss the legal and ethical questions related to drug testing.
- To discover the reasons employees engage in theft from their employer.
- To identify and analyze methods for dealing with employee dishonesty.

The Demise of Bob Brown

Bob Brown has been employed for ten years by the Chaffee Oil Company as an engineer in the company's southwestern district. His work has been satisfactory, although not particularly outstanding. He has been known as a congenial, extroverted worker. He was bypassed once for a promotion to the position of area engineer when the incumbent was killed in an automobile accident. An organization chart of the district, including Brown's position, is provided in Exhibit I.

Exhibit I—Organization Chart of Southwestern District of Chaffee Oil Company

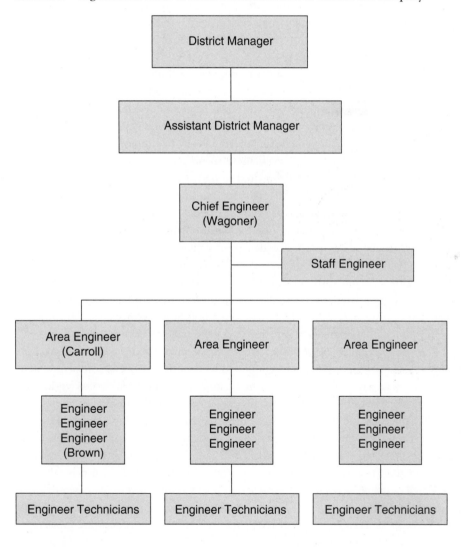

The district manager and the assistant district manager make major decisions concerning large expenditures or major policy changes. The chief engineer is responsible for major decisions in matters concerning engineering and the various technical aspects of oil production. The chief engineer is also responsible for the evaluation and deployment of the engineering personnel and the coordination of the entire engineering staff. The staff engineer serves as an advisor to the chief engineer. The area engineers are responsible for specific geographical territories. They are each supported by a staff of engineers. The size of this staff depends upon the number of wells for which the area engineer is responsible. Each staff of engineers is in turn supported by an adequate number of engineer technicians.

The distinction between the engineers and engineer technicians is an important factor in the case being considered. An engineer is a very technically oriented employee, usually holding a degree in petroleum engineering or a related engineering field. The responsibilities are numerous and varied, and the engineer essentially does very demanding engineering work, requiring all of the knowledge acquired as a result of education and work experience. The majority of the engineer's time is spent in the office.

The principal responsibility of the engineer technician is to serve as a go-between from the field to the office. The technician gathers data and supervises tests in the field and communicates with field personnel. Because these duties are less technically demanding, the position carries lower status value than does that of engineer. The typical engineer technician usually has some college experience but doesn't have a degree. Occasionally a technician will be a college graduate who holds a degree in a field not related to petroleum engineering. The engineer technician receives significantly less pay than the engineer.

Early last year, Bob Brown's attitude underwent a dramatic change. Instead of being outgoing and carefree, he became withdrawn and unsociable. He seemed unconcerned about his responsibilities as an engineer, and his work became less then satisfactory. His area engineer, Wiley Carroll, noticed the change in behavior and performance but took no immediate actions to identify the causes. Instead, Carroll's reaction primarily was to criticize the reports produced by Brown and then show his displeasure verbally whenever Brown made mistakes. Carroll took the position that "Bob had better shape up, or we're going to punish him."

The situation failed to improve. Brown's performance and general demeanor grew steadily worse. Brown began coming to work with hangovers. Some suspected he even drank while at work. Brown frequently missed a day or two of work. The entire district office became aware of his condition. Carroll still made no attempt to discover the causes of Brown's changed behavior. He continued to issue threats concerning Brown's work. Finally, Carroll confronted Brown in the hallway one Monday morning as Brown was coming to work two hours late. A shouting scene resulted that attracted the attention of most of the office. An hour later, Brown was called to the office of the chief engineer, Mel Wagoner. He was informed by Wagoner that his performance as an engineer wasn't meeting the standards of the company and that he was being demoted to engineer technician, with the resulting decrease in salary.

Wagoner's action was taken after hearing only Carroll's side of the story. Brown was never given the opportunity to present his version. The result of the demotion and verbal chastisement was an attitude of bitterness by Brown toward his bosses, his coworkers, and the company in general. Brown believed himself a victim of a grave injustice. The decrease in salary and the personal problems he was experiencing were a serious handicap to him. He suffered a substantial loss of status and professional pride. He felt that his career as an engineer was virtually ruined.

What no one bothered to discover was the cause for Brown's deteriorating attitude and performance. If the truth had been revealed, it would have been discovered that Brown's wife had filed for a divorce after almost twelve years of marriage. The separation was a very trying, emotional one, with bitter fighting occurring over the custody of the couple's only child. In addition, Brown was confronted with severe financial problems resulting from the division of the family's property.

Case Questions

1. Critique Carroll's performance as Brown's supervisor. What mistakes did he make?
2. Also evaluate Wagoner's actions.
3. What will the long-range effects of his supervisors' actions be upon Bob Brown? Upon Brown's fellow workers?
4. What responsibilities, if any, does a company such as Chaffee Oil have toward its employees? Discuss in detail.
5. Role play the counseling session between Carroll (or others) and Brown as it should have occurred.

While there are many employee-related problems that trouble today's managers, there are three in particular that make for costly, difficult-to-handle managerial concerns. Alcoholism, other drug abuse, and theft by employees are all major sources of anxiety for managers.

The Problems of Alcoholism

Throughout the years, many have regarded alcoholism and the problem drinker to be the number one human resource problem in business and industry. It is estimated that at least six million Americans come to work each day with the disease known as alcoholism.[1] An **alcoholic** is technically defined as a "person who consumes large amounts of alcohol over a considerable length of time, and whose addiction causes chronic, increasing incapacitation."[2] In addition, there are a number of **problem drinkers**—drinkers who may not be addicted to alcohol but whose behavior as a result of alcohol causes trouble for themselves and for others. At least one out of every sixteen workers has alcohol-related difficulties. The problems of alcoholism belong to every type of worker—white-collar, blue-collar, managerial, skilled, unskilled, and professional.

A conservative estimate of the cost of alcohol-related problems to American businesses would begin at thirty billion dollars annually. Losses occur through absenteeism, tardiness, injury, illness, deaths, property damage, poor quality performance, increased health insurance costs, higher workers' compensation

alcoholic
A person who consumes large amounts of alcohol over a considerable length of time and whose addiction causes chronic, increasing incapacitation.

problem drinkers
Individuals who may not be addicted to alcohol but whose behavior as a result of alcohol consumption causes trouble for themselves or for others.

costs, the cost of replacing and training new employees, as well as theft that sometimes is associated with alcohol and other drug problems.[3] The effects upon morale must also be acknowledged.

Absenteeism and tardiness for the heavy drinker tend to be fifteen to sixteen times more frequent than for the nondrinker or minimal drinker. The heavy drinker is involved in four times more accidents than is the nondrinker. Problem drinkers tend to work more slowly, do work of a poorer quality, make more bad decisions, and forget safety regulations more frequently than workers who have no alcohol problems. The identification of the problem drinker is frequently difficult. If you think back to the Bob Brown case, you will recall that his problem was never identified. For that and other reasons, he never got the help he needed. Like other problem areas, poor performance, careless actions, absences, and accidents may be behavior patterns that lead to the identification of an alcohol problem.

Other Drug Abuse Problems

A wide range of drugs other than alcohol are being abused by employees. Some of the drugs abused are legal prescription drugs such as tranquilizers. Other drugs being used illegally include cocaine, marijuana, heroin, PCP, codeine, and antidepressants. The estimates of the annual cost to industry resulting from the use of drugs (including alcohol) range between fifty billion to one hundred billion dollars.[4] As with alcohol, the abuse of other drugs affects health-care costs, decreased quality performance, absenteeism, accidents, and theft.

Cocaine usage has become a problem of major proportions.

The abuse of substances other that alcohol is especially alarming in that more than 90 percent of abusers admit having drugs with them and using them at work. Over 50 percent of the **drug abusers** studied admit to selling drugs to other workers on the work premises (a criminal offense), and more than 40 percent of the workers sampled admit to having stolen goods and materials from their employer to sell for personal profit. More than 30 percent of workers on drugs indicate they have stolen cash or checks from their employer or fellow employees.[5]

The detection of the worker with another kind of drug problem may be even more difficult than the discovery of the problem drinker. Supervisors seldom identify that the source of a drug abuser's problem is, in fact, drugs. Many times, drug abusers are codependent on alcohol and other substances. While a drug abuser may have symptoms such as dilated eyes, shaky coordination, and impaired depth perception, he or she is usually able to camouflage the symptoms under the guise of being too tired from overwork, lack of sleep, a personal problem, or even too much alcohol. An alcohol alibi, such as having a hangover, is more acceptable to a worker's supervisor in most cases than one based on another drug-related explanation.

Dealing with Alcohol and Other Drug Problems

Drug Testing

Obviously, the preferred way to solve the unpleasantness that results from problem drinking or other drug usage is to avoid hiring workers who are already experiencing problems. In many organizations, extensive screening occurs before a prospective employee is hired. Every applicant who is being considered seriously for a job may be given a thorough physical examination. Previous work records, educational records, and behavioral habits are scrutinized to uncover possible signs of alcohol or other drug abuse. **Drug testing** is increasingly being made a part of the evaluation process. In a survey done a few years ago, almost 50 percent of the Fortune 500 top organizations were found to use drug testing to screen prospective employees as well as for checking on existing employees.[6]

In a study done more recently, the percentage of companies testing for drug use remained fairly constant at 51.5 percent. Large companies (measured in volume of sales) do more testing than smaller organizations. In about one half of organizations with a sales volume of over five hundred million dollars, job applicants and current employees are both given drug tests.[7] Each drug test costs a firm from twenty-five dollars to thirty-five dollars.[8] Many employees say that they see alcohol as a bigger problem than other forms of drugs.

Most of the time a prospective employee who tests positive is given a second test to validate the findings. Urine samples are used predominately, but blood tests are being used more and more. Prospective employees who test positive usually are not hired. Existing employees who test positive are referred for counseling and treatment most of the time (69.6 percent). About one in five will be dismissed, and about the same percentage will be suspended, placed on probation, or given a leave of absence. A majority of all

drug abuser
An individual who uses any form of drug excessively beyond or against purposes for which the drug was intended.

drug testing
A method to evaluate the presence of (and to what degree) a drug is in the body systems of an individual.

Management in Action

Navy Program Succeeds with High-Quality Testing, Prompt Discipline

The granddaddy of all drug-detection programs is run by the Department of Defense. It started in the 1970s and was supposed to identify drug abusers, particularly returning Vietnam War veterans addicted to heroin, and get treatment for them before they returned to civilian life. A DOD-wide survey in 1980 discovered that nearly half the younger people in the military were using marijuana. As a result, each service began devising a drug-detection program.

The Navy, which had the highest percentage of marijuana users in the survey, was devising a ten-point plan for handling drug users when there was a fatal accident aboard the aircraft carrier U.S.S. *Nimitz* in the summer of 1981. An examination of the ship found widespread drug use among sailors and pushed the Navy's program full speed ahead.

Since then, the Navy testing program has evolved into the biggest and, many people would argue, the best in the country. Capt. Leo Cangianelli has been with the Navy program since its start and is pleased with the results. In the five years the program has been operating, Cangianelli says the level of drug use among personnel has been cut in half twice.

"Drug abuse has come down from the E1 to E5 group, basically the under-twenty-five population, from 47 percent in 1981, to about 22 percent in 1982, and to 10 percent in 1984," he says.

At least one outside consultant for the Navy's program says that positive tests are currently running only about 4 percent.

"The single most important factor in bringing down drug use in the Navy has been the urinalysis program," Cangianelli says. "And it has been the ability to take punitive action from a positive urinalysis."

When a sailor enters boot camp, he or she is tested immediately. If any drug is present other than marijuana, the sailor goes home. If marijuana is found,

companies (those who test and those who don't) conduct educational and awareness programs.[9]

Accuracy and Reliability   Screening and checking for drug use through blood and urine tests have raised a fair amount of controversy. One issue is over the accuracy and reliability of available tests. In answer to the charges that drug testing cannot be depended upon to be correct, some argue that drug testing can be very accurate. Hanson writes that drug testing is presently accurate as much as 95 percent of the time, with a 100 percent reliability possible if done properly.[10] The use of some drugs—marijuana, for example—can be detected up to a month after usage. A drug like cocaine, however, is eliminated more quickly and may not be identifiable three or four days after its use.

Legality   The other issue with drug testing is over the legality of such tests. Opponents often claim that the Fourth Amendment rights of employees and prospective employees are violated by the use of drug testing. The privacy amendment, however, protects individuals from illegal searches by agents of

Cangianelli says, the person will be tested again within 60 days; a second positive means a discharge. After the sixty-day period, if a person tests positive, the commanding officer has some discretion on the first offense.

"The CO can determine that this is a problem child, is not a good worker, and has not done very well, and can discharge the person for the single positive test," Cangianelli says. "Many of the younger ones are given two chances. The first time, the CO will counsel them, warn them, document the offense in their service record, fine them, and restrict them to the ship. If a second positive comes up the CO has no choice; the person is discharged."

Cangianelli says that for the ranks of chief petty officer and above, "anybody in khaki," the policy is one positive and you're out. The result of this policy is that about 6,000 enlisted men were discharged last year for drug abuse, and about thirty officers.

Today, the Navy has five laboratories doing drug analysis, and they run 1.8 million samples yearly. They test for marijuana, cocaine, barbiturates, amphetamines, PCP, and opiates. A test for LSD is being developed. Cangianelli says the Navy uses the Roche Radioimmunoassay and confirms all positive by GC-MS. Total cost of the program is about twenty-five million dollars per year, and averages about thirteen dollars per test.

In the past three years, the Navy claims it has not reported a single false positive. If true, it is because of the elaborate proficiency testing it uses. According to Cangianelli, every week each lab receives thirty-six open—that is knowingly containing reference drugs—samples for analysis. And each lab is sent thirty-six blind samples, twenty-four negative, and twelve positive, mixed in with regular samples each week. They are prepared by the Armed Forces Institute of Pathology, which takes the results and reports each month on the overall quality. In the more than 20,000 test samples, Cangianelli says no false positives have been reported.

Source: Reprinted with permission from *Chemical Engineering News,* June 2, 1986, 64(22), p. 8. Copyright 1986 American Chemical Society.

the government and excludes private employers. Some have cited the Fifth Amendment as a right that is broken by mandatory testing in that an employee or prospective employee is testifying against himself or herself when samples are used for evaluation, decision, and or disciplinary purposes. Thus far, however, most types of drug testing have stood up under court challenges.

Drug Policies and Procedures

With or without testing, every organization should develop a set of policies and procedures for handling alcohol and other drug abuse problems among employees. The development and application of rules and procedures should include the following:

1. A search of statutes and regulations established by federal and state governments to determine what is permissible in the way of inspection and control.

2. Clear definition and enforcement of rules. There should be rules about using drugs on the premises, reporting to work intoxicated or impaired, selling or providing drugs to other employees at work, and the right to administer tests or searches. The fact that tests will be used should be communicated. The consequences of identified violations should also be established.

3. Training and educating of supervisors in the knowledge of rules and regulations along with the methods of discovery of abuses and disciplinary action.

4. Development of rehabilitation or employee assistance programs.

5. The monitoring of performance to discover behavior that is sub-par, dangerous, or in other ways unacceptable.

6. Diagnosis of causes of inadequate or inappropriate performance. This may be done on a routine basis or on the basis of unique behavior. Drug testing may be included in this analysis.

7. Offering rehabilitation or employee assistance where appropriate.

8. Following appropriate disciplinary guidelines developed and communicated as they were formulated.[11]

Employee Rights

In all phases of the alcohol-drug abuse program, good employee relations techniques should be practiced. Confidentiality of information about employees and their problems should be observed, especially insofar as addiction to a drug is concerned. Reasonable steps should be taken to protect employees and others from harm caused by substance abuse.

Employee Philosophy and Attitudes

It is important that the employing organization have a positive philosophy toward alcoholism and other drug abuse. It is also important that supervisory personnel dealing with abusers have the support of their employer as they relate to problem workers. One of the big difficulties supervisors experience is the identification of the nature of an employee's problem (whether it is alcohol or other drug-related, a matter of some other health problem, or a psychological problem).

This positive attitude toward problem workers and supervisory personnel was pioneered by General Motors. In an early handbook to supervisors, GM stated its position on alcohol and the worker:

1. Alcoholism is recognized as a highly complex disease which is treatable. . . . Alcoholism is defined as a disease in which an employee's consumption of any alcoholic beverage definitely and repeatedly interferes with his or her performance and/or health.

2. Employee alcoholism becomes a concern when it interferes with the employee's job performance. To drink or not to drink socially is the prerogative of the employee. The social stigma often associated with alcoholism has no basis in fact. A realistic recognition of this illness will encourage employees to take advantage of available treatment. Employees with this illness will receive the same consideration and

referral for treatment that is presently extended to all employees having other illnesses.

3. Every effort should be made to identify the disease in its early stages, to work with and assist the employee, and to encourage him or her to obtain treatment without delay.

4. Early identification of the alcoholic employee should be based entirely on evidence of poor job performance and other related factors. The immediate supervisor should refer such an employee to the plant medical director or the designated representative for further evaluation.

5. A medically qualified individual will be available to consult with the employee about the nature of alcoholism and whether or not treatment is indicated. Medical records of employees will be maintained in a confidential manner.

6. The decision to undertake treatment is the responsibility of the individual . . . . The medical department is available to provide referral assistance if desired. Where a leave of absence for treatment is necessary, a sick leave will be granted and the employee will be eligible for company insurance benefits.

7. The employee should be assured that if he or she brings the illness under control and job performance becomes satisfactory, job security will not be jeopardized solely by the decision to seek treatment. However, the employee should also be advised that he or she may expect no special privileges or exemptions from standard personnel administration practices. Failure to obtain treatment and to improve in performance will result in a review of the employee's situation according to policies and rules.

8. Considerate and careful followup is vital for effective employee rehabilitation or continuance of corrective action, whichever is appropriate.

This set of statements and assumptions has served General Motors well through the years. Employees make a choice regarding whether or not to submit to treatment and rehabilitation, since substance abuse is treatable. Those agreeing to opt for treatment have a pretty good chance of successfully returning to stability and good performance. One study showed that 80 percent of the heavy drinkers who asked for help were assisted in overcoming their problems to the degree that they were able to retain their employment. The rate of dismissal for those who refused help, on the other hand, was high. Workers who accepted help reduced their absenteeism by 82 percent, while those turning down help had absenteeism increased by 121 percent.[12]

Rehabilitation Programs

While many companies have moved toward rehabilitation programs voluntarily, such programs may become mandatory in the future. California law now requires employers having twenty-five or more employees to reasonably accommodate employees by giving them the opportunity to enter and participate in an alcoholic rehabilitation program, providing the participation will not create a hardship on the employer's operations. Time off does not have to be paid, although accrued sick leave may be used. Employers are not prohibited from discharging or refusing to hire employees who, because of the use

Table 15–1

Test to Determine
Seriousness of
Alcohol Problems

The following questions will help to evaluate the degree to which alcohol might be a problem in a worker's life:

1. When did you first start drinking? (This question provides clues concerning the recency of an employee's involvement with alcohol.)
2. How often do you drink? (This helps to differentiate between the type of alcohol problems a worker may have.)
3. How much do you drink? (People who usually get drunk are not social drinkers in most cases.)
4. What happens when you drink? (If an individual's drinking has a detrimental effect on health, school, and work and the individual continues to drink, he or she has an alcohol problem.)
5. Is there any history of alcoholism in your family? (There appears to be a pattern of alcohol problems running in families. Children of alcoholics, for example, are more likely to have alcohol problems than children whose parents are not alcoholics.)
6. Do you use other drugs? (Many alcoholics are addicted to other drugs as well.)
7. Do you ever wake up in the morning and cannot remember what happened the night before? (Answers to this question show the stage to which an individual has progressed.)
8. Do you ever have a few drinks before you go to a party? (Alcohol-problem individuals often drink before going to a party so that it will be less obvious that they are drinking too much.)
9. Do you ever sneak drinks? (Alcohol-problem people frequently sneak a drink to avoid the appearance of drinking too much.)
10. Do you ever feel guilty about drinking? (Most people who are headed toward alcoholism begin to feel guilty at this time.)

of alcohol or other drugs, are unable to perform duties or who endanger the safety of self or others.[13]

One of the reasons rehabilitation programs are touted highly for use before disciplinary actions are considered (in addition to the high rehabilitation rates) is that helping an employee to overcome an alcohol or other drug problem is usually less expensive in the long run than dismissing a trained employee and then hiring and training someone new.

It is important that both the employer and the employee confront the problem. It is essential that the employee admit the problem and seek help. Employees seeking help stand an infinitely greater chance of success than employees who refuse to admit to their problem. Recovery rates on alcohol-related workers is somewhat higher than for other drug abusers, but there is hope for both types. The usual sequence for helping the alcohol or other drug abuser is this:

1. The worker with a problem is identified through the symptoms he or she exhibits.
2. The nature of the problem (whether it is alcohol, other drugs, or something else) is clarified by the worker, by the worker's supervisor, by a specialist, or by a combination of these people working together.

Table 15–1
continued

11. Does talking about alcoholism make you feel uncomfortable? (Most alcoholics would rather talk about anything else than alcoholism.)

12. Do you ever go out, plan to have just a couple of drinks, and then end up getting drunk? (This question addresses the loss of control.)

13. Do you ever make up excuses for getting drunk? (The alcoholic has an array of excuses for getting drunk every day.)

14. Do you find your mood changing quite a bit lately? (Alcoholics often have wide swings in moods in even short periods of time.)

15. What kinds of hobbies, sports, or other outside interests do you have? (Alcoholics gradually lose interest in things that were once fun and exciting.)

16. Have you had any health problems lately? (Alcoholics tend to have a wide range of health problems.)

17. Have you ever tried to stop drinking? (Almost every alcoholic has tried to stop to prove he or she has no alcohol problem.)

18. Do you ever find that you skip meals when drinking? (Many alcoholics do not eat breakfast or lunch because they find it difficult to keep anything down. Many start drinking early in the day, and eating just gets left out.)

19. Have you had any family problems, or has anyone in your family suggested that you drink too much? (With most alcoholics, this is a very sore point.)

20. Do you ever go on binges that last several days, or do you drink more or less constantly? (The alcohol-problem person often does.)

Source: "Diagnose Alcoholism," by J. Larry Goff, copyright May 1990. Reprinted with the permission of *Personnel Journal*, Costa Mesa, California; all rights reserved.

3. If the worker recognizes the problem and asks for help, the organization helps to outline a rehabilitation plan whereby the worker can overcome the problem. It is important that the worker commit self to doing his or her share if the process of rehabilitation is to be successful.

4. The organization lends its support to the success of a worker's fight with encouragement and understanding and through financial backing, where necessary. The organization makes a commitment to the worker to provide help throughout the difficulty.

The Test on Alcoholism (Table 15–1) lists some questions that help a person to identify the seriousness of an alcohol problem.

You as a Supervisor

Look back at the Bob Brown case. A pair of related issues in that case are of special importance to the manager. You'll notice that Brown's bosses never did really understand Brown's underlying problem. Instead, management reacted to Brown's poor work record. Many experienced managers reviewing a case like this will ask such questions as:

1. How much should I as a manager try to get involved in employees' personal problems?

2. What if the opposite of Brown's case comes up? Suppose I suspect personal problems, but those problems haven't yet affected the employee's work performance. Should I get involved?

At the heart of questions like these is the issue of the manager's job—should managers try to be counselors in matters outside of work performance? Managers usually aren't trained to be psychologists or psychotherapists, and really helping people with serious problems will likely involve the need for such training. Yet, as we review the case, most of us probably feel critical of Brown's management for not stepping in to do more to help. As you can see, there's a fine line. To give you an idea of how touchy the issue can be, the authors asked several experienced and highly effective managers to review the Bob Brown case and to talk to us about what they thought went wrong and what they would recommend. The responses were surprisingly similar. Here's how one executive put it:

> In a case like this, you really have to watch out. I'd say management was at fault for not giving Bob a chance to open up. Notice, though, that I'm saying "open up." What you *don't* do is to ask the guy if he's got a drinking problem, or worse yet, tell him he's got one. The kind of thing I'd do is this. I'd lay out some examples of what I'd seen—the tardiness and the work performance, for example. Then, I'd say "Bob, I've been around here long enough that I know this isn't like you. What's going on? If there's a problem, I want to help!" Now the ball is in Bob's court. He can either talk to me or deny it.

"What if he denies there's a problem?" we asked.

> Well then, there's not much I can do. I'd keep offering help, of course. But if Bob refuses to confront the problem and his work stays poor, I'm going to be faced with disciplinary action—demotion or firing—if necessary. Why? Well, because I've got other workers to think of. I can't have one set of standards for Bob and another for everyone else.

"Suppose he owns up to his problems," we asked. "After all, in this case there are several of them—marriage, drinking—maybe others as well. What now?"

> Now's the time to call in the pros. One thing you must remember is to try not to be an amateur psychologist. Otherwise you can become so involved in the employee's problems that you lose your effectiveness as a supervisor. Your job is to listen, offer support, and, most important, help the employee find professional help. In big companies, there may be someone inside the organization who does this. Otherwise the supervisor must be prepared.
>
> I have a list right in my desk drawer of county and state agencies that can help, and I pull it out when needed. If the employee seeks help, I do all I can to accommodate the recommendations from the treatment— just as I would for *any* employee with a treatable illness. But if treatment fails or if the employee doesn't try treatment, then it's back to my original guideline—take the actions justified by the work performance.

Is this cold-hearted? That's not an easy question. The bottom line is this. Management is partly a balancing act—balancing the employee's welfare, the rights of other employees, and the good of the organization.

Employee Dishonesty and Theft

Another chronic problem in organizations is the dishonest employee who acquires company cash or merchandise and willfully uses it for his or her own purposes. **Employee theft** may take many forms—padding an expense account, pocketing money from the cash register, taking home office supplies for personal use, and removing company products for the purpose of reselling them. In recent years, time theft has also received attention.[14] Time theft occurs when an employee willfully and habitually wastes or misuses the time for which he or she is being paid to work.

employee theft
Any form of stealing from one's employer, through such methods as time, materials, and money.

The cost of theft by employees is difficult to estimate. Literally, no one knows the amount of money, time, and merchandise that is lost, because many thefts are never discovered. Estimates range from thirty billion dollars to as much as two hundred billion dollars. One expert has said that the cost of theft from organizations is passed along to the customer to the tune of 15 percent of the cost of the merchandise being purchased. If employees did not steal from their employers, the cost of purchasing most goods could be reduced by that percentage.[15]

Who Steals and Why

Many explanations have been given for why employees steal. Employees who feel that they are not being paid enough may be more prone to steal. Hard

Employee theft is a problem in all types of occupations.

economic times may encourage theft. Weak value systems are another suggested explanation. Perceived or actual group norms may also foster theft—that is, the employee who steals usually feels that everyone engages in theft, so why shouldn't he or she do the same thing? It is said that theft is also more likely to occur when the opportunity is made available to individuals; i.e., lax controls make theft easy to accomplish. Employees may actually interpret lax control as a signal from management that theft is permissible. Employees who express a tolerance for the use for illegal drugs are higher theft risks than employees intolerant of drug use (drug abusers themselves have a high frequency of theft).

From a personality perspective, stubborn, sensation-seeking, aggressive, undependable quitters and habitual rule breakers are more likely to steal from their employer. Also, employees with few strong ties and an irresponsible outlook on life are more inclined toward theft.[16] Very often, the dishonest employee feels very little loyalty to the employer and feels little responsibility to deal fairly with bosses. Theft may even become a game among workers who contrive ways of getting things from their employer.

Management's Role in Employee Theft

Sometimes the actions of the management of the employing organization seem to encourage theft among employees. Supervisors who are dishonest themselves encourage their employees to follow in their footsteps. The design of buildings and plant facilities may contribute to the convenience and ease with which theft or other forms of dishonesty occur. While most organizations have policies designed to severely discipline (usually to discharge) the worker caught engaging in dishonest activities, these policies are seldom applied consistently. Managers or skilled employees are often thought to be too valuable to discipline. Poor publicity growing out of the organization's admission that it has dishonest employees is another excuse given to justify lack of disciplinary action. An organization's failure to apply disciplinary actions prescribed in stated policies and regulations appears to open the door to further dishonesty.

Dealing with Employee Theft

polygraph test
A means for evaluating the truthfulness of an individual through the use of electronic sensory devices attached to the individual's body to measure reactions to questions.

Lie Detector Tests   For many years, the **polygraph** (lie detector) **test** was a major force in the screening of prospective employees and the investigations of existing employees. At one time during the heyday of polygraph testing, employees (and prospective ones) were tested at the rate of about two million per year. Such testing was always controversial and sometimes was declared to be highly inaccurate. On December 27, 1988, federal legislation went into effect restricting the use of polygraphs. As of that date, the use of polygraphs was outlawed for use in screening prospective employees in all industries except security-oriented services and pharmaceuticals.

Lie detectors can still be used in a limited way for investigation for infractions that have occurred while an individual is employed in an organization. A test can be used along with other methods to investigate possible guilt but can never be used as the sole determinant of a misdeed. For a test to be used legally, an employee must have had access to a crime and must be under reasonable suspicion. The employee must receive a written statement indicating that he or she is under suspicion and telling him or her of his or her rights. Before the employee is attached to the machine, he or she should be allowed to see the list of questions to be asked. The employee can refuse to answer any questions felt to be too personal. In fact, the employee may terminate the polygraph activity at any point. The employee can't be asked questions related to his or her religious, political, or sexual beliefs.[17] These changes have severely altered the methods available to organizations for evaluating present and future employees.

Honesty Tests   A fairly recent substitute for the polygraph test as a screening device is the pencil-and-paper **honesty test.** (Take the Personal Feedback "How Honest Are You.") It is estimated that 5,000 or more organizations are already using honesty tests, which ask prospective employees to answer such questions as:

> **honesty tests**
> Some form of evaluation that checks the level of an employee's truthfulness or proneness to being truthful.

1. Should a person be fired if caught stealing $5.00?
2. Have you ever thought about taking company merchandise without actually taking any?
3. How easy would it be for a dishonest employee to steal from an employer?
4. What percentage of employee thieves are caught?
5. Do employers who pay people poorly have it coming to them when employees steal?

Personal Feedback

A Test of Your Honesty

Self Test

Answer each question in a straightforward manner. Assume in each case that you will not get caught in wrongdoing; being honest out of fear of being caught doesn't count. The directions for scoring the test are provided after you answer the questions.

1. As you are leaving a restaurant, the cashier totals your bill, which comes to $24. You give the cashier a 20-dollar and a 10-dollar bill. Instead of giving you back $6 in change, the cashier gives you $16 (perhaps thinking you gave him two 20-dollar bills). Do you keep the extra $10?

   No (✓)   Maybe ( )   Yes ( )

2. One of your employees asks you to write a letter of recommendation for her so that she can apply for a job with another company. She has not been a good employee, and you are anxious to get rid of her. Do you write her a letter of recommendation making her look better than she really is?

   No ( )   Maybe ( )   Yes (✓)

3. As you back out of a crowded parking lot you accidentally scrape the fender of another car. Do you leave a note telling the owner of the car what happened and how to get in touch with you?

   No ( )   Maybe ( )   Yes (✓)

Self Test
continued

4. You would like to have the day off to visit a friend who is to be in town. If you take the day off for anything other than health reasons you will not get paid. However, you still have some sick leave left. If you call in sick, your pay will not be docked. Would you call in sick?

   No (✓)   Maybe ( )   Yes ( )

5. You forgot to prepare for a big, important test you were to have at mid-morning. You know that you don't have time to prepare adequately. Would you call in and tell your professor you are sick and ask to take the test at another time?

   No ( )   Maybe ( )   Yes (✓)

6. You have an expense account you use when taking clients out to dinner. Would you take a friend who is not a client out to dinner and file an expense report as if business were discussed?

   No ( )   Maybe (✓)   Yes ( )

7. You buy a new coat that is selling for $100. When the clerk checks you out, she charges you for a coat that is selling for $69. Would you call the discrepancy to her attention?

   No (✓)   Maybe ( )   Yes ( )

8. An acquaintance is buying an old car from you for $500. He tells you that you can both save money on taxes by listing the price paid for the car as $300. He will pay you the rest ($200) in cash that won't be recorded. Would you agree to the transaction?

   No (✓)   Maybe ( )   Yes ( )

9. You are sent on a trip by your employer. You are gone four days, but you work only two and one-half days. The rest of the time you spend attending a major sporting event. Would you tell your employer?

   No ( )   Maybe ( )   Yes (✓)

10. It is time to write up your monthly performance report (on yourself) to turn in to your boss. There are some things in your past month's work that didn't go well and are embarrassing to you. You can avoid including them in your monthly report. Do you?

    No (✓)   Maybe ( )   Yes ( )

Scoring: To the right of every answer is a score. Add up the points from the answers you chose. The highest possible score is 20 points. If you score a 20 you are honest to the core. A score of 14 to 19 indicates you are to be trusted most of the time. A score of 8 to 13 shows your honesty is selective. A score of 1 to 7 shows you to be a self-seeker. A score of 0 says you look out for yourself.

1.	No	(✓)	2	Maybe	( )	1	Yes	( )	0
2.	No	( )	2	Maybe	( )	1	Yes	(✓)	0
3.	No	( )	0	Maybe	( )	1	Yes	(✓)	2
4.	No	(✓)	2	Maybe	( )	1	Yes	( )	0
5.	No	( )	2	Maybe	( )	1	Yes	(✓)	0
6.	No	( )	2	Maybe	(✓)	1	Yes	( )	0

7.	No	(✓)	0	Maybe	( )	1	Yes	( )	2
8.	No	(✓)	2	Maybe	( )	1	Yes	( )	0
9.	No	( )	0	Maybe	( )	1	Yes	(✓)	2
10.	No	(✓)	2	Maybe	( )	1	Yes	( )	0

Through the many answers given to a battery of questions, supporters say that a profile can be obtained that reveals a probable pattern of dishonesty. Pencil-and-paper honesty tests are promoted for their ease in application and measurement, their inexpensive cost, and the fact that they have not been outlawed in any states. Detractors, of course, point out that insightful prospective employees may be able to "fake" the tests.

Credit Reports   Another technique being used more frequently today to predict the integrity of prospective employees is the credit history of the individual. Equifax of Atlanta sold 350,000 reports to 15,000 different employers in a year. Trans Union Credit Information Company of Chicago sold 26,000 credit reports for personnel evaluation in one month alone. From the information gained from a credit report, many employers say that they can learn whether or not an individual will steal from them, will sell corporate secrets, or will otherwise act irresponsibly. Credit checks for this purpose usually cost five dollars or less.[18] The use of simple controls such as separation of duties, mandatory vacations, and the enforcement of existing internal controls can also cause many forms of fraud and theft to be discontinued.[19]

Promoting Positive Attitudes in Employees   Another avoidance method used *after* an employee is hired is the attempt to develop a positive attitude in each worker so that he or she will want to be honest. The following are some of the techniques used in the approach:

1. The decentralization of authority or the sharing of responsibility for decision making and control has the effect of helping the worker see his or her importance to the organization. A worker who feels that personal actions can make a difference in the success of the organization and feels that there will be adequate rewards for loyal performance usually will respond in a positive manner. In one study it was noted that one company experienced a great deal of success when it divided workers into work teams and gave each team authority to regulate and control itself and its members. The team was held accountable for its performance and rewarded when excellence occurred. One of the byproducts of this action was a marked reduction in theft. Workers felt responsible for their fellow team members and to the total organization.[20]

2. As a way of reinforcing the point, it is important for workers to be adequately rewarded for their good performance. Rewards for constructive effort create a desire to earn further rewards. At the same time, adequate compensation for performance reduces the need for stealing from the employer.

Insights

The Manager's Role in the Prevention of Theft

Two predominant approaches can be taken to dealing with theft by employees. One approach is to select the right employees—employees who will be unlikely to engage in stealing. The other is to limit the opportunities for employees to steal by controlling through security procedures.

The accompanying model describes the contributing factors and procedures that lead to theft. As the employee enters an organization, he or she brings a complex set of personal factors that may relate to theft, including characteristic deficiencies, psychological and physiological disorders, drug addictions, and peer group influences. The organization itself influences theft-related behavior through control and security procedures, theft policies, orientation programs, management's treatment of workers, and the behavior managers model to employees (see the accompanying model).

Much can be done by managers to improve performance and discourage theft. Managers can do the following:

1. Define theft and communicate a theft policy. Decisions must be made concerning what theft is. Does the use of the company copier for personal purposes constitute theft, for example? Such boundaries must be established and communicated.

2. Treat employees with dignity, respect, and trust. Employees who are treated as honest individuals are likely to behave that way.

3. Establish personal, caring, nonadversarial relationships with employees. It is more difficult to steal from a friend than it is from someone who doesn't care about you.

4. Provide feedback and reinforcement for nontheft behaviors. Participation, feedback, and praise are strong reinforcers, even when financial rewards are possible.

5. Provide theft alternatives. Whenever possible, employees should be given things they might steal anyway—such things as damaged goods, discontinued lines, used equipment.

6. Refer needy employees for assistance. When it is known that employees have psychological, emotional, and even economic problems, they may be referred to assistance programs or counselors.

7. Strive to improve employees' jobs by psychological enrichment and environmental improvement. Challenging, interesting tasks work against theft.

8. Let disgruntled employees vent their anger. The use of employee surveys, complaint sessions, and informal boss-subordinates meetings defuse dysfunctional aggression.

9. Provide good models of organizational integrity. Bosses who honor the organization's ownership of materials, tools, etc., set the right example for subordinates.

10. Eliminate oppressive control and selection procedures. Tact and restraint should be used to preserve employee dignity and reduce antiorganizational behavior.

Source: Robert R. Taylor, "Your Role in the Prevention of Employee Theft," *Management Solutions*, Volume 31, Number 8, August 1986, pp. 20–25. Reprinted by permission of publisher, from *Management Solutions*, August 1986 © 1986. American Management Association, New York. All rights reserved.

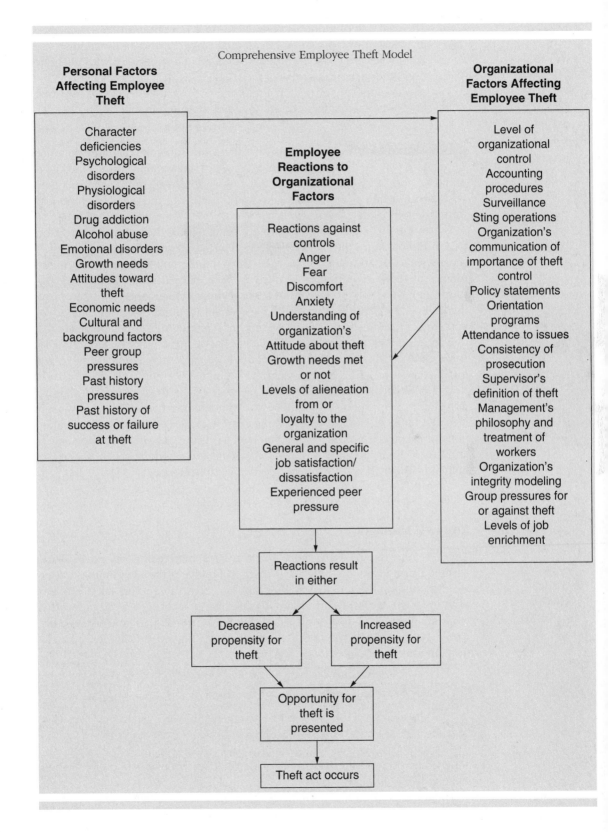

Comprehensive Employee Theft Model

Personal Factors Affecting Employee Theft

Character deficiencies
Psychological disorders
Physiological disorders
Drug addiction
Alcohol abuse
Emotional disorders
Growth needs
Attitudes toward theft
Economic needs
Cultural and background factors
Peer group pressures
Past history pressures
Past history of success or failure at theft

Employee Reactions to Organizational Factors

Reactions against controls
Anger
Fear
Discomfort
Anxiety
Understanding of organization's Attitude about theft
Growth needs met or not
Levels of alieneation from or loyalty to the organization
General and specific job satisfaction/ dissatisfaction
Experienced peer pressure

Organizational Factors Affecting Employee Theft

Level of organizational control
Accounting procedures
Surveillance
Sting operations
Organization's communication of importance of theft control
Policy statements
Orientation programs
Attendance to issues
Consistency of prosecution
Supervisor's definition of theft
Management's philosophy and treatment of workers
Organization's integrity modeling
Group pressures for or against theft
Levels of job enrichment

Reactions result in either

Decreased propensity for theft

Increased propensity for theft

Opportunity for theft is presented

Theft act occurs

3. The example of an honest boss who does not cheat on the company is an inspiration to associates to deal honesty and fairly themselves. Employees are inclined to follow the lead of a supervisor with integrity.
4. Any other action that makes the worker feel it is important that he or she act honestly for personal and organizational benefits will be a positive force in creating a desire to avoid engaging in theft.

Deterrents to Theft   More frequently, however, solutions that are suggested for dealing with the problem of employee theft concentrate on the negative, punitive type of action. Rules that threaten to discharge a worker (or otherwise penalize him or her) caught engaging in acts of theft are a deterrent to further actions if they are applied.

Organizational efforts to eliminate opportunities for theft may also be effective in discouraging theft. Television monitoring devices, frequent patrols by security officers, and other techniques for watching employees reduce opportunities to steal. Requiring employees to wear standardized, no-pockets uniforms may be a viable deterrent in some manufacturing concerns. Implementing policies where all checks and expense accounts must be signed or approved by more than one individual may reduce the temptation to cheat the organization out of funds. The location of the employees' parking lot some distance from the building in a supervised area may eliminate the carrying of some merchandise away from the premises.

It should be noted that preventive measures such as television monitoring, polygraph examinations, and the use of undercover agents are not warmly received by most employees. Even the honest employees who have no intentions of stealing from their employer tend to regard the constant checking as an insult to their integrity. Work under circumstances where there is a lack of mutual confidence and trust may negatively affect morale.

You as a Manager

There is one big message here for you as a manager. You can NEVER, NEVER afford to do anything to give your employees the idea that you tolerate dishonesty. One incident sums it up. Recently, the authors spent the day examining the workflow in an automobile manufacturing organization. After work, they spent a few moments talking to one of the employees, Ray, who'd been working the line that day. Ray was joined by Charlie, a friend, from another unit.

"Look what I got today," exclaimed Charlie, proudly showing a new car radio. It turned out that the radio had "walked," meaning that Charlie had stolen it from the line.

"Boy, are you ever lucky!" said Ray, the employee we knew. "My boss watches us like a hawk. We'd *never* be able to get away with that!"

As Charlie walked off, Ray looked at us, a bit sheepishly, we thought, and added this: "To tell the truth, I'm glad. I'd hate to be put in a spot where somebody would let me steal!"

The message is there, and managers and potential managers must heed it.

Summary

Most organizations, regardless of their size, can expect to encounter chronic employee problems related to alcoholism, other drug abuse, or employee dishonesty. If these problems are to be overcome, their sources must be identified and courses of action plotted. Managers must be committed to programs of prevention, rehabilitation, and elimination. Particularly in the cases of alcoholism and other drug abuse, the worker with the problem also is to be committed to a program of rehabilitation if the problem is to be corrected. Employers must be more willing to admit the possibility of such problems among employees and must be more courageous in engaging in improvement campaigns.

While control techniques such as television monitors, requiring two signatures on a check, and frequent polygraph tests serve to defer theft in the workplace, positive solutions lie in getting employees to feel personally responsible for the success of their work unit, their department, and the organization that employs them. The use of teams and teamwork concepts promote positive group norms. Both delegating authority and acceptance of responsibility encourage employee interest in organizational success. Employees quickly recognize that theft hinders organizational success. Making employees feel like owners is a useful technique. Actually, many employees who exercise stock options and are the recipients of stock in their employing company, are owners.

Questions to Consider

1. Why is it difficult for individuals with chronic alcohol or other drug problems to admit they have such a problem?
2. In what ways do organizations contribute to the development of alcohol, other drug, and theft problems?
3. Why is it sometimes difficult for managers to identify alcohol or other drug problems of employees?
4. Other than potential legal problems, what problems may the use of drug tests cause for employers?
5. What problems are to be expected when employers use honesty tests? What problems are to be anticipated with the use of lie detector tests where they can still be used?
6. The rehabilitation ratio of abusers of drugs other than alcohol is much lower than for problem drinkers. Should the probability of successful rehabilitation have an effect on what an employer is willing to do to help problem employees? Why or why not?
7. Should a prospective employee with a record of alcoholism, other drug abuse, or theft be given consideration equally with those who have no record of such problems even if he or she appears to have overcome the problem? Why or why not?

8. What actions not mentioned in the chapter could be taken to discourage theft?

Key Terms

alcoholic	honesty tests	polygraph test
drug abuser	problem	
drug testing	drinkers	
employee theft		

Chapter Case

Pat's Problem

"I almost wish Martin weren't such a nice guy," thought Pat Boyce, supervisor of a data analysis group for a large petroleum company. There was no doubt about it—Martin Stein was a nice guy. He had fit into the unit from the time he had arrived as a new hire and had done well in training. In fact, Boyce had thought at that time that Stein might have management potential.

"That surely hasn't worked out!" Boyce concluded sadly.

Unfortunately, Stein wasn't coming anywhere near to living up to his potential. He hadn't been out of training long when he started running into problems with lateness. When Boyce talked to him about it, Stein was extremely apologetic and said that he was having car trouble but would have things straightened out soon. In fact, the lateness improved, and things went along fine for a while. It wasn't long, however, until Stein's work performance started downhill. Boyce discussed the problem with Stein again. This time, Stein seemed upset and told Boyce that he was having family problems and couldn't keep his mind on his work.

Again, things improved for a while. Recently, Stein started having attendance problems. This time, when Boyce questioned him, he said that his wife had left him and he was trying to raise his two little daughters alone. One of them had health problems, and Stein had to stay home with her. Again, he "felt terrible" and promised to do better.

Most recently, the office scuttlebutt had it that Stein had started to have drinking problems—not during the week, though. Apparently, Stein had taken to starting his drinking on Friday evening and continuing through the weekend. Several of the female employees have told Boyce that they fear for the safety of Stein's young daughters during such times. Worse yet, Boyce has recently begun to wonder whether Stein is taking uppers of some kind to get him through the week.

"If only Stein weren't such a nice guy," Pat thought again. "I really believe that his story is true—but where does that leave me? I've got a unit to run and work to get out. I'm not sure I can count on Stein."

1. From a managerial perspective, what are the problems in this case?

2. If you were a coworker rather than Stein's boss, how (if any) would your perception of the problems differ?
3. What should Pat Boyce do? What are his options?
4. What should Stein's coworker who was aware of the problems do?
5. If you were a personal friend of Stein's but did not work with the same firm, what should you do?

Chapter
16

Equity for Minorities

Objectives

- To develop an awareness of the inequities existing for minority groups in work organizations.
- To become sensitive to the needs of members of minority groups at work.
- To identify the inequitable treatment given women as a minority group.
- To study the stereotypes that develop about minority group members.
- To discover the effects of stereotyping.
- To discuss age-group minorities and their experiences.
- To identify and consider the obstacles faced by minorities in the workplace.
- To discuss and evaluate what is known about AIDS and what the organizational response should be to workers with AIDS.
- To identify appropriate actions to provide fairness and equity in the workplace.

Ellen Crenshaw—
A Dissatisfied Banker

Ellen Crenshaw has been employed by Third State Bank since her graduation from State University five years ago. At State University she received a degree in general business and came to work for the bank in its management training program. The program, which lasted for one year, gave her an exposure to all phases of the bank's operation. From the training program, Crenshaw was assigned to the bookkeeping and records department as the assistant manager. Two years ago she was promoted to manager of the same department.

Several complaints and dissatisfactions have been building up in her mind since she completed the training program four years ago, but she has been reluctant to mention them. Her feelings have become so strong, however, that she has now sought out her supervisor, Parker Ferrell, assistant vice-president for bank operations, and is telling him several things she finds disturbing about her job with the bank. The following statements are a part of her conversation with Ferrell:

> I don't know about everyone's salary here at the bank, but I do know that my salary and some other women's salaries are somewhat lower than many of the men's salaries. I know for a fact that some of the male college graduates hired for the training program last month are being paid only a few dollars per month less than what I'm being paid, and I have five years of experience working with the bank. The pay scale seems to be unfair to women.
>
> It also seems to me that women are treated unfairly when job assignments are given out. Women always seem to get the secretarial, clerical, routine jobs, while the men get the more exciting, prestigious jobs. And it looks to me like women are being routinely diverted into staff jobs—where they are to act as "helpers"—while men are channeled into line jobs, where they have real decision-making authority. I think men believe all women enjoy routine work, but it just isn't true. Some women may, but I for one would enjoy something that challenges my abilities more fully.
>
> That brings me to another point. I think women are being bypassed for promotions to better jobs. I've applied for a transfer to the personal loan department and to the savings department on two different occasions, but I was turned down, and the jobs were given to men just coming out of the training program. I was given no reasons for the rejection of my requests except that I was needed in my present position.

Case Questions

1. Which of Ellen Crenshaw's complaints on the surface appear to be valid if they are true? Why? Which ones (if any) are not reasonable? Why?
2. What misconceptions does the case reveal in the attitudes many people have toward women at work?

3. If Mr. Ferrell uses the correct counseling techniques, what will be his attitude and comments during the conversation with Ellen?

4. If these complaints accurately portray the situation in the bank, what steps should the bank take to correct the problems? Please be specific.

equity
Fair treatment by managers and supervisory personnel. Equity includes fairness in wages, rewards, discipline, and any other type of attention given to workers.

minority
Any segment of the workforce that makes up less than one-half of the total population in the work environment or has less power than another group. The majority is usually considered to be dominant, while the minority is thought of as subservient. In this chapter, women, older workers, blacks, Hispanics, disabled people, and people with AIDS are viewed as minorities.

discrimination
Treating or giving attention to one person or group differently from other individuals or groups. Discrimination frequently is seen as giving attention to others in an unfavorable or unfair way.

Chapter 8 discussed equity theory as a force in keeping work performance at a satisfactory level. The inputs and outcomes of workers were compared to each other and to additional measurements to determine if outcomes were fair and equal. The comparison process resulted in psychological perceptions of equality or inequality which, in turn, resulted in specific behavior patterns. Equitable treatment led to differing levels of performance and satisfaction than did inequitable treatment. Where employees perceived that their treatment was equitable, high levels of performance resulted. Remember, too, that **equity** goes beyond fairness in salaries, wages, or rewards and carries over to virtually every part of an individual's work life. Most people want to be treated at least as well as other employees are treated.

What about the other side of the coin—the inequitable situation? While the effects of inequity are not always predictable, dissatisfaction, anxiety, insecurity, dissension, bitterness, and a lack of commitment are a few of the possible consequences where inequity is perceived. Clearly, organizations have a BIG stake in avoiding inequity.

While most people as individuals have felt that they have received unfair treatment at one time or another, there are groups of people who in sizeable numbers have felt inequity on a large scale and have felt it regularly. These groups represent **minorities** in the workforce. These are distinct units with something in common who are treated differently from other groups and subgroups. We will be looking at several groups of people who are classified as minorities at work to identify how they experience **discrimination** (different treatment from that of majorities).

Three important minority groups are classified as such as a result of their sex, age, or race. Women are described as the minority sex; older workers are usually the minority age classification; and blacks, Hispanics, Asians, and Native Americans, among others, are the minority races. Other groups that are gaining recognition as minorities are individuals who are disabled, including those with illnesses such as AIDS.

Gender: Women as a Minority

At the current rate increase, women may soon constitute the majority rather than the minority in the workplace. In the latest statistics available, women represented 45 percent of the workforce, whereas in 1970, women totaled only 37.7 percent (see Table 16–1) of workers. Of the civilian population in 1988, more than one out of every two women (55.9 percent) was employed, compared to fewer than one out of every three women of working age employed in 1948. As the ratio of working women to nonworking women has increased, the problems that employed women have encountered have grown (Table 16–1).[1]

Year	Total Labor Force	Number of Men	Percentage of Men	Number of Women	Percentage of Women
1970	78.7	49.0	62.3	29.7	37.7
1980	99.3	57.2	57.6	42.1	42.4
1988	115.0	63.3	55.0	51.7	45.0
2000 (est.)	138.8	73.1	52.7	65.6	47.3

Table 16–1

Structure of the Civilian Labor Force by Sex (In Millions)

Source: Adapted from *Statistical Abstract of the United States, 1990,* Washington, D.C.: U.S. Department of Commerce, Bureau of the Census, Volume 110, p. 380.

Problems of Employed Women

The problems women have faced as a minority in the workforce are numerous. Women, for example, have consistently earned less than their male counterparts. Recent figures reveal that women working full time average about 64 percent of the earnings received by men working full time. The average annual salary of the female full-time worker is $16,232, compared to the male average of $25,256 annually.[2] While women college graduates may have salary equity upon graduation, it lasts only for the first two years. Five years after graduation, 60 percent of women graduates and 40 percent of the men earn less than $30,000. At the same time, 14 percent of the males have earnings exceeding $50,000, while only 5 percent of the women earn this much.[3]

The lower salaries of women have been a concern for a long time. In one investigation (entitled "Why Do Women Earn Less?"), researchers concluded that in about one-third of the salary deficiencies, earnings are less because women have less work experience. They also found in a few situations that men have a little more education than women.

The investigators concluded, however, that there are three major reasons that women earn less. One is that some women aspire to lower paying jobs, perhaps because they have heavy family responsibilities and have decided to accept a lower paying job, which provides flexibility or permits working at home.

A second reason is that frequently the jobs women hold are not the ones where decisions about hiring, promoting, and paying others are made. In other words, women are often placed in STAFF, rather than LINE, jobs. Look at the complaint lodged by Ellen Crenshaw in our opening case, for example. When female employees are pushed into staff jobs, several things result. First, women are denied access to powerful, decision-making jobs and therefore get less opportunity to demonstrate their abilities. The result is that they are less likely to get promotions. Furthermore, staff jobs are almost always paid at a lower rate than line jobs at the same organizational level.

Finally, the researchers concluded that outright sex discrimination is the remaining cause of lower pay for women.[4]

Another problem women encounter is that they tend to climb the organizational ladder more slowly than do men and to reach a "glass ceiling," which prevents most of them from breaking into top management. The glass ceiling is a barrier that seems to keep women from being promoted. The majority of women are in lower level jobs.[5] Schein, in her study of why women seem less able than men to move up to middle management positions, suggests that

Self Test

Personal Feedback

Attitude Toward Women in Management
Women as Managers Scale

Using the numbers from 1 to 7 on the rating scale, mark your personal opinion about each statement in the blank that immediately precedes it. Give your *personal opinion* according to how much you agree or disagree with each item. Respond to all 21 items.

Rating Scale

1 = Strongly disagree   5 = Slightly agree
2 = Disagree   6 = Agree
3 = Slightly disagree   7 = Strongly agree
4 = Neither disagree nor agree

_____ 1. It is less desirable for women than men to have a job that requires responsibility.

_____ 2. Women have the objectivity required to evaluate business situations properly.

_____ 3. Challenging work is more important to men than it is to women.

_____ 4. Men and women should be given equal opportunity for participating in management training programs.

_____ 5. Women have the capability to acquire the necessary skills to be successful managers.

_____ 6. On the average, women managers are less capable of contributing to an organization's overall goals than are men managers.

_____ 7. It is not acceptable for women to assume leadership roles as often as men.

_____ 8. The business community should someday accept women in key managerial positions.

_____ 9. Society should regard work by female managers as valuable as work by male managers.

_____ 10. It is acceptable for women to compete with men for top executive positions.

_____ 11. The possibility of pregnancy does not make women less desirable employees than men.

_____ 12. Women would no more allow their emotions to influence their managerial behavior than would men.

_____ 13. Problems associated with menstruation should not make women less desirable than men as employees.

_____ 14. To be a successful executive, a woman does not have to sacrifice some of her femininity.

_____ 15. On the average, a woman who stays at home all the time with her children is a better mother than a woman who works outside the home at least half time.

_____ 16. Women are less capable of learning mathematical and mechanical skills than are men.

_____ 17. Women are not ambitious enough to be successful in the business world.

_____ 18. Women cannot be assertive in business situations that demand it.

_____ 19. Women possess the self-confidence required of a good leader.

_____ 20. Women are not competitive enough to be successful in the business world.

_____ 21. Women cannot be aggressive in business situations that demand it.

To determine your score on the Women as Managers Scale, add the points for the twenty-one items. Be sure to reverse score the answers marked with an asterisk. To reverse score, subtract the number you gave an answer from the number eight (8). For example, if for question number 1, you slightly agreed with the statement you would enter a 5 on your answer sheet. For purposes of determining your total score, subtract the 5 from 8 to come up with 3, which is your score on that item.

*1. _____
 2. _____
*3. _____
 4. _____
 5. _____
*6. _____
*7. _____
 8. _____
 9. _____
10. _____
11. _____
12. _____
13. _____
14. _____
*15. _____
*16. _____
*17. _____
*18. _____
19. _____
*20. _____
*21. _____

_____ Total Score

The range of possible scores is from 1 to 147. The higher your score, the more you look positively toward women as managers. The lower the score, the more negatively you view women in their roles as managers.

Source: L. H. Peters, J. R. Terborg, and J. Taynor, "Women as Managers Scale: A Measure of Attitudes Towards Women in Management," *Psychological Documents,* 4, 27, Manuscript # 585, 1974. Reprinted by permission of Select Press 415/924-1612.

Insights

The Imposter Syndrome

Carol is the vice-president/media director at a growing advertising agency. She has worked there for eight years, starting as an assistant out of college, advancing to copywriter, account executive, and her current position. In spite of her achievements, many successful ad campaigns, and the respect she has earned from clients and colleagues, Carol harbors a fear that one day she will be "unmasked" as an imposter, a person who really doesn't deserve success.

An organizational imposter is an individual who believes that he or she is not so qualified or capable as others seem to be. The imposter is likely to feel undeserving of the position he or she holds. The imposter feels he or she has somehow managed to slip through the system undetected, and it is just a matter of time until others will discover that he or she is a fraud.

Feeling like an unqualified person is a serious handicap for both the individual and the organization. For the individual, feeling like an imposter causes constant stress and limits the effectiveness of day-to-day performance. Career development, of course, is stymied because the person feels he or she has already gone beyond the level of competency. The person feels that further moves upward would only result in making the situation worse.

People who feel inadequate tend to procrastinate out of fear that when they do act, they will show their weaknesses. "Imposters" are unlikely to take risks that might benefit their employer. They sit on solutions for fear that suggesting an idea will show their ignorance. In other words, the imposter limits behavior to only those things that are established, comfortable, and non-risk oriented. Where creativity, innovation, and initiative are needed, the imposter is out of place.

Imposters can be identified in a number of ways. The imposter is often the person who:

1. Sits in meetings without saying things he or she was heard to say before the meeting began.
2. Endlessly delays doing things for no visible reason.
3. Has trouble shrugging off a mistake. Instead of being able to say "I will do better next time," the imposter wears failures for long periods of time.
4. Feels especially threatened by criticism. Criticism leads to chronic self-doubt.
5. Is often heard to use disclaimers, such as "this probably isn't right" or "this may be a dumb question, but . . . ."
6. Has difficulty accepting praise because it is felt that compliments are not deserved.

While men sometimes slip into the imposter syndrome, women are frequently more likely to experience the problem. Women often feel the need to outperform men so that they set higher expectations for themselves. Perfection is

stereotyping
Applying a generalization to all persons who are considered to be in a single category.

women face a dual problem that has its origins in **stereotyping**. Managerial jobs are often stereotyped as requiring "masculine" traits, such as forcefulness and decisiveness. To compound the situation, women are often stereotyped as possessing "feminine" traits, such as softness, which are believed not to be suitable for management. "It's like a 'double whammy'—stereotypes get women managers both coming and going," a female manager friend of the sometimes seen as the goal of women. Women in new positions frequently must do things correctly from the start. Women in traditionally male positions or professions are especially concerned about establishing their credibility and are likely to feel inadequate. All of the conditions lead to self-doubt.

Supervisors who wish to help imposters get back on the positive track can do a number of things. The supervisor can:

1. Help the employee to feel comfortable discussing concerns and securities.
2. Emphasize that job proficiency is a matter of acquiring and expanding skill and knowledge and not just innate ability.
3. Tell the employee that it is felt that he or she has the capacity to move up or do more challenging work.
4. Praise employees for good work. Praise helps to build confidence in employees.
5. Focus on the learning value of mistakes.
6. Help "imposters" to learn how to delegate to others. Those who feel they are imposters often find it difficult to turn loose of duties others can handle.
7. Encourage risk taking. The imposter needs to know that there is nothing wrong with failing if the employee has done the best he or she is capable of doing.
8. Ensure that self-doubters have the resources needed to perform successfully.

The employee who feels like an imposter can personally do any of several things:

1. Focus on each situation that triggers imposter feelings.
2. Take stock of thoughts, feelings, and actions during imposter situations.
3. Name the behavior pattern explicitly.
4. Determine how the process serves or protects him or her.
5. Find the "crusher" or negative belief about self.
6. Assess the price that is paid for this behavior.
7. Develop self-support and position-change strategy.
8. Brainstorm alternatives.

Each organization should do a self-audit to determine how it deals with (1) risk taking and mistake making, (2) people who ask for assistance when they don't know how to do a task, (3) norms that may be different for men and women, and (4) the way women's uniqueness with respect to achievement is treated.

Overcoming the imposter syndrome helps an employee to rise above insecurities, as doing so improves performance and profitability for the organization.

Source: Linda Garges, "Are You an Imposter?" Reprinted from *Managerial World*, Volume 15, Number 7, September/October 1986, pp. 11, 34. Copyright 1991, AMS, Washington, D.C., and "The Imposter Syndrome," *Managerial Solutions*, Volume 31, Number 8, August 1986, pp. 18–19, based upon interviews with Valerie Young.

authors ruefully concludes.[6] As a result, both men and women in upper management positions are more likely to choose men to move into middle management. Check your attitude toward women in the self test exercise.

Men also have tradition going for them when it comes to management positions, since in most types of management, men have been dominant through the years. Research conducted by Alexander found that women made

stereotyping
Stereotypes in this chapter refer in particular to generalizations made about sex, age, and race.

up 26.2 percent of all managers at any level in organizations with 100 or more employees.[7] In another study, it was discovered that length of tenure (frequently considered to be unbroken affiliation periods) with an organization is a good predictor of the number of promotions an employee will receive.[8] Women tend to have breaks in their employment patterns more than men because women usually bear more family responsibilities.

Women seem to be relegated primarily to jobs and careers that are labeled female in category. More than one-half of employed women are in jobs that are 80 percent dominated by women.[9] Many of these jobs have been continuously staffed by women. To some extent, women are likely to continue to fill these female-categorized positions, not only because they are ascribed as feminine but also because they are forecasted for heaviest growth in the next ten years. Jobs such as cashier, nurse, waitress, nurse's aide, retail salesperson, and teacher are projected for major expansion. All of these positions traditionally are staffed predominately by women.

One of the most important factors in the work careers of most women seems to be the family responsibilities that they bear. Much of the absenteeism by women is related to family responsibilities. Interruptions in careers occur for 72 percent of the women who enter the workforce (compared to only 26 percent for men).[10] This has led some to say that the most pressing problem facing working women today is the shortage of day care for children. Adequate day care would greatly reduce absenteeism as well as increase continuity of employment.

In response to a Gallup Poll, women executives said that one of their biggest disadvantages as women at work is male chauvinism. Not being taken seriously, not being included in social conversations and activities, and being patronized, especially by older men, are seen as other disadvantages.[11]

Research also shows that some psychological disadvantages exist for many women. Apparently, these disadvantages result from early socialization. While this is rapidly changing, many women are, in effect, "taught" by their parents and other significant adults during their childhood that they are "supposed to be" dependent and clinging. As a result, women are more likely than men to feel controlled by factors in the environment. This is called external locus of control.[12] Consequently, women are prone to downplay their own abilities and to feel like an imposter when they are successful.[13] When women do well, they may ignore the evidence of their own competence. Women are more likely to attribute success to luck and attribute failure to their own personal shortcomings (see Insights: The Imposter Syndrome).[14] Self-criticism among women is rather prevalent. Women often feel uncomfortable making demands that are in their own interests.[15] These characteristics make intrinsic satisfaction more difficult to achieve and may hinder initiative and motivation.

Another major disadvantage women experience in the workforce is stereotyping, mentioned earlier. Let's take a more detailed look now. It would appear that women are categorized concerning their intentions, skills, preferences, and most other areas of their lives. Some of the stereotypes may be generally valid, but most are false. As a result, women are often grouped together categorically and treated similarly, whether the treatment is appropriate or not. Stereotypes heavily influence the ways women are recruited, selected, placed, trained, rewarded, disciplined, and so forth. Let's compare truth with fiction related to some generalizations made about working women:

Fiction: *Women work primarily for supplementary income or for luxuries.*

Fact: *Two-thirds of employed women are self-supporting, and 30 percent to 40 percent of the women are the sole support of other family members as well.*

Fiction: *Women are better rote learners and are happier doing repetitive routine duties than men are.*

Fact: *Women, on the average, dislike repetitive tasks just as much as men do, although they seem to have a higher tolerance for them. They do not seem to do better at rote learning.*

Fiction: *Women are not especially concerned about the fulfillment of achievement needs and have a lower desire for promotions than do men.*

Fact: *Women have achievement and promotion desires as strong as those of men.*

Fiction: *Women are absent from work much more frequently than men are.*

Fact: *Women tend to be absent about 5.9 days a year, while men are away about 5.2 days (obviously not a meaningful difference).*

Fiction: *Women have a lower self-esteem than men do.*

Fact: *Women start work with self-esteem that is no different from that of men. If they develop a lower perception of themselves, it may be a result of their work experiences.*

Fiction: *Women are more susceptible to persuasive communication than are men.*

Fact: *Women and men do not differ in gullibility.*

Fiction: *Women are less aggressive than men.*

Fact: *Women are more oriented toward the win-win style, which many predict will lead the way in the global decade. Women are less inclined toward win-lose tactics than are men.*[16]

Research seems to support to some extent the generalizations that women have higher expectations of the work climate and are interested in a friendly work setting more than men tend to be.[17]

As can be seen, these generalizations do not serve to be a good description of women in many cases. Many other stereotypes are applied to women— many more than are applied to men. Each stereotype creates problems for those who use them and for those who are on the receiving end. Most stereotypes have done a disservice to women, especially hindering their progress in organizations. How? Look back to the Ellen Crenshaw case that started this chapter. Of course, *all* of Crenshaw's complaints may not be valid, but notice how many of the problems she mentions could have their origin in stereotypes such as those discussed here.

Advantages for Women Employees

Women have a number of areas to their advantage when compared to their male counterparts. The Gallup Poll mentioned earlier discovered that women felt that they have greater visibility than men (they are noticed more frequently). Women surveyed felt that they have skills superior to men's in getting along with other people. They viewed themselves as being more sensitive, patient, and compassionate than they believed men to be. It is often felt by women that they are able to relate to the needs of other workers better as a result of their own difficulties. Women indicate that they are treated with greater courtesy than are men. Also, people tend to trust women more than they do men and as a result tend to communicate more openly with women. Many of these advantages serve women well in people-related assignments. As noted earlier, there is also evidence that in the future, managers are going to need more and more of these people-oriented skills.

Many things are happening in business and industry today that are beneficial, especially for women. Child-care centers are opening in large numbers to help meet family needs. Flexible work hours (flexitime, for example) are being instituted to allow schedule planning around personal needs. Maternity leaves and related programs are being improved not only to provide security but also to protect career development. Workshops and other programs are being held to deal with subjects related to the stress of organizational and family responsibilities. Job sharing—where two people split a full-time job—is growing in popularity. Part-time employees (many of whom are women) are being recognized as a very valuable human resource.[18]

Dealing with the Problems Women Face

Along with the effort now being applied to overcome the inequities of women as a minority in the workforce, several other things can be done. We now know that all employees—men and women—derive great benefits from sponsorship by a mentor—someone to share past experiences, to point out pitfalls, and to help with ideas for career moves. Yet the male-dominated system in place in many organizations has hindered women from getting the mentoring they need. Some analysts also point out that as children, women had fewer experiences, such as team sports, that would lead them to recognize the need for finding a mentor. As a result, women may not search for mentors, and the organizations may be less likely to provide them. Recent evidence indicates that things are changing that could see more women getting the launch their careers require through the mentoring system. In the mentoring system, knowledgeable, more experienced managers or employees take newer, usually younger individuals under their wing and teach, challenge, and guide them to maturity and to more meaningful careers.

Programs and procedures designed to aid in the planning of a career will be especially important for women. Career planning enables each individual to develop a set of goals and then discover the step-by-step procedures needed to reach the goals. Assertiveness training can be provided to overcome reluctance to speak out. Policies toward absence and interruptions related to family responsibilities should be formulated so that they do not result in loss of seniority or in career penalties.[19]

Realistic job previews can help to make women's expectations more accurate. Also, colleges and universities need to give more descriptive information about careers and their opportunities for women. The use of experiential learning and case studies will make expectations more on target. Of course, a major step forward would be the curtailing of the use of stereotypes used to categorize women. Generalization should give way to more individualistic identification and treatment of each person.

Women will benefit from the holding of more responsible job assignments—particularly line positions where hiring, recruiting, selection, placement, and salary decisions are made. Women will also benefit from the development of support networks where male and female colleagues can give psychological and social boosts. Policies providing for equity in salaries and promotions are essential.

realistic job previews Accurate representations of both the good points and the negative features of a job given to a prospective employee. Weaknesses are shown graphically so that the prospective employee's perceptions of what to expect are not more positive than they should be.

Older Workers as an Age Minority

In recent years there has been a great deal of discussion about the age groupings present in the workforce. For example, younger workers, especially those in the baby boom generation, have received much attention. Often, the problems faced by older workers receive much less attention.

Problems of Older Workers

Older workers have received less attention than other age groups but seem to be a true minority at the workplace. What does it take to be considered an older worker? This is the group of workers who are 40 to 45 years of age and older (depending upon whose definition is used). The latest estimate available reveals that in today's workforce, the 45-and-above segment of workers represents about 27.7 percent of the total workforce (see Table 16–2). This group was extended some protection by the Age Discrimination Act of 1967 (amended in 1978), which states that unfair treatment of workers 40 years of age and above is prohibited unless age can be established as a bona fide requirement of a job. In spite of the regulations that exist, however, this group tends to encounter problems as decisions are made about hiring, placement, rewarding, promoting, and training workers.

No matter what your age may be, you are probably aware of some of the stereotypes about older people. Stereotypes are persistent and can be highly

Year	16–19	20–24	25–34	35–44	45–54	55–64	65 and over
1960	7.0	9.6	20.7	23.4	21.3	13.5	4.6
1970	8.8	12.8	20.6	19.9	20.5	13.6	3.9
1980	9.5	14.7	24.4	18.0	18.2	12.1	3.2
1988	6.6	11.9	29.4	23.7	15.2	9.9	2.6

Table 16–2

Percentage Distribution of the Labor Force by Age—1960–1988

Source: *Statistical Abstract of the United States, 1990,* Washington, D.C.: U.S. Department of Commerce, Bureau of the Census, Volume 110, p. 382.

damaging. Take a moment to think about how older people are categorized. As with women, there are many widely held generalizations made about older workers that tend to work to their detriment. We'll guess that you could think of several. Let's discuss the validity of some of the following types:

Fiction: *Older workers are poor training and promotion risks because they have fewer years left to work for an organization than do younger workers; as a result younger workers should be chosen.*

Fact: *It is true that older workers may have shorter total career spans in front of them, but they may stay with an employer longer than younger employees will. The average length of service with a single company for all employees in all industries is 3.6 years. Turnover is higher among younger workers than older workers. As a result, older workers typically show longer periods of service to a specific organization than do younger workers.*

Fiction: *Older workers are absent from work significantly more than are younger workers.*

Fact: *Usually, there is no difference in absences between older and younger workers. In fact, older workers often have much better attendance. At Hughes Tool Company in Houston, for example, the average absenteeism rate is 14 percent, while it is only one percent among older workers. Young workers tend to be absent more for nonhealth reasons.*

Fiction: *Operating costs will rise because health and retirement benefits will cost more when older workers are employed than when younger workers are present.*

Fact: *Overall, costs should not rise when older workers are hired. Even where costs of health coverage may rise, saving as a result of reduced turnover and training costs may more than offset increased fringe benefits.*

Fiction: *Older workers have more physical limitations than do younger workers. They are weaker, they hear and see less well, and they are sick more.*

Fact: *While physical problems may be associated with increasing age, most of the time physical limitations can be compensated for through the use of glasses, hearing devices, and the proper design of jobs. Typically, adjustments can be made for physical limitations.*

Fiction: *Older workers are more resistant to change and much slower to train.*

Fact: *There are wide differences in the abilities of older workers, and job requirements also vary greatly. It does appear that many older workers take longer to train and require more effort to change. Response time seems to decrease as age increases. Habits also become more established and ingrained. There are many jobs, however, that do not require abrupt change where the older workers' qualifications are quite appropriate. Some older workers are quick learners.*

Fiction: *Older workers have less education and less technical training.*

Fact: *Overall, older workers do have less formal education and sometimes have fallen behind in the development of technological skills. However, the high motivation and work ethic that is typical of many older workers can easily compensate in most jobs.*

Fiction: *Older workers are more conservative and cautious than are other workers and therefore should not be assigned to risk-involved jobs.*

Fact: *Older workers probably are more cautious in their decisions and actions. While these conservative responses may not be suited for some types of work, these traits are highly desirable for other types. Where safety and caution are desirable, slower, more deliberate actions are suitable.*

As shown in the discussion about women as a minority, older workers encounter problems on the job as a result of the generalizations made about them. Many of the stereotypes are untrue as a category, and others are true of only small parts of the group. Many of the supposed shortcomings of older workers can be overcome. In reality, many older workers are in good health, are open to change, are trainable, and are willing to take reasonable risks. In fact, what we have tried to show is that what may appear to be limitations are often assets. Older workers tend to have many strengths. They typically have greater experience than younger workers. They know their way around organizations. They have realisitic expectations of jobs as a result of their past experiences. Often they are easier to satisfy than are younger employees. They tend to respond to intrinsic reward opportunities more than do younger workers. They usually stay with their employer longer, and their absenteeism is often lower.

Dealing with the Problems of Older Workers

Employers obviously need to be aware of the legislation protecting older workers so that legislative requirements are met insofar as recruiting, selection, placement, dismissal, and retirement are concerned. (Of course, this is true of other minorities as well.) True characteristics of older workers need to be recognized. It would be preferable to discard the generalizations and begin to assess workers as individuals. The strengths that older workers bring to the organization need recognition. There will be areas where support and understanding may be required, but benefits for the extra effort will usually be forthcoming in increased loyalty and reduced absenteeism and turnover.

Here's an example that we feel illustrates the situation vividly. Mary Johnson was manager in charge of a telephone company operation services unit in a large northeastern city. Being a telephone operator involves working flexible shifts, including evening and night work. It has traditionally appealed to younger workers. For example, it's popular with students who can work evenings and go to school during the day. As you might expect, Mary was surprised to meet the new operator trainee who reported for work one day. The trainee, Olivia Wright, was nearly sixty.

More and more orga-
nizing the potential
of older workers.

"I think I retired too early," Olivia confided. "I was a teacher for over thirty years, and I felt that I really wasn't up to being on my feet all day any longer. But I can tell you this—I'm certainly NOT up to staying home and watching the soaps any longer. I'm used to a busy life and I'm not going to become a vegetable now!"

"Well," Mary laughed, "this may be just the thing for you!"

It turned out that it *was!* The physical demands of the operator's job were much less than the teaching job, and Olivia's pleasant personal style made her a fine operator. Olivia quickly became a confidante to many of the younger women—caring, providing a listening ear, and serving as a source of practical advice on how to manage a home and career. Furthermore, her savvy in dealing with the stresses of organizational life and her ability to tackle difficult human relations problems—all fine-tuned from her years of teaching experience—made her a valuable role model.

How about her ability to learn the work?

"Well," remarked Mary, "she honestly had no real trouble. All those years of teaching had kept her alert, and even more important, her willingness to work and her persistence got her through the rough spots during the training—for example, dealing with a computer, which she'd never done before. Overall, my impression is this—if Olivia's an older worker, I'll take 100 more just like her!"

Not every older worker is a success story, of course, but many are or can be. As this example illustrates, worker attitude, management attitude, and job match are essential elements.

Younger Employees—Their Strengths and Weaknesses

Even though younger employees are not considered to be a minority, a brief word about some of their qualities and concerns seems appropriate. Younger employees are seen as the antithesis of older workers in most respects. The young are seen as creative, idealistic, energetic, open to change, needs oriented, quick to learn, and more likely to take risks. While these generalizations are not descriptive of all younger employees, the description often holds. Organizational expenditures made on the younger worker usually seem appropriate, since a long future lies ahead for the average young employee. Barriers to hiring, training, and promotion seem relatively small for younger employees.

The typical complaints of younger workers lie in the areas of responsibility and opportunity. New employees, especially those with a college education, frequently complain that their jobs are those where little significance is attached to what they do. Important assignments are reserved for older workers. Immediate opportunities to climb the organizational ladder are often seen as limited, although long-range prospects may be good. In the first two years after graduation, more than half of all college graduates will switch to other organizations, giving responsibility and opportunity as their primary motivations for making a move.

Young employees need a better understanding of the responsibilities and opportunities before them. Management needs, for example, to carefully outline for new employees the company's promotion opportunities and career ladders. Usually, younger employees will also benefit from many of the suggestions identified earlier as helpful to women—organizational commitment to mentoring, better career planning, more realistic job previews, and the use of more experiential training techniques. Inequalities in wages and other benefits need reviewing also.

Younger workers tend to have many good things working for them. Overall they are better educated formally and technically than their older counterparts. They are more mobile and more frequently open to change. The strengths young workers bring to the workplace need encouraging and nurturing.[20]

Minorities Based upon Race

The two largest racial minorities in the U.S. workforce are blacks and Hispanics. Of the latest assessment of the total civilian workforce of more than 114,000,000 in 1988, about 82.7 percent were white, 10.1 percent were black, and 7.2 percent were Hispanics.[21]

Normally, the race to which an individual belongs does a number of things to and for the individual. Race usually contributes to the culture in which an individual lives. One's race usually determines the language the individual speaks. Race has much to do with influencing the religious affiliations and involvements of the individual. Race normally creates a set of behaviors that serve to differentiate one race from the others. People of similar racial backgrounds usually have stronger mutual affiliation and support relationships. Race provides not only a culture but also a set of traditions for its members. Race tends to unify group feelings of solidarity and uniqueness.[22]

Organizational Problems Faced by Racial Minorities

Of all the races employed, blacks, Hispanics, and, to some extent, Asians, are currently receiving the most active attention by management in organizations. Organizations are becoming more active in their work with these groups for several reasons. Blacks and Hispanics (good statistics are not available on Asians) tend to have less formal education than whites. Recent estimates of the average number of years of education for blacks showed 12.5 years, and the Hispanic average was 12.2 years. On the other hand, the average number of years of education for whites was 12.8 years. Even more revealing was the fact that 20.1 percent of all whites in the workforce were college graduates, compared with the 10.9 percent of blacks and 8.4 percent of Hispanics who had four or more years of college.

The level of education attained is important in a number of ways. One of the most affected areas of employees' lives is the ratio of unemployment to number of years of schooling. In 1988, for example, the average unemployment rate was about 4.7 percent. Unemployment of white men and women was about 4 percent. The unemployment percentage of college graduates was only 1.7 percent, while the unemployment rate of workers with nine to eleven years of formal schooling was 9.6 percent. Since many blacks and Hispanics were in the lesser educated ranks, they suffered the greatest amounts of unemployment. Black unemployment was 10 percent.[23]

In 1988, the median income for white households was $394 a week; the median income for the black household was $314 a week; and the median income for the Hispanic household was $290 a week. Many of the minority households had earnings of $200 or less for a week's work. Again, lower education rates are a contributing factor.[24]

The lower education rates serve to limit opportunities for many individuals and may be related to the lack of skill development. A look at where blacks and Hispanics are employed is revealing. Black workers, as Table 16–3 shows, represent 10.1 percent of the total labor force. They are underrepresented in the fields that require the most education and pay the highest wages. Blacks have only 6.1 percent of managerial and professional jobs, 7.5 percent of the precision-production-craft positions, and 9.1 percent of the technical, sales,

Table 16–3

Percentage of Blacks and Hispanics Employed in the Different Worker Classifications (1988)

Worker Classification	Percentage Black	Percentage Hispanic
Total part of the work force	10.1	7.2
Managerial and professional	6.1	3.7
Technical, sales, and administrative support	9.1	5.8
Service	17.6	10.2
Precision production and crafts	7.5	8.2
Operators, fabricators, laborers	15.0	11.1
Farming, forestry, and fishing	6.6	13.0

Source: *Statistical Abstract of the United States, 1990,* Washington, D.C.: U.S. Department of Commerce, Bureau of the Census, Volume 110, pp. 389–391.

administration-support jobs. On the other hand, blacks are overrepresented in service jobs (17.6 percent) and operator-fabricator-laborer positions (15.0 percent). A disturbing trend for blacks in particular is that many, if not most, workers are employed in the same occupational level in which their parents have been employed. There seems to be little, if any, upward movement for many black workers. In fact, some concern has been shown that blacks are experiencing a downward mobility where they are being employed in even lower paying, less-skilled jobs than their parents were.[25]

Hispanics experience much the same situation. Hispanics make up about 7.2 percent of the labor force. In management and professional jobs, Hispanics represent 3.7 percent of the total. In technical, sales, and administration support, Hispanics make up only 5.8 percent. In service jobs, Hispanics are 10.2 percent; in precision production and crafts, Hispanics are 8.2 percent; and in operators, fabricators, and laborers, Hispanics are 11.1 percent of the total.

The statistics on Hispanics are particularly important, since some estimate that the Hispanic segment of the total population and the workforce will experience the largest growth in the immediate future. Naisbitt, for example, feels that Hispanics will soon be the majority minority. This could result as rapidly as in the year 2000. In California and throughout the Southwest, it is estimated that 50 percent or more of the population will be Hispanic by 2000. If the trend is realized, Hispanics will have a bigger impact in the workplace.[26]

Organizations need to be aware of a serious consequence of lack of mobility, i.e., lack of trust in the system. One Hispanic high school student we talked to put it this way:

> You're talking to me about a CAREER? Well I'll tell you that you're crazy! What I'll have is a JOB—and a "go nowhere" job at that. There's no way I can break into the system. Look—I'm no fool, and I keep my eyes open. Everybody I know is going into a dead-end job, and I'll get one, too. What do big corporations care about people like me!

We hope you don't think these comments are an exception. In far too many cases, they are not. And what is the result? Young people who believe as this student does are less likely to expect and plan for productive, long-term careers, and they're less likely to continue their educations. Deep-seated beliefs are VERY difficult to change. The point is this: perceived lack of opportunities for promotion and growth has serious consequences. Where upward mobility seems to be the exception rather than the rule, the result is often a psychological adjustment that lowers expectations.

Other racial minorities make up part of the American workforce, also. Workers from Asian countries, for example, have made significant entries into the workforce. These minorities face some of the same problems that blacks and Hispanics do. Language problems often are severe. Some of the same cultural stumbling blocks must be overcome.

We haven't even touched on ethnic groups. While groups such as Jews and Armenians have achieved much success in the United States, they may still face some of the organizational problems we have discussed, and many are concerned about losing their heritage. Don't forget our earlier discussion of *perceptions*. It does not matter whether the perceptions are true or false—or how they came about. Perceptions can have a major impact on career planning. It would be nice to say that there is an easy solution—but there is not. Much hard work by schools, organizations, and community groups will be needed in the future.

What Can Be Done?

The Civil Rights Act of 1964 (as amended) was designed to initiate changes, particularly to eliminate hiring, selection, placement, training, and compensation problems experienced by racial minorities (and other minorities, including women). Subsequent legislation and court decisions have further added to the protection and pursuit of equity in the workplace. But it is obvious that this is only a starting point. Much more remains to be done, and as we have mentioned previously, the situation is so complex that easy solutions simply cannot be found. While we can't pretend to have either a magic wand or a crystal ball, we'd like to provide at least a sketch of our vision for the future. First, it is clear that minorities' perceptions that "the system" is set up so that they can't succeed is in itself, a major contributing factor to the problems minorities face. And, as we've said so often, perceptions are VERY difficult to change.

What can organizations do? An obvious starting point is to take a critical look inward. Policies and past practices need a thorough and diligent review to erase every trace of discrimination. Management's actions must support their commitment to a truly open workplace. Beyond this, though, positive, proactive steps are needed to get the message out.

Here are a few examples. Management can send representatives to talk to minority community and civic groups. Even more important are schools. Hosting "career opportunities" days—perhaps involving several organizations—could encourage minority students. To all groups, the message must be that there *are* career opportunities available. Management should show high school students not intending to go to college what jobs are good entry-level positions and what these students can do to advance from those jobs. Organizations should also consider tuition reimbursement programs for employees seeking college training. Work-study programs have been impressive. In one such program, students attend college for several semesters, take a semester off and work for an organization (gaining valuable experience as well as meeting financial needs), and then repeat the cycle until graduation.

Another innovative idea is the "shadow program" whereby students are offered the opportunity to spend a day "shadowing" a business leader to gain a realistic preview of both the excitement and the demands of managerial jobs. University educators are excited about such programs, but they don't want the program coverage to be limited to higher education. The logical next step is to get programs operating in high schools so that younger students can learn of the opportunities and challenges before they stop their education. The preview provided by a shadow program may keep some students in school.

Another alternative is the internship program that many universities have begun, in which a student (usually an upper-class student) receives college credit for working in an organization. Each student is placed in a meaningful job (usually a sort of management training position) in a carefully selected organization. A professor or internship program administrator and a representative of the employer oversee and supervise the work of the student on the job. The internship job is not to be a clerical or operative position but should be a position of responsibility where real decisions must be made. This provides not only skill development but also insight into the opportunities, responsibilities, and challenges of a career in a particular field. Employer and faculty liaison are responsible for the development of the student.

What does all of this mean? We think, in the final analysis, that the key ingredient must be *commitment*—by organizations, by professional groups, by minority organizations, and by schools.

Workers with Disabilities

Another segment of the workforce that will require increasing attention in the 1990s includes workers with disabilities. This segment is expected to assume particular importance as shortages of workers in the 1990s lead employers to look to disabled (many disabled prefer to be called disabled rather than handicapped) workers as a new pool of prospective employees. The entry of this group of workers into the workplace in large numbers will create challenges for managers, many of whom have never been involved with disabled workers.[27]

We need to look back at the Civil Rights Act of 1964 (as amended) for a definition of handicapped: a person is considered handicapped if he or she suffers from a mental or physical limitation or is *believed* to suffer from such a limitation. The element of *belief* is important because it protects workers such as those who have had cancer and have received successful treatment but are still *believed* to be ill by employers and other employees.[28] As we will see, it also may have implications for AIDS patients.

Note too, that both mental and physical limitations are included in the definition. Mental disabilities may include retardation, specific learning disabilities, and psychological problems. Physical handicaps may involve locomotion difficulties, blindness, deafness, and specialized problems such as epilepsy.[29] More recently, the passage in 1990 of the Americans with Disabilities Act has underscored these definitions and has added enforcement measures to support the rules.

A common thread that runs through any consideration of disabled status is the requirement for the employer to make reasonable effort to accommodate the needs of the worker. Most of us are familiar with ramps that permit access to buildings for people in wheelchairs, for example. Other, less obvious adjustments may also be involved. Lloyd Henry, a friend of the authors, is a disabled worker employed by a large governmental agency. Lloyd's disability is physical. When he was only 11 years old, Lloyd started to have dizzy spells and double vision. The diagnosis was a fast-growing but benign brain tumor.

A disability should not prevent someone from holding a job of significant responsibility.

An operation successfully removed the tumor but left Lloyd with severe reading and speaking problems.

"It's like a blockage," Lloyd explains. "I may know *exactly* what I want to say, but I just can't get the words out. Worse yet, I'll see a word or words on a page, and I can't think what they mean—and I mean simple, everyday words like *hat* and *book*. As a result, both speaking and reading are slow processes for me!"

What Lloyd doesn't tell you is that he is a person of outstanding courage and persistence. He graduated from college.

"Let me tell you, that was *tough!*" he reports. "Because of my reading problems, it seemed like I took three times longer than anyone else to study and prepare for class. It took a lot of hours, but I stuck with it. And the tests! Math classes were no trouble, because the blockage doesn't affect numbers, surprisingly enough. But English! My teachers were wonderful. The only way I got through was by either taking a lot of extra time on the exams or by dictating answers. Anyhow, I made it!"

After graduation, the agency Lloyd works for hired him as an analyst, and the agency and Lloyd cooperated to work around his problems. Much of

Lloyd's work is mathematical, and Lloyd is a whiz at that. But what about the reading demands of the job?

"There are ways around that too," Lloyd responds. "Believe it or not, large print helps; so I often use the blowup feature on our copy machine to enlarge pages I know I need to study carefully. Or I'll get a clerk to read a section to me. And, of course, I take a lot of work home. But the important thing is that I'm *here,* and making a contribution!"

Lloyd's boss agrees. "He's an inspiration," the boss tells us. "Lloyd's been here for nearly ten years and has an outstanding work record. I don't think of it in terms of *making accommodations.* As Lloyd's boss, I think that I'm his partner in seeing that he has what he needs to get the job done. After all, as a manager, that's a key responsibility of mine toward all of my employees—not just Lloyd."

It's attitudes like this that can make managers partners in success with employees like Lloyd.

The Americans with Disabilities Act of 1990

Legislation continues to provide a better set of conditions and opportunities for disabled individuals. The Americans with Disabilities Act of 1990 regulates employers in many ways. Employers may not discriminate against a disabled person qualified for a job either in hiring or firing. Employers may not inquire whether a prospective employee has a disability, but the employer may ask about ability to perform a job. An employer may not limit advancement opportunities or job classifications based upon disability. Tests or job requirements that tend to screen out the disabled may not be used. Employers may not enter into contractual agreements that discriminate against the disabled. Employers also may not deny opportunities to anyone in a relationship with a disabled person.

Employers are directed to provide reasonable accommodations to the disabled, including making existing facilities accessible, providing special equipment and training, arranging part-time modified work schedules, and providing readers for the blind. Employers are not, however, required to provide accommodations that impose an undue hardship on business operations. Employers with twenty-five or more employees must have met these requirements by 1992, while employers with fifteen or more people have until 1994 to meet the requirements.

Employees with AIDS

The issue of AIDS in the workplace has recently become a vital concern. What are the responsibilities of an organization toward an employee with AIDS? And what are the responsibilities toward other employees who are the coworkers of the person with AIDS?

Just what, exactly, is AIDS, anyway? Most of us at least have a little knowledge about this last question. AIDS stands for *acquired immune deficiency syndrome,* a technical term for a devastating virus that attacks the immune system, leaving the person vulnerable to a host of opportunistic diseases that

Insights

Sample Company AIDS Policy

Policy/Philosophy

Company ABC maintains the following philosophy regarding the welfare of its employees.

Employees with AIDS or any other life-threatening disease are treated with dignity and respect. The company strives to maintain an open and informed environment for all employees.

Employees with AIDS or any other life-threatening illness can continue to work as long as they are physically able to do so.

Employees are assured of complete confidentially when seeking counseling or medical referral assistance.

Commitment

Company ABC has an overall commitment to health education. AIDS is a national health problem, and the company feels a responsibility to educate its employees so that prejudice and unwarranted fear about the disease in the workplace can be eliminated.

Benefits

AIDS is treated like any other life-threatening condition with respect to medical coverage, disability leave, and life insurance.

Hiring

Company ABC does not test prospective employees for AIDS, and there are no AIDS screening questions on employment applications.

would normally be combatted by the immune system. While progress is being made toward a cure, AIDS must presently be considered fatal. According to the Surgeon General of the United States, between 1.5 and two million people are carrying the AIDS (HIV) virus. As of 1991, about 54,000 people have died as a result of AIDS. Consequently, considerable fear surrounds it. In fact, when an organization learns that an employee has AIDS, fear on the part of other employees is the biggest concern that must be faced. Newspapers contain frequent stories about parents' protests when a child with AIDS is sent to school, for example.[30]

What about the workplace? The fears center on whether AIDS can be transmitted by casual contact of the type to be expected in the school or work setting. Generally, experts agree that the dangers are minimal, though—primarily to guard against fears by the public—there is some agreement that AIDS patients should not handle food or work in a hospital setting. Fear remains, especially on the part of other employees. Some answers—such as a reliable cure—may be years away.

Education

Company ABC has undertaken a comprehensive education program. The education package includes a 23-minute videotape, brochures for employees, and managers' training materials. Sessions typically include an overview of the company's philosophy about AIDS, a discussion of how the disease is and is not contracted, a review of health benefits available to employees, an update on the latest information about AIDS, and a question-and-answer session.

Pamphlets, company newsletters with articles on AIDS, and fact sheets are available to employees through the employee assistance program (EAP) reference library. Samples of the health and fitness newsletter are included in this package.

Support Programs

Individual, family, or group counseling is available for employees, coworkers, and families through EAPs or can be arranged through outside agencies.

EAP staff has compiled a comprehensive list of agencies that assist people with AIDS and provides this information confidentially to any employee requesting it,

AIDS Task Force

An employee task force has been supporting a broad base of activities around education and other AIDS issues. The group—which meets monthly—is made up of employees from various divisions and departments throughout the company, such as personnel, communications, community affairs, operations, and office services.

The objectives of this task force include (1) developing a comprehensive employee education program, raising AIDS-related issues and proposing suggestions for action; (2) providing assistance to other employers or organizations seeking guidance in developing their own AIDS programs; and (3) obtaining support for AIDS organizations.

Source: Bill Patterson, "Managing with AIDS in the Workplace." Reprinted from *Management World*, Volume 18, Number 1, January–February 1989, pp. 44–47. Copyright 1991 AMS, Washington, D.C.

In light of this, what should organizations and managers do? A good starting place is the development of a statement of organization policy concerning AIDS. The sample policy included here covers most of the important areas. In general, most policy statements need to include the overall philosophy of the organization toward AIDS and those who have AIDS; a statement of commitment to both the virus carrier and healthy employees; a statement of medical, disability, and life insurance; a statement concerning hiring practices and continued employment; a description of what the organization will do to educate all employees and their families; a statement of support programs available, including individual and family counseling; and a statement affixing responsibilities for establishing, maintaining, and monitoring all AIDS programs.[31]

Most agree that openness and information are two crucial factors in dealing with AIDS. If an employee is hospitalized and you learn that it's AIDS, you'll need to do several things. First, what about the employee with AIDS? Does that individual want to return to work? If so, how do the employee—and the employee's doctors—prefer to deal with the situation? Management needs to

**Management
in Action**

A Businesslike Approach to AIDS

In the mid-80s, panic swept a General Motors plant in Clinton, Mississippi, when word leaked that a worker had been diagnosed with AIDS. Other workers refused to use bathrooms or phones the AIDS sufferer had touched; some even threatened to stay home if the infected employee returned to work. That kind of scare is unlikely to happen again—at least at GM. Spurned by the incident, the auto giant and the United Auto Workers launched a 2-million-dollar program to allay concerns about the disease and to safeguard the rights of AIDS victims.

"AIDS is not a threat to the workplace," says Patricia Houtteman, co-director of AIDS education at General Motors. "The *fear* of it is."

To combat the fear, the GM/UAW program concentrates on education. GM has mailed brochures and magazines on AIDS to all of its 500,000 employees and their families and provided classes for workers on the spread, prevention, and treatment of the disease. Through teleconferences, seminars, and written materials, the auto giant trains plant managers, union officials, health personnel, and counselors to deal with everything from discrimination against AIDS victims to safety issues. GM allows AIDS-infected employees to stay on the job as long as they are physically able to do the work. What's more, GM guarantees AIDS victims—including dependents of employees—confidentiality and continued access to the company's benefit plan. For example, GM paid medical bills for AIDS victim Ryan White, the Kokomo, Indiana, youth whose case received national attention in 1986 when neighbors tried to bar him from school; his mother works for a GM subsidiary.

A Frank Assessment For GM, the stakes are high. As the nation's largest employer after the federal government, it ensures 2.3 million workers and dependents—one percent of the U.S. population. If GM has a proportional share of the nation's AIDS cases at an average medical cost of $75,000 per case, it will face hundreds of millions—perhaps billions—of dollars in medical claims in the 1990s. And the rest of corporate America will share in the epidemic's costs. Last year alone, the 44,000 people diagnosed with AIDS incurred direct medical expenses of $3.3 billion, 40 percent of which was picked up by business and private insurers, according to an estimate by Fred Hellinger, an economist with the U.S. Department of Health and Human Services.

Faced with the Spread of AIDS, more and more firms are following GM's lead.

Source: Eva Pomice, "A Businesslike Approach to AIDS," *U.S. News & World Report,* April 2, 1990, p. 44. Copyright April 2, 1990, *U.S. News & World Report.*

be especially concerned about the grapevine. In many cases, it will be preferable to meet with the other employees prior to the AIDS patient's return to work. Get the facts out on the table and plan together to make any needed accommodations. In most cases, an employee's coworkers are concerned and anxious to be of support and help so long as factual information is supplied in advance of the rumor mill.

Steps Toward Equity

Let's think now of ways organizations can creatively overcome all of the problems of inequitable treatment of minorities, whoever they may be. While promoting the passage of more legislation may be appropriate, our viewpoint at the moment is what can be done *within* each organization.

As is true of almost any effort at improvement, each organization must have a purpose to bring about improvement and to shape its goals in the desired direction. This means that to achieve equitable treatment for minorities, specific goals need to be declared. A good beginning for an organization is the clear delineation of equity goals—equity in pay, promotions, benefits, supervisory treatment, and so forth. These goals need to be spelled out to focus the direction of the organization's energies. It is important that goals for equitable treatment have the support of upper management levels. Without top-level backing, goals are meaningless.

Specific individuals or groups need to be assigned the responsibility of seeing that the policies and provisions of the organization are designed for equity. Unless specific people are made accountable for the development and implementation of fair treatment, no one tends to feel personally obligated to see that improvements are made. To be effective, these individuals or groups need to be delegated the authority to initiate change. Designated individuals will be responsible for seeing that things such as day-care centers, job sharing, skill training, and career planning are made available where needed.

Evaluation procedures and standards must be designed to periodically check the success of the efforts to bring about equity. Jobs of equal skill requirements should be compared for equity in salaries and other treatment of employees. The ratios of promotions, hiring, training, and so forth, need to be checked to see if one or more of the sexes, ages, or races is being favored at the expense of others. Identified inequalities will call for revisions of practices and procedures. A part of this evaluation process should be the receiving and analyzing of complaints of inequality from employees, but the evaluation must also initiate investigations and seek data without waiting for complaints to be submitted. In other words, it must be proactive, not reactive.

Establishing support systems to help minority members of an organization is essential. Many of the successes at overcoming inequitable treatment seem to be linked to all of the things discussed earlier and centers on the organization's commitment to the development of active systems and programs for ensuring that minorities perceive that the organization is on their side. We are talking about community involvement, shadow programs, mentoring, and the like.

A very important step for each of us in reducing inequity is to set aside the use of stereotypes and sweeping generalizations, since many stereotypes are based upon mistakes and half-truths. A wise action here is to begin the treatment of personnel by taking each one separately—looking at his or her individual, unique traits, needs, and abilities. Recognition of the individuality will improve the understanding of others and will result in a better response to them. As Falkenberg says:

Decisions based upon inaccurate stereotypes lead to less qualified individuals being hired, assuming higher levels of responsibility, and receiving promotions. Inaccurate stereotypes may also prevent groups from implementing the most appropriate solution or system because input from qualified "out group" members is ignored. Because it is unfair to minorities and inefficient for organizations to take a passive approach and hope that over time stereotypes will change, organizations must attempt to improve the flow of accurate information and intentionally structure the membership of work groups.[32]

To avoid or overcome the effects of stereotypes, it is important that accurate information is distributed to more people to permit equitable treatment of employees. Both formal and informal networks need to be given correct data. Written communication should be provided to individuals, since written statements are less easily subject to misinterpretation. Putting messages in written form also helps avoid having important ideas overlooked. Accurate message interpretation can also be aided by giving message senders training in how to estimate the emotional reactions receivers will have to messages they are given. It is also important that messages be sent by credible individuals.

Where there is a lack of coordination between groups, team-building exercises (refer to Chapter 3) and the development of better interpersonal and intergroup communication are vital. The use of conflict resolution techniques, such as those mentioned in Chapter 13 (especially the team, win-win type techniques), may be needed where minorities are at odds with each other or with majorities. Activities that promote the development of good communication between individuals and groups tend to bring people to confront, not overlook, issues.

Also important in the bringing about of equitable opportunities is the better preparation and orientation of prospective employees. The formal educational program needs to equip individuals with adequate technical, interpersonal, and analytical skills for future careers. The education process is probably the best place to begin dealing with career-planning concepts, skills, and beliefs about organizations. Realistic job previews will also improve people's perceptions of job and career requirements.

Summary

Most organizations have minorities in them. Minorities may be based on gender, age, race, disability, or illness. Minority members are often disadvantaged whether the discrimination is related to salaries, training and promotion opportunities, acceptance into social groups, or in some other area. The treatment given to many minority groups is often based upon myth, misunderstanding, stereotyping, or fear.

The problems caused by discriminating attitudes and behaviors will not go away without confrontation. Most informal programs will be insufficient and ineffective. Individuals and groups must be officially appointed and held accountable for equity in treatment.

With a concerted effort, it is possible to remove many of the inequities. Some inequities based upon traditional cultural beliefs will be slower to rectify than others, but modification is possible in most situations. It is the responsibility of managers—and every employee—to be a positive force for change.

Questions to Consider

1. What stereotypes other than those mentioned in the chapter have you heard about women, men, older workers, younger workers, whites, blacks, and Hispanics? Is each of the stereotypes an accurate or inaccurate representation of the persons being described?
2. How do stereotypes of individuals and groups get started?
3. How can untrue stereotypes be dealt with so that they can lose their power?
4. In what ways, other than those mentioned in the chapter, can minorities be handled more equitably? What can be done to make treatment of minorities more fair?
5. Place yourself in the shoes of someone who is in a minority position in a work organization (other than those where you are presently a minority). How is your perspective changed as you empathize with those people who are in this minority?
6. Is there any justification for paying less money to workers performing the same job where there are differences in age, sex, or race? Discuss.
7. Do most majorities work to sustain their power at the expense of minorities? Is it common for majorities to guard and jealously apply the powers they possess?
8. What has been the rationale behind the paying of women less than men for doing the same job? Theoretically speaking, what rationalizing has been done to support the idea that men are entitled to more money than are women? What's wrong with this general concept?
9. What advice would you give to women, older workers, blacks, and other minorities in the workforce?
10. What ethical considerations are involved in the management of minority groups and individuals?

Key Terms

discrimination	realistic	stereotyping
equity	job previews	
minority		

Chapter Case

A New Breed of Nurse

"Please don't think I'm crazy," Joe Robles confided to his guidance counselor as they looked out the window onto the campus of the small state school that he attended. Joe was midway through his second year, and so far things were looking good for him, both academically and in terms of his outside activities. Not only had he participated in several sports, but he'd also played a lead in the recent campus play. He was paying his tuition through his grass-cutting and yard maintenance service.

"Overall, a most impressive young man," thought Marisa Dennehy, the counselor.

"Why should I think you're crazy?" Marisa inquired.

"Well," said Joe, "I know I certainly don't fit the traditional mold, but I've discovered I have a very strong interest in nursing."

"Don't you mean medical school?" queried Marisa. "I'm sure you'd make a fine doctor!"

"That's exactly what *everybody* says," moaned Joe. "But I mean just what I said. I want to be a nurse—not a doctor. I guess I haven't told you this, but both my uncle and my sister have had serious illnesses; so I've spent a lot of time in hospitals this past couple of years. And I've talked to both doctors and nurses about what they do. The doctor's job strikes me as too mechanical— you diagnose and prescribe, and that's it. It's the nurses who have the ongoing, hands-on patient care—and that's what I'm really interested in. I know it's not traditional, but why shouldn't I shoot for a career that I really want?"

1. Suppose you were in Marisa Dennehy's position and were asked to counsel Joe. What recommendations would you make, and why?
2. What problems could Joe encounter if he does decide on a career in nursing? What could he do to overcome them?

Managing Growth and Development

17. Planned and Unplanned Change,
and Organizational Development

18. A Look Toward the Future

Chapter 17

Planned and Unplanned Change, and Organizational Development

Objectives

- To review the reasons change occurs in an organization.
- To recognize the impact change has upon employees.
- To analyze the reasons change is frequently resisted by employees.
- To concentrate on management goals where change is called for.
- To identify the kinds of leadership needed during change.
- To learn how to get acceptance of change.
- To study the process for bringing about planned change through Organizational Development.
- To recognize the potential that Organizational Development has for organizations and individuals.

The Front Desk Worrier

Lucinda Montoya is a long-time employee of a medium-sized hotel chain. In fact, Montoya takes a lot of pride in being one of the originals—she's been there since the founder started things up, and she's been one of the people who's risen slowly to the position of front-desk manager, and that is as far as she wants to go. As Montoya puts it, "I LOVE the company, but I'm not sure I want the pressure of a high-level job." She has a group of eight front-desk employees reporting to her. Her job had been rewarding and full of satisfaction—until the change.

The change started with the organization's decision to computerize front-desk operations. The computer will be able to take care of room assignments, reservations, and a host of other functions. Now Montoya and her people won't have to be in constant telephone contact with the housekeeping and maintenance employees, making sure rooms are ready for incoming guests and that needed repairs have been made. The computer will track all of this.

"You must be excited about the new systems," commented Martin Edgeway, a supervisor at the front desk of a nearby hotel, who'd stopped by for an update on the changes.

"I wish I could say yes for sure," responded Montoya, "but I just don't know. Everybody says these systems are just great, but I really feel lost. Don't forget that I'm an old-timer—I didn't grow up on computers like these young people nowadays. Can I really do it? I know that I used to grumble about the time on the telephone with housekeeping and maintenance, but at least they were PEOPLE. When I talked to them, I felt certain about what was going on. But now, with a computer—well, who knows what's in there! Maybe if somebody from the home office would just come in and explain it all to us, I'd feel better. But they're all so busy; so all I've got to go by is this stack of manuals. We don't need more books and rules. We need some real human beings to tell us what's in all this for us."

Case Questions

1. What's Lucinda Montoya really afraid of?
2. What would have relieved Montoya's fears?
3. What do Montoya's bosses need to do now?
4. What should Montoya do now?

When **change** occurs in an organization, it means simply that something is different from the way it once was. Change usually implies that authority relationships, communication procedures, responsibilities, or employee behaviors must be revised. While not every change requires significant adjustments by employees, change is a daily event in most work climates. To illustrate the frequency and variety of changes that occur in work groups, consider the following situations:

change
A behavior, event, or condition that is different from a previous behavior, event, or condition.

Employee A is asked to cooperate with a newly formed decision-making team instead of acting independently in making decisions about the future of a specific product.

Employee B (who is a supervisor) is asked to try a new method of counseling with her department members in an attempt to improve organization communications.

Employee C is instructed to accept a new job description that requires him to increase his responsibilities and increase the rate of his daily performance.

Employee D is told that beginning the following week, she is being transferred to a new department.

Employees E, F, and G are informed that their present boss is being transferred and a new supervisor is being brought in.

The employees of a small branch store are informed that their store is being consolidated with the main store and that all personnel will be transferred to the larger store.

Each of the preceding changes requires adjustments and modifications in habits, procedures, and working relationships. Look, for example, at the Lucinda Montoya case used to start this chapter. Which of the aforementioned employee situations can be applied to Montoya's case? As the examples illustrate, the types of organizational changes that may occur are numerous. Furthermore, as the example also illustrates, change comes in many sizes and shapes. It can range from major, overall organizational change, possibly affecting every department and job in an organization, to smaller changes that may affect only an individual job. No matter what the magnitude of change, it's important to understand the change process and how to deal with change. This is the emphasis of this chapter.

Internal Change

planned change
Behavior, events, or conditions that are different as a result of deliberate actions. In this chapter, planned change takes place as a result of managerial planning.

The intentions of **planned change** are usually positive. Planned change has its beginnings *within* the organization and involves changes for the purpose of achieving previously unattainable things or achieving goals more effectively, more efficiently, or more satisfactorily. Planned change involves deliberate steps being taken at the initiative of the organization itself. Change can be a response to overcome existing problems. It has been suggested, for example, that managers should promote changes when necessary to improve the means for satisfying somebody's economic wants, to increase profitability, or to contribute to individual satisfaction and social well-being.

If change is planned within the context of these purposes, customers, shareholders, employees, and the public at large potentially may benefit from the results of change. All groups may benefit simultaneously. There are times, however, when change may appear to benefit one group at the expense of another.

External Change

There are also times when change is called for as a result of factors *external* to the organization. Such changes may result from economic, technological, legal, or social factors. These factors often result in **unplanned change**—change which was not predicted and, therefore, was not planned for. Some external events and conditions, of course, are planned for.

unplanned change Behavior, events, or conditions that are different as a result of unpredicted, spontaneous factors forcing alteration to occur.

The Economy and Its Effects

An illustration of an economic factor calling for change from an external source could be the oil glut followed by scarcity (or the supply-demand problems) of energy sources seen in recent years. As suppliers increased their capacity to produce petroleum and failed to limit production, the price of and demand for oil decreased significantly. As a result, energy companies were forced to revise their strategies, reduce production, and remove many employees from their payrolls. Some employees were retired early. Some workers were reassigned to other duties. Many were laid of as a result of the unfavorable conditions. Almost all petrochemical employees were required to make personal adjustments in one way or another.

For example, Sarah Johansen is an attorney who was hired at the height of the oil boom to do legal research into her company's (one of the top five oil producers) holdings and rights in offshore drilling.

"It was exciting work," Johansen reports sadly. "I worked long hours—and I mean LONG—fifty hours a week was minimal. But I was really challenged. It seemed like each site brought dozens of new legal questions, and I was in daily contact with all kinds of specialists, the courts, and you name it."

Unfortunately, with the oil bust, Johansen's company stopped most of its offshore drilling. While many of the lawyers specializing in offshore drilling were laid off, Johansen was "lucky." She was reassigned to do legal research into workers' compensation claims.

"Lucky?" says Johansen. "Sometimes I'm not sure. I'm grateful to the company for trying to find a slot for me, but the bottom line is that I'm unhappy. Compared to the excitement of offshore, workers' compensation is terribly routine. It's almost like clerical work. You just look up precedents—there's very little new coming out. I have so many years invested in the company that I hate to think of leaving, but I feel I'm just stagnating. What to do, that's the question."

Notice that in this case, change affects not only *what* Johansen does but also *how* she feels about herself as a person.

What About Technology?

A quick illustration of the effects of technology as a causal factor for change might be the availability of computers to monitor and control production processes. This computerization potential has forced employees to revise their skills, reorganized the socialization patterns within organizations, displaced some workers, and resulted in numerous additional modifications. Technology has created new products, processes, procedures, and personnel requirements. The decision of whether or not to take advantage of technological innovations may in part be voluntary, but the desire to be competitive and progressive may leave little choice to most organizations. Look at the Lucinda Montoya case. Notice that Montoya's problems have their origin in a technological decision—computerizing the front desk. What does this change mean for Montoya?

Legal Changes Cause Organization Change

An illustration of an organizational change with a legal origin might be the court decisions that forced the splitting up of American Telephone and Telegraph (AT&T) into many small, sometimes competing organizations. Understanding management's signals becomes important. After the AT&T breakup, it soon became apparent that a new kind of employee was wanted by the restructured companies. Older, long-service, loyal, but not particularly aggressive employees were passed over for promotion for younger people who were more active, vocal, and assertive. Some regarded this as good, while others became fearful. Regardless of the feeling, change had come to the telephone company. Look back at the Lucinda Montoya case. Is there a parallel? What "message" may the hotel be sending out about the kind of front-desk employees it wants in the future?

Society Calls for Changes

An illustration of an organizational change with a social origin might be the revision of an organization's wage policy to provide equal wages for equal performance regardless of the sex of the individual (refer to the previous chapter). The move for equity and other social forces may cause organizations to adjust and adopt policies and procedures in keeping with the evolution of social values. Changing social values can have an impact upon almost every phase of an organization's operations.

Kinds of Changes

Most organizations at this very moment are faced with pressure to change. What kinds of changes are being called for? Changes are pressuring for the need to:

1. Reduce pollutants.
2. Utilize biodegradable materials.
3. Comply with numerous standards and regulations from government agencies.
4. Modify the physical work setting.
5. Implement new management techniques.
6. Adjust to new accounting methods.
7. Deal with increasing external forces, such as consumer and environmental groups, a fluctuating economy, a freer trade.[1]

The Effects of Change upon Employees

Three types of adjustments must be made with change: behavioral alterations, psychological revisions, and social adaptations.

Behavioral Changes

Behavioral alterations are modifications in overt, physical routines by which work is performed. **Behavioral adjustments** for new regulations, procedures, and methods of operation are usually required. Look back at Lucinda Montoya's case. What behavioral changes were called for from Montoya and her workers? Will these changes be simple?

behavioral adjustment Modification of the actions of employees as a result of change.

Psychological Changes

The **psychological effect** of change might be defined as the attitude developed by the individual employee toward change. The attitude toward change is based upon an employee's ability to cope with the demands resulting from change. A worker who perceives self as capable of adjusting to change without an overwhelming degree of personal sacrifice and who views the end result of the change as largely beneficial may psychologically adopt a positive attitude toward the change. On the other hand, the employee who feels incapable and insecure and fails to see many personal benefits forthcoming from the change may have a negative attitude and will oppose the change.

A range of attitudes usually representative of workers reacting to change runs from open, complete acceptance of change to active resistance to it (see Figure 17–1). For example, management may want an employee to change a

psychological effect The results of change that causes mental strategies different from previous strategies.

Acceptance	Enthusiastic cooperation and support
	Cooperation
	Cooperation under pressure from management
	Acceptance
	Passive resignation
Indifference	Indifference
	Apathy; loss of interest in the job
	Doing only what is ordered
	Regressive behavior
Passive resistance	Nonlearning
	Protests
	Working to rule
	Doing as little as possible
Active resistance	Slowing down
	Personal withdrawal
	Committing "errors"
	Spoilage
	Deliberate sabotage

Figure 17–1
Range of Attitudes Toward Change and Resulting People's Behavior

Source: Arnold S. Judson, *A Manager's Guide to Making Changes,* London. Copyright 1966. Reprinted by permission of John Wiley & Sons, Ltd.

Some see equipment like the scanner to be a help, while others see it as a nuisance.

particular work behavior. Perhaps the need for the change has resulted from technology. Suppose a convenience store has installed an optical scanning system and cashiers must move the bar-code on an item over a scanner rather than ring up the sale. The result is change; employees no longer ring up items but now use the scanner. But will any particular clerk—Sammy Smith or Jane Elkins, for example—develop a positive or a negative attitude toward the change? The answer to that question depends on each employee's personal calculations of the pros and the cons of the change. Let's listen to Sammy's and Jane's reactions.

Sammy: *I think this whole thing is a terrible idea. Why? Well, it's the scanner. I can never get it to read right. Sometimes it seems like I've passed an item over it twenty-five times and it STILL won't register. In my opinion, all that so-called great new invention does is to make the work harder.*

Jane: *I don't see it that way at all. I really like the new system. I used to have a terrible time remembering prices—especially when items went on special. Now that's all done for me through the scanner's memory. My job's much easier now.*

Who's right and who's wrong? As you can tell, this example points to how different individual perceptions can lead to totally different attitudes toward change. In turn, as Figure 17–1 shows, attitudes result in behavioral patterns that may attempt to enhance the outcome of change, try to impede the progress of change, or take a neutral, more passive position toward it. In the above example, we would expect Sammy to actually resist the change, while Jane is much more likely to take a positive stance.

Social Changes

Look again at the opening case. Notice that Montoya has many years and a lot of loyalty invested in the status quo. How is that investment likely to affect her attitude toward the change to a new system? If you were her boss, what would you do? The **social adaptations** that change calls for involve alterations in the relationships between individual employees, their bosses, their colleagues, their workers, the informal groups to which they may belong, and new employees with whom they may come in contact. Change often affects the degree of social interaction between individuals. Change may also have an impact upon roles, status, cohesiveness, and patterns of identification and acceptance between people.

Change seldom leaves social patterns totally uninterrupted when it occurs. In the example with Sammy and Jane, Sammy may find that he has less time to spend talking to customers (because he's trying to get the scanner to work!), while Jane may find she has more time. In both cases, patterns of communication between the clerks and their customers will change. What do you suppose will happen with Lucinda Montoya and her relationship with the housekeeping and maintenance staffs in the opening case?

social adaptation
The result of change that causes new relationships and affiliations to be formed.

Additional Effects of Change

In addition to the categories already described, change may also result in new reward systems for employees, new job freedoms and constraints, new authority structures, new action-time schedules, and new working environments. Look again at the opening case. What are the potential benefits of the change? Is Montoya aware of the benefits?

Why Change Is Often Resisted

If all changes, regardless of their origins, were accepted and implemented enthusiastically by managers and other employees of every organization, this chapter would be unnecessary. There would be no problems of concern to the manager involving the development of a strategy for change. Change often results in resistance, however, and negative employee reactions may doom the success of programs of change if not handled properly. For a quick check on your own receptiveness to change, take the Personal Feedback Reaction to Change.

Why do employees sometimes resist changes within the organization? A number of explanations have been given as possible reasons for the development of attitudes and behavior patterns of resistance. At least two of the models discussed in Chapter 6 offer possible explanations. The success-failure model, for example, suggests that resistance to change, in part, is a function of previous experiences with change. Individuals who have experienced good results from previous change are likely to be receptive and open to future change. Individuals with bad experiences with previous change are more likely to resist future change (see Figure 17–2). In our discussion of Sammy's and Jane's reactions to the scanner, this theory suggests that one factor in Sammy's resistance may be that he has had negative experiences with past change. In the opening case, what about Lucinda Montoya? In terms of her past experience, why should she be a bit nervous about the new system?

Self Test

Personal Feedback

Reaction to Change

This group of questions will help you gain insight into how you think and what your behavior is when change takes place around you. Respond to each statement by putting the score to the left of each statement that represents your degree of agreement or disagreement with the statement.

A score of *5* means you *strongly agree* with the statement.
A score of *4* means you *agree* with the statement.
A score of *3* means you *neither agree nor disagree* with the statement.
A score of *2* means you *disagree* with the statement.
A score of *1* means you *strongly disagree* with the statement.

_____ 1. Change usually means that something better is going to result.
_____ 2. I'm willing to give new things a try.
_____ 3. My past experiences with change have been pleasant and positive.
_____ 4. It is difficult for me to accept new people when we first meet.
_____ 5. I have a strong, positive feeling about myself and what I am capable of doing.
_____ 6. I like to be given responsibility and to be held accountable for getting things done.
_____ 7. Something new usually means something not so good as something old.
_____ 8. Change for the sake of change is usually acceptable to me.
_____ 9. I am afraid of things I know nothing about.
_____ 10. I don't take risks unless I am pretty certain I can handle them.

When you have answered all ten of the questions record your answers in the following manner.

For the following questions write down the score you gave as an answer.

    1. _____
    2. _____
    3. _____
    5. _____
    6. _____
    8. _____
        Subtotal _____

Reverse score the following items by subtracting the score you gave the statement from 6. If, for example, you scored item 4 as a 2, subtract 2 from 6 to get your adjusted score of 4.

    4. (6-_____) = _____
    7. (6-_____) = _____
    9. (6-_____) = _____
   10. (6-_____) = _____
            Subtotal _____
            Total   _____

Now add your two subtotals together. The higher your score, the more positive you are toward change and the events calling for change. In other words, you have a good aptitude and openness toward change. The lower your score, the more you are disturbed by change and the threat of change. A score of 40 or above indicates a high confidence and receptivity to change. A score of 30 through 39 indicates some confidence and acceptance of change. A score of 20 to 29 indicates uncertain or neutral feelings toward change. A score of 10 to 19 indicates significant concern and reluctance to accept change.

The TA Approach

Chapter 6 presented the transactional analysis (TA) point of view. Drawing from TA, it is possible to say that people might be skeptical of future change for fear that stroking will be less likely from the new situation when compared to the stroking that they now receive. To say this in another way, future situations are sometimes seen as having fewer rewards or reinforcements than are presently being received. We know that stroking—i.e., rewards and reinforcements—is important to people. Maybe just talking to customers is the

Figure 17–2   Acceptance of Change Based Upon Previous Success or Failure

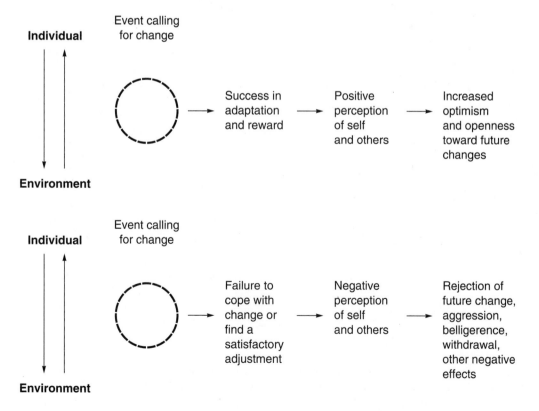

stroking that Sammy needs. When we think about Lucinda Montoya's situation, clearly she has taken a lot of pride in helping customers in the past. What about the future? Will the "strokes" belong to her or to the computer? What can management do to provide her with new strokes?

TA would also say that resistance to change may occur because the new situation is inconsistent with attitudes established by the parent and child parts of the personality. Only the adult part of the personality has the ability to look at change rationally and maturely. In Sammy's case, the child part of him may believe that he "looks stupid" to the customers when he can't get the system to work.

Tension

Other psychological concepts such as those advocated by Sigmund Freud operate on the basis of tension release.[2] Things that cause tension are uncomfortable, and the human organism tries to free itself of tension where it occurs. Change causes tension to develop. As tension develops, the individual either seeks ways to deal with it and get rid of it or neutralize it, or the individual attempts to erect a shield or barrier to avoid the stressful condition altogether. The ultimate goal is to minimize the time period between the creation of tension caused by change and the release of tension or to restore conditions to being tension-free if the change can't be avoided (see Figure 17–3). In Sammy's case, this theory would emphasize proper training so that Sammy becomes comfortable with the new system as quickly as possible. What about Lucinda Montoya?

Fear

In capturing a thread of unity from the previously described theories of resistance to change and adding a new dimension as well, it is clear that a large number of employees are afraid that change will result in the loss of something important to them. The anticipated loss suggests that a vacuum will be created in an area of personal value. Levinson has suggested that most of these fears are not based upon fictional imaginations but in fact usually result in real losses.

> All change—promotion, transfer, demotion, reorganization, merger, retirement, and most other managerial actions—produces loss. Despite the fact that change is necessary and is often for the better, the new always displaces the old, and at some level of consciousness, individuals experience the threat of this displacement or loss.[3]

Levinson goes further to say that personal losses because of change usually result in at least four areas of deprivation: the loss of love, the loss of support, the loss of sensory input, and the loss of the capacity to act. Others would add to these the fear of the loss of meaning and the loss of a future.[4] People are often afraid that respect, acceptance, help, the ability to influence others, power, and other things may be lost as a result of change.

Another way of looking at fears that develop because of the demands of change is simply to consider change as a threat to the personal needs and ambitions of the employee. Change may undermine the fulfillment of any or

Figure 17–3   Tensions and Reactions to Tensions Caused by Change

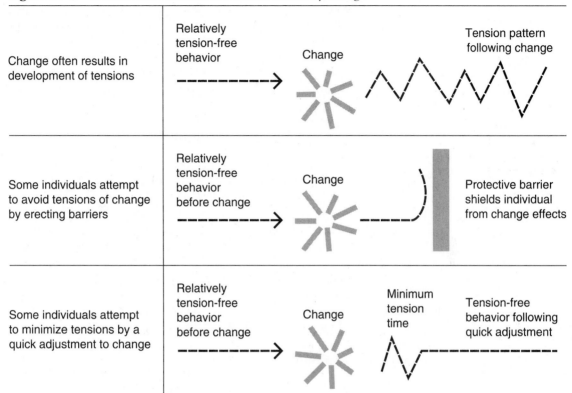

all human needs—physical maintenance, security, affiliation, social, esteem (recognition and reputation), competence, power, achievement, and hope. When a new supervisor comes on the scene, for example, an employee may immediately become concerned about the protection of sources for fulfillment of needs for security, social esteem, competence, and power. A worker who is asked to modify a job routine may instantly be afraid that he of she may suffer losses of security, affiliation, competency, power, and achievement as a direct result of the demands the change presents. Some fear connected with the demands that change may call for are only imaginary, while others are unmistakably real. The important fact, however, is that change is often resisted because of the anticipated threatening effects employees believe will result. In the Lucinda Montoya case, what fears has the new change called forth in Montoya? Do you think all of the employees feel the same way she does?

Other Factors Influencing Response to the Demands for Change

The Initiator of Change

Another important factor in the acceptance or rejection of change is the employee's attitude toward the individual(s) who decided that the change is

change agent
Often called the consultant. The individual with the responsibility for leading an organization in the process of renewal and growth, called Organizational Development. He or she serves as a catalyst to bring about innovation within an organization.

necessary and introduced it. If the **change agent** is respected and the employee has confidence that he or she will act in the employee's best interests when deciding upon and implementing a change, the employee may be more disposed to cooperate with the requested change. If, on the other hand, the employee lacks confidence and trust in the instigator of change, the resistance to change may be much greater. In the Lucinda Montoya case, notice that no one has explained why the change is needed or where it came from. What impact may this have had on Montoya and her workers?

The Risk-Taking Tendencies of the Employee

Each individual of whom change is demanded has a level of tolerance of change or degree of willingness to take risks involved in change. There are even methods for evaluating the risk-taking potential of employees through testing. The low risk taker sees mostly the negative consequences of the situation and no positive advantages. As a result, he or she is not receptive to change. The individual high in risk-taking tendencies, on the other hand, sees mostly the benefits of a risk (change) and is more open to events involving change. Previous experiences with change and confidence in one's own decision skills help to increase receptivity to the risk of change.[5] Think about the Sammy and Jane situation; then consider Lucinda Montoya. How have their experiences contributed to their willingness to take risks?

The Necessity of Change

Another dimension of acceptance of change is the urgency of the need for the change. If an organizational change *must* take place for the survival of the organization itself, workers will accept and implement change with less reluctance. If, for example, economic developments or competitive factors demand that a modification in work procedures must occur for a firm to continue in business, the adjustment may be made without too much foot dragging. Workers have been known to volunteer to work longer hours for less pay so that their employing organizations could continue operations.[6]

If organizational alterations appear unnecessary, employee receptiveness is not likely to be very high. If a manager, for example, asks his or her employees to stop taking the customary coffee break without supplying a good reason for the requested change, the employees typically will be nonreceptive to the request and will resist at great length. In such a situation, the workers may believe that the underlying forces necessitating the change are not really important, and they treat them accordingly. The required adjustments appear unnecessary and nonbeneficial to them. If there is an important reason for the change, however, acceptance may result quickly.

Management's Goals for Change

It is undeniable that change affects the people who work together within an organization. As change is being considered, the management of the organization must determine its goals and objectives for bringing about modifications and alterations. Some worthy objectives for change within organizations from a management point of view may include the following:

- ☐ Strive to make changes and alterations that are universally beneficial whenever possible. In other words, a change that results in gains for the organization, its owners, its employees, the public being served, and the community at large would be highly desirable We refer to such changes as "win/win" because everyone—the organization, employees, and customers—for example, comes out a winner.
- ☐ Initiate changes in such a way that employees are receptive to them and will be willing to give them a fair trial. Strive for acceptance and support of changes on the part of those who will be responsible for their successful completion.
- ☐ Anticipate the effects of change upon organizational members and, whenever possible, make adjustments for the impending effects.
- ☐ Attempt to minimize personal losses and fears that may develop as change approaches.

Leadership for Change

The leadership given in times of change is very important. Nadler and Tushman say that two general types of leadership activity are important in the change process. One set of activities involves what the authors call charismatic leadership, and the other is instrumental leadership. The charismatic part of leadership concentrates on bringing about changes in the values, goals, needs, and aspirations of the people involved in change. This type of charismatic leadership requires envisioning, energizing, and enabling. *Envisioning* is the creation of a picture showing what is possible and desirable for the future. *Energizing* is actually motivation—providing the desire to make a change. *Enabling* is psychologically helping people to perform the challenging new behaviors.[7]

Instrumental leadership makes it possible for people to do the things they are expected to do. Activities involved include building (structuring) teams of individuals to work together, developing and communicating goal expectations, and administering rewards and punishments so that individuals see that change is useful to themselves and the organization.

Managerial Guidelines

Keeping in mind the managerial objectives of beneficial achievement, employee acceptance and support, and minimization of fears and personal losses, it is appropriate to consider actions managers can take to make change in a way that accomplishes these objectives. Several things can be done.

Defining Objectives and Optimizing Mutual Benefits

It is essential to investigate overall organizational objectives to be certain that they support the philosophy of providing positive benefits for the organization, its owners, its employees, its customers, and the community in general. Unless organizational objectives specify the pursuit of mutually beneficial results, changes may fall short of providing fulfillment for everyone.

If objectives are outlined in a collectively advantageous manner, changes and innovations can be considered on the basis of whether or not they will contribute effectively to the reasonable fulfillment of needs and goals for all involved. Changes that do not have the interest of all in mind may be dismissed if the option lies within the organization. In the Lucinda Montoya case, the change was probably made so that the organization could compete better. Do Montoya and her employees know this? What difference would it make if they did?

Suppose change is forced on the organization from outside factors. Externally forced changes cannot, of course, be treated in the same manner. However, when external factors make change necessary, it is especially important for management to share the reasons for the change with those affected and to channel the modifications so that they can be useful to everyone. Carrying this thesis one step further, it can be said that only changes that promise desirable results should be implemented, except in the most unusual circumstances. Changes that offer minimal opportunities for success and desirable results normally will not be given serious consideration, because the adverse effects of adaptation to change will often overshadow the attainable merits.

Often change does offer benefits to the workers, but workers' perceptions enter in. If employees aren't shown how the change can benefit them, they may believe that it won't benefit them—especially if they've had negative experiences with past change. Earlier, we discussed Sammy's and Jane's reactions to the new scanning system in the convenience store. We can't help but wonder whether Sammy came to the conclusion that the new system wasn't beneficial because management hadn't shown him the benefits and trained him in how to use the system so he could obtain the benefits. These are management's responsibilities.

Enlisting Employee Participation

A particularly helpful managerial action in considering change is to allow and encourage employee participation in deciding whether or not the change should be made and how it should be made if a decision to change is reached. Early participation by employees affected by the change accomplishes a number of purposes. Change decisions that have overwhelmingly negative consequences on employees usually can be identified and eliminated or revised. Employee participation helps the new method or procedure to become the brainchild of the workers themselves. Workers feel personal responsibility for it, and they usually will support the change when it occurs. Employee participation aids in the full disclosure of the causes, consequences, and implications of the change so that uncertainties concerning the change are avoided. Control of change by those affected can reduce resistance.[8]

Employee participation in the change process is one of the most useful tools of management for the successful introduction and implementation of change.

Allowing for Early Planning and Advance Notification

When a change has officially been decided upon, early planning for the change and notification of those affected usually is helpful. Lead time for adjustment is important. An organization that knows a year in advance that it will be necessary to transfer several employees to new jobs can take the necessary steps to provide the reorientation, training, equipment realignment, social adjustment, and other actions necessary to be ready for the transfer when it finally happens. Employees appreciate advance notifications of changes that affect them personally so that they can begin to make physical, psychological, and social readjustments. Of course, not all changes allow for an advance warning signal; but when it is possible to sense a change in advance and communicate that fact, employees can prepare themselves more satisfactorily.

Guaranteeing Employee Protection

The adoption of organizational policies that provide protection and support for employees may add stability to the workforce when faced with change. A wage policy that guarantees that employees cannot be forced by any changing circumstance to accept jobs with lower pay scales within the organization removes some of the economic threat of change. A policy of utilizing seniority as the basis for making decisions on layoffs, position bidding and bumping, and in other important areas give security to the more established employees. A policy of providing adequate severance pay when an employee in good standing must be released from the organization also cushions economic fears. Informal policies of preserving status and upgrading positions when change occurs encourage workers to be more receptive to future change. A policy of retraining employees whose skills have become obsolete lends encouragement when technology forces change.

Most policies that provide protection from fears of loss will improve employees' attitudes toward impending changes. Looking back at the opening case, it's important that Montoya and her people feel certain that management has considered their job security when planning the change. If they have doubts about their security, full-scale resistance can be expected from them. Of course, getting back to the importance of perception, it's essential to remember that having policies such as these in place will be helpful ONLY if employees know about them. Again, this is a management responsibility. (See Insights: Methods for Dealing with Change.)

Providing Resources and Training

It is important that the organization commit resources that are sufficient to bring about the change satisfactorily. Knowledge of the availability of resources needs to be communicated to those who are expected to carry out the change. It is usually desirable that a slow pace be used with change. A slower pace reduces the complexity of change by allowing for adjustment time.

Insights

Methods for Dealing with Change

Approach	Commonly Used in Situations	Advantages	Drawbacks
Education & Communication Beforehand (helping people see the logic and need for change)	Where there is a lack of information or inaccurate information and analysis.	Once persuaded, people will often help with the implementation of the change.	Can be very time-consuming if lots of people are involved.
Participation & Involvement (initiators listen to those affected and use their advice)	Where the initiators do not have all the information they need to design the change and where others have considerable power to resist.	People who participate will be committed to implementing change, and any relevant information they have will be integrated into the change plan.	Can be very time-consuming if participators design an inappropriate change.
Facilitation & Support (providing training, allowing time off after a demanding period, listening)	Where people are resisting because of adjustment problems.	No other approach works as well with adjustment problems.	Can be time-consuming and expensive and can still fail.

Employees affected by change should be given adequate training on any new equipment or procedures involved. If training is not given, workloads should be temporarily reduced. As skills are developed, the work pace can be gradually increased.

Using Groups to Help Employees Overcome Their Fears

Identification of existing cohesive groups can be useful in helping employees to reduce their fear of an upcoming change. These groups are made of individuals who are bonded together firmly. They can be used as pilots of change. The grapevine can work effectively, too.

Approach	Commonly Used in Situations	Advantages	Drawbacks
Negotiation & Agreement (offer incentives to potential resisters—give something in return for something else)	Where someone or some group will clearly lose out in a change and where that group has considerable power to resist.	Sometimes it is a relatively easy way to avoid major resistance.	Can be too expensive in many cases if it alerts others to negotiate for compliance.
Manipulation & Cooptation (selective use of information and the consensus structuring of events. Cooptation is a form where the individual is given a role in the design and implementation of change.)	Where other tactics will not work or are too expensive	It can be a relatively quick and inexpensive solution to resistance problems.	Can lead to future problems if people feel manipulated.
Expect & Implicit Coercion (threatens someone with the loss of something)	Where speed is essential and the change initiators possess considerable power.	It is speedy and can overcome any kind of resistance.	Can be risky if it leaves people mad at the initiators.

Source: An exhibit from "Choosing Strategies for Change," by John P. Kotter and Leonard A. Schlesinger, Volume 57, Number 2, March–April 1979. © 1979 by the President and Fellows of Harvard College; all rights reserved.

Many steps can be taken to overcome or soften fears of loss of social rapport and affiliation. Whole groups of employees often are allowed to adjust to a change together so that social realignment will be as limited as is possible. Workers may be allowed to interact with future coworkers for long periods of time in advance of their actual working together so that affiliations can be made and fears overcome before the situation becomes binding.

Applying the Tentative Approach

An effective technique for overcoming fears is the use of the **tentative approach.** This technique is basically the establishment of a trial period of

tentative approach
A method of bringing about change where modifications done on a trial basis can be reversed if the employee doesn't like the adjustment after using it for a time.

change in which employees are asked to work under the new requirements or conditions without actually accepting the change and committing themselves to abide by its new demands. The tentative (trial) approach has several advantages:

1. Those involved are able to test their reactions to the new situation before committing themselves irrevocably.
2. Those involved are able to acquire more facts on which to base their attitudes and behavior toward the change.
3. Those involved who have strong preconceptions are in a better position to regard the change with greater objectivity. Consequently, they can review their preconceptions and perhaps modify some of them.
4. Those involved are less likely to regard the change as a threat.
5. Management is better able to evaluate the method of change and make any necessary modifications before carrying it out more fully.[9]

The tentative approach has a way of defusing potentially explosive rejection of change. Most individuals approaching a change on this basis discover that they are capable of the adjustment. Often they discover that the consequences are better than anticipated. There are, of course, some instances when a change is rejected after a trial, and management must be prepared to deal with that eventuality.

Additional Means of Encouraging Acceptance of Change

As mentioned earlier, the individual(s) selected to introduce change and to enlist employee cooperation will also have an effect upon the level of worker acceptance. Selecting individuals as change agents who are respected and who have the confidence of other workers improves the probabilities of successful reactions and adjustments to change.[10]

A very important part of the successful change process is to reward those who adjust to and accept change. Rewarding or reinforcing desirable behavior encourages the new behavior to continue.[11]

When the employees of an organization lose something as a result of unpreventable change (loss of wages, loss of desirable social climate, loss of freedom, and so forth), management can make an effort to substitute something else for the loss. The commission ratio of a salesperson who is transferred from a prime sales territory to one with less potential can be increased. The employee who is placed in an isolated, confining work position could be given shorter work hours or more coffee breaks to offset the restrictive environment. The manager who gives up a private office to another manager might receive other status symbols (preferred parking space, a fancy job title, etc.) to partially offset the losses sustained. It is true that not every loss can be compensated for, but efforts to do so often provide fruitful results.

Management should not overlook other possible sources of assistance in implementing change and getting its acceptance. Labor unions, for example, frequently work with managers in organizations to implement change when the change promises benefits to employees. Informal work groups within the formal organization may encourage members to respond favorably to change when the benefits of change are communicated and understood. Influential individuals both within and outside the organization may be persuasive in leading individuals to respond positively to change. Government agencies sometimes provide financial and advisory assistance in implementing organizational change.

Summary of Guidelines

This list of ways to enhance the positive side of organizational change and to minimize the negative consequences of change is by no means comprehensive. It does show, however, that many negative effects of change can be prevented or adjusted to if careful consideration is given to both the benefits and the negative consequences of change and if care and planning are included when implementing change. To summarize the suggested techniques, change can be facilitated by the following:

1. Defining organizational objectives that provide benefits for all parties related to the organization—the owners, employees, customers, and the community at large.
2. Choosing to make changes (whenever possible) that optimize the mutual benefits for all of these groups.
3. Allowing and encouraging participation by the employees to be affected by change in the decision-making and implementation stages of change.
4. Utilizing advance planning, notification, and communication of change and its anticipated effects.
5. Adopting organizational policies that provide maximum amounts of encouragement and support for organizational members when change occurs.
6. Committing resources sufficient to bring about successful change and then communicating this commitment to employees.
7. Giving adequate training or reduced workloads to employees so that adjustments can be made.
8. Considering a number of methods of facilitating the social adaptation demanded by change and utilizing the appropriate methods.
9. Utilizing the tentative trial technique whenever feasible.
10. Carefully selecting respected, valued individuals to serve as change agents (introducers of change).
11. Rewarding the performance that adjusts to change.
12. Compensating or substituting for personal losses that are unavoidable.[12]

Organizational Development

It is possible for the management team of an organization to establish a program of comprehensive change that we have come to label Organizational Development. **Organizational Development** (OD) is an attempt by the members of an organization with the help of a consultant to achieve the fullest potential of the organization as well as to correct any problems or shortcomings existing within it. Change could result in every area of the

Organizational Development
A form of planned change where the members of an organization, with the help of a consultant, audit themselves and their organization, then are led in a program of improvement and revitalization based upon the findings of the evaluation.

Employees who receive adequate notification of change along with helpful training are more likely to accept it.

organization—formal structure, informal relationships, goals and objectives, communication patterns, decision-making processes, relationship to the environment—as needed for optimum performance. In other words, when the organizational development effort begins, all phases of the organization are subject to review. Based upon the findings of the review, a program of change can be developed and implemented.

The concept known as Organizational Development got its start in the mid-1940s. Radical change after World War II meant that something more complete than simple training programs, isolated shuffling of authority, and other separate efforts were needed in many organizations. A comprehensive analysis and innovation was called for. Through the years, a procedure for bringing about a total review of an organization with the purposes of instituting planned change has developed. The steps to the process may include the following:

1. *Scouting.* Arriving at a decision of whether or not to have a change agent enter an organization for the purpose of applying organizational development.
2. *Entry.* Establishing a collaborative relationship for initial problem exploration and the selection of data-gathering/feedback methods.
3. *Data gathering.* Developing measures of organizational variables and processes.
4. *Data analysis and feedback.* Interpreting and organizing the data, feeding the data back to the system, and developing a shared understanding of the system and its problems in collaboration with the client.
5. *Action planning.* Developing specific action plans, including who will implement the plans and how their efforts will be evaluated.
6. *Action implementation.* Setting into motion specific action plans.
7. *Evaluation.* Determining effects and effectiveness of actions implemented, leading to further efforts or to termination.[13]

**Management
in Action**

Closing a Branch Office

A large engineering consulting firm decided to close one of its branches some years ago. The reasons for closure were primarily economic in that the demand for consulting services where the branch was located had weakened. The branch was in a community several hundred miles from the company's headquarters. The decision to close the branch had been made more than a year in advance of the planned closing date. Since there were no positions open at the headquarters or in other branch offices of the organization, the change, in effect, meant that most of the personnel at the office would be out of a job when the branch was actually shut down.

As soon as the decision was made, the manager of the branch office was authorized to tell the personnel (most of whom were engineers, technicians, and secretaries) what was about to happen, why it was occurring, and when it would take place. The manager extended a number of assurances to the staff, telling them that the company would initiate a placement service whereby employees' data sheets would be distributed to prospective employers of the employees' choice, an office would be opened within the branch office to allow recruiting representatives of other organizations to interview the employees concerning new jobs, other placement assistance would be given as needed, and appropriate severance pay would be provided for any employees who had not secured a job (if they were actively seeking one).

When the time came to close the office, every employee had received at least three offers from other employers, and most employees were able to move to higher paying, attractive positions. Not only were the displaced employees grateful for the interest and support of their old employer, but employees of the firm who worked at headquarters or in other branches had a greater respect for their employer and a higher level of security in the knowledge that their organization was sincerely concerned about the welfare of its employees.

Barczak et al. break the (OD) process into four major parts: pattern breaking, experimenting, visioning, and bonding and attunement. *Pattern breaking* is eliminating or unlearning the dysfunctional behavior that needs to be changed. *Experimenting* is the generating of new options, new ways of doing things. New systems, new methods, new products, and new personnel are considered. *Visioning* is the selection of new courses of action and new processes based upon the findings resulting from experimentation. *Bonding and attunement* is the process where a sense of community, trust, respect, and shared values is developed (see Table 17–1).[14]

Role of the Change Agent

A change agent or consultant is essential to this process. The change agent is an individual (often from outside the organization) who serves to lead the organization through the stages of OD until the review, implementation, and evaluation have taken place. The change agent serves primarily as a catalyst who assists the organization to discover its own solutions as much as possible. The change agent raises questions, encourages interaction, and supplements

Table 17–1

Assessing an
Organization's
Propensity to
Change

Key Variable	Indicators
Pattern Breaking	Is the organization willing and able to "let go" of approaches that no longer yield desired results?
	Are managers and departments rewarded for weeding out unproductive operations, products, and practices?
	Does the organization try to improve performance by challenging long-held traditions—e.g., large staff groups and layers of middle managers?
Experimenting	Does the organization encourage creativity and the implementation of new ideas and approaches? Are organizational mechanisms in place that facilitate experimentation and implementation, such as venture and project teams, basic research groups, and organizational simulation and modeling groups?
	What is the organization's track record in terms of innovation in products, manufacturing, processes, and managerial approaches?
Visioning	Is there a shared meaning throughout the organization that guides positive and purposeful action?
	Are concerted efforts made to periodically assess, update, and extend the organization's mission?
	Are departments, work units, managers, and personnel encouraged to suggest new strategic options for organizations? Are there methods of evaluating and acting on these options?
Bonding and Attunement	What is the quality of interpersonal relationships? Does the organization's culture promote diverse integration of members around important tasks?
	Do members share a "sense of inclusion"?
	What is the extent of "sandbox tending" by functional and staff managers? How permeable are organizational boundaries?
	Do informal organizations function in a positive, purposeful way?
	Does needed information flow via informed networks of experts or via the formal hierarchy?

Source: Gloria Barczak, Charles Smith, and David Wilemon, "Managing Large-scale Organizational Change," *Organizational Dynamics,* Volume 16, Number 2, Autumn 1987, pp. 23–35. Reprinted by permission of publisher, from *Organizational Dynamics,* Autumn/1987 © 1987. American Management Association, New York. All rights reserved.

knowledge so that a thorough review of problems, alternatives, and solutions occurs. Ideally, the change agent begins work without preconceived notions of what is wrong in an organization and what the solutions to the organization's problems are. The answers and the necessary actions are revealed as the organization's members perform the review the agent leads them to do.

Helping OD Work Properly

If the OD process is to work optimally, several conditions are needed:

1. Organizational members who can be candid with one another about their experiences in the organization.
2. People who take responsibility for their own actions.
3. Individuals who relate holistically (i.e., in terms of the whole person, not just aspects of the person, such as sex or age) to other organizational members.
4. Individuals who view other organizational personnel as equals.
5. Coordinated effort where there are shared plans and shared rewards.
6. Commitment by the members to the organization's welfare.
7. Commitment to humanistic management.[15]

A typical part of the data-gathering process would be the asking and answering of questions about every possible facet of the organization and the work groups within it (see Table 17-2). The managers and their subordinates develop their own answers individually or collectively to the questions asked them by the change agent. The change agent compiles answers and conveys findings back to the participants. At this stage, the consultant may allow the group to develop solutions to problems identified. In most cases, however, it will be necessary for the agent to use intervention techniques, such as team building or career planning, to get movement and change initiated. The change agent needs expertise to prescribe and conduct interventions that will produce positive results (see Table 17-3 for a list of frequently used intervention techniques).

The program of change that is established is based upon specific findings from the audit and not predetermined packages of answers. One of the keys to successful OD utilization seems to be the flexibility and the absence of predetermined solutions to anticipated problems. The ability and sensitivity of the consultant seem to be very important to the success of OD.[16]

OD, Attitude Change, and Training

The initial efforts of the action planning and action implementation concentrate on changing personal attitudes and habits of organizational members. Such changes affect the collective habits and attitudes of groups of people. As the groups are developed and integrated, organizational members become more capable of dealing with structural, technical, and operational problems. Organizational Development investigates the climate or surroundings in which people work as a forerunner to other changes.

Training or retraining individuals so that technical, interpersonal, and decision-making skills are cultivated or changed often is a part of the OD process. However, OD is very different in scope and application from simple training. Organizational Development focuses on all of an organization's problems. It may work with groups rather than with individuals. The role of the consultant is as a facilitator as the change agent works intensively over a long period of time with groups. The key to the success of OD often lies in the skill and sensitivity of the change agent. Solutions, usually based upon the findings of the organizational audit, determine the kinds of changes and interventions that will occur.

Table 17–2

Questions to Assist in the Location of Organizational and Group Problems

Structural Questions

1. What is the formalized authority structure of the group?
2. Is this structure adequate or inadequate?
3. To what degree is delegation of authority practiced?
4. Other than through formalized authority, in what ways have organizational members gained their authority?
5. In what ways do informal relationships differ from formalized ones?
6. Are there any rigid social class boundaries in the group?
7. What are the major paths of communication among the organization's members?
8. How extensive is the division of labor within the group?

Functional Questions

1. Do group activities have a positive or a negative effect upon organizational survival?
2. Is cooperation resulting or is competition being fostered? What factors are the critical influences?
3. How well are group tasks contributing to group cohesiveness?
4. If participative management is practiced, does it serve as a vehicle for involvement or as a source for feelings of incompetence?
5. If job enrichment is practiced, what is the attitude of the group members toward the group's major functions?
6. Does each member know the functional requirements of his or her team members?

Causal Questions

1. Is behavior induced by the group or by individuals within the group?
2. Do majority groups and minority groups exist among the members of the team?

Table 17–3

Interventions Used in OD Programs

Technique	Number Reporting Use
Team building	33
MBO (Management by Objective)	30
Systems analysis	20
Job enrichment/enlargement	20
Seminars	20
Mechanization/automation	17
Survey/feedback	13
Confrontation meetings	13
Lectures	12
Career planning	12
Grid training	8
Sensitivity training	5
Other	3

Source: William J. Heisler, "Patterns of OD in Practice," *Business Horizons,* Volume 17, Number 1, February 1975, Table 2, p. 82. Reprinted from *Business Horizons,* February 1975. Copyright 1975 by the Foundation for the School of Business at Indiana University. Used with permission.

Table 17–2
continued

3. What roles are played by the members of the group? How do the roles that are played influence the performance and behavior of the group?

4. Are there social cliques in the group? What effect do these groupings have upon the actions of the complete team?

5. Which members are the most influential in determining the group's goals and behavior norms?

6. Are the technological requirements of the task causing any feelings of incompetence among the group members?

7. Are the individuals encouraged to participate or are they discouraged from active involvement?

Interaction Questions

1. Do people communicate directly with each other or is the process one in which key individuals spread the information to other members?

2. On what basis is consensus reached—through persuasion, coercion, formal authority, charisma, or some other basis?

3. Do all members conform to group goals or are there several significant deviants?

4. How are protest actions channeled?

5. What happens during a group discussion? Who shows solidarity? Who shows antagonism? Who gives suggestions? Who asks for suggestions? Who moderates the discussion?

6. How are internal conflicts resolved?

7. How are conflicts with external forces handled?

Source: Excerpt from Z. S. Demirdjian, and O. Jeff Harris, "Revitalizing Work Teams: A Researched-Base Approach," *Current Business Perspectives,* Volume 1, Number 1, January 1981, pp. 9–11, 14–17, 23.

Summary

From an organizational point of view, change calls for modifications in the attitudes and behavior of the organization's members. Change frequently results from internal plans to improve the performance of the organization and to benefit organizational members and others. Change also may be a result of external influences, including economic, technological, and social factors.

Employees in organizations where change occurs are called upon to make several behavioral, psychological, or social adaptations. Worker reactions to these demands range from hearty acceptance to active resistance. The success-failure, transactional analysis, and fear theories provide explanations for the resistance and rejection of change that frequently occur. The individuals who serve as change agents also play a part in getting acceptance or rejection of change. The nature of a change (whether it is really necessary or only a luxury) may also influence the reactions organizational members exhibit toward the change.

It should be the purpose of every manager to maximize the positive effects of change and to minimize the negative consequences upon organizational members. If the guidelines suggested in this chapter are implemented, the results of change normally will be beneficial to both employees and the organization.

Organizational Development is a special form of planned change designed to help an organization become what it is capable of being. The change agent is particularly important here as he or she leads the self-analysis and innovation processes. Organizational Development makes use of many different intervention techniques as it seeks excellence. The interventions performed work best when they are a direct result of investigation of the organization's strengths and weaknesses rather than when they are prepackaged arrangements.

Questions to Consider

1. Why is it that so often change seems to benefit one individual or group at the expense of another?
2. Evaluate the statement, "Change that seems unavoidable is normally accepted more readily than change made when options are available." Is this statement valid? Why or why not?
3. Which types of adjustments are made most easily—the behavioral, the psychological, or the social?
4. Consider your own observations of change. Can you cite situations where change was handled adequately because individuals had successful previous experiences with change? Can you also recall instances where individuals have rejected change because of previous bad experiences?
5. "Changes should never be made unless there is a reasonable certainty that benefits will definitely result." Is this statement valid? Why or why not? What are the ethical considerations?
6. What problems exist with giving workers advance notice of impending changes?
7. "Preventive measures are always better than actions taken after problems develop." What is the meaning of this statement? Does it apply to the management of change?
8. Is it possible to forecast the effects of change? Please explain.
9. How is OD different from other forms of planned change?
10. How do training programs fit in with OD programs?
11. In your own words, state how OD and programs of training employees are different.
12. Please go back to the beginning of the chapter and answer the questions following the opening case.

Key Terms

behavioral adjustment	Organizational Development	social adaptation
change	planned change	tentative approach
change agent	psychological effect	unplanned change

Chapter Case

Making Something Happen at the School Board

Upon graduation, you take on what you quickly realize is the job challenge of a lifetime—you go to work for the City School Board of a large metropolitan area that is noted for problems with its school system. You are in a staff position. Officially, your title is Staff Analyst, Special Projects. You ask your boss what some of the special projects are expected to be.

"What you need to understand," your boss responds, "is that our staff is new and that we're in place to make some real changes. The mayor is really alarmed. You know, of course, that businesses in the city just lost a major contract for some work for the federal government. I'm sure that you've heard the 'official' position as well—that the low bid by Amalgamated Industries was the main reason. Well, the mayor's inside information is that the bid wasn't the main factor. The main factor is the state of education in this city. It's so bad that we aren't considered to have an educated workforce. The mayor, the governor, everybody, is determined that we must make an all-out effort to radically and totally revamp the entire public school system in this city to ensure that this never happens again. Your job will be to do the research that is needed to get things going."

You go home with a terrible headache and are worried that you're in way over your head—or anyone's head, for that matter. But the next morning you're feeling somewhat refreshed and decide to give it a try.

When you get to work the next day, the boss pulls you aside and says, "Now I've really got a tough assignment for you. I want you to try to persuade one of the district administrators to turn over control of one of his elementary schools to us so that we can run a study of a new experiential reading curriculum. You've got to do it—the guy won't even speak to me. The problem is that this particular administrator, John Harold, is strictly from the Stone Age. He's one year away from retirement and hasn't entertained a new idea in at least twenty years. Anyhow, give it a go. You're our last hope."

You aren't too optimistic, but you agree to try.

1. What can you, as a manager, do to get the new program accepted?
2. Suppose you determine that there's need to change the organization as a whole (a complete overhaul). How could OD be used in this situation? What steps would you take? Who should be involved?

Chapter 18

A Look Toward
the Future

Objectives

- To consider the challenges future managers will face.
- To identify the composition of the present and the future workforce.
- To anticipate what the organizations of the future will be in terms of structure and emphasis.
- To discern leadership trends and directions.
- To view patterns of movement in multinational activity.
- To consider the performance of management's role in multinational operations.
- To learn how to adjust to the cultural differences involved in multinational management.

I Need Advice!

Mary Staples is a young American visiting Austria for the first time. During her travels, she spends several days in Innsbruck, in Southwestern Austria, where she has distant relatives. Through her relatives, she meets Ulrich, a young banker from that area. Mary, too, works for a bank back in the United States, and their conversation quickly turns to their jobs.

It turns out that Ulrich is a manager in a large Austrian bank. The bank has grown rapidly over the past few years and currently has offices in every large Austrian city.

"Just for starters, that presents all sorts of problems," Ulrich laments. When asked why, he explains that beneath its serene appearance, Austria is a sharply divided country with a number of differing groups in its different regions.

"You know, of course, that the people in the Tyrol (a mountainous area in Western Austria) consider anyone else a foreigner," Ulrich explains. "But are you aware that the situation is at least as bad in the other regions? The Austrians of Italian origin who live in the Sudtyrol are forever trying to set up their own state. The lowlanders around Vienna look down on everyone else as a bunch of hicks. The people around Salzburg believe that they're the only cultured Austrians.

"I could go on and on, but it's a mess. As a result, a large bank that is national in scope meets with suspicion—and radically different local conditions—everywhere we operate. Worse yet, the government has all sorts of stringent regulations on banks, and those regulations often conflict with what the people in any particular area actually want. And speaking of regulations, there are also severe restrictions on what you can do in terms of personnel actions. The government makes it virtually impossible to fire anyone. And the labor unions! They're a major force all through Eastern Austria. The result is that we're paying steep wages in all of our regions, and in many locations, our payroll expenses are much higher than our local competition. Overall, we're under severe attack by local banks in over half of our areas. And the future! I shudder to think of the future!" Ulrich moans dramatically.

When Mary asks what the problem is with the future, Ulrich reminds her that Austria is poised on the brink of joining the European Economic Community (often referred to as the Common Market in the United States). Doing that, he explains, means that trade barriers will disappear entirely.

"People from other countries can come to Austria to work at will, and Austrians can go elsewhere. If we get French and Italians in—and I'm sure we will—labor unrest will go way up in Western Austria—the only place it's relatively calm now," he adds.

"But worse yet, think of the impact on prices, culture, competition, and who knows what else. Austria has traditionally used trade barriers to keep lower priced foreign competition out and to let Austrian-owned businesses flourish—and banks such as mine are no exception. Now we'll have a flood of competitors entering who can offer much more attractive prices and services than we can. I expect an enormous influx of foreigners and foreign business—and what will that do to our traditional Austrian cultures?"

"The immediate future really does sound pretty threatening," Mary remarks. "But is there any long-range hope?"

"Well," Ulrich responds, "the only thing I can see to do is to reorganize in some way to permit us to respond quickly to the pressures that I can see coming in the future. Furthermore, I'm convinced that the bank must assume an aggressive stance and face the competitors head on by going international. There's a lot of bank instability in both Southern France and Northern Italy, so I believe that there are opportunities in those places. In addition, the regime in Bulgaria has approached us as well, though I have no idea how we could set up anything with them. You Americans are creative thinkers," Ulrich concludes. "What should we do? Give me some advice."

Case Questions

1. Why does Ulrich feel that having to deal with several different cultural groups makes his job more complicated?
2. What problems with communication would you expect Ulrich to face?
3. What additional problems do you foresee for Ulrich?

We seldom pause to consider the future. We tend to be consumed by the present—what is taking place and what we need to do today. It can pay good dividends to consider the future and the steps we can take to prepare for it.

A decade ago, two books were published that reminded us we need to think about the future: *Megatrends* by John Naisbitt and *In Search of Excellence* by Thomas J. Peters and Robert H. Waterman, Jr. These books presented several strong points for us to consider. Naisbitt saw the impact of communication and computer technology as a significant influence in the workplace.

information float
The length of time it takes a message to move from the sender to the receiver.

He predicted that there would be a decrease in the **information float** that would require adjustments not only in communication patterns but also in organization structure. The information float, as Naisbitt described it, is the length of time required to get a message from a sender to a receiver. In addition to speeding up communication, computers make it possible for bosses to develop individually tailored arrangements with large numbers of employees.[1]

Megatrends described the movement to home computers with the many implications that go with it. We talked about some of these in Chapter 4. The cottage industry's rebirth is occuring as a result of this. Production sharing, a concept that has steadily developed, was also foreseen.

More and more companies, for example, make contributions separately toward a common product. One company provides the raw materials. Another company refines the raw materials. Another company provides the labor. Still another assembles the various parts, and yet another markets the product. A good illustration of this is the development of computer chips. The microprocessing of chips is done in the United States. The chips may be assembled in Singapore, further processed in India, and labeled in Japan. This example points up the importance of the development of global cooperation, discussed later in the chapter.

Characteristics of the Workforce of the Future

In Search of Excellence and *Megatrends* both saw the composition of the workforce itself as changing. More minorities, for example, were predicted to be visible in the workforce. As we saw in Chapter 16, more women and Hispanics in particular are projected for the workforce. In reality, there is another trend in the age composition of those who work. The main feature from an age perspective is the decrease of employees below the age of 25. As Chapter 16 showed, workers in the 25-to-44 age category make up at least 50 percent of the workforce. The challenge with regard to the shift in age groups lies in the different needs, experiences, and expectations of the workers.

In addition to the observations made in Chapter 16 about the inequities among age groups, Deutsch makes some important points. It is his position that age-related problems will be compounded in the future. Age-related issues will go far beyond simple explanations. In his very revealing article, Deutsch states that the structure of the workforce of the future will be made up of three very distinct generations of workers laboring side by side but who have very different sets of experiences and values.

Deutsch sees a struggle coming between three groups he has labeled as the **pre-World War II group** (born before 1945), the **post-World War II group** (born between 1945 and 1965), and the **entrants** (born between 1966 and 1975). In most situations today, the pre-War individuals born before the Depression make up the very top level positions on organizations' ladders; the post-War generation makes up the middle-management ranks; and the entrants, the most recent workers to enter the marketplace, occupy the lower rungs. Deutsch calls the post-War classification of people TV babies because he feels that they were brought up on television and were all fed the same information. TV babies grew up in an era where prosperity and economic expansion were key factors.

In contrast, most workers now entering the workforce (the computer babies) grew up in a declining economy, where family structures were changing toward single-parent households, stepfamilies, and fewer siblings. Since the computer babies were not all fed the same information, they are a less homogenous group than the TV babies.

As Table 18–1 shows, there are many differences in the values, expectations, and behavior patterns of the members of the different age groups. The differences can only spell challenge to future managers.

As seen by Deutsch, today's workforce has a significant amount of differentiation in what it wants and what it is willing to accept. Since the pre-World War II group makes up most of the upper management ranks, it is this group that is comfortable with the traditional top-down organizational structure. Loyalty to the organization is high. Routine 9-to-5 work schedules are seen as the rule, and overtime is accepted without a struggle. Patterns of consumption and information seeking are simplistic, with past experiences serving as a major determinant of behavior. Employees from this age group for the most part follow bosses without asking many questions or posing challenges. Top-down authority is accepted and demanded. Accomplishment is a motivational factor.

post-World War II group
That segment of the workforce born between 1945 and 1965. This group is also called the TV babies. Those in this age category are most likely to fill the ranks of middle management.

pre-World War II group
The part of today's workforce who were born before 1945 so that its members are now in their middle forties or older. The members of this group are most likely to have risen to the tops of organizations making up upper management.

entrants
That segment of the workforce born between 1966 and 1975. These individuals are just beginning to go to work or will be doing so in the next few years. Deutsch calls this group the computer babies.

Table 18–1

Key Characteristics of the Workforce for the Present and Future

	Age Group		
	Pre-WWII Babies (born before 1945)	*TV Babies (1945–1965)*	*Computer Babies (1966–1975)*
Goals to be achieved from work	Accomplish work because it is good for the organization and the country.	Have a meaningful experience from doing the job; personal growth.	Get job done so that personal leisure time can be used more satisfactorily.
Preferred work environment	Traditional structure with power hierarchy; can work up the ladder.	Quality circles and teams; under participatory management.	Autonomy; working alone with the least amount of supervision.
Work medium	Assembly line; human labor.	Mainframe computers.	Personal (desktop) computers.
Time values	9-to-5; overtime.	9-to-5; flexitime begins.	Flexitime, flexiplace.
Information and enculturation sources	Radio in living room; newsreels at movie theater.	Television news; rock and roll; transistor radios.	Walkman; VCRs; music videos.
Consumption	Brand-name buying; few choices available, few demanded.	More choices available.	More choices demanded.

Source: R. Eden Deutsch, "Tomorrow's Work Force," *The Futurist,* Volume 19, Number 6, December 1985, pp. 8–11. Used with permission.

flexitime
A technique for scheduling work that allows employees some freedom to choose the hours within which they will work.

flexiplace
A method for scheduling work that allows employees to choose if they wish to work at the organization's location, at home, or at some other site.

The TV baby group of the post-War generation, on the other hand, is seen in a very different light. As middle managers, these workers often have rejected traditional values and have demanded more from their jobs than accomplishing the goals of the organization. They seek intrinsic, through-the-job satisfaction. To be motivated, this group needs work that is meaningful. Personal growth is important. Participation in the process of making decisions is considered vital. It is to this group that quality circles and teamwork have the greatest appeal. While traditional work hours are not rejected, **flexitime** is welcomed wherever practical.

The most recent addition to the workforce—the computer baby generation born between 1966 and 1975—is seen by Deutsch to be much more self-oriented. These workers want autonomy in work and seek independence from supervision and team participation. Organizational goals are less important to this group, who view work as a means of earning money to provide for the basic necessities of life so that they can have more personal leisure time. Flexitime and **flexiplace** jobs (people can work at the office, at home, or elsewhere outside the organization's offices) are highly sought after. These workers question and often reject traditional authority. Restlessness is common within this group.

As can be seen, if these descriptions of the workforce of the present and near future are accurate, behavior patterns are likely to be varied. Those who manage will find it necessary to give a variety of direction and support. Leadership, motivation, control mechanisms, and other managerial duties will all need to consider the differences individuals bring to the workplace. Heterogeneity (being different) will become the rule rather than the exception. Managing behavior will become even more complicated and adaptive than it is now.[2]

Organizations of the Future

Dynamic Networks and Interorganizational Cooperation

Not only are the people who make up the workforce changing, but the organizations in which they work are being modified. It appears that manager-employee relationships will become more flexible and more complicated.

Instead of the familiar organization structure, where a single company engages in a number of performance functions to accomplish its goals, **dynamic networking** (interaction) will develop. There will be more joint ventures, subcontracting, and licensing across international borders, with new ventures spinning off from established companies. In other words, organizations will become more interdependent.

The dynamic network that is now taking shape will have several unique characteristics, including vertical disaggregation, brokers, market mechanisms, and full-disclosure information systems. Vertical disaggregation means that business functions such as product design and development, manufacturing, marketing, and distribution that have typically been performed in a single organization are being done more by independent organizations within a network. Each unit will perform its specialty contributing to the accomplishment of overall results. Environmental and competitive circumstances will determine the functions that need to be performed.[3]

Because each function will not necessarily be performed by a single organization, **brokers** (independent coordinators) will assemble the necessary groups so that cooperative goals can be achieved. Sometimes a single broker will play a lead role and will subcontract for the necessary services. In other cases, linkages between equal partners specializing in different services may be created by brokers. Coordination and cooperation will become more important and more difficult. Authority relationships will be more uncertain and will require greater flexibility.

Market mechanisms such as patterns of selling, advertising, and distribution will hold units together more than will planning and control. Contracts and payments for results will be used more than progress reports and traditional supervision.

There will be full-disclosure information systems, Miles and Snow predict. That is, broad-access, computerized information systems will become the substitutes for trust-building processes based upon experience that takes time to accomplish. The value of contributions will be predetermined by participants, who will then hook themselves together in a continuously updated information system so that contributions can be mutually and instantly verified.

dynamic networking
A method of structuring organizations whereby a broker coordinates the efforts of several separate organizations so that they complement each other's actions. Individual organizations specialize in their functions and contribute certain things toward the purposes of the unit that are thus bonded together.

broker
The person who assembles individual organizations so that they can accomplish cooperative goals.

Components making up the dynamic network will complement rather than compete with one another. Individual units can become more competent in what they do through specialization. Each component will be held in check by other components. More complex situations can be handled by networks than by a single organization.

This preview of future organizations is just one of several, but a common thread among all forecasts is the prediction of a more complicated climate in which work behavior will take place.

Structure, Power, and Authority in Future Organizations

Internal structure and power relationships are expected to change as well. Two predictions about structures of the future suggest that organizations will be flatter and middle management positions will be greatly reduced. Organizations are seen as flattening themselves to provide quicker, more competitive actions. Where there are a few levels of authority, decisions can be made quickly as communication becomes more streamlined. Fewer bottlenecks in the flow of message and authority exist in the flat structure.

The reduction of the number of managers in mid-level positions is in keeping with the flatness trend. Removal of these positions in the hierarchy provides for faster and easier communication. Reasons given by organizations that are shrinking mid-level positions are that the move reduces costs and makes the organization competitive. Other reasons given include the consideration that it is no longer necessary to have middle managers as links in the lines of authority. The ease and speed of electronic (and other forms of) communications have made it possible to have efficient exchange between upper and lower levels of personnel and to establish control mechanisms without the intervention of middle managers.[4]

In a related matter, Houston also sees power relationships and sources changing. "From chief executive to frontline supervisor, managers are finding themselves defrocked of the prerogative of power once conferred upon them as an inalienable right."[5] Power today is defined as the ability to achieve an intended mission. Instead of force and command, the words used to describe power today are collaboration, consensus, and cooperation. Power has changed from coercion to influence and persuasion. Power comes by being able to gain the confidence of people.

Why has the role and nature of power changed? There's a very logical explanation that fits right in with the contingency-situational messages of Chapter 10. People who are more educated, want responsibility, will accept delegation, and desire participation respond to involvement more than do the less educated who need guidance and prefer to have others make decisions for them.

A Leadership Trend

As discussed earlier, leadership in today's organizations is flexible and adaptive. To meet the dynamic structures and the variables in workers' experiences and expectations, it seems likely that leadership must continue to be of a contingency nature. Recent literature has also talked about the importance of the **transformational leader.** In many ways, the concept of the transformational leader is a throwback to the trait and behavior schools of the past.

The transformational leader displays a type of leadership that promotes change, innovation, and entrepreneurship. This type of leader will show up at the top of organizations more than at the middle and lower levels. As Table 18–2 shows, transformational leaders tend to identify themselves as change agents. They are courageous individuals who are not afraid to take a stand and stay with it. This leader has a set of values that are considered vital and basic. The transformational leader is a lifelong learner continuing to develop even after becoming well experienced. He or she has the ability to deal with complexity, ambiguity, and uncertainty. This leader is a visionary, able to shape future goals effectively.[6] We see in the transformational leader a person who knows where he or she is going, with the capacity to adjust and adapt leadership styles to fit the needs of the situation.

A look at Table 18–2 shows that being a transformational leader requires more dynamic traits and abilities than most individuals possess. It is the rare person who can live up to all of these attributes, but developing many of these skills and abilities may be crucial in the complex world of the future. This type of individual will indeed be an asset in tomorrow's workforce.

transformational leader
A recent categorization of leadership based upon bringing about change in organizations. These leaders are labeled as courageous, forceful, value-driven shapers of the destiny of the organizations of the future.

Table 18–2
Characteristics of Transformational Leaders

1. They identify themselves as change agents. That is, transformational leaders take on the role of seeing that transitions take place so that improvement can occur.
2. They are courageous individuals. Courage does not mean that they are stupid. They are prudent risk takers—individuals who can take a stand. Taking a stand may mean going against the status quo or telling the truth to people who may not want the truth. They can withstand ridicule and social pressure when needed.
3. They believe in people. They are not dictators. They are powerful, yet sensitive and ultimately work toward the empowerment of others. They have a keen understanding of motivation, emotion, pain, trust, and loyalty.
4. They are value driven. They are able to articulate a set of core values and to exhibit behavior congruent with their value positions.
5. They are lifelong learners. They can talk about mistakes they have made. Mistakes are viewed as learning experiences rather than failures. They have the ability to be self-reflective. They have self-renewal skills which they are able to impart to other people.
6. They have the ability to deal with complexity, ambiguity, and uncertainty. They can cope with and frame problems. This ability includes the capacity to build theories, articulate principles, and examine assumptions.
7. They are visionaries able to dream and to translate dreams and images so others can share them.

Source: Adapted from Noel Tichey and Mary Anne Devanna, "The Transformational Leader," *Training and Development Journal,* Volume 40, Number 7, July 1986, pp. 27–32.

A Managerial Challenge—The Multinational Movement

One trend everyone agrees upon is the increase in the global interaction of organizations and their employees. More and more firms are increasing their scope of activities to reach out to other nations. Many nations, such as Japan, are already a force within the United States. From a management perspective, the intertwining of cultures has major repercussions because every culture has different norms and expectations. If we do not take culture into consideration, leader-follower relations, productivity, and a number of additional elements will not function well.

Consider the culture of a nation and what it determines. A nation's culture defines the operating environment managers will face in establishing direction for their organizations. In the past, understanding other cultures wasn't a problem. Firms in the United States, for example, were managed by U.S. citizens. That may be less and less true in the future as citizens of other countries come to the United States as managers and as U.S. citizens find themselves relocated to other countries to manage firms there. Managing in an international setting means that the manager must become adept at responding to subtle points in a different culture. Culture, for example, establishes the work ethic employees bring with them to their jobs. This work ethic determines what employees expect from their jobs and what kind of effort they are willing to give. The culture establishes the level of respect employees have for the authority of their supervisors at work. The kind of authority they respect is also determined by the culture.

Cultural Values

multinational
Anything in which the cultures of more than one nation are involved.

individualism
A cultural value in which individuals show more concern for themselves and their immediate family than they show for groups and others outside their close circle.

collectivism
A cultural value in which individuals are strongly concerned for groups and other social units around them.

Managers must learn a number of things about the society and culture of the country or countries where they may work. A good starting place in the analysis of a particular country or region and its culture is to identify the value systems of the people in the area. A major researcher in **multinational** matters, Geert Hofstede, suggests that the cultural analysis should begin with a look at some specific dimensions (dimensions that have shown very different priorities between compared countries). These dimensions include attitudes of culture related to individualism-collectivism, power distance, uncertainty avoidance, and masculinity-femininity.[7]

The basic questions on the **individualism-collectivism** dimension are, Do the people define themselves as individuals or as members of a group? and Do people look after themselves and their family primarily, or do they concern themselves with groups and teams? Individualistic people are only loosely tied to other individuals. They care more about themselves and their immediate family and do not concern themselves much with others. Where the collectivism attitude prevails, individuals concern themselves strongly with the groups or social units to which they belong.

In his research, Hofstede determined that people from the United States, Australia, and Great Britain are very individualistic in their thinking, while people from Colombia, Venezuela, and Pakistan are very collectivistic in their thinking. People from other cultures seem to fall in between these two extremes on the individualism-collectivism scale. In our opening case, Ulrich, the Austrian manager, points out that he faces a special challenge as a result of the distinct cultures found in Austria. What differences would you expect to find in terms of individualism-collectivism between the "Italian-oriented" Austrians in the South and those in the rest of the country?

A second value explored—**power distance**—is defined as the extent to which less powerful members of an organization accept the unequal distribution of power, i.e., how much do employees accept the fact that their boss has more authority than they do? Employees who do what the boss says because he or she is considered to have superior authority would be high power-distance people. Hofstede concluded that the Philippines, Venezuela, and Mexico are among the high power-distance nations, while Austria, Israel, and Denmark are among the lowest in power distance. The United States rates toward the middle of the power-distance distribution. In our opening case, what differences would you expect to see in the power distance values between Mary and Ulrich?

A third value—**uncertainty avoidance**—describes how the people in a specific society react to ambiguous situations. Those who feel very threatened tend to establish formal rules, seek stability in their careers, and reject deviant ideas. Study results show Greece, Portugal, Japan, and Belgium to be nations where ambiguity is considered very threatening. Singapore, Hong Kong, and Denmark are the least concerned about avoidance of uncertainty. The United States tends to be somewhat low in concern for uncertain and ambiguous situations.

The fourth value—**masculinity-femininity**—describes masculinity as the emphasis in society on assertiveness and the acquisition of money and material things. Femininity is seen as the emphasis on relationships among people, concern for others, and concern for the overall quality of life. Japan, Australia, and Venezuela seem to be the most masculine in orientation, while Sweden, Norway, and Denmark rate highest in femininity. The United States was rated as somewhat more masculine than feminine.[8] Looking again at our case, should Ulrich expect the Southern (Italian) Austrians to be more masculine or more feminine than the others?

Many additional values need to be investigated. Each culture gives its own priority to things like the urgency of time or timeliness in getting things done (in such areas as making decisions and meeting deadlines). Each culture tends to concentrate on a time period (past, present, or future). Personal space (how much distance physically and psychologically indviduals in a culture prefer to keep between themselves and others) is another differentiating factor.[9] Other values include attitude toward material possessions, family roles and relationships, religious beliefs, and the degree to which personal achievement is desirable. Religious beliefs influence not only perceptions of what is right or wrong behavior but also decisions about diets and social activities and holidays.

Societal Procedures and Methods

Most cultures develop their own operational procedures or modes of operation that reflect their values. For example, each culture has its own negotiating

power distance
The degree to which nonpowerful individuals accept the unequal distribution of power around them—the acceptance of the fact that others have more authority than they have.

uncertainty avoidance
The degree to which members of a specific culture feel threatened by ambiguous situations. High uncertainty avoidance cultures are those that feel much stress when ambiguity develops.

masculinity
A cultural value that shows the degree to which people are assertive and interested in the acquisition of money and material things.

femininity
A cultural value that shows concern for relationships, the welfare of others, and the overall quality of life.

style (method for making decisions). Negotiating is one of the most important international activities in that multinational managers spend more than 50 percent of their time negotiating. Table 18–3 shows that cultures differ in how emotions are to be handled, whether decisions are to be made by individuals or groups, what the major decision criteria will be, and how much and what kind of documentation should occur.

As is shown in Table 18–3, the North American negotiating method includes straightforward, impersonal discussion; analysis on a cost/benefit basis; argumentation when differences of opinion are discovered; and careful documentation of available evidence.[10] In contrast, Japanese negotiating is highly sensitive, with strong loyalty shown for the employer. Face saving is important so that those involved will be spared embarrassment. Special interests are considered, and what is for the group good is the priority. Think again about our opening case. Ulrich believes that there may be some opportunities in Southern France, Northern Italy, and Bulgaria. What differences would you expect he will face when he begins to negotiate in those three areas?

When persuasion is needed, there are culturally based ways of doing it. The North American approach is to use facts and to appeal to the logic of the decision participants. Objectivity is important. Small concessions may be made early to help establish a working relationship. Pressure is applied to make timely decisions. Deadlines for reaching an agreement are highly important. By comparison, the persuasion style of Arabs appeals to emotions and uses subjective feelings. Concessions are made throughout bargaining, and concessions made by an opponent are usually reciprocated. Deadlines are not of major concern.[11] (See Table 18–4.)

Many additional procedures and behavioral patterns need to be learned as well. Managers in different cultures need to learn when to conduct business (during business hours? in the evenings? on holidays? on Sunday?). Should business relationships be formal or informal? (The American approach is to be informal, with first names being used quickly, while the French rarely use first names, even after long relationships.) Should eye contact be maintained or avoided? (The American procedure accepts eye contact as a sign of honesty, courage, and determination, while the Japanese consider eye contact to be impolite.) How should affirmation or agreement and acceptance be communicated? (In Malaya, a sharp, forward thrust of the head indicates agreement; in Ethiopia, it's a backward movement of the head; and in Borneo, a raised eyebrow says yes.)[12]

Discovering the value systems and codes of operational conduct can be a difficult task. The use of a questionnaire such as the one developed by Harris and Moran can be very helpful as a starting point. Their predeployment questionnaire has questions in over fiteen specific areas, including general considerations, political factors, geographic-demographic data, nonverbal communication, daily life patterns, religious beliefs, social structure (includes class levels, dress practices, etc.), educational matters, roles expected of men and women, business customs and values, food and drink habits, methods and attitudes about mass communication, the use of humor, and the way Americans are to be considered.[13] Get personal feedback from the sample questions from the Harris-Moran survey to see how prepared you are for a multinational job.

Japanese	*North American*	*Latin American*
Emotional sensitivity highly valued.	Emotional sensitivity not highly valued.	Emotional sensitivity valued.
Hiding of emotions.	Dealing straight-forwardly or impersonally.	Emotionally passionate.
Subtle power plays; conciliation.	Litigation; not as much conciliation.	Great power plays; use of weakness.
Loyalty to employer; employer taking care of employees.	Lack of commitment to employer; breaking of ties by either if necessary.	Loyalty to employer (who is often family).
Group decision making by consensus.	Teamwork provides input to a decision maker.	Decisions come down from one individual.
Face-saving crucial decisions often made; basis of saving someone from embarrassment.	Decisions made on a cost-benefit basis; face saving does not always matter.	Face saving crucial in decision making to preserve honor, dignity.
Decision makers openly influenced by special interests.	Decision makers influenced by special interest but often not considered ethical.	Execution of special interests of decision maker expected, condoned.
Not argumentative; quiet when right.	Argumentative when right or wrong, but impersonal.	Argumentative when right or wrong; passionate.
What is down in writing must be accurate, valid.	Great importance given to documentation as evidential proof.	Impatient with documentation, seen as obstacle to under-standing general principles.
Step-by-step approach to decision making.	Methodically organized decision making.	Impulsive, spontaneous decision making.
Good of group is the ultimate aim.	Profit motive or good of individual ultimate aim.	What is good for group is good for the individual.
Cultivate a good emotional social setting for decision making; get to know decision makers.	Decision making impersonal; avoid involvements, conflict of interest.	Personalism necessary for good decision making.

Table 18–3

Negotiation Styles from a Cross-cultural Perspective

Source: Pierre Casee, *Training for the Multicultural Manager: A Practical and Cross-Cultural Approach to the Management of People,* Washington, D.C.: Society for Intercultural Training and Research, 1982., SIETAR International, 733 15th St. N.W., Suite 900, Washington, D.C. 20005 U.S.A.

Table 18–4

National Styles
of Persuasion

	North Americans	*Arabs*	*Russians*
Primary Negotiating style and process	Factual: Appeals made to logic	Affective: Appeals made to emotions	Axiomatic: Appeals made to ideals
Conflict: Opponent's arguments countered with . . .	Objective facts	Subjective feelings	Asserted Ideals
Making concessions	Small concessions made early to establish a relationship	Concessions made throughout as a part of the bargaining process	Few, if any small concessions made
Response to opponent's concessions	Usually reciprocate opponent's concessions	Almost always reciprocate opponent's concessions	Opponent's concessions viewed as weakness and almost never reciprocated
Relationship	Short-term	Long-term	No continuing relationship
Authority	Broad	Broad	Limited
Initial position	Moderate	Extreme	Extreme
Deadline	Very important	Casual	Ignored

Source: E.S. Glenn, D. Witmeyer, and K.A. Stevenson, "Cultural Styles of Persuasion," *International Journal of Intercultural Relations,* Volume 1, 1984., Used by permission.

The complete Harris-Moran test has ninety-two questions; the questions in the Self-Test are only representative questions. By taking the test, you can begin to appreciate the importance of preparation before moving into a different cultural setting.[14] Speaking of preparation, in the opening case, Ulrich has obviously given some thought to the regional and multinational differences he'll be facing. At least he's aware that there ARE differences! But it's clear that he'll need to know much more to be successful. We would bet that answering the questions on the Harris-Moran test would be an invaluable aid to him.

Managing in the multinational area provides a good argument for the use of contingency-situational practices. American techniques and theories (things that work in the United States) frequently are inappropriate for use in other cultures.

Personal Feedback

Sample Questions from the Harris-Moran
Predeployment Area Questionnaire

Think of a nation other than your home nation [e.g. the United States] you think you know the most about. Now answer the questions from the Moran-Harris test to see if you are well prepared to go to that country to work. If you can't think of a country that you are familiar with, attempt to answer the questions about either of our neighbors—Canada or Mexico.

1. Who are the prominent contemporary people in this country—people such as politicians, poets, religious leaders, business/corporate leaders?
2. What are the names of the political parties and their beliefs, functions, and symbols?
3. What are the geographic divisions of the country? How is the country divided up?
4. Are there any nonverbal behavior patterns you see that may be interpreted as offensive in this country? If so, what are they?
5. What work practices are typical? How many days a week do people work? What days? What hours? Are business and social situations mixed?
6. Is there a state religion? Are other religions tolerated?
7. Do you know what the class divisions are? What are they?
8. How is discipline administered at school? At home? By whom?
9. Are female and male children equally desired?
10. Do bosses invite subordinates into their homes?
11. What rules govern dining at a restaurant? What determines who pays?
12. What are the mass media policies? Which media are most popular?
13. What medical facilities are available?
14. What kind of humor is understood and appreciated?
15. Presently, what is the relationship between this country and the U.S.?

How well did you do? How many questions did you not know the answer to? What do you need to learn?

Source: These are a few of the cultural evaluation questions put together by Philip R. Harris and Robert T. Moran in *Managing Cultural Differences,* Third edition, Houston: Gulf, 1991. From *Managing Cultural Differences,* Third Edition by Philip R. Harris and Robert T. Moran. Copyright 1991 by Gulf Publishing Company, Houston, Texas. Used with permission. All rights reserved.

International managers must decide to use autocratic or democratic styles of leadership, individual- or group-oriented motivational schemes, long-term or short-term criterion for decision making. Their decisions, to be most effective and most appropriate, must depend on the particular industry, organization, individual, and culture involved. Far from being useless, theoretical models guide the questions we ask. Only observation

Different cultures conduct business in different manners and settings.

and analysis of the particular culture and situation involved can guide our answers.[15]

Through observation, studying the experiences of others, and feedback from those who have worked previously in another culture, it is possible to develop a general set of behavioral guidelines. Wall, for example, in his study of Chinese cultural values and norms, suggests that the managers should do the following:

1. Know people in high places. Power and prestige are important factors in the Chinese culture.
2. Cultivate friendships. Try to get on good terms with coworkers and others. Feel free to call upon these friendships whenever something is needed. Don't be afraid to ask favors.
3. If someone requests more from you than you can give, simply say no. This statement will be respected.
4. Identify the chain of command in a China-based organization and climb the ladder to the top when needed. Authority is respected, and going over the heads of other people is acceptable.
5. If a request is turned down, ask again. Persistence indicates to those in the Chinese culture that something is important.
6. Bring communications from your own superiors to those with whom you are in contact. Representatives of higher powers are respected.
7. If negotiating for something with the Chinese, negotiate general rather than specific things. Establish general guidelines first.
8. Common interests are important. Try to establish these before moving to other issues.
9. Keep your own commitments general, too. Details can be worked out after an overall position is agreed upon.
10. Negotiate slowly. Commitments are serious; therefore, haste should be avoided.[16]

In the same way, Moffatt suggests that Americans working with Japanese companies should *not* do the following:

1.   Assume that all Japanese companies are alike.
2.   Expect to become a star. Instead, think consensus.
3.   Look for large numbers of pats on the back. External encouragement is infrequent.
4.   Think that pay will be based upon merit.
5.   Expect to rise to the top of Japanese organizations. The Japanese are not ready for foreigners to head their organizations.

On the other hand, Americans should:

6.   Be ready to deal with a certain level of vagueness.
7.   Be willing to work long hours.
8.   Expect slow progress in moving upward in an organization.
9.   Accept the Japanese process rather than fight it.
10. Expect many activities to be performed in groups and teams.[17]

Just as American workers must learn about the cultures they may be moving into, so must managers from other countries learn about American values and ways of doing things when they come to the United States. Getting the right fit between managers and workers from different cultures is sometimes difficult. Probably the largest number of owners and managers in the United States who are from other cultures are the Japanese. An increasing number of organizations are being founded or purchased by companies from Japan. Acceptance of some Japanese-originated ideas, such as quality circles, is being achieved, but there are many cultural differences. Take a look at the description in Management in Action of events at the Kotobuki Electronics Industries in Vancouver, Washington, as Atsushi Kageyama tells us what happened.

As an organization member of the future, you obviously need to keep your multicultural skills sharp.

Multinational Language and Communication

Think for a minute about all of the rules and decisions discussed in the earlier chapter on communication (Chapter 11). It's important to evaluate the needs of the receiver. It's helpful to select the right communication medium. On the other hand, there may be problems with filtering, distortion, timing, actions inconsistent with words, and the like. All of these problems and factors exist in multinational communication, and there are many additional items involved as well.

Even if the communication takes place in a common language such as English, the language is subject to cultural interpretation. In the short run, it may be possible to have an interpreter to help with the language as well as with cultural awareness and understanding. Interpreters could be inadequate in many ways, and they would be impractical in the long run. Knowing the rules, meanings, media, and symbols of the multicultural situation is invaluable.

Suppose you received the following message from one of your coworkers. Would you have problems understanding the message?

Management in Action

The Kotobuki Electronics Story

I (Atsushi Kageyama) was part of the Japanese team that established the Panasonic subsidiary Kotobuki Electronics Industries in Vancouver, Washington, in 1986. When we celebrated our first anniversary, I asked our American employees how they enjoyed working with us. For the most part, they were happy, but I was surprised by some of the criticisms they made:

—Japanese managers don't trust American workers and are too secretive.
—American managers (in this company) have many responsibilities but little decision-making authority.
—The Japanese do not give their employees clear job descriptions.
—Japanese managers are too negative; they criticize but never praise.

I hadn't realized until then that my American workers were experiencing cultural shock. Cultural shock in the work context can be a source of damaging misunderstandings and intolerable frustrations. It became clear to me that I had a formidable management challenge to communicate the reason for our Japanese ways to our American employees.

So that our American employees could better understand the Japanese management style an explanation is needed.

Do Japanese managers mistrust Americans and keep secrets from them? I don't think so. The problem lies more in the fact that, in American terms, the Japanese are simply poor communicators.

In Japanese culture silence is golden, and the real messages are often communicated nonverbally. Japanese speak with great reserve, and their messages are often communicated subtly. Japanese value a listener who uses his perceptiveness to understand the speaker's meaning. From a small bit of information—perhaps from a simple gesture or the speaker's tone of the voice—the Japanese listener gleans the whole meaning. The Japanese have learned from a very early age how to understand one another without direct verbal communication.

Americans understandably interpret this behavior as secretive; and they think that Japanese consciously withhold information because they don't trust them. I think the problem lies rather on the level of a misunderstanding because of different communication styles.

But perhaps Americans also feel mistrusted because they don't have the authority that the same level of responsibility of job title would give them in an American company. Again this has nothing to do with Japanese mistrust. Authority to make decisions is shared in Japanese companies in ways Americans are unused to. And whether a manager is American or Japanese, the authority he is

Dear Kim:

Because of the on-again/off-again haggling with one of our subcontractors, we have been putting off getting in touch with you. Frankly, we were turned off by their shoddy merchandise, the excuses they made up, and the way they put down some of our customers. Since we have our good name to keep up, we have decided to touch base with you and see if you would be interested in bidding on the contract for spare parts.

granted is more a function of time than of his job title. Authority is a reward for loyalty and a consistent demonstration of responsibility.

Before being promoted to manager, Japanese employees are assigned to different departments over the course of ten to fifteen years. During this time they work alongside many different people to give them the chance to develop extensive working relationships based on trust and respect. This is why job descriptions are not specific; a manager in a Japanese company is expected to be a generalist, an all-round player. At the end of this long process, a manager—whether Japanese or American—is granted a degree of authority because he has proven himself trustworthy.

But even when a manager earns this trust, he is rarely given the kind of individual authority that is common in American companies. Americans value an aggressive, quick, individualistic decision-making style. But for the Japanese it is more important to have consensus than to have a quick decision. Working relationships in Japanese companies are long-term, and loyalty, cooperation, and harmonious interpersonal relationships are very important. A participative management style has developed in Japan to induce better cooperation. This means less individual authority and a much longer decision-making process than Americans are used to. In this system the nail that sticks out tends to get hammered down.

Maybe some Americans who were used to standing out and who expected praise as a result were bewildered when no praise came. But it is important for Americans to understand that Japanese rarely praise others because they are uncomfortable when others praise them. Praise is confused with flattery, and flattery is a cause of mistrust.

Japanese children are raised in a way many Americans would find severe. After a wonderfully frivolous early childhood, they are exposed to rigid discipline as soon as they enter school. They are continuously indoctrinated to avoid shame and disgrace. They know they are expected to do well, and they do not expect to be praised unless their work is truly outstanding. Perhaps one could say that the Japanese are motivated more by fear of shame than by desire for praise, but there is also a profound desire to excel and to do a better job. For this reason the Japanese always look for a better way to do something. This is the motive for criticism—not to be negative, but to find a better way.

So there is an understandable truth at the root of each of the American criticisms. The Japanese do not communicate clearly. They do not give much individual authority. They make decisions slowly. They do not praise. But there are deep cultural reasons for the behaviors and policies—not an anti-American bias.

If you are interested in playing ball with us, please give it your best shot and fire off your choice price list ASAP.
Sincerely,

Pat

Since American English is a language you speak, you probably would have no trouble with it. But if you speak the English of the United Kingdom or

Table 18–5
Multi-phrase
Combinations and
Interpretations

Multi-phrase Combination	Meaning(s) or Interpretation
Die down	Diminish
Let down	Disappoint
Narrow down	Eliminate, reduce
Carry out	Complete, transport
Rule out	Eliminate
Fall through	Discontinue, cease
Pan out	Develop
Work out	Develop

Source: Rose Knotts, "If You Understand American English You Can Learn International English," *Proceedings,* Association of Business Communicators, 1990. Used by permission.

some other principality, you might not comprehend all of the important messages. If English is not your primary language, you might have even more problems with the proper interpretation. Several factors make American English unique for others to interpret. American English is difficult because it uses numerous multi-phrase combinations, slang expressions, acronyms, and idioms.[18]

multi-phrase combination
A communication term where there is the use of more than one word in a situation where one word could be sufficient.

Multi-phrase Combinations One of the most routine problems for the non-American is the usage of **multi-phrase combinations** of words that could, in most cases, be replaced by one word. Americans commonly use the phrase "put off" instead of "delay" or "keep up" instead of "maintain." (See Table 18–5.) The problem with these multi-phrase combinations lies both in their informality and in the difficulty of developing an accurate interpretation by the individual receiving the communication who isn't familiar with American English. While the international individual could locate all of the words in a dictionary, the sender's intended meaning might not be accurately interpreted. As a matter of fact, some Americans might by baffled by some of the commonly used multi-phrase terms.

slang
The jargon (terminology) of a particular class or society that is often unknown by outsiders.

Slang Every cultural and social group generates its own personalized vocabulary of **slang** words and phrases. Common and frequent usage of slang may cause people to become insensitive to its incorrectness. Though some slang words are "universally" accepted—such as O.K.—slang is inappropriate in international communication because of the strong probability that it will be misinterpreted. An amusing incident was related about a provincial businessman who ended his letter asking for an order: "The ball is now in your court." The Chinese vendor replied by ending his letter, "Sir, the ball is back on your knee!" It appeared that the Chinese gentleman understood roughly what the American meant but did not know the appropriate slang reply.

Common slang words and phrases are illustrated in Table 18–6.

Table 18–6

Illustration of Slang Words/Phrases and Interpretations

Slang Word/Phrase	Interpretation
Get a pink slip	Fired, terminated
Big time	Massive
Touch base with	Contact
Arena	Businessplace, marketplace
Play it by ear	Remain flexible
Play ball	Cooperate

Source: Rose Knotts, "If You Understand American English You Can Learn International English," *Proceedings,* Association of Business Communicators, 1990. Used by permission.

Acronyms   Numerous **acronyms** have also gained popularity in the business world and media over the past few years. While many Americans could quote the meaning of ASAP, LBO, PDQ, LCD, etc., these acronyms could be confusing in international communication. If an acronym is used, its meaning should be designated. Some common acronyms are shown in Table 18–7.

Idioms   An **idiom** is the usual way in which words of a language are joined to express understanding or an accepted phrase or expression having a meaning separate from the literal. For example, Americans use the phrase to "move up the organizational ladder" to mean career promotions in rank; they refer to a fashionably dressed but incompetent executive as an "empty suit." Usage of idioms with international employees may prove to be confusing and threatening. At best, these types of phrases should be avoided; at the least, they should be kept to a minimum. Table 18–8 outlines some common idioms used among various American cultures.

A more satisfactory version of the letter from Pat to Kim might read something like this:

Dear Kim:

Because of sporadic negotiations with one of our subcontractors, we delayed getting in contact with you. Finally we were discouraged by their defective merchandise, the excuses they fabricated, and the way

acronym

A series of letters used as an abbreviation for a sequence of words. For example, the acronym ASAP replaces the four words *as soon as possible.*

idioms

A sequence of words placed together to have a unique meaning different from the meanings the words have when used separately.

Table 18–7

Acronyms and Interpretations

Acronyms	Meanings
ASAP	As soon as possible
LBO	Leveraged buyout
MIS	Management information system
PDQ	Pretty darn quick
LCD	Light conducting diode

Source: Rose Knotts, "If You Understand American English You Can Learn International English," *Proceedings,* Association of Business Communicators, 1990. Used by permission.

Table 18–8

Idioms and
Interpretations

Idiom	Interpretation
Empty suit	Stylishly dressed but incompetent executive
Move up the corporate ladder	Career progression
Airhead; lightweight	Person possessing little substance
Raw meat	Devastated

Source: Rose Knotts, "If You Understand American English You Can Learn International English," *Proceedings,* Association of Business Communicators, 1990. Used by permission.

they humiliated some of our customers. Since we have our reputation to maintain, we have decided to contact you and see if you would be interested in bidding on the contract for spare parts.

If you are interested in negotiating with us, please send us your choice price list as soon as possible.
Sincerely,

Pat

The problems and challenges we've seen with multinational management are formidable, but in our mobile, dynamic world, global interaction appears to be the future. Most problems are not insurmountable, and dividends appear to be great.

Summary

Several trends about the future of organizations and the people in them are clarifying themselves. For one thing, the average age of the employee is slowly increasing. There are growing numbers of women in the workplace. Organizations themselves are changing. Dynamic networks are replacing separate units in many cases. Structure, authority, and power in traditional organizations are also changing. There is a trend to flatness and away from tall arrangements. Pressure is being applied in some situations to reduce the number of middle-level managers. Power is coming more from collaboration, consensus, and participation and less from force and command.

A new kind of leadership is emerging where leaders are not satisfied with the status quo but seek to take employees to new heights of performance and personal satisfaction. This type of leadership is not yet commonplace, but the concept seems to be catching on.

The single most talked about future concern probably is the multinational movement. More Americans are being assigned abroad, while more internationals are being sent to the United States. More organizations are exchanging business as well as people. The cultures of the countries involved are different, just as the cultures within the organizations are different. Different cultures mean different values. Different cultures have varying methods of operation. Languages and communication are different. All of these require different managerial actions and responses.

Personal Challenges and Opportunities

Now that you are armed with a good bit of knowledge and several skills, review your strengths and weaknesses and then decide what you need to change about yourself and which strengths you want to build up. Lay out a course of action for yourself. Consult with people you have confidence in if you're not sure how to go about retraining or redirecting yourself in areas that need improvement.

The workplace of the future will be a challenge—that's for sure. But it's a challenge you can meet. Find a way to keep up with, and how to manage the latest knowledge and research on behavior in organizations. Find professional groups in the field of work you choose. Subscribe to periodicals that present new ideas, new theories, and new applications. It might be helpful to review the periodicals used in the writing of this book (refer to the endnotes for each chapter) as a source of future ideas.

Do some career planning for yourself. Ask yourself questions such as Where have I been (what is my previous work history)? Where am I now (in terms of skills and knowledge)? Where do I want to go from here (what are my ambitions for this year, next year, five years from now, ten years away)? How can I get to where I want to go? What kinds of skills, experience, support, and opportunities will I need to achieve my ambitions?

Individuals from different cultural backgrounds may find working together to be interesting and challenging.

Then plan a course of action, including what training you plan to participate in, what transfers you need to make in terms of organizations, if any, and so forth. The more tangible you can be in formulating the plan, the easier you will find your actual completion of the plan. Look at any setbacks you experience along the way as learning experiences.

Remember that your actions as a leader, a subordinate, or a peer can make a difference in the behavior of others around you. Relating to other people has a ripple-in-the-pond effect. When you do something correctly and positively, you affect someone else favorably. They, in turn, touch other people constructively.

Your thoughts and actions do make a difference!

Questions to Consider

1. What is your assessment of the dynamic network of organizations? What are its strengths? Its weaknesses?
2. In what ways will managers probably find themselves treating pre-War, post-War, and entrants groups differently? What problems will be experienced in managing the groups?
3. Why does Deutsch use the term TV babies for the post-War generation? What are the effects of this?
4. Is the transformational leader concept really something new? Why or why not? Is the concept practical for use at all levels in the organization?
5. How are the goals of the age groupings different?
6. How similar are the codes of ethics in countries such as the United States, Japan, and Russia? Support your answer.
7. How would you treat people if they affirm themselves to be individualists? Collectivists?
8. How does the negotiating style used in a country affect the way the country's managers would handle conflict?
9. What advice would you give to a company just beginning multinational operations about managing employees in different countries?

Key Terms

acronym	idioms	power distance
broker	individualism	pre-World War II
collectivism	information float	group
dynamic	masculinity	slang
networking	multinational	transformational
entrants	multi-phrase	leader
femininity	combination	uncertainty
flexiplace	post-World War II	avoidance
flexitime	group	

Chapter Case

Case of the Wrong Mangoes

In due course, you find yourself out of school and holding a good "normal" job working for a firm that specializes in producing canned fruit. Your boss calls you in and announces that the firm has made a major decision—it will be moving immediately to set up a subsidiary in Jamaica to produce canned mangoes.

"It's a whole new concept," your boss explains. "Nobody else is canning mangoes, so we should make a fortune. Did you know that the Jamaicans grow over thirty varieties of mangoes?"

You didn't, and furthermore you don't even like mangoes, but you agree to go and help with the startup.

When you reach Jamaica, however, it's clear that all is not well. The firm is getting ready to start production—and the employees and the management team (consisting of a group of British, Austrian, and American managers from the firm's home location) are already at odds. You discover that while the top management team was regarded as excellent at home, none of the team has even been to Jamaica before.

"Shouldn't be a problem, though," remarks the British general manager. "After all, Jamaica was a colony of ours for years. They've inherited our laws and customs, and they even speak our language."

The last comment, you soon discover, is something of an overstatement. In fact, the Jamaicans speak a patois, a combination of French, Spanish, African, and English, the result of their slave heritage. They can understand "standard" English when it is spoken slowly and clearly but are also past masters at not understanding when it seems convenient.

As for the customs and manner of thinking of the people, you are somewhat at a loss. As best you can tell, their religion consists of a veneer of Christianity overlaying several forms of voodoo-like worship stemming from their African heritage. In addition, Rastafarianism has taken on an important role. It is a highly passive-seeming worship—the "Rastas" simply smoke the local "ganga" all day and await the second coming of Christ, who is to be incarnated in the form of an emperor of Ethiopia.

A similarly passive approach appears in many aspects of Jamaican life, but you can't tell whether the seeming passivity is real or whether it disguises a deep-felt resentment of the British—and, by extension, of all whites—for the many years of exploitation and prejudice you sense the Jamaicans feel they have endured. Certainly, this combination of passivity and resentment is exemplified by the government, under Michael Manly. Manly appears to be highly socialistic and emphasizes "taking care" of the people from cradle to grave, but he is also strongly anti-Western and uses anti-Western slogans as a way of uniting the people against a common enemy.

Things reach a crisis when the first canning operation is an utter failure. The mangoes taste all right (though you still don't like mangoes), but the texture is terrible—a ghastly, stringy, and soupy mixture. You are present when the general manager holds a "fact-finding" meeting. The few Jamaicans who are present say nothing. Finally, under tense questioning, one of them offers, "Well, saar (this is how they refer to anyone perceived as a "boss"), the problem is the mangoes, you know."

"What on earth do you mean?" bellows the general manager. "They were plenty fresh and ripe, because we checked carefully."

"Of course, saar," replies the subordinate, "but they were the wrong kind, you know. Those were sucking mangoes, not chewing mangoes. The chewing ones are the only kind you can eat."

"Insubordination!" responds the general manager.

"What now," you wonder.

1. There's clearly a communication problem in the Jamaican operation. What factors are contributing to the lack of communication between the Jamaicans and the management team? What should be done?
2. Perhaps differences in values are creating problems. How would you guess that the Jamaicans would rate on the values that Hofstede talks about? What about the British general manager?
3. The British general manager believes that the Jamaican subordinate is "insubordinate." Is this true? Why does the manager believe it? Explain in terms of the attribution process and communication.

Endnotes

Chapter One

1. Rosabeth Moss Kanter, "The New Managerial World," *Harvard Business Review,* Volume 89, Number 6, November–December 1989, pp. 85–92.
2. Bruce D. Fisher, "Positive Law As the Ethic of Our Time," *Business Horizons,* Volume 33, Number 5, September–October 1990, pp. 28–39.
3. Reprinted from "Creating Ethical Corporate Structures," by Patrick E. Murphy, *Sloan Management Review,* Volume 30, Number 2, Winter 1989, pp. 81–87, by permission of publisher. Copyright 1989 by the Sloan Management Review Association. All rights reserved.
4. Donald Robin, Michael Giallourakis, Fred R. David, and Thomas E. Moritz, "A Different Look at Codes of Ethics," *Business Horizons,* January–February 1989, Table 1, p. 68. Reprinted from *Business Horizons,* January–February 1989. Copyright 1989 by the Foundation for the School of Business at Indiana University. Used with permission.
5. Amanda Bennett, "Ethics Codes Spread Despite Skepticism," *Wall Street Journal,* July 15, 1988.
6. Kenneth R. Andrews, "Ethics in Practice," *Harvard Business Review,* Volume 89, Number 5, September–October 1989, pp. 99–104.
7. Justin G. Longenecker, Joseph A. McKinney, and Carlos W. Moore, "The Generation Gap in Business Ethics," *Business Horizons,* Volume 32, Number 5, September–October 1989, pp. 9–14.
8. Justin G. Longenecker, Joseph A. McKinney, and Carlos W. Moore, "Do Smaller Firms Have Higher Codes of Ethics?" *Business and Society Review,* Number 71, Fall 1989, pp. 19–21.
9. Kenneth H. Blanchard and Norman V. Peale, in their book entitled *The Power of Ethical Management,* New York: William Morrow and Company, 1988, provide some additional ethical guidelines.
10. Andrews, 1989.
11. Richard E. Wokutch, "Corporate Social Responsibility Japanese Style," *Academy of Management Executive,* Volume 4, Number 2, May 1990, pp. 56–74.
12. Wokutch, 1990.
13. Archie B. Carroll, *Social Responsibility of Management,* Chicago: Science Research Associates, 1984.

Chapter Two

1. Ralph H. Kilmann, "Corporate Cultures: Managing the Intangible Style of Corporate Life May Be the Key to Avoiding Stagnation," *Psychology Today,* April 1985, pp. 62–68.
2. Stephen P. Robbins, *Essentials of Organizational Behavior,* Second Edition, Englewood Cliffs, N.J.: Prentice-Hall, 1988, pp. 205–220. Cass Bettinger, "Use Cor-

porate Culture to Trigger Performance," *Journal of Business Strategy,* Volume 10, Number 2, March/April 1989, pp. 38–42.

3. See Rensis Likert, *The Human Organization,* New York: McGraw-Hill, 1967, Ralph H. Kilmann, 1985, and Stephen P. Robbins, 1988, for a more detailed discussion of idealistic norms and positions for an organization's culture.

4. Ralph H. Kilmann, 1985, pp. 65–66.

5. Yoash Weiner, "Forms of Value Systems: A Focus on Organizational Effectiveness and Cultural Change and Maintenances," *Academy of Management Review,* Volume 13, Number 4, October 1988, pp. 534–545.

6. Joe G. Thomas and Ricky Griffin, "The Power of Social Information in the Workplace," *Organizational Dynamics,* Volume 18, Number 2, Autumn 1989, pp. 63–74.

7. See Fred E. Katz, "Explaining Informal Work Groups in Complex Organizations: The Case for Autonomy in Structure," *Administrative Science Quarterly,* Volume 10, Number 2, September 1965, pp. 204–233, for a more complete discussion of the difference between formal and informal organizations.

8. Carroll E. Izard, "Personality Similarity and Friendship," *Journal of Abnormal Psychology,* Volume 61, Number 1, July 1960, pp. 50–51.

9. S. A. Stouffer et. al., *The American Soldier: Combat and Its Aftermath,* Princeton, N.J.: Princeton University Press, 1949.

10. See Donald F. Roy, "Banana Time, Job Satisfaction and Information Interaction," *Human Organization,* Volume 18, Number 4, Winter 1960, pp. 158–168, for a good article revealing goals and activities of informal organizations.

11. See H. K. Baker, "Tapping into the Power of the Informal Groups," *Supervisory Management,* Volume 25, Number 10, October 1980, pp. 41–43, for additional ideas and explanations.

12. John A. Pearce III, and Fred R. David, "A Social Network Approach to Organizational Design–Performance," *Academy of Management Review,* Volume 8, Number 3, July 1983, pp. 436–444.

13. See John P. Wanous and Arnon E. Reichers, "Organizational Socialization and Group Development: Toward an Integrative Perspective," *Academy of Management Review,* Volume 9, Number 4, December 1984, pp. 670–683, for further discussion.

14. Daniel C. Feldman, "The Development and Enforcement of Group Norms," *Academy of Management Review,* Volume 9, Number 1, January 1984, pp. 47–53.

15. Lyman C. Porter, Edward E. Lawler, and J. R. Hackman, *Behavior in Organizations,* New York: McGraw-Hill, 1975, pp. 392–393.

16. Orlando Behling and Chester Schriesheim, *Organizational Behavior,* Boston: Allyn and Bacon, 1976, pp. 157–158.

17. Behling and Schriesheim, 1976.

18. Bernice M. Lott, "Group Cohesiveness: A Learning Phenomenon," *Journal of Social Psychology,* Volume 55, Second Half, December 1961.

19. Marvin E. Shaw, *Group Dynamics,* New York: McGraw-Hill, 1971.

20. Keith Davis, "Management Communication and the Grapevine," *Harvard Business Review,* Volume 31, Number 5, September–October 1953, p. 45, and "The Care and Cultivation of the Corporate Grapevine," *Dun's Review,* Volume 102, July 1973, pp. 44–47.

21. Davis, 1953, p. 16.

Chapter Three

1. "The Lure of Team Production," *Business Week,* August 24, 1987, pp. 54–55.

2. John Rohbaugh, "Improving the Quality of Group Judgement: Social Judgement Analysis and the Nominal Group Technique," *Organizational Behavior and Human Performance,* Volume 28, Number 2, October 1981, pp. 272–288.

3. Andrew H. Van de Ven and Andre L. Delbecq, "The Effectiveness of Nominal, Delphi, and Interacting Group Decision Making Process," *Academy of Management Journal,* Volume 17, Number 4, December 1974, pp. 605–620, deals with some specific group decision techniques in arriving at this conclusion.

4. Frank V. Cespedes, Stephen X. Doyle, and Robert J. Freedman, "Teamwork for Today's Selling," *Harvard Business Review,* Volume 67, Number 2, January–February 1989, pp. 44–55.

5. Kevin M. Paulsen, "Gain Sharing: A Group Motivator," *Managment World,* Volume 18, Number 3, May–June 1989, pp. 24–25.

6. Charles E. Miller, Patricia Jackson, Jonathan Mueller, and Cynthia Schersching, "Some Social Psychological Effects of Group Decisions," *Journal of Personality and Social Psychology,* Volume 52, Number 2, February 1987, pp. 325–332.

7. Irving L. Janis, *Groupthink,* 2nd Edition. Copyright © 1982 by Houghton Mifflin Company. Used with permission.

8. Glen Whyte, "Groupthink Revisited," *Academy of Management Review,* Volume 14, Number 1, January 1989, pp. 40–56.

9. James P. Gustafson, Lowell Garner, Nancy Lathrop, Karen Ringler, Fredric A. Seldin, and Marcia K. Wright, "Cooperative and Clashing Interests in Some Groups, Part I," *Human Relations,* Volume 34, Number 4, April 1981, pp. 315–338.

10. David R. Hampton, Charles E. Summer, and Ross A. Webber, *Organizational Behavior and the Practice of Management,* revised edition, Glenwood, Ill: Scott Foresman, 1973, p. 285.

11. Edwin M. Bridges, Wayne F. Doyle, and David F. Mahan, "Effects of Hierarchical Differentiation on Group Productivity," *Administration Science Quarterly,* Volume 13, Number 2, September 1968, pp. 305–319.

12. Philip Slater, "Contrasting Correlates of Group Size," *Sociometry,* Volume 21, Number 2, June 1958, pp. 129–139.

13. Robert M. Bray, Norbert L. Kerr, and Robert S. Atkin, "Effects of Group Size, Problem Difficulty, and Sex on Group Performance and Member Relations," *Journal of Personality and Social Psychology,* Volume 36, Number 11, November 1978, pp. 1224–1240.

14. Robert F. Bales, Fred L. Strodbeck, Theodore M. Mills, and Mary E. Roseborough, "Channels of Communication in Small Groups," *American Sociological Review,* Volume 16, Number 4, August 1951, pp. 461–469.

15. Steven E. Markham, Fred Dansereau, Jr., and Joseph A. Alutto, "Group Size and Absenteeism Rates: A Longitudinal Analysis," *Academy of Management Journal,* Volume 25, Number 4, December 1982, pp. 921–927.

16. See Kenneth R. Hammond, John Rohrbaugh, J. Manpower, and L. Adelman, "Social Judgment Theory: Applications in Policy Formulation," in *Human Judgment and Decision Processes in Applied Settings,* M. K. Kaplan and S. Schwartz (Eds.), New York: Academic Press, 1977; and K. R. Hammond, T. R. Steward, T. R. Brehmer, and D. Steinmann, *Social Judgment Theory, Human Judgment and Decision Process: Formal and Mathematical Approaches,* M. K. Kaplan and S. Schwartz (Eds.), New York: Academic Press, 1975, for more detailed discussion of social judgment analysis.

17. See Andre L. Delbecq, Andrew H. Van de Ven, and David H. Gustafson, *Group Techniques for Program Planning,* Glenwood, Ill.: Scott, Foresman, 1975; or Van de Ven and Delbecq, 1974, for more details on NGT.

18. Norman C. Dalkey, *Experiment in Group Production,* Santa Monica, Calif.: Rand Corporation, 1968; and Norman C. Dalkey, *The Delphi Technique: An Experimental Study of Group Opinion,* Santa Monica, Calif.: Rand Corporation, 1969.

19. Van de Ven and Delbecq, 1974, p. 620.

20. Ed Yager, "Quality Circles: A Tool for the 80's," *Training and Development Journal,* Volume 34, Number 8, August 1980, pp. 60–62.
21. Robert E. Cole, *Work, Mobility, and Anticipation,* Berkeley: Univeristy of California Press, 1979, p. 138.
22. George Munchus III, "Employer-Employee Based Quality Circles in Japan: Human Resource Policy Implementation for American Firms," *Academy of Management Review,* Volume 8, Number 2, April 1983, pp. 255–261.
23. Cole, 1979, p. 138.
24. Stephen C. Harper, "Now That the Dust Has Settled: Learning from Japanese Management," *Business Horizons,* Volume 31, Number 4, July–August 1988, evaluates Japanese style management, which has brought to the United States a whole package of organizational concepts, including quality circles. Harper concludes that the emphasis on group effort may not be well-suited for many American organizations. He even points out that many Japanese organizations do not subscribe completely to what we call Japanese style management.
25. Edgar F. Huse, *Organizational Development and Change,* 2nd edition, St. Paul: West, 1980, p. 343.
26. William G. Dyer, *Team Building, Issues and Alternatives,* Reading, Mass.: Addison-Wesley, 1977, 41–50.
27. Huse, 1980, pp. 101-126.

Chapter Four

1. William Taylor, "The Business of Innovation: An Interview with Paul Cook," *Harvard Business Review,* Volume 68, Number 2, March–April 1990, pp. 97–106.
2. Y. Sankar, "Organizational Culture and New Technology," *Journal of Systems Management,* Volume 39, Number 4, April 1988, pp. 10–18.
3. Paul Adler and Ferdows Kasra, "The Chief Technology Officer," *California Management Review,* Volume 22, Number 3, Spring 1990, pp. 35–62.
4. Adler and Kasra, 1990.
5. Joel E. Goldhar and Mariann Jelinek, "Plan for Economies of Scope," *Harvard Business Review,* Volume 61, Number 6, November–December 1983, pp. 141–153.
6. Hamid Noori, *Managing the Dynamics of New Technology,* Englewood Cliffs, N. J.: Prentice Hall, 1990.
7. Jack R. Meredith, "The Strategic Advantages of the Factory of the Future," *California Management Review,* Volume 29, Number 3, Spring 1987, 27–41.
8. Clark Holloway and Herbert H. Hand, "Who's Running the Store Anyway? Artificial Intelligence!!!," *Business Horizons,* Volume 31, Number 2, March–April 1988, Figure 2, p. 71. Reprinted from *Business Horizons,* March–April 1988. Copyright 1988 by the Foundation for the School of Business at Indiana University. Used with permission.
9. Holloway and Hand, 1988.
10. Holloway and Hand, 1988.
11. Michael G. Ashmore, "Applying Expert Systems to Business Strategy," *The Journal of Business Strategy,* Volume 10, Number 5, September–October 1989, pp. 46–49. Reprinted from *Journal of Business Strategy* (New York: Warren, Gorham & Lamont) © 1989. Warren, Gorham & Lamont Inc. Used with permission.
12. Ashmore, 1989.
13. Julie Solomon, "As Electronic Mail Loosens Inhibitions, Impetuous Senders Feel Anything Goes," *Wall Street Journal,* October 12, 1990, p. B1.
14. Laurence Hooper, "Future Shock," *Wall Street Journal,* June 4, 1990, pp. R19 and R22.
15. Richard C. Huseman and Edward W. Miles, "Organizational Communication— The Information Age: Implications of Computer-Based Systems," *Journal of Management,* Volume 14, Number 2, June 1988, pp. 181–204.

16. Stephen Kreider Yoder, "Putting It All Together," *Wall Street Journal,* June 4, 1990, p. 24.
17. Cynthia Crossen, "Workplace—Where We'll Be—At Home," *Wall Street Journal,* June 4, 1990, pp. R6–R8, R10.
18. William H. Bulkeley, "Gearing Up," *Wall Street Journal,* June 4, 1990, p. R12.
19. Cathy Trost, "Where We'll Be: Close To You," *Wall Street Journal,* March 4, 1990, pp. R14 and R15.
20. Willis J. Goldsmith, "Workplace Ergonomics: A Safety and Health Issue of the 90's," *Employee Relations Labor Journal,* Volume 15, Number 2, Autumn 1989, p. 291; and Linda B. Samuels, Ella P. Gardner, and Susan C. Fouts, "Video Display Terminals: Health Problems Raise Possibility of New Regulation," *Business and Society,* Number 73, Spring 1989, pp. 23–31.
21. Goldsmith, (1989, p. 293).
22. Robert H. Sand, "Employer Obligations with Respect to Video Display Terminals, Bad Backs, and Smoking in the Workplace," *Employee Labor Relations Journal,* Volume 14, Number 3, Winter 1989, pp. 459–466.
23. Willis J. Goldsmith, "Forecast of the 90's: Increased Workplace Regulation by OSHA and EPA," *Employee Labor Relations Journal,* Volume 15, Number 4, Spring 1990, pp. 595–605.

Chapter Five

1. Franklin D. Becker, *Workspace: Creating Environments in Organizations,* New York: Praeger Publishers, 1981.
2. Stephen Rosen, *Weathering: How the Atmosphere Conditions Your Body, Your Mind, Your Moods, and Your Health,* New York: M. Evans, 1979; and "How Weather Can Fool Your Mood," *U.S. News and World Report,* July 2, 1979, pp. 37–40.
3. C. R. Bell amd A. J. Watts, "Thermal Limits for Industrial Workers," *British Journal of Industrial Medicine,* Volume 28, Number 3, July 1971, pp. 259–264.
4. M. P. Wyon, "The Effects of Moderate Heat Stress on Typewriting Performances," *Ergonomics,* Volume 17, Number 3, May 1974, pp. 309–318.
5. John M. Lockhart, Harold O. Kiess, and Thomas J. Clegg, "Effects of Rate and Level of Lowered Finger Surface Temperature on Manual Performance," *Journal of Applied Psychology,* Volume 67, Number 1, February 1982, pp. 97–102.
6. Stephen C. Vickroy, James B. Shaw, and Cynthia D. Fisher, "Effects of Temperature, Clothing, and Task Complexity on Task Performance and Satisfaction," *Journal of Applied Psychology,* Volume 67, Number 1, February 1982, pp. 97–102.
7. James Rotton, "Angry, Sad, Happy? Blame the Weather," *U.S. News and World Report,* Volume 95, Number 5, August 1983, pp. 52–53.
8. Rotton, 1983.
9. Alexander Schauss, as quoted from Leslie Kane, "The Power of Color," *Health,* Volume 14, Number 7, July 1982, pp. 36–37.
10. Kane, 1982.
11. Abraham Maslow and Norbert L. Mintz, "Effects of Aesthetic Surroundings: I. Initial Effects of Three Aesthetic Conditions upon Perceiving 'Energy' and 'Well-Being' in Faces," *Journal of Psychology,* Volume 41, Second Half, April 1956, pp. 247–254.
12. Norbert L. Mintz, "Effects of Aesthetic Surroundings: II. Prolonged and Repeated Experience in a 'Beautiful' and an 'Ugly' Room," *Journal of Psychology,* Volume 41, Second Half, April 1956, pp. 459–466.
13. Becker, 1981, p. 117.
14. "Lighting and Colors," *Industrial Management,* Volume 21, Number 9, September 1979, pp. 21–24.
15. Mary C. Finnegan and Linda Z. Solomon, "Work Attitudes in Windowed Versus Nonwindowed Environments," *Journal of Social Psychology,* Volume 15, Second Half, December 1981, pp. 291–292.

16. James Trunzo, "Office Computers Create Glaring Problems," *Wall Street Journal,* October 5, 1987, p. 18.

17. Joachim Wohlwill, Jack L. Nasar, David D. DeJoy, and Hossein H. Foruzani, "Behavioral Effects of a Noisy Environment: Task Involvement Versus Passive Exposure," *Journal of Applied Psychology,* Volume 61, Number 1, January 1976, pp. 67–74.

18. D. C. Glass and Jerome E. Singer, *Urban Stress: Experiments on Noise and Social Stressors,* New York: Academic Press, 1972.

19. See Sheldon Cohen, "Sound Effects on Behavior," *Psychology Today,* Volume 15, Number 5, October 1981, pp. 38, 41–49, for a complete discussion of studies about noise and its effects.

20. Cohen, 1981.

21. Tim R. V. Davis, "The Influence of the Physical Environment in Offices," *Academy of Management Review,* Volume 9, Number 2, April 1984, pp. 271–273.

22. Greg Oldham and Dan Brass, "Employee Reaction to an Open-Plan Office: A Naturally Occurring Quasi-Experiment," *Administrative Science Quarterly,* Volume 24, Number 2, June 1979, pp. 267–284.

23. Y. Clearwater, "A Comparison of Open and Closed Office Design on Job Satisfaction and Productivity." Unpublished dissertation, University of California, Davis, 1980.

24. Fritz Steele, "The Ecology of Executive Teams: A New View of the Top," *Organizational Dynamics,* Volume 11, Number 4, Spring 1983, pp. 65–78.

25. Robert Sommer, *Personal Space: The Behavioral Basis of Design,* Englewood Cliffs, N.J.: Prentice-Hall, 1969.

26. Becker, 1981, p. 48.

27. Becker, 1981.

28. Becker, 1981.

29. Jerald G. Bachman and Lloyd D. Johnston, "Drug Use," *ISR Newsletter,* Volume 15, Numbers 2 and 3, Fall–Winter 1987–88, pp. 3, 6.

30. ASH Special Report, *The Economics of Employee Smoking,* undated, 4 pp.

31. From the study done by William L. Weis, "Can You Afford to Hire Smokers?" *Personnel Administrator,* Volume 27, Number 4, May 1981, as reported in Elizabeth M. Crocker, "Controlling Smoking in the Workplace," *Labor Law Journal,* Volume 38, Number 12, December 1987, pp. 739–746.

32. Glenwood Regional Medical Center, *Smoking Cessation Programs in the Workplace,* undated working paper, 2 pp.

33. Richard H. Deane, "Smoking in the Workplace—A Growing Dilemma," *Business,* Volume 37, Number 4, November–December 1987, pp. 30–34.

34. "Smoking Is Costly for Employers as Well as Employees," *Employee Health and Fitness,* Volume 9, Number 6, August 1987, pp. 85–96.

35. William M. Timmons, "Smoking Versus Nonsmoking at Work," *Public Personnel Management,* Volume 16, Number 3, Fall 1987, pp. 221–231.

Chapter Six

1. Stanley Coopersmith, *The Antecedents of Self-Esteem,* San Francisco: Freeman, 1967.

2. Kevin W. Mossholder, Arthur G. Bedian, and Achilles A. Armenakis, "Group Process-Work Outcome Relationships: A Note on the Moderating Impact of Self-Esteem," *Academy of Management Journal,* Volume 25, Number 3, September 1982, pp. 575–585.

3. Jonathan D. Quick, "Successful Executives: How Independent?" *Academy of Management Executive,* Volume 1, Number 2, May 1987, pp. 139–145.

4. Arthur W. Combs and Donald Snygg, *Individual Behaviors: A Perceptual Approach to Behavior,* revised edition, New York: Harper and Brothers, 1959, pp. 240 ff.

5. Combs and Snygg, pp. 243–257.

6. Eric Berne, *Games People Play,* New York: Grove Press, 1964.

7. Excerpts from *I'm OK—You're OK* by Thomas A. Harris. Copyright © 1967, 1968, 1969 by Thomas A. Harris. Reprinted by permission of HarperCollins Publishers.

8. See Phyllis Tharehou, "Employee Self-Esteem: A Review of the Literature," *Journal of Vocational Behavior,* December 1979, Volume 15, Number 3, pp. 316–346 for further ideas.

9. Anat Rafaeli, "When Clerks Meet Customers: A Test of Variables Related to Emotional Expressions on the Job," *Journal of Applied Psychology,* Volume 74, Number 3, June 1989, pp. 385–394.

10. Marilyn E. Gist, "Self Efficacy: Implications for Organizational Behavior and Human Resource Management," *Academy of Management Review,* Volume 12, Number 3, July 1987, pp. 472–485.

11. J. B. Rotter, "Generalized Expectancies for Internal Versus External Control of Reinforcement," *Psychological Monographs,* Volume 80, Number 1, 1966, pp. 1–28.

12. See Terence R. Mitchell, Charles M. Smyser, and Stan E. Weed, "Locus of Control: Supervision and Work Satisfaction," *Academy of Management Journal,* Volume 18, Number 3, September 1975, for some ideas about the effects of locus of control on behavior. See also M. W. Pryer and M. K. Distefano, "Perceptions of Leadership Behavior, Job Satisfaction, and Internal-External Control Across Three Nursing Levels," *Nursing Research,* Volume 20, Number 6, November–December 1971, pp. 534–537; and L. A. Broedling, "Relationship of Internal-External Control to Work Motivation and Performance in an Expectancy Model, *Journal of Applied Psychology,* Volume 60, Number 1, February 1975, pp. 65–70.

Chapter Seven

1. Jeremiah J. Sullivan, "Human Nature, Organizations, and Management Theory," *Academy of Management Review,* Volume II, Number 3, July 1986, pp. 534–549.

2. Henry A. Murray, *Explorations in Personality,* New York: Oxford University Press, 1938.

3. See Abraham H. Maslow, "A Theory of Human Motivation," *Psychological Review,* Volume 50, Number 1, January 1943, pp. 370–396; and Abraham H. Maslow, *Toward a Psychology of Being,* Princeton, N.J.: Van Nostrand, 1962, for more information about the Maslow approach.

4. Clayton P. Alderfer, *Existence, Relatedness, and Growth: Human Needs in Organizational Settings,* New York: Free Press, 1972.

5. Frederick Herzberg, "Workers' Needs: The Same Around the World," *Industry Week,* September 21, 1987, pp. 29–31.

6. Earl Ubell, "Is Your Job Killing You?" *Parade,* January 8, 1989, quotes J. Paul Leigh, "Job Related Deaths in 347 Occupations," a study done at San Jose State University.

7. O. Jeff Harris, "The Expectations of Young College Graduates—Is Expectancy Motivational Theory Relevant to Them?" In *Managment Perspectives on Organizational Effectiveness,* Dennis F. Ray and Thad B. Green (Eds.), Southern Management Association, 1975, pp. 88–90.

8. Elizabeth G. French, "Effects of the Interaction of Motivation and Feedback on Task Performance." In J. W. Atkinson (Ed.), *Motives in Fantasy, Actions, and Society,* Princeton. N.J.: Van Nostrand, 1958.

9. John R. P. French and Bertram Raven, "The Bases of Social Power." In Donovan Cartwright (Ed.), *Studies in Social Power,* Ann Arbor, Mich.: Institute for Social Research, 1959.

10. David C. McClelland, "The Business Drive and National Achievement," *Harvard Business Review,* Volume 40, Number 4, July–August 1962, p. 104.

11. Robert N. Beck, "Visions, Values, and Strategies: Changing Attitudes and Culture," *Academy of Management Executive,* Volume 1, Number 1, February 1987, pp. 33–41, includes a discussion of some of the effects of willingness to take risks.

12. Ron Zemke, "What Are High-Achieving Managers Really Like?" *Training and Human Resource Development,* Volume 76, Number 3, February 1979, pp. 35–36.

13. Neal Q. Herrick, "Who's Happy at Work and Why?" *Manpower,* U.S. Department of Labor, January 1972, p. 5.

14. Mitchell Fein, "The Real Needs and Goals of Blue Collar Workers," *The Conference Board Record,* Volume 10, Number 3, February 1973, pp. 26–33.

15. Geert H. Hofstedt, "The Color of Collars," *Columbia Journal of World Business,* Volume 7, Number 5, September–October 1972, p. 78.

16. Vance F. Mitchell, "Need Satisfaction of Military Commanders and Staff," *Journal of Applied Psychology,* Volume 54, Number 3, June 1970, pp. 284–285.

17. Joan L. Kelly, "Employers Must Recognize That Older People Want to Work," *Personnel Journal,* Volume 69, Number 1, January 1990, pp. 44–52.

18. Kenneth A. Kovach, "What Motivates Employees? Workers and Employees Give Different Answers," *Businenss Horizons,* Volume 30, Number 5, September–October 1987, pp. 58–65.

19. Henry A. Murray, *Thematic Apperception Test Manual,* Cambridge: Harvard University Press, 1943.

20. Larry Reibstein, "A Finger on the Pulse: Companies Expand Use of Employee Surveys," *Wall Street Journal,* October 27, 1986, p. 23.

Chapter Eight

1. For more discussion of this, see Lawrence M. Miller, *Behavior Management: The New Science of Managing People at Work,* New York: John Wiley and Sons, 1978.

2. Lyman W. Porter and Edward E. Lawler III, *Managerial Attitudes and Performance,* Homewood, Ill.: Richard D. Irwin, 1968.

3. Porter and Lawler, 1968, p. 10.

4. See Robert M. Madigan, "Complete Worth Judgments: A Measurement Properties Analysis," *Journal of Applied Psychology,* Volume 70, Number 1, February 1985, pp. 137–147; R. D. Pritchard, Marvin D. Dunnette, and D. O. Jorgensen, "Effects of Perceptions of Equity and Inequity on Worker Performances and Satisfaction," *Journal of Applied Psychology,* Volume 56, Number 1, February 1972, pp. 75–94; and Jerald Greenberg and Suzyn Ornstein, "High States Job Title as Compensation for Underpayment: A Test of Equity Theory," *Journal of Applied Psychology,* Volume 68, Number 2, May 1983, pp. 285–297, for examples.

5. Edwin A. Locke, "Toward a Theory of Task Motivation and Incentives," *Organizational Behavior and Human Performance,* Volume 3, Number 1, February 1968, pp. 157–189.

6. Edwin A. Locke, K. N. Shaw, L. M. Saari, and G. P. Latham, "Goal Setting and Task Performance," *Psychological Bulletin,* Volume 90, Number 1, July 1981, pp. 125–152.

7. Gary P. Latham and Gary A. Yukl, "A Review of Research on the Application of Goal Setting in Organization," *Academy of Management Journal,* Volume 18, Number 4, December 1975, pp. 824–845.

8. Latham and Yukl, 1975, p. 835.

9. Latham and Yukl, 1975.

10. Grace Shing-Yung Chang and Peter Lorenzi, "The Effects of Participative Versus Assigned Goal Setting on Intrinsic Motivation," *Journal of Managment,* Volume 9, Number 1, Spring–Summer 1983, pp. 55–64.

11. Shing-Yung Chang and Lorenzi, 1983, p. 62.

12. Richard M. Steers, "Factors Affecting Job Attitudes in a Goal Setting Environment," *Academy of Management Journal,* Volume 19, Number 1, March 1976, pp.
6–16.
13. R. S. Schuler and J. S. Kim, "Interactive Effects of Participation in Decision-Making;
the Goal Setting Process and Feedback on Employee Satisfaction and Performance," *Academy of Management Proceedings,* 1976, pp. 114–117.
14. Dennis D. Umstot, Terence R. Mitchell, and Cecil H. Bell, Jr., "Goal Setting and
Job Enrichment: An Integrated Approach to Job Design," *Academy of Management Review,* Volume 3, Number 4, October 1978, pp. 867–879.
15. J. Richard Hackman and Greg R. Oldham, *Work Redesign,* © 1980 by Addison-
Wesley Publishing Company. Reprinted with permission of the publisher.
16. Hackman and Oldham, 1980, p. 79.
17. Hackman and Oldham, 1980, p. 80.

Chapter Nine

1. E. L. Thorndike, *Animal Intelligence,* New York: Macmillan, 1911.
2. William F. Whyte, "Skinnerian Theory in Organizations," *Psychology Today,* Volume 5, Number 11, April 1972, pp. 67–68, 96, 98, 100. See also B. F. Skinner,
Contingencies of Reinforcement, New York: Appleton, Century, Crofts, 1969.
3. A. Bandura, *Principles of Behavior Modification,* New York: Holt, Rinehart and
Winston, 1969.
4. W. Clay Hammer and Dennis M. Organ, *Organizational Behavior: An Applied
Psychological Approach,* Dallas: Business Publications, 1978, pp. 49–51.
5. Stephen C. Bushardt, Aubrey R. Fowler, Jr., and Art Sekumar, "Sales Force Motivations," *Human Relations,* Volume 41, Number 12, December 1989, pp. 901–913.
6. B. F. Skinner, 1969.
7. Hammer and Organ, 1978.
8. Leonard R. Sayles and George Strauss, in *Human Behavior in Organization,*
Englewood Cliffs, N.J.: Prentice-Hall, 1966, state that the hot stove rule originated
with Douglas McGregor.

Chapter Ten

1. David G. Bowers and Stanley E. Seashore, "Predicting Organizational Effectiveness with a Four-Factor Theory of Leadership," *Administrative Science Quarterly,*
Volume 11, Number 2, September 1966, p. 240.
2. Henry P. Sims, Jr., "The Leader as a Manager of Reinforcement Contingencies: An
Empirical Example and Model." In J. G. Hunt and L. L. Larson (Eds.), *Leadership:
The Cutting Edge,* Carbondale, Ill.: Southern Illinois University Press, 1977, pp.
121–127.
3. Henri Fayol, *General and Industrial Management,* Storrs (Trans.), London: Sir
Isaac Pitman and Sons, 1949 (originally written in 1916).
4. William G. Scott and Terence R. Mitchell, *Organization Theory: A Structural and
Behavioral Analysis,* Homewood, Ill.: Richard D. Irwin and the Dorsey Press, 1972.
5. R. M. Stogdill, "Personal Factors Associated with Leadership: A Survey of the Literature," *Journal of Psychology,* Number 25, January 1948, pp. 35–72.
6. Robert J. House, "A 1976 Theory of Charismatic Leadership." In *Leadership: The
Cutting Edge,* Chicago: Southern Illinois University Press, 1977.
7. Stogdill, 1948, p. 64.
8. E. A. Fleishman, E. F. Harris, and H. E. Burtt, *Leadership and Supervision in Industry,* Columbus: Ohio State University, Bureau of Educational Research, 1955.

9. Daniel Katz and Robert L. Kahn, "Human Organization and Worker Motivation," *Industrial Productivity,* L. R. Tripp (Ed.), Madison, Wisc.: Industrial Relations Research Association, 1952.

10. Rensis Likert, *The Human Organization,* New York: McGraw-Hill, 1967.

11. Robert R. Blake and Anne Adams McCanse, *Leadership Dilemmas—Grid Solutions,* Houston: Gulf Publishing Company, p. 29. Copyright 1991 by Scientific Methods, Inc. Published by permission of the owners.

12. Blake and McCanse, 1991, p. 29.

13. See Fred E. Fiedler, "Engineer the Job to Fit the Manager," *Harvard Business Review,* Volume 43, Number 4, 1965, pp. 115–122; and Fred E. Fiedler, *A Theory of Leadership Effectiveness,* New York: McGraw-Hill, 1962, for samples of Fiedler's work.

14. Fred E. Fiedler and Martin E. Chemers, *Leadership and Effective Management,* Glenview, Ill.: Scott, Foresman, 1974.

15. Fred E. Fiedler and Joseph E. Garcia, *New Approaches to Effective Leadership,* New York: John Wiley, 1987.

16. Victor Vroom and Phillip W. Yetton, *Leadership and Decision-Making,* Pittsburgh: University of Pittsburgh Press, 1973.

17. Paul Hersey and Kenneth H. Blanchard, *Management of Organizational Behavior* (5th edition), Englewood Cliffs, N.J.: Prentice-Hall, 1988.

18. Robert J. House and Terence R. Mitchell, "Path-Goal Theory of Leadership," *Journal of Contemporary Business,* Volume 3, Number 4, 1976.

19. Some of the most recent studies on participative leadership include J. L. Cotton, D. A. Vollrath, K. L. Froggatt, M. L. Lengnick-Hall, and K. R. Jennings, "Employee Participation: Diverse Forms and Different Outcomes," *Academy of Management Review,* Volume 13, Number 1, January 1988, pp. 8–22; J. L. Cotton, D. A. Vollrath, M. L. Lengnick, and K. L. Froggatt, "Fact: The Form of Participation Does Matter—A Rebuttal to Leana, Locke, and Schweiger," *Academy of Management Review,* Volume 15, Number 1, January 1990, pp. 147–153; C. R. Leana, E. A. Locke, and D. A. Schweiger, "Fact and Fiction in Analyzing Research on Participative Decision-Making: A Critique of Cotton, Vollrath, Froggatt, Lengnick-Hall, and Jennings," *Academy of Management Review,* Volume 15, Number 1, January 1990, pp. 137–146.

20. Some of the more recent studies of the vertical dyad include those by Richard M. Dienesch and Robert C. Liden, "Leader-Member Exchange Model of Leadership," *Academy of Management Review,* Volume 11, Number 3, July 1986, pp. 618–634; R. P. Vecchio and B. C. Gobel, "The Vertical Dyad Linkage Model of Leadership," *Organization Behavior and Human Performance,* Volume 34, Number 1, 1984, pp. 5–20; and G. R. Ferris, "Role of Leadership in the Employee Withdrawal Process," *Journal of Applied Psychology,* Volume 70, Number 4, 1985, pp. 777–781.

Chapter Eleven

1. Lee Thayer, *Communication and Communication Systems,* Homewood, Ill.: Richard D. Irwin, 1968, pp. 187, 205, 220, 239.

2. Howard H. Greenbaum, "The Audit of Organizational Communication," *Academy of Management Journal,* Volume 17, Number 4, December 1974, pp. 739–754.

3. Thayer, 1968. p. 226; and Cal M. Logue, "Persuasion in a Competitive Society." In Richard C. Huseman, Cal M. Logue, and Dwight L. Freshly, *Readings in Interpersonal and Organizational Communication,* Boston: Holbrook Press, 1977.

4. Thayer, 1968, p. 239.

5. Thayer, 1968, pp. 239–240.

6. See Jerie McArthur and D. W. McArthur, "The Pitfalls (and Pratfalls) of Corporate Communications, *Management Solutions,* Volume 32, Number 12, December 1987, pp. 15–19, for other helpful suggestions about the communication process.

7. "Slang of the Skyway," *Monroe News Star,* Gannett Publications, April 4, 1987, p. B1.

8. Alicia Swasy, "This Could Be Your Only Chance to Call Your Boss 'Maniac' and Live," *Wall Street Journal,* June 1, 1989, p. B1.

9. John O. Greene and H. E. Lindsey, "Encoding Processes in the Production of Multiple-Goal Messages," *Human Communication Research,* Volume 16, Number 1, Fall 1989, pp. 120–140.

10. G. Michael Barton, "Manage Words Effectively," copyright January 1990. Reprinted with the permission of *Personnel Journal,* Costa Mesa, Calif. All rights reserved.

11. Robert H. Lengel and Richard L. Daft, "The Selection of Communication Media as an Executive Skill," *Academy of Management Executive,* Volume 2, Number 3, August 1988, pp. 225–232.

12. Lengel and Daft, 1988.

13. Richard C. Huseman and Edward W. Miles, "Organizational Communication in the Information Age: Implications of Computer-Based Systems," *Journal of Management,* Volume 14, Number 2, June 1988, pp. 181–204.

14. Leonard R. Sayles and George Strauss, *Human Behavior in Organizations,* Englewood Cliffs, N.J.: Prentice-Hall, 1966, p. 363.

15. For a more complete analysis of upward communication problems, see William M. Pride and O. Jeff Harris, "Psychological Barriers in the Upward flow of Communication," *Atlanta Economic Review,* Volume 21, Number 3, March 1971, pp. 30–32.

16. Arthur Gemmill, "Managing Upward Communication," *Personnel Journal,* Volume 49, Number 2, February 1970, pp. 107–110.

17. Marshall H. Brenner and Norman B. Sigband, "Organizational Communication—An Analysis Based on Empirical Data," *Academy of Management Journal,* Volume 16, Number 2, June 1973, pp. 323–325.

18. Pride and Harris, 1971, pp. 30–32; and Ronald J. Burke and Douglas S. Wilcox, "Effects of Different Patterns and Degrees of Openness in Superior-Subordinate Communication on Subordinate Job Satisfaction," *Acadmeny of Management Journal,* Volume 12, Number 3, September 1969, pp. 319–326.

19. Charles E. Beck and Elizabeth A. Beck, "The Manager's Open Door and the Communication Climate," January–February 1986, adaptation, pp. 15–19. Reprinted from *Business Horizons,* January–February 1986. Copyright 1986 by the Foundation for the School of Business at Indiana University. Used with permission. And Jack E. Gibb, "Defensive Communication," *Journal of Communication,* September 1961, pp. 141–148.

20. See Harold H. Dawley, Jr. and W. W. Wenrich, *Achieving Assertive Behavior,* Monterey, Calif.: Brooks/Cole, 1976; and Arthur Lange and Patricia Jakubowski, *Response Assertive Behavior,* Champaign, Ill.: Research Press, 1976.

21. Lange and Jakubowski, 1976.

22. Dawley and Wenrich, 1976.

Chapter Twelve

1. Wilbert R. Sykes and Douglas T. Lind, "Rolling the Therapist's Couch into the Executive Suite," *Business and Society Review,* Number 69, Spring 1989, pp. 48–51.

2. Marvin D. Dunnette and Wayne K. Kirchner, *Psychology Applied to Industry,* New York: Appleton-Century-Crofts, 1965.

3. M. I. Gould, "Counseling for Self-Development," *Personnel Journal,* Volume 49, Number 3, March 1970, pp. 226–234.

4. Allen J. Schuh and Milton D. Hakel, "The Counselor in Organizations: A Look to the Future," *Personnel Journal,* Volume 51, Number 5, May 1972, p. 358.

5. Joseph P. Zima, "Counseling Concepts for Supervisors," *Personnel Journal*, Volume 50, Number 6, June 1971, p. 482.
6. Alfred Benjamin, *The Helping Interview*, Boston: Houghton Mifflin, 1969, p. 3.
7. A. W. Combs, et. al., F*lorida Studies in the Helping Professions*, Monograph Number 37, Gainesville: University of Florida, 1969, pp. 21–27.
8. Douglas McGregor, *Human Side of Enterprise*, New York: McGraw-Hill, 1960.
9. I. L. Heckmann, Jr. and S. G. Huneryager (Eds.), *Human Relations in Management*, Cincinnati: South-Western Publishing Company, 1960, pp. 508–509.
10. Carl R. Rogers, "The Characteristics of a Helping Relationship," *Personnel and Guidance Journal*, Volume 37, Number 1, September 1985, pp. 6–16.
11. Heckmann and Huneryager, 1960, pp. 505–506.
12. William A. Ruch, "The Why and How of Nondirective Interviewing," *Supervisory Management*, Volume 18, Number 1, January 1973, pp. 13–19.
13. W. J. Dickson, *Understanding and Training Employees*, Personnel Series, Number 35, 1936.
14. Ann Vernon, "Assessment and Treatment of Child Problems: Application of Rational-Emotional Therapy," *Counseling and Development*, Volume 22, Number 4, December 1989, pp. 1–12.
15. Carl A. Rogers and Richard E. Farson, "Active Listening." In Richard C. Huseman, Cal M. Logue, and Dwight L. Freshley (Eds.), *Readings in Inter-Personal and Organizational Communication*, Boston: Holbrook Press, 1977.
16. G. Michael Barton, "Manage Words Effectively," *Personnel Journal*, Volume 69, Number 1, January 1990, pp. 32, 34, 36, 38, 40.
17. *Interviewer's Manual*, Ann Arbor: Institute for Social Research, University of Michigan Research Center, 1969, pp. 113–114.
18. Benjamin, pp. 113–114.
19. Gerald D. Cook, "Employee Counseling Session," *Supervision*, Volume 50, Number 8, August 1989, pp. 3–5, gives several helpful suggestions for use in directive counseling.
20. Thomas C. Froehle and Gilda Broadwell, "Therapy Duration: Independence of Field Practitioners," *Counseling and Human Development*, Volume 21, Number 5, January 1989, pp. 1–16.

Chapter Thirteen

1. Joseph A. Litterer, "Managing Conflict in Organizations," *Proceedings of the Eighth Annual Midwest Management Conference*," Carbondale, Ill.: Southern Illinois University Bureau of Business Research, 1965.
2. Mary Parker Follett, *Dynamic Administration: The Colllected Papers of Mary Parker Follett*, edited by Henry C. Metcalf and Lyndall Urwick, New York: Harper and Brothers, Publishers, 1940.
3. Kenneth Thomas and Ralph H. Kilmann, adapted from "Conflict and Conflict Management," in *The Handbook of Industrial and Organizational Psychology*, Marvin Dunnette (Ed.), Chicago: Rand McNally, 1975.
4. Karen R. Krupar and Joseph J. Krupar, "Jerks at Work," *Personnel Journal*, Volume 67, Number 6, June 1988, pp. 69–75.
5. Gordon Cliff, "Managing Organization Conflict," *Management Review*, Volume 76, Number 5, May 1987, pp. 51–53.
6. See Rosemary S. Cafarella, "Managing Conflict: An Analytical Tool," *Training and Development Journal*, Volume 38, Number 2, February 1984, pp. 34–37, for some additional thoughts about causes of conflict.
7. Ronald C. Phillips, "Manage Differences Before They Destroy Your Business," *Training and Development Journal*, Volume 42, Number 9, September 1988, pp. 66–71.

8. Stephen P. Robbins, *Managing Organizational Conflict: A Nontraditional Approach,* Englewood Cliffs, N. J.: Prentice-Hall, 1974.

9. Robert R. Blake and Anne Adams McCanse, *Leadership Dilemmas—Grid Solutions,* Houston: Gulf Publishing Company, p. 29. Copyright 1991 by Scientific Methods, Inc. Published by permission of the owners.

10. See Maria Alicia Jones, Stephen C. Bushardt, and Gary Cadenhead, "A Paradigm for Effective Resolution of Interpersonal Conflict," *Nursing Management,* Volume 21, Number 12, February 1990, pp. 64B–64L.

11. See Patricia B. Link, "How to Cope with Conflict Between the People Who Work for You," *Supervision,* Volume 51, Number 5, January 1990, pp. 7–9, for some other ideas.

12. William G. Scott, *The Management of Conflict,* Homewood, Ill.: Richard D. Irwin, Inc. 1965, contains an excellent review of workers' right to appeal unjust actions.

13. Robbins, *Managing Organizational Conflict,* 1974.

Chapter Fouteen

1. Terry A. Beehr and John E. Newman, "Job Stress, Employee Health, and Organizational Effectiveness: A Facet Analysis, Model, and Literature Review," *Personal Psychology,* Volume 31, Number 3, Autumn 1978, pp. 669–670.

2. D. K. Caplan, et al., "Job Demands and Worker Health: Main Effects and Occupational Differences," Washington, D.C.: U.S. Government Printing Office, 1975.

3. "Stress: The Test Americans Are Flunking," *Business Week,* April 18, 1988, pp. 74–78.

4. A. K. Matthews, "Psychological Perspectives on the Type A Behavior Pattern," *Psychological Bulletin,* Volume 91, Number 2, March 1982, pp. 293–323.

5. K. J. Hennigan and A. W. Wortham, "Analysis of Workday Stresses on Industrial Managers Using Heart Rate as a Criterion," *Ergonomics,* Volume 18, Number 6, November 1975, pp. 675–681.

6. M. S. Sales, "Some Effects of Role Overload and Underload," *Organizational Behavior and Human Performance,* Volume 5, Number 6, November 1970, pp. 592–608.

7. Alan A. McLean, "Job Stress and the Psychosocial Pressures of Change," *Personnel,* Volume 53, Number 1, January–February 1976, pp. 40–49.

8. T. Theorall, "Selected Illnesses and Somatic Factors in Relation to Two Psychosocial Stress Indices—A Prospective Study on Middle-aged Construction Workers," *Journal of Psychosomatic Reasearch,* Volume 20, Number 1, January–February 1976, pp. 7–20.

9. Karl Albrecht, *Stress and the Manager,* Englewood Cliffs, N.J.: Prentice-Hall, 1979. Much of the discussion related to overload and underload factors and stressors is drawn from the Albrecht publication.

10. Mark Robichoux, "Business First, Family Second," *Wall Street Journal,* May 12, 1989, p. B1.

11. Roger Rickles and Udayan Gupta, "Traumas of a New Entrepreneur," *Wall Street Journal,* May 10, 1989, p. B6.

12. Pamela R. Johnson and Julie Indrik, "The Role Communication Plays in Developing and Reducing Organizational Stress and Burnout," *Bulletin of the Association of Business Communication,* Volume 53, Number 1, March 1990, pp. 5–9.

13. Susan E. Jackson, Randall S. Schurer, and Richard Schwold, "Toward an Understanding of the Burnout Phenomenon," *Journal of Applied Psychology,* Volume 71, Number 4, August 1986, pp. 630–640.

14. Manuel A. Tipgos, "The Things That Stress Us," *Management World,* Volume 16, Number 4, June–August 1987, pp. 17–18.

15. Don Hellriegel, John W. Slocum, Jr., and Richard W. Woodman, *Organizational Behavior* (4th edition), St. Paul: West, 1986.

16. John M. Ivancevich and M. T. Matteson, *Stress and Work: A Managerial Perspective,* Glenview, Ill.: Scott, Foresman, 1980.

17. See Beehr and Newman, 1978, pp. 672–674; and J. M. Ivancevich and M. T. Matteson, *Stress and Work: A Managerial Perspective,* Glenview, Ill.: Scott Foresman, 1980, pp. 10–11, for discussions of the process of coping with stress.

18. Frank Harwood, "Seven Successful Stress Managers: Their Strategies/Tactics," *Bulletin of the Association of Business Communication,* Volume 53, Number 1, March 1990, pp. 10–13.

Chapter Fifteen

1. "Dealing with Alcoholism on the Job," *Management Review,* Volume 74, Number 7, July 1985, pp. 4–5.

2. Marion Sadler and James F. Horst, "Company-Union Programs for Alcoholics," *Harvard Business Review,* Volume 50, Number 5, September–October 1971, p. 23.

3. Thomas E. Geidt, "Drug and Alcohol Abuse in the Work Place: Balancing Employer and Employee Rights," *Employee Labor Law Journal,* Volume 11, Number 2, Autumn 1985, pp. 181–205.

4. David J. Hanson, "Drug Abuse Testing Programs Gaining Acceptance in the Workplace," *Chemical and Engineering News,* Volume 64, Number 22, June 2, 1986, pp. 7–14.

5. Quoted by Stephen J. Levy, "Drug Abuse in Business: Telling It Like It Is," *Personnel,* Volume 49, Number 5, September–October 1972, p. 8.

6. Abby Brown, "Employment Test: Issues Without Clear Answers: Today's Tests Screen Well, But Raise Some Tough Issues as Well," *Personnel Administrator,* Volume 30, Number 9, September 1985, pp. 58–65.

7. Hanson, 1986.

8. Eric Rolfe Greenburg, "Workplace Testing: The 1990 AMA Survery, Part 2, *Personnel,* Volume 67, Number 7, July 1990, pp. 26–29.

9. Allen Hanson, "What Employees Say About Drug Testing," *Personnel,* Volume 67, Number 7, July 1990, pp. 32–36.

10. Greenburg, 1990.

11. Geidt, 1985, discusses the evaluation and control process in detail.

12. "Alcoholism and the Workplace: An I L O View," *Industrial Relations Research Reports,* Volume 4, Number 5, May–June 1980.

13. Geidt, 1985.

14. "Time Theft Hits $161 billion in 1987," *Management World,* Volume 15, Number 1, January 1986, p. 5.

15. Norman Jaspan, "Why Employees Steal," *The Office,* Volume 76, Number 3, September 1972, p. 58.

16. William Terris, as quoted in Ron Zemke, "Employee Theft: How to Cut Your Losses," *Training,* Volume 23, Number 5, May 1986, pp. 74–78.

17. Susan Gardner, "Congress Regulates Truth Verification in the Workplace," *Labor Law Journal,* Volume 40, Number 2, February 1989, pp. 122–127; and "Polygraph Tests Banned," *Inc.,* Volume 10, Number 9, September 1988, p. 121.

18. Gilbert Fuchsberg, "More Employers Check Credit Histories of Job Seekers to Judge Their Character," *Wall Street Journal,* May 30, 1989, p. B1.

19. W. Steve Albrecht and David W. Schmoldt, "Employee Fraud," *Business Horizons,* Volume 31, Number 4, July/August 1988, pp. 16–18.

20. "The Drive to Make Dull Jobs More Interesting," *U.S. News and World Report,* Volume 70, Number 3, July 17, 1972, p. 53.

Chapter Sixteen

1. *Statisical Abstract of the United States, 1990,* Washington, D.C.: U.S. Department of Commerce, Bureau of the Census, Volume 110, p. 384.
2. "Business Starts Tailoring Itself to Suit Working Women," *Business Week,* October 6, 1986, pp. 50–54.
3. Jacqueline Landou and Lisa Amoss, "Myths, Dreams, and Disappointments: Preparing for the Future." In Lynda L. Moore, *Not as Far as You Think,* Lexington, Mass.: Lexington Books, 1986, pp. 13–24.
4. Mary E. Corcoran and Greg J. Duncan, "Why Do Women Earn Less?" *Institute of Social Research Newsletter,* Volume 11, Number 1, Spring/Summer, 1983, pp. 4–5, 8.
5. Moshe Semyonov, "The Social Context of Women's Labor Force Participation," *American Journal of Sociology,* Volume 86, Number 3, November 1980, pp. 534–550.
6. Virginia Schein, "Relationships Between Sex Role Stereotypes and Requisite Management Characteristics Among Female Managers," *Journal of Applied Psychology,* Volume 60, Number 3, June 1975, pp. 340–344.
7. Keith L. Alexander, "Both Racism and Sexism Block the Path to Management for Minority Women," *Wall Street Journal,* July 25, 1990, p. B1.
8. Lea P. Stewart and William B. Gudykunst, "Differential Factors Influencing the Hierarchial Level and Number of Promotions of Males and Females Within an Organization," *Academy of Management Journal,* Volume 25, Number 3, September 1982, pp. 586–597.
9. "Business Starts Tailoring Itself to Suit Working Women," 1986.
10. "Work Interruptions and the Female-Male Earnings Gap," *Monthly Labor Review,* February 1985, pp. 50–51.
11. "Women Executives Feel That Men Both Aid and Hinder Their Careers," *Wall Street Journal,* October 29, 1985, p. 31, 44.
12. Landou and Amoss, 1986.
13. Lee Bell and Valerie Young, "Imposters, Fakes, and Frauds." In Lynda L. Moore, *Not as Far as You Think,* Lexington, Mass.: Lexington Books, 1986, pp. 25–51.
14. N. T. Feather, "Attribution of Responsibility and Valence of Success and Failure in Relation to Initial Confidence and Task Performance," *Journal of Abnormal and Social Psychology,* Volume 13, Number 2, 1969, pp. 129–144.
15. John F. Viega, "Women in Management: An Endangered Species?" *M.S.U. Business Topics,* Volume 25, Number 3, Summer 1977, pp. 31–35.
16. Information about these and other stereotypes of women can be found in Eleanor E. Maccoby and Carol N. Jacklin, "What We Know and Don't Know About Sex Differences," *Psychology Today,* Volume 8, Number 7, December 1974, pp. 189–191; Bette A. Stead, *Women in Management,* Englewood Cliffs, N.J.: Prentice-Hall, 1978; Joan E. Crowley, Teresa Levitin and Robert P. Quinn, *IRS Newsletter,* Volume 1, Number 16; and O. Jeff Harris, "Is Self-Concept a Limiting Factor for Women?" *Proceedings of the Southern Management Association,* 1978, pp. 42–44.
17. "Women Executives Feel That Men Both Aid and Hinder Their Careers," 1985.
18. "Business Starts Tailoring Itself to Suit Working Women," 1986.
19. These generalizations are discussed in "Job Tenure," *Economic Road Map,* Number 1888, New York: The Conference Board, October 1980; Benson Rosen and Thomas H. Jerdee, "The Influence of Age Stereotypes in Management Decisions," *Journal of Applied Psychology,* Volume 61, Number 4, August 1976, pp. 428–432; and D. Baugher, *Aging and Work,* Volume 1, Number 4, Fall 1978.
20. Barbara A. Price, "What the Baby Boomer Believes," *American Demographics,* Volume 6, Number 5, May 1984, pp. 31–33.

21. *Statistical Abstract of the United States, 1990,* p. 389.

22. Berry Brewton, *Race and Ethnic Relations,* 3rd edition, Boston: Houghton-Mifflin, 1965.

23. *Statistical Abstract of the United States, 1990,* p. 397.

24. *Statistical Abstract of the United States, 1990,* p. 409.

25. *Statistical Abstract of the United States, 1990,* p. 390-391.

26. John Naisbitt, *The Year Ahead,* Washington D.C.: The Naisbitt Group, 1985, pp.13–17.

27. Cheryl Russell, "Trouble Ahead," *American Demographics,* Volume 12, Number 3, March 1990, p. 2.

28. D. J. Jackson, "Update on Handicapped Discrimination," *Personnel Journal,* Volume 57, Number 9, September 1978, pp. 488–491.

29. B. Griss, *Access to Health Care,* Volume 1, Berkeley, Calif.: World Institute on Disability, 1988.

30. "AIDS Compromise Clears Way for Bill to Aid Disabled," *Times Picayune,* July 13, 1990.

31. Bill Patterson, "Managing with AIDS in the Workplace," *Management World,* Volume 18, Number 1, January–February 1989, pp. 44–47.

32. Loren Falkenberg, "Improving the Accuracy of Stereotypes Within the Workplace," *Journal of Management,* Volume 16, Number 1, 1990, pp. 107–118.

Chapter Seventeen

1. J. Trevor Leathem, "Managing Organizational Change," *Business Quarterly,* Volume 54, Number 1, Summer 1989, pp. 39–43, identifies several pressures and trends regarding change.

2. See Sigmund Freud, *An Outline of Psychoanalysis* (translated by J. Strachey), New York: W. W. Norton, 1949.

3. Harry Levinson, "Easing the Pain of Personal Loss," *Harvard Business Review,* Volume 50, Number 5, September–October 1972, p. 81.

4. William Bridges, "How to Manage Organizational Transition," *Training—The Magazine of Human Resource Development,* Volume 22, Number 9, September 1985, pp. 28–32.

5. Maggie Moore and Paul Gergen, "Risk Taking and Organizational Change," *Training and Development Journal,* Volume 39, Number 6, June 1985, pp. 72–76.

6. See Douglas T. Hall and Roger Mansfield, "Organizational Stress and Individual Response to External Stress," *Administrative Science Quarterly,* Volume 16, Number 4, December 1971, pp. 535–547, for an interesting analysis of employees' receptivity to change resulting from forces external to the organizations.

7. David A. Nadler and Michael L. Tushman, "Beyond the Charismatic Leader, Leadership and Organizational Change," *California Management Review,* Volume 32, Number 2, Winter 1990, pp. 77–97.

8. John Lawrie, "The ABC's of Change Management," *Training and Development Journal,* Volume 44, Number 3, March 1990, pp. 87–89.

9. Arnold S. Judson, *A Manager's Guide to Making Changes,* Copyright 1966. Reprinted by permission of John Wiley and Sons, Limited.

10. J. Trevor Leathem, 1989.

11. John Lawrie, March 1990.

12. See Homer H. Johnson and Alan Fredian, "Simple Rules for Complex Change," *Training and Development Journal,* Volume 40, Number 8, August 1986, pp. 47–49; and Tommy Moore, "Making Changes Smoothly," *Management World,* Volume 15, Number 5, June 1986, pp. 26–28, for helpful suggestions for implementing change.

13. See Paul F. Buller, "For Successful Strategic Change: Blend OD Practices with Strategic Management," *Organizational Dynamics,* Volume 16, Number 3, Winter 1988, pp. 42–45, for a list of OD activities.

14. Gloria Barczak, Charles Smith, and David Wilemon, "Managing Large-Scale Organizational Change," *Organizational Dynamics,* Volume 16, Number 2, Autumn 1987, pp. 23–25.
15. Eric H. Nielsen, *Becoming an OD Practitioner,* Englewood Cliffs, N.J.: Prentice-Hall, 1984.
16. D. E. Terpstra, "Relationship Between Methodical Rigor and Reported Outcomes in Organization Development Evaluation Research," *Journal of Applied Psychology,* Volume 66, Number 5, October 1981, pp. 541–543.

Chapter Eighteen

1. John Naisbitt, *Megatrends: Ten New Directions Transforming Our Lives,* New York: Warner Books, 1982; and Thomas J. Peters and Robert H. Waterman, Jr., *In Search of Excellence,* New York: Warner Books, 1984.
2. R. Eden Deutsch, "Tomorrow's Work Force," *The Futurist,* Volume 19, Number 6, December 1985, pp. 8–11.
3. Raymond E. Miles and Charles C. Snow, "Organizations: New Concepts for New Forms," *California Management Review,* Volume 28, Number 3, Spring 1986, pp. 62–73.
4. Patrick Houston, "High Anxiety," *Business Month,* Volume 136, Number 6, June 1990, pp. 32–41.
5. Patrick Houston, 1990, p. 34.
6. Noel Tichey and Mary Anne Devanna, "The Transformational Leader," *Training and Development Journal,* Volume 40, Number 7, July 1986, pp. 27–32.
7. Geert Hofstede, *Culture's Consequences: International Differences in Work Related Values,* Beverly Hills: Sage Publications, 1980.
8. The Hofstede study is discussed at length in Nancy J. Adler, *International Dimensions of Organizational Behavior,* 2nd edition, Boston: PWS-Kent Publishing Company, 1991; and Philip B. Harris and Robert T. Moran, *Managing Cultural Differences,* 3rd edition, Houston: Gulf, 1991.
9. Rose Knotts, "Cross-Cultural Managment: Transformations and Adaptations," *Business Horizons,* Volume 32, Number 1, January–February 1989, pp. 29–33.
10. Pierre Casse, *Training for the Multicultural Manager: A Practical and Cross-Cultural Approach to the Management of People,* Washington, D.C.: Society of Intercultural Education, Training, and Research, 1982.
11. E. S. Glenn, D. Witmeyer, and K. A. Stevenson, "Cultural Styles of Persuasion," *International Journal of Intercultural Relations,* Volume 1, 1984.
12. Rose Knotts and Sandra J. Hartman, "Proper Protocol in International Business: What's a Person to Do?," *Proceedings,* Western Academy of International Business, 1990.
13. Philip R. Harris and Robert T. Moran, *Managing Cultural Differences,* 2nd edition, Houston: Gulf, 1987, pp. 528–535.
14. Harris and Moran, 1987.
15. Nancy J. Adler, 1991.
16. James A. Wall, Jr., "Managers in the People's Republic of China," *Academy of Management Executive,* Volume 4, Number 2, May 1990, pp. 19–32. Used with permission.
17. Susan Moffatt, "Should You Work for the Japanese?," *Fortune,* December 3, 1990, pp. 107–108, 112, 116, 120.
18. Much of the communication materials in the chapter are taken from a paper by Rose Knotts entitled "If You Can Understand American English You Can Learn International English," *Proceedings,* Association of Business Communicators, 1990. We are grateful to her for the use of the material.

Glossary

achievement need The desire to accomplish feats or tasks that are very challenging. The desire to do things that have an element of risk involved.

acronym A series of letters used as an abbreviation for a sequence of words. For example, the acronym ASAP replaces the four words *as soon as possible.*

active listening Making a concentrated effort to hear what the communicator is attempting to convey rather than passively absorbing the message. Seeking the purpose and intent of someone else's messages.

affiliation need The desire to belong, to be accepted, to be able to associate with others.

aggressiveness Directly standing up for one's own rights at the expense of others' rights.

alcoholic A person who consumes large amounts of alcohol over a considerable length of time and whose addiction causes chronic, increasing incapacitation.

artificial intelligence The capacity of computers to make humanlike decisions.

assertiveness Communication in which the rights of self and others are respected. As a result, communication is honest and forthright.

authority relationships The situation in which an individual has the right to give orders and instructions to another individual and can expect the orders to be followed.

beautiful room As applied here, a beautiful work area—one that has pleasing colors, lights, and furnishings.

behavior theories of leadership Explanations of why individuals are followed by others based on the concept that successful leaders perform activities or duties differently from other less successful individuals.

behavioral adjustment Modification of the actions of employees as a result of change.

broker The person who assembles individual organizations so that they can accomplish cooperative goals.

change A behavior, event, or condition that is different from a previous behavior, event, or condition.

change agent Often called the consultant. The individual with the responsibility for leading an organization in the process of renewal and growth, called Organizational Development. He or she serves as a catalyst to bring about innovation within an organization.

CIM (computer integrated manufacturing) CIM is achieved when computers and other technological devices coordinate the activities involved in a production process from the beginning of the process (planning and scheduling) to the end of the process (distribution).

cluster approach The technique most frequently used by the grapevine (informal communication network) in which one person tells a few others (one cluster) and each subsequent person tells a few other members forming additional clusters.

code of conduct A set of guidelines specifying how the members of a unit (organization, profession) should behave.

coercive power The right to dominate people or things based upon the ability to give out undesirable reinforcements.

cognitive motivation The view of how people are stimulated to action that believes that individuals make rational choices based on the incentive opportunities they will respond to. Cognitive motivation is needs oriented, looking to future fulfillment.

cohesiveness The degree of strength or attractiveness a group has for its members. Where members find their group to be highly attractive, the cohesiveness level is said to be high.

collaboration (nine, nine—9, 9—conflict handling) A technique for achieving positive results from conflict through bringing together people with disagreements, encouraging open discussion, confronting differences, and seeking outcomes beneficial to the parties as well as for the organization.

485

collectivism A cultural value in which individuals are strongly concerned for groups and other social units around them.

command and instruction function A function of communication that makes an employee aware of his or her obligations to the organization.

communication channel The path through which messages are expected to pass within an organization.

communication The transfer of a mental concept from the brain of one person to the brain of another.

competence need The desire to feel adequate to meet the expectations and requirements that one must face.

complementary transaction An exchange between two individuals where both parties are correctly aware of the personality parts doing the communicating.

conformity The acceptance of group values and norms to the point that behavior is consistent with group directives.

contemporary view An attitude that considers conflict to be inevitable when people work together. The role of the manager, therefore, is to attempt to turn conflict into desirable consequences with constructive results for the organization and its people.

conventional design A floor plan or design where people are separated from one another by walls and other permanent partitions. In this procedure, the work locations of individuals and some groups of people will be set apart from the work areas of others by structural dividers.

corrective counseling A type of interpersonal communication where the listener seeks to discover a counselee's problems and the underlying causes, with the goal of eliminating or overcoming the problems.

cottage industry A development in which individuals work in their own homes to produce or process products, materials, services, or information rather than working at a central location.

crossed transaction An exchange between two individuals where the parties involved incorrectly determine the personality part doing the sending, the receiving, or both.

CTD (cumulative trauma disorders) Pain and stiffness of wrist, arm, and shoulder resulting from data input into computers over an extended period of time.

CTO (chief technology officer) The CTO in an organization is responsible for seeing that the technology appropriate for the organization is identified, implemented, and correctly utilized. This person's responsibilities are organizationwide.

culture The social setting in which people live, including the values, norms, and procedures to be utilized. The culture develops over a period of time as individuals and groups interact and experience personal and social change.

decibel (dB) The unit used to measure the loudness of sounds.

decision-making group A team formally assigned to work together to solve a problem or make a decision.

decoding The process by which the receiver of a message takes the symbols communicated and gives meaning to them.

delphi technique A technique for making group decisions where experts are chosen as participants. Group members never meet together directly. They receive information, respond in written form, receive written feedback, vote, and so forth, until a consensus is reached.

deontology The view that social responsibility is a duty—an obligation to be fulfilled.

developmental counseling The activity of a counselor that attempts to help the counselee perform up to the level of his or her capabilities.

directive counseling A structured communicative interaction where the counselor leads in the identification of problems, alternatives, and solutions by asking questions and giving answers.

discipline The process by which an individual learns self-control that leads him or her to do the correct things so that rewards are earned and penalties are avoided.

discrimination Treating or giving attention to one person or group differently from other individuals or groups. Discrimination frequently is seen as giving attention to others in an unfavorable or unfair way.

distortion Giving an incorrect meaning to communicated symbols. Is sometimes the result of misleading conditions or circumstances.

drug abuser An individual who uses any form of drug excessively beyond or against purposes for which the drug was intended.

drug testing A method to evaluate the presence of (and to what degree) a drug is in the body systems of an individual.

dynamic networking A method of structuring organizations whereby a broker coordinates the efforts of several separate organizations so that they complement each other's actions. Individual organizations specialize in their functions and contribute certain things toward the purposes of the units that are thus bonded together.

economies of integration Computer technology enables organizations to concentrate on the production of one product efficiently and then switch to production of another product without costly retooling and setup. In this way economies of scale and economies of scope can both be achieved.

economies of scale Production of a larger quantity of units so that the cost per unit is reduced as fixed costs are spread over more units.

economies of scope Economies of scope occur when an organization can produce two or more products at a cost less than or equal to the cost of producing only one product.

electronic mail Written information is exchanged between individuals at different locations by sending messages through their computers.

employee theft Any form of stealing from one's employer, through such methods as time, materials, and money.

encoding The process where the sender of a message selects symbols to communicate to the receiver so that a message will be integrated correctly.

enlightened self-interest The belief that if an organization acts in a socially responsible way, everyone, including the organization itself, will benefit. The greatest good for the greatest number of people will be achieved.

entrants That segment of the workforce born between 1966 and 1975. These individuals are just beginning to go to work or will be doing so in the next few years. Deutsch calls this group the computer babies.

equity Fair treatment by managers and supervisory personnel. Equity includes fairness in wages, rewards, discipline, and any other type of attention given to workers.

equity theory A concept of motivation in which each performer evaluates rewards received against the rewards received by other employees as well as against inputs required to earn the rewards. Outcomes (rewards) equal to inputs are considered against the outcomes and inputs of others. Where outcomes and inputs differ from those of reference persons, results will be perceived as inequitable.

ergonomics The study of the relationship between the worker and the workplace. In particular, the goal of ergonomics is to increase health, comfort, and productivity for each employee.

esteem need The desire to be respected (considered to be valuable) by self and others.

ethical behavior Actions consistent with society's code of conduct. Doing what is considered morally right.

ethics A set of values representing what a particular society believes to be right as well as what it considers to be wrong.

executive row Usually a series of offices occupied by managerial personnel. All managers are located within the series, and the offices are usually set apart from nonmanagerial personnel.

expectancy theory The model of motivation that operates on the premise that people do the things they do because they believe their actions will result in future rewards to fulfill their important needs. People "expect" their efforts to result in good things they will earn.

expert power Respect earned by an individual based upon the possession of supervisor skills, knowledge, or abilities.

expert system A knowledge-based program whereby rules, probabilities, facts, and relationships are entered into a computer database by a human expert in a particular field. The computer can then give expertlike responses to questions and problems that arise.

external person An individual who thinks things happening to him or her are controlled by external factors, such as the boss or the economy.

extinction A form of conditioning where behavior goes unrewarded as a method of getting that behavior discontinued.

fast track The career path designed to let an employee climb the organizational ladder in a short timespan or the quickest way possible. In this track, the employee is expected to place first priority on doing whatever his or her job requires to benefit the organization most.

femininity A cultural value that shows concern for relationships, the welfare of others, and the overall quality of life.

filtering The action of a receiver in which the receiver hears only what he or she wishes to hear.

flexiplace A method for scheduling work that allows employees to choose if they wish to work at the organization's location, at home, or at some other site.

flexitime A technique for scheduling work that allows employees some freedom to choose the hours within which they will work.

functional duties In this context, sources of conflict result from varying job responsibilities, disputes over access to limited resources, intraorganizational competition, and goal incompatibility related to the job being performed.

grapevine The informal communication network through which information is spread.

groupthink The cohesiveness that develops in a group causing its members to seek a unanimous decision at the risk of failing to identify or consider factors that might result in a better decision.

honesty tests Some form of evaluation that checks the level of an employee's truthfulness or proneness to being truthful.

hope need The desire to be able to believe that future conditions or circumstances will be better than those existing presently or in the past.

hot stove disciplining The process used by an organization to get "correct" behaviors from employees by the use of immediate, consistent, impersonal, prewarned penalties.

human need A personal, unfilled vacancy that exists within an individual.

idioms A sequence of words placed together to have a unique meaning different from the meanings the words have when used separately.

incentive The reward offered to a worker to stimulate him or her to act.

individual differences In this context, variances in temperament, background, and philosophy of employees are seen as sources of conflict.

individualism A cultural value in which individuals show more concern for themselves and their immediate family than they show for groups and others outside their close circle.

influence and persuasion function One of the purposes of communication primarily known as motivation, used to encourage individuals to perform or behave in specific ways.

informal work organizations The unplanned groups that develop spontaneously as workers interact. Sets of relationships not bound by formal authority that provide important support and fulfillment of needs for members.

information float The length of time it takes a message to move from the sender to the receiver.

information function One of the purposes of communication that provides knowledge to individuals, including data concerning jobs, the organization, and other related materials.

informational counseling Communication between two or more persons primarily to convey ideas.

innovation function The purpose of communication intending to help the organization and its members to adapt to internal and external influences as they occur.

integrative function The purpose of communication used to relate the activities of workers so that they complement rather than detract from one another.

internal person An individual who feels that his or her own behavior and the consequences are controlled by himself or herself.

latent need A need, according to Murray, that lies dormant because nothing has happened to stimulate it.

leadership approaches or styles A pattern of interacting with others for leadership purposes that consistently uses the same methods or techniques.

Leadership Grid ® A leadership style concept developed by Robert Blake and Anne McCanse for purposes of diagnosing leadership styles and proposing an idealistic style (the 9,9 approach).

legitimate power The right to dominate and control based upon an offered role or position held.

life position A form of perception where interpretations of one's previous performance and the manner and amount of stroking received from others lead to interpretations of self and others.

locus of control An individual's perception of who or what controls the events in his or her life and affects the outcomes related to his or her efforts.

love need Sometimes called the social need. The desire to give and receive affection from others. Belongingness and acceptance by others are important here.

manifest need A need, according to Murray, that has been activated by a stimulus or cue.

masculinity A cultural value that shows the degree to which people are assertive and interested in the acquisition of money and material things.

minority Any segment of the workforce that makes up less than one-half of the total population in the work environment or has less power than another group. The majority is usually considered to be dominant, while the minority is thought of as subservient. In this chapter, women, older workers, blacks, Hispanics, disabled people, and people with AIDS are viewed as minorities.

mommy track A term used to describe situations where employees—usually mothers—choose to temporarily slow down their organizational career progress while raising small children. During the time of being away from the fast track, the woman works part-time. She returns to the fast track when the children no longer need constant care.

motivating potential score A number arrived at by using the Hackman-Oldham test of job design that reveals the degree of skill variety, task identity, task significance, autonomy, and feedback of a specific job. The larger the number of these characteristics of a job, the greater the motivating potential score.

motive An inner state that energizes, activates, moves, directs, or channels behavior toward goals.

multinational Anything in which the cultures of more than one nation are involved.

multi-phrase combination A communication term where there is the use of more than one word in a situation where one word could be sufficient.

negative motivational process A view of the way to stimulate people to action where fear is used as the incentive. Employees are threatened with punitive action if they do not perform successfully. If performance is successful, the penalty is avoided. If performance is not successful, the penalty is applied.

negative stress The state or condition wherein the pressures applied to an individual cause a threatening, fearful sort of tension within the individual. Often in this kind of stress, the individual feels incapable and inadequate to meet the challenges lying ahead.

neighborhood work center A building located away from headquarters where people go to work rather than commute to the headquarters. Equipment and services are provided. Employees of several different organizations may go to a single work center.

nine-nine (9,9) leadership The idealistic style of leadership proposed in the Leadership Grid® in which the best leader pursues task and human goals to the fullest degree possible.

Nominal Group Technique (NGT) A group decision-making approach where individuals identify solutions, share them in round-robin fashion, and eventually vote to select the best choice. At certain points during the group's effort, members may discuss the votes before making other votes.

nonassertiveness (passive behavior) Communication where the rights of self or others are infringed upon. Passive behavior tends to be self-denying. Inactivity rather than activity tends to occur.

nondirective counseling Communication between counselor and counselee in which the counselor listens and encourages the counselee to identify problems, alternatives, and solutions. The role of the counselor is supportive rather than dominating.

norms Standards of behavior to which group members are expected to conform.

ombudsman An individual who listens to the needs and complaints of employees (or other groups and individuals) and represents the employees or groups to management.

open office The office or room plan where there are no permanent partitions or dividers separating employees in a working area. Partial partitions may be used, but in most cases the plan is to allow people to be free to interact with others without structural interference.

operational group A team of individuals formally assigned to perform a specific function or set of functions in an organization. This type of group may be a department or a set of functionally interrelated individuals.

organizational characteristics Sources of conflict resulting from size, departmentation, spans of supervision, and other structural factors.

Organizational Development A form of planned change where the members of an organization, with the help of a consultant, audit themselves and their organization, then are led in a program of improvement and revitalization based upon the findings of the evaluation.

overload A situation in the workplace wherein the demands made by a work-related component are so high that tensions develop.

perception A sensory experience in which an individual observes (experiences) a behavior, event, or condition, forms his or her own interpretation of the experience, develops an attitude or frame of reference toward the object observed, and allows the interpretation to be a factor influencing behavior.

perceptual differences In this concept, perceptual differences are assessments individuals make about the authority they possess, the role they play, the treatment they receive from others, the status they possess, the rights that accompany their status, and the goals being pursued that may be construed in ways that would put individuals at odds with each other.

physical climate The environment in the workplace. The elements surrounding employees as they work, including such things as air, temperature, noise, lighting, and humidity, as well as the physical objects, including furniture, machinery, and windows.

physical maintenance (or physiological) need The seeking of biological survival for food, clothing, and shelter.

planned change Behavior, events, or conditions that are different as a result of deliberate actions. In this chapter, planned change takes place as a result of managerial planning.

polygraph test A means for evaluating the truthfulness of an individual through the use of electronic sensory devices attached to the individual's body to measure reactions to questions.

positive motivational model A view of the way to stimulate people to action that is very similar to expectancy theory. Behavior results from the perception that incentives offered are worthwhile and attainable. Satisfaction occurs after rewards are received and evaluated favorably.

post-World War II group That segment of the workforce born between 1945 and 1965. This group is also called the TV babies. Those in this age category are most likely to fill the ranks of middle management.

power distance The degree to which nonpowerful individuals accept the unequal distribution of power around them—the acceptance of the fact that others have more authority than they have.

power need The seeking of the capacity to control people or things in one's environment. To wish to be dominant, influential.

pre-World War II group The part of today's workforce who were born before 1945 so that its members are now in their middle forties or older.

The members of this group are most likely to have risen to the tops of organizations making up upper management.

primary reinforcer Basic items such as food, clothing, and shelter that are used to provide the continuation of a desirable behavior or the elimination of an undesirable behavior.

probe An effort to get the counselee to talk about problems, alternatives, and solutions that seeks to be stimulating without being too demanding.

problem drinkers Individuals who may not be addicted to alcohol but whose behavior as a result of alcohol consumption causes trouble for themselves or for others.

problem solving Terminology used for the technique of managing conflict in which causes are identified, alternative solutions are sought, and a course of action believed to be optimal for everyone is chosen.

psychological effect The results of change that causes mental strategies different from previous strategies.

punishment A form of reinforcement where penalties are applied to get a behavior decreased or stopped.

Pygmalion effect A concept named after a character in Greek mythology in which people give back to others performance consistent with the others' expectations. Those who sense high expectations give back high performance, for example. This concept is also known as the self-fulfilling prophecy.

quality circle A voluntary grouping of a small number of individuals who work together within an organization. The group is joined together to pursue ways of improving and protecting the quality of the product on which they work. The circle originated in Japan.

realistic job previews Accurate representations of both the good points and the negative features of a job given to a prospective employee. Weaknesses are shown graphically so that the prospective employee's perceptions of what to expect are not more positive than they should be.

receiver The person in the organization who takes in a message issued by the sender in the communication process.

referent power The ability to dominate others based upon attractiveness such that the person(s) dominated want to be associated with the power holder on a continuing basis even when the cost is heavy.

reinforcement Providing either a reward or a penalty following an employee's behavior to encourage the continuation of desirable behavior or the elimination of an undesirable behavior.

reinforcement schedule A designated pattern by which behaviors will be rewarded or penalized. The sequence and frequency is determined usually by ratio or interval on a variable or fixed basis.

reputation need The desire to have the respect of others, to have one's competencies recognized by others.

restatement A technique used by the counselor to get the counselee to talk more by repeating what the counselee has just said.

reward power The right to dominate people or things as a result of control over desirable reinforcements.

robotics The creation of mechanical units that act like humans and take the place of humans in the production process of an organization.

role A pattern of behavior expected of an individual by others.

role ambiguity An individual's uncertainty about what he or she is expected to do for other individuals or groups.

role perception An individual's view of the obligations he or she has to fulfill the expectations of others.

roles A pattern of behavior expected of an individual.

sanity track The career path where an employee usually deliberately opts to take a slower route in moving up within the organization. The path is usually taken to eliminate some of the stress involved in being on the fast track. Other personal goals are often given priority.

secondary reinforcer Reward or penalty following a behavior where the reward takes the form of a promotion, praise, or recognition.

security need The yearning for safety or for the ability to overcome threats and dangers.

self-actualization need The desire or yearning to become self-fulfilled, to achieve one's potential, to excel at something.

self-esteem An attitude of approval or disapproval or an indication of the extent to which the individual believes self to be capable, sufficient, and worthy.

sender The person in an organization who begins the communication process by issuing symbols with meaning.

service need The desire to do things that will be helpful or supportive of other people.

situational leadership The view of leadership activities that suggests that there is no single best way leaders should perform. Each leadership situation must be judged and responded to based upon its own unique needs.

slang The jargon (terminology) of a particular class or society that is often unknown by outsiders.

smoothing A technique for handling conflict where common interests are talked about but discussions of differences are avoided so that conflict can be minimized.

social adaptation The result of change that causes new relationships and affiliations to be formed.

social responsibility The obligations a specific unit—an organization, for example—is perceived to have to act beneficially for the community at large.

span of supervision The number of people who are directly accountable to an individual supervisor or manager.

specialization The structuring of a job that results in an individual's doing a small number of tasks repetitively. Only a limited number of skills are required. Training is simplified as a result of the use of this procedure.

stars (informal leaders) Frequently those who are the center of much communication.

status A form of recognition in which an individual is esteemed in a way that distinguishes him or her from other individuals and groups. A high-status person is held in positive esteem. A low-esteem person is given little recognition.

stereotyping Applying a generalization to all persons who are considered to be in a single category. Stereotypes in this chapter refer in particular to generalizations made about sex, age, and race.

stress A state or condition wherein external factors (time pressures, social norms, success-failure conditions, and so forth) interact with an individual psychologically or physiologically so that tensions develop inside the individual.

stressor Factor that causes tensions to build within an individual to the point that stress occurs. A strong command from a superior or a rapid decline in the market may be an externally caused stressor. A strong achievement need or a demanding growth need may be an internally originated stressor.

stroking The giving of attention psychologically, physically, or both to another individual. Stroking can be positive when the attention given is supportive and rewarding, and it can be negative when the attention is in a chastising or penalizing form. Stroking fulfills a common need among human beings.

superordinate goals A way of avoiding, reducing, or handling conflict where the sharing of common purposes unifies the efforts of the parties involved.

system 4 A leadership style proposed by Rensis Likert that calls for participative leadership using a team-oriented concept of people in organizations.

team building A concept including many stages where the intention is to improve the quality and effectiveness of performance in a specific group. Several exercises may be performed to build group cohesiveness as well as to produce more goal-oriented behavior.

tentative approach A method of bringing about change where modifications done on a trial basis can be reversed if the employee doesn't like the adjustment after using it for a time.

therapeutic counseling Consultation between counselor and counselee in which problems are diagnosed and "healing" solutions are provided.

traditional interacting group The most typical decision-making group, where group discussion is used as the method for reaching a decision.

traditional view An attitude toward conflict that anticipates that each situation of dispute and disagreement can have only bad results. Since this is expected, conflict is considered to be something to avoid or eliminate.

trait approach The theory of leadership that states that individuals are granted the right to give direction because they possess certain respected traits, such as physical and mental qualities, knowledge, and skills.

transformational leader A recent categorization of leadership based upon bringing about change in organizations. These leaders are labeled as courageous, forceful, value-driven shapers of the destiny of the organizations of the future.

transactional analysis A method of studying and analyzing behavior that concentrates on the type of interactions an individual has with other individuals. Three parts of the human personality (parent, adult, and child) provide the mechanism for looking at past and present behavior. Recordings of past experiences are stored away for future reference.

Type A personality The nature and disposition of an individual to be fast living, impatient, self-preoccupied, competitive, accepting of more and more responsibility, and so forth. The Type A person drives himself or herself to the point that health is threatened.

Type B personality The nature and disposition of an individual to take things slowly, to avoid unrealistic demands, and to be deliberate rather than reactive.

ugly room A work location where the colors and other decorations are unattractive, the lighting is inadequate, and furnishings are poorly suited to the work situation.

ulterior transaction An exchange between two individuals where one or both parties deliberately hide personality parts sending and receiving a message.

uncertainty avoidance The degree to which members of a specific culture feel threatened by ambiguous situations. High uncertainty avoidance cultures are those that feel much stress when ambiguity develops.

underload A situation in the workplace wherein the demands of a work-related component are less than normal or expected so that tensions develop.

unplanned change Behavior, events, or conditions that are different as a result of unpredicted, spontaneous factors forcing alteration to occur.

video display terminal (VDT) A technical term describing the screen on which desktop computer operators view the work they have put into the computer system.

visual stimuli Things seen by the eye that cause reactions, moods, or behaviors in individuals.

voice mail Through a network (usually of telephone lines), messages are sent using pushbutton telephones. Machines record, store, replay, forward, or distribute messages for the appropriate individuals.

Name Index

A

Adelman, L., 469n
Adler, Nancy J., 483n
Adler, Paul, 470n
Alberti, Robert E., 278
Albrecht, Karl, 345, 479n
Albrecht, W. Steve, 480n
Alderfer, Clayton P., 145, 473n
Alexander, Keith L., 481n
Alutto, Joseph A., 469n
Amoss, Lisa, 481n
Anderson, Joyce, 273
Andrews, Kenneth R., 467n
Armenakis, Achilles A., 472n
Ashmore, Michael G., 470n
Atkins, Robert S., 469n

B

Bachman, Jerald G., 472n
Baker, H. K., 468n
Bales, Robert F., 56, 469n
Bandura, A., 475n
Barczak, Gloria, 435–436, 483n
Barton, G. Michael, 258, 477n, 478n
Baugher, D., 481n
Beck, Charles E., 269, 477n
Beck, Elizabeth A., 269, 477n
Beck, Robert N., 474n
Becker, Franklin D., 105, 471n
Bedean, Arthur G., 472n
Beeby, Robert H., 76–77
Beehr, Terry A., 479n, 480n
Behling, Orlando, 468n
Bell, C. R., 471n
Bell Jr., Cecil H., 475n
Bell, Lee, 481n
Benjamin, Alfred, 478n
Bennett, Amanda, 467n
Berkowitz, L., 229
Berne, Eric, 121, 473n
Blake, Robert R., 225–227, 324, 476n, 479n
Blanchard, Kenneth H., 234, 236, 299, 467n, 476n
Bowers, David G., 475n
Brass, Dan, 101, 472n
Bray, Robert M., 56, 469n

Brehmer, T. R., 469n
Brenner, Marshall H., 477n
Brewton, Berry, 482n
Bridges, Edwin M., 469n
Bridges, William, 482n
Broadwell, Gilda, 301, 304, 478n
Broedling, L. A., 131, 473n
Brown, Abby, 480n
Bulkeley, William H., 471n
Buller, Paul F., 482n
Burke, Ronald J., 477n
Burtt, H. E., 475n
Bushardt, Stephen C., 475n, 479n

C

Cadenhead, Gary, 479n
Cafarella, Rosemary S., 478n
Campion, Michael A., 192
Caplan, D. K., 479n
Carroll, Archie B., 467n
Casse, Pierre, 452, 483n
Caudron, Shari, 288
Cespedes, Frank V., 51, 469n
Chang, Grace Shing-Yung, 187, 474n
Chemers, M. M., 229
Chemers, Martin E., 476n
Claytor, Graham W., 243
Clearwater, Y., 472n
Clegg, Thomas J., 471n
Cliff, Gordon, 478n
Cohen, Sheldon, 472n
Cole, Robert E., 470n
Combs, Arthur W., 115, 472n, 478n
Cook, Gerald D., 478n
Cook, Paul, 71
Coopersmith, Stanley, 472n
Corcoran, Mary E., 481n
Cotton, J. L., 476n
Crandell, James E., 35
Crocker, Elizabeth M., 472n
Crossen, Cynthia, 81, 471n
Crowley, Joan E., 481n

D

Daft, Richard L., 257, 259, 477n
Dalkey, Norman C., 60, 469n
Dansereau Jr., Fred, 469n
David, Fred R., 8, 467n, 468n

Davis, Keith, 39, 468n
Davis, Tim R. V., 472n
Dawley, Jr., Harold H., 271, 477n
Deane, Richard H., 472n
DeJoy, David D., 472n
Delbecq, Andre L., 60, 469n
Deming, Edward, 61
Demirdjean, Z. S., 439
Deutsch, R. Eden, 445–446, 483n
Devanna, Mary Anne, 449, 483n
Dickson, W. J., 478n
Dienesch, Richard M., 476n
Distefano, M. K., 131, 473n
Doyle, Stephen X., 469n
Doyle, Wayne F., 469n
Dumaine, Brian, 26, 50
Duncan, Greg J., 481n
Dunnette, Marvin D., 474n, 477n
Dyer, William G., 62, 63, 470n

E

Emmons, Michael L., 278

F

Falkenberg, Loren, 409–410, 482n
Frason, Richard E., 478n
Fayol, Henri, 475n
Feather, N. T., 481n
Fein, Mitchell, 156–157, 474n
Feldman, Daniel C., 468n
Ferris, G. R., 476n
Fiedler, Fred E., 228, 230, 476n
Filley, Alan C., 237
Finnegan, Mary C., 471n
Fisher, Bruce D., 467n
Fisher, Cynthia D., 471n
Fleishman, E. A., 475n
Follett, Mary Parker, 312, 478n
Foruzani, Hossein H., 472n
Fouts, Susan C., 471n
Fowler, Jr., Aubrey R., 475n
Fredian, Alan, 482n
Freedman, Robert J., 469n
French, Elizabeth G., 473n
French, John R. P., 153, 473n
Freshley, Dwight L., 476n, 478n
Freud, Sigmund, 424, 482n
Froehle, Thomas C., 301, 304, 478n

Froggatt, K. L., 476n
Fuchsberg, Gilbert, 480n

G

Galle, William P. Jr., 318
Garcia, Joseph E., 476n
Gardner, Ella P., 471n
Gardner, Susan, 480n
Garges, Linda, 341
Garner, Lowell, 469n
Geidt, Thomas E., 480n
Gemmill, Arthur, 268, 477n
Gergen, Paul, 482n
Giallourakis, Michael, 8, 467n
Gibb, Jack E., 477n
Gilbreth, Frank, 2
Gist, Marilyn E., 473n
Glass, D. C., 472n
Glenn, E. S., 454, 483n
Glidden, Priscilla A., 329
Gobel, B. C., 476n
Goff, J. Larry, 371
Goldhar, Joel E., 470n
Goldsmith, Willis J., 471n
Good, Katherine C., 13
Good, Lawrence R., 13
Gould, M. I., 286, 477n
Gould, Richard, 321
Greenbaum, Howard H., 253, 476n
Greenberg, Jerald, 474n
Greenburg, Eric Rolfe, 480n
Greene, John O., 477n
Griffin, Ricky, 468n
Griss, B., 482n
Gudykunst, William B., 481n
Gupta, Udayan, 355, 479n
Gustafson, David H., 469n
Gustafson, James P., 469n

H

Hackman, J. Richard, 188–191, 468n, 475n
Hakel, Milton D., 286, 477n
Hall, Douglas T., 482n
Hall, R. Vance, 205
Hammer, W. Clay, 475n
Hammond, Kenneth R., 60, 469n
Hampton, David R., 469n
Hand Herbert H., 79, 470n
Hanson, Allen, 306, 480n
Hanson, David J., 480n
Harper, Stephen C., 470n
Harris, E. J., 475n
Harris, O. Jeff, 439, 473n, 477n, 481n
Harris, Phillip R., 454–455, 483n
Harris, Thomas A., 121–122, 473n
Hartman, Sandra J., 483n
Harwood, R. Frank, 347, 480n
Heckman, Jr., I. L., 298–301, 478n

Heisler, William J., 438
Hellriegel, Don, 479n
Hennigan, K. J., 479n
Herrick, Neal Q., 474n
Hersey, Paul, 234, 236, 299, 476n
Herzberg, Frederick, 145–146, 473n
Higgins, James M., 117
Hofstede, Geert H., 156–158, 450, 474n, 483n
Holloway, Clark, 79, 470n
Holmes, Thomas H., 344
Hooper, Laurence, 470n
Horst, James F., 480n
House, Robert J., 223, 237, 475n, 476n
Houston, Patrick, 483n
Hovey, David H., 214
Howard, G. S., 304
Huneryager, S. G., 298–301, 478n
Huse, Edgar F., 470n
Huseman, Richard C., 470n, 477n, 478n
Hymowitz,Carol, 355

I

Indrik, Julie, 348, 479n
Ingham, Harry, 120
Ivancevich, John M., 480n
Izard, Carroll E., 468n

J

Jacklin, Carol N., 481n
Jackson, D. J., 482n
Jackson, Patricia, 469n
Jackson, Susan E., 479n
Jacobs, Stanford I., 105
Jakubowski, Patricia, 271, 274, 477n
Janis, Irving L., 54–55, 469n
Jaspan, Norman, 480n
Jelinek, Mariann, 470n
Jennings, K. R., 476n
Jerdee, Thomas H., 481n
Johnson, Homer H., 482n
Johnson, Pamela R., 348, 479n
Johnston, Lloyd D., 472n
Jones, Maria Alicia, 479n
Jorgensen, D. O., 474n
Judson, Arnold S., 419, 482n
Juran, Joseph, 61

K

Kageyama, Atsushi, 457–459
Kahn, Robert L., 476n
Kane, Leslie, 471n
Kanter, Roseabeth Moss, 4, 467n
Kaplan, M. K., 469n
Kasra, Ferdows, 470n
Katz, Daniel, 476n
Katz, Fred E., 468n
Kay, Ira, 202
Kelly, Joan L., 474n

Kerr, Norbert L., 469n
Kerr, Steven, 237
Kiess, Harold O., 471n
Kilmann, Jr., Ralph H., 23, 325–326, 333, 467n, 468n, 478n
Kim, J. S., 187, 475n
Kirchner, Wayne K., 477n
Knotts, Rose, 460–462, 483n
Kolb, Deborah, 329
Koontz, Harold, 2
Kotter, John P., 431
Kovach, Kenneth A., 159, 474n
Krupar, Karen R., 314–315, 478n
Krupar, Joseph J., 314–315, 478n

L

Landou, Jacqueline, 481n
Lange, Arthur, 271 274, 477n
Latham, Gary P., 181, 186–187, 474n
Lathrop, Nancy, 469n
Lawler, Edward E., 468n, 474n
Lawrie, John, 482n
Leana, C. R., 476n
Leathem, J. Trevor, 482n
Leibowitz, Zandy B., 127
Leigh, J. Paul, 473n
Lengel, Robert H., 257, 259, 477n
Lengnick-Hall, M. L., 476n
Levinson, Harry, 424, 482n
Levitin, Teresa, 481n
Levy, Stephen J., 480n
Lewy, Alfred, 92
Liden, Robert C., 476n
Likert, Rensis, 23, 225, 254–255, 468n, 476n
Lind, Douglas T., 477n
Lindsey, H. E., 477n
Link, Patricia B., 479n
Litterer, Joseph A., 478n
Locke, Edwin A., 181, 474n, 476n
Lockhart, John M., 471n
Logue, Cal M., 476n, 478n
Longenecker, Justin G., 467n
Lord, Mary, 148
Lorenzi, Peter, 187, 474n
Lott, Bernice M., 468n
Luft, Joseph, 120

M

Maccoby, Eleanor E., 481n
Machalaba, Daniel, 243
Madigan, Robert J., 474n
Mahan, David F., 469n
Manpower, J., 469n
Mansfield, Roger, 482n
Markham, Steven E., 56, 469n
Marriott, J. W., 25
Maslow, Abraham, 94, 143–145, 471n, 473n

Matteson, M. T., 480n
Matthews, A. K., 479n
McArthur, D. W., 476n
McArthur, Jerie, 476n
McCanse, Anne Adams, 225–227, 324, 476n, 479n
McClelland, David C., 154, 473n
McDonald, Angus, 25
McGregor, Douglas, 211, 291, 475n, 478n
McKinney, Joseph A., 467n
McLean, Alan A., 479n
Meredith, Jack R., 470n
Metcalf, Henry C., 478n
Miles, Edward W., 470n, 477n
Miles, Raymond E., 447, 483n
Miller, Charles E., 469n
Miller, Lawrence M., 474n
Mills, Theodore M., 469n
Mintz, Norbert L., 94, 471n
Mitchell, Terence R., 131, 473, 475n, 476n
Mitchell, Vance F., 157, 474n
Moffatt, Susan, 457, 483n
Moore, Carlos W., 467n
Moore, Lynda L., 481n
Moore, Maggie, 482n
Moore, Tommy, 482n
Moran, Robert T., 454–455, 483n
Moritz, Thomas E., 8, 467n
Mossholder, Kevin W., 472n
Mueller, Jonathan, 469n
Munchus, III, George, 470n
Murphy, Patrick E., 7, 467n
Murray, Henry A., 143, 160, 473n, 474n
Myers, P., 304

N

Nadler, David A., 427, 482n
Naisbitt, John, 444, 482n, 483n
Nance, D. W., 304
Nasar, Jack L., 472n
Newman, John E., 479n, 480n
Nielsen, Eric H., 483n
Noori, Hamid, 470n
Nordstrom, Rodney R., 209

O

Oldham, Greg R., 101, 188–191, 472n, 475n
Organ, Dennis M., 475n
Ornstein, Suzyn, 474n

P

Patterson, Bill, 407, 482n
Paulsen, Kevin M., 52, 469n
Peale, Norman V., 467n
Pearce, III, John A., 468n
Peters, L. H., 389
Peters, Thomas J., 444, 483n

Phillips, Ronald C., 322–323, 333, 478n
Pomice, Eva, 408
Porter, Lyman W., 468n, 474n
Price, Barbara A., 481n
Pride, William M., 477n
Pritchard, R. D., 474n
Pryer, Mildred W., 131
Pryor, M. W., 473n

Q

Quick, Jonathon, D., 472n
Quinn, Robert P., 481n

R

Rafaeli, Anat, 473n
Raloff, Janet, 96–97
Raven, Bertram, 153, 473n
Reibstein, Larry, 474n
Reichers, Arnon E., 468n
Rickles, Roger, 355, 479n
Ringler, Karen, 469n
Robbins, Stephen P., 23, 325, 467n, 468n, 479n
Robichoux, Mark, 479n
Robin, Donald, 8, 467n
Rogers, Carl, 291–292, 478n
Rohrbaugh, John, 60, 468n, 469n
Roppel, Charles, 352, 354
Roseborough, Mary E., 469n
Rosen, Benson, 481n
Rosen, Stephen, 91, 471n
Rotter, Julian B., 132–133, 473n
Rotton, James, 471n
Roy, Donald F., 468n
Ruch, William A., 478n
Russell, Cheryl, 482n

S

Saari, L. M., 474n
Sadler, Marion, 480n
Sales, M. S., 479n
Samuels, Linda B., 471n
Sand, Robert H., 471n
Sankar, Y., 470n
Sayles, leonard R., 261, 475n, 477n
Schauss, Alexander, 471n
Schein, Virginia, 387, 481n
Schersching, Cynthia, 469n
Schlesinger, Leonard A., 431
Schlossberg, Nancy K., 127
Schmoldt, David W., 480n
Schriesheim, Chester, 468n
Schuh, Allen J., 286, 477n
Schuler, R. S., 187, 475n
Schurer, Randall S., 479n
Schwadel, Francine, 185
Schwartz, S., 469n
Schweiger, David M., 181
Schweiger, D. A., 476n

Schwold, Richard, 479n
Scott, William G., 475n, 479n
Seashore, Stanley E., 475n
Sekumar, Art, 475n
Seldin, Fredric, A., 469n
Semyonov, Moshe, 481n
Shaw, James B., 471n
Shaw, K. N., 474n
Shaw, Marvin E., 468n
Shore, Jane E., 127
Sigband, Norman B., 477n
Sims, Jr., Henry P., 475n
Singer, Jerome E., 472n
Skinner, B. F., 290, 475n
Slater, Philip, 56, 469n
Slocum, Jr., John W., 479n
Smith, Charles, 435–436, 483n
Smyser, Charles M., 131, 473n
Snow, Charles C., 447, 483n
Snygg, Donald, 115, 472n
Solomon, Judy, 470n
Solomon, Linda Z., 471n
Sommer, Robert, 103–104, 472n
Stead, Bette A., 481n
Steele, Fritz, 472n
Steers, Richard M., 187, 475n
Steinmann, D., 469n
Stevenson, K. A., 454, 483n
Steward, T. R., 469n
Stewart, Lea P., 481n
Stogdill, R. M., 223–224, 475n
Stouffer, S. A., 468n
Strauss, George, 261, 475n, 477n
Strodbeck, Fred L., 469n
Sullivan, Jeremiah J., 473n
Summer, Charles E., 469n
Swasy, Alicia, 477n
Sykes, Wilbert R., 477n

T

Taylor, Frederick, 2
Taylor, Robert R., 378
Taylor, William, 470n
Taynor, J., 389
Terborg, J. R., 389
Terpstra, D. E., 483n
Terris, William, 480n
Tharehou, Phyllis, 473n
Thayer, Paul W., 192
Thayler, Lee, 253, 476n
Theorall, T., 479n
Thomas, Joe G., 468n
Thomas, Kenneth, 325–326, 333, 478n
Thorndike, E. L., 199, 475n
Tichey, Noel, 449, 483n
Timmons, William M., 472n
Tipgos, Manuel A., 479n
Templin, Neal, 288
Tracy, Brian S., 125
Trost, Cathy, 471n

Trunzo, James, 472n
Tushman, Michael L., 427, 482n

U

Ubell, Earl, 473n
Umstot, Dennis D., 475n
Urwick, Lyndall, 478n

V

Van de Ven, Andrew H., 60, 469n
VanEpps, Pamela D., 318
Vecchio, R. P., 476n
Vernon, Ann, 478n
Vickroy, Stephen C., 471n
Viega, John F., 481n
Vollrath, D. A. 476n
Vroom, Victor, 230–237, 476n

W

Wall, Jr., James A., 456, 483n
Wanous, John P., 468n
Waterman, Jr., Robert H., 444, 483n
Watts, A. J., 471n
Webber, Ross A., 469n
Weed, Stan E., 131, 473n
Weiner, Yoash, 468n
Weis, William L., 106, 472n
Wenrich, W. W., 271, 477n
Whyte, Glen, 469n
Whyte, William F., 209, 475n
Wilcox, Douglas S., 477n
Wilemon, David, 435–436, 483n
Witmeyer, D., 454, 483n
Wohlwill, Joachim, 97, 472n
Wokutch, Richard E., 467n

Woodman, Richard W., 479n
Wortham, A. W., 479n
Wright, Marcia K., 469n
Wyon, M. P., 471n

Y

Yager, Ed, 470n
Yetton, Phillip W., 230–237, 235, 476n
Yoder, Stephen Kreider, 75, 471n
Young, Valerie, 391, 481n
Yukl, Gary A., 186–187, 474n

Z

Zemke, Ron, 155, 474n, 480n
Zima, Joseph P., 478n

Subject Index

A

Achievement need, 154–155
Acronym, 461
Affiliation need, 149–150
Aggressiveness, 271
AIDS, employees with, 405–408
Alcoholic, 363
Alcoholism and other drug problems, 363–372
  alcoholism, 363–364
  drug policies and procedures, 367–368
  employee rights, philosophy, and attitudes, 368–369
  General Motors guidelines, 368–369
  other drug problems, 364–365
  rehabilitation programs, 369–371
  supervisor's role in, 371–372
  tests to determine seriousness of, 370–371
Alcoholism, problems of, 363
  alcoholic, 363
  problem drinker, 363
Alderfer's ERG approach, 145
Americans with Disabilities Act of 1990, 405
Artificial intelligence, 75
  expert system, 76–78
Assertiveness, 271
  aggressiveness, 271
  nonaggressiveness, 271
Auditory factors, 95–99
  decibels, 96
  effects of noise, 95, 97–98
  reducing noise levels, 99
Authority relationship, 26–27

B

Beautiful room, 94–95
Behavioral adjustment, 419
Behavior concept of leadership, 224
  behavior theories of leadership, 224
Broker, 447

C

Centralization for decision making, 29
Change agent, 426

Change, effects upon employees, 419–421
  behavioral changes, 419
  psychological changes, 418–419
  social changes, 421
Change, the management of, 426–433
  early planning and notification,
  enlisting participation, 428
  management's goals and guidelines, 426–429
  overcoming fears, 430–431
  providing employee protection, 429
  providing resources and training, 429
  the tentative approach, 431–432
Change, other factors influencing response to, 425–426
  initiator of change, 425
  change agent, 426
  necessity of change, 426
  risk-taking tendencies of employees, 426
Change, reasons for resistance to, 421–425
  fear, 424
  TA Approach, 423
  tension, 424
Chief technology officer (CTO), 73
Civil Rights Act of 1964, 5
Coercive power, 153
Cognitive motivation, 170
  model of, 172
Cohesiveness of groups, 36
Collaboration, 331
Collectivism, 450
Color, effects of, 93–94
Communication channels, 28
Communication functions, 253
  command and instruction, 253
  influence and persuasion, 254
  information, 253
  innovation, 254
  integrative, 254
Communication process, 255–266
  analysis of the receiver, 256
  choice of symbols, 256
  deciding on a message, 255
  decoding, 260

encoding, 257
  problems of the, 260–266
  receiver responsibilities, 259–260
  selection of a medium, 257
Communication process, problems of, 260–264
  complementary transactions, 262
  crossed transactions, 262
  distortion, 261
  filtering, 260–261
  inconsistent actions and messages, 262–263
  receiver's state of mind, 263–264
  timing, 261–262
  ulterior transactions, 263
Communication style indicator, 58–59
Comparison of reinforcement motivation with cognitive motivation, 207
Competence need, 150
Complementary transactions, 262
Computer integrated manufacturing (CIM), 74
Conduct, Code of, 6
Conflict, contemporary view of, 310
Conflict development, degree of, 322–324
Conflict, management's goal when it arises, 311–313
  accomplishing real and permanent solutions, 313
  achieving unity, 313
  identifying what's behind the conflict, 311
  integration of ideas, 312
  redirecting tensions and hostilities, 312
Conflict, sources of, 314–315, 317–322
  functional duties, 322
  individual differences, 314
  organization characteristics and functional differences, 319–322
  organizational characteristics, 319
  perceptual differences, 318–319
Conflict, techniques for dealing with, 324–332
  choosing an appropriate approach, 330–332
  collaboration, 331

Leadership Grid R approach, 324
mediation and arbitration, 329–330
problem solving, 324
Robbins' approach, 324
smoothing, 324
subordinate goals, 324
Thomas-Kilmann conflict mode, 325–328
Conflict, traditional view, 310
Conventional office design, 99
Correctional interview, 214–216
conducting the, 214–216
Cottage industries, 81
Counseling,
applying contingency theory to, 298–302
conditions for effective, 287–291
corrective, 283
developmental, 283
ethics and obligations of, 299–302
informational, 283
person to handle, 285, 287
techniques, 291–298
therapeutic, 283
Counseling conditions, 287–291
people, 288–289
place, 288
preparation, 289–291
Counseling techniques, 291–298
directive, 291–292
nondirective, 292–298
Crossed transactions, 262
Cultural realities, 24
Culture(s), 5
characteristics of, 21–23
ideals, 23
management's role in, 24
organization structure's effects on, 25
organizational, 20
Cumulative trauma disorders (CTD), 83

D

Data accumulation, 74
Decentralization for decision-making, 29
Decibels, 96
Decision-making groups, 49, 50
groupthink, 53
problems of, 52
Delphi, technique, 60
Deontology, 11
Directive counseling, 291–292
Disabilities, workers with, 403–405
Americans with Disabilities Act of 1990, 405
Disciplinary action, 208, 211
fairness in, 211
hot stove disciplining, 211

philosophy of, 209–210
Dow Chemical Company, 108
Drug abuse problems, 364–365
drug abuser, 365
Drug abuser, 365
Drug testing, 365–367
Dynamic networking, 447

E

Economics of integration, 74
Economics of scale, 73
Economics of scope, 73
Effective communication, conditions for, 266–269
Electronic mail, 80
Employee dishonesty (*See* theft)
Enlightened self-interest, 10
Entrants, 445
Equity for minorities, 386
discrimination, 386
steps toward, 409–410
Equity theory, 179–182
Ergonomics, 83
Esteem need, 144
Ethics,
codes of, 8, 14
in the workplace, 4
Executive row, 103
Expectancy theory, 173–179
Expert power, 153
Expert systems (ES), 76–78
External factors causing change, 417–418
economy and its effects, 417
legally-based changes, 418
technology, 417–418
unplanned change, 417
External person, 130–133
Extinction, 200

F

Femininity, 451
Fiedler contingency approach, 228–230
Filtering, 260
Flexible leadership, 236
determining needs for, 238
problem of consistency, 242
Flexiplace, 446
Flexitime, 446–447
Formal groups and teams, 48

G

Gender (*See* women as a minority)
Goal setting, 185–187
Grapevine communication, 32, 38–40
cluster approach, 39
Grapevine and its problems, 269–271
Groups
nontraditional, 54

operational, 64
traditional, 49
Groupthink, 53–55

H

Hawthorne studies, 2
Hersey-Blanchard situational approach, 234, 236
Honesty test, 375–377
Hope need, 155–156
Hot stove disciplining, 211
Human needs, 142
specific needs, 146–156
urgency of, 156–159

I

Idioms, 461
Incentive, 171
Individualism, 450
Informal groups and organizations, 30–31
characteristics and activities, 33
conformity, 36
functions of, 32
grapevine communication, 38–40
management's relationship to, 40–42
norms of, 34
stars (leaders), 34
work organizations, 30–31
Information float, 444
Integrating devices, 80
Internal change, 416
planned change, 416
Internal person, 130–131, 133

J

Johari Window, 120

L

Latent need, 143
Leadership
style approaches, 225
Leadership Grid R, 226–227
nine-nine leadership, 227–228
system 4, 225–226
Leadership, situational contingency view of, 228
factors in the selection of, 240–241
Fiedler contingency approach, 228–230
Hersey-Blanchard situational approach, 234, 236
path-goal view of leadership, 236
Vroom-Yetton decision tree approach, 230–235
Legitimate power, 153
Life position, 121
Lighting and work performance, 95
Locus of control, 130–133

external person, 130–133
internal person, 130–133
Love need, 144

M

Manifest need, 143
Masculinity, 451
McDonald's, 13
Monsanto Pledge of social responsibility, 11
Motivation, 171
 incentive, 171
 motive, 171
Motivational potential of jobs, 187–191
 motivating potential score, 189–191
Motives, 171
Multinational language and communication, 457–462
 acronym, 461
 idioms, 461
 multi-phase combinations, 460
 slang, 458
Multinational movement, 450–463
 cultural values, 450
 collectivism, 450
 femininity, 451
 individualism, 450
 masculinity, 451
 multinational, 450
 power distance, 451
 societal procedures and methods, 451
 uncertainty avoidance, 451
Multi-phase combinations, 460

N

Need theories, 143–146
 Alderfer's ERG, 145
 Herzberg's two-factor, 145–146
 Maslow's need hierarchy, 143–145
 Murray's latent and manifest, 143
Needs-based motivation, 170
 assumptions underlying, 170
 cognitive motivation, 170
Negative Motivational Model, 182–184
 negative motivational process, 182
 process of, 182
 role of boss in, 184
Negative reinforcement, 208
Neighborhood work centers, 82–83
Noise levels, 95–99
 high levels of, 97–98
 reduction of, 99
Nominal group technique (NRG), 60
Nonaggressiveness, 271
Nondirective counseling, 292–298
 active listening, 293–294
 closing, 296
 example of, 297–298

probes, 294
restatement, 294–296
steps to, 296–297
Nontraditional groups, 54
 Delphi technique, 60
 Interacting conference groups, 54
 Normal group technique, 60
 Quality circle, 61
 Traditional interacting group, 54
Norms, 21

O

Occupational Safety and Health Administration (OSHA), 83–84, 96
Older workers as an age minority, 395–398
 dealing with problems of, 397–398
 problems of, 395–397
Ombudsman, 11
Open office, 99
 working with, 102
Operational groups, 64
Organizational Development, 433–439
 change agent's role in, 435–436
 optimal conditions for, 437
 the process of, 434–435
Organizations of the future, 447–449
 broker, 447
 dynamic networks and,
  international cooperation, 447
 leadership trends, 448–449
 structure, power, and authority, 448
 transformational leaders, 449

P

Path-goal leadership view, 236
Perception, 114
Perception about self and others, 115
 managerial actions for better, 123, 126
 perception, 114
 self esteem, 115
 success-failure, 117
Physical climate, 90, 105–106
 status impact, 105–106
Physical location and placement, 99
 centralization, 103
 conventional design, 99
 open office, 99
 other causes, 103–104
 placement of management, 103
 and results, 103–104
 status impact, 105–106
Physical maintenance need, 146
Physical surroundings
 climate and humidity, 90
 effects of nature, 91
 implications for managers, 92
 temperature, 91
Physiological need, 144

Planned change, 416
Polygraph tests, 374–375
Positive motivational model, 172–182
 equity theory, 179–182
 expectancy theory, 173–179
 probabilities of successful performance, 175
 self test, 177–178
Power distance, 451
Power need, 152–154
Primary reinforcer, 199
Problem drinker, 363
Punishment, 200
Pygmalion effect, 134–135
 perceptual process of, 135

Q

Quality circle, 49, 61–62

R

Racial minorities, 399–403
 actions to benefit, 402–403
 organizational problems faced by, 400–402
Realistic job previews, 395
Referent power, 153
Reinforcement, 198–208
 extinction, 200
 guidelines, 201–203
 negative reinforcement, 208
 primary reinforcer, 199
 punishment, 200
 secondary reinforcer, 199
Reinforcement schedules, 203–207
 fixed interval, 204
 fixed ratio, 206
 variable interval, 205
 variable ratio, 206
Reputation need, 151–152
Restatement, 294–295
 exercise in the use of, 295
Reward power, 153
Robbins' approach for conflict management, 324
Robotics, 74
Role, 127–129
Role ambiguity, 128–129
Role perception, 127–130
 process of, 128–129
 role, 127–128
 role ambiguity, 128–129
 role perceptions, 127
 ways to improve, 129–130
Roles, 21
Rotary International four-way test, 9
Rotter Locus of Control Scale, 132–133

S

Scale of social interest, 35, 44–45
Secondary reinforcer, 199

Security need, 147–149
Security Pacific Corporation Credo, 6–7
Self-actualization need, 144
Self esteem, 115
  test for, 116–117
Service need, 154
Slang, 458
Smoking in the workplace, 106–108
  Brooks vs Trans World Airlines, 107
  cost of, 106
  Glasper vs La. Stadium and, Exposition District, 107
  management of, 107–108
Smoothing, 324
Social responsibility, 10, 13
Span of supervision, 29
Specialization, 29
Stereotyping, 390
Stress, factors influencing, 340–344
  age and education, 343–344
  experiences with family and friends, 343
  health as a factor, 342–343
  personality types, 341
  role of managers and coworkers, 351–355
  self concept, 343
  Type A, 341
  Type B, 341
Stress, managerial actions to help, 351–355
Stressors, 344–349
  job-related, 345–348
  other stressors, 348–349
  overload, 345
  underload, 345
Stroking, 121
Success-failure model, 117–119
Superfund Amendments and Reauthorization Act, 84
Superordinate goals, 324
System 4 leadership, 225–226
Systems view of organizations, 2–3, 12

T

Technology
  artificial intelligence, 75–78
  chief technology officer (CTO), 73
  computer integrated manufacturing, 74
  economics of integration, 74
  economies of scale, 73
  economics of scope, 73
  expert systems, 76–78
  impact on production, 73
  manager's role, 84
  robotics, 74
Team building, 62
  checklist, 63
Team building and problem solving, 62
  team building, 62
Team decision-making process, 49–50
Technology and communication, 79
  electronic mail, 80
  integrating devices, 80
  voice mail, 81
Technology-health and safety problems, 83–84
  clean air activities, 84
  cumulative trauma disorders, 83
  ergonomics, 83
  video display terminal, 83
Temperature and humidity, 91–92
Tentative approach to getting change expected, 431
Theft and employee dishonesty, 373–380
  dealing with, 374–375
  honesty tests, 375–377
  management's role in, 374
  polygraph tests, 374–375
  who steals and why, 373–374
Thematic Apperception Test, 160
Thomas-Kilmann conflict mode, 325–327
Traditional groups and teams, 49
  decision-making group, 49
  quality circle, 49

Traditional interacting group, 54
Trait approach, 223–224
Transactional analysis model, 121
  life position, 121
  stroking, 121
Transformational leader, 449
Type A personality, 341
Type B personality, 341

U

Ugly room, 94
Ulterior transactions, 263
Unplanned change, 417
Utilitarianism, 10

V

Video display terminal, 83
Visual stimuli, 93
  beauty vs ugliness, 94
  effect of color, 93
  impact of, 93
  lighting and work performance, 95
Voice mail, 81
Vroom-Yetton decision tree approach, 230–235

W

Weather, 91–92
Women as a minority, 386–395
  advantages for women employees, 394
  dealing with problems women face, 394
  problems of employed women, 387
  realistic job previews, 395
  stereotyping, 390–393
Workforce of the future, 445
  characteristics of, 445
  entrants, 445
  post-World War II group, 445
  pre-World War II group, 445

Y

Younger employees' strengths and weaknesses, 398–399

Assign #1 - Chapt 1   p 1-16
            7   p 140-146
        Case study @ 141

                                          do self test
#2   Chapt 16   384-409   @ 161 fmi
(minorities) case study p 385

#3   Chapt 15   360-380
(Alcoholism + Drug Abuse) Case study p 382

#4   Chapt 7   146-165   Case St 339
            14   338-351   "   +
                                     443
    Personal needs
    Stress